Legal and Ethical Responsibilities in Business

16 E

Halbert/Ingulli/Mann/Roberts

CENGAGE
Learning·

Australia • Brazil • Japan • Korea • Mexico • Singapore • Spain • United Kingdom • United States

CENGAGE
Learning·

Legal and Ethical Responsibilities in Business 16 E

Senior Manager, Student Engagement:

Linda deStefano

Manager, Student Engagement:

Julie Dierig

Marketing Manager:

Rachael Kloos

Manager, Premedia:

Kim Fry

Manager, Intellectual Property Project Manager:

Brian Methe

Senior Manager, Production:

Donna M. Brown

Manager, Production:

Terri Daley

For product information and technology assistance, contact us at
Cengage Learning Customer & Sales Support, 1-800-354-9706
For permission to use material from this text or product,
submit all requests online at **cengage.com/permissions**
Further permissions questions can be emailed to
permissionrequest@cengage.com

This book contains select works from existing Cengage Learning resources and was produced by Cengage Learning Custom Solutions for collegiate use. As such, those adopting and/or contributing to this work are responsible for editorial content accuracy, continuity and completeness.

Compilation © 20XX Cengage Learning

ISBN: 978-1-305-76960-1

WCN: 01-100-101

Cengage Learning
20 Channel Center Street
Boston, MA 02210
USA

Cengage Learning is a leading provider of customized learning solutions with office locations around the globe, including Singapore, the United Kingdom, Australia, Mexico, Brazil, and Japan. Locate your local office at:
www.international.cengage.com/region.

Cengage Learning products are represented in Canada by Nelson Education, Ltd.

For your lifelong learning solutions, visit **www.cengage.com/custom.**

Visit our corporate website at **www.cengage.com.**

Brief Contents

CHAPTER 1

INTRODUCTION TO LAW

CHAPTER OUTCOMES

After reading and studying this chapter, you should be able to:

- Identify and describe the basic functions of law.

- Distinguish between (1) law and justice and (2) law and morals.

- Distinguish between (1) substantive and procedural law, (2) public and private law, and (3) civil and criminal law.

- Identify and describe the sources of law.

- Explain the principle of *stare decisis*.

Law concerns the relations of individuals with one another as such relations affect the social and economic order. It is both the product of civilization and the means by which civilization is maintained. As such, law reflects the social, economic, political, religious, and moral philosophy of society. The laws of the United States influence the lives of every U.S. citizen. At the same time, the laws of each State influence the lives of its citizens and the lives of many noncitizens as well. The rights and duties of all individuals, as well as the safety and security of all people and their property, depend upon the law.

The law is pervasive. It interacts with and influences the political, economic, and social systems of every civilized society. It permits, forbids, or regulates practically every human activity and affects all persons either directly or indirectly. Law is, in part, prohibitory: certain acts must not be committed. For example, one must not steal; one must not murder. Law is also partly mandatory: certain acts must be done or be done in a prescribed way. Taxes must be paid; corporations must make and file certain reports with State or Federal authorities; traffic must keep to the right. Finally, law is permissive: individuals may choose to perform or not to perform certain acts. Thus, one may or may not enter into a contract; one may or may not dispose of one's estate by will.

Because the areas of law are so highly interrelated, an individual who intends to study the several branches of law known collectively as business law should first consider the nature, classification, and sources of law as a whole. This enables the student not only to comprehend better any given branch of law but also to understand its relation to other areas of law.

NATURE OF LAW

The law has evolved slowly, and it will continue to change. It is not a pure science based upon unchanging and universal truths. Rather, it results from a continuous effort to balance, through a workable set of rules, the individual and group rights of a society. In *The Common Law*, Oliver Wendell Holmes wrote,

> The life of the law has not been logic; it has been experience. The felt necessities of the time, the prevalent moral and political theories, avowed or unconscious, even the prejudices which judges share with their fellowmen, have had a good deal more to do than the syllogism in determining the rules by which men should be governed. The law embodies the story of a nation's development through many centuries, and it cannot be dealt with as if it contained only the axioms and corollaries of a book of mathematics.

DEFINITION OF LAW

A fundamental but difficult question regarding law is this: what is it? Numerous philosophers and jurists (legal scholars) have attempted to define it. American jurists and Supreme Court Justices Oliver Wendell Holmes and Benjamin Cardozo defined law as predictions of the way that a court will decide specific legal questions. William Blackstone, an English jurist, on the other hand, defined law as "a rule of civil conduct prescribed by the supreme power in a state, commanding what is right, and prohibiting what is wrong."

Similarly, Austin, a nineteenth-century English jurist, defined law as a general command that a state or sovereign makes to those who are subject to its authority by laying down a course of action enforced by judicial or administrative tribunals.

Because of its great complexity, many legal scholars have attempted to explain the law by outlining its essential characteristics. Roscoe Pound, a distinguished American jurist and former dean of the Harvard Law School, described law as having multiple meanings:

> First, we may mean the legal order, that is, the regime of ordering human activities and relations through systematic application of the force of politically organized society, or through social pressure in such a society backed by such force. We use the term "law" in this sense when we speak of "respect for law" or for the "end of law."
>
> Second, we may mean the aggregate of laws or legal precepts; the body of authoritative grounds of judicial and administrative action established in such a society. We may mean the body of received and established materials on which judicial and administrative determinations proceed. We use the term in this sense when we speak of "systems of law" or of "justice according to law."
>
> Third, we may mean what Mr. Justice Cardozo has happily styled "the judicial process." We may mean the process of determining controversies, whether as it actually takes place, or as the public, the jurists, and the practitioners in the courts hold it ought to take place.

FUNCTIONS OF LAW

At a general level the primary function of law is to maintain stability in the social, political, and economic system while simultaneously permitting change. The law accomplishes this basic function by performing a number of specific functions, among them dispute resolution, protection of property, and preservation of the state.

Disputes, which inevitably arise in a society as complex and interdependent as ours, may involve criminal matters, such as theft, or noncriminal matters, such as an automobile accident. Because disputes threaten the stability of society, the law has established an elaborate and evolving set of rules to resolve them. In addition, the legal system has instituted societal remedies, usually administered by the courts, in place of private remedies such as revenge.

The recognition of private ownership of property is fundamental to our economic system, based as it is upon the exchange of goods and services among privately held units of consumption. Therefore, a second crucial function of law is to protect the owner's use of property and to facilitate voluntary agreements (called contracts) regarding exchanges of property and services. Accordingly, a significant portion of law, as well as this text, involves property and its disposition, including the law of property, contracts, sales, commercial paper, and business associations.

A third essential function of the law is preservation of the state. In our system, law ensures that changes in leadership and the political structure are brought about by political actions such as elections, legislation, and referenda, rather than by revolution, sedition, and rebellion.

LEGAL SANCTIONS

A primary function of the legal system is to make sure that legal rules are enforced. **Sanctions** are the means by which the law enforces the decisions of the courts. Without sanctions, laws would be ineffectual and unenforceable.

An example of a sanction in a civil (noncriminal) case is the seizure and sale of the property of a debtor who fails to pay a court-ordered obligation, called a judgment. Moreover, under certain circumstances, a court may enforce its order by finding an offender in contempt and sentencing him to jail until he obeys the court's order. In criminal cases, the principal sanctions are the imposition of a fine, imprisonment, and capital punishment.

LAW AND MORALS

Although moral and ethical concepts greatly influence the law, morals and law are not the same. They may be considered as two intersecting circles, as shown in *Figure 1-1*. The more darkly shaded area common to both circles includes the vast body of ideas that are both moral and legal. For instance, "Thou shall not kill" and "Thou shall not steal" are both moral precepts and legal constraints.

On the other hand, the part of the legal circle that does not intersect the morality circle includes many rules of law that are completely unrelated to morals, such as the rules stating that you must drive on the right side of the road and that you must register before you can vote. Likewise, the portion of the morality circle which does not intersect the legal circle includes moral precepts not enforced by law, such as the moral principle that you should not silently stand by and watch a blind man walk off a cliff or that you should provide food to a starving child.

◆ SEE FIGURE 1-1: **Law and Morals**

LAW AND JUSTICE

Law and justice represent separate and distinct concepts. Without law, however, there can be no justice. Although justice has at least as many definitions as law does, justice may be defined as fair, equitable, and impartial treatment of the competing interests and desires of individuals and groups with due regard for the common good.

◆ **FIGURE 1-1:** **Law and Morals**

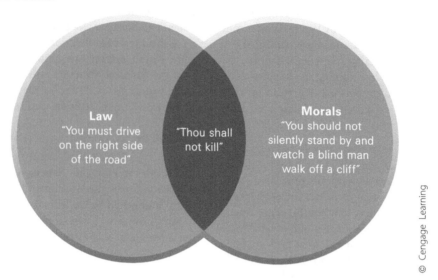

On the other hand, law is no guarantee of justice. Some of history's most monstrous acts have been committed pursuant to "law." Examples include the actions of Nazi Germany during the 1930s and 1940s and the actions of the South African government under apartheid from 1948 until 1994. Totalitarian societies often have shaped formal legal systems around the atrocities they have sanctioned.

CLASSIFICATION OF LAW

Because the subject is vast, classifying the law into categories is helpful. Though a number of classifications are possible, the most useful categories are (1) substantive and procedural, (2) public and private, and (3) civil and criminal.

Basic to understanding these classifications are the terms *right* and *duty*. A **right** is the capacity of a person, with the aid of the law, to require another person or persons to perform, or to refrain from performing, a certain act. Thus, if Alice sells and delivers goods to Bob for the agreed price of $500 payable at a certain date, Alice has the capability, with the aid of the courts, of enforcing the payment by Bob of the $500. A **duty** is the obligation the law imposes upon a person to perform, or to refrain from performing, a certain act. Duty and right are correlatives: no right can rest upon one person without a corresponding duty resting upon some other person or, in some cases, upon all other persons.

◆ **SEE FIGURE 1-2:** **Classification of Law**

◆ **FIGURE 1-2:** **Classification of Law**

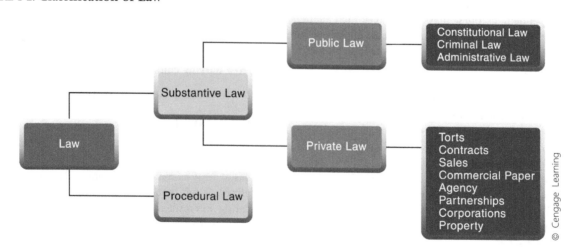

SUBSTANTIVE AND PROCEDURAL LAW

Substantive law creates, defines, and regulates legal rights and duties. Thus, the rules of contract law that determine when a binding contract is formed are rules of substantive law. This book is principally concerned with substantive law. On the other hand, **procedural law** establishes the rules for enforcing those rights that exist by reason of substantive law. Thus, procedural law defines the method by which one may obtain a remedy in court.

PUBLIC AND PRIVATE LAW

Public law is the branch of substantive law that deals with the government's rights and powers in its political or sovereign capacity and in its relation to individuals or groups. Public law consists of constitutional, administrative, and criminal law. **Private law** is that part of substantive law governing individuals and legal entities (such as corporations) in their relations with one another. Business law is primarily private law.

CIVIL AND CRIMINAL LAW

The **civil law** defines duties the violation of which constitutes a wrong against the party injured by the violation. In contrast, the **criminal law** establishes duties the violation of which is a wrong against the whole community. Civil law is a part of private law, whereas criminal law is a part of public law. (The term *civil law* should be distinguished from the concept of a civil law *system*, which is discussed later in this chapter.) In a civil action the injured party **sues** to recover **compensation** for the damage and injury he has sustained as a result of the defendant's wrongful conduct. The party bringing a civil action (the **plaintiff**) has the burden of proof, which he must sustain by a **preponderance** (greater weight) of the evidence. Whereas the purpose of criminal law is to punish the wrongdoer, the purpose of civil law is to compensate the injured party. The principal forms of relief the civil law provides are a judgment for money damages and a decree ordering the defendant to perform a specified act or to desist from specified conduct.

A crime is any act or omission that public law prohibits in the interest of protecting the public and that the government makes punishable in a judicial proceeding brought (**prosecuted**) by it. The government must prove criminal guilt **beyond a reasonable doubt**, which is a significantly higher burden of proof than that required in a civil action. The government prohibits and punishes crimes upon the ground of public policy, which may include the safeguarding of the government itself, human life, or private property. Additional purposes of criminal law include deterrence and rehabilitation.

◆ SEE FIGURE 1-3: **Comparison of Civil and Criminal Law**

SOURCES OF LAW

The sources of law in the U.S. legal system are the Federal and State constitutions, Federal treaties, interstate compacts, Federal and State statutes and executive orders, the ordinances of countless local municipal governments, the rules and regulations of Federal and State administrative agencies, and an ever-increasing volume of reported Federal and State court decisions.

The *supreme law* of the land is the U.S. Constitution. The Constitution provides that Federal statutes and treaties shall be the supreme law of the land. Federal legislation and treaties are, therefore, paramount to State constitutions and statutes. Federal legislation is of great significance as a source of law. Other Federal actions having the force of law are executive orders of the President and rules and regulations of Federal administrative officials, agencies, and commissions. The Federal courts also contribute considerably to the body of law in the United States.

◆ FIGURE 1-3: **Comparison of Civil and Criminal Law**

	Civil Law	Criminal Law
Commencement of Action	Aggrieved individual (plaintiff) sues	State or Federal government prosecutes
Purpose	Compensation Deterrence	Punishment Deterrence Rehabilitation Preservation of peace
Burden of Proof	Preponderance of the evidence	Beyond a reasonable doubt
Principal Sanctions	Monetary damages Equitable remedies	Capital punishment Imprisonment Fines

◆ **FIGURE 1-4: Hierarchy of Law**

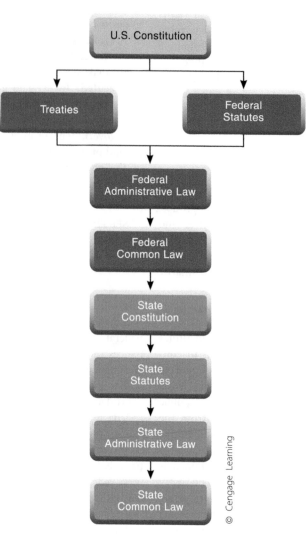

The same pattern exists in every State. The paramount law of each State is contained in its written constitution. (Although a State constitution cannot deprive citizens of Federal constitutional rights, it can guarantee rights beyond those provided in the U.S. Constitution.) State constitutions tend to be more specific than the U.S. Constitution and, generally, have been amended more frequently. Subordinate to the State constitution are the statutes that the State's legislature enacts and the case law that its judiciary develops. Likewise, State administrative agencies issue rules and regulations having the force of law, as do executive orders promulgated by the governors of most States. In addition, cities, towns, and villages have limited legislative powers within their respective municipal areas to pass ordinances and resolutions.

◆ **SEE FIGURE 1-4: Hierarchy of Law**

CONSTITUTIONAL LAW

A **constitution**—the fundamental law of a particular level of government—establishes the governmental structure and allocates power among the levels of government, thereby defining political relationships. One of the fundamental principles on which our government is founded is that of separation of powers. As detailed in the U.S. Constitution, this means that the government consists of three distinct and independent branches: the Federal judiciary, the Congress, and the executive branch.

A constitution also restricts the powers of government and specifies the rights and liberties of the people. For example, the Constitution of the United States not only specifically states what rights and authority are vested in the national government but also specifically enumerates certain rights and liberties of the people. Moreover, the Ninth Amendment to the U.S. Constitution makes it clear that this enumeration of rights does not in any way deny or limit other rights that the people retain.

All other law in the United States is subordinate to the Federal Constitution. No law, Federal or State, is valid if it violates the Federal Constitution. Under the principle of **judicial review**, the Supreme Court of the United States determines the constitutionality of *all* laws.

JUDICIAL LAW

The U.S. legal system is a **common law system**, first developed in England. It relies heavily on the judiciary as a source of law and on the **adversary system** for the adjudication of disputes. In an adversary system the parties, not the court, must initiate and conduct litigation. This approach is based upon the belief that the truth is more likely to emerge from the investigation and presentation of evidence by two opposing parties, both motivated by self-interest, than from judicial investigation motivated only by official duty. Other English-speaking countries, including England, Canada, and Australia, also use the common law system.

In distinct contrast to the common law system are civil law systems, which are based on Roman law. **Civil law systems** depend on comprehensive legislative enactments (called codes) and an inquisitorial method of adjudication. In the **inquisitorial system**, the judiciary initiates litigation, investigates pertinent facts, and conducts the presentation of evidence. The civil law system prevails in most of Europe, Scotland, the State of Louisiana, the province of Quebec, Latin America, and parts of Africa and Asia.

COMMON LAW The courts in common law systems have developed a body of law, known as "case law," "judge-made law," or "common law," that serves as precedent for determining later controversies. In this sense, common law is distinguished from other sources of law such as legislation and administrative rulings.

To evolve steadily and predictably, the common law has developed by application of *stare decisis* (to stand by the decisions). Under the principle of ***stare decisis***, courts, in deciding cases, adhere to and rely on rules of law that they or superior courts announced and applied in prior decisions involving similar cases. Judicial decisions thus have two uses: (1) to determine with finality the case currently being decided and (2) to indicate how the courts will decide similar cases in the future. *Stare decisis* does not, however, preclude courts from correcting erroneous decisions or from choosing among conflicting precedents. Thus, the doctrine allows sufficient flexibility for the common law to change.

The strength of the common law is its ability to adapt to change without losing its sense of direction. As Justice Cardozo said, "The inn that shelters for the night is not the journey's end. The law, like the traveler, must be ready for the morrow. It must have a principle of growth."

EQUITY As the common law developed in England, it became overly rigid and beset with technicalities. Consequently, in many cases the courts provided no remedies because the judges insisted that a claim must fall within one of the recognized forms of action. Moreover, courts of common law could provide only limited remedies; the principal type of relief obtainable was a monetary judgment. Consequently, individuals who could not obtain adequate relief from monetary awards began to petition the king directly for justice. He, in turn, came to delegate these petitions to his chancellor.

Gradually, there evolved a supplementary system of judicial relief for those who had no adequate remedy at common law. This new system, called **equity**, was administered by a court of chancery presided over by a chancellor. The chancellor, deciding cases on "equity and good conscience," afforded relief in many instances in which common law judges had refused to act or in which the remedy at law was inadequate. Thus, two systems of law administered by different tribunals developed side by side: the common law courts and the courts of equity.

An important difference between law and equity was that the chancellor could issue a **decree**, or order, compelling a defendant to do or refrain from doing a specific act. A defendant who did not comply with the order could be held in contempt of court and punished by fine or imprisonment. This power of compulsion available in a court of equity opened the door to many needed remedies not available in a court of common law.

Equity jurisdiction, in some cases, recognized rights that were enforceable at common law but for which equity provided more effective remedies. For example, in a court of equity, for breach of a land contract, the buyer could obtain a decree of **specific performance** commanding the defendant seller to perform his part of the contract by transferring title to the land. Another powerful and effective remedy available only in the courts of equity was the **injunction**, a court order requiring a party to do or refrain from doing a specified act. Still another remedy not available elsewhere was **reformation**, in which case, upon the ground of mutual mistake, contracting parties could bring an action to reform or change the language of a written agreement to conform to their actual intentions. Finally, an action for **rescission** of a contract allowed a party to invalidate a contract under certain circumstances.

Although courts of equity provided remedies not available in courts of law, they granted such remedies only at their discretion, not as a matter of right. The courts exercised this discretion according to the general legal principles, or

maxims, that they formulated over the years. A few of these familiar maxims of equity are the following: equity will not suffer a wrong to be without a remedy. Equity regards the substance rather than the form. Equity abhors a forfeiture. Equity delights to do justice and not by halves. He who comes into equity must come with clean hands. He who seeks equity must do equity.

In nearly every jurisdiction in the United States, courts of common law and courts of equity have united to form a single court that administers both systems of law. Vestiges of the old division remain, however. For example, the right to a trial by jury applies only to actions at law but not, under Federal law and in almost every State, to suits filed in equity.

Restatements of Law The common law of the United States results from the independent decisions of the State and Federal courts. The rapid increase in the number of decisions by these courts led to the establishment of the American Law Institute (ALI) in 1923. The ALI was composed of a distinguished group of lawyers, judges, and law professors who set out to prepare

> an orderly restatement of the general common law of the United States, including in that term not only the law developed solely by judicial decision, but also the law that has grown from the application by the courts of statutes that were generally enacted and were in force for many years. Wolk in, "Restatements of the Law: Origin, Preparation, Availability," 21 *Ohio B.A. Rept.* 663 (1940).

Currently the ALI is made up of more than 4,300 lawyers, judges, and law professors.

Regarded as the authoritative statement of the common law of the United States, the Restatements cover many important areas of the common law, including torts, contracts, agency, property, and trusts. Although not law in themselves, they are highly persuasive and frequently have been used by courts in support of their opinions. Because they state much of the common law concisely and clearly, relevant portions of the Restatements are frequently relied upon in this book.

LEGISLATIVE LAW

Since the end of the nineteenth century, legislation has become the primary source of new law and ordered social change in the United States. The annual volume of legislative law is enormous. Justice Felix Frankfurter's remarks to the New York City Bar in 1947 are even more appropriate in the twenty-first century:

> Inevitably the work of the Supreme Court reflects the great shift in the center of gravity of law-making.

Broadly speaking, the number of cases disposed of by opinions has not changed from term to term. But even as late as 1875 more than 40 percent of the controversies before the Court were common-law litigation, fifty years later only 5 percent, while today cases not resting on statutes are reduced almost to zero. It is therefore accurate to say that courts have ceased to be the primary makers of law in the sense in which they "legislated" the common law. It is certainly true of the Supreme Court that almost every case has a statute at its heart or close to it.

This modern emphasis upon legislative or statutory law has occurred because common law, which develops evolutionarily and haphazardly, is not well suited for making drastic or comprehensive changes. Moreover, courts tend to be hesitant about overruling prior decisions, whereas legislatures frequently repeal prior enactments. In addition, legislatures are independent and able to choose the issues they wish to address, while courts may deal only with issues that arise in actual cases. As a result, legislatures are better equipped to make the dramatic, sweeping, and relatively rapid changes in the law that enable it to respond to numerous and vast technological, social, and economic innovations.

While some business law topics, such as contracts, agency, property, and trusts, still are governed principally by the common law, most areas of commercial law have become largely statutory, including partnerships, corporations, sales, commercial paper, secured transactions, insurance, securities regulation, antitrust, and bankruptcy. Because most States enacted statutes dealing with these branches of commercial law, a great diversity developed among the States and hampered the conduct of commerce on a national scale. The increased need for greater uniformity led to the development of a number of proposed uniform laws that would reduce the conflicts among State laws.

The most successful example is the **Uniform Commercial Code** (UCC), which was prepared under the joint sponsorship and direction of the ALI and the Uniform Law Commission (ULC), which is also known as the National Conference of Commissioners on Uniform State Laws (NCCUSL). (Selected provisions of the Code are set forth in Appendix B of this book.) All fifty States (although Louisiana has adopted only part of it), the District of Columbia, and the Virgin Islands have adopted the UCC. The underlying purposes and policies of the Code are as follows:

1. simplify, clarify, and modernize the law governing commercial transactions;
2. permit the continued expansion of commercial practices through custom, usage, and agreement of the parties; and
3. make uniform the law among the various jurisdictions.

The ULC has drafted more than three hundred uniform laws, including the Uniform Partnership Act, the Uniform Limited Partnership Act, and the Uniform Probate Code. The ALI has developed a number of model statutory formulations, including the Model Code of Evidence, the Model Penal Code, a Model Land Development Code, and a proposed Federal Securities Code. In addition, the American Bar Association has promulgated the Model Business Corporation Act.

TREATIES A **treaty** is an agreement between or among independent nations. Article II of the U.S. Constitution authorizes the President to enter into treaties with the advice and consent of the Senate, "providing two thirds of the Senators present concur."

Only the Federal government, not the States, may enter into treaties. A treaty signed by the President and approved by the Senate has the legal force of a Federal statute. Accordingly, a Federal treaty may supersede a prior Federal statute, while a Federal statute may supersede a prior treaty. Like statutes, treaties are subordinate to the Federal Constitution and subject to judicial review.

EXECUTIVE ORDERS In addition to his executive functions, the President of the United States also has authority to issue laws, which are called **executive orders**. Typically, Federal legislation specifically delegates this authority. An executive order may amend, revoke, or supersede a prior executive order. An example of an executive order is the one issued by President Johnson in 1965 prohibiting discrimination by Federal contractors on the basis of race, color, sex, religion, or national origin in employment on any work the contractor performed during the period of the Federal contract.

The governors of most States enjoy comparable authority to issue executive orders.

ADMINISTRATIVE LAW

Administrative law is the branch of public law that is created by administrative agencies in the form of rules, regulations, orders, and decisions to carry out the regulatory powers and duties of those agencies. Administrative functions and activities concern matters of national safety, welfare, and convenience, including the establishment and maintenance of military forces, police, citizenship and naturalization, taxation, coinage of money, elections, environmental protection, and the regulation of transportation, interstate highways, waterways, television, radio, trade and commerce, and, in general, public health, safety, and welfare.

To accommodate the increasing complexity of the social, economic, and industrial life of the nation, the scope of administrative law has expanded enormously. Justice Jackson stated that "the rise of administrative bodies has been the most significant legal trend of the last century, and perhaps more values today are affected by their decisions than by those of all the courts, review of administrative decisions apart." *Federal Trade Commission v. Ruberoid Co.*, 343 U.S. 470 (1952). This is evidenced by the great increase in the number and activities of Federal government boards, commissions, and other agencies. Certainly, agencies create more legal rules and adjudicate more controversies than all the legislatures and courts combined.

LEGAL ANALYSIS

Decisions in State trial courts generally are not reported or published. The precedent a trial court sets is not sufficiently weighty to warrant permanent reporting. Except in New York and a few other States where selected trial court opinions are published, decisions in trial courts are simply filed in the office of the clerk of the court, where they are available for public inspection. Decisions of State courts of appeals are published in consecutively numbered volumes called "reports." Court decisions are found in the official State reports of most States. In addition, West Publishing Company publishes State reports in a regional reporter, called the National Reporter System, composed of the following: Atlantic (A., A.2d, or A.3d), South Eastern (S.E. or S.E.2d), South Western (S.W., S.W.2d, or S.W.3d), New York Supplement (N.Y.S. or N.Y.S.2d), North Western (N.W. or N.W.2d), North Eastern (N.E. or N.E.2d), Southern (So., So.2d, or So.3d), Pacific (P., P.2d, or P.3d), and California Reporter (Cal.Rptr., Cal.Rptr.2d, or Cal.Rptr.3d). At least twenty States no longer publish official reports and have designated a commercial reporter as the authoritative source of State case law. After they are published, these opinions, or "cases," are referred to ("cited") by giving (1) the name of the case; (2) the volume, name, and page of the official State report, if any, in which it is published; (3) the volume, name, and page of the particular set and series of the National Reporter System; and (4) the volume, name, and page of any other selected case series. For instance, *Lefkowitz v. Great Minneapolis Surplus Store, Inc.*, 251 Minn. 188, 86 N.W.2d 689 (1957) indicates that the opinion in this case may be found in Volume 251 of the official Minnesota Reports at page 188; and in Volume 86 of the North Western Reporter, Second Series, at page 689.

The decisions of courts in the Federal system are found in a number of reports. U.S. District Court opinions appear in the Federal Supplement (F.Supp. or F.Supp.2d). Decisions of the U.S. Court of Appeals are found in the Federal Reporter (Fed., F.2d, or F.3d), and the U.S. Supreme Court's opinions are published in the U.S. Supreme Court Reports (U.S.), Supreme Court Reporter (S.Ct.), and Lawyers Edition (L.Ed.).

While all U.S. Supreme Court decisions are reported, not every case decided by the U.S. District Courts and the U.S. Courts of Appeals is reported. Each circuit has established rules determining which decisions are published.

In reading the title of a case, such as "*Jones v. Brown*," the "v." or "vs." means "versus" or "against." In the trial court, Jones is the **plaintiff**, the person who filed the suit, and Brown is the **defendant**, the person against whom the suit was brought. When a case is appealed, some, but not all, courts of appeals place the name of the party who appeals, or the **appellant**, first, so that "*Jones v. Brown*" in the trial court becomes, if Brown loses and becomes the appellant, "*Brown v. Jones*" in the appellate court. But because some appellate courts retain the trial court order of names, determining from the title itself who was the plaintiff and who was the defendant is not always possible. The student must read the facts of each case carefully and clearly identify each party in her mind to understand the discussion by the appellate court. In a criminal case, the caption in the trial court will first designate the prosecuting government unit and then will indicate the defendant, as in "*State v. Jones*" or "*Commonwealth v. Brown*."

The study of reported cases requires the student to understand and apply legal analysis. Normally, the reported opinion in a case sets forth (1) the essential facts, the nature of the action, the parties, what happened to bring about the controversy, what happened in the lower court, and what pleadings are material to the issues; (2) the issues of law or fact; (3) the legal principles involved; (4) the application of these principles; and (5) the decision.

A serviceable method by which students may analyze and brief cases after reading and comprehending the opinion is to write a brief containing the following:

1. the facts of the case,
2. the issue or question involved,
3. the decision of the court, and
4. the reasons for the decision.

By way of example, the edited case of *Ryan v. Friesenhahn* (see *Case 1-1*) is presented after the chapter summary and then briefed using the suggested format.

◆ SEE CASE 1-1

You can and should use this same legal analysis when learning the substantive concepts presented in this text and applying them to the end-of-chapter questions and case problems. By way of example, in a number of chapters throughout the text we have included a boxed feature called **Applying the Law**, which provides a systematic legal analysis of a single concept learned in the chapter. This feature begins with the **facts** of a hypothetical case, followed by an identification of the broad legal **issue** presented by those facts. We then state the **rule of law**—or applicable legal principles, including definitions, which aid in resolving the legal issue—and **apply** it to the facts. Finally we state a legal **conclusion**, or decision in the case. An example of this type of legal analysis follows.

APPLYING THE LAW

Introduction to Law

FACTS Jackson bought a new car and planned to sell his old one for about $2,500. But before he did so, he happened to receive a call from his cousin, Trina, who had just graduated from college. Among other things, Trina told Jackson she needed a car but did not have much money. Feeling generous, Jackson told Trina he would give her his old car. But the next day a coworker offered Jackson $3,500 for his old car, and Jackson sold it to the coworker.

ISSUE Did Jackson have the right to sell his car to the coworker, or legally had he already made a gift of it to Trina?

RULE OF LAW A gift is the transfer of ownership of property from one person to another without anything in return. The person making the gift is called the donor, and the person receiving it is known as the donee. A valid gift requires (1) the donor's present intent to transfer the property and (2) delivery of the property.

APPLICATION In this case, Jackson is the would-be donor and Trina the would-be donee. To find that Jackson had already made a gift of the car to Trina, both Jackson's intent to give it to her and delivery of the car to Trina would need to be demonstrated. It is evident from their telephone conversation that Jackson did intend at that point to give the car to Trina. It is equally apparent from his conduct that he later changed his mind, because he sold it to someone else the next day. Consequently, he did not deliver the car to Trina.

CONCLUSION Because the donor did not deliver the property to the donee, legally no gift was made. Jackson was free to sell the car.

CHAPTER SUMMARY

NATURE OF LAW	**Definition of Law** "a rule of civil conduct prescribed by the supreme power in a state, commanding what is right, and prohibiting what is wrong" (William Blackstone) **Functions of Law** to maintain stability in the social, political, and economic system through dispute resolution, protection of property, and the preservation of the state, while simultaneously permitting ordered change **Legal Sanctions** are means by which the law enforces the decisions of the courts **Law and Morals** are different but overlapping; law provides sanctions, while morals do not **Law and Justice** are separate and distinct concepts; justice is the fair, equitable, and impartial treatment of competing interests with due regard for the common good

CLASSIFICATION OF LAW	**Substantive and Procedural Law** • *Substantive Law* law creating rights and duties • *Procedural Law* rules for enforcing substantive law **Public and Private Law** • *Public Law* law dealing with the relationship between government and individuals • *Private Law* law governing the relationships among individuals and legal entities **Civil and Criminal Law** • *Civil Law* law dealing with rights and duties the violation of which constitutes a wrong against an individual or other legal entity • *Criminal Law* law establishing duties which, if violated, constitute a wrong against the entire community

SOURCES OF LAW	**Constitutional Law** fundamental law of a government establishing its powers and limitations **Judicial Law** • *Common Law* body of law developed by the courts that serves as precedent for determination of later controversies • *Equity* body of law based upon principles distinct from common law and providing remedies not available at law **Legislative Law** statutes adopted by legislative bodies • *Treaties* agreements between or among independent nations • *Executive Orders* laws issued by the President or by the governor of a State **Administrative Law** body of law created by administrative agencies to carry out their regulatory powers and duties

CASES

RYAN v. FRIESENHAHN
Court of Appeals of Texas, 1995
911 S.W.2d 113
http://scholar.google.com/scholar_case?q=911+S.W.2d+113&hl=en&as_sdt=2,34
&case=5075518384525866053&scilh=0

Rickhoff, J.

This is an appeal from a take-nothing summary judgment granted the defendants in a social host liability case. Appellants' seventeen-year-old daughter was killed in a single-car accident after leaving appellees' party in an intoxicated condition. While we hold that the appellants were denied an opportunity to amend their pleadings, we also find that their pleadings stated a cause of action for negligence and negligence per se. We reverse and remand.

Todd Friesenhahn, son of Nancy and Frederick Friesenhahn, held an "open invitation" party at his parents' home that encouraged guests to "bring your own bottle." Sabrina Ryan attended the party, became intoxicated, and was involved in a fatal accident after she left the event. According to the Ryans' petition, Nancy and Frederick Friesenhahn were aware of this activity and of Sabrina's condition.

Sandra and Stephen Ryan, acting in their individual and representative capacities, sued the Friesenhahns for wrongful death, negligence, and gross negligence. * * *

* * *

a. The Petition The Ryans pled, in their third amended petition, that Todd Friesenhahn planned a "beer bust" that was advertised by posting general invitations in the community for a party to be held on the "Friesenhahn Property." The invitation was open and general and invited persons to "B.Y.O.B." (bring your own bottle). According to the petition, the Friesenhahns had actual or constructive notice of the party and the conduct of the minors in "possessing, exchanging, and consuming alcoholic beverages."

The Ryans alleged that the Friesenhahns were negligent in (1) allowing the party to be held on the Friesenhahn property; (2) directly or indirectly inviting Sabrina to the party; (3) allowing the party to continue on their property "after they knew that minors were in fact possessing, exchanging, and consuming alcohol"; (4) failing "to provide for the proper conduct at the party"; (5) allowing Sabrina to become intoxicated and failing to "secure proper attention and treatment"; (6) and allowing Sabrina to leave the Friesenhahn property while driving a motor vehicle in an intoxicated state. * * *

b. Negligence Per Se Accepting the petition's allegations as true, the Friesenhahns were aware that minors possessed and

consumed alcohol on their property and specifically allowed Sabrina to become intoxicated. The Texas Alcoholic Beverage Code provides that one commits an offense if, with criminal negligence, he "makes available an alcoholic beverage to a minor." [Citation.] The exception for serving alcohol to a minor applies only to the minor's adult parent. [Citation.]

An unexcused violation of a statute constitutes negligence per se if the injured party is a member of the class protected by the statute. [Citation.] The Alcoholic Beverage Code was designed to protect the general public and minors in particular and must be liberally construed. [Citation.] We conclude that Sabrina is a member of the class protected by the Code.

In viewing the Ryans' allegations in the light most favorable to them, we find that they stated a cause of action against the Friesenhahns for the violation of the Alcoholic Beverage Code.

c. Common Law Negligence The elements of negligence include (1) a legal duty owed by one person to another; (2) breach of that duty; and (3) damages proximately caused by the breach. [Citation.] To determine whether a common law duty exists, we must consider several factors, including risk, foreseeability, and likelihood of injury weighed against the social utility of the defendant's conduct, the magnitude of the burden of guarding against the injury and consequences of placing that burden on the defendant. [Citation.] We may also consider whether one party has superior knowledge of the risk, and whether one party has the right to control the actor whose conduct precipitated the harm. [Citation.]

As the Supreme Court in [citation] explained, there are two practical reasons for not imposing a third-party duty on social hosts who provide alcohol to adult guests: first, the host cannot reasonably know the extent of his guests' alcohol consumption level; second, the host cannot reasonably be expected to control his guests' conduct. [Citation.] The Tyler court in [citation] relied on these principles in holding that a minor "had no common law duty to avoid making alcohol available to an intoxicated guest [another minor] who he knew would be driving." [Citation.]

We disagree with the Tyler court because the rationale expressed [by the Supreme Court] in [citation] does not apply to the relationship between minors, or adults and minors. The adult social host need not estimate the extent of a minor's alcohol consumption because serving minors any amount of alcohol is a criminal offense. [Citation.] Furthermore, the social host may control the minor, with whom there is a special relationship, analogous to that of parent-child. [Citation.]

* * *

As this case demonstrates, serving minors alcohol creates a risk of injury or death. Under the pled facts, a jury could find that the Friesenhahns, as the adult social hosts, allowed open invitations to a beer bust at their house and they could foresee, or reasonably should have foreseen, that the only means of arriving at their property would be by privately operated vehicles; once there, the most likely means of departure would be by the same means. That adults have superior knowledge of the risk of drinking should be apparent from the legislature's decision to allow persons to become adults on their eighteenth birthday for all purposes but the consumption of alcohol. [Citations.]

While one adult has no general duty to control the behavior of another adult, one would hope that adults would exercise special diligence in supervising minors—even during a simple swimming pool party involving potentially dangerous but legal activities. We may have no special duty to watch one adult to be sure he can swim, but it would be ill-advised to turn loose young children without insuring they can swim. When the "party" is for the purpose of engaging in dangerous and illicit activity, the consumption of alcohol by minors, adults certainly have a greater duty of care. [Citation.]

* * * Accordingly, we find that the Ryans' petition stated a common-law cause of action.

* * *

We reverse and remand the trial court's summary judgment.

Brief of Ryan v. Friesenhahn

I. Facts
Todd Friesenhahn, son of Nancy and Frederick Friesenhahn, held an open invitation party at his parents' home that encouraged guests to bring their own bottle. Sabrina Ryan attended the party, became intoxicated, and was involved in a fatal accident after she left the party. Sandra and Stephen Ryan, Sabrina's parents, sued the Friesenhahns for negligence, alleging that the Friesenhahns were aware of underage drinking at the party and of Sabrina's condition when she left the party. The trial court granted summary judgment for the Friesenhahns.

II. Issue
Is a social host who serves alcoholic beverages to a minor liable in negligence for harm suffered by the minor as a result of the minor's intoxication?

III. Decision
In favor of the Ryans. Summary judgment reversed and case remanded to the trial court.

IV. Reasons
Accepting the Ryans' allegations as true, the Friesenhahns were aware that minors possessed and consumed alcohol on their property and specifically allowed Sabrina to become intoxicated. The Texas Alcoholic Beverage Code provides that a person commits an offense if, with criminal negligence, he "makes available an alcoholic beverage to a minor." A violation of a statute constitutes negligence per se if the injured party is a member of the class protected by the statute. Since the Alcoholic Beverage Code was designed to protect the general public and minors in particular, Sabrina is a member of the class protected by the Code. Therefore, we find that the Ryans stated a cause of action against the Friesenhahns for the violation of the Alcoholic Beverage Code.

In considering common-law negligence as a basis for social host liability, the Texas Supreme Court has held that there are two practical reasons for not imposing a third-party duty on social hosts who provide alcohol to adult guests: first, the host cannot reasonably know the extent of his guests' alcohol consumption level; second, the host cannot reasonably be expected to control his guests' conduct. However, this rationale does not apply where the guest is a minor. The adult social host need not estimate the extent of a minor's alcohol consumption because serving minors any amount of alcohol is a criminal offense. Furthermore, the social host may control the minor, with whom there is a special relationship, analogous to that of parent-child.

CHAPTER 2

CIVIL DISPUTE RESOLUTION

CHAPTER OUTCOMES

After reading and studying this chapter, you should be able to:

- List and describe the courts in the Federal court system and in a typical State court system.

- Distinguish among exclusive Federal jurisdiction, concurrent Federal jurisdiction, and exclusive State jurisdiction.

- Distinguish among (1) subject matter jurisdiction and jurisdiction over the parties and (2) the three types of jurisdiction over the parties.

- List and explain the various stages of a civil proceeding.

- Compare and contrast litigation, arbitration, conciliation, and mediation.

As discussed in *Chapter 1*, substantive law establishes the rights and duties of individuals and other legal entities while procedural law determines the means by which these rights are asserted. Procedural law attempts to accomplish two competing objectives: (1) to be fair and impartial, and (2) to operate efficiently. The judicial process in the United States represents a balance between these two objectives as well as a commitment to the adversary system.

The first part of this chapter describes the structure and function of the Federal and State court systems. The second part of this chapter deals with jurisdiction; the third part discusses civil dispute resolution, including the procedure in civil lawsuits.

THE COURT SYSTEM

Courts are impartial tribunals (seats of judgment) established by government bodies to settle disputes. A court may render a binding decision only when it has jurisdiction over the dispute and the parties to that dispute; that is, when it has a right to hear and make a judgment in a case. The United States has a dual court system: The Federal government has its own independent system, as does each of the fifty States plus the District of Columbia.

THE FEDERAL COURTS

Article III of the U.S. Constitution states that the judicial power of the United States shall be vested in one Supreme

Court and such lower courts as Congress may establish. Congress has established a lower Federal court system consisting of a number of special courts, district courts, and courts of appeals. The Federal court system is staffed by judges who receive lifetime appointments from the President, subject to confirmation by the Senate.

◆ **SEE FIGURE 3-1: Federal Judicial System**

DISTRICT COURTS

The district courts are the general trial courts in the Federal system. Most cases begin in a district court, and it is here that issues of fact are decided. The district court is generally presided over by *one* judge, although in certain cases three judges preside. In a few cases, an appeal from a judgment or decree of a district court is taken directly to the Supreme Court. In most cases, however, appeals go to the Circuit Court of Appeals of the appropriate circuit, the decision of which, in most cases, is final.

Congress has established ninety-four judicial districts, each of which is located entirely in a particular State. All States have at least one district, whereas certain States contain more than one. For instance, New York has four districts, Illinois has three, and Wisconsin has two, whereas a number of less populated States each make up a single district.

COURTS OF APPEALS

Congress has established twelve judicial circuits (eleven numbered circuits plus the D.C. Circuit), each having a

◆ **FIGURE 3-1: Federal Judicial System**

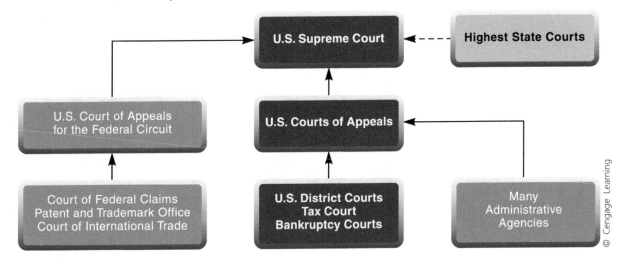

court known as the Court of Appeals, which primarily hears appeals from the district courts located within its circuit. In addition, these courts review decisions of many administrative agencies, the Tax Court, and the Bankruptcy Court. Congress has also established the U.S. Court of Appeals for the Federal Circuit, which is discussed in the section on "Special Courts." The U.S. Courts of Appeals generally hear cases in panels of *three* judges, although in some instances all of the judges of the circuit will sit *en banc* to decide a case.

The function of appellate courts is to examine the record of a case on appeal and to determine whether the trial court committed prejudicial error. If so, the appellate court will **reverse** or **modify** the judgment and if necessary **remand** it (send it back) to the lower court for further proceeding. If no prejudicial error exists, the appellate court will **affirm** the decision of the lower court.

◆ **SEE FIGURE 3-2: Circuit Courts of the United States**

THE SUPREME COURT

The nation's highest tribunal is the U.S. Supreme Court, which consists of nine justices (a Chief Justice and eight Associate Justices) who sit as a group in Washington, D.C. A quorum consists of any six justices. In certain types of cases, the U.S. Supreme Court has original jurisdiction (the right to hear a case first). The Court's principal function, nonetheless, is to review decisions of the Federal Courts of Appeals and, in some instances, decisions involving Federal law made by the highest State courts. Cases reach the Supreme Court under its appellate jurisdiction by one of two routes. Very few come by way of **appeal by right**—cases the Court must hear should a party request the review. In 1988, Congress

enacted legislation that almost completely eliminated the right to appeal to the U.S. Supreme Court.

The second way in which the Supreme Court may review a decision of a lower court is by the discretionary **writ of certiorari**, which requires a lower court to produce the records of a case it has tried. Now almost all cases reaching the Supreme Court come to it by means of writs of *certiorari*. The Court uses the writ as a device to choose the cases it wishes to hear. The Court grants writs for cases involving a Federal question of substantial importance or a conflict in the decisions of the U.S. Circuit Courts of Appeals. Only a small percentage of the petitions to the Supreme Court for review by *certiorari* are granted, however. The vote of four justices is required to grant a writ.

SPECIAL COURTS

The special courts in the Federal judicial system include the U.S. Court of Federal Claims, the U.S. Tax Court, the U.S. Bankruptcy Courts, and the U.S. Court of Appeals for the Federal Circuit. These courts have jurisdiction over particular subject matter. The U.S. Court of Federal Claims has national jurisdiction to hear claims against the United States. The U.S. Tax Court has national jurisdiction over certain cases involving Federal taxes. The U.S. Bankruptcy Courts have jurisdiction to hear and decide certain matters under the Federal Bankruptcy Act, subject to review by the U.S. District Court. The U.S. Court of Appeals for the Federal Circuit has nationwide jurisdiction and reviews decisions of the Court of Federal Claims, the Patent and Trademark Office, the U.S. Court of International Trade, the Merit Systems Protection Board, and the U.S. Court of Veterans Appeals, as well as patent cases decided by the U.S. District Court.

◆ **FIGURE 3-2: Circuit Courts of the United States**

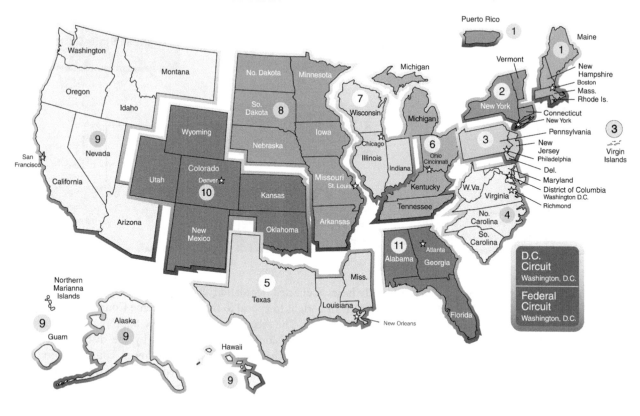

Source: Administrative Office of The United States Courts, January 1983

STATE COURTS

Each of the fifty States and the District of Columbia has its own court system. In most States the voters elect judges for a stated term.

◆ **SEE FIGURE 3-3: State Court System**

INFERIOR TRIAL COURTS

At the bottom of the State court system are the **inferior trial courts**, which decide the least serious criminal and civil matters. Usually, inferior trial courts do not keep a complete written record of trial proceedings. Such courts, which are referred to as municipal courts, justice of the peace courts, or traffic courts, hear minor criminal cases such as traffic offenses. They also conduct preliminary hearings in more serious criminal cases.

Small claims courts are inferior trial courts that hear civil cases involving a limited amount of money. Usually there is no jury, the procedure is informal, and neither side employs an attorney. An appeal from small claims court is taken to the trial court of general jurisdiction, where a new trial (called a trial *de novo*), in which the small claims court's decision is given no weight, is begun.

TRIAL COURTS

Each State has trial courts of general jurisdiction, which may be called county, district, superior, circuit, or common pleas courts. (In New York the trial court is called the Supreme Court.) These courts do not have a dollar limitation on their jurisdiction in civil cases and hear all criminal cases other than minor offenses. Unlike the inferior trial courts, these trial courts of general jurisdiction maintain formal records of their proceedings as procedural safeguards.

SPECIAL COURTS

Many States have special courts that have jurisdiction over particular areas. For example, many States have probate courts with jurisdiction over the administration of wills and estates. Many States also have family courts, which have jurisdiction over divorce and child custody cases. Appeals from these special courts go to the general State appellate courts.

APPELLATE COURTS

At the summit of the State court system is the State's court of last resort, a reviewing court generally called the Supreme Court of the State. Except for those cases in which review by

◆ **FIGURE 3-3: State Court System**

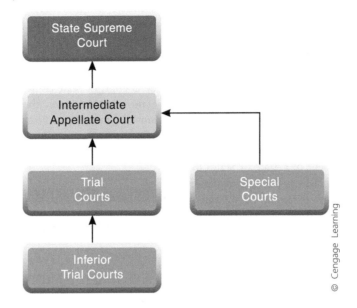

the U.S. Supreme Court is available, the decision of the highest State tribunal is final. Most States also have created intermediate appellate courts to handle the large volume of cases seeking review. Review by such a court is usually by right. Further review is in most cases at the highest court's discretion.

JURISDICTION

Jurisdiction means the power or authority of a court to hear and decide a given case. To resolve a lawsuit, a court must have two kinds of jurisdiction. The first is subject matter jurisdiction. Where a court lacks jurisdiction over the subject matter of a case, no action it takes in the case will have legal effect.

The second kind of jurisdiction is over the parties to a lawsuit. This jurisdiction is required for the court to render an enforceable judgment that affects the rights and duties of the parties to the lawsuit. A court usually may obtain jurisdiction over the defendant if she lives and is present in the court's territory or if the transaction giving rise to the case has a substantial connection to the court's territory. The court obtains jurisdiction over the plaintiff when he voluntarily submits to the court's power by filing a complaint with the court.

SUBJECT MATTER JURISDICTION

Subject matter jurisdiction refers to the authority of a particular court to adjudicate a controversy of a particular kind. Federal courts have *limited* subject matter jurisdiction, as set forth in the U.S. Constitution, Article III, Section 2. State courts have jurisdiction over *all* matters that the Constitution or Congress has not given exclusively to the Federal courts or expressly denied the State courts.

FEDERAL JURISDICTION

The Federal courts have, to the exclusion of the State courts, subject matter jurisdiction over some areas. Such jurisdiction is called **exclusive Federal jurisdiction**. Federal jurisdiction is exclusive only if Congress so provides, either explicitly or implicitly. If Congress does not so provide and the area is one over which Federal courts have subject matter jurisdiction, they share this jurisdiction with the State courts. Such jurisdiction is known as **concurrent Federal jurisdiction**.

EXCLUSIVE FEDERAL JURISDICTION The Federal courts have exclusive jurisdiction over Federal criminal prosecutions; admiralty, bankruptcy, antitrust, patent, trademark, and copyright cases; suits against the United States; and cases arising under certain Federal statutes that expressly provide for exclusive Federal jurisdiction.

CONCURRENT FEDERAL JURISDICTION The two types of concurrent Federal jurisdiction are Federal question jurisdiction and diversity jurisdiction. The first arises whenever there is a Federal question over which the Federal courts do not have exclusive jurisdiction. A **Federal question** is any case arising under the Constitution, statutes, or treaties of the United States. For a case to be treated as "arising under" Federal law, either Federal law must create the plaintiff's cause of action or the plaintiff's right to relief must depend upon the resolution of a substantial question of Federal law in dispute between the parties. There is no minimum dollar requirement in Federal question cases. When a State court hears a concurrent Federal question case, it applies Federal substantive law, but its own procedural rules.

The second type of concurrent jurisdiction—diversity jurisdiction—arises in cases in which there is "diversity of citizenship" *and* the amount in controversy exceeds $75,000. Then private litigants may bring an action in a Federal district court or a State court. **Diversity of citizenship** exists (1) when the plaintiffs are all citizens of a State or States different from the State or States of which the defendants are citizens; (2) when a foreign country brings an action against citizens of the United States; or (3) when the controversy is between citizens of a State and citizens of a foreign country. The citizenship of an individual litigant is the State in which the litigant resides or is domiciled, whereas that of a corporate litigant is both the State of incorporation and the State in which its principal place of business is located. For example, if the amount in controversy exceeds $75,000, then diversity of citizenship jurisdiction would be satisfied if Ada, a citizen of California, sues Bob, a citizen of Idaho. If, however, Carol, a citizen of Virginia, and Dianne, a citizen of North Carolina, sue Evan, a citizen of Georgia, and Farley, a citizen of North Carolina, diversity of citizenship would not exist because both Dianne, a plaintiff, and Farley, a defendant, are citizens of North Carolina.

The $75,000 jurisdictional requirement is satisfied if the plaintiff makes a good faith claim to the amount in the complaint, unless it is clear to a legal certainty that the claim does not exceed the required amount.

When a Federal district court hears a case solely under diversity of citizenship jurisdiction, no Federal question is involved, and, accordingly, the Federal court must apply substantive State law. The conflict of laws rules of the State in which the district court is located determine which State's substantive law the court will use. (Conflict of laws is discussed later.) Federal courts apply Federal procedural rules in diversity cases.

In any case involving concurrent jurisdiction, the plaintiff has the choice of bringing the action in either an appropriate Federal court or State court. If the plaintiff brings the case in a State court, however, the defendant usually may have it **removed** (shifted) to a Federal court for the district in which the State court is located.

◆ SEE CASE 3-1

PRACTICAL ADVICE

If you have the option, consider whether you want to bring your lawsuit in a Federal or State court.

STATE JURISDICTION

EXCLUSIVE STATE JURISDICTION The State courts have exclusive jurisdiction over *all other matters* not granted to the Federal courts in the Constitution or by Congress. Accordingly, exclusive State jurisdiction would include cases involving diversity of citizenship where the amount in controversy is $75,000 or less. In addition, the State courts have exclusive jurisdiction over all cases to which Federal judicial power does not reach. These matters include, but are by no means limited to, property, torts, contracts, agency, commercial transactions, and most crimes.

◆ SEE FIGURE 3-4: **Federal and State Jurisdiction**

◆ SEE FIGURE 3-5: **Subject Matter Jurisdiction**

CHOICE OF LAW IN STATE COURTS A court in one State may be a proper forum for a case even though some or all of the relevant events occurred in another State. For example, a

◆ FIGURE 3-4: **Federal and State Jurisdiction**

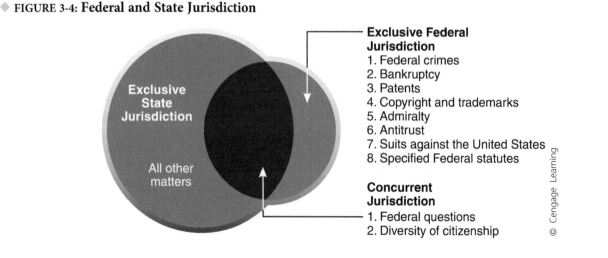

◆ FIGURE 3-5: **Subject Matter Jurisdiction**

Types of Jurisdiction	Court	Substantive Law Applied	Procedural Law Applied
Exclusive Federal	Federal	Federal	Federal
Concurrent: Federal Question	Federal	Federal	Federal
	State	Federal	State
Concurrent: Diversity	Federal	State	Federal
	State	State	State
Exclusive State	State	State	State

© Cengage Learning

California plaintiff may sue a Washington defendant in Washington over a car accident that occurred in Oregon. Because of Oregon's connections to the accident, Washington may choose, under its **conflict of laws rules**, to apply the substantive law of Oregon. Conflict of laws rules vary from State to State.

PRACTICAL ADVICE

Consider including in your contracts a choice-of-law provision specifying which jurisdiction's law will apply.

STARE DECISIS IN THE DUAL COURT SYSTEM

The doctrine of *stare decisis* presents certain problems when there are two parallel court systems. Consequently, in the United States, *stare decisis* functions approximately as follows:

1. The U.S. Supreme Court has never held itself to be bound rigidly by its own decisions, and lower Federal courts and State courts have followed that course with respect to their own decisions.
2. A decision of the U.S. Supreme Court on a Federal question is binding on all other courts, Federal or State.
3. On a Federal question, although a decision of a Federal court other than the Supreme Court may be persuasive in a State court, the decision is not binding.
4. A decision of a State court may be persuasive in the Federal courts, but it is not binding except in cases in which Federal jurisdiction is based on diversity of citizenship. In such a case the Federal courts must apply State law as determined by the highest State court.
5. Decisions of the Federal courts (other than the U.S. Supreme Court) are not binding upon other Federal courts of equal or inferior rank, unless the latter owe obedience to the deciding court. For example, a decision of the Fifth Circuit Court of Appeals binds district courts in the Fifth Circuit but binds no other Federal court.

6. A decision of a State court is binding upon all courts inferior to it in its jurisdiction. Thus, the decision of the highest court in a State binds all other courts in that State.
7. A decision of a State court is not binding on courts in other States except in cases in which the latter courts are required, under their conflict of laws rules, to apply the law of the former State as determined by the highest court in that State. For example, if a North Carolina court is required to apply Virginia law, it must follow decisions of the Supreme Court of Virginia.

◆ SEE FIGURE 3-6: *Stare Decisis* **in the Dual Court System**

JURISDICTION OVER THE PARTIES

In addition to subject matter jurisdiction, a court also must have jurisdiction over the parties, which is the power to bind the parties involved in the dispute. The court obtains jurisdiction over the *plaintiff* when she voluntarily submits to the court's power by filing a complaint with the court. A court may obtain jurisdiction over the *defendant* in three possible ways: (1) *in personam* jurisdiction, (2) *in rem* jurisdiction, or (3) attachment jurisdiction. In addition, the exercise of jurisdiction over a defendant must satisfy the constitutionally imposed requirements of due process: reasonable notification and a reasonable opportunity to be heard. Moreover, the court's exercise of jurisdiction over a defendant is valid under the Due Process Clause of the U.S. Constitution only if the defendant has minimum contacts with the State sufficient to prevent the court's assertion of jurisdiction from offending "traditional notions of fair play and substantial justice." For a court constitutionally to assert jurisdiction over a defendant, the defendant must have engaged in either purposeful acts in the State or acts outside the State that are of such a nature that the defendant could reasonably foresee being sued in that State. This overriding limitation on jurisdictional power

◆ **FIGURE 3-6:** *Stare Decisis* **in the Dual Court System**

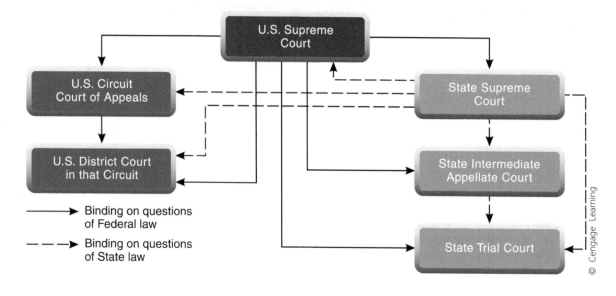

is imposed upon the Federal and State courts through the U.S. Constitution, as discussed more fully in *Chapter 4*.

What notice is due depends on several factors but generally must be "notice reasonably calculated, under the circumstances, to apprise interested parties of the pendency of the action and afford them the opportunity to present their objections."

◆ **SEE CASE 3-2**

IN PERSONAM JURISDICTION

In personam jurisdiction, or **personal jurisdiction**, is jurisdiction of a court over the parties to a lawsuit, in contrast to jurisdiction over their property. A court obtains *in personam* jurisdiction over a defendant either (1) by serving process on the party within the State in which the court is located, or (2) by reasonable notification to a party outside the State in those instances where a "long-arm statute" applies. To *serve process* means to deliver a summons, which is an order to respond to a complaint lodged against a party. (The terms *summons* and *complaint* are explained more fully later in this chapter.)

Personal jurisdiction may be obtained by personally serving a person within a State if that person is domiciled in that State. The U.S. Supreme Court has held that a State may exercise personal jurisdiction over a nonresident defendant who is temporarily present if the defendant is personally served in that State. Personal jurisdiction also may arise from a party's consent. For example, parties to a contract may agree that any dispute concerning that contract will be subject to the jurisdiction of a specific court.

Most States have adopted **long-arm statutes** to expand their jurisdictional reach beyond those persons who may be personally served within the State. These statutes allow courts to obtain jurisdiction over nonresident defendants whose contacts with the State in which the court is located are such that the exercise of jurisdiction does not offend traditional notions of fair play and substantial justice. The typical long-arm statute permits a court to exercise jurisdiction over a defendant, even though process is served beyond its borders, if the defendant (1) has committed a tort (civil wrong) within the State, (2) owns property within the State and that property is the subject matter of the lawsuit, (3) has entered into a contract within the State, or (4) has transacted business within the State and that business is the subject matter of the lawsuit.

PRACTICAL ADVICE

Consider including in your contracts a choice-of-forum provision specifying what court will have jurisdiction over any litigation arising from the contract.

IN REM JURISDICTION

Courts in a State have the jurisdiction to adjudicate claims to property situated within the State if the plaintiff gives those persons who have an interest in the property reasonable notice and an opportunity to be heard. Such jurisdiction over property is called *in rem* jurisdiction, from the Latin word *res*, which means "thing." For example, if Carpenter and Miller are involved in a lawsuit over property located in Kansas, then an appropriate court in Kansas would have *in rem* jurisdiction to adjudicate claims with respect to this property so long as both parties are given notice of the lawsuit and a reasonable opportunity to contest the claim.

ATTACHMENT JURISDICTION

Attachment jurisdiction, or **quasi *in rem* jurisdiction**, is jurisdiction over property rather than over a person. Attachment jurisdiction is invoked by seizing the defendant's property located within the State to obtain payment of a claim against the defendant that is *unrelated* to the property seized. For example, Allen, a resident of Ohio, has obtained a valid judgment in the amount of $20,000 against Bradley, a citizen of Kentucky. Allen can attach Bradley's automobile, which is located in Ohio, to satisfy his court judgment against Bradley.

◆ SEE FIGURE 3-7: **Jurisdiction**

VENUE

Venue, which often is confused with jurisdiction, concerns the geographic area in which a lawsuit *should* be brought. The purpose of venue is to regulate the distribution of cases within a specific court system and to identify a convenient forum. In the Federal court system, venue determines the district or districts in a given State in which a suit may be brought. State rules of venue typically require that a suit be initiated in a county where one of the defendants resides. In matters involving real estate, most venue rules require that a suit be initiated in the county where the property is situated. A defendant, however, may object to the venue for various reasons.

CIVIL DISPUTE RESOLUTION

As mentioned in *Chapter 1*, one of the primary functions of law is to provide for the peaceful resolution of disputes. Accordingly, our legal system has established an elaborate set of government mechanisms to settle disputes. The most prominent of these is judicial dispute resolution, called *litigation*. The rules of civil procedure, discussed in the first part of this section, govern judicial resolution of civil disputes. Judicial resolution of criminal cases is governed by the rules of criminal procedure, which are covered in *Chapter 6*. Dispute resolution by administrative agencies, which is also common, is discussed in *Chapter 5*.

As an alternative to government dispute resolution, several nongovernment methods of dispute resolution, such as arbitration, have developed. These are discussed in the second part of this section.

PRACTICAL ADVICE
If you become involved in litigation, make full disclosure to your attorney and do not discuss the lawsuit without consulting your attorney.

CIVIL PROCEDURE

Civil disputes that enter the judicial system must follow the rules of civil procedure. These rules are designed to resolve the dispute justly, promptly, and inexpensively.

To acquaint the student with civil procedure, it will be helpful to carry a hypothetical action through the trial court to the highest court of review in the State. Although there are

◆ FIGURE 3-7: **Jurisdiction**

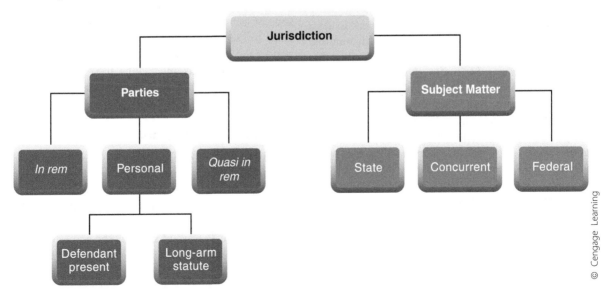

technical differences in trial and appellate procedure among State and Federal courts, the following example will provide a general understanding of the trial and appeal of cases. Assume that Pam Pederson, a pedestrian, while crossing a street in Chicago, is struck by an automobile driven by David Dryden. Pederson suffers serious personal injuries, incurs heavy medical and hospital expenses, and is unable to work for several months. Pederson desires that Dryden pay her for the loss and damages she sustained. After attempts at settlement fail, Pederson brings an action at law against Dryden. Pederson is the plaintiff, and Dryden the defendant. Each is represented by a lawyer. Let us follow the progress of the case.

THE PLEADINGS

The **pleadings** are a series of responsive, formal, written statements in which each side to a lawsuit states its claims and defenses. The purpose of pleadings is to give notice and to establish the issues of fact and law that the parties dispute. An "issue of fact" is a dispute between the parties regarding the events that gave rise to the lawsuit. In contrast, an "issue of law" is a dispute between the parties as to what legal rules apply to these facts. Issues of fact are decided by the jury, or by the judge when there is no jury, whereas issues of law are decided by the judge.

COMPLAINT AND SUMMONS   A lawsuit commences when Pederson, the plaintiff, files with the clerk of the trial court a **complaint** against Dryden which contains (1) a statement of the claim and supporting facts showing that she is entitled to relief, and (2) a demand for that relief. Pederson's complaint alleges that while exercising due and reasonable care for her own safety, she was struck by Dryden's automobile, which was negligently being driven by Dryden, causing her personal injuries and damages of $50,000, for which Pederson requests judgment.

Once the plaintiff has filed a complaint, the clerk issues a **summons** to be served upon the defendant to notify him that a suit has been brought against him. If the defendant has contacts with the State sufficient to show that the State's assertion of jurisdiction over him is constitutional, proper service of the summons establishes the court's jurisdiction over the person of the defendant. The sheriff of the county or a deputy sheriff serves a summons and a copy of the complaint upon Dryden, the defendant, commanding him to file his appearance and answer with the clerk of the court within a specific time, usually thirty days from the date the summons was served. A number of States permit the server to leave a copy of the summons at the defendant's home with a person of "suitable age and discretion." Most long-arm statutes allow service of the summons to be sent to out-of-state defendants by registered mail. If the defendant is a corporation, the statutes typically authorize actual service to the company's general or managing agent. When direct methods of notifying the defendant are unavailable, service by publication may be allowed.

RESPONSES TO COMPLAINT   At this point Dryden has several options. If he fails to respond at all, a **default judgment** will be entered against him for the relief the court determines in a hearing. He may make **pretrial motions** contesting the court's jurisdiction over him or asserting that the action is barred by the statute of limitations, which requires suits to be brought within a specified time. Dryden also may move that the complaint be made more definite and certain, or that the complaint be dismissed for failure to state a claim upon which the court may grant relief. Such a motion, sometimes called a **demurrer**, essentially asserts that even if all of Pederson's allegations were true, she still would not be entitled to the relief she seeks, and that, therefore, there is no need for a trial of the facts. The court rules on this motion as a matter of law. If it rules in favor of the defendant, the plaintiff may appeal the ruling.

If he does not make any pretrial motions, or if they are denied, Dryden will respond to the complaint by filing an **answer**, which may contain admissions, denials, affirmative defenses, and counterclaims. Thus, Dryden might answer the complaint by denying its allegations of negligence and stating, on the other hand, that he, Dryden, was driving his car at a low speed and with reasonable care (a **denial**) when his car struck Pederson (an **admission**), who had dashed across the street in front of Dryden's car without looking in any direction to see whether cars or other vehicles were approaching; that, accordingly, Pederson's injuries were caused by her own negligence (an **affirmative defense**); and that, therefore, she should not be permitted to recover any damages. Dryden might further state that Pederson caused damages to his car and request a judgment for $2,000 (a **counterclaim**). These pleadings create an issue of fact regarding whether Pederson or Dryden, or both, failed to exercise due and reasonable care under the circumstances and were thus negligent and liable for their carelessness.

If the defendant counterclaims, the plaintiff must respond by a **reply**, which may also contain admissions, denials, and affirmative defenses.

PRETRIAL PROCEDURE

JUDGMENT ON PLEADINGS   After the pleadings, either party may move for **judgment on the pleadings**, which requests the judge to rule as a matter of law whether the facts as alleged in the pleadings, which for the purpose of the motion are taken to be as the nonmoving party alleges them, form a sufficient basis to warrant granting the requested relief.

DISCOVERY   In preparation for trial and even before completion of the pleadings stage, each party has the right to obtain relevant evidence, or information that may lead to evidence, from the other party. This procedure is known as **discovery**. It includes (1) pretrial **depositions** consisting of sworn testimony, taken out of court, of the opposing party or other witnesses; (2) sworn answers by the opposing party to **written interrogatories**; (3) **production** of documents and physical objects in the possession of the opposing party or, by a court-ordered subpoena, in the possession of nonparties; (4) a relevant court-ordered physical and/or mental **examination**, by a physician, of the opposing party; and (5) admissions of facts obtained by a **request for admissions** submitted to the opposing party. By properly using discovery, each party may become fully informed of relevant evidence and avoid surprise at trial. Another purpose of this procedure is to encourage and facilitate settlements by providing both parties with as much relevant information as possible.

PRETRIAL CONFERENCE Also furthering these objectives is the **pretrial conference** between the judge and the attorneys representing the parties. The basic purposes of the pretrial conference are (1) to simplify the issues in dispute by amending the pleadings, admitting or stipulating facts, and identifying witnesses and documents to be presented at trial; and (2) to encourage settlement of the dispute without trial. (More than 90 percent of all cases are settled before going to trial.) If no settlement occurs, the judge will enter a pretrial order containing all of the amendments, stipulations, admissions, and other matters agreed to during the pretrial conference. The order supersedes the pleadings and controls the remainder of the trial.

SUMMARY JUDGMENT The evidence disclosed by discovery may be so clear that a trial to determine the facts becomes unnecessary. Thus, after discovery, either party may move for a summary judgment, which requests the judge to rule that, because there are no issues of fact to be determined by trial, the party thus moving should prevail as a matter of law. A **summary judgment** is a final binding determination on the merits made by the judge before a trial.

◆ **SEE CASE 3-3**

TRIAL

In all Federal civil cases at common law involving more than $20, the U.S. Constitution guarantees the right to a jury trial. In addition, nearly every State constitution provides a similar right. In addition, Federal and State statutes may authorize jury trials in cases not within the constitutional guarantees. Under Federal law and in almost all States, jury trials are *not* available in equity cases. Even in cases in which a jury trial is available, the parties may waive (choose not to have) a trial by jury. When a trial is conducted without a jury, the judge serves as the fact finder and will make separate findings of fact and conclusions of law. When a trial is conducted with a jury, the judge determines issues of law and the jury determines questions of fact.

JURY SELECTION Assuming a timely demand for a jury has been made, the trial begins with the selection of a jury. The jury selection process involves a *voir dire*, an examination by the parties' attorneys (or, in some courts, by the judge) of the potential jurors. Each party may make an unlimited number of **challenges for cause**, which prevent a prospective juror from serving if the juror is biased or cannot be fair and impartial. In addition, each party has a limited number of **peremptory challenges**, which allow the party to disqualify a prospective juror without showing cause. The Supreme Court has held that the U.S. Constitution prohibits discrimination in jury selection on the basis of race or gender.

CONDUCT OF TRIAL After the jury has been selected, both attorneys make an **opening statement** concerning the facts that they expect to prove in the trial. The plaintiff and her witnesses then testify upon **direct examination** by the plaintiff's attorney. Each is then subject to **cross-examination** by the defendant's attorney. Thus, in our hypothetical case, the plaintiff and her witnesses testify that the traffic light at the street intersection where Pederson was struck was green for traffic in the direction in which Pederson was crossing but changed to yellow when she was about one-third of the way across the street.

During the trial the judge rules on the admission and exclusion of evidence on the basis of its relevance and reliability. If the judge does not allow certain evidence to be introduced or certain testimony to be given, the attorney must make an offer of proof to preserve the question of admissibility for review on appeal. An **offer of proof** consists of oral statements of counsel or witnesses showing for the record the evidence that the judge has ruled inadmissible; it is not regarded as evidence and is not heard by the jury.

After cross-examination, followed by redirect examination of each of her witnesses, Pederson rests her case. At this point, Dryden may move for a directed verdict in his favor. A **directed verdict** is a final binding determination on the merits made by the judge after a trial but before the jury renders a verdict. If the judge concludes that the evidence introduced by the plaintiff, which is assumed for the purposes of the motion to be true, would not be sufficient for the jury to find in favor of the plaintiff, then the judge will grant the directed verdict in favor of the defendant. In some States, the judge will deny the motion for a directed verdict if there is *any* evidence on which the jury might possibly render a verdict for the plaintiff. If a directed verdict is reversed on appeal, a new trial is necessary.

If the judge denies the motion for a directed verdict, the defendant then has the opportunity to present evidence. The defendant and his witnesses testify that Dryden was driving his car at a low speed when it struck Pederson and that Dryden at the time had the green light at the intersection.

After the defendant has presented his evidence, the plaintiff and the defendant may be permitted to introduce rebuttal evidence. Once both parties have rested (concluded), either party may move for a directed verdict. By this motion the party contends that the evidence is so clear that reasonable persons could not differ as to the outcome of the case. If the judge grants the motion for a directed verdict, he takes the case away from the jury and enters a judgment for the party making the motion.

If the judge denies the motion, the plaintiff's attorney makes a **closing argument** to the jury, reviewing the evidence and urging a verdict in favor of Pederson. Dryden's attorney then makes a closing argument, summarizing the evidence and urging a verdict in favor of Dryden. Pederson's attorney is permitted to make a short argument in rebuttal.

JURY INSTRUCTIONS The attorneys previously have tendered possible written jury instructions on the applicable law to the trial judge, who gives to the jury those instructions he approves and denies those he considers incorrect. The judge also may give the jury instructions of his own. **Jury instructions** (called "charges" in some States) advise the jury of the particular rules of law that apply to the facts the jury determines from the evidence.

VERDICT The jury then retires to the jury room to deliberate and to reach a **general verdict** in favor of one party or the other. If it finds the issues in favor of the defendant, its verdict is that the defendant is not liable. If, however, it finds the issues for the plaintiff and against the defendant, its verdict will hold the defendant liable and will specify the amount of the plaintiff's damages. In this case, the jury found that Pederson's damages were $35,000. Upon returning to the jury box, the foreman either announces the verdict or hands it in written form to the clerk to give to the judge, who reads the general verdict in open court. In some jurisdictions, the jury must reach a **special verdict** by making specific written findings on each factual issue. The judge then applies the law to these findings and renders a judgment. In the United States the prevailing litigant is ordinarily *not* entitled to collect attorneys' fees from the losing party, unless otherwise provided by statute or an enforceable contract allocating attorney's fees.

MOTIONS CHALLENGING THE VERDICT The unsuccessful party then may file a written motion for a new trial or for judgment notwithstanding the verdict. The judge may grant a **motion for a new trial** if (1) the judge committed prejudicial error during the trial, (2) the verdict is against the weight of the evidence, (3) the damages are excessive, or (4) the trial was not fair. The judge has the discretion to grant a motion for a new trial (on grounds 1, 3, or 4) even if substantial evidence supports the verdict. On the other hand, he must deny a motion for judgment notwithstanding the verdict (also called a judgment n.o.v.) if any substantial evidence supports the verdict. This motion is similar to a motion for a directed verdict, only it is made *after* the jury's verdict. To grant the **motion for judgment notwithstanding the verdict**, the judge must decide that the evidence is so clear that reasonable people could not differ as to the outcome of the case. If a judgment n.o.v. is reversed on appeal, a new trial is *not* necessary, and the jury's verdict is entered. If the judge denies the motions for a new trial and for a judgment n.o.v., he enters **judgment on the verdict** for $35,000 in favor of Pederson.

APPEAL

The purpose of an **appeal** is to determine whether the trial court committed prejudicial error. Most jurisdictions permit an appeal only from a final judgment. As a general rule, an appellate court reviews only errors of law. Errors of law include the judge's decisions to admit or exclude evidence; the judge's instructions to the jury; and the judge's actions in denying or granting a motion for a demurrer, a summary judgment, a directed verdict, or a judgment n.o.v. Appellate courts review errors of law *de novo*. An appellate court will reverse errors of fact only if they are so clearly erroneous that the court considers them to constitute an error of law.

Assume that Dryden directs his attorney to appeal. The attorney files a notice of appeal with the clerk of the trial court within the prescribed time. Later, Dryden, as appellant, files in the reviewing court the record on appeal, which contains the pleadings, transcript of the testimony, rulings by the judge on motions made by the parties, arguments of counsel, jury instructions, the verdict, posttrial motions, and the judgment from which the appeal is taken. In States having an intermediate court of appeals, such court usually will be the reviewing court. In States having no intermediate courts of appeal, a party may appeal directly from the trial court to the State supreme court.

Dryden, as appellant, is required to prepare a condensation of the record, known as an abstract, or pertinent excerpts from the record, which he files with the reviewing court together with a brief and argument. His **brief** contains a statement of the facts, the issues, the rulings by the trial court that Dryden contends are erroneous and prejudicial, grounds for reversal of the judgment, a statement of the applicable law, and arguments on his behalf. Pederson, the appellee, files an answering brief and argument. Dryden may, but is not required to, file a reply brief. The case is now ready for consideration by the reviewing court.

The appellate court does not hear any evidence; rather, it decides the case upon the record, abstracts, and briefs. After **oral argument** by the attorneys, if the court elects to hear one, the court takes the case under advisement and makes a decision based upon majority rule, after which the court prepares a written opinion containing the reasons for its decision, the applicable rules of law, and its judgment. The judgment may **affirm** the judgment of the trial court, or, if the appellate court finds that reversible error was committed, the judgment may be **reversed**, or the case may be **reversed and remanded** for a new trial. In some instances the appellate court will affirm the lower court's decision in part and reverse it in part. The losing party may file a petition for rehearing, which is usually denied.

If the reviewing court is an intermediate appellate court, the party losing in that court may decide to seek a reversal of its judgment by filing within a prescribed time a notice of appeal, if the appeal is by right, or a petition for leave to appeal to the State supreme court, if the appeal is by discretion. This petition corresponds to a petition for a writ of *certiorari* in the U.S. Supreme Court. The party winning in the appellate court may file an answer to the petition for leave to appeal. If the petition is granted or if the appeal is by right, the record is certified to the State supreme court, where each party files a new brief and argument. Oral argument may be held, and the case is taken under advisement. If the supreme court concludes that the judgment of the appellate court is correct, it affirms. If it decides otherwise, it reverses the judgment of the appellate court and enters a reversal or an order of remand. The unsuccessful party may again file a petition for a rehearing, which is likely to be denied. Barring the remote possibility of an application for still further review by the U.S. Supreme Court, the case either has reached its termination or, upon remand, is about to start its second journey through the courts, beginning, as it did originally, in the trial court.

ENFORCEMENT

If Dryden does not appeal or if the reviewing court affirms the judgment if he does appeal and Dryden does not pay the judgment, the task of enforcement remains. Pederson must request the clerk to issue a **writ of execution**, demanding payment of the judgment, which is served by the sheriff upon the defendant. If the writ is returned "unsatisfied," Pederson may post bond or other security and order a levy on and sale of specific nonexempt property belonging to Dryden, which is then seized by the sheriff, advertised for sale, and sold at public sale under the writ of execution. If the proceeds of the sale do not produce sufficient funds to pay the judgment,

plaintiff Pederson's attorney may institute a supplementary proceeding in an attempt to locate money or other property belonging to Dryden. In an attempt to collect the judgment, Pederson's attorney also may proceed by **garnishment** against Dryden's employer to collect from Dryden's wages or against a bank in which Dryden has an account.

If Pederson cannot satisfy the judgment with Dryden's property located within Illinois (the State where the judgment was obtained), Pederson will have to bring an action on the original judgment in other States where Dryden owns property. Because the U.S. Constitution requires each State to accord judgments of other States **full faith and credit**, Pederson will be able to obtain a local judgment that may be enforced by the methods described previously.

◆ SEE FIGURE 3-8: **Stages in Civil Procedure**

ALTERNATIVE DISPUTE RESOLUTION

Litigation is complex, time-consuming, and expensive. Furthermore, court adjudications involve long delays, lack special expertise in substantive areas, and provide only a limited range of remedies. In addition, the litigation process offers little opportunity for compromise and often causes or exacerbates animosity between the disputants. Consequently, in an attempt to overcome some of the disadvantages of litigation, several nonjudicial methods of dealing with disputes have developed. The most important of these alternatives to litigation is arbitration. Others include conciliation, mediation, "mini-trials," and summary jury trials.

The various techniques differ in a number of ways, including (1) whether the process is voluntary, (2) whether the process is binding, (3) whether the disputants represent themselves or are represented by attorneys, (4) whether the decision is made by the disputants or by a third party, (5) whether the procedure used is formal or informal, and (6) whether the basis for the decision is law or some other criterion.

Which method of civil dispute resolution—litigation or one of the nongovernmental methods—is better for a particular dispute depends on several factors, including the financial circumstances of the disputants, the nature of their relationship (commercial or personal, ongoing or limited), and the urgency of their need for a quick resolution. Alternative dispute resolution methods are especially suitable in cases in which privacy, speed, preservation of continuing relations, and control over the process—including the flexibility to compromise—are important to the parties. Nevertheless, the disadvantages of using alternative dispute mechanisms may make court adjudication more appropriate. For example, except for arbitration, only courts can compel participation and provide a binding resolution. In addition,

◆ **FIGURE 3-8: Stages in Civil Procedure**

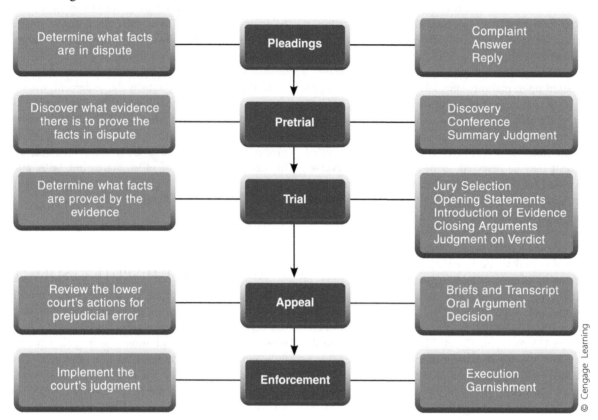

only courts can establish precedents and create public duties. Furthermore, the courts provide greater due process protections and uniformity of outcome. Finally, the courts are independent of the disputants and are publicly funded.

◆ **SEE FIGURE 3-9: Comparison of Court Adjudication, Arbitration, and Mediation/Conciliation**

PRACTICAL ADVICE

Consider including in your contracts a provision specifying what means of dispute resolution will apply to the contract.

ARBITRATION

In **arbitration**, the parties select a neutral third person or persons (the arbitrator[s]) who render(s) a binding decision after hearing arguments and reviewing evidence. Because the presentation of the case is less formal and the rules of evidence are more relaxed, arbitration usually takes less time and costs less than litigation. Moreover, in many arbitration cases the parties are able to select an arbitrator with special expertise concerning the subject of the dispute. Thus, the quality of the arbitrator's decision may be higher than that available through the court system. In addition, arbitration

normally is conducted in private, which enables the parties to avoid unwanted publicity. Arbitration is commonly used in commercial and labor management disputes.

TYPES OF ARBITRATION Arbitration is of two basic types—consensual, which is by far the most common, and compulsory. **Consensual arbitration** occurs whenever the parties to a dispute agree to submit the controversy to arbitration. They may do this in advance by agreeing in their contract that disputes arising out of the contract will be resolved by arbitration. Or, after a dispute arises, they may agree to submit the dispute to arbitration. In either instance, such agreements are enforceable under the Federal Arbitration Act (FAA) and State statutes. Forty-nine States adopted the Uniform Arbitration Act of 1956 (UAA). (In 2000, the Uniform Law Commission, also known as the National Conference of Commissioners on Uniform State Laws, promulgated the Revised UAA to provide State legislatures with a more up-to-date statute to resolve disputes through arbitration. To date, at least seventeen States have adopted the Revised UAA.) In **compulsory arbitration**, which is relatively infrequent, a Federal or State statute requires arbitration for specific types of disputes, such as those involving public employees like police officers, teachers, and firefighters.

◆ FIGURE 3-9: **Comparison of Court Adjudication, Arbitration, and Mediation/Conciliation**

	Court Adjudication	Arbitration	Mediation/Conciliation
Binding	Yes	Yes	No
Public Proceedings	Yes	No	No
Special Expertise	No	Yes	Yes
Publicly Funded	Yes	No	No
Precedents Established	Yes	No	No
Time Consuming	Yes	No	No
Long Delays	Yes	No	No
Expensive	Yes	No	No

© Cengage Learning

PROCEDURE Usually the parties' agreement to arbitrate specifies how the arbitrator or arbitrators will be chosen. If it does not, the FAA and State statutes provide methods for selecting arbitrators. Although the requirements for arbitration hearings vary from State to State, they generally consist of opening statements, case presentation, and closing statements. Case presentations may include witnesses, documentation, and site inspections. The parties may cross-examine witnesses and the parties may be represented by attorneys.

The decision of the arbitrator, called an **award**, is binding on the parties. Nevertheless, it is subject to very limited judicial review. Under the FAA and the Revised UAA, grounds for review include (1) the award was procured by corruption, fraud, or other undue means; (2) the arbitrators were partial or corrupt; (3) the arbitrators were guilty of misconduct prejudicing the rights of a party to the arbitration proceeding; and (4) the arbitrators exceeded their powers. Historically, the courts were unfriendly to arbitration; now, however, they favor the procedure.

INTERNATIONAL ARBITRATION Arbitration is a commonly used means for resolving international disputes. The United Nations Committee on International Trade Law (UNCITRAL) and the International Chamber of Commerce have promulgated arbitration rules that have won broad international adherence. The FAA has provisions implementing the United Nations Convention on the Recognition and Enforcement of Foreign Arbitral Awards. A number of States have enacted laws specifically governing international arbitration; some of the statutes have been based on the Model Law on International Arbitration drafted by UNCITRAL.

COURT-ANNEXED ARBITRATION A growing number of Federal and State courts have adopted court-annexed arbitration in civil cases in which the parties seek limited amounts of damages. The arbitrators are usually attorneys. Appeal from this type of *nonbinding* arbitration is by trial *de novo*.

Many States have enacted statutes requiring the arbitration of medical malpractice disputes. Some States provide for mandatory nonbinding arbitration before bringing a case to court. Other States provide for voluntary but binding arbitration agreements, which patients sign before receiving medical treatment.

◆ SEE CASE 3-4

CONCILIATION

Conciliation is a nonbinding, informal process in which the disputing parties select a neutral third party (the conciliator) who attempts to help them reach a mutually acceptable agreement. The duties of the conciliator include improving communications, explaining issues, scheduling meetings, discussing differences of opinion, and serving as an intermediary between the parties when they are unwilling to meet.

MEDIATION

Mediation is a process in which a neutral third party (the mediator) selected by the disputants helps them to reach a voluntary agreement resolving their disagreement. In addition to employing conciliation techniques to improve communications, the mediator, unlike the conciliator, proposes possible solutions for the parties to consider. Like the conciliator, the mediator lacks the power to render a binding decision. Because it is a voluntary process and has lower costs than a formal legal proceeding or arbitration, mediation has become one of the most widespread forms of dispute resolution in the United States. Mediation commonly is used by the judicial system in such tribunals as small claims courts, housing courts, family courts, and neighborhood justice centers. In 2001 the Uniform Law Commission promulgated the Uniform Mediation Act, which was amended in 2003. The Act establishes a privilege of confidentiality for mediators and participants. At least eleven States have adopted it.

Sometimes the techniques of arbitration and mediation are combined in a procedure called "med-arb." In med-arb, the neutral third party serves first as a mediator. If all issues are not resolved through such mediation, she then serves as an arbitrator authorized to render a binding decision on the remaining issues.

MINI-TRIAL

A mini-trial is a structured settlement process that combines elements of negotiation, mediation, and trials. Mini-trials are most commonly used when both disputants are corporations. In a mini-trial, attorneys for the two corporations conduct limited discovery and then present evidence to a panel consisting of managers from each company, as well as a neutral third party, who may be a retired judge or other attorney. After the lawyers complete their presentations, the managers try to negotiate a settlement without the attorneys. The managers may consult the third party on how a court might resolve the issues in dispute.

SUMMARY JURY TRIAL

A summary jury trial is a mock trial in which the parties present their case to an advisory jury. Though not binding, the jury's verdict does influence the negotiations in which the parties must participate following the mock trial. If the parties do not reach a settlement, they may have a full trial *de novo*.

NEGOTIATION

Negotiation is a consensual bargaining process in which the parties attempt to reach an agreement resolving their dispute. Negotiation differs from other methods of alternate dispute resolution in that no third parties are involved.

CHAPTER SUMMARY

THE COURT SYSTEM

FEDERAL COURTS **District Courts** trial courts of general jurisdiction that can hear and decide most legal controversies in the Federal system
Courts of Appeals hear appeals from the district courts and review orders of certain administrative agencies
The Supreme Court the nation's highest court, whose principal function is to review decisions of the Federal Courts of Appeals and the highest State courts
Special Courts have jurisdiction over cases in a particular area of Federal law and include the U.S. Court of Federal Claims, the U.S. Tax Court, the U.S. Bankruptcy Courts, and the U.S. Court of Appeals for the Federal Circuit

STATE COURTS **Inferior Trial Courts** hear minor criminal cases, such as traffic offenses, and civil cases involving small amounts of money; conduct preliminary hearings in more serious criminal cases
Trial Courts have general jurisdiction over civil and criminal cases
Special Courts trial courts, such as probate courts and family courts, having jurisdiction over a particular area of State law
Appellate Courts include one or two levels; the highest court's decisions are final except in those cases reviewed by the U.S. Supreme Court

JURISDICTION

SUBJECT MATTER JURISDICTION **Definition** authority of a court to decide a particular kind of case
Federal Jurisdiction
- *Exclusive Federal Jurisdiction* Federal courts have sole jurisdiction over Federal crimes, bankruptcy, antitrust, patent, trademark, copyright, and other specified cases

- *Concurrent Federal Jurisdiction* authority of more than one court to hear the same case; State and Federal courts have concurrent jurisdiction over (1) Federal question cases (cases arising under the Constitution, statutes, or treaties of the United States) that do not involve exclusive Federal jurisdiction, and (2) diversity of citizenship cases involving more than $75,000

State Jurisdiction State courts have exclusive jurisdiction over all matters to which the Federal judicial power does not reach

---

JURISDICTION OVER THE PARTIES

Definition the power of a court to bind the parties to a suit

In Personam **Jurisdiction** jurisdiction based upon claims against a person, in contrast to jurisdiction over the person's property

In Rem **Jurisdiction** jurisdiction based on claims against property

Attachment Jurisdiction jurisdiction over a defendant's property to obtain payment of a claim not related to the property

Venue geographic area in which a lawsuit should be brought

CIVIL DISPUTE RESOLUTION

CIVIL PROCEDURE

Pleadings a series of statements that give notice and establish the issues of fact and law presented and disputed
- *Complaint* initial pleading by the plaintiff stating his case
- *Summons* notice given to inform a person of a lawsuit against her
- *Answer* defendant's pleading in response to the plaintiff's complaint
- *Reply* plaintiff's pleading in response to the defendant's answer

Pretrial Procedure process requiring the parties to disclose what evidence is available to prove the disputed facts; designed to encourage settlement of cases or to make the trial more efficient
- *Judgment on Pleadings* a final ruling in favor of one party by the judge based on the pleadings
- *Discovery* right of each party to obtain evidence from the other party
- *Pretrial Conference* a conference between the judge and the attorneys to simplify the issues in dispute and to attempt to settle the dispute without trial
- *Summary Judgment* final ruling by the judge in favor of one party based on the evidence disclosed by discovery

Trial determines the facts and the outcome of the case
- *Jury Selection* each party has an unlimited number of challenges for cause and a limited number of peremptory challenges
- *Conduct of Trial* consists of opening statements by attorneys, direct and cross-examination of witnesses, and closing arguments
- *Directed Verdict* final ruling by the judge in favor of one party based on the evidence introduced at trial
- *Jury Instructions* judge gives the jury the particular rules of law that apply to the case
- *Verdict* the jury's decision based on those facts the jury determines the evidence proves
- *Motions Challenging the Verdict* include motions for a new trial and a motion for judgment notwithstanding the verdict

Appeal determines whether the trial court committed prejudicial error

Enforcement plaintiff with an unpaid judgment may resort to a writ of execution to have the sheriff seize property of the defendants and to garnishment to collect money owed to the defendant by a third party

<table>
<tr><td>ALTERNATIVE DISPUTE
RESOLUTION</td><td>**Arbitration** a nonjudicial proceeding in which a neutral party selected by the disputants renders a binding decision (award)
Conciliation a nonbinding process in which a third party acts as an intermediary between the disputing parties
Mediation a nonbinding process in which a third party acts as an intermediary between the disputing parties and proposes solutions for them to consider
Mini-Trial a nonbinding process in which attorneys for the disputing parties (typically corporations) present evidence to managers of the disputing parties and a neutral third party, after which the managers attempt to negotiate a settlement in consultation with the third party
Summary Jury Trial mock trial followed by negotiations
Negotiation consensual bargaining process in which the parties attempt to reach an agreement resolving their dispute without the involvement of third parties</td></tr>
</table>

CASES

CASE 3-1

(Concurrent Federal Jurisdiction)
MIMS v. ARROW FINANCIAL SERVICES, LLC
Supreme Court of the United States, 2012
565 U.S. ___, 132 S.Ct. 740, 181 L.Ed.2d 881
http://scholar.google.com/scholar_case?q=132-4S.Ct.+740&hl=en&as_sdt=2,34&case=15936914266018909724&scilh=0

Ginsburg, J.

This case concerns enforcement * * * of the Telephone Consumer Protection Act of 1991 (TCPA or Act), [citation]. Voluminous consumer complaints about abuses of telephone technology—for example, computerized calls dispatched to private homes—prompted Congress to pass the TCPA. Congress determined that federal legislation was needed because telemarketers, by operating interstate, were escaping state-law prohibitions on intrusive nuisance calls. The Act bans certain practices invasive of privacy and directs the Federal Communications Commission (FCC or Commission) to prescribe implementing regulations. It authorizes States to bring civil actions to enjoin prohibited practices and to recover damages on their residents' behalf. The Commission must be notified of such suits and may intervene in them. Jurisdiction over state-initiated TCPA suits, Congress provided, lies exclusively in the U.S. district courts. Congress also provided for civil actions by private parties seeking redress for violations of the TCPA or of the Commission's implementing regulations.

Petitioner Marcus D. Mims, complaining of multiple violations of the Act by respondent Arrow Financial Services, LLC (Arrow), a debt-collection agency, commenced an action for damages against Arrow in the U.S. District Court for the Southern District of Florida. Mims invoked the court's "federal question" jurisdiction, *i.e.*, its authority to adjudicate claims "arising under the … laws … of the United States," [citation]. The District Court, affirmed by the U.S.

Court of Appeals for the Eleventh Circuit, dismissed Mims's complaint for want of subject-matter jurisdiction. Both courts relied on Congress' specification, in the TCPA, that a private person may seek redress for violations of the Act (or of the Commission's regulations thereunder) "in an appropriate court of [a] State," "if [such an action is] otherwise permitted by the laws or rules of court of [that] State." [Citation.]

* * *

We granted certiorari, [citation], to resolve a split among the Circuits as to whether Congress granted state courts exclusive jurisdiction over private actions brought under the TCPA. [Citations.] We now hold that Congress did not deprive federal courts of federal-question jurisdiction over private TCPA suits.

Federal courts, though "courts of limited jurisdiction," [citation], in the main "have no more right to decline the exercise of jurisdiction which is given, then to usurp that which is not given." [Citation.] Congress granted federal courts general federal-question jurisdiction in 1875. [Citation.] * * * "The district courts shall have original jurisdiction of all civil actions arising under the Constitution, laws, or treaties of the United States." 28 U.S.C. § 1331. * * *

Because federal law creates the right of action and provides the rules of decision, Mims's TCPA claim, in 28 U.S.C. § 1331's words, plainly "aris[es] under" the "laws … of the United States." * * *

Arrow agrees that this action arises under federal law, [citation], but urges that Congress vested exclusive adjudicatory authority over private TCPA actions in state courts. In cases "arising under" federal law, we note, there is a "deeply rooted presumption in favor of concurrent state court jurisdiction," rebuttable if "Congress affirmatively ousts the state courts of jurisdiction over a particular federal claim." [Citation.] * * *

* * *

Arrow's arguments do not persuade us that Congress has eliminated § 1331 jurisdiction over private actions under the TCPA.

The language of the TCPA—"A person or entity may, if otherwise permitted by the laws or rules of court of a State, bring [an action] in an appropriate court of that State," 47 U.S.C. § 227(b)(3)—Arrow asserts, is uniquely state-court oriented. [Citation.] That may be, but "[i]t is a general rule that the grant of jurisdiction to one court does not, of itself, imply that the jurisdiction is to be exclusive." [Citation.]

Nothing in the permissive language of § 227(b)(3) makes state-court jurisdiction exclusive, or otherwise purports to oust federal courts of their 28 U.S.C. § 1331 jurisdiction over federal claims. * * *

Title 47 U.S.C. § 227(b)(3) does not state that a private plaintiff may bring an action under the TCPA "only" in state court, or "exclusively" in state court. * * *

* * *

Nothing in the text, structure, purpose, or legislative history of the TCPA calls for displacement of the federal-question jurisdiction U.S. district courts ordinarily have under 28 U.S.C. § 1331. In the absence of direction from Congress stronger than any Arrow has advanced, we apply the familiar default rule: Federal courts have § 1331 jurisdiction over claims that arise under federal law. Because federal law gives rise to the claim for relief Mims has stated and specifies the substantive rules of decision, the Eleventh Circuit erred in dismissing Mims's case for lack of subject-matter jurisdiction.

* * *

For the reasons stated, the judgment of the United States Court of Appeals for the Eleventh Circuit is reversed, and the case is remanded for further proceedings consistent with this opinion.

CASE 3-2

Jurisdiction

WORLD-WIDE VOLKSWAGEN CORP. v. WOODSON

Supreme Court of the United States, 1980
444 U.S. 286, 100 S.Ct 559, 62 L.Ed.2d 490
http://scholar.google.com/scholar_case?q=100+S.CT.+559&hl=en&as_sdt=2,34&case=2649456870546423871&scilh=0

White, J.

The issue before us is whether, consistently with the Due Process Clause of the Fourteenth Amendment, an Oklahoma court may exercise *in personam* jurisdiction over a nonresident automobile retailer and its wholesale distributor in a products-liability action, when the defendants' only connection with Oklahoma is the fact that an automobile sold in New York to New York residents became involved in an accident in Oklahoma.

Respondents Harry and Kay Robinson purchased a new Audi automobile from petitioner Seaway Volkswagen, Inc. (Seaway), in Massena, N.Y., in 1976. The following year the Robinson family, who resided in New York, left that State for a new home in Arizona. As they passed through the State of Oklahoma, another car struck their Audi in the rear, causing a fire which severely burned Kay Robinson and her two children.

The Robinsons subsequently brought a products-liability action in the District Court for Creek County, Okla., claiming that their injuries resulted from defective design and placement of the Audi's gas tank and fuel system. They joined as defendants the automobile's manufacturer, Audi NSU Auto Union Aktiengesellschaft (Audi); its importer, Volkswagen of America, Inc. (Volkswagen); its regional distributor, petitioner World-Wide Volkswagen Corp. (World-Wide); and its retail

dealer, petitioner Seaway. Seaway and World-Wide entered special appearances, claiming that Oklahoma's exercise of jurisdiction over them would offend the limitations on the State's jurisdiction imposed by the Due Process Clause of the Fourteenth Amendment.

The facts presented to the District Court showed that World-Wide is incorporated and has its business office in New York. It distributes vehicles, parts, and accessories, under contract with Volkswagen, to retail dealers in New York, New Jersey, and Connecticut. Seaway, one of these retail dealers, is incorporated and has its place of business in New York. Insofar as the record reveals, Seaway and World-Wide are fully independent corporations whose relations with each other and with Volkswagen and Audi are contractual only. Respondents adduced no evidence that either World-Wide or Seaway does any business in Oklahoma, ships or sells any products to or in that State, has an agent to receive process there, or purchases advertisements in any media calculated to reach Oklahoma. In fact, as respondents' counsel conceded at oral argument, [citation], there was no showing that any automobile sold by World-Wide or Seaway has ever entered Oklahoma with the single exception of the vehicle involved in the present case.

* * *

The Supreme Court of Oklahoma [held] that personal jurisdiction over petitioners was authorized by Oklahoma's "long-arm" statute, [citation]. * * *

* * *

The Due Process Clause of the Fourteenth Amendment limits the power of a state court to render a valid personal judgment against a nonresident defendant. [Citation.] A judgment rendered in violation of due process is void in the rendering State and is not entitled to full faith and credit elsewhere. [Citation.] Due process requires that the defendant be given adequate notice of the suit, [citation], and be subject to the personal jurisdiction of the court, [citation]. In the present case, it is not contended that notice was inadequate; the only question is whether these particular petitioners were subject to the jurisdiction of the Oklahoma courts.

As has long been settled, and as we reaffirm today, a state court may exercise personal jurisdiction over a nonresident defendant only so long as there exist "minimum contacts" between the defendant and the forum State. [Citation.] The concept of minimum contacts, in turn, can be seen to perform two related, but distinguishable, functions. It protects the defendant against the burdens of litigating in a distant or inconvenient forum. And it acts to ensure that the States, through their courts, do not reach out beyond the limits imposed on them by their status as coequal sovereigns in a federal system.

The protection against inconvenient litigation is typically described in terms of "reasonableness" or "fairness." We have said that the defendant's contacts with the forum State must be such that maintenance of the suit "does not offend 'traditional notions of fair play and substantial justice.'" [Citation.] The relationship between the defendant and the forum must be such that it is "reasonable * * * to require the corporation to defend the particular suit which is brought there." [Citation.] Implicit in this emphasis on reasonableness is the understanding that the burden on the defendant, while always a primary concern, will in an appropriate case be considered in light of other relevant factors, including the forum State's interest in adjudicating the dispute, [citation]; the plaintiff's interest in obtaining convenient and effective relief, [citation], at least when that interest is not adequately protected by the plaintiff's power to choose the forum, [citation]; the interstate judicial system's interest in obtaining the most efficient resolution of controversies; and the shared interest of the several States in furthering fundamental substantive social policies, [citation].

* * *

Thus, the Due Process Clause "does not contemplate that a state may make binding a judgment in personam against an individual or corporate defendant with which the state has no contacts, ties, or relations." [Citation.]

* * *

Applying these principles to the case at hand, we find in the record before us a total absence of those affiliating circumstances that are a necessary predicate to any exercise of state-court jurisdiction. Petitioners carry on no activity whatsoever in Oklahoma. They close no sales and perform no services there. They avail themselves of none of the privileges and benefits of Oklahoma law. They solicit no business there either through salespersons or through advertising reasonably calculated to reach the State. Nor does the record show that they regularly sell cars at wholesale or retail to Oklahoma customers or residents or that they indirectly, through others, serve or seek to serve the Oklahoma market. In short, respondents seek to base jurisdiction on one, isolated occurrence and whatever inferences can be drawn therefrom: the fortuitous circumstance that a single Audi automobile, sold in New York to New York residents, happened to suffer an accident while passing through Oklahoma.

* * *

Because we find that petitioners have no "contacts, ties, or relations" with the State of Oklahoma, [citation], the judgment of the Supreme Court of Oklahoma is Reversed.

CASE 3-3

Pretrial Procedure: Summary Judgment

PARKER v. TWENTIETH CENTURY-FOX CORP.

Supreme Court of California, 1970
3 Cal.3d 176, 89 Cal.Rptr. 737, 474 P.2d 689
http://scholar.google.com/scholar_case?q=474+P.2d+689&hl=en&as_sdt=2,34&case=8204943341098207403&scilh=0

Burke, J.

Defendant Twentieth Century-Fox Film Corporation appeals from a summary judgment granting to plaintiff [Shirley MacLaine Parker] the recovery of agreed compensation under a written contract for her services as an actress in a motion picture. As will appear, we have concluded that the trial court correctly ruled in plaintiff's favor and that the judgment should be affirmed.

Plaintiff is well known as an actress, and in the contract between plaintiff and defendant is sometimes referred to as the "Artist." Under the contract, dated August 6, 1965, plaintiff was to play the female lead in defendant's contemplated production of a motion picture entitled "Bloomer Girl." The contract provided that defendant would pay plaintiff a minimum "guaranteed compensation" of $53,571.42 per week for 14 weeks commencing May 23, 1966, for a total of $750,000.

Prior to May 1966 defendant decided not to produce the picture and by a letter dated April 4, 1966, it notified plaintiff of that decision and that it would not "comply with our obligations to you under" the written contract.

By the same letter and with the professed purpose "to avoid any damage to you," defendant instead offered to employ plaintiff as the leading actress in another film tentatively entitled "Big Country, Big Man" (hereinafter, "Big Country"). The compensation offered was identical, as were 31 of the 34 numbered provisions or articles of the original contract. Unlike "Bloomer Girl," however, which was to have been a musical production, "Big Country" was a dramatic "western type" movie. "Bloomer Girl" was to have been filmed in California; "Big Country" was to be produced in Australia. Also, certain terms in the proffered contract varied from those of the original. Plaintiff was given one week within which to accept; she did not and the offer lapsed. Plaintiff then commenced this action seeking recovery of the agreed guaranteed compensation.

The complaint sets forth two causes of action. The first is for money due under the contract; the second, based upon the same allegations as the first, is for damages resulting from defendant's breach of contract. Defendant in its answer admits the existence and validity of the contract, that plaintiff complied with all the conditions, covenants and promises and stood ready to complete the performance, and that defendant breached and "anticipatorily repudiated" the contract. It denies, however, that any money is due to plaintiff either under the contract or as a result of its breach, and pleads as an affirmative defense to both causes of action plaintiff's allegedly deliberate failure to mitigate damages, asserting that she unreasonably refused to accept its offer of the leading role in "Big Country."

Plaintiff moved for summary judgment under Code of Civil Procedure section 437c, the motion was granted, and summary judgment for $750,000 plus interest was entered in plaintiff's favor. This appeal by defendant followed.

The familiar rules are that the matter to be determined by the trial court on a motion for summary judgment is whether facts have been presented which give rise to a triable factual issue. The court may not pass upon the issue itself. Summary judgment is proper only if the affidavits or declarations in support of the moving party would be sufficient to sustain a judgment in his favor and his opponent does not by affidavit show facts sufficient to present a triable issue of fact. The affidavits of the moving party are strictly construed, and doubts as to the propriety of summary judgment should be resolved against granting the motion. Such summary procedure is drastic and should be used with caution so that it does not become a substitute for the open trial method of determining facts. The moving party cannot depend upon allegations in his own pleadings to cure deficient affidavits, nor can his adversary rely upon his own pleadings in lieu or in support of affidavits in opposition to a motion; however, a party can rely on his adversary's pleadings to establish facts not contained in his own affidavits. [Citations.] Also, the court may consider facts stipulated to by the parties and facts which are properly the subject of judicial notice. [Citations.]

* * *

Applying the foregoing rules to the record in the present case, with all intendments in favor of the party opposing the summary judgment motion—here, defendant—it is clear that the trial court correctly ruled that plaintiff's failure to accept defendant's tendered substitute employment could not be applied in mitigation of damages because the offer of the "Big Country" lead was of employment both different and inferior, and that no factual dispute was presented on that issue. The mere circumstance that "Bloomer Girl" was to be a musical review calling upon plaintiff's talents as a dancer as well as an actress, and was to be produced in the City of Los Angeles, whereas "Big Country" was a straight dramatic role in a "Western type" story taking place in an opal mine in Australia, demonstrates the difference in kind between the two employments; the female lead as a dramatic actress in a western style motion picture can by no stretch of imagination be considered the equivalent of or substantially similar to the lead in a song-and-dance production.

Additionally, the substitute "Big Country" offer proposed to eliminate or impair the director and screenplay approvals accorded to plaintiff under the original "Bloomer Girl" contract * * * and thus constituted an offer of inferior employment. No expertise or judicial notice is required in order to hold that the deprivation or infringement of an employee's rights held under an original employment contract converts the available "other employment" relied upon by the employer to mitigate damages, into inferior employment which the employee need not seek or accept. [Citation.]

* * *

The judgment is affirmed.

CASE
3-4

Arbitration

NITRO-LIFT TECHNOLOGIES, LLC v. HOWARD

Supreme Court of the United States, 2012
568 U.S. ___, 133 S.Ct. 500, 184 L.Ed.2d 328
http://scholar.google.com/scholar_case?q=133+S.Ct.+500&hl=en&as_sdt=4,60&as_ylo=2012&
case=12798986269666351327&scilh=0

Per Curiam

State courts rather than federal courts are most frequently called upon to apply the Federal Arbitration Act (FAA), [citation], including the Act's national policy favoring arbitration. It is a matter of great importance, therefore, that state supreme courts adhere to a correct interpretation of the legislation. * * *

This dispute arises from a contract between petitioner Nitro-Lift Technologies, L.L.C., and two of its former employees. Nitro-Lift contracts with operators of oil and gas wells to provide services that enhance production. Respondents Eddie Lee Howard and Shane D. Schneider entered a confidentiality and noncompetition agreement with Nitro-Lift that contained the following arbitration clause:

> "'Any dispute, difference or unresolved question between Nitro-Lift and the Employee (collectively the "Disputing Parties") shall be settled by arbitration by a single arbitrator mutually agreeable to the Disputing Parties in an arbitration proceeding conducted in Houston, Texas in accordance with the rules existing at the date hereof of the American Arbitration Association.'" [Citation.]

After working for Nitro-Lift on wells in Oklahoma, Texas, and Arkansas, respondents quit and began working for one of Nitro-Lift's competitors. Claiming that respondents had breached their noncompetition agreements, Nitro-Lift served them with a demand for arbitration. Respondents then filed suit in the District Court of Johnston County, Oklahoma, asking the court to declare the noncompetition agreements null and void and to enjoin their enforcement. The court dismissed the complaint, finding that the contracts contained valid arbitration clauses under which an arbitrator, and not the court, must settle the parties' disagreement.

The Oklahoma Supreme Court retained respondents' appeal and ordered the parties to show cause why the matter should not be resolved by application of Okla. Stat., Tit. 15, § 219A (West 2011), which limits the enforceability of noncompetition agreements. Nitro-Lift argued that any dispute as to the contracts' enforceability was a question for the arbitrator. It relied for support—as it had done before the trial court—upon several of this Court's cases interpreting the FAA, and noted that under [citation], "this arbitration law applies in both state and federal courts." [Citation.]

The Oklahoma Supreme Court was not persuaded. It held that despite the "[U.S.] Supreme Court cases on which the employers rely," the "existence of an arbitration agreement in an employment contract does not prohibit judicial review of the underlying agreement." [Citation.] * * * Finding the arbitration clauses no obstacle to its review, the court held that the noncompetition agreements were "void and unenforceable as against Oklahoma's public policy," expressed in Okla. Stat., Tit. 15, § 219A. [Citation.]

The Oklahoma Supreme Court declared that its decision rests on adequate and independent state grounds. [Citation.] If that were so, we would have no jurisdiction over this case. [Citation.] It is not so, however, because the court's reliance on Oklahoma law was not "independent"—it necessarily depended upon a rejection of the federal claim, which was both "'properly presented to'" and "'addressed by'" the state court. [Citation.] Nitro-Lift claimed that the arbitrator should decide the contract's validity, and raised a federal-law basis for that claim by relying on Supreme Court cases construing the FAA. * * * The Oklahoma Supreme Court acknowledged the cases on which Nitro-Lift relied, as well as their relevant holdings, but chose to discount these controlling decisions. Its conclusion that, despite this Court's jurisprudence, the underlying contract's validity is purely a matter of state law for state-court determination is all the more reason for this Court to assert jurisdiction.

The Oklahoma Supreme Court's decision disregards this Court's precedents on the FAA. That Act, which "declare[s] a national policy favoring arbitration," [citation], provides that a "written provision in … a contract evidencing a transaction involving commerce to settle by arbitration a controversy thereafter arising out of such contract or transaction … shall be valid, irrevocable, and enforceable, save upon such grounds as exist at law or in equity for the revocation of any contract." [Citation.] It is well settled that "the substantive law the Act created [is] applicable in state and federal courts." [Citations.] And when parties commit to arbitrate contractual disputes, it is a mainstay of the Act's substantive law that attacks on the validity of the contract, as distinct from attacks on the validity of the arbitration clause itself, are to be resolved "by the arbitrator in the first instance, not by a federal or state court." [Citations.] * * *

This principle requires that the decision below be vacated. The trial court found that the contract contained a valid arbitration clause, and the Oklahoma Supreme Court did not hold otherwise. It nonetheless assumed the arbitrator's role by declaring the noncompetition agreements null and void.

The state court insisted that its "[own] jurisprudence controls this issue" and permits review of a "contract submitted to arbitration where one party assert[s] that the underlying agreement [is] void and unenforceable." [Citation.] But the Oklahoma Supreme Court must abide by the FAA, which is "the supreme Law of the Land," U.S. Const., Art. VI, cl. 2, and by the opinions of this Court interpreting that law. "It is this Court's responsibility to say what a statute means, and once the Court has spoken, it is the duty of other courts to respect that understanding of the governing rule of law." [Citation.] Our cases hold that the FAA forecloses precisely this type of "judicial hostility towards arbitration." [Citation.]

The state court reasoned that Oklahoma's statute "addressing the validity of covenants not to compete, must govern over the more general statute favoring arbitration." [Citation.] But the ancient interpretive principle that the specific governs the general (*generalia specialibus non derogant*) applies only to conflict between laws of equivalent dignity. Where a specific statute, for example, conflicts with a general constitutional provision, the latter governs. And the same is true where a specific state statute conflicts with a general federal statute. There is no general-specific exception to the Supremacy Clause, U.S. Const. Art. VI, cl. 2. "'[W]hen state law prohibits outright the arbitration of a particular type of claim, the analysis is straightforward: The conflicting rule is displaced by the FAA.'" [Citation.] Hence, it is for the arbitrator to decide in the first instance whether the covenants not to compete are valid as a matter of applicable state law. [Citation.]

For the foregoing reasons, the petition for certiorari is granted. The judgment of the Supreme Court of Oklahoma is vacated, and the case is remanded for proceedings not inconsistent with this opinion.

It is so ordered.

QUESTIONS

1. On June 15, a newspaper columnist predicted that the coast of State X would be flooded on the following September 1. Relying on this pronouncement, Gullible quit his job and sold his property at a loss so as not to be financially ruined. When the flooding did not occur, Gullible sued the columnist in a State X court for damages. The court dismissed the case for failure to state a cause of action under applicable State law. On appeal, the State X Supreme Court upheld the lower court. Three months after this ruling, the State Y Supreme Court heard an appeal in which a lower court had ruled that a reader could sue a columnist for falsely predicting flooding.

   a. Must the State Y Supreme Court follow the ruling of the State X Supreme Court as a matter of *stare decisis*?
   b. Should the State Y lower court have followed the ruling of the State X Supreme Court until the State Y Supreme Court issued a ruling on the issue?
   c. Once the State X Supreme Court issued its ruling, could the U.S. Supreme Court overrule the State X Supreme Court?
   d. If the State Y Supreme Court and the State X Supreme Court rule in exactly opposite ways, must the U.S. Supreme Court resolve the conflict between the two courts?

2. State Senator Bowdler convinced the legislature of State Z to pass a law requiring all professors to submit their class notes and transparencies to a board of censors to be sure that no "lewd" materials were presented to students at State universities. Professor Rabelais would like to challenge this law as violating his First Amendment rights under the U.S. Constitution.
   a. May Professor Rabelais challenge this law in the State Z courts?
   b. May Professor Rabelais challenge this law in a Federal district court?

3. While driving his car in Virginia, Carpe Diem, a resident of North Carolina, struck Butt, a resident of Alaska. As a result of the accident, Butt suffered more than $80,000 in medical expenses. Butt would like to know, if he personally serves the proper papers to Diem, whether he can obtain jurisdiction against Diem for damages in the following courts:
   a. Alaska State trial court
   b. Federal Circuit Court of Appeals for the Ninth Circuit (includes Alaska)
   c. Virginia State trial court
   d. Virginia Federal district court
   e. Federal Circuit Court of Appeals for the Fourth Circuit (includes Virginia and North Carolina)
   f. Virginia equity court
   g. North Carolina State trial court

4. Sam Simpleton, a resident of Kansas, and Nellie Naive, a resident of Missouri, each bought $85,000 in stock at local offices in their home States from Evil Stockbrokers, Inc. ("Evil"), a business incorporated in Delaware, with its principal place of business in Kansas. Both Simpleton and Naive believe that they were cheated by Evil Stockbrokers and would like to sue Evil for fraud. Assuming that no Federal question

is at issue, assess the accuracy of the following statements:

  a. Simpleton can sue Evil in a Kansas State trial court.

  b. Simpleton can sue Evil in a Federal district court in Kansas.

  c. Naive can sue Evil in a Missouri State trial court.

  d. Naive can sue Evil in a Federal district court in Missouri.

5. The Supreme Court of State A ruled that, under the law of State A, pit bull owners must either keep their dogs fenced or pay damages to anyone bitten by the dogs. Assess the accuracy of the following statements:

  a. It is likely that the U.S. Supreme Court would issue a writ of *certiorari* in the "pit bull" case.

  b. If a case similar to the "pit bull" case were to come before the Supreme Court of State B in the future, the doctrine of *stare decisis* would leave the court no choice but to rule the same way as the "pit bull" case.

6. The Supreme Court of State G decided that the U.S. Constitution requires professors to warn students of their right to remain silent before questioning the students about cheating. This ruling directly conflicts with a decision of the Federal Court of Appeals for the circuit that includes State G.

  a. Must the Federal Circuit Court of Appeals withdraw its ruling?

  b. Must the Supreme Court of State G withdraw its ruling?

CASE PROBLEMS

7. Thomas Clements brought an action to recover damages for breach of warranty against defendant Signa Corporation. (A warranty is an obligation that the seller of goods assumes with respect to the quality of the goods sold.) Clements had purchased a motorboat from Barney's Sporting Goods, an Illinois corporation. The boat was manufactured by Signa Corporation, an Indiana corporation with its principal place of business in Decatur, Indiana. Signa has no office in Illinois and no agent authorized to do business on its behalf within Illinois. Clements saw Signa's boats on display at the Chicago Boat Show. In addition, literature on Signa's boats was distributed at the Chicago Boat Show. Several boating magazines, delivered to Clements in Illinois, contained advertisements for Signa's boats. Clements also had seen Signa's boats on display at Barney's Sporting Goods Store in Palatine, Illinois, where he eventually purchased the boat. A written warranty issued by Signa was delivered to Clements in Illinois. Although Signa was served with a summons, it failed to enter an appearance in this case. The court entered a default order and, subsequently, a judgment of $6,220 against Signa. Signa appealed. Decision?

8. Mariana Deutsch worked as a knitwear mender and attended a school for beauticians. The sink in her apartment collapsed on her foot, fracturing her big toe and making it painful for her to stand. She claims that as a consequence of the injury she was compelled to abandon her plans to become a beautician because that job requires long periods of standing. She also asserts that she was unable to work at her current job for a month. She filed a tort claim against Hewes Street Realty for negligence in failing properly to maintain the sink. She brought the suit in Federal district court, claiming damages of $25,000. Her medical expenses and actual loss of salary were less than $1,500; the rest of her alleged damages were for loss of future earnings as a beautician. Hewes Street moved to dismiss the suit on the basis that Deutsch's claim fell short of the jurisdictional requirement, which then was $10,000, and that the Federal court therefore lacked subject matter jurisdiction over her claim. Decision?

9. Vette sued Aetna under a fire insurance policy. Aetna moved for summary judgment on the basis that the pleadings and discovered evidence showed a lack of an insurable interest in Vette. (An "insurable interest" exists where the insured derives a monetary benefit or advantage from the preservation or continued existence of the property or would sustain an economic loss from its destruction.) Aetna provided ample evidence to infer that Vette had no insurable interest in the contents of the burned building. Vette also provided sufficient evidence to put in dispute this factual issue. The trial court granted the motion for summary judgment. Vette appealed. Decision?

10. Mark Womer and Brian Perry were members of the U.S. Navy and were stationed in Newport, Rhode Island. On April 10, Womer allowed Perry to borrow his automobile so that Perry could visit his family in New Hampshire. Later that day, while operating Womer's vehicle, Perry was involved in an accident in Manchester, New Hampshire. As a result of the accident, Tzannetos Tavoularis was injured. Tavoularis brought action against Womer in a New Hampshire superior court,

contending that Womer was negligent in lending the automobile to Perry when he knew or should have known that Perry did not have a valid driver's license. Womer sought to dismiss the action on the ground that the New Hampshire courts lacked jurisdiction over him, citing the following facts: (a) he lived and worked in Georgia; (b) he had no relatives in New Hampshire; (c) he neither owned property nor possessed investments in New Hampshire; and (d) he had never conducted business in New Hampshire. Did the New Hampshire courts have jurisdiction?

11. Kenneth Thomas brought suit against his former employer, Kidder, Peabody & Company, and two of its employees, Barclay Perry and James Johnston, in a dispute over commissions on sales of securities. When he applied to work at Kidder, Peabody & Company, Thomas had filled out a form, which contained an arbitration agreement clause. Thomas had also registered with the New York Stock Exchange (NYSE). Rule 347 of the NYSE provides that any controversy between a registered representative and a member company shall be settled by arbitration. Kidder, Peabody & Company is a member of the NYSE. Thomas refused to arbitrate, relying on Section 229 of the California Labor Code, which provides that actions for the collection of wages may be maintained "without regard to the existence of any private agreement to arbitrate." Perry and Johnston filed a petition in a California State court to compel arbitration under Section 2 of the Federal Arbitration Act. Should the petition of Perry and Johnston be granted?

12. Steven Gwin bought a lifetime Termite Protection Plan for his home from the local office of Allied-Bruce, a franchise of Terminix International Company. The plan provided that Allied-Bruce would "protect" Gwin's house against termite infestation, reinspect periodically, provide additional treatment if necessary, and repair damage caused by new termite infestations. Terminix International guaranteed the fulfillment of these contractual provisions. The plan also provided that all disputes arising out of the contract would be settled exclusively by arbitration. Four years later Gwin had Allied-Bruce reinspect the house in anticipation of selling it. Allied-Bruce gave the house a "clean bill of health." Gwin then sold the house and transferred the Termite Protection Plan to Dobson. Shortly thereafter, Dobson found the house to be infested with termites. Allied-Bruce attempted to treat and repair the house, using materials from out of state, but these efforts failed to satisfy Dobson. Dobson then sued Gwin, Allied-Bruce, and Terminix International in an Alabama state court. Allied-Bruce and Terminix International asked for a stay of these proceedings until arbitration could be carried out as stipulated in the contract. The trial court refused to grant the stay. The Alabama Supreme Court upheld that ruling, citing a state statute that makes predispute arbitration agreements unenforceable. The court found that the Federal Arbitration Act, which preempts conflicting state law, did not apply to this contract because its connection to interstate commerce was too slight. Was the Alabama Supreme Court correct? Explain.

TAKING SIDES

John Connelly suffered personal injuries when a tire manufactured by Uniroyal failed while his 1969 Opel Kadett was being operated on a highway in Colorado. Connelly's father had purchased the automobile from a Buick dealer in Evanston, Illinois. The tire bore the name "Uniroyal" and the legend "made in Belgium" and was manufactured by Uniroyal, sold in Belgium to General Motors, and subsequently installed on the Opel when it was assembled at a General Motors plant in Belgium. The automobile was shipped to the United States for distribution by General Motors. It appears that between the years 1968 and 1971 more than four thousand Opels imported into the United States from Antwerp, Belgium, were delivered to dealers in Illinois each year; that in each of those years between 600 and 1,320 of the Opels delivered to Illinois dealers were equipped with tires manufactured by Uniroyal, and that the estimated number of Uniroyal tires mounted on Opels delivered in Illinois within each of those years ranged from 3,235 to 6,630. Connelly brought suit in Illinois against Uniroyal to recover damages for personal injuries. Uniroyal asserted that it was not subject to the jurisdiction of the Illinois courts because it is not registered to do business and has never had an agent, employee, representative, or salesperson in Illinois; that it has never possessed or controlled any land or maintained any office or telephone listing in Illinois; that it has never sold or shipped any products into Illinois, either directly or indirectly; and that it has never advertised in Illinois.

a. What arguments could Connelly make in support of its claim that Illinois courts have jurisdiction over Uniroyal?

b. What arguments could Uniroyal make in support of its claim that Illinois courts do not have jurisdiction over it?

c. Who should prevail? Explain.

CHAPTER 3

INTENTIONAL TORTS

CHAPTER OUTCOMES

After reading and studying this chapter, you should be able to:

- Identify and describe the torts that protect against intentional harm to personal rights.

- Explain the application of the various privileges to defamation suits and how they are affected by whether the plaintiff is (1) a public figure, (2) a public official, or (3) a private person.

- Describe and distinguish the four torts comprising invasion of privacy.

- Identify and describe the torts that protect against harm to property.

- Distinguish among interference with contractual relations, disparagement, and fraudulent misrepresentation.

All forms of civil liability are either (1) voluntarily assumed, as by contract, or (2) involuntarily assumed, as imposed by law. Tort liability is of the second type. Tort law gives persons redress from civil wrongs or injuries to their person, property, and economic interests. Examples include assault and battery, automobile accidents, professional malpractice, and products liability. The law of torts has three principal objectives: (1) to compensate persons who sustain harm or loss resulting from another's conduct, (2) to place the cost of that compensation only on those parties who should bear it, and (3) to prevent future harms and losses. The law of torts therefore reallocates losses caused by human misconduct. In general, a tort is committed when:

1. a duty owed by one person to another
2. is breached and
3. proximately causes
4. injury or damage to the owner of a legally protected interest.

Each person is legally responsible for the damages his tortious conduct proximately causes. Moreover, as discussed in *Chapter 20*, businesses that conduct their business activities through employees are also liable for the torts their employees commit in the course of employment. The tort liability of employers makes the study of tort law essential to business managers.

Injuries may be inflicted intentionally, negligently, or without fault (strict liability). This chapter will discuss intentional torts; the following chapter will cover negligence and strict liability.

The same conduct may, and often does, constitute both a crime and a tort. An example would be an assault and battery committed by Johnson against West. For the commission of this crime, the State may take appropriate action against Johnson. In addition, however, Johnson has violated West's right to be secure in his person and so has committed a tort against West, who may, regardless of the criminal action by the State against Johnson, bring a civil action against Johnson for damages. On the other hand, an act may be criminal without being tortious, and, by the same token, an act may be a tort but not a crime.

In a tort action, the injured party *sues* to recover *compensation* for the injury sustained as a result of the defendant's wrongful conduct. The primary purpose of tort law, unlike criminal law, is to compensate the injured party, not to punish the wrongdoer. In certain cases, however, courts may award **punitive** or exemplary damages, which are damages over and above the amount necessary to compensate the plaintiff. In cases in which the defendant's tortious conduct has been intentional—or, in some States, reckless—and outrageous, exhibiting "malice" or a fraudulent or evil motive, most courts permit a jury to award punitive damages. The allowance of punitive damages is designed to deter the defendant and others from similar conduct by punishing and making an example of the defendant.

◆ SEE CASE 7-1

When bringing a lawsuit for an intentional tort, consider whether it is appropriate to ask for punitive damages.

Tort law is primarily common law. The Restatement of Torts provides an orderly presentation of this law. From 1934 to 1939, the American Law Institute (ALI) adopted and promulgated the first Restatement. Since then, the Restatement has served as a vital force in shaping the law of torts. Between 1965 and 1978, the institute adopted and promulgated a second edition of the Restatement of Torts, which revises and supersedes the first Restatement. This text will refer to the second Restatement simply as the Restatement.

In 1996, the ALI approved the development of a new Restatement, called Restatement Third, Torts: Liability for Physical and Emotional Harm, which addresses the general or basic elements of the tort action for liability for accidental personal injury, property damage, and emotional harm but does not cover liability for economic loss. This work replaces comparable provisions in the Restatement Second, Torts. The final work is published in two volumes. Volume 1 was released in 2010 and primarily covers liability for negligence causing physical harm, duty, strict liability, factual cause, and scope of liability (traditionally called proximate cause). Volume 2 covers affirmative duties, emotional harm, land possessors' liability, and liability of actors who retain independent contractors. Volume 2 was approved in 2011 and published in 2012.

Because this new Restatement primarily applies to nonintentional torts, it will be covered extensively in the next chapter, and it will be cited as the "Third Restatement." A few of its provisions, however, do apply to intentional torts and will be included in this chapter. Comment c to Section 5 of the Third Restatement provides that the Second Restatement remains largely authoritative in explaining the details of specific intentional torts and their related defenses. However, the Institute has begun work on the Restatement Third, Torts: Intentional Torts to Persons, which is the latest installment of the ALI's ongoing revision of the Restatement Second of Torts. This new project will complete the major avenues of recovery for physical and emotional harm to persons.

The Institute's Restatement Third, Torts: Economic Torts and Related Wrongs will update coverage on torts that involve economic loss or pecuniary harm *not* resulting from physical harm or physical contact to a person or property. The project will update coverage of economic torts in Restatement Second, Torts and address some topics not covered in prior Restatements. The Institute began this project in 2004 and, after several years of inactivity, the project was resumed in 2010. In 2012, a portion of Chapter 1 of the Tentative Draft was approved.

State legislatures and, to a lesser extent, courts have actively assessed the need for **tort reform**. In general, tort reform has focused on limiting liability by restricting damages or narrowing claims. The majority of States have enacted at least one piece of legislation that falls into the broad category of tort reform, but these States have enacted different changes or different combinations of changes affecting specific aspects of tort law. Approaches to tort reform that have been taken at the State level include the following:

1. Laws that address specific types of claims; for example, limits on medical malpractice awards or on the liability of providers of alcohol.
2. Laws abolishing joint and several liability or limiting the application of this rule. Where joint and several liability is abolished, each one of the several defendants is liable only for his share of the plaintiff's damages.
3. Laws adding defenses to certain types of tort actions.
4. Laws capping noneconomic damages—so-called pain and suffering awards.
5. Laws to abolish or limit punitive damages, or to raise the standard of proof beyond the preponderance of the evidence.
6. Laws aimed at attorneys' fees; for example, laws that directly regulate contingent fees.

INTENT

Intent, as used in tort law, does not require a hostile or evil motive; rather, the term denotes either that the actor desires to cause the consequences of his act or that he believes that those consequences are substantially certain to result from it. Restatement, Section 8A. The Third Restatement provides that "[a] person acts with the intent to produce a consequence if: (a) the person acts with the purpose of producing that consequence; or (b) the person acts knowing that the consequence is substantially certain to result." Section 1.

The following examples illustrate the definition of intent: (1) If A fires a gun in the middle of the Mojave Desert, he intends to fire the gun; but when the bullet hits B, who is in the desert without A's knowledge, A does not intend that result. (2) A throws a bomb into B's office to kill B. A knows that C is in B's office and that the bomb is substantially certain to injure C, although A has no desire to harm C. A, nonetheless, is liable to C for any injury caused C. A's intent to injure B is *transferred* to C.

Infants (persons who have not reached the age of majority, which is eighteen years in almost all States) are held liable for their intentional torts. The infant's age and knowledge, however, are critical in determining whether the infant had sufficient intelligence to form the requisite intent. Incompetents, like infants, are generally held liable for their intentional torts.

A number of established and specifically named torts protect an individual from various intentional interferences with his person, dignity, property, and economic interests. Because the law of torts is dynamic, new forms of relief continue to develop. To guide the courts in determining when they should impose liability for intentionally inflicted harm that does not fall within the requirements of an established tort, Section 870 of the Restatement provides a general catch-all intentional tort: "One who intentionally causes injury to another is subject to liability to the other for that injury, if his conduct is generally culpable and not justifiable under the circumstances. This liability may be imposed although the actor's conduct does not come within a traditional category of tort liability."

This section also provides a unifying principle both for long-established torts and for those that have developed more recently. The Third Restatement has a similar provision. Section 5.

◆ **SEE FIGURE 7-1: Intent**

HARM TO THE PERSON

The law provides protection against intentional harm to the person. The primary interests protected by these torts are freedom from bodily contact (by the tort of battery), freedom from apprehension (assault), freedom from confinement (false imprisonment), and freedom from mental distress (infliction of emotional distress). Generally, intentional torts to the person entitle the injured party to recover damages for

bodily harm, emotional distress, loss or impairment of earning capacity, reasonable medical expenses, and harm the tortious conduct caused to property or business.

BATTERY

Battery is an intentional infliction of harmful or offensive bodily contact. It may consist of contact causing serious injury, such as a gunshot wound or a blow to the head with a club. Or it may involve contact causing little or no physical injury, such as knocking a hat off of a person's head or flicking a glove in another's face. Bodily contact is offensive if it would offend a reasonable person's sense of dignity, even if the defendant intended the conduct only as a joke or a compliment. Restatement, Section 19. For instance, kissing another without permission would constitute a battery. Bodily contact may be accomplished by the use of objects, such as Arthur's throwing a rock at Bea with the intention of hitting her. If the rock hits Bea or any other person, Arthur has committed a battery. Nonetheless, in a densely populated society one cannot expect complete freedom from personal contact with others. Accordingly, neither casually bumping into another in a congested area nor gently tapping that other on the shoulder to get her attention would constitute a battery.

ASSAULT

Assault is intentional conduct by one person directed at another that places the other in apprehension of imminent (immediate) bodily harm or offensive contact. It is usually

◆ **FIGURE 7-1: Intent**

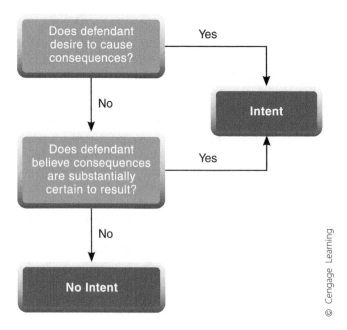

committed immediately preceding a battery, but if the intended battery fails, the assault remains. Assault is principally a mental rather than a physical intrusion. Accordingly, damages for assault may include compensation for fright and humiliation. The person in danger of immediate bodily harm must have *knowledge* of the danger and be apprehensive of its imminent threat to his safety. For example, if Joan aims a loaded gun at Kelly's back, but Pat subdues her before Kelly becomes aware of the danger, Joan has not committed an assault upon Kelly.

Historically, it has been said that words alone do not constitute an assault. Nonetheless, spoken words must be taken in context, and if as taken cause apprehension, these spoken words will constitute an assault. On the other hand, words sometimes will negate an apparent threat so that there is no assault. This does not mean that a defendant can avoid liability for an assault by making his threat conditional. The threat "If you do not give me your book, I will break your arm" constitutes an assault.

FALSE IMPRISONMENT

The tort of **false imprisonment**, or false arrest, is the intentional confining of a person against her will within fixed boundaries if the person is conscious of the confinement or is harmed by it. Merely obstructing a person's freedom of movement is not false imprisonment so long as a reasonable alternative exit is available. False imprisonment may be brought about by physical force, by the threat of physical force (both express and implied), by physical barriers, or by force directed against the plaintiff's property. For instance, an individual who remains in a store after his wallet is confiscated or who remains on a train after the conductor refuses to allow her suitcase to be removed are both examples of false imprisonment through the use of force against personal property. Damages for false imprisonment may include compensation for loss of time, physical discomfort, inconvenience, physical illness, and mental suffering.

Merchants occasionally encounter potential liability for false imprisonment when they seek to question a suspected shoplifter. A merchant who detains an innocent person may face a lawsuit for false imprisonment. Nonetheless, most States have statutes protecting the merchant, provided she detains the suspect upon probable cause, in a reasonable manner, and for not more than a reasonable time.

◆ **SEE CASE 7-2**

PRACTICAL ADVICE

When detaining a suspected shoplifter, be careful to conform to the limitations of your State's statutory privilege.

INFLICTION OF EMOTIONAL DISTRESS

Under the Second and Third Restatements, a person is liable for **infliction of emotional distress** when that person by extreme and outrageous conduct intentionally or recklessly causes severe emotional distress to another. The person is liable for that emotional distress and, if the emotional distress causes bodily harm, also for the resulting bodily harm. **Recklessness** is conduct that evidences a conscious disregard of or an indifference to the consequences of the act committed. With respect to infliction of emotional distress, the Third Restatement explains that an

> actor acts recklessly when the actor knows of the risk of severe emotional disturbance (or knows facts that make the risk obvious) and fails to take a precaution that would eliminate or reduce the risk even though the burden is slight relative to the magnitude of the risk, thereby demonstrating the actor's indifference.

Damages may be recovered for severe emotional distress even in the absence of any physical injury. Liability for infliction of emotional distress, however, arises only when the person seeking recovery has suffered *severe* emotional disturbance and when a reasonable person in the same circumstances would suffer severe disturbance. Thus, the Third Restatement imposes an objective—not a subjective—test. Accordingly, there is no liability for mental harm suffered by an unusually vulnerable plaintiff, unless the defendant knew of the plaintiff's special vulnerability. Under the "extreme and outrageous" requirement, a person is liable only if the conduct goes beyond the bounds of human decency and would be regarded as intolerable in a civilized community. Ordinary insults and indignities are not enough for liability to be imposed, even if the person desires to cause emotional disturbance. Examples of this tort would include sexual harassment on the job and outrageous, prolonged bullying tactics employed by creditors or collection agencies attempting to collect a debt or by insurance adjusters trying to force a settlement of an insurance claim.

◆ **SEE CASE 7-2**

HARM TO THE RIGHT OF DIGNITY

The law also protects a person against intentional harm to his right of dignity. This protection includes a person's reputation, privacy, and right to freedom from unjustifiable litigation.

DEFAMATION

The tort of defamation is a false communication that injures a person's reputation by disgracing him and diminishing the respect in which he is held. An example would be the publication of a false statement that a person had committed a crime or had a loathsome disease. In *Beckman v. Dunn*, 276 Pa.Super. 527, 419 A.2d 583 (1980), the court stated, "A communication is defamatory if it tends to harm the reputation of another so as to lower him in the estimation of the community or deter third persons from associating or dealing with him, and necessarily involves the idea of disgrace."

ELEMENTS OF DEFAMATION The elements of a defamation action are (1) a false and defamatory statement concerning another; (2) an unprivileged publication (communication) to a third party; (3) depending on the status of the defendant, negligence or recklessness on her part in knowing or failing to ascertain the falsity of the statement; and (4) in some cases, proof of special harm caused by the publication. Restatement, Section 558. The burden of proof is on the plaintiff to prove the falsity of the defamatory statement.

If a defamatory communication is handwritten, typewritten, printed, pictorial, or in another medium with like communicative power, such as a television or radio broadcast, it is designated **libel**. If it is spoken or oral, it is designated **slander**. Restatement, Sections 568 and 568A. In either case, it must be communicated to a person or persons other than the one who is defamed, a process referred to as *publication*. If Maurice hands or mails to Pierre a defamatory letter he has written about Pierre's character, this is not a publication, as it is intended only for Pierre. The publication must have been intentional or the result of the defendant's negligence.

Any living person, as well as corporations, partnerships, and unincorporated associations, may be defamed. Restatement, Sections 561 and 562. Unless a statute provides otherwise, no action may be brought for defamation of a deceased person. Restatement, Section 560.

A significant trend affecting business has been the bringing of defamation suits against former employers by discharged employees. It has been reported that such suits account for approximately one-third of all defamation lawsuits.

◆ SEE CASE 7-3

PRACTICAL ADVICE

Consider whether you should provide employment references for current and former employees, and if you decide to do so, take care in what you say.

DEFENSES TO DEFAMATION **Privilege** is immunity from tort liability granted when the defendant's conduct furthers a societal interest of greater importance than the injury inflicted upon the plaintiff. Three types of privileges apply to defamation: absolute, conditional, and constitutional.

Absolute privilege protects the defendant regardless of his motive or intent. This type of privilege, which has been confined to those few situations in which public policy clearly favors complete freedom of speech, includes (1) statements made by participants in a judicial proceeding regarding that proceeding, (2) statements made by members of Congress on the floor of Congress and by members of State and local legislative bodies, (3) statements made by certain executive branch officers in the discharge of their government duties, and (4) statements regarding a third party made between spouses when they are alone.

Qualified or **conditional privilege** depends upon proper use of the privilege. A person has conditional privilege to publish defamatory matter to protect his own legitimate interests or, in some cases, the interests of another. Conditional privilege also extends to many communications in which the publisher and the recipient have a common interest, such as in letters of reference. A publisher who acts in an excessive manner, without probable cause, or for an improper purpose forfeits conditional privilege.

The First Amendment to the U.S. Constitution guarantees freedom of speech and freedom of the press. The U.S. Supreme Court has applied these rights to the law of defamation by extending a form of constitutional privilege to defamatory and false statements regarding public officials or public figures so long as it is done without malice. Restatement, Section 580A. For these purposes, *malice* is not ill will but clear and convincing proof of the publisher's knowledge of falsity or reckless disregard of the truth. Thus, under **constitutional privilege** the public official or public figure must prove that the defendant published the defamatory and false comment with knowledge or in reckless disregard of the comment's falsity and its defamatory character. In a defamation suit brought by a private person (one who is neither a public official nor a public figure) the plaintiff must prove that the defendant published the defamatory and false comment with malice *or* negligence.

Congress enacted Section 230 of the **Communications Decency Act of 1996 (CDA)**, granting immunity to Internet service providers (ISPs) from liability for defamation when publishing information originating from a third party. A court has interpreted this provision of the CDA as immunizing an ISP that refused to remove or retract an allegedly defamatory posting made on its bulletin board. The immunity granted by the CDA to ISPs has spawned a number of lawsuits urging ISPs to reveal the identities of subscribers who have posted allegedly defamatory statements. To date, ISPs have complied, generating additional litigation by angry ISP patrons attempting to keep their identities protected by asserting that their right to free speech is being compromised.

Because Section 230 of the CDA grants immunity only to ISPs, there is the possibility that employers will be held liable for some online defamatory statements made by an employee. Section 577(2) of the Restatement of Torts provides that a person who intentionally and unreasonably fails to remove defamatory matter that she knows is exhibited on property in her possession or under her control is liable for its continued publication. Therefore, employers in control of e-forums, such as electronic bulletin boards and chat rooms, should act quickly to remove any defamatory statement brought to their attention.

INVASION OF PRIVACY

The invasion of a person's right to privacy actually consists of four distinct torts: (1) appropriation of a person's name or likeness, (2) unreasonable intrusion upon the seclusion of another, (3) unreasonable public disclosure of private facts, or (4) unreasonable publicity that places another in a false light in the public eye. Restatement, Section 652A.

It is entirely possible and not uncommon for a person to invade another's right of privacy in a manner entailing two or more of these related torts. For example, Cindy forces her way into Ozzie's hospital room, takes a photograph of Ozzie, and publishes it to promote Cindy's cure for Ozzie's illness along with false statements about Ozzie that a reasonable person would consider highly objectionable. Ozzie would be entitled to recover on any or all of the four torts comprising invasion of privacy.

◈ SEE FIGURE 7-2: **Privacy**

APPROPRIATION Appropriation is the unauthorized use of the plaintiff's name or likeness for the defendant's benefit, as, for example, in promoting or advertising a product or service. Restatement, Section 652C. The tort of appropriation, also known as the **right of publicity**, seeks to protect the individual's right to the exclusive use of his identity. In the earlier example, Cindy's use of Ozzie's photograph to promote Cindy's business constitutes the tort of appropriation.

◆ SEE CASE 7-4

When using another person's identity for your own purposes, be sure to obtain that person's written consent.

INTRUSION Intrusion is the unreasonable and highly offensive interference with the solitude or seclusion of another. Restatement, Section 652B. Such unreasonable interference would include improper entry into another's dwelling, unauthorized eavesdropping upon another's private conversations, and unauthorized examination of another's private papers and records. The intrusion must be highly offensive or objectionable to a reasonable person and must involve matters that are private. Thus, there is no liability if the defendant examines public records or observes the plaintiff in a public place. This form of invasion of privacy is committed once the intrusion occurs, as publicity is not required.

PUBLIC DISCLOSURE OF PRIVATE FACTS Under the tort of public disclosure of private facts, the courts impose liability for publicity given to private information about another if the matter made public would be highly offensive and objectionable to a reasonable person. Like intrusion, this tort applies only to private, not public, information regarding an individual; unlike intrusion, it requires publicity. Under the Restatement, the publicity required differs in degree from the "publication" required under the law of defamation. This tort requires that private facts be communicated to the public at large or that they become public knowledge, whereas publication of a defamatory statement need only be made to a single third party. Section 652D, Comment a. Some courts, however, have allowed recovery where the disclosure was made to only one person. Thus, under the Restatement approach, Kathy, a creditor of Gary, will not invade Gary's privacy by writing a letter to Gary's employer to inform the employer of Gary's failure to pay a debt, but Kathy would be liable if she posted in the window of her store a statement that Gary will not pay the debt he owes to her. Also, unlike defamation, this tort applies to truthful private information if the matter published would be offensive and objectionable to a reasonable person of ordinary sensibilities.

◈ FIGURE 7-2: **Privacy**

	Appropriation	Intrusion	Public Disclosure	False Light
Publicity	Yes	No	Yes	Yes
Private Facts	No	Yes	Yes	No
Offensiveness	No	Yes	Yes	Yes
Falsity	No	No	No	Yes

FALSE LIGHT The tort of false light imposes liability for publicity that places another in a false light that is highly offensive if the defendant *knew* or acted in *reckless disregard* of the fact that the matter publicized was false. Restatement, Section 652E. For example, Linda includes Keith's name and photograph in a public "rogues' gallery" of convicted criminals. Because Keith has never been convicted of any crime, Linda is liable to him for placing him in a false light. Other examples include publicly and falsely attributing to a person an opinion, statement, or written work, as well as the unauthorized use of a person's name on a petition or on a complaint in a lawsuit.

Like defamation, the matter must be untrue; unlike defamation, it must be "publicized," not merely "published." Restatement, Section 652D, Comment a. Although the matter must be objectionable to a reasonable person, it need not be defamatory. In many instances, the same facts will give rise to actions both for defamation and for false light.

DEFENSES The defenses of absolute, conditional, and constitutional privilege apply to publication of any matter that is an invasion of privacy to the same extent that such defenses apply to defamation.

MISUSE OF LEGAL PROCEDURE

Three torts comprise the misuse of legal procedure: malicious prosecution, wrongful civil proceedings, and abuse of process. Each protects an individual from being subjected to unjustifiable litigation. Malicious prosecution and wrongful civil proceedings impose liability for damages caused by improperly brought proceedings, including harm to reputation, credit, or standing; emotional distress; and the expenses incurred in defending against the wrongfully brought lawsuit. Abuse of process is a tort consisting of the use of a legal proceeding (criminal or civil) to accomplish a purpose for which the proceeding is not designed. Abuse of process applies even when there is probable cause or when the plaintiff or prosecution succeeds in the litigation.

HARM TO PROPERTY

The law also provides protection against invasions of a person's interests in property. Intentional harm to property includes the torts of (1) trespass to real property, (2) nuisance, (3) trespass to personal property, and (4) conversion.

REAL PROPERTY

Real property is land and anything attached to it, such as buildings, trees, and minerals. The law protects the possessor's rights to the exclusive use and quiet enjoyment of the land. Accordingly, damages for harm to land include compensation for the resulting diminution in the value of the land, the loss of use of the land, and the discomfort caused to the possessor of the land. Restatement, Section 929.

TRESPASS Section 158 of the Restatement provides:

One is subject to liability to another for trespass, irrespective of whether he thereby causes harm to any legally protected interest of the other, if he intentionally

(a) enters land in the possession of the other, or causes a thing or a third person to do so, or

(b) remains on the land, or

(c) fails to remove from the land a thing which he is under a duty to remove.

It is no defense that the intruder acted under the mistaken belief of law or fact that he was not trespassing. If the intruder intended to be upon the particular property, his reasonable belief that he owned the land or had permission to enter upon the land is irrelevant. Restatement, Section 164. An intruder is not liable if his own actions do not cause his presence on the land of another. For example, if Carol throws Ralph onto Tim's land, Ralph is not liable to Tim for trespass, although Carol is.

A trespass may be committed on, beneath, or above the surface of the land, although the law regards the upper air, above a prescribed minimum altitude for flight, as a public highway. Therefore, no aerial trespass occurs unless the aircraft enters into the lower reaches of the airspace and substantially interferes with the landowner's use and enjoyment. Restatement, Section 159.

NUISANCE A nuisance is a nontrespassory invasion of another's interest in the private use and enjoyment of land. Restatement, Section 821D. In contrast to trespass, nuisance does not require interference with another's right to exclusive possession of land, but rather imposes liability for significant and unreasonable harm to another's use or enjoyment of land. Examples of nuisances include the emission of unpleasant odors, smoke, dust, or gas, as well as the pollution of a stream, pond, or underground water supply. In one case, a computer's serious disturbance of a television retailer's signal reception was considered a nuisance.

PRACTICAL ADVICE

In using, manufacturing, and disposing of dangerous, noxious, or toxic materials take care not to create a nuisance.

PERSONAL PROPERTY

Personal property, or chattel, is any type of property other than an interest in land. The law protects a number of interests in the possession of personal property, including an interest in the property's physical condition and usability, an interest in the retention of possession, and an interest in its availability for future use.

TRESPASS Trespass to personal property consists of the intentional dispossession or unauthorized use of the personal property of another. Though the interference with the right to exclusive use and possession may be direct or indirect, liability is limited to instances in which the trespasser (1) dispossesses the other of the property; (2) substantially impairs the condition, quality, or value of the property; (3) deprives the possessor of the use of the property for a substantial time; or (4) causes harm to the possessor or to some person or thing in which the possessor has a legally protected interest. Restatement, Section 218. For example, Albert parks his car in front of his house. Ronald pushes Albert's car around the corner. Albert subsequently looks for his car but cannot find it for several hours. Ronald is liable to Albert for trespass.

CONVERSION Conversion is an intentional exercise of dominion or control over another's personal property that so seriously interferes with the other's right of control as to justly require the payment of full value for the property. Restatement, Section 222A. Thus, all conversions are trespasses, but not all trespasses are conversions.

Conversion may consist of the intentional destruction of personal property or the use of property in an unauthorized manner. For example, Ken entrusts an automobile to Barbara, a dealer, for sale. After she drives the car eight thousand miles on her own business, Barbara is liable to Ken for conversion. On the other hand, in the example in which Ronald pushed Albert's car around the corner, Ronald would *not* be liable to Albert for conversion. Moreover, a person who buys stolen property is liable to the rightful owner for conversion even if the buyer acquires the property in good faith and without knowledge that it was stolen. Restatement, Section 229.

HARM TO ECONOMIC INTERESTS

Economic interests account for a fourth set of interests the law protects against intentional interference. Economic or pecuniary interests include a person's existing and prospective contractual relations, a person's business reputation, a person's name and likeness (previously discussed under the section titled "Appropriation"), and a person's freedom from deception. Business torts—those torts that protect a person's economic interests—are discussed in this section under the following headings: (1) interference with contractual relations, (2) disparagement, and (3) fraudulent misrepresentation.

INTERFERENCE WITH CONTRACTUAL RELATIONS

To conduct business it is necessary to establish trade relations with employees, suppliers, and customers. Though these relations may or may not be contractual, those that are, or are capable of being established by contract, receive legal protection against interference. Section 766 of the Restatement provides:

> One who intentionally and improperly interferes with the performance of a contract (except a contract to marry) between another and a third person by inducing or otherwise causing the third person not to perform the contract, is subject to liability to the other for the pecuniary loss resulting to the other from the failure of the third person to perform the contract.

The law imposes similar liability for intentional and improper interference with another's prospective contractual relation, such as a lease renewal or financing for construction. Restatement, Section 766B.

In either case, the rule requires that a person act with the purpose or motive of interfering with another's contract or with the knowledge that such interference is substantially certain to occur as a natural consequence of her actions. The interference may occur by threats or by prevention through the use of physical force. Frequently, interference is accomplished through inducement, such as the offer of a better contract. For instance, Edgar may offer Doris, an employee of Frank, a salary of $5,000 more per year than the contractual arrangement between Doris and Frank. If Edgar is aware that a contract exists between Doris and Frank and of the fact that his offer to Doris will interfere with that contract, then Edgar is liable to Frank for intentional interference with contractual relations.

To be distinguished is the situation in which the contract may be terminated at will or in which the contractual relation is only prospective. In these cases, competition is a proper basis for interference; for if one party is pursuing a contractual relation, others also are free to pursue a similar arrangement. For example, Amos and Brenda are competing distributors of transistors. Amos induces Carter, a prospective customer of Brenda, to buy transistors from Amos instead of Brenda. Amos has no liability to Brenda because his interference with Brenda's prospective contract with Carter is justified on the basis of competition, so long as Amos does not use predatory means such as physical violence, fraud, civil suits, or criminal prosecution to persuade Carter to deal with him.

Damages for interference with contractual relations include the pecuniary loss of the benefits of the contract, consequential losses caused by the interference, and emotional distress or actual harm to reputation. Restatement, Section 774A. In one case, Pennzoil had orally entered into a contract to merge with Getty Oil. Before the merger was consummated, however, Texaco induced Getty to merge with Texaco instead. Pennzoil sued Texaco for tortious interference with the merger contract and was awarded $7.53 billion in compensatory damages and $3 billion in punitive damages. *Texaco, Inc. v. Pennzoil, Co.*, 729 S.W.2d 768 (1987).

PRACTICAL ADVICE

Recognize that inducing another person's employees to breach a valid agreement not to compete or not to disclose confidential information may be improper interference with contractual relations.

DISPARAGEMENT

The tort of **disparagement** or injurious falsehood imposes liability upon a person who publishes a false statement that results in harm to another's interests which have pecuniary value, if the publisher knows that the statement is false or acts in reckless disregard of its truth or falsity. This tort most commonly involves false statements that the publisher intends to cast doubt upon the title or quality of another's property or products. Thus, Adam, while contemplating the purchase of merchandise that belongs to Barry, reads a newspaper advertisement in which Carol falsely asserts she owns the merchandise. Carol has disparaged Barry's property in the goods. Similarly, Marlene, knowing her statement to be false, tells Lionel that Matthew, an importer of wood, does not deal in mahogany. As a result, Lionel, who had intended to buy mahogany from Matthew, buys it elsewhere. Marlene is liable to Matthew for disparagement.

Absolute, conditional, and constitutional privileges apply to the same extent to the tort of disparagement as they do to defamation. In addition, a competitor has conditional privilege to compare her products favorably with those of a rival, even though she does not believe that her products are superior. No privilege applies, however, if the comparison contains false assertions of specific unfavorable facts about the competitor's property. For example, a manufacturer who advertises that his goods are the best in the market, even though he knows that a competitor's product is better, is not liable for disparagement. If he goes further, however, by falsely stating that his product is better because his competitor uses shoddy materials, then his disparagement would no longer be privileged, and he would be liable to his competitor for disparagement.

The pecuniary loss an injured person may recover is that which directly and immediately results from impairment of the marketability of the property disparaged. The injured party also may recover damages for expenses necessary to counteract the false publication, including litigation expenses, the cost of notifying customers, and the cost of publishing denials. Thus, Ursula publishes in a magazine an untrue statement that cranberries grown during the current season in a particular area are unwholesome. Shortly thereafter, the business of Victor, a jobber who has contracted to buy the entire output of cranberries grown in this area, falls off by 50 percent. If no other facts account for this decrease in his business, Victor is entitled to recover the amount of his loss from Ursula, plus the expenses necessary to counteract the misinformation published.

PRACTICAL ADVICE

When commenting on the products or services offered by a competitor, take care not to make any false statements.

FRAUDULENT MISREPRESENTATION

With respect to intentional, or fraudulent, misrepresentation, Section 525 of the Restatement provides:

> One who fraudulently makes a misrepresentation of fact, opinion, intention, or law for the purpose of inducing another to act or to refrain from action in reliance upon it, is subject to liability to the other in deceit for pecuniary loss caused to him by his justifiable reliance upon the misrepresentation.

For example, Smith represents to Jones that a tract of land in Texas is located in an area where oil drilling had recently commenced. Smith makes this statement knowing it to be false. In reliance upon the statement, Jones purchases the land from Smith, who is liable to Jones for fraudulent misrepresentation. Although fraudulent misrepresentation is a tort action, it is closely connected with contractual negotiations; the effects of such misrepresentation on assent to a contract are discussed in *Chapter 11.*

◆ SEE FIGURE 7-3: **Intentional Torts**

PRACTICAL ADVICE

When describing your products or services, take care not to make any false statements.

DEFENSES TO INTENTIONAL TORTS

Even though the defendant has intentionally invaded the interests of the plaintiff, the defendant will not be liable if such conduct was privileged. A defendant's conduct is

◆ **FIGURE 7-3: Intentional Torts**

Interest Protected	Tort
Person	
Freedom from contact	Battery
Freedom from apprehension	Assault
Freedom of movement	False imprisonment
Freedom from distress	Infliction of emotional distress
Dignity	
Reputation	Defamation
Privacy	Appropriation
	Intrusion
	Public disclosure of private facts
	False light
Freedom from wrongful legal actions	Misuse of legal procedure
Property	
Real	Trespass
	Nuisance
Personal	Trespass
	Conversion
Economic	
Contracts	Interference with contractual rights
Goodwill	Disparagement
Freedom from deception	Fraudulent misrepresentation

© Cengage Learning

privileged if it furthers an interest of such social importance that the law confers immunity from tort liability for the damage the conduct causes to others. Examples of privilege include self-defense, defense of property, and defense of others. In addition, the plaintiff's consent to the defendant's conduct is a defense to intentional torts.

CONSENT

If one consents to conduct resulting in damage or harm to his own person, dignity, property, or economic interests, no liability will generally attach to the intentional infliction of injury. **Consent**, which signifies that one is willing for an act to occur, negates the wrongfulness of the act. A person may manifest consent expressly or impliedly, by words or by conduct.

Consent must be given by an individual with capacity to do so. Consent given by a minor, mental incompetent, or intoxicated individual is invalid if he is not capable of appreciating the nature, extent, or probable consequences of the conduct to which he has consented. Consent is not effective if given under duress, by which one constrains another's will by compelling that other to give consent unwillingly.

PRIVILEGE

A person who would otherwise be liable for a tort is *not* liable if he acts pursuant to and within the limits of a privilege. Restatement, Section 890. Conditional privileges, as discussed in the section on defamation, depend upon proper use of the privilege. Absolute privilege, on the other hand, protects the defendant regardless of his purpose. Examples of absolute privilege include untrue, defamatory statements made by participants during the course of judicial proceedings, by legislators, by certain governmental executives, and between spouses. Absolute immunity also protects a public prosecutor from civil liability for malicious prosecution.

One conditional privilege—self-defense—entitles an individual to injure another's person without the other's consent. The law created the privilege of **self-defense** to enable an individual to protect himself against tortious interference. By virtue of this privilege an individual may inflict or impose what would otherwise constitute battery, assault, or false imprisonment.

Section 63 of the Restatement provides: "An actor is privileged to use reasonable force, not intended or likely to cause death or serious bodily harm, to defend himself against unprivileged harmful or offensive contact or other bodily harm which he reasonably believes that another is about to inflict intentionally upon him."

The privilege of self-defense exists whether or not the danger actually exists, provided that the defendant reasonably believed self-defense was necessary. The reasonableness of the defendant's actions is based upon what a person of average courage would have thought under the circumstances. A possessor of property is also permitted to use reasonable force, not intended or likely to cause death or serious bodily harm, to protect his real and personal property.

CHAPTER SUMMARY

HARM TO THE PERSON
Battery intentional infliction of harmful or offensive bodily contact
Assault intentional infliction of apprehension of immediate bodily harm or offensive contact
False Imprisonment intentional confining of a person against her will
Infliction of Emotional Distress extreme and outrageous conduct intentionally or recklessly causing severe emotional distress

HARM TO THE RIGHT OF DIGNITY
Defamation false communication that injures a person's reputation
- *Libel* written or electronically transmitted defamation
- *Slander* spoken defamation
- *Defenses* truth, absolute privilege, conditional privilege, and constitutional privilege are defenses to a defamation action
Invasion of Privacy
- *Appropriation* unauthorized use of a person's identity
- *Intrusion* unreasonable and highly offensive interference with the seclusion of another
- *Public Disclosure of Private Facts* highly offensive publicity of private information
- *False Light* highly offensive and false publicity about another
Misuse of Legal Procedure torts that protect an individual from unjustifiable litigation

HARM TO PROPERTY
Real Property land and anything attached to it
- *Trespass* wrongfully entering on land of another
- *Nuisance* a nontrespassory interference with another's use and enjoyment of land
Personal Property any property other than land
- *Trespass* an intentional taking or use of another's personal property
- *Conversion* intentional exercise of control over another's personal property

HARM TO ECONOMIC INTERESTS
Interference with Contractual Relations intentionally causing one of the parties to a contract not to perform
Disparagement publication of false statements about another's property or products
Fraudulent Misrepresentation a false statement, made with knowledge of its falsity, intended to induce another to act

DEFENSES TO INTENTIONAL TORTS
Consent a person may not recover for injury to which he willingly and knowingly consents
Self-Defense a person may take appropriate action to prevent harm to himself where time does not allow resort to the law

CASES

Punitive Damages
Philip Morris USA v. Williams
Supreme Court of the United States, 2007
549 U.S. 346, 127 S.Ct. 1057, 166 L.Ed.2d 940
http://scholar.google.com/scholar_case?case=3002949669360902078&q=549+U.S.+346&hl=en&as_sdt=2,34

Breyer, J.

This lawsuit arises out of the death of Jesse Williams, a heavy cigarette smoker. Respondent [plaintiff at trial], Williams' widow, represents his estate in this state lawsuit for negligence and deceit against Philip Morris, the manufacturer of Marlboro, the brand that Williams favored. A jury found that Williams' death was caused by smoking; that Williams smoked in significant part because he thought it was safe to do so; and that Philip Morris knowingly and falsely led him to believe that this was so. The jury ultimately found that Philip Morris was negligent (as was Williams) and that Philip Morris had engaged in deceit. In respect to deceit, the claim at issue here, it awarded compensatory damages of about $821,000 (about $21,000 economic and $800,000 noneconomic) along with $79.5 million in punitive damages.

The trial judge subsequently found the $79.5 million punitive damages award "excessive," [citation], and reduced it to $32 million. Both sides appealed. The Oregon Court of Appeals rejected Philip Morris' arguments and restored the $79.5 million jury award. Subsequently, [the State Supreme Court rejected Philip Morris' arguments that the trial court should have instructed the jury that it could not punish Philip Morris for injury to persons not before the court, and that the roughly 100-to-1 ratio the $79.5 million award bore to the compensatory damages amount indicated a "grossly excessive" punitive award].

* * *

Philip Morris then sought certiorari. It asked us to consider, among other things, (1) its claim that Oregon had unconstitutionally permitted it to be punished for harming nonparty victims; and (2) whether Oregon had in effect disregarded "the constitutional requirement that punitive damages be reasonably related to the plaintiff's harm." [Citation.] We granted certiorari limited to these two questions.

* * *

This Court has long made clear that "punitive damages may properly be imposed to further a State's legitimate interests in punishing unlawful conduct and deterring its repetition." [Citations.] At the same time, we have emphasized the need to avoid an arbitrary determination of an award's amount. Unless a State insists upon proper standards that will cabin the jury's discretionary authority, its punitive damages system may deprive a defendant of "fair notice … of the severity of the penalty that a State may impose," [citation]; it may threaten "arbitrary punishments," *i.e.*, punishments that reflect not an "application of law" but "a decision maker's caprice," [citation]; and, where the amounts are sufficiently large, it may impose one State's (or one jury's) "policy choice," say as to the conditions under which (or even whether) certain products can be sold, upon "neighboring States" with different public policies, [citation].

For these and similar reasons, this Court has found that the Constitution imposes certain limits, in respect both to procedures for awarding punitive damages and to amounts forbidden as "grossly excessive." [Citation] (requiring judicial review of the size of punitive awards); [citation] (review must be de novo); [citation] (excessiveness decision depends upon the reprehensibility of the defendant's conduct, whether the award bears a reasonable relationship to the actual and potential harm caused by the defendant to the plaintiff, and the difference between the award and sanctions "authorized or imposed in comparable cases"); [citation] (excessiveness more likely where ratio exceeds single digits). Because we shall not decide whether the award here at issue is "grossly excessive," we need now only consider the Constitution's procedural limitations.

In our view, the Constitution's Due Process Clause forbids a State to use a punitive damages award to punish a defendant for injury that it inflicts upon nonparties or those whom they directly represent, *i.e.*, injury that it inflicts upon those who are, essentially, strangers to the litigation. * * *

* * *

* * * [W]e can find no authority supporting the use of punitive damages awards for the purpose of punishing a defendant for harming others. We have said that it may be appropriate to consider the reasonableness of a punitive damages award in light of the *potential* harm the defendant's conduct could have caused. But we have made clear that the potential harm at issue was harm potentially caused *the plaintiff*. [Citation.] ("We have been reluctant to identify concrete constitutional limits on the ratio between harm, or potential harm, *to the plaintiff* and the punitive damages award"). * * *

* * * Evidence of actual harm to nonparties can help to show that the conduct that harmed the plaintiff also posed a

substantial risk of harm to the general public, and so was particularly reprehensible—although counsel may argue in a particular case that conduct resulting in no harm to others nonetheless posed a grave risk to the public, or the converse. Yet for the reasons given above, a jury may not go further than this and use a punitive damages verdict to punish a defendant directly on account of harms it is alleged to have visited on nonparties.

* * * We therefore conclude that the Due Process Clause requires States to provide assurance that juries are not asking the wrong question, *i.e.*, seeking, not simply to determine reprehensibility, but also to punish for harm caused strangers.

* * *

The instruction that Philip Morris said the trial court should have given distinguishes between using harm to others as part of the "reasonable relationship" equation (which it would allow) and using it directly as a basis for punishment. The instruction asked the trial court to tell the jury that "you *may* consider the extent of harm suffered by others *in determining what [the] reasonable relationship is*" between Philip Morris' punishable misconduct and harm

caused to Jesse Williams, "*[but] you are not to punish the defendant for the impact of its alleged misconduct on other persons, who may bring lawsuits of their own* in which other juries can resolve their claims…" [Citation.] And as the Oregon Supreme Court explicitly recognized, Philip Morris argued that the Constitution "prohibits the state, acting through a civil jury, from using punitive damages to punish a defendant for harm to nonparties." [Citation.]

* * *

As the preceding discussion makes clear, we believe that the Oregon Supreme Court applied the wrong constitutional standard when considering Philip Morris' appeal. We remand this case so that the Oregon Supreme Court can apply the standard we have set forth. Because the application of this standard may lead to the need for a new trial, or a change in the level of the punitive damages award, we shall not consider whether the award is constitutionally "grossly excessive." We vacate the Oregon Supreme Court's judgment and remand the case for further proceedings not inconsistent with this opinion.

It is so ordered.

CASE 7-2

False Imprisonment/Infliction of Emotional Distress

Ferrell v. Mikula

Court of Appeals of Georgia, 2008, reconsideration denied, 2008

295 Ga.App. 326, 672 S.E.2d

http://scholar.google.com/scholar_case?case=12901711244406213270&hl=en&as_sdt=2&as_vis=1&oi=scholarr

Barnes, C. J.

Racquel Ferrell and the parents of Kristie Ferrell sued Ruby Tuesday, Inc. and its manager Christian Mikula for false imprisonment, intentional infliction of emotional distress, * * * . After extensive discovery, the defendants moved for summary judgment on all counts. In a one-page order stating only that no genuine issues as to any material fact existed, the trial court granted the motion, and the Ferrells' appeal. For the reasons that follow, we affirm the trial court's grant of summary judgment to the defendants on the Ferrells' claim for intentional infliction of emotional distress * * * but reverse the grant on the false imprisonment claim.

* * *

* * * [T]he evidence shows that on Friday night, August 6, 2006, 18-year-old Racquel Ferrell and 13-year-old Kristie Ferrell went to Ruby Tuesday. After they ate and paid their bill, the girls left the restaurant, got into their car, and drove out of the parking lot. As they began to enter the highway, Racquel noticed a black truck following her very closely with its headlights on high. She could not see well out of her rearview mirror with the bright lights behind her, so she changed lanes, but the truck changed lanes with her and stayed close behind. She switched lanes again, and the truck did too.

A marked police car by the side of the road pulled onto the highway between the girls' car and the following truck and pulled the car over. After asking Racquel if she had any drugs or weapons, the officer pulled her out of the car, placed her in handcuffs, and put her in the back seat of his patrol car. Another officer removed Kristie from the car, placed her in handcuffs, and put her in the back of another patrol car.

All of the police officers gathered to talk to the driver of the truck that had been following the Ferrells, who turned out to be a uniformed off-duty police officer working as a security guard for Ruby Tuesday. The officer who arrested Racquel returned to the patrol car where she was being held and told her if she had not paid her Ruby Tuesday bill she was going to jail. She protested, and the officer conferred again with the other officers, then returned to the car and said, "It was a mistake." He explained that the manager at the restaurant had sent the off-duty officer after them because he said the girls had not paid their bill, but they did not fit the description of the two people who had walked out without paying. The officers removed the handcuffs from Racquel and Kristie and returned them to their car. After asking for Racquel's driver's license and obtaining information about both girls, the officer told them they were free to go.

Mikula had been an assistant manager for about a month, and was the only manager at Ruby Tuesday that night. One of the servers, Robert, reported that his customers at Table 24 had a complaint, so Mikula talked to the couple and told them he would "take care of" the food item in question. The customers were a man and a woman in their late 20s to early 30s. Mikula left the table to discuss the matter with Robert, after which server Aaron told Mikula that the patrons at Table 24 had left without paying. Mikula looked at the table, confirmed they had not left any money for the bill, and went out the main entrance. He saw a car pulling out of the parking lot, and said to the off-duty officer, "Hey, I think they just left without paying." The officer said, "Who, them?" Mikula said, "I think so," and the officer got up and went to his vehicle.

* * *

Mikula knew the officer was going to follow the people in the car and would stop them, but did not ask the officer if he had seen who got into the car. He did not give the officer a description of the people at Table 24, and did not know the race, age, gender, or number of people in the car being followed. He did not know if there were people in any of the other cars in the parking lot. He did not ask any other people in the restaurant if they had seen the people at Table 24 leave the building, which had two exits. He did not know how long the people had been gone before Aaron told him they left, or whether another customer had picked up money from Table 24. He could have tried to obtain more information to determine whether the people in the car he pointed out were the people who had been sitting at Table 24, but did not do so.

* * *

In this case, the Ferrells were detained without a warrant, and thus have a claim for false imprisonment * * * . [Citation.] "False imprisonment is the unlawful detention of the person of another, for any length of time, whereby such person is deprived of his personal liberty." [Citation.] "The only essential elements of the action being the detention and its unlawfulness, malice and the want of probable cause need not be shown." [Citations.]

The evidence in this case clearly establishes that the Ferrells were detained. " * * * under modern tort law an individual may be imprisoned when his movements are restrained in the open street, or in a traveling automobile." [Citation.] Ruby Tuesday does not argue otherwise, but instead argues that the evidence established sufficient probable cause and the plaintiffs failed to establish that Mikula acted with malice. But malice is not an element of false imprisonment, * * * . Further, * * * the mere existence of probable cause standing alone has no real defensive bearing on the issue of liability [for false imprisonment]. [Citation.]

* * *

Arresting or procuring the arrest of a person without a warrant constitutes a tort, "unless he can justify under some of the exceptions in which arrest and imprisonment without a warrant are permitted by law, [citations]." Generally, one "who causes or directs the arrest of another by an officer without a warrant may be held liable for false imprisonment, in the absence of justification, and the burden of proving that such imprisonment lies within an exception rests upon the person…causing the imprisonment." [Citations.] * * *

Accordingly, as the Ferrells have established an unlawful detention, the next issue to consider is whether Mikula "caused" the arrest. Whether a party is potentially liable for false imprisonment by "directly or indirectly urg[ing] a law enforcement official to begin criminal proceedings" or is not liable because he "merely relates facts to an official who then makes an independent decision to arrest" is a factual question for the jury. [Citation.] The party need not expressly request an arrest, but may be liable if his conduct and acts "procured and directed the arrest." [Citation.]

* * *

Here, Mikula told the officer that the car leaving the parking lot contained people who left without paying for their food, although he did not know or try to ascertain who was in the car. He also knew the officer was going to detain the people in the car and could have tried to stop him, but made no attempt to do so. Accordingly, the trial court erred in granting summary judgment to the defendants on the plaintiffs' false imprisonment claim.

* * *

The Ferrells also contend that the trial court erred in granting summary judgment to the defendants on their claim for intentional infliction of emotional distress. The elements of a cause of action for intentional infliction of emotional distress are: (1) intentional or reckless conduct; (2) that is extreme and outrageous; (3) a causal connection between the wrongful conduct and the emotional distress; and (4) severe emotional distress. [Citation.] Further,

> [l]iability for this tort has been found only where the conduct has been so outrageous in character, and so extreme in degree, as to go beyond all possible bounds of decency, and to be regarded as atrocious, and utterly intolerable in a civilized community. Generally, the case is one in which the recitation of the facts to an average member of the community would arouse his resentment against the actor, and lead him to exclaim, "Outrageous!"

[Citation.]

In this case, the action upon which the Ferrells base their emotional distress claim is being stopped by the police, placed in handcuffs, and held in a patrol car for a short period of time before being released. While this incident was unfortunate, the question raised by the evidence was whether the restaurant manager's actions were negligent, not whether he acted maliciously or his conduct was extreme, atrocious, or utterly intolerable. Accordingly, the trial court did not err in granting the defendants' motion for summary judgment

on the Ferrells' claim for intentional infliction of emotional distress.

* * *

Judgment affirmed in part and reversed in part.

<table>
<tr><td>CASE
7-3</td><td>Defamation
FRANK B. HALL & CO., INC. v. BUCK
Court of Appeals of Texas, Fourteenth District, 1984
678 S.W.2d 612, cert. denied, 472 U.S. 1009, 105 S.Ct. 2704, 86 L.Ed.2d 720 (1985)
http://scholar.google.com/scholar_case?q=678+S.W.2d+612&hl=en&as_sdt=2,34&case=17495651340574040653&scilh=0</td><td></td></tr>
</table>

Junell, J.

[On June 1, 1976, Larry W. Buck, an established salesman in the insurance business, began working for Frank B. Hall & Co. In the course of the ensuing months, Buck brought several major accounts to Hall and produced substantial commission income for the firm. In October 1976, Mendel Kaliff, then president of Frank B. Hall & Co. of Texas, informed Buck that his salary and benefits were being reduced because of his failure to generate sufficient income for the firm. On March 31, 1977, Kaliff and Lester Eckert, Hall's office manager, fired Buck. Buck was unable to procure subsequent employment with another insurance firm. He hired an investigator, Lloyd Barber, to discover the true reasons for his dismissal and for his inability to find other employment.

Barber contacted Kaliff, Eckert, and Virginia Hilley, a Hall employee, and told them he was an investigator and was seeking information about Buck's employment with the firm. Barber conducted tape-recorded interviews with the three in September and October of 1977. Kaliff accused Buck of being disruptive, untrustworthy, paranoid, hostile, untruthful, and of padding his expense account. Eckert referred to Buck as "a zero" and a "classical sociopath" who was ruthless, irrational, and disliked by other employees. Hilley stated that Buck could have been charged with theft for certain materials he brought with him from his former employer to Hall. Buck sued Hall for damages for defamation and was awarded over $1.9 million by a jury—$605,000 for actual damages and $1,300,000 for punitive damages. Hall then brought this appeal.]

Any act wherein the defamatory matter is intentionally or negligently communicated to a third person is a publication. In the case of slander, the act is usually the speaking of the words. Restatement (Second) Torts § 577 comment a (1977). There is ample support in the record to show that these individuals intentionally communicated disparaging remarks to a third person. The jury was instructed that "Publication means to communicate defamatory words to some third person in such a way that he understands the words to be defamatory. A statement is not published if it was authorized, invited or procured by Buck and if Buck knew in advance

the contents of the invited communication." In response to special issues, the jury found that the slanderous statements were made and published to Barber.

Hall argues that Buck could and should have expected Hall's employees to give their opinion of Buck when requested to do so. Hall is correct in stating that a plaintiff may not recover for a publication to which he has consented, or which he has authorized, procured or invited, [citation]; and it may be true that Buck could assume that Hall's employees would give their opinion when asked they do so. However, there is nothing in the record to indicate that Buck knew Hall's employees would defame him when Barber made the inquiries. The accusations made by Kaliff, Eckert and Hilley were not mere expressions of opinion but were false and derogatory statements of fact.

* * *

A defamer cannot escape liability by showing that, although he desired to defame the plaintiff, he did not desire to defame him to the person to whom he in fact intentionally published the defamatory communication. The publication is complete although the publisher is mistaken as to the identity of the person to whom the publication is made. Restatement (Second) of Torts § 577 comment e (1977). Likewise, communication to an agent of the person defamed is a publication, unless the communication is invited by the person defamed or his agent. Restatement § 577 comment e. We have already determined that the evidence is sufficient to show that Buck did not know what Kaliff, Eckert or Hilley would say and that he did not procure the defamatory statements to create a lawsuit. Thus, the fact that Barber may have been acting at Buck's request is not fatal to Buck's cause of action. There is absolutely no proof that Barber induced Kaliff, Eckert or Hilley to make any of the defamatory comments.

* * *

When an ambiguity exists, a fact issue is presented. The court, by submission of proper fact issues, should let the jury render its verdict on whether the statements were fairly susceptible to the construction placed thereon by the plaintiff. [Citation.] Here, the jury found (1) Eckert made a statement calculated to convey that Buck had been terminated because of serious misconduct; (2) the statement was slanderous or libelous; (3) the statement was made with malice; (4) the statement was published; and (5) damage directly resulted from the statement. The jury also found the statements were not substantially true. The jury thus determined that these statements, which were capable of a defamatory meaning, were understood as such by Burton.

* * *

We hold that the evidence supports the award of actual damages and the amount awarded is not manifestly unjust.

Furthermore, in responding to the issue on exemplary damages, the jury was instructed that exemplary damages must be based on a finding that Hall "acted with ill will, bad intent, malice or gross disregard to the rights of Buck." Although there is no fixed ratio between exemplary and actual damages, exemplary damages must be reasonably apportioned to the actual damages sustained. [Citation.] Because of the actual damages [$605,000] and the abundant evidence of malice, we hold that the award of punitive damages [$1,300,000] was not unreasonable.

The judgment of the trial court is affirmed.

CASE 7-4

Appropriation
WHITE v. SAMSUNG ELECTRONICS AMERICA, INC.
United States Court of Appeals, Ninth Circuit, 1992
971 F.2d 1395, cert. denied, 508 U.S. 951, 113 S.Ct. 2443, 124 L.Ed.2d 660 (1993)
http://scholar.google.com/scholar_case?case=15763501998860364615&q=971+F.2d+1395&hl=en&as_sdt=2,34

Goodwin, J.

This case involves a promotional "fame and fortune" dispute. In running a particular advertisement without Vanna White's permission, defendants Samsung Electronics America, Inc. (Samsung) and David Deutsch Associates, Inc. (Deutsch) attempted to capitalize on White's fame to enhance their fortune. White sued, alleging infringement of various intellectual property rights, but the district court granted summary judgment in favor of the defendants. We affirm in part, reverse in part, and remand.

Plaintiff Vanna White is the hostess of "Wheel of Fortune," one of the most popular game shows in television history. An estimated forty million people watch the program daily. Capitalizing on the fame which her participation in the show has bestowed on her, White markets her identity to various advertisers.

The dispute in this case arose out of a series of advertisements prepared for Samsung by Deutsch. The series ran in at least half a dozen publications with widespread, and in some cases national, circulation. Each of the advertisements in the series followed the same theme. Each depicted a current item from popular culture and a Samsung electronic product. Each was set in the twenty-first century and conveyed the message that the Samsung product would still be in use by that time. By hypothesizing outrageous future outcomes for the cultural items, the ads created humorous effects. For example, one lampooned current popular notions of an unhealthy diet by depicting a raw steak with the caption: "Revealed to be health food, 2010 A.D." Another depicted irreverent "news"-show host Morton Downey Jr. in front of an American flag with the caption: "Presidential candidate. 2008 A.D."

The advertisement which prompted the current dispute was for Samsung videocassette recorders (VCRs). The ad depicted a robot, dressed in a wig, gown, and jewelry which Deutsch consciously selected to resemble White's hair and dress. The robot was posed next to a game board which is instantly recognizable as the Wheel of Fortune game show set, in a stance for which White is famous. The caption of the ad read: "Longest running game show. 2012 A.D." Defendants referred to the ad as the "Vanna White" ad. Unlike the other celebrities used in the campaign, White neither consented to the ads nor was she paid.

Following the circulation of the robot ad, White sued Samsung and Deutsch in federal district court under: * * * the California common law right of publicity; * * * . The district court granted summary judgment against White on each of her claims. White now appeals.

* * *

White * * * argues that the district court erred in granting summary judgment to defendants on White's common law right of publicity claim. In *Eastwood v. Superior Court*, [citation], the California court of appeal stated that the common law right of publicity cause of action "may be pleaded by alleging (1) the defendant's use of the plaintiff's identity; (2) the appropriation of plaintiff's name or likeness to defendant's advantage, commercially or otherwise; (3) lack of consent, and (4) resulting injury." [Citation.] The district court dismissed White's claim for failure to satisfy *Eastwood*'s second prong, reasoning that defendants had not appropriated White's "name or likeness" with their robot ad. We agree that the robot ad did not make use of White's name or likeness. However, the common law right of publicity is not so confined.

The *Eastwood* court did not hold that the right of publicity cause of action could be pleaded only by alleging an appropriation of name or likeness. *Eastwood* involved an unauthorized use of photographs of Clint Eastwood and of his name. Accordingly, the *Eastwood* court had no occasion to consider the extent beyond the use of name or likeness to which the right of publicity reaches. That court held only that the right of publicity cause of action "may be" pleaded by alleging, *inter alia*, appropriation of name or likeness, not that the action may be pleaded only in those terms.

The "name or likeness" formulation referred to in *Eastwood* originated not as an element of the right of publicity cause of action, but as a description of the types of cases in which the cause of action had been recognized. The source of this formulation is Prosser, *Privacy*, 48 Cal.L.Rev. 383, 401–07 (1960), one of the earliest and most enduring articulations of the common law right of publicity cause of action. In looking at the case law to that point, Prosser recognized that right of publicity cases involved one of two basic factual scenarios: name appropriation, and picture or other likeness appropriation. [Citation.]

Even though Prosser focused on appropriations of name or likeness in discussing the right of publicity, he noted that "[i]t is not impossible that there might be appropriation of the plaintiff's identity, as by impersonation, without use of either his name or his likeness, and that this would be an invasion of his right of privacy." [Citation.] At the time Prosser wrote, he noted however, that "[n]o such case appears to have arisen." [Citation.]

Since Prosser's early formulation, the case law has borne out his insight that the right of publicity is not limited to the appropriation of name or likeness. In *Motschenbacher v. R.J. Reynolds Tobacco Co.*, [citation], the defendant had used a photograph of the plaintiff's race car in a television commercial. Although the plaintiff appeared driving the car in the photograph, his features were not visible. Even though the defendant had not appropriated the plaintiff's name or likeness, this court held that plaintiff's California right of publicity claim should reach the jury.

In *Midler*, this court held that, even though the defendants had not used Midler's name or likeness, Midler had stated a claim for violation of her California common law right of publicity because "the defendants * * * for their own profit in selling their product did appropriate part of her identity" by using a Midler sound-alike. [Citation.]

In *Carson v. Here's Johnny Portable Toilets, Inc.*, [citation], the defendant had marketed portable toilets under the brand name "Here's Johnny"—Johnny Carson's signature "Tonight Show" introduction—without Carson's permission. The district court had dismissed Carson's Michigan common law right of publicity claim because the defendants had not used Carson's "name or likeness." [Citation.] In reversing the district court, the sixth circuit found "the district court's conception of the right of publicity * * * too narrow" and held that the right was implicated because the defendant had

appropriated Carson's identity by using, *inter alia*, the phrase "Here's Johnny." [Citation.]

These cases teach not only that the common law right of publicity reaches means of appropriation other than name or likeness, but that the specific means of appropriation are relevant only for determining whether the defendant has in fact appropriated the plaintiff's identity. The right of publicity does not require that appropriations of identity be accomplished through particular means to be actionable. It is noteworthy that the *Midler* and *Carson* defendants not only avoided using the plaintiff's name or likeness, but they also avoided appropriating the celebrity's voice, signature, and photograph. The photograph in *Motschenbacher* did include the plaintiff, but because the plaintiff was not visible the driver could have been an actor or dummy and the analysis in the case would have been the same.

Although the defendants in these cases avoided the most obvious means of appropriating the plaintiffs' identities, each of their actions directly implicated the commercial interests which the right of publicity is designed to protect. As the *Carson* court explained,

> [t]he right of publicity has developed to protect the commercial interest of celebrities in their identities. The theory of the right is that a celebrity's identity can be valuable in the promotion of products, and the celebrity has an interest that may be protected from the unauthorized commercial exploitation of that identity. * * * If the celebrity's identity is commercially exploited, there has been an invasion of his right whether or not his "name or likeness" is used.

[Citation.] It is not important how the defendant has appropriated the plaintiff's identity, but whether the defendant has done so. *Motschenbacher, Midler*, and *Carson* teach the impossibility of treating the right of publicity as guarding only against a laundry list of specific means of appropriating identity. A rule which says that the right of publicity can be infringed only through the use of nine different methods of appropriating identity merely challenges the clever advertising strategist to come up with the tenth.

Indeed, if we treated the means of appropriation as dispositive in our analysis of the right of publicity, we would not only weaken the right but effectively eviscerate it. The right would fail to protect those plaintiffs most in need of its protection. Advertisers use celebrities to promote their products. The more popular the celebrity, the greater the number of people who recognize her, and the greater the visibility for the product. The identities of the most popular celebrities are not only the most attractive for advertisers, but also the easiest to evoke without resorting to obvious means such as name, likeness, or voice.

Consider a hypothetical advertisement which depicts a mechanical robot with male features, an African-American complexion, and a bald head. The robot is wearing black hightop Air Jordan basketball sneakers, and a red basketball uniform with black trim, baggy shorts, and the number 23 (though not revealing "Bulls" or "Jordan" lettering). The ad depicts the robot dunking a basketball one-handed, stiff-armed, legs extended like open scissors, and tongue hanging out. Now envision that this ad is run on television during professional basketball games. Considered individually, the robot's physical attributes, its dress, and its stance tell us little. Taken together, they lead to the only conclusion that any sports viewer who has registered a discernible pulse in the past five years would reach: the ad is about Michael Jordan.

Viewed separately, the individual aspects of the advertisement in the present case say little. Viewed together, they leave little doubt about the celebrity the ad is meant to depict. The female-shaped robot is wearing a long gown, blond wig, and large jewelry. Vanna White dresses exactly like this at times, but so do many other women. The robot is in the process of turning a block letter on a game-board.

Vanna White dresses like this while turning letters on a game-board but perhaps similarly attired Scrabble-playing women do this as well. The robot is standing on what looks to be the Wheel of Fortune game show set. Vanna White dresses like this, turns letters, and does this on the Wheel of Fortune game show. She is the only one. Indeed, defendants themselves referred to their ad as the "Vanna White" ad. We are not surprised.

Television and other media create marketable celebrity identity value. Considerable energy and ingenuity are expended by those who have achieved celebrity value to exploit it for profit. The law protects the celebrity's sole right to exploit this value whether the celebrity has achieved her fame out of rare ability, dumb luck, or a combination thereof. We decline Samsung and Deutsch's invitation to permit the evisceration of the common law right of publicity through means as facile as those in this case. Because White has alleged facts showing that Samsung and Deutsch had appropriated her identity, the district court erred by rejecting, on summary judgment, White's common law right of publicity claim.

QUESTIONS

1. The Penguin intentionally hits Batman with his umbrella. Batman, stunned by the blow, falls backwards, knocking Robin down. Robin's leg is broken in the fall, and he cries out, "Holy broken bat bones! My leg is broken." Who, if anyone, is liable to Robin? Why?

2. CEO was convinced by his employee, M. Ploy, that a coworker, A. Cused, had been stealing money from the company. At lunch that day in the company cafeteria, CEO discharges Cused from her employment, accuses her of stealing from the company, searches through her purse over her objections, and finally forcibly escorts her to his office to await the arrival of the police, which he has his secretary summon. Cused is indicted for embezzlement but subsequently is acquitted upon establishing her innocence. What rights, if any, does Cused have against CEO?

3. Ralph kisses Edith while she is asleep but does not waken or harm her. Edith sues Ralph for battery. Has a battery been committed?

4. Claude, a creditor seeking to collect a debt, calls on Dianne and demands payment in a rude and insolent manner. When Dianne says that she cannot pay, Claude calls Dianne a deadbeat and says that he will never trust her again. Is Claude liable to Dianne? If so, for what tort?

5. Lana, a ten-year-old child, is run over by a car negligently driven by Mitchel. Lana, at the time of the accident, was acting reasonably and without negligence. Clark, a newspaper reporter, photographs Lana while she is lying in the street in great pain. Two years later, Perry, the publisher of a newspaper, prints Clark's picture of Lana in his newspaper as a lead to an article concerning the negligence of children. The caption under the picture reads: "They ask to be killed." Lana, who has recovered from the accident, brings suit against Clark and Perry. What result?

6. In 1963 the *Saturday Evening Post* featured an article entitled "The Story of a College Football Fix," characterized in the subtitle as "A Shocking Report of How Wally Butts and Bear Bryant Rigged a Game Last Fall." Butts was athletic director of the University of Georgia, and Bryant was head coach of the University of Alabama. The article was based on a claim by one George Burnett that he had accidentally overheard a long-distance telephone conversation between Butts and Bryant in the course of which Butts divulged information on plays Georgia would use in the upcoming game against Alabama. The writer assigned to the story by the *Post* was not a football expert, did not interview either Butts or Bryant, and did not personally see the notes Burnett had made of the telephone conversation. Butts admitted that he had a long-distance telephone conversation with Bryant but denied that any advance information on prospective football plays was given. Has Butts been defamed by the *Post*?

7. Joan, a patient confined in a hospital, has a rare disease that is of great interest to the public. Carol, a television reporter, requests Joan to consent to an interview. Joan refuses, but Carol, nonetheless, enters Joan's room over her objection and photographs her. Joan brings a suit against Carol. Is Carol liable? If so, for what tort?

8. Owner has a place on his land where he piles trash. The pile has been there for three months. John, a neighbor of Owner and without Owner's consent or knowledge, throws trash onto the trash pile. Owner learns that John has done this and sues him. What tort, if any, has John committed?

9. Chris leaves her car parked in front of a store. There are no signs that say Chris cannot park there. The store owner, however, needs the car moved to enable a delivery truck to unload. He releases the brake and pushes Chris's car three or four feet, doing no harm to the car. Chris returns and sees that her car has been moved and is very angry. She threatens to sue the store owner for trespass to her personal property. Can she recover?

10. Carr borrowed John's brand-new car for the purpose of going to the store. He told John he would be right back. Carr then decided, however, to go to the beach while he had the car. Can John recover from Carr the value of the automobile? If so, for what tort?

CASE PROBLEMS

11. Marcia Samms claimed that David Eccles had repeatedly and persistently called her at various hours, including late at night, from May to December, soliciting her to have illicit sexual relations with him. She also claimed that on one occasion Eccles came over to her residence to again solicit sex and indecently exposed himself to her. Mrs. Samms had never encouraged Eccles but had continuously repulsed his "insulting, indecent, and obscene" proposals. She brought suit against Eccles, claiming she suffered great anxiety and fear for her personal safety and severe emotional distress, demanding actual and punitive damages. Can she recover? If so, for what tort?

12. National Bond and Investment Company sent two of its employees to repossess Whithorn's car after he failed to complete the payments. The two repossessors located Whithorn while he was driving his car. They followed him and hailed him down to make the repossession. Whithorn refused to abandon his car and demanded evidence of their authority. The two repossessors became impatient and called a wrecker. They ordered the driver of the wrecker to hook Whithorn's car and move it down the street while Whithorn was still inside the vehicle. Whithorn started the car and tried to escape, but the wrecker lifted the car off the road and progressed seventy-five to one hundred feet until Whithorn managed to stall the wrecker. Has National Bond committed the tort of false imprisonment?

13. In March, William Proxmire, a U.S. senator from Wisconsin, initiated the "Golden Fleece of the Month Award" to publicize what he believed to be wasteful government spending. The second of these awards was given to the Federal agencies that had for seven years funded Dr. Hutchinson's research on stress levels in animals. The award was made in a speech Proxmire gave in the Senate; the text was also incorporated into an advance press release that was sent to 275 members of the national news media. Proxmire also referred to the research in two subsequent newsletters sent to one hundred thousand constituents and during a television interview. Hutchinson then brought this action alleging defamation resulting in personal and economic injury. Assuming that Hutchinson proved that the statements were false and defamatory, would he prevail?

14. Capune was attempting a trip from New York to Florida on an eighteen-foot-long paddleboard. The trip was being covered by various media to gain publicity for Capune and certain products he endorsed. By water, Capune approached a pier owned by Robbins, who had posted signs prohibiting surfing and swimming around the pier. Capune was unaware of these notices and attempted to continue his journey by passing under the pier. Robbins ran up yelling and threw two bottles at Capune. Capune was frightened and tried to maneuver his paddleboard to go around the pier. Robbins then threw a third bottle that hit Capune in the head. Capune had to be helped out of the water and taken to the hospital. He suffered a physical wound that required twenty-four sutures and, as a result, had to discontinue his trip. Capune brought suit in tort against Robbins. Is Robbins liable? If so, for which tort or torts?

15. Ralph Nader, who has been a critic of General Motors Corp. for several years, claims that when General Motors learned that Nader was about to publish a book entitled *Unsafe at Any Speed*, criticizing one of its automobiles, it decided to conduct a campaign of intimidation against

him. Specifically, Nader claims that GMC (a) conducted a series of interviews with Nader's acquaintances, questioning them about his political, social, racial, and religious views; (b) kept him under surveillance in public places for an unreasonable length of time, including close observation of him in a bank; (c) caused him to be accosted by women for the purpose of entrapping him into illicit relationships; (d) made threatening, harassing, and obnoxious telephone calls to him; (e) tapped his telephone and eavesdropped by means of mechanical and electronic equipment on his private conversations with others; and (f) conducted a "continuing" and harassing investigation of him. Nader brought suit against GMC for invasion of privacy. Which, if any, of the alleged actions would constitute invasion of privacy?

16. Bill Kinsey was charged with murdering his wife while working for the Peace Corps in Tanzania. After waiting six months in jail, he was acquitted at a trial that attracted wide publicity. Five years later, while a graduate student at Stanford University, Kinsey had a brief affair with Mary Macur. He abruptly ended the affair by telling Macur he would no longer be seeing her because another woman, Sally Allen, was coming from England to live with him. A few months later, Kinsey and Allen moved to Africa and were subsequently married. Soon after Bill ended their affair, Macur began a letter-writing campaign designed to expose Bill and his mistreatment of her. Macur sent several letters to both Bill and Sally Kinsey, their parents, their neighbors, their parents' neighbors, members of Bill's dissertation committee, other faculty, and the president of Stanford University. The letters contained statements accusing Bill of murdering his first wife, spending six months in jail for the crime, being a rapist, and other questionable behavior. The Kinseys brought an action for invasion of privacy, seeking damages and a permanent injunction. Will the Kinseys prevail? If so, for what tort?

17. The Brineys (defendants) owned a large farm on which was located an abandoned farmhouse. For a ten-year period the house had been the subject of several trespassings and housebreakings. In an attempt to stop the intrusions, Briney boarded up the windows and doors and posted "no trespassing" signs. After one break-in, however, Briney set a spring gun in a bedroom. It was placed over the bedroom window so that the gun could not be seen from outside, and no warning of its presence was posted. The gun was set to hit an intruder in the legs. Briney loaded the gun with a live shell, but he claimed that he did not intend to injure anyone.

Katko (plaintiff) and a friend, McDonough, had broken into the abandoned farmhouse on an earlier occasion to steal old bottles and fruit jars for their antique collection. They returned for a second time after the spring gun had been set, and Katko was seriously wounded in the leg when the gun discharged as he entered the bedroom. He then brought action for damages. Decision?

18. Plaintiff, John W. Carson, was the host and star of *The Tonight Show*, a well-known television program broadcast by the National Broadcasting Company. Carson also appeared as an entertainer in nightclubs and theaters around the country. From the time he began hosting *The Tonight Show*, he had been introduced on the show each night with the phrase "Here's Johnny." The phrase "Here's Johnny" is still generally associated with Carson by a substantial segment of the television viewing public. To earn additional income, Carson began authorizing use of this phrase by outside business ventures.

   Defendant, Here's Johnny Portable Toilets, Inc., is a Michigan corporation engaged in the business of renting and selling "Here's Johnny" portable toilets. Defendant's founder was aware at the time he formed the corporation that "Here's Johnny" was the introductory slogan for Carson on *The Tonight Show*. He indicated that he coupled the phrase with a second one, "The World's Foremost Commodian," to make "a good play on a phrase." Carson brought suit for invasion of privacy. Should Carson recover? If so, for which tort?

19. Susan Jungclaus Peterson was a twenty-one-year-old student at Moorhead State University who had lived most of her life on her family farm in Minnesota. Though Susan was a dean's list student during her first year, her academic performance declined after she became deeply involved in an international religious cult organization known locally as The Way of Minnesota, Inc. The cult demanded an enormous psychological and monetary commitment from Susan. Near the end of her junior year, her parents became alarmed by the changes in Susan's physical and mental well-being and concluded that she had been "reduced to a condition of psychological bondage by The Way." They sought help from Kathy Mills, a self-styled "deprogrammer" of minds brainwashed by cults.

   On May 24, Norman Jungclaus, Susan's father, picked up Susan at Moorhead State. Instead of returning home, they went to the residence of Veronica Morgel, where Kathy Mills attempted to deprogram Susan. For the first few days of her stay, Susan was unwilling to discuss her involvement. She lay curled in a fetal position in her bedroom, plugging her ears and hysterically screaming and crying while her father pleaded with her to listen. By the third day, however, Susan's demeanor changed completely. She became friendly and vivacious and communicated with her father. Susan also went roller-skating and played softball at a nearby park over the following weekend. She spent the next week in Columbus, Ohio, with a former cult member who had shared her experiences of the previous week. While in Columbus, she spoke daily by telephone with her fiancé, a member of The Way, who begged her to return to the cult. Susan expressed the desire to get her fiancé out of the organization, but a meeting between them could not be arranged outside the presence of other members of The Way. Her parents attempted to persuade Susan to sign an agreement releasing them from liability for their actions, but Susan refused. After nearly sixteen days of "deprogramming" Susan left the Morgel residence and returned to her fiancé and The Way. Upon the direction of The Way ministry, she brought this action against her parents for false imprisonment. Will Susan prevail? Explain.

20. Debra Agis was a waitress in a restaurant owned by the Howard Johnson Company. On May 23, Roger Dionne, manager of the restaurant, called a meeting of all waitresses at which he informed them that "there was some stealing going on." Dionne also stated that the identity of the party or parties responsible was not known and that he would begin firing all waitresses in alphabetical order until the guilty party or parties were detected. He then fired Debra Agis, who allegedly "became greatly upset, began to cry, sustained emotional distress, mental anguish, and loss of wages and earnings." Mrs. Agis brought a complaint against the Howard Johnson Company and Roger Dionne, alleging that the defendants acted recklessly and outrageously, intending to cause emotional distress and anguish. The defendants argued that damages for emotional distress are not recoverable unless physical injury occurs as a result of the distress. Will Agis be successful on her complaint?

21. On July 31, Amanda Vaughn and Jason Vaughn accompanied their mother, Emma Simpson Vaughn, to a Walmart store. Amanda's friend, Kimberly Dickerson, was also with them. Once they entered the store, Mrs. Vaughn and Jason went into separate areas of the store. The two girls remained together in the front of the store and selected a stamp album to purchase. Kimberly

took the album to the checkout register, and while she was at the register, she also selected a pack of gum. Once Kimberly paid for her two items, they were placed in a bag and she was given her change. Kimberly testified that she did not immediately put the change in her wallet while she was at the register. Instead, Kimberly walked back into the merchandise area where Amanda had remained. Kimberly was in the merchandise area, away from the registers, when she placed her change in her purse. Kimberly proceeded to place her hand in the Walmart bag to retrieve the gum she had just purchased.

At this time, Ms. Clara Lynn Neal, a customer service manager, observed Kimberly's hand coming out of her Walmart bag. According to Ms. Neal, because the two girls were in a somewhat-secluded area of the store, Ms. Neal walked past the two girls twice to observe them before she walked over to them.

Ms. Neal testified that she asked Kimberly if she could see her bag and her receipt and that Kimberly voluntarily gave her the bag. Plaintiffs alleged that Ms. Neal "detained the girls, snatched Kimberly's bag from her, searched the bag, discovered a receipt, tied the bag, and then personally escorted the girls to an area near the front door away from the registers." However, Kimberly's testimony stated that "[Ms. Neal] said she was going to have to check my bag because she doesn't know if I'm stealing something. So I didn't say anything. I didn't really give it to her because I was shocked. So she took it, and she was like searching through it."

Once Ms. Neal checked the purchases with the receipt, the girls were told to go to the front of the store and wait for their party. The girls were never told that they could not leave the store and the girls were not detained by anyone else. According to all parties, from the time Ms. Neal walked up to the girls, verified the purchases, and returned the bag to Kimberly, the entire incident only lasted about one minute. While the girls were waiting at the front of the store, Jason was asked by his mother to inform the girls that she was ready to go. Jason approached the girls, and they responded that they could not leave. When Jason reported to his mother that the girls stated they could not leave the area, Mrs. Vaughn then went to the front of the store to investigate. Before Mrs. Vaughn took the children home, she explained to a store manager what had occurred. Do the girls have a cause of action against Walmart?

Edith Mitchell, accompanied by her thirteen-year-old daughter, went through the checkout at Walmart and purchased several items. As they exited, the Mitchells passed through an electronic antitheft device, which sounded an alarm. Robert Canady, employed by Walmart as a "people greeter" and security guard, forcibly stopped Edith Mitchell at the exit, grabbed her bag, and told her to step back inside. The security guard never touched Edith or her daughter and never threatened to touch either of them. Nevertheless, Edith Mitchell described the security guard's actions in her affidavit as "gruff, loud, rude behavior." The security guard removed every item Mitchell had just purchased and ran it through the security gate. One of the items still had a security code unit on it, which an employee admitted could have been overlooked by the cashier. When the security guard finished examining the contents of Mitchell's bag, he put it on the checkout counter. This examination of her bag took ten or fifteen minutes. Once her bag had been checked, no employee of Walmart ever told Mitchell she could not leave. Mitchell was never threatened with arrest. Mitchell brought a tort action against Walmart.

a. Explain on which torts should Mitchell base her claim against Walmart.

b. What arguments would support Walmart denial of liability for these torts?

c. Which party should prevail? Explain.

CHAPTER 4

Privacy and Technology

© Ryan McVay/The Image Bank/Getty Images

A wonderful fact to reflect upon, that every human creature is constituted to be that profound secret and mystery to every other. A solemn consideration, when I enter a great city by night, that every one of those darkly clustered houses encloses its own secret; that every room in every one of them encloses its own secret; that in every beating heart in the hundreds of thousands of breasts there is, in some of its imaginings, a secret to the heart nearest to it!

—CHARLES DICKENS

Ladies and gentlemen, progress is like a storekeeper. You can have anything you want, but you have to pay the price. You can have the telephone, but you will lose some of your privacy, and the charm of distance. You can have the airplane, but the birds will lose their wonder and the clouds will smell of gasoline.

—CLARENCE DARROW in *Inherit the Wind*

You already have zero privacy—get over it.

—SCOTT MCNEALY, CEO, Sun Microsystems

Human beings must experience a degree of privacy to thrive. Yet, as they act inside organizations, they frequently need information about one another, information that may be sensitive and confidential. Employers want to find out if their workers are productive and loyal. Corporations want to know the preferences of potential customers or the strategies of their competitors. Governments want to thwart terrorists. Tension between privacy and the need to know is heightened as computer technology revolutionizes information gathering. The process has never been so fast, so efficient, or so omnipresent.

This chapter highlights the conflict between the sweeping power of technology to access and assemble information and the ongoing concerns we all share about privacy. Opening with a case involving the interception of e-mail by an employer, it broadens to look at electronic surveillance more generally, and at the legal framework that might address it. We read about the value of privacy, both for individuals and for communities. Next, we look at efforts to control employees' off-the-job behavior. Should employers be able to fire you for smoking, drinking, or other unhealthy habits? For dating someone who is married? We then explore, for employees in the public sector, the limits of privacy for text messaging, and read about the expectations Millennials have about employer access to social media. We learn about the Genetic Information Nondiscrimination Act (GINA) and end the chapter with a case in which corporations claim that, under the Pennsylvania

Constitution, they should be able to prevent disclosure of the chemicals they use to hydro-frack for natural gas.

⦿ SURVEILLANCE AT WORK

E-mail Interception

In the United States, billions of e-mails are sent every day from business settings. Because they use pass-codes, employees may believe their e-mail messages are private, but the reality is that they are not. Even deleted messages are stored in archives easily accessible to employers and others.

■ ■ ■

In 1996, a district court in Philadelphia was faced with the following situation. A Pillsbury employee and his supervisor were sending e-mail messages to one another. One message, referring to sales management, mentioned plans to "kill the back-stabbing bastards." Another message described a holiday party as the "Jim Jones Kool-Aid affair." These messages fell into their boss's hands, and both men were fired for sending "inappropriate and unprofessional comments" over Pillsbury's e-mail system. One of the employees sued, claiming he was "wrongfully discharged" when he lost his well-paid position as a regional manager.

Michael A. Smyth v. The Pillsbury Company
United States District Court, 1996
914 F. Supp. 97

WEINER, District Judge.

Defendant [Pillsbury Company] maintained an electronic mail communication system ("e-mail") in order to promote internal corporate communications between its employees. Defendant repeatedly assured its employees, including plaintiff, that all e-mail communications would remain confidential and privileged. Defendant further assured its employees, including plaintiff, that e-mail communications could not be intercepted and used by defendant against its employees as grounds for termination or reprimand.

In October 1994, plaintiff [Michael Smyth] received certain e-mail communications from his supervisor over defendant's e-mail system on his computer at home. In reliance on defendant's assurances regarding defendant's e-mail system, plaintiff responded and exchanged e-mails with his supervisor. At some later date, contrary to the assurances of confidentiality made by defendant, defendant, acting through its agents, servants, and employees, intercepted plaintiff's private e-mail messages made in October 1994. On January 17, 1995, defendant notified plaintiff that it was terminating his employment ... for transmitting what it deemed to be inappropriate and unprofessional comments over defendant's e-mail system....

[Smyth argued wrongful discharge, claiming his employer had violated public policy by committing a tort known as "invasion of privacy." One version of invasion of privacy is called "intrusion." In the first step of his analysis, the judge defines the tort of "intrusion":]

One who intentionally intrudes, physically or otherwise, upon the solitude or seclusion of another or his private affairs or concerns, is subject to liability to the other for invasion of his privacy, if the intrusion would be highly offensive to a reasonable person....

[To determine if the facts of the case fit the definition above, the judge uses a "balancing test," weighing the employee's privacy interests against the employer's need to discover information.]

[W]e do not find a reasonable expectation of privacy in e-mail communications voluntarily made by an employee to his supervisor over the company e-mail system notwithstanding any assurances that such communications would not be intercepted by management. Once plaintiff communicated the alleged unprofessional comments to a second person (his supervisor) over an e-mail system which was apparently utilized by the entire company, any reasonable expectation of privacy was lost. Significantly, the defendant did not require plaintiff, as in the case of a urinalysis or personal property search, to disclose any personal information about himself. Rather, plaintiff voluntarily communicated the alleged unprofessional comments over the company e-mail system. We find no privacy interests in such communications.

Secondly, even if we found that an employee had a reasonable expectation of privacy in the contents of his e-mail communications over the company e-mail system, we do not find that a reasonable person would consider the defendant's interception of these communications to be a substantial and highly offensive invasion of his privacy.... [T]he company's interest in preventing inappropriate and unprofessional comments or even illegal activity over its e-mail system outweighs any privacy interest the employee may have in those comments.

In sum, we find that the defendant's actions did not tortiously invade the plaintiff's privacy and, therefore, did not violate public policy.

QUESTIONS

1. How does Judge Weiner explain why Michael Smyth lost any "reasonable expectation of privacy" in his e-mail comments?

2. Is there any difference between a password-protected message sent on company e-mail and a handwritten memo sealed in an envelope marked "private" sent through company mail? Consider the judge's reasons for his ruling. Would they also apply to the memo? Suppose Pillsbury began covert audio monitoring of the area near the coffee station in order to screen employee conversations on break time. How would the judge's reasoning apply?

3. Corporate culture varies, and with it, corporate surveillance policies. Some companies give notice to employees that their e-mail communications are not private. Kmart's policy, for example, introduced at every employee orientation, states that "misuse of the e-mail system could result in denial of access to the Kmart computing environment or dismissal." Apple, on the other hand, has an explicit policy of not monitoring employee e-mail. What might be the advantages and disadvantages of such policies from an employee's viewpoint? An employer's?

4. Nearly half of American workers bring work home with them regularly, according to *American Sociological Review* in December 2009. Technology allows us to do increasing amounts of work outside the office, during hours that were once considered reserved for leisure time. At the same time, people often find themselves handling personal chores while they are at work. According to a study by the Center for Business Ethics at Bentley College, by 2003, virtually all (92 percent of) employers allow office computers to be used—within reason—for personal purposes. As the division between work and the rest of life becomes ever more blurred, should the balancing of interests articulated in the *Pillsbury* case change?

5. Marina Stengart worked with Loving Care Agency, Inc., which provided services for children and adults. She resigned in 2007 because of gender issues, and would then sue for sex discrimination. Before she resigned, Stengart had used her employer's laptop to send e-mails to her lawyer from her password-protected Yahoo account, describing her situation at work. Once she was gone Loving Care hired a computer expert to create a forensic image of the laptop's hard drive, including temporary Internet files with the e-mails Stengart had exchanged with her lawyer. At the bottom of each e-mail sent by Stengart's lawyer, a warning stated that the information was a "privileged and confidential" attorney-client communication. Compare and contrast the facts of this case with *Smyth v. Pillsbury*. Do you think the judge in Smyth would decide that the way these e-mails were accessed violated Marina Stengart's right to privacy? Find out what happened in this case. **Research:** *Stengart v. Loving Care Agency Inc.* (New Jersey Supreme Court, 2010).

6. Should educational institutions be free to randomly monitor student and faculty e-mail? What is your school's policy on e-mail privacy? Review it and discuss it with others. Are there elements of the policy that you would change, in light of what you have read? Rewrite it.

■ ■ ■

Electronic Surveillance: The Debate

Employers have long had an interest in scrutinizing their workforces. In the 1880s, Frederick Taylor invented an approach to industrial efficiency that broke each job into many separate, measurable components. He monitored every part of the process—time per task; hand and eye movements; spacing between workers, machines, and products—and developed a system that gave managers the ability to track both the speed and the intensity of work very closely. And in the early twentieth century, Ford Motor Company hired social workers to investigate employees, to check that they had the right habits of cleanliness, thriftiness, and churchgoing to deserve what was then an impressive $5/day wage. What is different about present-day workplace oversight is the use of technology that allows workers to be observed secretly and in newly intrusive ways. Also, the rate of electronic monitoring of employees has scaled up dramatically over recent years. In 1998, the congressional Office of Technology Assessment found that only eight percent of firms were conducting monitoring. Just five years later, by 2003, nearly all (92 percent) of employers were using some form of electronic surveillance.[1]

---

[1]2003 Center for Business Ethics at Bentley College, "Survey: You've Got Mail, and the Boss Knows."

SURVEY DATA SHOW INCREASING WORKPLACE SURVEILLANCE

Since 2001 the American Management Association (AMA) has been conducting biannual studies of the employee monitoring practices of hundreds of firms. Their 2007 survey indicated that workplace surveillance—from videotaping to monitoring of blogsites to GPS (Global Positioning System) tracking of vehicles—was on the rise. While AMA data from 2005 showed 25 percent of respondents reporting they had fired employees for misuse of e-mail, by 2007, 28 percent reported having done so. In the 2005 AMA survey, 26 percent of respondents reported firing employees for misuse of the Internet; by 2007 that number had increased to 30 percent. Further 2007 findings: Nearly half of employers surveyed tracked keystrokes, content, and time spent on computers. Twelve percent monitored blogs to check for comments about the company, and 10 percent monitored social networking sites. In 2001, when the AMA did its first electronic monitoring survey, 33 percent of employers reported using video surveillance to counter theft or sabotage. By 2007 nearly half did so—48 percent—with 7 percent reporting video monitoring of job performance. According to the latest AMA survey, 12 percent of the companies that monitor do not notify their employees.

Interest in the use of software to track employee activity online is growing. Filtering software is evolving quickly and becoming increasingly sophisticated. These programs can take surreptitious "screen shots" of employee computers; track Web usage; rank individuals according to their rates of traffic to game, joke, pornography, shopping, or job-hunting sites; or examine images attached to e-mails for anything that looks like flesh. Consider for example SpectorSoft's flagship product, Spector 360, which "takes the recorded Internet and computer activities from each of your employees, feeds that information into a database, and provides you with more than 50 built-in reports and unlimited customization." About $2,000 will pay for installation on 15 computers, allowing a company to discover:

- *Which employees spend the most time surfing websites*
- *Which employees chat the most*
- *Who sends the most e-mails with attachments*
- *Who arrives to work late and leaves early*
- *What ... employees [are] searching for on the Internet*

This software product promises "through a first of its kind surveillance-like camera recording tool" to reveal a "level of detail so precise that you can see what an employee does each and every second."[2]

Businesses justify electronic surveillance in a number of ways. It enables supervisors to observe and improve employee performance. It both measures and encourages efficiency. It enhances the completeness and fairness of personnel evaluations. It can uncover employee disloyalty, which can take the form of stealing tangible items, such as products and supplies, or intangibles, such as trade secrets. It can flag racially or sexually harassing e-messages.

Countering all this, employees claim that electronic monitoring puts them under dehumanizing pressure with computers instead of people judging their performance.

---

[2]http://www.spectorsoft.com, last visited June 18, 2010.

Because computers measure quantity better than quality, employees who work fast might look better than those who work best. The "electronic sweatshop," they say, causes psychological stress and physical symptoms.[3] For example, a study of employees in financial institutions and government agencies found that subjecting people to monitoring negatively affected the quality of their work. And a 1993 Rutgers University study found that employees subjected to video surveillance were less able to solve complex problems.[4] Apart from the more measurable costs, employees emphasize their need to preserve at work what they expect to maintain elsewhere—a sense of dignity and self-respect.

Electronic Surveillance: The Law

America lacks a comprehensive and uniform legal standard protecting privacy. No express "right to privacy" was written into the U.S. Constitution, although the Supreme Court has interpreted the First, Fourth, Fifth, Ninth, and Fourteenth Amendments as creating certain privacy rights that cannot be violated by the government. (Later in this chapter, we explore one aspect: the right to be free of unreasonable government searches and seizures.)

In the private sector, privacy law is determined by a variety of federal and state statutes and by the common law of torts.[5] Employees may claim that electronic monitoring amounts to "intrusion," a variation on the tort of invasion of privacy. As the *Pillsbury* case indicates, intrusion involves invading another person's solitude in a manner considered highly offensive—unauthorized prying into a personal bank account or a landlord bugging the wall of his tenants' bedroom, for example. Most courts consider two main factors: (1) the obnoxiousness of the means used to intrude, that is, whether it is a deviation from the normal, accepted means of discovering the relevant information; and (2) the reasons for intruding. In one Alabama case, a man had multiple surgeries after he fell while working as a winch-truck driver. In preparation for a worker's compensation trial, and in order to collect evidence regarding the extent of his actual injuries, the employer had him videotaped secretly while he was at home. The court dismissed his claim for intrusion, stating "Because the activities [the injured worker] carried on in his front yard could have been observed by any passerby," the employer's investigation was not offensive or objectionable.[6] As electronic monitoring becomes increasingly commonplace, and increasingly taken for granted, and as long as employers can point to a legitimate purpose for monitoring, it will be difficult for employees to convince courts that their privacy was invaded.

The 1968 Federal Wiretap Law, as amended by the Electronic Communications Privacy Act 1986 (ECPA), making it illegal to intercept, disclose, or access messages without authorization, would appear to protect workers from electronic eavesdropping. But there are a number of exemptions to the ECPA. For example, there is no protection for communications that are "readily accessible to the general public," such as public chat room

---

[3]Peter Blackman and Barbara Franklin, "Blocking Big Brother: Proposed Law Limits Employers' Right to Snoop," *New York Law Journal*, August 19, 1993, p. 5, citing University of Wisconsin study finding monitored telecommunications workers suffered more depression, anxiety, and fatigue than their nonmonitored counterparts in the same facility.

[4]Lewis Maltby, *Can They Do That? Retaking our Fundamental Rights at the Workplace* (New York: Penguin Publishing, 2009), p. 27.

[5]Connecticut and Delaware have passed laws to protect employees against electronic monitoring without notice. *Conn. Gen. Stat.* Sec 31-48d, *Del. Code* tit. 19 Sec. 705.

[6]*5ICU Investigations, Inc. v. Charles R. Jones,* 780 So.2d 685 (2000).

exchanges. The law does not apply to the extent that employees give "consent" to monitoring, which would seem to eliminate ECPA coverage in the many workplaces where people are told that their communications are not private. The ECPA also allows employers to listen in on communications made in the "ordinary course of business." In other words, where business interests such as efficiency or legal liability are at stake, the surveillance would be allowed.

THE VALUE OF PRIVACY

Privacy is much more than just a possible social technique for assuring this or that substantive interest ... it is necessarily related to ends and relations of the most fundamental sort: respect, love, friendship, and trust. Privacy is not merely a good technique for furthering these fundamental relations, rather without privacy they are simply inconceivable. They require a context of privacy or the possibility of privacy for their existence.... To respect, love, trust, feel affection for others, and to regard ourselves as the objects of love, trust, and affection is at the heart of our notion of ourselves as persons among persons, and privacy is the necessary atmosphere for those attitudes and actions, as oxygen is for combustion.

—CHARLES FRIED, "Privacy," 77 Yale L.J. 475 (1968)

The following excerpt describes how privacy serves a set of important human needs. The author, Alan Westin (1930–2013), was a Columbia University Professor Emeritus and a corporate consultant on privacy issues, and in the forefront of research on the effects of technology on privacy in our society, particularly in the workplace.

The Functions of Privacy

Alan Westin[7]

[T]he functions privacy performs for individuals in democratic societies ... can [be] ... grouped conveniently under four headings—personal autonomy, emotional release, self-evaluation, and limited and protected communication....

Personal Autonomy

In democratic societies there is a fundamental belief in the uniqueness of the individual, in his basic dignity and worth as a creature of God and a human being, and in the need to maintain social processes that safeguard his sacred individuality. Psychologists and sociologists have linked the development and maintenance of this sense of individuality to the human need for autonomy—the desire to avoid being manipulated or dominated wholly by others.

[Scholars describe a] "core self,"... pictured as an inner circle surrounded by a series of larger concentric circles. The inner circle shelters the individual's "ultimate secrets"—those hopes, fears, and prayers that are beyond sharing with anyone unless the individual comes under such stress that he must pour out these ultimate secrets to secure emotional relief.... The next circle outward contains "intimate

---

[7]Reprinted with the permission of Simon and Schuster, Inc. from *Privacy and Freedom* by Alan F. Westin. Copyright © 1967 by the Association of the Bar of the City of New York. All rights reserved.

secrets," those that can be willingly shared with close relations, confessors, or strangers who pass by and cannot injure. The next circle is open to members of the individual's friendship group. The series continues until it reaches the outer circles of casual conversation and physical expression that are open to all observers.

The most serious threat to the individual's autonomy is the possibility that someone may penetrate the inner zone and learn his ultimate secrets, either by physical or psychological means. Each person is aware of the gap between what he wants to be and what he actually is, between what the world sees of him and what he knows to be his much more complex reality. In addition, there are aspects of himself that the individual does not fully understand but is slowly exploring and shaping as he develops. Every individual lives behind a mask in this manner; indeed, the first etymological meaning of the word "person" was "mask."...

Emotional Release

Life in society generates such tensions for the individual that both physical and psychological health demand periods of privacy for various types of emotional release. At one level, such relaxation is required from the pressure of playing social roles.... On any given day a man may move through the roles of stern father, loving husband, car-pool comedian, skilled lathe operator, union steward, water-cooler flirt, and American Legion committee chairman—all psychologically different roles.... [N]o individual can play indefinitely, without relief, the variety of roles that life demands. There have to be moments "off stage" when the individual can be "himself": tender, angry, irritable, lustful, or dream-filled. Such moments may come in solitude; in the intimacy of family, peers, or woman-to-woman and man-to-man relaxation; in the anonymity of park or street; or in a state of reserve while in a group. Privacy in this aspect gives individuals, from factory workers to presidents, a chance to lay their masks aside for rest....

Another form of emotional release is provided by the protection privacy gives to minor noncompliance with social norms.... [A]lmost everyone does break some social or institutional norms—for example, violating traffic laws, breaking sexual mores, cheating on expense accounts, overstating income tax deductions, or smoking in restrooms when this is prohibited. Although society will usually punish the most flagrant abuses, it tolerates the great bulk of the violations as "permissible" deviations.... [I]f all transgressions were known—most persons in society would be under organizational discipline or in jail, or could be manipulated by threats of such action. The firm expectation of having privacy for permissible deviations is a distinguishing characteristic of life in a free society. At a lesser but still important level, privacy also allows individuals to deviate temporarily from social etiquette when alone or among intimates, as by putting feet on desks, cursing, letting one's face go slack, or scratching wherever one itches.

Another aspect of release is the "safety valve" function afforded by privacy. Most persons need to give vent to their anger at "the system," "city hall," "the boss," and various others who exercise authority over them, and to do this in the intimacy of family or friendship circles, or in private papers, without fear of being held responsible for such comments. This is very different from freedom of speech or press, which involves publicly voiced criticism without fear of interference by government....

Still another aspect of release through privacy arises in the management of bodily and sexual functions....

Self-Evaluation

Every individual needs to integrate his experiences into a meaningful pattern and to exert his individuality on events. To carry on such self-evaluation, privacy is essential. At the intellectual level, individuals need to process the information that is constantly bombarding them, information that cannot be processed while they are still "on the go." This is particularly true of creative persons. Studies of creativity show that it is in reflective solitude and even "daydreaming" during moments of reserve that most creative "nonverbal" thought takes place. At such moments the individual runs ideas and impressions through his mind in a flow of associations; the active presence of others tends to inhibit this process....

The evaluative function of privacy also has a major moral dimension—the exercise of conscience by which the individual "repossesses himself." While people often consider the moral consequences of their acts during the course of daily affairs, it is primarily in periods of privacy that they take a moral inventory of ongoing conduct and measure current performance against personal ideals. For many persons this process is a religious exercise.... Even for an individual who is not a religious believer, privacy serves to bring the conscience into play, for, when alone, he must find a way to continue living with himself.

Limited and Protected Communication

The greatest threat to civilized social life would be a situation in which each individual was utterly candid in his communications with others, saying exactly what he knew or felt at all times. The havoc done to interpersonal relations by children, saints, mental patients, and adult "innocents" is legendary.

In real life, among mature persons all communication is partial and limited.... Limited communication is particularly vital in urban life, with its heightened stimulation, crowded environment, and continuous physical and psychological confrontations between individuals who do not know one another in the extended, softening fashion of small-town life....

Privacy for limited and protected communication has two general aspects. First, it provides the individual with the opportunities he needs for sharing confidences and intimacies with those he trusts.... "A friend," said Emerson, "is someone before ... [whom] I can think aloud." In addition, the individual often wants to secure counsel from persons with whom he does not have to live daily after disclosing his confidences. He seeks professionally objective advice from persons whose status in society promises that they will not later use his distress to take advantage of him. To protect freedom of limited communication, such relationships—with doctors, lawyers, ministers, psychiatrists, psychologists, and others—are given varying but important degrees of legal privilege against forced disclosure. In its second general aspect, privacy through limited communication serves to set necessary boundaries of mental distance in interpersonal situations ranging from the most intimate to the most formal and public. In marriage, for example, husbands and wives need to retain islands of privacy in the midst of their intimacy if they are to preserve a saving respect and mystery in the relation.... In work situations, mental distance is necessary so that the relations of superior and subordinate do not slip into an intimacy which would create a lack of respect and an impediment to directions and correction....

Psychological distance is also used in crowded settings.... [A] complex but well-understood etiquette of privacy is part of our social scenario.... We learn to ignore people and to be ignored by them as a way of achieving privacy in subways, on streets, and in the "nonpresence" of servants or children....

QUESTIONS

1. What are the functions of privacy, as described by Westin? For each, can you think of examples from your own experience?

2. Law professor and journalist Jeffrey Rosen, author of *The Unwanted Gaze: The Destruction of Privacy in America*,[8] offers this description of one of the primary values of privacy:

> *Privacy protects us from being misdefined and judged out of context.... [W]hen your browsing habits or e-mail messages are exposed to strangers, you may be reduced, in their eyes, to nothing more than the most salacious book you once read or the most vulgar joke you once told. And even if your Internet browsing isn't in any way embarrassing, you run the risk of being stereotyped as the kind of person who would read a particular book or listen to a particular song. Your public identity may be distorted by fragments of information that have little to do with how you define yourself. In a world where citizens are bombarded with information, people form impressions quickly, based on sound bites, and these brief impressions tend to oversimplify and misrepresent our complicated and often contradictory characters.*

   Does Westin come close to mentioning this aspect of privacy?

3. Which functions of privacy may have been served by the e-mail messages that Michael Smyth sent while working for Pillsbury?

4. To what extent can we describe privacy as an ethical imperative? Think of the *Smyth v. Pillsbury* scenario. Who are the most affected stakeholders? Under the utilitarian approach to ethics, was intercepting the e-mail the right thing to do? Now consider the case from the deontological perspective. Again, was Pillsbury's action ethical?

● LIFESTYLE CONTROL

If you have something that you don't want anyone to know maybe you shouldn't be doing it in the first place.

—ERIC SCHMIDT, CEO, Google

During the early phase of the Industrial Revolution, it was not unusual for "company towns" to be built, communities where a single company constructed, owned, and operated the entire town—not only the business enterprise itself, but also the stores, roads, parks, recreational and medical facilities, and homes for the workers. Firms would also pay for services normally provided by government, such as sewage treatment and garbage collection. In the mid-1800s, company towns were created out of self-interest, in often-remote locations where relatively dangerous operations in coal mining, timber, or construction required a stable workforce. With the many amenities came pervasive social control. Drinking, gambling, smoking, cleanliness, and morals were tightly regulated. Employees were closely watched in public and in private, and were fired for "straying from the path of virtue."[9] They could also be disciplined for minor infringements: Frank Gilchrist, the entrepreneur who built Gilchrist, Oregon, "drove around town,

---

[8]New York: Random House, 2000.

[9]James B. Allen, *The Company Town in the American West* (Oklahoma 1966), 189.

upbraiding those whose yards weren't clean and tidy."[10] One mill owner would walk around the workers' houses at 9:00 p.m. every night, knocking on doors to hurry people to turn off their lights and go to bed![11]

When he opened up his assembly line in the early twentieth century, Henry Ford issued a booklet, called *Helpful Hints and Advice to Employees*, warning against drinking, gambling, borrowing money, taking in boarders, and poor hygiene (advising workers to "use plenty of soap and water in the home and upon their children, bathing frequently"). Ford deployed a vast "Sociology Department," with 150 door-to-door investigators to check the conduct of workers who were not living in houses or shopping in stores that Ford built, but whose well-being was of great interest to the entrepreneur. Once Ford instituted the famous $5 a day wage, he worried that workers would splurge their windfall; his goal was to maintain maximum productivity at the factory by keeping them healthy and stable. The company established a savings and loan to encourage thrift, and had doctors available at all times for workers and their families.[12]

Today we find such a story quaint. We might think we have reached some sort of societal consensus that what employees do on their own time, away from the workplace, should be entirely their own business. Yet we see in the twenty-first century a wave of corporate efforts to control employees' off-site, off-duty conduct. Rather than paternalism, this is driven by the hard facts surrounding health care in the United States. Expenses are skyrocketing, and employers carry many of them. Escalating insurance costs as well as lost productivity are affecting global competitiveness: Average health-care costs to U.S. companies are 13 percent of total payroll, while countries like Germany, Japan, or the United Kingdom spend half that proportion. In 2013, corporate spending on health care in the United States averaged more than $12,000 per employee per year.

Smoking and obesity, for example, are the major causes of poor health in the United States. According to a 2011 Gallup survey, obese or overweight workers miss an added 450 million days of work annually, costing more than $153 billion in lower productivity. The Centers for Disease Control (CDC) study found that annual health care and productivity losses traceable to smoking were $3,391 per smoker. Consider what this means for a company like Wal-Mart, with 2 million workers. If they smoked at the average U.S. rate, each year they would cost the firm $1.4 billion in health-care costs. Companies have tried to cut such losses with a number of strategies. Some are voluntary. IBM, for example, offers a range of rebates, and employees who agree to exercise, to eat healthy, and not to smoke are paid $150 per year—$300 if their whole family follows suit. At the other end of the spectrum, some employers find that penalties work better than rewards. Michelin North America, for example, had been giving its employees $600 credits toward deductibles if they participated in wellness programs, but when health-care costs spiked in 2012, they changed their policy. As of 2014, if you work for Michelin North America and your blood pressure is too high or your waist measures more than 40 inches, you could pay as much as $1,000 more per year for health insurance.[13] Scotts employees take a long, extremely personal health-risk assessment, which asks, for instance,

---

[10]Id. at 193.

[11]Margaret Crawford and Earle S. Draper, "The Company Town in the American South," 146 in Garner, ed., *The Company Town: Architecture and Society in the Early Industrial Age* 3, 4 (Oxford 1992).

[12]Steven Watts, *The People's Tycoon: Henry Ford and the American Century* 204-05 (Knopf, 2005).

[13]"When Your Boss Make You Pay For Being Fat," *Wall Street Journal*, April 5, 2013.

"Do you smoke? Drink? What did you parents die of? Do you feel down, sad, hopeless? Burned out? How is your relationship with your spouse? Your kids?" If they refuse to take the test, employees pay added premium costs each month.[14] Weyco, a Michigan-based, health-benefits management company, not only refuses to hire smokers, but fires every employee who fails the mandatory nicotine test. Recently Weyco expanded this program to include workers' spouses; if the spouse fails the monthly nicotine test, the worker pays $80 monthly until the spouse quits. Policies like these have been aimed at a range of behaviors: Workers must keep their blood pressure and cholesterol at healthy levels, wear seat belts, and join corporate wellness programs. One Georgia developer will not employ anyone who engages in "high risk" recreational activities such as motorcycling or skydiving. At the Borgata Casino in Atlantic City, New Jersey, bartenders and waitresses can be fired if they gain more than 7 percent of their body weight. Weigh-ins are mandatory, with 90-day unpaid suspensions for violators. Exceptions are made for pregnancy and other valid medical reasons. "Borgata Babes" who miss their target weight after 90 days are fired.

Whereas companies say they are cutting health-care costs and lowering rates of absenteeism in these ways, organizations such as the American Civil Liberties Union (ACLU) are troubled by this drift to control off-site behavior. Former ACLU president Ira Glasser has said:

> If an employer believes your capacity to take care of yourself is in his interest, then you become like a piece of equipment. He gets to lock it up at night and control the temperature and make sure dust doesn't get into the machine, because what happens when it's not working affects how long it's going to last.

In fact, an interesting alliance between the ACLU and the tobacco industry was extremely effective in lobbying state legislatures for laws that protect employees who smoke when they are not at work.[15] Today, a majority of states have some version of off-the-job privacy protection laws. In New York, for instance, it is illegal to fire an employee for engaging in off-hours sports, games, hobbies, exercise, reading, movie- or TV-watching. This is the statute at issue in the next case.

■ ■ ■

Laurel Allen was married, but separated from her husband when she began dating Samuel Johnson, a coworker at Walmart. When the store manager found out, they were both fired. Walmart's anti-fraternization policy prohibited such relationships as inconsistent with the company's "strongly held belief in and support of the family unit." The New York attorney general entered the case on behalf of the dating couple, alleging that firing them violated the state law protecting the employees' right to engage in off-duty, off-premises recreational activity.

---

[14]The company will analyze each set of test results and will then arrange a coach and action plan for each at-risk employee.

[15]By 1996, such laws were in effect in 28 states. Virginia, a "tobacco state," was the first to pass one. It reads: "No employee or applicant ... shall be required ... to smoke or use tobacco products on the job, or to abstain from smoking or using tobacco products outside of the course of his employment." *VA Code Ann.* 15.1-29, 18 (1990).

State of New York v. Walmart Stores, Inc.

N.Y. App. Div., 1995
621 N.Y.S.2d 158

MERCURE, Justice.

In February 1993, defendant discharged two of its employees for violating its "fraternization" policy, which is codified in defendant's 1989 Associates Handbook and prohibits a "dating relationship" between a married employee and another employee, other than his or her own spouse. In this action, plaintiff seeks reinstatement of the two employees with back pay upon the ground that their discharge violated [New York] Labor Law § 201-d(2)(c), which forbids employer discrimination against employees because of their participation in "legal recreational activities" pursued outside of work hours....

[The court must decide whether "a dating relationship" is meant to be included within the statutory definition of "recreational activities."]

[NY] Labor Law § 201-d(1)(b) defines "recreational activities" as meaning:

> *... any lawful, leisure-time activity, for which the employee receives no compensation and which is generally engaged in for recreational purposes, including but not limited to sports, games, hobbies, exercise, reading, and the viewing of television, movies, and similar material.*

In our view, there is no justification for proceeding beyond the fundamental rule of construction that "[w]here words of a statute are free from ambiguity and express plainly, clearly and distinctly the legislative intent, resort may not be had to other means of interpretation," ... To us, "dating" is entirely distinct from and, in fact, bears little resemblance to "recreational activity." Whether characterized as a relationship or an activity, an indispensable element of "dating," in fact its raison d'etre, is romance, either pursued or realized. For that reason, although a dating couple may go bowling and under the circumstances call that activity a "date," when two individuals lacking amorous interest in one another go bowling or engage in any other kind of "legal recreational activity," they are not "dating."

Moreover, even if [NY] Labor Law § 201-d(1)(b) was found to contain some ambiguity, application of the rules of statutory construction does not support [the trial court's] interpretation. We agree with defendant that ... the voluminous legislative history to the enactment, including memoranda issued in connection with the veto of two earlier more expansive bills, [shows] an obvious intent to limit the statutory protection to certain clearly defined categories of leisure-time activities. Further, in view of the specific inclusion of "sports, games, hobbies, exercise, reading, and the viewing of television, movies, and similar material" within the statutory definition of "recreational activities," ... personal relationships fall outside the scope of legislative intent....

[Order modified to grant defendant's motion to dismiss.]

YESAWICH, Justice, dissenting.

I respectfully dissent, for I find defendant's central thesis, apparently accepted by the majority, that the employment policy at issue only prohibits romantic entanglements and not other types of social interactions, to be wholly without merit. While the majority encumbers the word "dating" with an "amorous interest" component, there is nothing in defendant's fraternization policy, its application—defendant does not allege that its two former employees manifested an intimate or amatory attitude toward each other—or even in defendant's own definition of a "date," "a social engagement between persons of opposite sex" (Webster's Ninth New Collegiate Dictionary, 325 [1988]), that leads to such a conclusion.

More importantly, I do not agree that "dating," whether or not it involves romantic attachment, falls outside the general definition of "recreational activities" found in [the law]. The statute, by its terms, appears to encompass social activities, whether or not they have a romantic element, for it includes any lawful activity pursued for recreational purposes and undertaken during leisure time. Though no explicit definition of "recreational purposes" is contained in the statute, "recreation" is, in the words of one dictionary, "a means of refreshment or diversion" (Webster's Ninth New Collegiate Dictionary, 985 [1985]); social interaction surely qualifies as a "diversion."...

In my view, given the fact that the Legislature's primary intent in enacting Labor Law § 201-d was to curtail employers' ability to discriminate on the basis of activities that are pursued outside of work hours, and that have no bearing on one's ability to perform one's job, and concomitantly to guarantee employees a certain degree of freedom to conduct their lives as they please during nonworking hours, the narrow interpretation adopted by the majority is indefensible. Rather, the statute, and the term "recreational activities" in particular, should be construed as broadly as the definitional language allows, to effect its remedial purpose.... Here, the list, which includes vast categories such as "hobbies" and "sports," as well as very different types of activities (e.g., exercise, reading), appears to have been compiled with an eye toward extending the reach of the statute. This, coupled with the explicit directive that the definition is not to be limited to the examples given, provides further indication that the term "recreational activities" should be construed expansively.

QUESTIONS

1. The judges in this case—both majority and dissenting—are engaging in what is called statutory construction; they are determining the outcome of the case by trying to understand the meaning of the law passed by New York's legislature. Note the differences between them. One gives the statute a "broad" reading, the other gives it a "narrow" one. Which is which? What tools do the two judges use to interpret the law? Which interpretation do you think is most in keeping with the intent of the legislators?

2. Try to imagine yourself in Albany as this New York law was being debated. What policy issues might have been raised in favor of passing the law? Against?

3. Suppose you had the ability to rewrite the New York law, or even delete it from the statute books. How would you change it?

4. **Research**: For your state, find out if there is any legislation protecting employees' rights to engage in off-site activities. If so, are there any cases interpreting the law? Then go back to the Montana Wrongful Discharge statute in Chapter 2. What similarities can you see between it and your state's law? What differences?

As Lewis Maltby, president and founder of the National Workrights Institute, explains in the following excerpt from his 2010 book, American citizens may have constitutional protection from privacy invasions by their government, but when it comes to similar invasions by their bosses, the picture is very different.

Can They Do That?:
Retaking Our Fundamental Rights in the Workplace

Lew Maltby[16]

If the government wants to tap your phone or read your e-mail, it needs to have evidence that you are doing something illegal. In most cases, it needs a court order. But employers routinely monitor telephone calls, e-mail, Web site visits, and virtually every other type of electronic communication....

Under the doctrine of employment at will, your boss can fire you for any reason, or no reason at all. Some employers use this power to control the private lives of their employees....

You lose your rights before you even get a job. Many employers now conduct extensive investigations into prospective employees. If you've ever been arrested, you probably won't get the job, even if you weren't found guilty. If your credit history is spotty, it can cost you a job, even if the job has nothing to do with handling money. Other employers turn down people because of their driving record, even for jobs that don't involve driving. And even if your background is spotless, you can still lose the job because the information broker gets you mixed up with someone else with a similar name.

If you survive this gauntlet, the drug test is waiting for you. No sensible employer wants to hire a drug abuser, but drug tests can't tell if someone is an abuser, only that someone used drugs at some point in the past. If you've ever smoked marijuana at a party, you could be in for trouble. When your body metabolizes something you ingest, the chemicals it creates (called metabolites) stay in your body for days, or even weeks. Even if you've never touched drugs, you're not safe. Some employers use cheap tests that mistake Advil, Sudafed, NyQuil, and other over-the-counter medications for illegal drugs. Even if proper testing is used, labs often make mistakes. A study by the Centers for Disease Control found that 37 percent of drug test results were wrong; the samples labeled positive were actually clean. And don't count on having any privacy for the test; some employers have "urination monitors" watch everyone while they fill the cup to make sure nobody is cheating.

Finally there are the psychological tests. Some are designed to test your honesty. The only problem with those is that most of the people who fail are honest. Others ask about your sex life, religious beliefs, and other highly personal matters having nothing to do with your ability to do the job.

You may have already lost a job because of one of these pre-employment screenings without even knowing it. The law does not require employers to tell unsuccessful applicants why they weren't hired, and most employers don't. Some employers lie about why you weren't hired. The bottom line is, you'll never know why you were turned down.

As bad as things are, they are going to get worse. All new cell phones are now required by federal law to come equipped with the Global Positioning System (GPS). Some employers who issue company cell phones use this technology to track employees during their private lives, often in secret. Recently developed genetic tests allow employers to determine whether you carry the genes linked to breast cancer, Alzheimer's, and other serious illnesses. Employers are starting to use this knowledge to keep people out of the workforce to save money on corporate medical costs. Some biometric security systems, such as retina scans (which chart the blood vessels in your eye), reveal sensitive medical information such as whether you are diabetic, and facilitate identity theft.

Even in the few areas of employment where you do have legal rights, it can be nearly impossible to enforce them. Almost 20 percent of employers today require all employees to agree in advance not to go to court if the company violates their legal rights, and to take their dispute to a private arbitration system selected (and sometimes run) by the employer. If you don't agree, you don't get the job. Some of these programs are fair. But others are kangaroo courts in which employers may handpick the arbitrators and deny employees the right to have a lawyer, or whose rules don't require the arbitrator to follow the law.

Traditionally, employees who are being treated unfairly have been able to protect themselves by joining a union. Union contracts generally prohibit most of these abuses. But joining a union has become a dangerous undertaking. Over eight thousand employees are fired every year simply for trying to join one. Technically, this kind of firing is illegal, but the penalties are so trivial that employers just pay the fines and keep breaking the law.

There is something profoundly disturbing, almost schizophrenic, about our approach to human rights. We have fought wars, millions of us have served in the military, and several hundred thousand Americans have died, defending our country and protecting our freedom of speech and other rights. Yet we have created a legal system that leaves those rights in the wastebasket when we go to work.

QUESTIONS

1. Elsewhere in his book Maltby suggests an alternative to drug testing—impairment testing. He thinks this makes sense, even for those jobs where safety is a critical factor. For example, he writes:

   [We should] test pilots for what really counts: their ability to fly a plane safely. The reason stoned pilots are dangerous is that their vision, reflexes, coordination and judgment are impaired. Systems are available that will test whether someone is impaired in this way in a matter of minutes. The technology for these systems was originally developed by NASA for testing astronauts. Taking the test is a lot like paying a video game. You take the test a few times to establish a baseline. Every time you take the test later, the system compares your score to the baseline. If your score is significantly lower than the baseline, the system reports that you are impaired.[17]

   Maltby points out that scores indicating impairment can be caused by any number of factors beyond drug-taking—being sleep-deprived, ill, or going through a divorce, for example—but whatever the reason, the test will determine that you shouldn't fly the plane.

   Although workplace drug testing occurs less frequently—the practice peaked in 1996 at 81 percent of firms—it is still prevalent. What do you think of Lew Maltby's suggestion? Can you imagine impairment testing for various jobs instead of drug testing?

2. The multimillion dollar psychological testing industry has been criticized for unreliability. And recent studies reveal a very low correlation between good tests results and effective performance at work. Given these problems what might be a better way for employers to screen job applicants?

---

[17]Id. at 105.

Privacy under the Constitution

The right of the people to be secure in their persons, houses, papers, and effects, against unreasonable searches and seizures, shall not be violated.

—FOURTH AMENDMENT, U.S. Constitution

What are the legal boundaries of an employee's privacy in this interconnected, electronic-communication age, one in which thoughts and ideas that would have been spoken personally and privately in ages past are now instantly text-messaged to friends and family via hand-held, computer-assisted electronic devices?

—DISTRICT JUDGE LARSON, *Quon v. Arch Wireless Operating Co., Inc.,* (9th Cir. 2006)

Although the word "privacy" cannot be found in the Constitution, over the years, the Supreme Court has created three types of privacy rights through its interpretation of various Constitutional Amendments. One stops the government from interfering in the choices you make about your private family and sexual life—to use or not use birth control or (for adults) to engage in consensual homosexual activity, for example—without government interference. Another prevents the government from publicizing the kind of information about ourselves that we consider most intimate—our medical and sexual histories, for example. Finally, and of most importance to business, the Fourth Amendment protects the "reasonable expectations of privacy" of both individual and corporations against unwarranted and unreasonable government searches or seizures. When police frisk for drugs or test for alcohol, when a health department inspects a restaurant, or when a regulatory agency searches a business for evidence of illegal activity, there is a potential Fourth Amendment "privacy" claim.

While the Fourth Amendment does protect citizens from "unreasonable searches," it is triggered only when the government is conducting a search; there is no constitutional protection against unwarranted invasion of privacy by private corporations, as Maltby explained. And while government employees might argue that electronic surveillance is a "search" in violation of the Fourth Amendment, their constitutional rights are limited by a balancing test: judges must decide which counts more weightly, an employee's privacy interest or the need of the government (as employer) to conduct a search.

In 1987, the Supreme Court decided a case involving the search of a public employee's office. Magno Ortega, a psychiatrist at a state hospital, was suspected of stealing a computer and of sexually harassing female workers. While he was on vacation, his desk and file cabinets were searched thoroughly. Investigators found, among other items, a valentine card, a book of love poetry, and a seminude photograph of a female doctor. The Court found that this search did not violate the Fourth Amendment. It explained that the employment context itself both (1) lowered the employee's legitimate privacy expectations, and (2) created a special need on the employer's part to discover work-related misconduct:

> *An office is seldom a private enclave free from entry by supervisors, other employees, and business and personal invitees. Instead in many cases offices are continually entered by fellow employees and other visitors during the workday for conferences, consultations, and other work-related visits....*
>
> *While police ... conduct searches for the primary purpose of obtaining evidence for use in criminal ... proceedings, employers most frequently need to enter the offices*

and desks of their employees for legitimate work-related reasons wholly unrelated to illegal conduct. Employers and supervisors are focused primarily on the need to complete the government agency's work in a prompt and efficient manner. An employer may have need for correspondence, or a file or report available only in an employee's office while the employee is away.... Or, as is alleged to have been the case here, employers may need to safeguard or identify state property or records in an office in connection with a pending investigation into suspected employee malfeasance.[18]

■ ■ ■

In June 2010, using *O'Connor v. Ortega* as precedent, the Supreme Court decided the case that follows. Jeff Quon, a member of the police special-weapons and tactics (SWAT) team in Ontario, California, had been given a text-messaging pager by his department. In an effort to determine whether it should raise its quota of free messages for employees, the department obtained a transcript of Quon's texting, and discovered that most were sexually explicit communications to his wife and mistress. Sergeant Quon challenged this search as violating his Fourth Amendment rights.

City of Ontario, California v. Quon
Supreme Court of the United States, 2010
130 S.Ct. 2619

Justice Kennedy delivered the opinion of the Court.

... In October 2001, the City acquired 20 alphanumeric pagers capable of sending and receiving text messages. Arch Wireless Operating Company provided wireless service for the pagers. Under the City's service contract with Arch Wireless, each pager was allotted a limited number of characters sent or received each month. Usage in excess of that amount would result in an additional fee. The City issued pagers to Quon and other SWAT Team members in order to help the SWAT Team mobilize and respond to emergency situations.

Before acquiring the pagers, the City announced a "Computer Usage, Internet, and E-Mail Policy" (Computer Policy) that applied to all employees. Among other provisions, it specified that the City "reserves the right to monitor and log all network activity, including e-mail and Internet use, with or without notice. Users should have no expectation of privacy or confidentiality when using these resources." In March 2000, Quon signed a statement acknowledging that he had read and understood the Computer Policy.

The Computer Policy did not apply, on its face, to text messaging. Text messages share similarities with e-mails, but the two differ in an important way. In this case, for instance, an e-mail sent on a City computer was transmitted through the City's own data servers, but a text message sent on one of the City's pagers was transmitted using wireless radio frequencies from an individual pager to a receiving station owned by Arch Wireless. It was routed through Arch Wireless' computer network.... After delivery, Arch Wireless retained a copy on its computer servers. The message did not pass through computers owned by the City....

---

[18]*O'Connor v. Ortega*, 480 U.S. 709 (1987).

At an April 18, 2002, staff meeting at which Quon was present, Lieutenant Steven Duke, the OPD officer responsible for the City's contract with Arch Wireless, told officers that messages sent on the pagers "are considered e-mail messages. This means that [text] messages would fall under the City's policy as public information and [would be] eligible for auditing." Duke's comments were put in writing in a memorandum....

Within the first or second billing cycle after the pagers were distributed, Quon exceeded his monthly text message character allotment. Duke told Quon about the overage, and reminded him that messages sent on the pagers were "considered e-mail and could be audited." Duke said, however, that "it was not his intent to audit [an] employee's text messages to see if the overage [was] due to work related transmissions." Duke suggested that Quon could reimburse the City for the overage fee rather than have Duke audit the messages. Quon wrote a check to the City for the overage. Duke offered the same arrangement to other employees who incurred overage fees.

Over the next few months, Quon exceeded his character limit three or four times. Each time he reimbursed the City. Quon and another officer again incurred overage fees for their pager usage in August 2002. At a meeting in October, Duke told Scharf that he had become " 'tired of being a bill collector.' " [Chief] Scharf decided to determine whether the existing character limit was too low—that is, whether officers such as Quon were having to pay fees for sending work-related messages—or if the overages were for personal messages. Scharf told Duke to request transcripts of text messages sent in August and September by Quon and the other employee who had exceeded the character allowance....

Duke reviewed ... transcripts [provided by Arch Wireless] and discovered that many of the messages sent and received on Quon's pager were not work related, and some were sexually explicit. Duke reported his findings to Scharf, who, along with Quon's immediate supervisor, reviewed the transcripts himself. After his review, Scharf referred the matter to OPD's internal affairs division for an investigation into whether Quon was violating OPD rules by pursuing personal matters while on duty.

The officer in charge of the internal affairs review ... used Quon's work schedule to redact the transcripts in order to eliminate any messages Quon sent while off duty. He then reviewed the content of the messages Quon sent during work hours. [His] report noted that Quon sent or received 456 messages during work hours in the month of August 2002, of which no more than 57 were work related; he sent as many as 80 messages during a single day at work; and on an average workday, Quon sent or received 28 messages, of which only 3 were related to police business. The report concluded that Quon had violated OPD rules. Quon was allegedly disciplined.

[Quon, his then wife, his mistress (who worked for the police department), and another member of the SWAT team brought suit against the city for violating their Fourth Amendment rights by obtaining and reading the transcript of text messages. The progress of this case through the federal courts up to the Supreme Court displays a range of interpretations of the Constitution.]

The Fourth Amendment states: "The right of the people to be secure in their persons, houses, papers, and effects, against unreasonable searches and seizures, shall not be violated." The Court discussed this principle in *O'Connor*.... All Members of the Court agreed with the general principle that "[i]ndividuals do not lose Fourth Amendment rights merely because they work for the government instead of a private employer." [Because it would be impracticable to require government employees to get a warrant to search government office, we instead established a two-step analysis.] First, because "some government offices may be so open to fellow employees or the public that no expectation of privacy is reasonable," a court must consider "[t]he operational realities of the workplace" in order to determine whether an employee's Fourth Amendment rights are implicated. On this view, "the question whether an employee has a reasonable expectation of privacy must be addressed on a case-by-case basis." Next, where an employee has a legitimate privacy expectation, an employer's intrusion on that expectation "for non-investigatory, work-related purposes, as well as for investigations of work-related misconduct, should be judged by the standard of reasonableness under all the circumstances."...

The Court must proceed with care when considering the whole concept of privacy expectations in communications made on electronic equipment owned by a government employer.... In [a case from 1967] the Court relied on its own knowledge and experience to conclude that there is a reasonable expectation of privacy in a telephone booth. It is not so clear that courts at present are on so sure a ground. Prudence counsels caution before the facts in the instant case are used to establish far-reaching premises that define the existence, and extent, of privacy expectations enjoyed by employees when using employer-provided communication devices....

Rapid changes in the dynamics of communication and information transmission are evident not just in the technology itself but in what society accepts as proper behavior. As one *amici* [Electronic Frontier Foundation] brief notes, many employers expect or at least tolerate personal use of such equipment by employees because it often increases worker efficiency. Another *amicus* points out that the law is beginning to respond to these developments, as some States have recently passed statutes requiring employers to notify employees when monitoring their electronic communications. At present, it is uncertain how workplace norms, and the law's treatment of them, will evolve....

[T]he Court would have difficulty predicting how employees' privacy expectations will be shaped by those changes or the degree to which society will be prepared to recognize those expectations as reasonable. Cell phone and text message communications are so pervasive that some persons may consider them to be essential means or necessary instruments for self-expression, even self-identification. That might strengthen the case for an expectation of privacy. On the other hand, the ubiquity of those devices has made them generally affordable, so one could counter that employees who need cell phones or similar devices for personal matters can purchase and pay for their own. And employer policies concerning communications will of course shape the reasonable expectations of their employees, especially to the extent that such policies are clearly communicated....

[Continuing its analysis, the Court assumes Sergeant Quon had a reasonable expectation of privacy in the text messages, and that the city's review of those messages amounted to a "search" under the Fourth Amendment. Guided by its *O'Connor* decision, the Court now must determine whether the search was yet "reasonable."]

Although as a general matter, warrantless searches "are *per se* unreasonable under the Fourth Amendment," there are "a few specifically established and well-delineated exceptions" to that general rule. The Court has held that the "special needs" of the workplace justify one such exception. Under the *[O'Connor]* approach, when conducted for a "non-investigatory, work-related purpose" or for the "investigation of work-related misconduct," a government employer's warrantless search is reasonable if it is "justified at its inception" and if "the measures adopted are reasonably related to the objectives of the search and not excessively intrusive in light of" the circumstances giving rise to the search.

The search was justified at its inception because there were "reasonable grounds for suspecting that the search [was] necessary for a non-investigatory work-related purpose." As a jury found, Chief Scharf ordered the search in order to determine whether the character limit on the City's contract with Arch Wireless was sufficient to meet the City's needs.... The City and OPD had a legitimate interest in ensuring that employees were not being forced to pay out of their own pockets for work-related expenses, or on the other hand that the City was not paying for extensive personal communications.

As for the scope of the search, reviewing the transcripts was reasonable because it was an efficient and expedient way to determine whether Quon's overages were the result of work-related messaging or personal use. The review was also not "excessively intrusive." Although Quon had gone over his monthly allotment a number of times, OPD requested transcripts for only the months of August and September 2002. While it may have been reasonable as well for OPD to review transcripts of all the months in which Quon exceeded his allowance, it was certainly reasonable for OPD to review messages for just two months.... And it is worth noting that during his internal affairs investigation, [the investigating officer] redacted all messages Quon sent while off duty, a measure which reduced the intrusiveness....

[A]gain on the assumption that Quon had a reasonable expectation of privacy in the contents of his messages, the extent of an expectation is relevant to assessing whether the search was too intrusive. Even if he could assume some level of privacy would inhere in his messages, it would not have been reasonable for Quon to conclude that his messages were in all circumstances immune from scrutiny. Quon was told that his messages were subject to auditing. As a law enforcement officer, he would or should have known that his actions were likely to come under legal scrutiny, and that this might entail an analysis of his on-the-job communications. Under the circumstances, a reasonable employee would be aware that sound management principles might require the audit of messages to determine whether the pager was being appropriately used. Given that the City issued the pagers to Quon and other SWAT Team members in order to help them more quickly respond to crises—and given that Quon had received no assurances of privacy—Quon could have anticipated that it might be necessary for the City to audit pager messages to assess the SWAT Team's performance in particular emergency situations.

Because the search was motivated by a legitimate work-related purpose, and because it was not excessive in scope, the search was reasonable ... [The city] did not violate respondents' Fourth Amendment rights, and the court below erred by concluding otherwise. The judgment of the Court of Appeals for the Ninth Circuit is reversed, and the case is remanded for further proceedings consistent with this opinion.

It is so ordered.

QUESTIONS

1. Trace the Fourth Amendment analysis made by Justice Kennedy. Based on that, and what you know about the law of privacy from this chapter, tell how the following would be resolved:

   (a) You work as a car salesperson. One day your boss walks over to your desk and sees that you are playing Grand Theft Auto. She says nothing about it, but later, using surveillance software, reviews your online activities over recent months and finds many more visits to video game sites. There has been no communication about whether you would be monitored. You are fired.

(b) You work for an investment bank. You have been issued a Blackberry to do business, on- and off-site. The bank, without warning, decides to review your cell phone use and determines you have been spending too much time manipulating your own stock portfolio. You are fired.

(c) You work for the local library. You have been told that your use of the Internet will not be monitored without notice. However, your supervisors have decided to use surveillance software anyway, without notice, and have discovered that you are having e-mail correspondence with a homeless individual who frequently sits amongst the periodicals, making strange grunting noises that sometime disturb other visitors. You are fired.

2. **Research:** As Justice Kennedy notes, "Many employers expect or at least tolerate personal use of [electronic communications] equipment by employees because it often increases worker efficiency." To what extent are employees taking care of personal matters during working hours? What can you find out about the causes of this trend and the rate at which it might be increasing? Start by looking at the Web sites of some of the organizations who filed *amicus* ("friend of the court" advisory) briefs in this case: The Electronic Frontier Foundation, The Center for Democracy & Technology, The Electronic Privacy Information Center, the ACLU, etc.

3. **Research:** Daniel R. Carter Jr. worked for the Sheriff's Office in Hampton Virginia. He alleged he was fired for posting a Facebook "like" for the candidate running against the Sheriff in the 2009 election. Should a public employee's Facebook "like" be protected under the Fourth Amendment? Research: Bland v. Roberts, Fourth Circuit Court of Appeals, 2013.

4. In gauging the intrusiveness of the search in this case, Justice Kennedy states, "[T]he audit of messages on Quon's employer-provided pager was not nearly as intrusive as a search of his personal e-mail account or pager, or a wiretap on his home phone line, would have been." Given the trend to use employer-provided communications equipment to accomplish private tasks both at work and from home, does the distinction Justice Kennedy draws make sense? What are the ethical considerations that come up when law is trying to form itself on the cusp of technological change?

■ ■ ■

Social Media and Privacy

The tidy distinctions ... between the workplace and professional affairs, on the one hand, and personal possessions and private activities, on the other, do not exist in reality.

—JUSTICE BLACKMUN, Dissenting in *Ortega v. O'Connor*, 1987

How can we be creeped out by the increasing invasiveness of security cameras or the collection of market research on every family member yet simultaneously be drawn to any opportunity to share the most intimate facts about ourselves with the world at large? ....

And this goal—this almost instinctive push toward gaining access to one another—far outweighs our concern over how this data might be used.

—DOUGLAS RUSHKOFF, "Invading Our Own Privacy," 2009

The Supreme Court in *Quon* displayed a reluctance to rule on reasonable privacy expectations in modern communication devices. Finding that the police department had not violated officer Quon's Fourth Amendment rights to privacy because it had a work-related purpose for the search of his pager, the Court ducked the question of whether Quon had a reasonable expectation of privacy in his text messages. Acknowledging that "rapid changes in the dynamics of communication and information transmission [are] evident not just in the technology itself but in what society accepts as proper behavior," the justices admitted having trouble predicting how to analyze privacy expectations on an "emerging technology before its role in society has become clear."

The next reading can be seen as an attempt to shed light on the role in society of one aspect of emerging technology. Business law professors Patricia Abril and Avner Levin joined with Alissa Del Rioego, who earned her law degree in 2012, to survey college students on their attitudes about employers accessing information taken from social media sites like Facebook. These students were business undergraduates about to enter the workforce. The results were paradoxical. In general, the Millennials wanted privacy from employer eyes, yet they shared a considerable amount of personal information online, knowing that employers could gain access to it. The authors ask: "What is at the core of this seemingly contradictory behavior? Is it just an adolescent 'have my cake and eat it too' mentality, or does it reveal something deeper about privacy and social performances?

Viewing the data in the light of relevant law, the authors conclude by offering recommendations to better align workplace policies with privacy expectations in a digital world.

Blurred Boundaries:
Social Media Privacy and the 21st Century Employee

Patricia Sanchez Abril, Avner Levin, and Alissa Del Riego[19]

...Today, technology makes the boundaries between the professional and personal more porous.... Personal blogs, social media profiles, Tweets, and other online fora allow individuals to publicly express multiple facets of themselves, including their private lives and their opinions. Employer-provided laptops and mobile devices do not discriminate between private and professional communications or locations. These "boundary-crossing" technologies blur the already elusive line between the private and the public, the home and the workplace.... While legislatures and courts have waffled in characterizing privacy expectations in social media, the rising generation of workers already manifests certain beliefs about the technology as it plays out in work life....

Whether it involves using employer computers to check personal e-mail and social network profiles or sending text messages on employer-provided communications devices, employee use of boundary-crossing technologies in the workplace for personal purposes is prevalent. Social media, in particular, has permeated modern culture and the daily lives of the incoming workforce. Both businesses and individuals view sites like Facebook and Twitter as valuable marketing and

[19]By Patricia Sanchez Abril, Avner Levin, and Alissa Del Riego from the *American Business Law Journal*, Spring 2012. Reprinted by permission of the authors.

communication tools. However, given these sites' relative newness and the ill-defined norms surrounding them, their use across work/life contexts raises numerous legal, ethical, and business-related questions.

Accounts of employees discrediting themselves and their employers via postings on social networking and media sites have become ubiquitous. A high school teacher was dismissed after posting on her Facebook page that she thought residents of the school district were "arrogant and snobby" and that she was "so not looking forward to another year [at the school]." A flight attendant was fired for posting suggestive pictures of herself in her company uniform. A study reported medical students engaged in unprofessional banter and disclosure about patients on their social networking profiles. Two pizza chain employees were fired after posting a "prank" video on YouTube that showed them preparing sandwiches at work while one put cheese up his nose and mucus on the food. Whether these well-documented anecdotes reflect ill-advised judgment of employees or overly aggressive responses by employers, they exemplify the tension between employer interests and employee privacy and speech rights.

[Summarizing the legal landscape regarding employer monitoring of social media profiles of employees and prospective employees, as well as employer-imposed restrictions on off-duty social media activity, the authors write:]

U.S. law currently provides feeble protection to the electronic social communications of employees—whether on or off the job. Fourth Amendment case law suggests that, while expectations of privacy in digital communication may be recognized as reasonable in the future, several factors usually cut against a finding of reasonableness, including employer interests, the logistical demands of the workplace, and the general accessibility of the information. In fact, every U.S. law touching upon employee privacy grants significant deference to the legitimate business interests of employers. Statutes that specifically govern the intersection of social media and workplace privacy have yet to be enacted. In their absence, it seems that U.S. employers may legally canvass social media sites for information on employees and candidates and act on the basis of the information found therein. Employers do not have an obligation to disclose their methods of gaining information....

The Privacy Expectations of Millennial Employees: A Survey

Much has been forecast about the role [the demographic group sometimes called the Millennials] will play in shaping the workplace of the twenty-first century. Scholars have described the new generation of employees as ambitious—having high expectations for salary and career promotions—while perhaps incongruously placing a premium on private life, flexibility, and work/life balance. They are reported to value a "fun" and relaxed workplace atmosphere and tend to perplex employers with the "casualness of their e-mail and texting language" and their furtive participation on social media while on company time. Regarding privacy, they have been characterized as having "few qualms about sharing information that [others] might consider sensitive or private," as evidenced by their copious digital dossiers. For them, identity seems to be a "synthesis of real-space and online expressions of self." Paradoxically, as a whole this group reports being unnerved by the idea of "someone aggregating, searching through, and acting on the basis of [the] information" they share online....

[Next, the authors review the results of their survey of some 2,500 American and Canadian undergraduates. Ninety-two percent of respondents used Facebook. Seventy-two percent of respondents used privacy settings to restrict access to their profiles.]

A. Employer Monitoring of Employee OSN [Online Social Networking] Profiles

....[S]ome respondents reported voluntarily posting information about traditionally private or sensitive topics such as political preferences (24%) or their partner's name (25%). Interestingly, 62% posted their relationship status and 40% disclosed dating interests.... It is unsurprising that this cohort, which has been characterized as valuing a casual and social work environment, would be inclined to share facts relating to private life with employers. This sharing reflects perhaps a population that does not construct the traditional segregation between social or home and work contexts on the basis of such facts.

....[Fifty-four percent] agreed with the statement, "It is not right when people can have access to information not intended for them." This response suggests that respondents generally disapprove of unintended audiences learning information about them posted on social media profiles.

Overall, respondents disapproved of employer monitoring or accessing employees' OSN profiles. Seventy-five percent found this practice to be somewhat or very inappropriate....

Respondents were slightly less perturbed, however, by employers checking on job applicants online without the applicant's knowledge. Fifty-six percent of respondents considered it somewhat or very inappropriate for employers to access OSNs to check the character of a job candidate. The greater disapproval of intrusions in the private life of employees versus applicants may stem from a shared sentiment that judging a person based on his or her private life is more appropriate before hiring. After all, the purpose of the hiring process is to vet applicants based in part on their character and reputation....

B. Work/Personal Life Separation

While a majority of respondents reported not inviting their employers or supervisors to be part of their OSN, many respondents considered it appropriate to blend worlds in that manner. Nearly one-third (29%) of respondents included their immediate supervisor as an online "friend." ... [S]ome welcomed their employers' participation in their social networks; others reported being required to give their employers access to their profiles. These data are consistent with the conclusion above regarding the openness and transparency of millennial employees vis-a-vis their workplace cohorts, as well as the characterization of Millennials as valuing casual and social work environments.

....Despite the fact that approximately one-third of respondents included supervisors or senior company executives or both in their OSNs, respondents tended to disassociate work life from personal life. Fifty-four percent of those surveyed strongly or somewhat agreed that "work life is completely separate from personal life, and what you do in one should not affect the other." Eighteen percent of respondents somewhat or strongly disagreed with that statement. Further, 56% disagreed that "knowing how a person behaves outside of work hours gives managers insight into whether that person is ready for a promotion." Only 16% of respondents agreed that off-duty behavior is evidence of career readiness or potential, which is highly consistent with a separatist view of professional and personal life....

[Respondents were asked to imagine themselves in the following hypothetical scenario, and to decide who was responsible for its consequences:]

You called in sick to work because you really wanted to go to your friend's all day graduation party. The next day you see several pictures of you having a great time at the party. Because the pictures are dated you start to worry about whether you might be caught in your lie about being sick. You contact the developers of the social network and ask that the pictures be taken down because the tagging goes so far, it would take you too long to find all the pictures. There was no response from the network. You are stunned to be called in by your supervisor a week later to be advised that you were being "written up" for taking advantage of sick leave and put on notice that if it happened again you would be terminated.

When attributing responsibility to the various parties for the adverse consequences, 78% assumed personal responsibility, while the rest laid blame on the "snooping" supervisor. Nearly half (47%) of respondents were concerned that material *about* them was not posted *by* them. Seventy-one percent respondents agreed that "real harm"—defined as physical, economic, or reputational injury—could arise from this occurrence. Respondents reported experiencing an invasion of privacy when information moved, uncontrolled by participants, across networks and contexts....

These statistics suggest the same contradiction that we have seen above: the respondents were willing to give digital access to their personal lives but resist being judged on the basis of what they disclose. They expect their work and personal lives to be segregated regardless of their unified and publicly accessible digital identity.

The Future of Digital Privacy in the Workplace

....While a majority of the surveyed Millennials found employer monitoring of employee online profiles inappropriate, an employee's remedy in U.S. law is contingent on whether the information obtained by the employer was publicly available. The "reasonable expectations of privacy" bar is high. More often than not, the large number of OSN friends with whom Millennials share information would clearly eliminate any reasonable expectation of privacy. Computer usage policies, which employers broadly adopt and employees often thoughtlessly accept, also inform the reasonable expectation analysis. Though our survey respondents generally expect the information they post on their OSNs will remain private from unauthorized parties, their expectation is not currently recognized by U.S. law as reasonable and legally protectable.

Millennials' online participation appears inconsistent with their stated expectations of privacy and audience segregation. However, what seems at first glance as incongruous is readily understandable as an attempt to achieve some control in a world where individuals will inevitably amass a public digital dossier. The only way to control the dossier is to participate actively in shaping it, rather than to renounce entirely online participation.

A picture emerges of a society that is, surprisingly, less free, in which tools for self-expression turn oppressive in the absence of normative, technological, and legal controls. Normative controls may come in the form of social acceptance of certain types of disclosures or skeletons in the online closet. Some have suggested that businesses and society in general will necessarily become more forgiving of unseemly personal disclosures eventually, because so many individuals will have online evidence of some purportedly inappropriate behavior. Technological controls, which have not yet been widely perfected, could one day give individuals the capacity to shield unwanted audiences from their online expression and identities.

[The authors note that while normative and technological controls are maturing, and in the light of the cumbersome, "messy, reactionary" process of lawmaking, businesses should lead the way by adopting best practices.]

Clear and Communicated Employer Policies on Technology and Internet Participation

To achieve buy-in from employees ... technology and Internet participation policies must be specific and clearly articulated in a manner consistent with the organization's culture, while reflecting emerging society-wide norms. [They] should contain a high level of detail specific to the type of communication (cell phones, text messages, computer), the character of the medium (company e-mail versus Internet-based e-mail), the nature of the online forum (chat rooms, blogs, etc.), the location of the message sender (on the employer premises versus at home, on employer time or off duty), and the effect of the hardware and transmitting systems' ownership on the message's privacy. Employees also should be informed about the types of information they are prohibited from transmitting (such as harassment or libel about a coworker, confidential and proprietary information, unauthorized expressions of endorsement using the company logo or affiliation, and the like). Further, such policies should remind employees that digital information is fluid and difficult to control and that employees must comply with Web sites' terms of service.

An Employee's Right to Respond and Rebut

In the event online information either suggests employee involvement in criminal or unethical activity or evidences a breach of loyalty, employers should be free to take action against the employee only after revealing the source of the discrediting information and offering the employee a meaningful opportunity to respond or to prove the information inaccurate.

Finally, technology and Internet participation policies should realistically reflect the stated perceptions and common expectations of employees. Employers should consider polling employees regarding their views or inviting representative employees to give input on proposed policies.

QUESTIONS

1. Elsewhere in this article the authors note that almost half of the resurvey respondents were concerned that the information posted about them online was not posted by them, and could cast a negative light on them, harming them economically, or even physically. The European Parliament is considering legislation that creates a "right to be forgotten," a "right to delete." This law would allow users to force websites, including social networking sites, to remove personal information upon request. If this law existed in the United States, Millennials would be gaining "nothing more than the right of forgetting that the natural frailty of human memory gave to past generations." What would some of the advantages of such a law be for situations where online behavior negatively affects the workplace? Can you see any disadvantages?

2. **Research:** Can you find any case law dealing with employees or prospective employees alleging privacy violations due to employers accessing information about them posted on social media?

3. Many colleges and universities are trawling social media to find information relevant to admissions decisions. What do you think about this practice? How is it different/similar to the employment context? Analyze it through the lens of ethical theory.

4. **Research:** California and Illinois are two of the handful of states that have passed legislation barring companies from asking employees or prospective employees for their social media passwords. How does an employer's request for such passwords look when viewed through the different lenses of ethical theory?

AMERICA vs. EUROPE: LIBERTY v. DIGNITY

Yale law professor James Q. Whitman makes this broad distinction between conceptions of privacy in American versus Europe:

The American right to privacy still takes much of the form that it took in the eighteenth century: It is the right to freedom from intrusions by the state, especially in one's own home. The prime danger, from the American point of view, is that the ... [home] will be breached by government actors. American anxieties ... tend to be about maintaining a kind of private sovereignty within our own walls. [In contrast, European] privacy protections are, at their core, a form of protection of a right to respect and personal dignity. [They] … are rights to one's image, name, and reputation, and … to informational self-determination—the right to control the sorts of information disclosed about one-self … all rights to control your public image—to guarantee that people see you the way you want to be seen. They are, as it were, rights to be shielded against unwanted public exposure….[20]

The European perspective on privacy, shaped by the way information was collected and used under Communism and by dictators like Franco and Hitler, is expressed in the strength of the protections of European Privacy Directive. Since 1995, under the Privacy Directive each member nation must pass laws guaranteeing that personal data gathered are accurate, up-to-date, relevant, and not excessive. Information collected may be used only for the purpose for which it was collected, and can be processed only with the consent of the subject, when required by law, or to protect the "public interest" or the "legitimate interests" of a third party, unless those interests are superseded by the "fundamental rights and freedoms of the data subject." The Directive sharply limits the collection of information about "racial or ethnic origin, political opinions, religious or philosophical beliefs, trade-union membership, [or] concerning health or sex life." Data subjects must be informed that data will be taken about them, and must be notified how it will be used.

The European Union (EU) Directive also gives Europeans the right to access and correct inaccuracies to the information collected about themselves. In the United States—except for certain regulated industries like credit—consumer information can be kept by the companies that process it, but Europeans have the right to withdraw permission for companies to continue to hold their personal data. Most starkly distinct from the U.S. perspective is the European notion of the "right to oblivion—" the right to be forgotten. In 2011, two German citizens who had committed murder and served their prison sentences sued Wikipedia to drop the entry about their crime.

Privacy in Genetic Information

Whatsoever things I see or hear concerning the life of men, in my attendance on the sick or even apart therefrom, which ought not to be noised about, I will keep silence thereon, counting such things to be as sacred secrets.

—HIPPOCRATIC OATH

Genetic testing of tiny amounts of human tissue—strands of hair or a few drops of blood—can reveal tremendous amounts of sensitive health data. In 2007, a Johns Hopkins University survey indicated that 93 percent of respondents believed that insurers and employers should be prevented from accessing predictive genetic test results.

---

[20]"The Two Western Cultures of Privacy: Dignity v. Liberty," *Yale Law Journal* 113, 2004, p. 1151.

While a variety of laws addressing genetic discrimination exist in most states—some forbidding preemployment testing, some prohibiting discrimination only against persons with certain specific genetic traits, some regulating the use of test results—they make up a patchwork quilt offering inconsistent protection. Until recently, federal legislation dealt only tangentially with genetic information. The 2004 *Health Information Portability and Accountability Act* (HIPAA), for example, requires consent for medical information to be accessed and shared, but does not address discrimination. The *Americans with Disabilities Act* covers those with "perceived" disability or with symptoms of inherited disability, but does not protect anyone from requests to provide genetic information to employers as part of a post-offer medical exam.

Widespread public concern gave a boost to privacy advocates, who had been working toward a comprehensive federal statute for 18 years. Their efforts finally bore fruit in the form of the *Genetic Information Nondiscrimination Act* (GINA). This law represents a rare bipartisan effort: It passed in the House of Representatives 414 to 1; in the Senate it passed unanimously.

Before GINA, federal laws addressing discrimination were designed to end particular forms of existing harm. In the debates preceding their passage, statutes like the Civil Rights Act of 1964 looked back at lengthy histories of discrimination—300 years of legal ownership of Africans as slaves, for example. Yet when GINA passed in 2008, the technology for mining genetic data was new, and there was relatively little evidence indicating that genetic-information discrimination posed a historical—or even a current—problem. As one commentator stated, "While GINA's opponents saw the absence of a history of discrimination as a major flaw, its advocates embraced the slim record as an exciting opportunity to preempt discrimination for the first time in American history."[21]

Genetic Information Nondiscrimination Act of 2008

Sec. 201. Definitions.
(1) GENETIC INFORMATION.
   The term "genetic information" means, with respect to any individual, information about—
   (a) such individual's genetic tests,
   (b) the genetic tests of family members of such individual, and
   (c) the manifestation of a disease or disorder in family members of such individual.
(2) GENETIC MONITORING.
   The term "genetic monitoring" means the periodic examination of employees to evaluate acquired modifications to their genetic material, such as chromosomal damage or evidence of increased occurrence of mutations, that may have developed in the course of employment due to exposure to toxic substances in the workplace, in order to identify, evaluate, and respond to the effects of or control adverse environmental exposures in the workplace.
(3) GENETIC SERVICES.
   The term "genetic services" means
   (a) a genetic test,
   (b) genetic counseling (including obtaining, interpreting, or assessing genetic information).

[21]Jessica L. Roberts, "Preemptive Discrimination: The Genetic Information Nondiscrimination Act," *Vanderbilt Law Review* 63, Spring 2010, p. 440.

Sec. 202. Employer Practices.

(A) DISCRIMINATION BASED ON GENETIC INFORMATION.
It shall be an unlawful employment practice for an employer:—

(1) to fail or refuse to hire, or to discharge, any employee, or otherwise to discriminate against any employee with respect to the compensation, terms, conditions or privileges of employment because of genetic information with respect to the employee; or

(2) to limit, segregate, or classify employees … in any way that would deprive or tend to deprive any employee of employment opportunities or otherwise adversely affect the status of the employee …, because of genetic information with respect to the employee.

(B) ACQUISITION OF GENETIC INFORMATION. It shall be unlawful for an employer to request, require, or purchase genetic information related to employees or their families.

There are several exceptions to this, including:

(1)   Where an employer inadvertently requests or requires family medical history of the employee or family member of the employee;

(2)(a) where health or genetic services are offered by the employer, including such services offered as part of a wellness program;

(2)(b) where the employee provides prior, knowing, voluntary, and written authorization;

(2)(c) where only the employee and the licensed health care professional or board certified genetic counselor involved in providing such services receive individually identifiable information concerning the results of such services, and the employer receives aggregate, not individually identified, genetic information;

(3)   [where medical history is requested in regard to a claim for Family and Medical Leave];

(5)   where the information involved is to be used for genetic monitoring of the biological effects of toxic substances in the workplace, but only if [employees are given notice, sign consent forms, and are told the results, and the monitoring is either required by law or the employee gives prior knowing, voluntary and written authorization.]

Sec. 206. Confidentiality of Genetic Information.

(A) TREATMENT OF INFORMATION AS PART OF CONFIDENTIAL MEDICAL RECORD. If an employer … possesses genetic information about an employee or member, such information shall be maintained on separate forms and in separate medical files and be treated as a confidential medical record of the employee....

(B) LIMITATION ON DISCLOSURE.—An employer … shall not disclose genetic information concerning an employee or member except—

(1) to the employee … (or family member if the family member is receiving the genetic services) at the written request of the employee;

(2) to an occupational or other health researcher …

(3) in response to an order of a court.

[GINA similarly restricts insurers from discriminating, forbidding them from raising premiums or denying coverage on the basis of genetic information. GINA does not, however, prevent an insurance company from raising an employer's premium if an insured individual in the group actually manifests a disease or disorder.]

QUESTIONS

1. Has anyone in the following scenarios violated GINA? If so, what part of the law was violated?

   (a) Supervisor overhears Employee A say she and her sister share the same gene predictive of developing breast cancer. Supervisor gives Employee A a lower performance rating than she deserves, in preparation for letting her go with the next round of lay-offs.

   (b) A health professional working learns that Employee B has family members with breast cancer as a result of a medical interview in which Employee B participated as a requirement for joining the company's wellness program. He shares that information with Employee B's supervisor over lunch.

   (c) Employer asks Employee C, who has requested Family and Medical Leave, to certify the health status of the family member she will care for, and Employee C provides evidence that her mother has breast cancer.

   (d) Employee D reads the obituary of Employee C's mother, describing that she died after a long struggle with breast cancer for which she carried a predictive gene. She shares this information with Supervisor, who asks Employee C to take a genetic test.

   (e) A drilling company uses vast quantities of water containing toxic chemicals in a "fracking" operation, which forces water deep underground to fracture rock and release natural gas. During routine medical check-ups given by the company that normally do not contain genetic testing, workers' blood is analyzed to find out if exposure to toxic chemicals in this process might be causing health problems. Three employees are discovered to have a genetic tendency to develop lymphoma and are given desk jobs that pay less.

   (f) Same as (e), but the tests are mandated by state law, the employees are given notice, sign consent forms, and are told the results and why they have been reassigned.

2. In May 2013, the agency responsible for enforcing GINA, the Equal Employment Opportunity Commission (EEOC), brought its first case. It involved the following facts: Rhonda Jones was working for Fabricut as a temporary memo clerk. As her temp job was ending, she applied for a permanent job. Fabricut initially offered Jones the position, but asked her questions about her family medical history as part of a preemployment medical exam. Based on her answers, the company then required Jones to take more tests to rule out carpal tunnel syndrome (CTS). Although these further tests showed Jones did not have CTS, Fabricut rescinded its job offer. This case was settled for $50,000 the same day it was filed in federal court. How did Fabricut arguably violate GINA?

3. In 1927, the Supreme Court legitimized state-sponsored sterilization of a young woman with alleged mental disabilities. Carrie Buck, an 18-year-old described as having the mental age of nine, was sent to the State Colony of Epileptics and the Feeble-Minded in Virginia to deliver a baby who was conceived after she had been raped by the nephew of her foster parents. At that time, Virginia allowed sterilization of people who suffered hereditary forms of insanity or imbecility, a law designed to prevent "mentally defective" people from reproducing. Against her will, Buck was ordered to be sterilized. The superintendent of the state facility petitioned the courts to enforce Virginia law, arguing that compulsory sterilization was simply analogous to compulsory vaccination.

In an 8–1 decision, the Court agreed, stating that Carrie Buck was "feeble-minded" and "promiscuous." Justice Oliver Wendell Holmes, Jr. argued that a "pure" gene pool outweighed an individual's interest in bodily integrity:

> We have seen more than once that the public welfare may call upon the best citizens for their lives. It would be strange if it could not call upon those who already sap the strength of the State for these lesser sacrifices, often not felt to be such by those concerned, to prevent our being swamped with incompetence. It is better for all the world, if instead of waiting to execute degenerate offspring for crime, or to let them starve for their imbecility, society can prevent those who are manifestly unfit from continuing their kind. The principle that sustains compulsory vaccination is broad enough to cover cutting the Fallopian tubes.

Holmes infamously concluded that "Three generations of imbeciles are enough."[22]

In the 40 years following the Court's decision, the pseudoscience of eugenics permitted the forcible sterilization of some 60,000 Americans. What has happened to change societal attitudes (as reflected in change in the law) so significantly?

4. The 1000 Genomes Project collects genetic information from people around the world and posts it online for researchers to use. It includes the genetic sequence, and regions where participants live, but shields their identity. In 2013, using genealogical sites and other DNA databases, human genetics researcher Yaniv Erlich was able to identify five individuals who were part of the study, and through them, their entire families. (a) Would publishing their names violate GINA? (b) What might possibly be done to better protect the privacy of those participating in scientific studies such as the Genomes Project?[23]

PRIVACY AND CORPORATE PERSONHOOD

As we learned in Chapter 1, the courts treat corporations as "persons" with a constitutional right to free speech protected by the First Amendment. And, while the Supreme Court has applied the Fourth Amendment to limit government searches of businesses, insisting that there is "no doubt that proprietors of commercial premises, including corporations, have the right to conduct their business free from unreasonable official intrusion,"[24] the full parameters of a corporation's constitutional right to privacy are not clear. That has not stopped corporate lawyers from asserting broad rights, as the next case demonstrates.

Hydrogen-fracturing (fracking) is a process by which natural gas is forced from deep underground by the high pressure injection of a mixture of water and chemicals. Although natural gas is a cheaper and cleaner form of energy than other fossil fuels, fracking is a highly controversial process. Concerns about water pollution and harm to humans living near the drill-sites have intensified as the companies refuse to provide

---

[22]*Buck v. Bell*, 274 U.S. 200, at 270 (1927). In 1979, researchers determined that Carrie Buck, her sister, who was also sterilized, and her daughter, were all of average intelligence. Virginia's sterilization procedures were not repealed until 1974.

[23]Gina Kolata, "Web Hunt for DNA Sequences Leaves Privacy Compromised," *The New York Times*, January 18, 2013.

[24]*Dow Chemical Company v. United States*, 476 U.S. 227 (1986).

detailed information about the chemicals they use, doing what they can to keep this "proprietary" information secret.

A family in Western Pennsylvania sued a group of corporations that had been fracking near their home, alleging that the gas drilling had contaminated their water supply and created health risks. They settled the case for $750,000. Then several newspapers sued to make this confidential settlement public, so that journalists, environmentalists, and community rights advocates could learn more about the consequences of fracking.

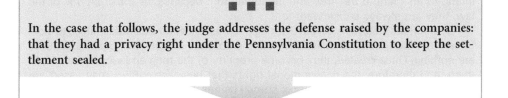

In the case that follows, the judge addresses the defense raised by the companies: that they had a privacy right under the Pennsylvania Constitution to keep the settlement sealed.

Hallowich v. Range Resources Corp.

Pennsylvania Court of Common Pleas, Washington County, 2013

DEBBIE O'DELL-SENECA, Judge.

Defendants ground their claimed right of privacy in Article I of Pennsylvania's constitution, specifically, sections 1 and 8.... Those sections provide:

§ I. Inherent Rights of Mankind

All men are born equally free and independent, and have certain inherent and indefeasible rights, among which are those of enjoying and defending life and liberty, of acquiring, possessing and protecting property and reputation, and of pursuing their own happiness.

and:

§ 8. Security from Search and Seizure

The people shall be secure in their persons, houses, papers and possessions from unreasonable searches and seizures ...

Neither these provisions nor any other part of the constitution explicitly announce a right of privacy. Even so, courts of this Commonwealth have extrapolated the right of privacy from these clauses and others like them.

After [the 1965 U.S. Supreme Court case of *Griswold v. Connecticut,* holding that a married couple's right to privacy was violated by a state law outlawing birth control], the Supreme Court of Pennsylvania began to ... develop privacy protections, and, nearly 30 years later, an unanimous court would remark that "the right of privacy is a well-settled part of the jurisprudential tradition in this Commonwealth ... " [cite omitted] However, nothing in that jurisprudence indicates that that right is available to business entities.

Article I, § 1 of our constitution, entitled "Inherent Rights of Mankind," opens with a particularly striking phrase: "All men are born ...." Through [Pennsylvania's Equal Rights Amendment] the people of this Commonwealth extended legal rights, ... to women, as well as men. Consequently, women and men come into this world with "certain inherent and indefeasible rights ..."

There are no men or women defendants in the instant case; they are various business entities. Range Resources Corporation is a corporation; Williams Gas/Laurel Mountain Midstream and MarkWest Energy Group, L.L.C. are limited-liability companies; and MarkWest Energy Partners, L.P. is a limited partnership. These are all legal fictions, existing not by natural birth but by operations of state statutes. For example, Range Resource Corporation is a publicly-traded, Texas-based corporation, formed under the laws of Delaware. Such business entities cannot have been "born equally free and independent," because they were not *born* at all. Indeed, the framers of our constitution could not have intended for them to be "free and independent," because, as the creations of the law, they are always subservient to it.

The various states, via acts of their legislatures, allow for business entities to exist but are not required to establish them. In the absence of state law, business entities are nothing. Once created, they become property of the men and women who own them, and therefore, the constitutional rights that business entities may assert are not coterminous ... with the rights of human beings. Were they so, the chattel would become the co-equal to its owners, the servant on par with its masters, the agent the peer of its principals, and the legal fabrication superior to the law that created and sustains it. Surely, what the people have incorporated, the text of Article I, § 1 does not prohibit them from disincorporating or otherwise circumscribing its activities.

[At this point Judge Seneca acknowledges that the U.S. Supreme Court has found that corporations have rights under the federal Constitution. She notes that the mid-19th century congressional authors of the 14th Amendment understood the word "person" as applicable to business entities, but she contrasts that with the language and history of the Pennsylvania Constitution, in the following analysis.]

....Critically, the exact opposite conclusion is derived from plain language of Article X of the Constitution of the Commonwealth of Pennsylvania. It provides, in pertinent part:

§ 2. Certain Charters to Be Subject to the Constitution

Private corporations which have accepted or accept the Constitution of this Commonwealth or the benefits of any law passed by the General Assembly ... shall hold their charters subject to the provisions of the Constitution of this Commonwealth.

§ 3. Revocation, Amendment, and Repeal of Charters

All charters of private corporations and all ... powers, rights, duties or liabilities of private corporations or their officers, directors or shareholders may be revoked, amended or repealed.

Not only did our framers know how to employ the names of business entities when and where they wanted them (as the above text demonstrates), they used those words to subjugate business entities to the constitution. Unlike "all men (and women)," who are "born equally free," ... the framers permitted the Commonwealth to revoke, amend, and repeal "[a]ll charters of private corporations" and any "powers, *rights,* duties or liabilities" of corporations. Thus, the constitution vests in business entities no special rights that the laws of this Commonwealth cannot extinguish. In sum, Defendants cannot assert the protections of Article I, § 1, because they are not mentioned in its text.

....If the framers had intended this section to shield corporations, limited-liability corporations, or limited partnerships, this Court presumes that they could and would have used those words. The plain meaning of "people" is the living, breathing humans in this Commonwealth.

[To shed more light on Article I of the Pennsylvania Constitution, the judge looks back to the Commonwealth's constitutional convention, which pre-dated the U.S. constitutional convention by 11 years.]

The majority of the 1776 constitutional convention delegates was comprised of poorer Pennsylvanians from the agrarian, western counties, because that convention had been called by the [men in the countryside who] suspected the wealthier Philadelphians of holding British loyalties. Thus, the constitution they created "was one of the most liberal and influential" of the new nation. Dr. Benjamin Franklin presided over that convention, and his theories on government, as well as those of William Penn, greatly influenced the delegates.

In 1682, Pennsylvania, like all American colonies, began as a business venture on behalf of the Crown: *i.e.,* as a proprietorship under Penn's absolute control, in which "some 600 investors bought shares."...

[Judge O'Dell-Seneca suggests that while Penn conceded that Pennsylvania could not divest its settlers of rights they had already under the *Magna Carta*], ... nothing in his writings on liberty suggests that Penn thought that those rights inured to businesses.

Penn also had a strong respect for privacy of the individual, as a crucial ingredient of true happiness and enjoyment of life....

It is highly improbable that Penn founded Pennsylvania with an eye toward securing liberty for business entities or to grant them a right of privacy.

An even more dubious proposition is that the framers of the Constitution of 1776, given their egalitarian sympathies, would have concerned themselves with vesting, for the first time in history, indefeasible rights in such entities. This Court has found no documentation from the era indicating that they were so inclined. Moreover, given that a majority of the delegates who authored Article I were farmers from the young Commonwealth's frontier, with little or no ties to institutionalized business, it seems most likely that they intended their words in the Article to convey solely and precisely their plain-language meanings. As stated above, that language therein extends only to natural persons. Thus, the history of the 1776 convention and legislative intent that that history indicates point away from the constitutional interpretation urged by the Defendants.

....[T]he right of privacy was invoked to protect people, not businesses....

Justice Brandeis wrote in] his famous dissent in *Olmstead v. United States,* (1928):

The makers of our Constitution undertook to secure conditions favorable to the pursuit of happiness. They recognized the significance of man's spiritual nature, of his feelings and of his intellect. They knew that only a part of the pain, pleasure and satisfactions of life are to be found in material things. They sought to protect Americans in their beliefs, their thoughts, their emotions and their sensations. They conferred, as against the government, the right to be let alone—the most comprehensive of rights and the right most valued by civilized men.

... [C]orporations, companies, and partnership have no "spiritual nature," "feelings," "intellect," "beliefs," "thoughts," "emotions," or "sensations," because they do not exist in the manner that humankind exists.... They cannot be "let alone" by government, because businesses are but grapes, ripe upon the vine of the law, that the people of this Commonwealth raise, tend, and prune at their pleasure and need.

[Judge Seneca orders the settlement between the fracking companies and the Hallowich family unsealed.]

QUESTIONS

1. What happens when patients come to doctors with symptoms that might be related to fracking? Under a law passed in Pennsylvania in 2011, drillers must disclose the chemicals used to frack on a public website that doctors can access. But some chemicals are not listed because they are considered trade secret—the companies don't want their competitors finding out about them. Doctors can access those too, but only if they sign nondisclosure agreements promising to use the information to treat patients, and not share it. This law, dubbed the "doctor gag rule," leaves physicians uncertain as to whether they can notify other doctors, community health officials, or even their patients about the trade-secret chemicals. Many are worried that the rule, known as Act 13, will hamper research into the public health aspects of fracking.

   Research: A lawsuit has been filed against the PA EPA by Dr. Alfonso Rodriguez, alleging that the law is vague and violates physicians' First Amendment rights. In addition, some Pennsylvania legislators have introduced a bill to remove the requirement that doctors sign the confidentiality agreement. Update the "doctor gag rule" in Pennsylvania and find out whether your state has been the site of a similar controversy.

2. In this case, Judge Seneca interprets Article I of the Pennsylvania Constitution. In the Wal-Mart case earlier in this chapter, New York judges interpret a state statute. What tools do these judges say they are using to analyze the work of lawmakers? Do you think that other factors might influence the way judges interpret the law, factors that remain unmentioned? Can you point to anything in the *Hallowich* case that indicates other factors at play?

3. In the *Hallowich* case, Judge Seneca jumped right into the controversy about corporate personhood, which has been raging since the Supreme Court decided *Citizens United* in 2010. **Research:** Find out if *Hallowich v. Range Resources* has been reversed on appeal.

■ ■ ■

CHAPTER PROBLEMS

1. We have seen that, in general, workplace e-mail monitoring is legal. In the landmark *Smyth v. Pillsbury* case at the start of this chapter, employees fired for messages sent through the employer's server, even when password-protected, and even when the employer had issued assurances that they would not be read for retaliatory purposes, had no recourse. But what if the employer monitors messages sent on company-owned computers through a personal e-mail account, such as Yahoo? In 2008, Scott Sidell allegedly forgot to sign off his Yahoo account when he was fired from his job at Structured Settlement Investments. During the next week or so, the company read his still-accessible private e-mail, including confidential messages between Sidell and his attorney regarding his termination. Under these circumstances, did Sidell have a reasonable expectation of privacy? Was it violated by SSI?

2. Google recently developed Google Glass, an accessory worn on a person's face, which places a small computer above one eye, allowing people to take photos and videos by

touching the device or by speaking commands. "Glass" is, in effect, a wearable extension of a smartphone. In 2013, some privacy advocates, like Justin Brookman of the Center for Democracy and Technology, believed the device "doesn't do anything more than your phone can already do—it's just a new hands-free interface." Others, like Marc Rotenberg of the Electronic Privacy Information Center, saw major problems: "The number one concern is whether Google is capturing the data stream generated by the user." What are the pros and cons of this new wearable computer? **Research:** What is the latest on the privacy implications of Google Glass?

3. A restaurant employee, Brian Pietrylo, created a private MySpace forum to vent about work. The site was full of personal information—about illegal drug use, for example—and contained sexual comments about the restaurant's customers and managers. One of the members of the MySpace group was a hostess at the restaurant. She showed the site to a manager. Another one of the restaurant's managers then asked her to divulge her login and password so that management could access the group directly. The hostess complied. Brian and another employee were fired. In the ensuing lawsuit, they argued that their privacy was violated under the ECPA statute and under tort law. At the trial, the hostess testified that she felt under pressure to give her password up to management. When asked whether she felt that something would happen to her if she did not, she answered "I felt that I probably would have gotten in trouble." Do you think the terminated employees would win? Find out. **Research:** *Pietrylo v. Hillstone Restaurant Group*, a 2009 New Jersey case.

4. Do Americans have a reasonable expectation of privacy that is violated when they are videotaped on public streets? In store dressing rooms? In motel rooms? In coffee bars? When cybercafés began to proliferate in Garden Grove, California, they seemed to bring with them gang activity. The police chief pushed for some control, and the city council responded by passing a law requiring cybercafés to install video-surveillance systems that could be inspected by the city during business hours. When a California court denied a constitutional challenge to the video-surveillance law, one judge dissented:

> *Cybercafes allow people who cannot afford computers ... the freedom of the press. They can post messages to the whole world, and, in theory (if they get enough "hits") can reach more people than read the hard copy of* The New York Times *every morning.... Logging on is an exercise of free speech.*
>
> *Consider that totalitarian governments have always cracked down on unrestricted access to the means of communication. When the Communists were in control of countries such as Albania and Bulgaria, each typewriter was licensed....*
>
> *And consider that the governments of both Communist China and Vietnam have recently cracked down on cybercafes in an effort to curb the freedom of ideas that they promote—an effort that has entailed learning the identity of cybercafe owners.... Given the constitutional ramifications of the very nature of cybercafes, I will go so far as to say that there is an expectation of privacy even as to one's identity when using a cybercafé.... Vo v. City of Garden Grove, 9 Cal.Rptr.3d 257 (Court of Appeal, 2004).*

(a) Create a constitutional analysis of Garden Groves' video-surveillance requirement.

(b) **Research:** The ubiquitous cameras that provide the images for Google's Street View caused a stir in Europe recently. What happened?

(c) **Research:** Along with street photos, Google scooped up passwords, e-mails, and other personal information from nearby computer users. Thirty-eight states sued Google for violating the privacy rights of their citizens. Find out what happened to this Street View suit 2013. What actions has Google taken since then to better protect privacy?

5. The cost of errors in inventory management may be as high as $500 billion a year in the United States. Radio Frequency Identification (RFID), the technology which enabled British flight controllers in World War II to distinguish between friendly and enemy planes and which makes possible the EZ Pass and similar systems through highway tollbooths, is the likely successor to bar code scanning. Tags can be almost as small as a grain of sand. Unlike the Universal Product Code used by bar code scanners, RFID does not require that the scanning device "see" the bars. Some RFID sensors can operate at 100 meters. And, unlike the Universal Product Code used by bar code scanners, the Electronic Product Code (EPC) can be programmed to add specific information that may have uses in product handling prior to sale and even in research concerning customer behavior after the purchase. It is the use of RFID technology to study customer behavior that has privacy groups concerned. In 2003, Procter & Gamble used RFID to trigger hidden cameras, enabling researchers in Cincinnati to watch female customers handling lipstick in a Wal-Mart store in Oklahoma. As a California state senator said in reference to that incident, "How would you like it if … one day you realized your underwear was reporting on your whereabouts?" What are the ethical pros and cons of RFID?

6. As we have seen, there is an ongoing controversy over the status of corporations as "persons"—and whether or not a corporation's privacy rights are coextensive with those of human beings. Consider this example: Under the Freedom of Information Act (FOIA) federal agencies must make records and documents publicly available upon request, unless they fall within one of several statutory exemptions. One of those exemptions covers law enforcement records, the disclosure of which "could reasonably be expected to constitute an unwarranted invasion of personal privacy." In 2004, competitors to AT&T requested documents related to an investigation by the Federal Communications Commission (FCC) into possible overcharging by AT&T. The investigation had been settled, and AT&T asserted that some of the documents should not be turned over because they were "exempt" under FOIA's "personal privacy exemption." **Research:** Find out whether the Supreme Court agreed when it ruled in *Federal Communications Commission v. AT&T*, 131 S. Ct. 1171 (2012).

7. Early in 2013, a French court found that pseudonymous Twitter postings violated French law against racist speech. The court ordered Twitter to identify the people who had posted the anti-Semitic and racist remarks. Twitter refused, explaining that it protects the identities of users except when a U.S. court orders disclosure. (a) Why do you suppose that French laws would outlaw such speech when U.S. laws do not? Should it? (b) **Research:** Find out what happened in this controversy.

8. After the tragic school shooting in Newtown Connecticut in 2013, one New York newspaper mapped the names and addresses of more than 33,000 handgun permit holders in nearby counties. Although they gleaned that information from public sources, its publication raised hackles. Using the ethical theories outlined in Chapter 1, consider the ethics of posting the following on a newspaper website: (a) the personal details of all employees of local clinics that perform abortions; (b) police records of arrests for drunk driving; (c) The names and addresses of food stamp recipients in your community; (d) the donors to a group that promotes L.G.B.T. rights.[25]

9. Should the police be allowed to routinely take DNA samples when they arrest someone? Maryland police did just that. When Alonzo Jay King, Jr. was arrested for assault in 2009,

---

[25]Based on hypotheticals posed by Bill Keller, "Invasion of the Data Snatchers," *The New York Times*, Op. Ed., January 14, 2013.

police swabbed his cheek and checked the King's DNA against evidence from a 2003 rape. He was convicted, and challenged the practice as a violation of his privacy. (a) How would you analyze DNA sampling under the Fourth Amendment? (b) Would it be illegal under GINA? (c) How did the Supreme Court rule in the actual case?

10. In 2012, the Obama administration proposed a Consumer Privacy Bill of Rights:

   — Individual Control: Consumers have a right to exercise control over what personal data companies collect from them and how they use it.
   — Transparency: Consumers have a right to easily understandable and accessible information about privacy and security practices.
   — Respect for Context: Consumers have a right to expect that companies will collect, use, and disclose personal data in ways that are consistent with the context in which consumers provide the data.
   — Security: Consumers have a right to secure and responsible handling of personal data.
   — Access and Accuracy: Consumers have a right to access and correct personal data in usable formats, in a manner that is appropriate to the sensitivity of the data and the risk of adverse consequences to consumers if the data are inaccurate.
   — Focused Collection: Consumers have a right to reasonable limits on the personal data that companies collect and retain.
   — Accountability: Consumers have a right to have personal data handled by companies with appropriate measures in place to assure they adhere to the Consumer Privacy Bill of Rights.

   Research: Find out what action has been taken to adopt this action.

CHAPTER PROJECT

Team Exercise: Writing a Model Corporate Privacy Policy

Begin with students working in teams of five. Within each group, the following roles should be represented:

- Upper management
- Mid-management
- Production/office workers
- Human resources
- Public relations

Each team should first discuss and try to reach consensus on a set of guiding values. From there, it should hammer out specific policies addressing electronic monitoring, Internet usage, mixing work and personal activities, testing policies, and so on.

Groups should write their final versions and present them to one another, arguing in support of their privacy policies to their classmates, taking questions and challenges.

A final task might be to vote on the "best" corporate privacy policy, and to compare it to the one recommended by the National Workrights Institute.

CHAPTER 5

NEGLIGENCE AND STRICT LIABILITY

CHAPTER OUTCOMES

After reading and studying this chapter, you should be able to:

- List and describe the three required elements of an action for negligence.

- Explain the duty of care that is imposed on (1) adults, (2) children, (3) persons with a physical disability, (4) persons with a mental deficiency, (5) persons with superior knowledge, and (6) persons acting in an emergency.

- Differentiate among the duties that possessors of land owe to trespassers, licensees, and invitees.

- Identify the defenses that are available to a tort action in negligence and those that are available to a tort action in strict liability.

- Identify and describe those activities giving rise to a tort action in strict liability.

Whereas intentional torts deal with conduct that has a substantial certainty of causing harm, negligence involves conduct that creates an unreasonable risk of harm. The basis of liability for negligence is the failure to exercise reasonable care, under given circumstances, for the safety of another person or his property, which failure causes injury to such person or damage to his property, or both. Thus, if the driver of an automobile intentionally runs down a person, she has committed the intentional tort of battery. If, on the other hand, the driver hits and injures a person while driving without reasonable regard for the safety of others, she is negligent.

Strict liability is not based upon the negligence or intent of the defendant but rather upon the nature of the activity in which he is engaging. Under this doctrine, defendants who engage in certain activities, such as keeping animals or carrying on abnormally dangerous conditions, are held liable for the injuries they cause, even if they have exercised the utmost care. The law imposes this liability to effect a just reallocation of loss, given that the defendant engaged in the activity for his own benefit and is in a better position to manage, by insurance or otherwise, the risk inherent in the activity.

As mentioned in Chapter 7, the American Law Institute (ALI) has published the Restatement Third, Torts: Liability for Physical and Emotional Harm (the "Third Restatement"). This new Restatement addresses the general or basic elements of the tort action for liability for accidental personal injury, property damage, and emotional harm, but does not

cover liability for economic loss. "Physical harm" is defined as bodily harm (physical injury, illness, disease, and death) or property damage (physical impairment of real property or tangible personal property). The Third Restatement replaces comparable provisions in the Restatement Second, Torts. However, the Third Restatement does not cover the following matters, which remain governed by the Second Restatement: protection of reputation or privacy, economic loss, or domestic relations; determination of the recoverable damages and their amount; and the standards for liability of professionals for malpractice. Otherwise, this chapter reflects the Third Restatement's provisions.

The ALI's Restatement Third, Torts: Economic Torts and Related Wrongs will update coverage on torts that involve economic loss or pecuniary harm *not* resulting from physical harm or physical contact to a person or property. This project will update coverage of economic torts in Restatement Second, Torts and address some topics not covered in prior Restatements. The ALI began this project in 2004, and after several years of inactivity, the project was resumed in 2010. In 2012, a portion of Chapter 1 of the Tentative Draft was approved.

NEGLIGENCE

A person acts negligently if the person does not exercise reasonable care under all the circumstances. Third Restatement, Section 3. Moreover, the general rule is that a person is under a duty to all others at all times to exercise reasonable care for the safety of the others' person and property. Third Restatement, Section 7.

An action for negligence consists of five elements, each of which the plaintiff must prove:

1. **Duty of care:** that a legal duty required the defendant to conform to the standard of conduct established for the protection of others;
2. **Breach of duty:** that the defendant failed to exercise reasonable care;
3. **Factual cause:** that the defendant's failure to exercise reasonable care in fact caused the harm the plaintiff sustained;
4. **Harm:** that the harm sustained is of a type protected against negligent conduct; and
5. **Scope of liability:** that the harm sustained is within the "scope of liability," which historically has been referred to as "proximate cause." Third Restatement, Section 6, comments.

The first two elements will be discussed in the next section, "Breach of Duty of Care"; the last three elements will be covered in subsequent sections.

BREACH OF DUTY OF CARE

Negligence consists of conduct that creates an unreasonable risk of harm. In determining whether a given risk of harm was unreasonable, the law considers the following factors: (1) the foreseeable probability that the person's conduct will result in harm, (2) the foreseeable gravity or severity of any harm that may follow, and (3) the burden of taking precautions to eliminate or reduce the risk of harm. Third Restatement, Section 3. Thus, the standard of conduct, which is the basis for the law of negligence, is usually determined by a cost-benefit or risk-benefit analysis.

REASONABLE PERSON STANDARD

The duty of care imposed by law is measured by the degree of carefulness that a reasonable person would exercise in a given situation. The reasonable person is a fictitious individual who is always careful and prudent and never negligent. What the judge or jury determines a reasonable person would have done in light of the facts disclosed by the evidence in a particular case sets the standard of conduct for that case. The reasonable person standard is thus external and *objective*, as described by Justice Holmes:

> If, for instance, a man is born hasty and awkward, is always hurting himself or his neighbors, no doubt his congenital defects will be allowed for in the courts of Heaven, but his slips are no less troublesome to his neighbors than if they sprang from guilty neglect. His neighbors accordingly require him, at his peril, to come up to their standard, and the courts which they establish decline to take his personal equation into account. Holmes, *The Common Law.*

CHILDREN   A child is a person below the age of majority, which in almost all States has been lowered from twenty-one to eighteen. The standard of conduct to which a child must conform to avoid being negligent is that of a reasonably careful person of the same age, intelligence, and experience under all the circumstances. Third Restatement, Section 10. For example, Alice, a five-year-old girl, was walking with her father on the crowded sidewalk along Main Street when he told her that he was going to take her to Disney World for her birthday next week. Upon hearing the news, Alice became so excited that she began to jump up and down and run around. During this fit of exuberance, Alice accidentally ran into and knocked down an elderly woman who was passing by. Alice's liability, if any, would be determined by whether a reasonable five-year-old person of like age, intelligence, and experience under like circumstances would have the capacity and judgment to understand the increased risk her enthusiastic display of joy caused to others.

The law applies an individualized test because children do not possess the judgment, intelligence, knowledge, and experience of adults. Moreover, children as a general rule do not engage in activities entailing high risk to others, and their conduct normally does not involve a potential for harm as great as that of adult conduct. A child who engages in a dangerous activity that is characteristically undertaken by adults, however, such as flying an airplane or driving a boat or car, is held in almost all States to the standard of care applicable to adults. Finally, some States modify this individualized test by holding that under a minimum age, most commonly the age of seven, a child is incapable of committing a negligent act. The Third Restatement further provides that a child less than five years of age is incapable of negligence. Section 10.

PHYSICAL DISABILITY   If a person is ill or otherwise physically disabled, the standard of conduct to which he must conform to avoid being negligent is that of a reasonably careful person with the same disability. Third Restatement, Section 11(a). Thus, a blind man must act as a reasonable man who is blind, and a woman with multiple sclerosis must act as a reasonable woman with multiple sclerosis. However, the conduct of a person during a period of sudden incapacitation or loss of consciousness resulting from physical illness is negligent only if the sudden incapacitation or loss of consciousness was reasonably foreseeable to the actor. Examples of sudden incapacitation include heart attack, stroke, epileptic seizure, and diabetes. Third Restatement, Section 11(b).

MENTAL DISABILITY A person's mental or emotional disability is not considered in determining whether conduct is negligent unless the person is a child. Third Restatement, Section 11(c). The defendant is held to the standard of conduct of a reasonable person who is *not* mentally or emotionally disabled, even though the defendant is, in fact, incapable of conforming to the standard. Thus, an adult with the mental acumen of a six-year-old will be held liable for his negligent conduct if he fails to act as carefully as a reasonable adult of normal intelligence. In this case the law may demand more of the individual than his mental limitations permit him to accomplish. When a person's intoxication is voluntary, it is not considered as an excuse for conduct that is otherwise lacking in reasonable care. Third Restatement, Section 12, Comment c.

SUPERIOR SKILL OR KNOWLEDGE If a person has skills or knowledge beyond those possessed by most others, these skills or knowledge are circumstances to be taken into account in determining whether the person has acted with reasonable care. Third Restatement, Section 12. Thus, persons who are qualified and who practice a profession or trade that calls for special skill and expertise are required to exercise that care and skill that members in good standing of their profession or trade normally possess. This standard applies to such professionals as physicians, surgeons, dentists, attorneys, pharmacists, architects, accountants, and engineers and to those who perform skilled trades, such as airline pilots, electricians, carpenters, and plumbers. A member of a profession or skilled trade who possesses greater skill than that common to the profession or trade is required to exercise that skill.

EMERGENCIES An emergency is a sudden and unexpected event that calls for immediate action and permits no time for deliberation. In determining whether a defendant's conduct is reasonable, the law takes into consideration the fact that he was at the time confronted with a sudden and unexpected emergency. Third Restatement, Section 9. The standard is still that of a reasonable person under the circumstances—the emergency is simply part of the circumstances. If, however, the defendant's own negligent or tortious conduct created the emergency, he is liable for the consequences of this conduct even if he acted reasonably in the resulting emergency situation. Moreover, failure to anticipate an emergency may itself constitute negligence.

VIOLATION OF STATUTE The reasonable person standard of conduct may be established by legislation or administrative regulation. Third Restatement, Section 14. Some statutes expressly impose civil liability upon violators. Absent such a provision, courts may adopt the requirements of the statute as the standard of conduct if the statute is designed to protect against the type of accident the defendant's conduct causes and the accident victim is within the class of persons the statute is designed to protect.

If the statute is found to be applicable, the majority of the courts hold that an unexcused violation is **negligence *per se***; that is, the violation conclusively constitutes negligent conduct. In a minority of States, the violation is considered merely to be evidence of negligence. In either event, the plaintiff must also prove legal causation and injury.

For example, a statute enacted to protect employees from injuries requires that all factory elevators be equipped with specified safety devices. Arthur, an employee in Freya's factory, and Carlos, a business visitor to the factory, are injured when the elevator fails because the safety devices have not been installed. The court may adopt the statute as a standard of conduct as to Arthur and hold Freya negligent *per se* to Arthur, but not as to Carlos, because Arthur, not Carlos, is within the class of persons the statute is intended to protect. Carlos would have to establish that a reasonable person in the position of Freya under the circumstances would have installed the safety device.

On the other hand, compliance with a legislative enactment or administrative regulation does not prevent a finding of negligence if a reasonable person would have taken additional precautions. Third Restatement, Section 16. For instance, driving at the speed limit may not constitute due care when traffic or road conditions require a lower speed. Legislative or administrative rules normally establish *minimum* standards.

◆ **SEE FIGURE 8-1: Negligence and Negligence *Per Se***

◆ **SEE CASE 1-1**

> **PRACTICAL ADVICE**
> *Assess the potential liability for negligence arising from your activities and obtain adequate liability insurance to cover your exposure.*

DUTY TO ACT

As stated previously, the general rule is that a person is under a duty to all others at all times to exercise reasonable care for the safety of the others' person and property. On the other hand, subject to several exceptions, a person (A) does not have a duty of care when the other's (B's) person or property is at risk for reasons other than the conduct of A. Third Restatement, Section 37. This rule applies even though the person may be in a position to help another in peril. As William Prosser, an authority on tort law, has stated, "The law has persistently refused to recognize the moral obligation

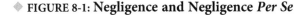

◆ FIGURE 8-1: **Negligence and Negligence** *Per Se*

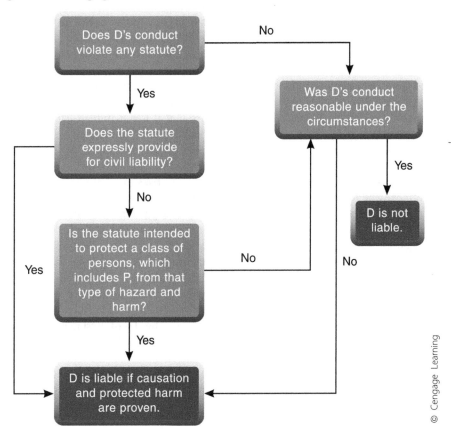

of common decency and common humanity, to come to the aid of another human being who is in danger, even though the outcome is to cost him his life." For example, Toni, an adult standing at the edge of a steep cliff, observes a baby carriage with a crying infant in it slowly rolling toward the edge and certain doom. Toni could easily prevent the baby's fall at no risk to her own safety. Nonetheless, Toni does nothing, and the baby falls to his death. Toni is under no legal duty to act and, therefore, incurs no liability for failing to do so.

Nonetheless, special relations between the parties may impose an affirmative duty of reasonable care upon the defendant to aid or protect the other with respect to risks that arise within the scope of the relationship. Thus, if in the previous example, Toni were the baby's mother or babysitter, Toni would be under a duty to act and therefore would be liable for not taking action. The special relations giving rise to an affirmative duty to aid or protect another include (1) a common carrier with its passengers, (2) an innkeeper with its guest, (3) an employer with its employees, (4) a school with its students, (5) a landlord with its tenants with respect to common areas under the landlord's control, (6) a business open

to the public with its customers, and (7) a custodian with those in its custody including parents with their children. Third Restatement, Section 40. The Third Restatement leaves it to the courts whether to recognize additional relationships as sufficient to impose an affirmative duty. Furthermore, State and Federal statutes and administrative regulations as well as local ordinances may impose an affirmative duty to act for the protection of another.

In addition, when a person's prior conduct, even though not tortious, creates a continuing risk of physical harm, the person has a duty to exercise reasonable care to prevent or minimize the harm. Third Restatement, Section 39. For example, Dale innocently drives her car into Bob, rendering him unconscious. Dale leaves Bob lying in the middle of the road, where he is run over by a second car driven by Chen. Dale is liable to Bob for the additional injuries inflicted by Chen.

Moreover, a person who voluntarily begins a rescue by taking charge of another who is imperiled and unable to protect himself incurs a duty to exercise reasonable care under the circumstances. Furthermore, a person who discontinues aid or protection is under a duty of reasonable care not to leave the other in a worse position. Third Restatement, Section 44. For example, Ann finds Ben drunk and stumbling along a dark sidewalk. Ann leads Ben halfway up a steep and unguarded stairway, where she abandons him. Ben attempts to climb the stairs but trips and falls, suffering serious injury. Ann is liable to Ben for having left him in a worse position. Most States have enacted Good Samaritan statutes to encourage voluntary emergency care. These statutes vary considerably, but they typically limit or disallow liability for some rescuers under specified circumstances.

There are special relationships in which one person has some degree of control over another person, including (1) a parent with dependent children, and (2) an employer with employees when the employment facilitates the employee's causing harm to third parties. The parent and the employer each owe a duty of reasonable care under the circumstances to third persons with regard to foreseeable risks that arise within the scope of the relationship. Third Restatement, Section 41. Depending on the circumstances, reasonable care may require controlling the activities of the other person or merely providing a warning. Generally, the duty of parents is limited to dependent children; thus when children reach majority or are no longer dependent, parents no longer have control and the duty of reasonable care ceases.

The duty of employers includes the duty to exercise reasonable care in the hiring, training, supervision, and retention of employees. This duty of employers is independent of the vicarious liability of an employer for an employee's tortious conduct during the course of employment, and extends to conduct by the employee that occurs both inside and outside the scope of employment so long as the employment facilitates the employee causing harm to third parties. The Third Restatement provides the following example of an employer's duty:

> Don is employed by Welch Repair Service, which knows that Don had several episodes of assault in his previous employment. Don goes to Traci's residence, where he had previously been dispatched by Welch, and misrepresents to Traci that he is there on Welch business to check repairs that had previously been made in Traci's home. After Traci admits Don, he assaults Traci. Welch is subject to a duty under this subsection with regard to Don's assault on Traci.

◆ SEE CASE 8-1

DUTIES OF POSSESSORS OF LAND

The right of possessors of land to use that land for their own benefit and enjoyment is limited by their duty to do so in a reasonable manner; that is, by the use of their land, they cannot cause unreasonable risks of harm to others. Liability for

breach of this obligation may arise from conduct in any of the three areas of torts discussed in this and the preceding chapter: intentional harm, negligence, or strict liability. Most of these cases fall within the classification of negligence.

In conducting activities on her land, the possessor of land is required to exercise reasonable care to protect others who are not on her property. For example, a property owner who constructs a factory on her premises must take reasonable care that it is not unreasonably dangerous to people off the site. Moreover, a business or other possessor of land that holds its premises open to the public owes those who are lawfully on the premises a duty of reasonable care with regard to risks that arise within the scope of the relationship.

In most States and under the Second Restatement, the duty of a possessor of land to persons who come upon the land depends on whether those persons are trespassers, licensees, or invitees. In about fifteen States, however, licensees and invitees are owed the same duty. In addition, at least nine States have abandoned these distinctions and simply apply ordinary negligence principles of foreseeable risk and reasonable care to all entrants on the land including trespassers. The Third Restatement has adopted this last—the unitary—approach.

SECOND RESTATEMENT In accordance with the historical—and still majority—approach to the duties of possessors of land, the Second Restatement provides for varying duties depending on the status of the entrant on the land.

A **trespasser** is a person who enters or remains on the land of another without the possessor's consent or a legal privilege to do so. The possessor of the land is not liable to adult trespassers for her failure to maintain the land in a reasonably safe condition. Nonetheless, trespassers are not criminals, and the possessor is not free to inflict intentional injury on them. Moreover, most courts hold that upon discovering the presence of trespassers on her land, the lawful possessor is required to exercise reasonable care for their safety in carrying on her activities and to warn the trespassers of potentially highly dangerous conditions that the trespassers are not likely to discover.

A **licensee** is a person who is privileged to enter or remain upon land only by virtue of the lawful possessor's consent. Restatement, Section 330. Licensees include members of the possessor's household, social guests, and salespersons calling at private homes. A licensee will become a trespasser, however, if he enters a portion of the land to which he is not invited or remains upon the land after his invitation has expired. The possessor owes a higher duty of care to licensees than to trespassers. The possessor must warn a licensee of dangerous activities and conditions (1) of which the possessor has knowledge or has reason to know and (2) which the licensee does not and is not likely to discover. A licensee who is not warned may recover if the activity or dangerous condition resulted from the possessor's failure to exercise reasonable care to protect him from the danger. Restatement, Section 342. To illustrate: Jose invites a friend, Julia, to his place in the country at 8:00 P.M. on a winter evening. Jose knows that a bridge in his driveway is in a dangerous condition that is not noticeable in the dark. Jose does not inform Julia of this fact. The bridge gives way under Julia's car, causing serious harm to Julia. Jose is liable to Julia.

An **invitee** is a person invited upon land as a member of the public or for a business purpose. An invitee is either a public invitee or a business visitor. Restatement, Section 332. A *public invitee* is a person invited to enter or remain on land as a member of the public for a purpose for which the land is held open to the public. Such invitees include those who use public parks, beaches, or swimming pools, as well as those who use government facilities, such as a post office or office of the Recorder of Deeds, where business with the public is transacted openly. A *business visitor* is a person invited to enter or remain on the premises for a purpose directly or indirectly concerning business dealings with the possessor of the land, such as one who enters a store or a tradesperson who enters a residence to make repairs. With respect to the condition of the premises, the possessor of land is under a duty to exercise reasonable care to protect invitees against dangerous conditions they are unlikely to discover. This liability extends not only to those conditions of which the possessor knows but also to those she would discover by the exercise of reasonable care. Restatement, Section 343. For example, at the front of Tilson's supermarket is a large glass front door that is well lit and plainly visible. Johnson, a customer, nonetheless mistakes the glass for an open doorway and walks into it, injuring himself. Tilson is not liable to Johnson. If, on the other hand, the glass was difficult to see and a person might foreseeably mistake the glass for an open doorway, then Tilson would be liable to Johnson if Johnson crashed into the glass while exercising reasonable care.

THIRD RESTATEMENT The status-based duty rules just discussed have been rejected by the Third Restatement, which adopts a unitary duty of reasonable care to people entering the land. Section 51.

[Except for "flagrant trespassers,"] a land possessor owes a duty of reasonable care to entrants on the land with regard to:

(1) conduct by the land possessor that creates risks to entrants on the land;

(2) artificial conditions on the land that pose risks to entrants on the land;

(3) natural conditions on the land that pose risks to entrants on the land;…

This rule is similar to the duty land possessors owed to invitees under the Second Restatement except that it extends the duty to all who enter the land, including trespassers, with the exception of "flagrant trespassers." This rule requires a land possessor to use reasonable care to investigate and discover dangerous conditions and to use reasonable care to eliminate or improve those dangerous conditions that are known or should have been discovered by the exercise of reasonable care. However, some risks cannot reasonably be discovered, and the land possessor is not subject to liability for those risks. In addition, a land possessor is not liable to an ordinary trespasser whose unforeseeable presence results in an unforeseeable risk.

A different rule applies to "flagrant trespassers." The Third Restatement requires that a land possessor only (1) refrain from intentional, willful, or wanton conduct that harms a flagrant trespasser and (2) exercise reasonable care on behalf of flagrant trespassers who are imperiled and helpless. Third Restatement, Section 52. The Third Restatement does not define "flagrant trespassers" but instead leaves it to each State to determine at what point an ordinary trespasser becomes a "flagrant trespasser." Comment a to Section 52 of the Third Restatement explains:

The idea behind distinguishing particularly egregious trespassers for different treatment is that their presence on another's land is so antithetical to the rights of the land possessor to exclusive use and possession of the land that the land possessor should not be subject to liability for failing to exercise the ordinary duty of reasonable care otherwise owed to them as entrants on the land. It stems from the idea that when a trespass is sufficiently offensive to the property rights of the land possessor it is unfair to subject the possessor to liability for mere negligence.

The Third Restatement provides an illustration of a flagrant trespasser: "Herman engaged in a late-night burglary of the Jacob liquor store after it had closed. While leaving the store after taking cash from the store's register, Herman slipped on a slick spot on the floor, fell, and broke his arm. Herman is a flagrant trespasser."

PRACTICAL ADVICE

Take care to inspect your premises regularly to detect any dangerous conditions and either remedy the danger or post prominent warnings of any dangerous conditions you discover.

◆ SEE CASE 8-2

RES IPSA LOQUITUR

A rule of circumstantial evidence has developed that permits the jury to infer both negligent conduct and causation from the mere occurrence of certain types of events. This rule, called *res ipsa loquitur*, meaning "the thing speaks for itself," applies "when the accident causing the Plaintiffs physical harm is a type of accident that ordinarily happens as a result of the negligence of a class of actors of which the defendant is the relevant member." Third Restatement, Section 17.

For example, Abrams rents a room in Brown's motel. During the night a large piece of plaster falls from the ceiling and injures Abrams. In the absence of other evidence, the jury may infer that the harm resulted from Brown's negligence in permitting the plaster to become defective. Brown is permitted, however, to introduce evidence to contradict the inference of negligence.

FACTUAL CAUSE

Liability for the negligent conduct of a defendant requires that the conduct in fact caused harm to the plaintiff. The Third Restatement states: "Tortious conduct must be a factual cause of physical harm for liability to be imposed." Section 26. A widely applied test for causation in fact is the **but-for test**: A person's conduct is a cause of an event if the event would not have occurred *but for* the person's negligent conduct. That is, conduct is a factual cause of harm when the harm would not have occurred absent the conduct. Third Restatement, Section 26. For instance, Arnold fails to erect a barrier around an excavation. Doyle is driving a truck when its accelerator becomes stuck, and he and the truck plummet into the excavation. Arnold's negligence is not a cause in fact of Doyle's death if the runaway truck would have crashed through the barrier that Arnold could have erected. Similarly, the failure to install a proper fire escape on a hotel is not the cause in fact of the death of a person who is suffocated by smoke while sleeping in bed during a hotel fire.

If the tortious conduct of Adam is insufficient by itself to cause Paula's harm, but when Adam's conduct is combined with the tortious conduct of Barry, the combined conduct is sufficient to cause Paula's harm, then Adam and Barry are each considered a factual cause of Paula's harm. Third Restatement, Section 26, Comment c.

The but-for test, however, is not satisfied when there are two or more causes, each of which is sufficient to bring about the harm in question and each of which is active at the time the harm occurs. For example, Wilson and Hart negligently set fires that combine to destroy Kennedy's property. Either fire would have destroyed the property. Under the but-for test, either Wilson or Hart, or both, could argue that the fire caused by the other would have destroyed the property and that he, therefore, is not liable. The Third Restatement addresses this problem of multiple *sufficient* causes by providing, "If multiple acts exist, each of which alone would have been a factual cause under [the but-for test] of the

physical harm at the same time, each act is regarded as a factual cause of the harm." Section 27. Under this rule, the conduct of both Wilson and Hart would be found to be a factual cause of the destruction of Kennedy's property.

SCOPE OF LIABILITY (PROXIMATE CAUSE)

As a matter of social policy, legal responsibility has not followed all the consequences of a negligent act. Tort law does not impose liability on a defendant for all harm factually caused by the defendant's negligent conduct. Liability has been limited—to a greater extent than with intentional torts—to those harms that result from the risks that made the defendant's conduct tortious. Third Restatement, Section 29. This "risk standard" limitation on liability also applies to strict liability cases. Third Restatement, Section 29, Comment l. The Third Restatement provides the following example:

> Richard, a hunter, finishes his day in the field and stops at a friend's house while walking home. His friend's nine-year-old daughter, Kim, greets Richard, who hands his loaded shotgun to her as he enters the house. Kim drops the shotgun, which lands on her toe, breaking it. Although Richard was negligent for giving Kim his shotgun, the risk that made Richard negligent was that Kim might shoot someone with the gun, not that she would drop it and hurt herself (the gun was neither especially heavy nor unwieldy). Kim's broken toe is outside the scope of Richard's liability, even though Richard's tortious conduct was a factual cause of Kim's harm.

FORESEEABILITY

Determining the liability of a negligent defendant for unforeseeable consequences has proved to be troublesome and controversial. The Second Restatement and many courts have adopted the following position:

1. If the actor's conduct is a substantial factor in bringing about harm to another, the fact that the actor neither foresaw nor should have foreseen the extent of the harm or the manner in which it occurred does *not* prevent him from being liable.
2. The actor's conduct may be held not to be a legal cause of harm to another where, after the event and looking back from the harm to the actor's negligent conduct, it appears to the court highly extraordinary that it should have brought about the harm. Restatement, Section 435.

Comment j to Section 29 of the Third Restatement explains that

> the foreseeability test for proximate cause is essentially consistent with the standard set forth in this Section.

Properly understood, both the risk standard and a foreseeability test exclude liability for harms that were sufficiently unforeseeable at the time of the actor's tortious conduct that they were not among the risks—potential harms—that made the actor negligent. Negligence limits the requirement of reasonable care to those risks that are foreseeable.

For example, Albert, while negligently driving an automobile, collides with a car carrying dynamite. Albert is unaware of the contents of the other car and has no reason to know about them. The collision causes the dynamite to explode, shattering glass in a building a block away. The shattered glass injures Betsy, who is inside the building. The explosion also injures Calvin, who is walking on the sidewalk near the collision. Albert would be liable to Calvin because Albert should have realized that his negligent driving might result in a collision that would endanger pedestrians nearby. Betsy's harm, however, was beyond the risks posed by Albert's negligent driving and he, accordingly, is not liable to Betsy.

◆ SEE CASE 8-3

SUPERSEDING CAUSE

An intervening cause is an event or act that occurs after the defendant's negligent conduct and, together with the defendant's negligence, causes the plaintiff's harm. If the intervening cause is deemed a superseding cause, then it relieves the defendant of liability for harm to the plaintiff caused in fact by both the defendant's negligence and the intervening event or act. For example, Carol negligently leaves in a public sidewalk a substantial excavation without a fence or warning lights, into which Gary falls at night. Darkness is an intervening, but not a superseding, cause of harm to Gary because it is a normal consequence of the situation caused by Carol's negligence. Therefore, Carol is liable to Gary. In contrast, if Carol negligently leaves an excavation in a public sidewalk into which Barbara intentionally shoves Gary, under the Second Restatement as a matter of law, Carol is not liable to Gary because Barbara's conduct is a superseding cause that relieves Carol of liability. The Third Restatement rejects this exception to liability, stating,

> Whether Gary's harm is within the scope of Carol's liability for her negligence is an issue for the factfinder. The factfinder will have to determine whether the appropriate characterization of the harm to Gary is falling into an unguarded excavation site or being deliberately pushed into an unguarded excavation site and, if the latter, whether it is among the risks that made Carol negligent. Section 34, Comment e.

An intervening cause that is a foreseeable or normal consequence of the defendant's negligence is not a superseding cause.

Thus, a person who negligently places another person or his property in imminent danger is liable for the injury sustained by a third-party rescuer who attempts to aid the imperiled person or his property. Third Restatement, Section 32. The same is true of attempts by the endangered person to escape the peril, as, for example, when a person swerves off the road to avoid a head-on collision with an automobile driven negligently on the wrong side of the road. It is commonly held that a negligent defendant is liable for the results of necessary medical treatment of the injured party, even if the treatment itself is negligent. Third Restatement, Section 35.

HARM

The plaintiff must prove that the defendant's negligent conduct proximately caused harm to a legally protected interest. Certain interests receive little or no protection against such conduct, while others receive full protection. The courts determine the extent of protection for a particular interest as a matter of law on the basis of social policy and expediency. For example, negligent conduct that is the proximate cause of harmful contact with the person of another is actionable. Thus, if Bob, while driving his car, negligently runs into Julie, a pedestrian who is carefully crossing the street, Bob is liable for physical injuries Julie sustains as a result of the collision. On the other hand, if Bob's careless driving causes the car's side-view mirror to brush Julie's coat but results in no physical injuries to her or damage to the coat, thus causing only offensive contact with Julie's person, Bob is not liable because Julie did not sustain harm to a legally protected interest.

The courts traditionally have been reluctant to allow recovery for negligently inflicted emotional distress. Nevertheless, this view has changed gradually during this century, and the majority of courts now hold a person liable for negligently causing emotional distress if bodily harm—such as a heart attack—results from the distress. Restatement, Section 436. In the majority of States, a defendant is not liable for negligent conduct resulting solely in emotional disturbance. Restatement, Section 436A. Some courts, however, have recently allowed recovery of damages for negligently inflicted emotional distress even in the absence of resultant physical harm when a person's negligent conduct places another in immediate danger of bodily harm. The Third Restatement follows the minority approach: a person whose negligent conduct places another in immediate danger of bodily harm is subject to liability to the other for serious emotional disturbance caused by reaction to the danger even though the negligent conduct did not cause any impact or bodily harm to the other. Third Restatement, Section 46. Furthermore, in a majority of States and under the Third Restatement liability for negligently inflicted emotional distress arises in the following situation: Aldana negligently causes serious bodily injury to Bernard.

If Charlize is a close family member of Bernard and witnesses the injury to Bernard, then Aldana is liable to Charlize for serious emotional disturbance she suffers from witnessing the event. Third Restatement, Section 47.

DEFENSES TO NEGLIGENCE

A plaintiff who has established by the preponderance of the evidence all the required elements of a negligence action may, nevertheless, be denied recovery if the defendant proves a valid defense. As a general rule, any defense to an intentional tort is also available in an action in negligence. In addition, contributory negligence, comparative negligence, and assumption of risk are three defenses available in negligence cases that are not defenses to intentional torts.

CONTRIBUTORY NEGLIGENCE

The Restatement, Section 463, defines contributory negligence as "conduct on the part of the plaintiff which falls below the standard to which he should conform for his own protection, and which is a legally contributing cause cooperating with the negligence of the defendant in bringing about the plaintiff's harm." The Third Restatement's definition of negligence as the failure of a person to exercise reasonable care under all the circumstances applies to the contributory negligence of the plaintiff. Section 3, Comment b. In those few States that have not adopted comparative negligence (Alabama, Maryland, North Carolina, and Virginia, as well as Washington, D.C.), the contributory negligence of the plaintiff, whether slight or extensive, prevents him from recovering *any* damages from the defendant.

Notwithstanding the contributory negligence of the plaintiff, if the defendant had a **last clear chance** to avoid injury to the plaintiff but did not avail himself of such chance, the plaintiff's contributory negligence does not bar his recovery of damages. Restatement, Section 479.

COMPARATIVE NEGLIGENCE

The harshness of the contributory negligence doctrine has caused all but a few States to reject its all-or-nothing rule and to substitute the doctrine of comparative negligence, which is also called comparative fault or comparative responsibility. (In States adopting comparative negligence, the doctrine of last clear chance has also been abandoned.) Approximately a dozen States have judicially or legislatively adopted "pure" comparative negligence systems. (The Third Restatement of Torts: Apportionment of Liability advocates this form of comparative negligence.) Under **pure comparative negligence**, the law apportions damages between the parties in proportion to the degree of fault or negligence found against them. For instance, Matthew negligently drives his automobile into Nancy, who is crossing against the light. Nancy sustains damages in the amount of $10,000 and sues Matthew. If the trier of fact determines that Matthew's negligence contributed 70 percent to Nancy's injury and that Nancy's contributory negligence contributed 30 percent to her injury, then Nancy would recover $7,000.

Most States have adopted the doctrine of "modified" comparative negligence. Under modified comparative negligence the plaintiff recovers as in pure comparative negligence unless her contributory negligence was "as great as" or "greater than" that of the defendant, in which case the plaintiff recovers nothing. Thus, in the example above, if the trier of fact determined that Matthew's negligence contributed 40 percent to Nancy's injury and Nancy's contributory negligence contributed 60 percent, then Nancy would recover nothing from Matthew.

ASSUMPTION OF RISK

A plaintiff who has *voluntarily* and *knowingly* assumed the risk of harm arising from the negligent or reckless conduct of the defendant cannot recover from such harm. Restatement, Section 496A. In **express** assumption of the risk, the plaintiff expressly agrees to assume the risk of harm from the defendant's conduct. Usually, but not always, such an agreement is by contract. Courts usually construe these exculpatory contracts strictly and will hold that the plaintiff has assumed the risk only if the terms of the agreement are clear and unequivocal. Moreover, some contracts for assumption of risk are considered unenforceable as a matter of public policy. See *Chapter 13*.

In **implied** assumption of the risk, the plaintiff voluntarily proceeds to encounter a known danger. Thus, a spectator entering a baseball park may be regarded as consenting that the players may proceed with the game without taking precautions to protect him from being hit by the ball. Most States have abolished or modified the defense of implied assumption of risk. Some have abandoned it entirely while others have merged implied assumption of risk into their comparative negligence systems.

Reflecting this general trend, the Third Restatement of Torts: Apportionment of Liability has abandoned the doctrine of implied voluntary assumption of risk: it is no longer a defense that the plaintiff was aware of a risk and voluntarily confronted it. But if a plaintiff's conduct in the face of a known risk is unreasonable, it might constitute contributory negligence, thereby reducing the plaintiff's recovery under comparative negligence. This new Restatement limits the defense of assumption of risk to express assumption of risk, which consists of a contract between the plaintiff and another person to absolve the other person from liability for future harm. Section 2. Contractual assumption of risk may occur by written agreement, express oral agreement, or conduct that creates an implied-in-fact contract, as determined

◆ FIGURE 8-2: **Defenses to a Negligence Action**

© Cengage Learning

by the applicable rules of contract law. Some contractual assumptions of risk, however, are not enforceable under other areas of substantive law or as against public policy.

◆ SEE FIGURE 8-2: **Defenses to a Negligence Action**

◆ SEE CASE 8-4

PRACTICAL ADVICE

Consider having customers and clients sign waivers of liability and assumption of risk forms, but realize that many courts limit their effectiveness.

STRICT LIABILITY

In some instances, people may be held liable for injuries they have caused even though they have not acted intentionally or negligently. Such liability is called strict liability, absolute liability, or liability without fault. The law has determined

that because certain types of otherwise socially desirable activities pose sufficiently high risks of harm regardless of how carefully they are conducted, those who perform these activities should bear the cost of any harm they cause. The doctrine of strict liability is not predicated upon any particular fault of the defendant, but rather upon the nature of the activity in which he is engaging.

ACTIVITIES GIVING RISE TO STRICT LIABILITY

The following activities giving rise to strict liability will be discussed in this section: (1) activities that are, in themselves, abnormally dangerous, and (2) the keeping of animals. In addition, strict liability is imposed upon other activities. Nearly all States have imposed a limited form of strict product liability upon manufacturers and merchants who sell goods in a *defective condition* unreasonably dangerous to the user or consumer. This topic is covered in *Chapter 24*. All States have enacted workers' compensation statutes that make employers liable to employees for injuries arising out of the course of employment. Because the law imposes this liability without regard to the employer's negligence, it is a form of strict liability. Workers' compensation is discussed in *Chapter 42*. Moreover, the liability imposed upon an employer for torts that employees commit in the scope of their employment is a type of strict liability, as discussed in *Chapter 20*. Additional instances of strict liability include carriers and innkeepers (*Chapter 47*), innocent misrepresentation (*Chapter 11*), and some violations of the securities laws (*Chapter 43*).

ABNORMALLY DANGEROUS ACTIVITIES

A person who carries on an abnormally dangerous activity is subject to strict liability for physical harm resulting from the activity. Third Restatement, Section 20(a). "An activity is abnormally dangerous if: (1) the activity creates a foreseeable and highly significant risk of physical harm even when reasonable care is exercised by all actors; and (2) the activity is not one of common usage." Third Restatement, Section 20(b). The court determines whether an activity is abnormally dangerous by applying these factors. Activities to which the rule has been applied include collecting water or sewage in such quantity and location as to make it dangerous; storing explosives or flammable liquids in large quantities; blasting or pile driving; crop dusting; drilling for or refining oil in populated areas; and emitting noxious gases or fumes into a settled community. On the other hand, courts have refused to apply the rule where the activity is a "natural" use of the land, such as drilling for oil in the oil fields of Texas, collecting water in a stock watering tank, or transmitting gas through a gas pipe or electricity through electric wiring.

◆ SEE CASE 8-5

PRACTICAL ADVICE

Determine whether any of your activities involve abnormally dangerous activities for which strict liability is imposed and be sure to obtain adequate insurance.

KEEPING OF ANIMALS

Strict liability for harm caused by animals existed at common law and continues today with some modification. As a general rule, those who possess animals for their own purposes do so at their peril and must protect against the harm those animals may cause to people and property.

TRESPASSING ANIMALS Owners and possessors of animals, except for dogs and cats, are subject to strict liability for physical harm their animals cause by trespassing on the property of another. Third Restatement, Section 21. There are two exceptions to this rule: (1) keepers of animals are not strictly liable if those animals incidentally stray upon land immediately adjacent to a highway on which they are being lawfully driven, although the owner may be liable for negligence if he fails to properly control them; and (2) keepers of farm animals, typically cattle, in some western States are not strictly liable for harm caused by their trespassing animals that are allowed to graze freely.

NONTRESPASSING ANIMALS Owners and possessors of wild animals are subject to strict liability for physical harm caused by such animals, whether they are trespassing or not. Third Restatement, Section 22(b). Accordingly the owner or possessor is liable even if she has exercised reasonable care in attempting to restrain the wild animal. **Wild animals** are defined as those that, in the particular region in which they are kept, are known to be likely to inflict serious damage and cannot be considered safe, no matter how domesticated they become. The Third Restatement has a similar definition: "A wild animal is an animal that belongs to a category of animals that have not been generally domesticated and that are likely, unless restrained, to cause personal injury." Section 22(b). The court determines whether a category of animals is wild. Animals that have been determined to be wild include bears, lions, elephants, monkeys, tigers, wolves, zebras, deer, and raccoons. On the other hand, iguanas, pigeons, and manatees are not considered wild animals because they do not pose a risk of causing substantial personal injury. Third Restatement, Section 22, Comment b.

Domestic animals are those that are traditionally devoted to the service of humankind and that as a class are considered safe. Examples of domestic animals are dogs, cats, horses, cattle, and sheep. Owners and possessors of domestic animals are subject to strict liability if they knew, or had reason to know, of an animal's dangerous tendencies abnormal for the animal's category. Restatement, Section 509; Third Restatement, Section 23. The animal's dangerous propensity must be the cause of the harm. For example, merely because he knows that a dog has a propensity to fight with other dogs, a keeper is not liable when the dog bites a human. On the other hand, a person whose 150-pound sheepdog has a propensity to jump enthusiastically on visitors would be liable for any damage caused by the dog's playfulness. About half of the States statutorily impose strict liability in dog cases even where the owner or possessor does not know, and did not have reason to know, of the dog's dangerous tendencies.

◆ SEE CASE 8-6

DEFENSES TO STRICT LIABILITY

This section will discuss the availability in a strict liability action for abnormally dangerous activities and keeping of animals of the following defenses: (1) contributory negligence, (2) comparative negligence, and (3) assumption of risk.

CONTRIBUTORY NEGLIGENCE

Because the strict liability of one who carries on an abnormally dangerous activity or keeps animals is not based on his negligence, the ordinary contributory negligence of the plaintiff is not a defense to such liability. In imposing strict liability, the law places on the defendant the full responsibility for preventing harm. For example, Adrian negligently fails to observe a sign on a highway warning of a blasting operation conducted by Benjamin. As a result, Adrian is injured by these operations; nonetheless, he may recover from Benjamin.

COMPARATIVE NEGLIGENCE

Despite the rationale that disallows contributory negligence as a defense to strict liability, some States apply the doctrine of comparative negligence to some types of strict liability. The Third Restatement provides that if the plaintiff has been contributorily negligent in failing to take reasonable precautions, the plaintiff's recovery in a strict-liability claim for physical harm caused by abnormally dangerous activities or keeping of animals is reduced in accordance with the share of comparative responsibility assigned to the plaintiff. Section 25.

ASSUMPTION OF RISK

Under the Second Restatement of Torts voluntary assumption of risk is a defense to an action based upon strict liability. If the owner of an automobile knowingly and voluntarily parks the vehicle in a blasting zone, he may not recover for harm to his automobile. The assumption of risk, however, must be voluntary. For example, the possessor of land located near a blasting operation is not required to move away; she may, in fact, recover for harm she suffers because of the operation.

The more recent Third Restatement of Torts: Apportionment of Liability has abandoned the doctrine of implied voluntary assumption of risk in tort actions generally: it is no longer a defense that the plaintiff was aware of a risk and voluntarily confronted it. This new Restatement limits the defense of assumption of risk to express assumption of risk, which consists of a contract between the plaintiff and another person to absolve the other person from liability for future harm. Section 2.

The Third Restatement: Liability for Physical and Emotional Harm recognizes a limitation on strict liability for abnormally dangerous activities and keeping of animals when the victim suffers harm as a result of exposure to the animal or activity resulting from the victim's securing some benefit from that exposure. Section 24(a). The Third Restatement gives the following example: "if the plaintiff is a veterinarian or a groomer who accepts an animal such as a dog from the defendant, the plaintiff is deriving financial benefits from the acceptance of the animal, and is beyond the scope of strict liability, even if the dog can be deemed abnormally dangerous."

CHAPTER SUMMARY

NEGLIGENCE

BREACH OF DUTY OF CARE	**Definition of Negligence** conduct that falls below the standard established by law for the protection of others against unreasonable risk of harm **Reasonable Person Standard** degree of care that a reasonable person would exercise under all the circumstances • *Children* must conform to conduct of a reasonable person of the same age, intelligence, and experience under all the circumstances • *Physical Disability* a disabled person's conduct must conform to that of a reasonable person under the same disability • *Mental Disability* a mentally disabled person is held to the reasonable person standard • *Superior Skill or Knowledge* if a person has skills or knowledge beyond those possessed by most others, these skills or knowledge are circumstances to be taken into account in determining whether the person has acted with reasonable care • *Emergencies* the reasonable person standard applies, but an unexpected emergency is considered part of the circumstances • *Violation of Statute* if the statute applies, the violation is negligence *per se* in most States **Duty to Act** a person is under a duty to all others at all times to exercise reasonable care for the safety of the others' person and property; however, except in special circumstances, no one is required to aid another in peril

Duties of Possessors of Land
- *Second Restatement* a land possessor owes the following duties: (1) not to injure intentionally *trespassers*, (2) to warn *licensees* of known dangerous conditions licensees are unlikely to discover for themselves, and (3) to exercise reasonable care to protect *invitees* against dangerous conditions land possessor should know of but invitees are unlikely to discover
- *Third Restatement* adopts a unitary duty of reasonable care to all entrants on the land except for flagrant trespassers: a land possessor must use reasonable care to investigate and discover dangerous conditions and must use reasonable care to eliminate or improve those dangerous conditions that are known or should have been discovered by the exercise of reasonable care

Res Ipsa Loquitur permits the jury to infer both negligent conduct and causation

FACTUAL CAUSE AND SCOPE OF LIABILITY	**Factual Cause** the defendant's conduct is a factual cause of the harm when the harm would not have occurred absent the conduct **Scope of Liability (Proximate Cause)** liability is limited to those harms that result from the risks that made the defendant's conduct tortious • *Foreseeability* excludes liability for harms that were sufficiently unforeseeable at the time of the defendant's tortious conduct that they were not among the risks that made the defendant negligent • *Superseding Cause* an intervening act that relieves the defendant of liability
HARM	**Harm to Legally Protected Interest** courts determine which interests are protected from negligent interference **Burden of Proof** plaintiff must prove that defendant's negligent conduct caused harm to a legally protected interest
DEFENSES TO NEGLIGENCE	**Contributory Negligence** failure of a plaintiff to exercise reasonable care for his own protection, which in a few States prevents the plaintiff from recovering anything **Comparative Negligence** damages are divided between the parties in proportion to their degree of negligence; applies in almost all States **Assumption of Risk** plaintiff's express consent to encounter a known danger; some States still apply implied assumption of the risk

STRICT LIABILITY

ACTIVITIES GIVING RISE TO STRICT LIABILITY	**Definition of Strict Liability** liability for nonintentional and nonnegligent conduct **Abnormally Dangerous Activity** strict liability is imposed for any activity that (1) creates a foreseeable and highly significant risk of harm and (2) is not one of common usage **Keeping of Animals** strict liability is imposed for wild animals and usually for trespassing domestic animals
DEFENSES TO STRICT LIABILITY	**Contributory Negligence** is not a defense to strict liability **Comparative Negligence** some States apply this doctrine to some strict liability cases **Assumption of Risk** express assumption of risk is a defense to an action based upon strict liability; some States apply implied assumption of risk to strict liability cases

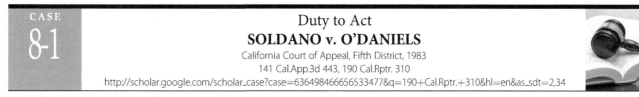

CASES

CASE
8-1

Duty to Act
SOLDANO v. O'DANIELS
California Court of Appeal, Fifth District, 1983
141 Cal.App.3d 443, 190 Cal.Rptr. 310
http://scholar.google.com/scholar_case?case=636498466656533477&q=190+Cal.Rptr.+310&hl=en&as_sdt=2,34

Andreen, J.

Does a business establishment incur liability for wrongful death if it denies use of its telephone to a good samaritan who explains an emergency situation occurring without and wishes to call the police?

This appeal follows a judgment of dismissal of the second cause of action of a complaint for wrongful death upon a motion for summary judgment. The motion was supported only by a declaration of defense counsel. Both briefs on appeal adopt the defense averments:

> This action arises out of a shooting death occurring on August 9, 1977. Plaintiff's father [Darrell Soldano] was shot and killed by one Rudolph Villanueva on that date at defendant's Happy Jack's Saloon. This defendant owns and operates the Circle Inn which is an eating establishment located across the street from Happy Jack's. Plaintiff's second cause of action against this defendant is one for negligence.
>
> Plaintiff alleges that on the date of the shooting, a patron of Happy Jack's Saloon came into the Circle Inn and informed a Circle Inn employee that a man had been threatened at Happy Jack's. He requested the employee either call the police or allow him to use the Circle Inn phone to call the police. That employee allegedly refused to call the police and allegedly refused to allow the patron to use the phone to make his own call. Plaintiff alleges that the actions of the Circle Inn employee were a breach of the legal duty that the Circle Inn owed to the decedent.

We were advised at oral argument that the employee was the defendant's bartender. The state of the record is unsatisfactory in that it does not disclose the physical location of the telephone—whether on the bar, in a private office behind a closed door or elsewhere. The only factual matter before the trial court was a verified statement of the defense attorney which set forth those facts quoted above. Following normal rules applicable to motions for summary judgment, we strictly construe the defense affidavit. [Citation.] Accordingly, we assume the telephone was not in a private office but in a position where it could be used by a patron without inconvenience to the defendant or his guests. We also assume the call was a local one and would not result in expense to defendant.

There is a distinction, well rooted in the common law, between action and nonaction. [Citation.] It has found its way into the prestigious Restatement Second of Torts (hereafter cited as "Restatement"), which provides in section 314: "The fact that the actor realizes or should realize that action on his part is necessary for another's aid or protection does not of itself impose upon him a duty to take such action." * * *

* * *

As noted in [citation], the courts have increased the instances in which affirmative duties are imposed not by direct rejection of the common law rule, but by expanding the list of special relationships which will justify departure from that rule. * * *

* * *

Section 314A of the Restatement lists other special relationships which create a duty to render aid, such as that of a common carrier to its passengers, an innkeeper to his guest, possessors of land who hold it open to the public, or one who has a custodial relationship to another. A duty may be created by an undertaking to give assistance. [Citation.]

Here there was no special relationship between the defendant and the deceased. It would be stretching the concept beyond recognition to assert there was a relationship between the defendant and the patron from Happy Jack's Saloon who wished to summon aid. But this does not end the matter.

It is time to re-examine the common law rule of nonliability for nonfeasance in the special circumstances of the instant case.

* * *

We turn now to the concept of duty in a tort case. The [California] Supreme Court has identified certain factors to be considered in determining whether a duty is owed to third persons. These factors include:

> the foreseeability of harm to the plaintiff, the degree of certainty that the plaintiff suffered injury, the closeness of the connection between the defendant's conduct and the injury suffered, the moral blame attached to the defendant's conduct, the policy of preventing future harm, the

extent of the burden to the defendant and consequences to the community of imposing a duty to exercise care with resulting liability for breach, and the availability, cost, and prevalence of insurance for the risk involved. [Citation.]

We examine those factors in reference to this case. (1) The harm to the decedent was abundantly foreseeable; it was imminent. The employee was expressly told that a man had been threatened. The employee was a bartender. As such he knew it is foreseeable that some people who drink alcohol in the milieu of a bar setting are prone to violence. (2) The certainty of decedent's injury is undisputed. (3) There is arguably a close connection between the employee's conduct and the injury: the patron wanted to use the phone to summon the police to intervene. The employee's refusal to allow the use of the phone prevented this anticipated intervention. If permitted to go to trial, the plaintiff may be able to show that the probable response time of the police would have been shorter than the time between the prohibited telephone call and the fatal shot. (4) The employee's conduct displayed a disregard for human life that can be characterized as morally wrong: he was callously indifferent to the possibility that Darrell Soldano would die as the result of his refusal to allow a person to use the telephone. Under the circumstances before us the bartender's burden was minimal and exposed him to no risk: all he had to do was allow the use of the telephone. It would have cost him or his employer nothing. It could have saved a life. (5) Finding a duty in these circumstances would promote a policy of preventing future harm. A citizen would not be required to summon the police but would be required, in circumstances such as those before us, not to impede another who has chosen to summon aid. (6) We have no information on the question of the availability, cost, and prevalence of insurance for the risk, but note that the liability which is sought to be imposed here is that of employee negligence, which is covered by many insurance policies. (7) The extent of the burden on the defendant was minimal, as noted.

* * *

We acknowledge that defendant contracted for the use of his telephone, and its use is a species of property. But if it exists in a public place as defined above, there is no privacy or ownership interest in it such that the owner should be permitted to interfere with a good faith attempt to use it by a third person to come to the aid of another.

* * *

We conclude that the bartender owed a duty to the plaintiff's decedent to permit the patron from Happy Jack's to place a call to the police or to place the call himself.

It bears emphasizing that the duty in this case does not require that one must go to the aid of another. That is not the issue here. The employee was not the good samaritan intent on aiding another. The patron was.

* * *

We conclude there are sufficient justiciable issues to permit the case to go to trial and therefore reverse.

CASE
8-2

Duty to Invitees
LOVE v. HARDEE'S FOOD SYSTEMS, INC.
Court of Appeals of Missouri, Eastern District, Division Two, 2000
16 S.W.3d 739
http://scholar.google.com/scholar_case?case=12304910341505965816&hl=en&as_sdt=2&as_= 1&oi=scholarr

Crane, J.

At about 3:15 P.M. on November 15, 1995, plaintiff, Jason Love, and his mother, Billye Ann Love, went to the Hardee's Restaurant in Arnold, Missouri, which is owned by defendant, Hardee's Food Systems, Inc. There were no other customers in the restaurant between 3:00 P.M. and 4:00 P.M., but two or three workmen were in the back doing construction. The workmen reported that they did not use the restroom and did not see anyone use the restroom. After eating his lunch, plaintiff, who was wearing rubber-soled boat shoes, went to use the restroom. He opened the restroom door, took one step in, and, upon taking his second step, slipped on water on the restroom floor. Plaintiff fell backwards, hit his head, and felt a shooting pain down his right leg. He found himself lying in an area of dirty water, which soaked his clothes. There were no barricades, warning cones, or anything else that would either restrict access to the bathroom or warn of the danger.

Plaintiff crawled up to the sink to pull himself up and made his way back to the table and told his mother that his back and leg were "hurting pretty bad." His mother reported the fall to another employee. Plaintiff's mother went back to the men's restroom and looked at the water on the floor. She observed that the water was dirty. The restaurant supervisor came out and interviewed plaintiff and viewed the water in the restroom. * * * The supervisor then filled out an accident report form, which reported that the accident occurred at 3:50 P.M. The supervisor testified that the water appeared to have come from someone shaking his hands after washing them. The supervisor told plaintiff he could not recall the last time the restroom had been checked. Plaintiff was taken to a hospital emergency room. As a result of his injuries, plaintiff underwent two back surgeries, missed substantial time from work, and suffered from continuing pain and limitations on his physical activities.

Defendant had a policy requiring that the restroom was to be checked and cleaned every hour by a maintenance man. The maintenance man was scheduled to work until 3:00 P.M., but normally left at 1:00 P.M. The supervisor could not recall whether the maintenance man left at 1:00 P.M. or 3:00 P.M. on November 15. The time clock activity report would show when the maintenance man clocked out, but defendant was unable to produce the time clock report for November 15.

It was also a store policy that whenever employees cleaned the tables, they would check the restroom. The restrooms were used by customers and employees. If an employee had to use the restroom, then that employee was also supposed to check the restroom. The restaurant supervisor did not ask if any employees had been in the restroom, or if they had checked it in the hour prior to the accident, and did not know if the restroom was actually inspected or cleaned at 3:00 P.M.

The restaurant had shift inspection checklists on which the manager would report on the cleanliness of the restrooms and whether the floors were clean and dry. However, the checklists for November 15 were thrown away. * * *

Plaintiff subsequently filed the underlying lawsuit against defendant to recover damages for negligence. The jury returned a verdict in plaintiff's favor in the amount of $125,000. * * *

* * * [Defendant] argues that plaintiff failed to make a submissible case of negligence because plaintiff failed to prove that defendant had actual or constructive notice of the water on the restroom floor in that there was no evidence showing the source of the water or the length of time the water had been on the floor.

* * *

In order to have made a submissible case, plaintiff had to show that defendant knew or, by using ordinary care, could have known of the dangerous condition and failed to use ordinary care to remove it, barricade it, or warn of it, and plaintiff sustained damage as a direct result of such failure. [Citation.]

"In order to establish constructive notice, the condition must have existed for a sufficient length of time or the facts must be such that the defendant should have reasonably known of its presence." [Citation.] [Prior] cases * * * placed great emphasis on the length of time the dangerous condition had been present and held that times of 20 or 30 minutes, absent proof of other circumstances, were insufficient to establish constructive notice as a matter of law. [Citations.]

* * *

Defendant's liability is predicated on the foreseeability of the risk and the reasonableness of the care taken, which is a question of fact to be determined by the totality of the circumstances, including the nature of the restaurant's business and the method of its operation. [Citations.]

In this case the accident took place in the restaurant's restroom which is provided for the use of employees and customers. The cause of the accident was water, which is provided in the restroom. The restaurant owner could reasonably foresee that anyone using the restroom, customers or employees, would use the tap water provided in the restroom and could spill, drop, or splash water on the floor. Accordingly, the restaurant owner was under a duty to use due care to guard against danger from water on the floor.

There was substantial evidence to support submissibility. First, there was evidence from which the jury could infer that the water came from the use of the restroom. It was on the floor of the restroom and the supervisor testified it appeared that someone had shaken water from his hands on the floor.

Next, there was evidence from which the jury could infer that, if the water was caused by a non-employee, the water was on the floor for at least 50 minutes, or longer, because there was evidence that no other customers were in the store to use the restroom after 3:00 P.M. and the workmen on the site advised that they had not used the restroom.

In addition, plaintiff adduced evidence from which the jury could have found that defendants' employees had the opportunity to observe the hazard. The restroom was to be used by the employees and was supposed to be checked by them when they used it; employees cleaning tables were supposed to check the restroom when they cleaned the tables; and a maintenance man was supposed to check and clean the restroom every hour.

There was evidence from which the jury could have inferred that the maintenance man charged with cleaning the restroom every hour did not clean the restroom at 3:00 P.M. as scheduled on the day of the accident. There was testimony that the maintenance man usually left at 1:00 P.M. * * * This could have created a span of 2 hours and 50 minutes during which there was no employee working at the restaurant whose primary responsibility was to clean the restroom. [Citation.]

There was also evidence from which the jury could have inferred that the restroom was not inspected by any employee who had the responsibility to inspect it during that same time period. The supervisor testified that he could not recall the last time the restroom had been checked and did not ask any employees if they had been in the restroom or had checked it in the hour before the accident. * * *

* * *

The judgment of the trial court is affirmed.

CASE 8-3

Scope of Liability (Proximate Cause)
PALSGRAF v. LONG ISLAND RAILROAD CO.
Court of Appeals of New York, 1928
248 N.Y. 339, 162 N.E. 99
http://www.nycourts.gov/reporter/archives/palsgraf_lirr.htm

Cardozo, C. J.

Plaintiff was standing on a platform of defendant's railroad after buying a ticket to go to Rockaway Beach. A train stopped at the station, bound for another place. Two men ran forward to catch it. One of the men reached the platform of the car without mishap, though the train was already moving. The other man, carrying a package, jumped aboard the car, but seemed unsteady as if about to fall. A guard on the car, who had held the door open, reached forward to help him in, and another guard on the platform pushed him from behind. In this act, the package was dislodged, and fell upon the rails. It was a package of small size, about fifteen inches long, and was covered by a newspaper. In fact it contained fireworks, but there was nothing in its appearance to give notice of its contents. The fireworks when they fell exploded. The shock of the explosion threw down some scales at the other end of the platform many feet away. The scales struck the plaintiff, causing injuries for which she sues.

The conduct of the defendant's guard, if a wrong in its relation to the holder of the package, was not a wrong in its relation to the plaintiff, standing far away. Relatively to her it was not negligence at all. Nothing in the situation gave notice that the falling package had in it the potency of peril to persons thus removed. Negligence is not actionable unless it involves the invasion of a legally protected interest, the violation of a right. "Proof of negligence in the air, so to speak, will not do." [Citations.] "Negligence is the absence of care, according to the circumstances." [Citations.]

* * *

If no hazard was apparent to the eye of ordinary vigilance, an act innocent and harmless, at least to outward seeming, with reference to her, did not take to itself the quality of a tort because it happened to be a wrong, though apparently not one involving the risk of bodily insecurity, with reference to someone else. "In every instance, before negligence can be predicated of a given act, back of the act must be sought and found a duty to the individual complaining, the observance of which would have averted or avoided the injury." [Citations.]

* * *

A different conclusion will involve us, and swiftly too, in a maze of contradictions. A guard stumbles over a package which has been left upon a platform. It seems to be a bundle of newspapers. It turns out to be a can of dynamite. To the eye of ordinary vigilance, the bundle is abandoned waste, which may be kicked or trod on with impunity. Is a passenger at the other end of the platform protected by the law against the unsuspected hazard concealed beneath the waste? If not, is the result to be any different, so far as the distant passenger is concerned, when the guard stumbles over a valise which a truckman or a porter has left upon the walk? The passenger far away, if the victim of a wrong at all, has a cause of action, not derivative, but original and primary. His claim to be protected against invasion of his bodily security is neither greater nor less because the act resulting in the invasion is a wrong to another far removed. In this case, the rights that are said to have been violated, the interests said to have been invaded, are not even of the same order. The man was not injured in his person nor even put in danger. The purpose of the act, as well as its effect, was to make his person safe. If there was a wrong to him at all, which may very well be doubted, it was a wrong to a property interest only, the safety of his package. Out of this wrong to property, which threatened injury to nothing else, there has passed, we are told, to the plaintiff by derivation or succession a right of action for the invasion of an interest of another order, the right to bodily security. The diversity of interests emphasizes the futility of the effort to build the plaintiff's right upon the basis of a wrong to someone else. * * * One who jostles one's neighbor in a crowd does not invade the rights of others standing at the outer fringe when the unintended contact casts a bomb upon the ground. The wrongdoer as to them is the man who carries the bomb, not the one who explodes it without suspicion of the danger. Life will have to be made over, and human nature transformed, before prevision so extravagant can be accepted as the norm of conduct, the customary standard to which behavior must conform.

* * *

The judgment of the Appellate Division and that of the Trial Term should be reversed, and the complaint dismissed, with costs in all courts.

CASE
8-4

Contributory Negligence
MOORE v. KITSMILLER
Court of Appeals of Texas, Twelfth District, Tyler, 2006
201 S.W.3d 147, review denied
http://scholar.google.com/scholar_case?q=201+S.W.3D+147&hl=en&as_sdt=2,34&case=5663712118613187322&scilh=0

Worthen, C. J.

In the spring of 2001, Kitsmiller purchased a house in Van Zandt County to use as rental property. In mid-June, he hired B&H Shaw Company, Inc. ("B&H") to install a replacement septic tank in the back yard. The septic tank was located about two or three feet from a concrete stoop at the back door of the garage. B&H mounded dirt over the septic tank and the lateral lines going out from it upon completion. Sometime after B&H installed the septic tank, Kitsmiller smoothed out the mounds of dirt over the septic tank and lateral lines using the box blade on his tractor. Kitsmiller then leased the property to Moore and his wife on July 27. Kitsmiller testified that he viewed the back yard about a week or ten days prior to leasing the property to the Moores and stated that the dirt around the septic system looked firm.

On August 7, the Moores moved in. On August 11, Moore and his wife ventured into the back yard for the first time, carrying some trash bags to a barrel. Moore testified that his wife led the way and he followed her about a foot and a half behind. Moore testified that at the time, his right arm was in a sling and a bag of trash was in his left hand. He stated that as he stepped off the stoop, he was unable to see the ground and could only see his wife and the bag of trash in his left arm. His wife testified that the ground looked flat as she walked toward the barrel. Moore testified that he had only taken a few steps off the stoop when his left leg sank into a hole, causing him to fall forward into his wife. As he tried to steady himself with his right foot, it hung and then sank, causing him to fall backward on his head and back. Moore testified that the injury to his back required surgery and affected his ability to earn a living.

Moore filed suit against Kitsmiller and B&H. He sought damages for past and future pain and suffering, past and future mental anguish, past and future physical impairment, and past and future loss of earning capacity. In their answers to Moore's suit, both Kitsmiller and B&H pleaded the affirmative defense of contributory negligence. [Citation.] B&H specifically pleaded that Moore was negligent for not having kept a proper lookout when stepping into the back yard and looking for obstructions, such as erosion or soft soil.

During the jury trial, Moore testified Kitsmiller should have notified him where the septic tank and lateral lines were located and that the dirt should have remained mounded over the tank and lines. On August 13, Moore asked Ken Martin to inspect the site of the fall (the "occurrence"). Martin is an on-site septic tank complaint investigator for both the Texas Commission on Environmental Quality and Van Zandt County. Martin testified that dirt should have been mounded over the septic tank and lateral lines, so that when the dirt settled, there would be no holes in the ground around the septic tank or lateral lines. However, there was no dirt mounded over the septic tank or lines when he inspected the site. Martin's photographs of the site also indicated that there were no mounds of dirt over the septic tank. Further, the photographs showed sunken ground around the septic tank, including, but not limited to, the area where Moore fell. Martin testified that it was common for sinkholes to develop around a septic tank. He also testified that he had observed situations where dirt around a septic tank or lateral line looked to be solid, but sank when a person stepped on it. Martin testified that the photographs showed an obvious depression around the septic tank. Bill Shaw, president of B&H, testified that Moore should have been watching where he was going as he stepped into the back yard. Shaw stated that Martin's photographs indicated to him that the depressions in the ground around the septic tank were visible at the time of the occurrence.

The first question for the jury was whose negligence caused the occurrence. The jury responded that both Kitsmiller and Moore were negligent, but B&H was not. In the second question, the jury determined that Kitsmiller was 51% negligent and Moore was 49% negligent. In the third question, the jury determined that Moore was entitled to $210,000.00 in damages. On September 29, 2004, the trial court entered a judgment in favor of Moore and against Kitsmiller in the amount of $210,000.00 plus interest and costs.

On October 14, 2004, Kitsmiller asked that the trial court modify the judgment to $107,100.00 based upon Moore's contributory negligence. The trial court entered a modified final judgment on November 1, 2004 awarding Moore $107,100.00 plus interest and costs. On November 23, 2004, a partial satisfaction and release of judgment filed with the court showed that Kitsmiller had paid the amount awarded in the modified judgment to Moore. However, Moore reserved the right to appeal all issues involving his contributory negligence to this court. Moore then timely filed his notice of appeal.

* * *

* * * Moore contends the evidence is legally insufficient to support the judgment. Moore argues that his wife and Kits-miller testified that the back yard was flat at the time of the occurrence. He contends that no one could have anticipated any danger from walking into the yard. Therefore, Moore argues that there is no evidence in the record to support the jury's determination that he was contributorily negligent.

Contributory negligence contemplates an injured person's failure to use ordinary care regarding his or her own safety. [Citation.] This affirmative defense requires proof that the plaintiff was negligent and that the plaintiff's negligence proximately caused his or her injuries. [Citation.] Negligence requires proof of proximate cause. [Citation.] Proximate cause requires proof of both cause in fact and foreseeability. [Citation.] The test for cause in fact is whether the negligent act or omission was a substantial factor in bringing about an injury without which the harm would not have occurred. [Citation.] Foreseeability requires that a person of ordinary intelligence should have anticipated the danger created by a negligent act or omission. [Citation.]

Because comparative responsibility involves measuring the party's comparative fault in causing the plaintiff's injuries, it necessitates a preliminary finding that the plaintiff was in fact contributorily negligent. [Citation.] The standards and tests for determining contributory negligence ordinarily are the same as those for determining negligence, and the rules of law applicable to the former are applicable to the latter. [Citation.] The burden of proof on the whole case is on the plaintiff. [Citation.] However, on special issues tendered by the defendant presenting an affirmative defense such as contributory negligence, the burden of proof is on the defendant to prove the defense by a preponderance of the evidence. [Citation.]

When attacking the legal sufficiency of an adverse finding on an issue on which the party did not have the burden of proof, that party must demonstrate there is no evidence to support the adverse finding. [Citation.] To evaluate the legal sufficiency of the evidence to support a finding, we must determine whether the proffered evidence as a whole rises to a level that would enable reasonable and fair minded people to differ in their conclusions. [Citation.] We sustain a no evidence issue only if there is no more than a scintilla of evidence proving the elements of the claim. [Citation.] In making this determination, we must view the evidence in the light most favorable to the verdict, crediting favorable evidence if reasonable jurors could and disregarding contrary evidence unless reasonable jurors could not. [Citation.] The trier of fact may draw reasonable and logical inferences from the evidence. [Citation.] It is within the province of the jury to draw one reasonable inference from the evidence although another inference could have been made. [Citation.]

* * *

Moore testified that when he stepped off the stoop into the back yard for the first time on August 11, 2001, he could only see his wife and the plastic bag of trash he was carrying in his left hand. The jury was allowed to draw an inference from this evidence that Moore was not watching where he was walking. An individual must keep a proper lookout where he is walking, and a jury is allowed to make a reasonable inference that failure to do so was the proximate cause of his injuries. [Citation.] It was reasonable for the jury to make an inference from Moore's testimony that his failure to keep a proper lookout where he was walking contributed to the occurrence.

Moore contends that the only reasonable inference the jury could have made was that, even if he had been watching where he was walking, he would not have been able to avoid stepping in the holes because they were not visible to the naked eye. The jury could have made that inference, but chose not to do so. Shaw's testimony that Martin's photographs showed the depressions could have been present at the time of the occurrence could have led the jury to believe that Moore's contention was not a reasonable inference. We conclude that the jury made a reasonable inference from the evidence in finding Moore contributorily negligent.

* * *

* * * [T]he judgment of the trial court is affirmed.

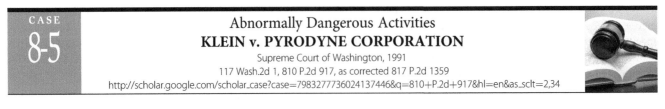

CASE 8-5

Abnormally Dangerous Activities
KLEIN v. PYRODYNE CORPORATION
Supreme Court of Washington, 1991
117 Wash.2d 1, 810 P.2d 917, as corrected 817 P.2d 1359
http://scholar.google.com/scholar_case?case=7983277736024137446&q=810+P.2d+917&hl=en&as_sclt=2,34

Guy, J.
[Pyrodyne Corporation contracted to conduct the fireworks display at the Western Washington State Fairgrounds in

Puyallup, Washington, on July 4, 1987. During the fireworks display, one of the five-inch mortars was knocked into a horizontal position. A shell inside ignited and discharged, flying five hundred feet parallel to the earth and exploding near the crowd of onlookers. Danny and Marion Klein were injured by the explosion. Mr. Klein suffered facial burns and serious injuries to his eyes. The parties provided conflicting explanations for the improper discharge, and because all the evidence had exploded, there was no means of proving the cause of the misfire. The Kleins brought suit against Pyrodyne under the theory of strict liability for participating in an abnormally dangerous activity.]

Analysis
Fireworks Displays as Abnormally Dangerous Activities
The Kleins contend that strict liability is the appropriate standard to determine the culpability of Pyrodyne because Pyrodyne was participating in an abnormally dangerous activity. * * *

The modern doctrine of strict liability for abnormally dangerous activities derives from *Fletcher v. Rylands*, [citation], in which the defendant's reservoir flooded mine shafts on the plaintiff's adjoining land. *Rylands v. Fletcher* has come to stand for the rule that "the defendant will be liable when he damages another by a thing or activity unduly dangerous and inappropriate to the place where it is maintained, in the light of the character of that place and its surroundings." [Citation.]

The basic principle of *Rylands v. Fletcher* has been accepted by the Restatement (Second) of Torts (1977). [Citation.] Section 519 of the Restatement provides that any party carrying on an "abnormally dangerous activity" is strictly liable for ensuing damages. The test for what constitutes such an activity is stated in section 520 of the Restatement. Both Restatement sections have been adopted by this court, and determination of whether an activity is an "abnormally dangerous activity" is a question of law. [Citations.]

Section 520 of the Restatement lists six factors that are to be considered in determining whether an activity is "abnormally dangerous." The factors are as follows: (a) existence of a high degree of risk of some harm to the person, land or chattels of others; (b) likelihood that the harm that results from it will be great; (c) inability to eliminate the risk by the exercise of reasonable care; (d) extent to which the activity is not a matter of common usage; (e) inappropriateness of the activity to the place where it is carried on; and (f) extent to which its value to the community is outweighed by its dangerous attributes. Restatement (Second) of Torts § 520 (1977). As we previously recognized in [citation], the comments to section 520 explain how these factors should be evaluated:

> Any one of them is not necessarily sufficient of itself in a particular case, and ordinarily several of them will be

required for strict liability. On the other hand, it is not necessary that each of them be present, especially if others weigh heavily. Because of the interplay of these various factors, it is not possible to reduce abnormally dangerous activities to any definition. The essential question is whether the risk created is so unusual, either because of its magnitude or because of the circumstances surrounding it, as to justify the imposition of strict liability for the harm that results from it, even though it is carried on with all reasonable care.

Restatement (Second) of Torts § 520, Comment f (1977). Examination of these factors persuades us that fireworks displays are abnormally dangerous activities justifying the imposition of strict liability.

We find that the factors stated in clauses (a), (b), and (c) are all present in the case of fireworks displays. Any time a person ignites aerial shells or rockets with the intention of sending them aloft to explode in the presence of large crowds of people, a high risk of serious personal injury or property damage is created. That risk arises because of the possibility that a shell or rocket will malfunction or be misdirected. Furthermore, no matter how much care pyrotechnicians exercise, they cannot entirely eliminate the high risk inherent in setting off powerful explosives such as fireworks near crowds.

* * *

The factor expressed in clause (d) concerns the extent to which the activity is not a matter "of common usage." The Restatement explains that "[a]n activity is a matter of common usage if it is customarily carried on by the great mass of mankind or by many people in the community." Restatement (Second) of Torts § 520, Comment i (1977). As examples of activities that are not matters of common usage, the Restatement comments offer driving a tank, blasting, the manufacture, storage, transportation, and use of high explosives, and drilling for oil. The deciding characteristic is that few persons engage in these activities. Likewise, relatively few persons conduct public fireworks displays. Therefore, presenting public fireworks displays is not a matter of common usage.

* * *

The factor stated in clause (e) requires analysis of the appropriateness of the activity to the place where it was carried on. In this case, the fireworks display was conducted at the Puyallup Fairgrounds. Although some locations—such as over water—may be safer, the Puyallup Fairgrounds is an appropriate place for a fireworks show because the audience can be seated at a reasonable distance from the display. Therefore, the clause (e) factor is not present in this case.

The factor stated in clause (f) requires analysis of the extent to which the value of fireworks to the community outweighs its dangerous attributes. We do not find that this factor is present here. This country has a long-standing tradition of fireworks on the 4th of July. That tradition suggests that we as a society have decided that the value of fireworks on the day celebrating our national independence and unity outweighs the risks of injuries and damage.

In sum, we find that setting off public fireworks displays satisfies four of the six conditions under the Restatement test; that is, it is an activity that is not "of common usage" and that presents an ineliminably high risk of serious bodily injury or property damage. We therefore hold that conduct-

ing public fireworks displays is an abnormally dangerous activity justifying the imposition of strict liability.

* * *

Conclusion

We hold that Pyrodyne Corporation is strictly liable for all damages suffered as a result of the July 1987 fireworks display. Detonating fireworks displays constitutes an abnormally dangerous activity warranting strict liability * * * . This establishes the standard of strict liability for pyrotechnicians. Therefore, we affirm the decision of the trial court.

CASE 8-6

Keeping of Animals
PALUMBO v. NIKIRK
Supreme Court, Appellate Division, Second Department, New York, 2009
59 A.D.3d 691, 874 N.Y.S.2d 222, 2009 N.Y. SLIP OP. 01454
http://scholar.google.com/scholar_case?case=7266290354304468850&q=2009+NY+Slip+Op+1454&hl=en&as_sdt=2,34

Per Curiam

The plaintiff, a mail carrier, sustained injuries when he allegedly was bitten and attacked by a dog on the front steps of the defendants' house as he attempted to deliver the mail. The plaintiff, who crossed over the defendants' lawn and driveway from the house next door, and whose view of the dog was obstructed by a bush, did not see the dog or hear it bark until he opened the lid of the mailbox and was bitten. [The plaintiff brought an action to recover damages for personal injuries. The Supreme Court, Nassau County, granted the defendants' motion for summary judgment dismissing the complaint. The plaintiff appealed.]

To recover upon a theory of strict liability in tort for a dog bite or attack, a plaintiff must prove that the dog had vicious propensities and that the owner of the dog, or person in control of the premises where the dog was, knew or should have known of such propensities [citations]. "Vicious propensities include the 'propensity to do any act that might

endanger the safety of the persons and property of others in a given situation'" [citations].

Here, the defendants established their *prima facie* entitlement to judgment as a matter of law by presenting evidence that the dog had never bitten, jumped, or growled at anyone prior to the incident in question, nor had the dog exhibited any other aggressive or vicious behavior [citations]. In opposition, the plaintiff failed to come forward with any proof in evidentiary form that the dog had ever previously bitten anyone or exhibited any vicious propensities. Furthermore, the presence of a "Beware of Dog" sign on the premises, the breed of the dog, and the owner's testimony that the dog was always on a leash were insufficient to raise a triable issue of fact as to the dog's vicious propensities in the absence of any evidence that prior to this incident the dog exhibited any fierce or hostile tendencies [citations].

[Summary judgment is affirmed.]

QUESTIONS

1. A statute requiring railroads to fence their tracks is construed as intended solely to prevent animals that stray onto the right-of-way from being hit by trains. B&A Railroad Company fails to fence its tracks. Two of Calvin's cows wander onto the track. Nellie is hit by a train. Elsie is poisoned by weeds growing beside the track. For which cow(s), if any, is B&A Railroad Company liable to Calvin? Why?

2. Martha invites John to come to lunch. Though she knows that her private road is dangerous to travel, having been heavily eroded by recent rains, Martha

doesn't warn John of the condition, reasonably believing that he will notice the deep ruts and exercise sufficient care. While John is driving over, his attention is diverted from the road by the screaming of his child, who has been stung by a bee. He fails to notice the condition of the road, hits a rut, and skids into a tree. If John is not contributorily negligent, is Martha liable to John?

3. Nathan is run over by a car and left lying in the street. Sam, seeing Nathan's helpless state, places him in his car for the purpose of taking him to the hospital. Sam drives

negligently into a ditch, causing additional injury to Nathan. Is Sam liable to Nathan?

4. Led Foot drives his car carelessly into another car. The second car contains dynamite, which Led had no way of knowing. The collision causes an explosion, which shatters a window of a building half a block away on another street. The flying glass inflicts serious cuts on Sally, who is working at a desk near the window. The explosion also harms Vic, who is walking on the sidewalk near the point of the collision. Toward whom is Led Foot negligent?

5. A statute requires all vessels traveling on the Great Lakes to provide lifeboats. One of Winston Steamship Company's boats is sent out of port without a lifeboat. Perry, a sailor, falls overboard in a storm so strong that had there been a lifeboat, it could not have been launched. Perry drowns. Is Winston liable to Perry's estate?

6. Lionel is negligently driving an automobile at excessive speed. Reginald's negligently driven car crosses the centerline of the highway and scrapes the side of Lionel's car, damaging its fenders. As a result, Lionel loses control of his car, which goes into the ditch. Lionel's car is wrecked, and Lionel suffers personal injuries. What, if anything, can Lionel recover?

7. Ellen, the owner of a baseball park, is under a duty to the entering public to provide a reasonably sufficient number of screened seats to protect those who desire such protection against the risk of being hit by batted balls. Ellen fails to do so.
   a. Frank, a customer entering the park, is unable to find a screened seat and, although fully aware of the risk, sits in an unscreened seat. Frank is struck and injured by a batted ball. Is Ellen liable?

   b. Gretchen, Frank's wife, has just arrived from Germany and is viewing baseball for the first time. Without asking any questions, she follows Frank to a seat. After the batted ball hits Frank, it caroms into Gretchen, injuring her. Is Ellen liable to Gretchen?

8. Negligent in failing to give warning of the approach of its train to a crossing, CC Railroad thereby endangers Larry, a blind man who is about to cross. Mildred, a bystander, in a reasonable effort to save Larry, rushes onto the track to push Larry out of danger. Although Mildred acts as carefully as possible, she is struck and injured by the train.
   a. Can Mildred recover from Larry?
   b. Can Mildred recover from CC Railroad?

9. Vance was served liquor while he was an intoxicated patron of the Clear Air Force Station Non-Commissioned Officers' Club. He later injured himself as a result of his intoxication. An Alaska State statute makes it a crime to give or to sell liquor to intoxicated persons. Vance has brought an action seeking damages for the injuries he suffered. Could Vance successfully argue that the United States was negligent *per se* by its employee's violation of the statute?

10. Timothy keeps a pet chimpanzee, which is thoroughly tamed and accustomed to playing with its owner's children. The chimpanzee escapes, despite every precaution to keep it upon its owner's premises. It approaches a group of children. Wanda, the mother of one of the children, erroneously thinking the chimpanzee is about to attack the children, rushes to her child's assistance. In her hurry and excitement, she stumbles and falls, breaking her leg. Can Wanda recover for her personal injuries?

CASE PROBLEMS

11. Hawkins slipped and fell on a puddle of water just inside the automatic door to the H. E. Butt Grocery Company's store. The water had been tracked into the store by customers and blown through the door by a strong wind. The store manager was aware of the puddle and had mopped it up several times earlier in the day. Still, no signs had been placed to warn store patrons of the danger. Hawkins brought an action to recover damages for injuries sustained in the fall. Was the store negligent in its conduct?

12. Escola, a waitress, was injured when a bottle of soda exploded in her hand while she was putting it into the restaurant's cooler. The bottle came from a shipment

that had remained under the counter for thirty-six hours after being delivered by the bottling company. The bottler had subjected the bottle to the method of testing for defects commonly used in the industry, and there is no evidence that Escola or anyone else did anything to damage the bottle between its delivery and the explosion. Escola brought an action against the bottler for damages. As she is unable to show any specific acts of negligence on its part, she seeks to rely on the doctrine of *res ipsa loquitur*. Should she be able to recover on this theory? Explain.

13. Hunn injured herself when she slipped and fell on a loose plank while walking down some steps. The night

before, while entering the hotel, she had noticed that the steps were dangerous, and although she knew from her earlier stays at the hotel that another exit was available, she chose that morning to leave via the dangerous steps. The hotel was aware of the hazard, as one of the other guests who had fallen that night had reported his accident to the desk clerk then on duty. Still, the hotel did not place cautionary signs on the steps to warn of the danger, and they were not roped off or otherwise excluded from use. Hunn brought an action against the hotel for injuries she sustained as a result of her fall. Should she recover? Explain.

14. Fredericks, a hotel owner, had a dog named "Sport" that he had trained as a watchdog. When Vincent Zarek, a guest at the hotel, leaned over to pet the dog, it bit him. Although Sport had never bitten anyone before, Fredericks was aware of the dog's violent tendencies and, therefore, did not allow it to roam around the hotel alone. Vincent brought an action for injuries sustained when the dog bit him. Is Fredericks liable for the actions of his dog? Explain.

15. Two thugs in an alley in Manhattan held up an unidentified man. When the thieves departed with his possessions, the man quickly gave chase. He had almost caught one when the thief managed to force his way into an empty taxicab stopped at a traffic light. The Peerless Transport Company owned the cab. The thief pointed his gun at the driver's head and ordered him to drive on. The driver started to follow the directions while closely pursued by a posse of good citizens, but then suddenly jammed on the brakes and jumped out of the car to safety. The thief also jumped out, but the car traveled on, injuring Mrs. Cordas and her two children. The Cordases then brought an action for damages, claiming that the cab driver was negligent in jumping to safety and leaving the moving vehicle uncontrolled. Was the cab driver negligent? Explain.

16. A foul ball struck Marie Uzdavines on the head while she was watching the Metropolitan Baseball Club ("The Mets") play the Philadelphia Phillies at the Mets' home stadium in New York. The ball came through a hole in a screen designed to protect spectators sitting behind home plate. The screen contained several holes that had been repaired with baling wire lighter in weight than the wire used in the original screen. Although the manager of the stadium makes no formal inspections of the screen, his employees do try to repair the holes as they find them. Weather conditions, rust deterioration, and baseballs hitting the screen are the chief causes of these holes. The owner of the stadium, the city of New York, leases the stadium to "The Mets" and replaces the entire

screen every two years. Uzdavines sued The Mets for negligence under the doctrine of *res ipsa loquitur*. Is this an appropriate case for *res ipsa loquitur*? Explain.

17. Two-year-old David Allen was bitten by Joseph Whitehead's dog while he was playing on the porch at the Allen residence. Allen suffered facial cuts, a severed muscle in his left eye, a hole in his left ear, and scarring over his forehead. Through his father, David sued Whitehead, claiming that, as owner, Whitehead is responsible for his dog's actions. Whitehead admitted that (1) the dog was large, mean looking, and frequently barked at neighbors; (2) the dog was allowed to roam wild; and (3) the dog frequently chased and barked at cars. He stated, however, that (1) the dog was friendly and often played with his and neighbors' children; (2) he had not received previous complaints about the dog; (3) the dog was neither aggressive nor threatening; and (4) the dog had never bitten anyone before this incident. Is Whitehead liable?

18. Larry VanEgdom, in an intoxicated state, bought alcoholic beverages from the Hudson Municipal Liquor Store in Hudson, South Dakota. An hour later, VanEgdom, while driving a car, struck and killed Guy William Ludwig, who was stopped on his motorcycle at a stop sign. Lela Walz, as special administrator of Ludwig's estate, brought an action against the city of Hudson, which operated the liquor store, for the wrongful death of Ludwig. Walz alleged that the store employee was negligent in selling intoxicating beverages to VanEgdom when he knew or could have observed that VanEgdom was drunk. Decision?

19. The *MacGilvray Shiras* was a ship owned by the Kinsman Transit Company. During the winter months, when Lake Erie was frozen, the ship and others moored at docks on the Buffalo River. As oftentimes happened, one night an ice jam disintegrated upstream, sending large chunks of ice downstream. Chunks of ice began to pile up against the *Shiras*, which at that time was without power and manned only by a shipman. The ship broke loose when a negligently constructed "deadman" to which one mooring cable was attached pulled out of the ground. The "deadman" was operated by Continental Grain Company. The ship began moving down the S-shaped river stern first and struck another ship, the *Tewksbury*. The *Tewksbury* also broke loose from its mooring, and the two ships floated down the river together. Although the crew manning the Michigan Avenue Bridge downstream had been notified of the runaway ships, they failed to raise the bridge in time to avoid a collision because of a mix-up in the shift change-over. As a result, both ships crashed into the bridge and were wedged against the bank of the river. The two

vessels substantially dammed the flow of the river, causing ice and water to back up and flood installations as far as three miles upstream. The injured parties brought this action for damages against Kinsman, Continental, and the city of Buffalo. Who, if any, is liable? Explain.

20. Carolyn Falgout accompanied William Wardlaw as a social guest to Wardlaw's brother's camp. After both parties had consumed intoxicating beverages, Falgout walked onto a pier that was then only partially completed. Wardlaw had requested that she not go on the pier. Falgout said, "Don't tell me what to do," and proceeded to walk on the pier. Wardlaw then asked her not to walk past the completed portion of the pier. She ignored his warnings and walked to the pier's end. When returning to the shore, Falgout got her shoe caught between the boards. She fell, hanging by her foot, with her head and arms in the water. Wardlaw rescued Falgout, who had seriously injured her knee and leg. She sued Wardlaw for negligence. Decision?

21. Joseph Yania, a coal strip-mine owner, and Boyd Ross visited a coal strip-mining operation owned by John Bigan to discuss a business matter with Bigan. On Bigan's property there were several cuts and trenches he had dug to remove the coal underneath. While there, Bigan asked the two men to help him pump water from one of these cuts in the earth. This particular cut contained water eight to ten feet in depth with sidewalls or embankments sixteen to eighteen feet in height. The two men agreed, and the process began with Ross and Bigan entering the cut and standing at the point where the pump was located. Yania stood at the top of one of the cut's sidewalls. Apparently, Bigan taunted Yania into jumping into the water from the top of the sidewall—a height of sixteen to eighteen feet. As a result, Yania drowned. His widow brought a negligence action against Bigan. She claims that Bigan was negligent "(1) by urging, enticing, taunting, and inveigling Yania to jump into the water; (2) by failing to warn Yania of a dangerous condition on the land; and (3) by failing to go to Yania's rescue after he jumped into the water." Was Bigan negligent?

TAKING SIDES

Rebecca S. Dukat arrived at Mockingbird Lanes, a bowling alley in Omaha, Nebraska, at approximately 6:00 P.M. to bowl in her league game. The bowling alley's parking lot and adjacent sidewalk were covered with snow and ice. Dukat proceeded to walk into the bowling alley on the only sidewalk provided in and out of the building. She testified that she noticed the sidewalk was icy. After bowling three games and drinking three beers, Dukat left the bowling alley at approximately 9:00 P.M. She retraced her steps on the same sidewalk, which was still covered with ice and in a condition that, according to Frank Jameson, general manager of Mockingbird Lanes, was "unacceptable" if the bowling alley were open to customers. As Dukat proceeded along the sidewalk to her car, she slipped, attempted to catch herself by reaching toward a car, and fell. She suffered a fracture of both bones in her left ankle as well as a ruptured ligament. Dukat sued Mockingbird Lanes, seeking damages for her for personal injuries. Mockingbird denied liability for Dukat's personal injuries.

a. What arguments would support Dukat's claim for her personal injuries?

b. What arguments would support Mockingbird's denial of liability for Dukat's personal injuries?

c. Which side should prevail? Explain.

CHAPTER 6

Allocating Risk and Responsibilities in the Global Marketplace Products Liability

... [The role tort law plays in this country] is uniquely American. A mass tort case is a passion or morality play. It speaks to the conscience of the country and asks whether we have gone badly astray. It examines values and probes motives; and when it is completed, it has a cathartic effect. When courts speak of punitive damages as reflecting a sense of outrage, they utter an important truth: when society bears witness to truly outrageous conduct it must react. Swift and certain justice is necessary not only because it will deter future wrongdoers, but also because it substantiates society's intolerance for malevolent corporate behavior that brings injury to thousands.

—AARON TWERSKI 1994[1]

Virtually every product is dangerous in some manner and to some extent, at least when put to certain uses. But most such dangers are simple facts of physics, chemistry, or biology. There is no reasonable way to avoid them. For such natural risks of life, product users, rather than product suppliers, properly bear responsibility for avoiding and insuring against any injuries that may result.

—DAVID OWEN (2004)[2]

For centuries, the phrase *caveat emptor* ("buyer beware") dominated the law in Britain and the United States, warning that most sellers made no enforceable promises with regard to their goods. By the middle of the twentieth century, the common law had shifted, allowing those injured by dangerous products to hold both sellers and manufacturers accountable. Today, government agencies such as the **Food and Drug Administration (FDA)**, the **Consumer Product Safety Commission (CPSC)**, and the **National Highway Transportation Safety Agency (NHTSA)** are charged with setting safety standards. And buyers and sellers can distribute risks—with some constraints—when they enter contracts under the **Uniform Commercial Code (UCC).** When harm is widespread—when millions of Toyotas have sudden-acceleration problems, for example—those injured may now turn to the courts to hold manufacturers and sellers liable. In recent decades class action suits on behalf of thousands, sometimes hundreds of

---

[1]Aaron Twerski, Introduction to "Symposium on Punitive Damages Awards in Products Liability Litigation: Strong Medicine or Poison Pill?" *Villanova Law Review* 39, 1994, p. 353.

[2]David G. Owen, "Proof of Product Defect," *Kentucky Law Journal* 93, 2004–2005, p. 1.

thousands, of injured plaintiffs have been brought against entire industries found to have hidden the known risks of their products: asbestos, tobacco, and lead.

The chapter opens with a recent Supreme Court case that illustrates the ongoing contest over who among the various players—federal agencies, state court juries, legislators—has primary responsibility to set safety standards for the products we use. We then explore the complexities of assuring the safety of globally sourced products consumed in the United States, such as a loaf of Sara Lee whole grain white bread containing ingredients from India, the Netherlands, China, Switzerland, honey from Vietnam, Brazil, Uruguay, Canada, or Mexico, and wheat gluten from France, Poland, Russia, or Australia. We observe how safety is differently prioritized in the United States versus the European Union (EU) when it comes to oversight of genetically modified organisms (GMOs). After a consideration of tort suits—especially class actions—we turn to contract law, and warranties made under the UCC. The chapter ends with a reading that offers a public-health perspective on the most deadly of consumer products: tobacco, drugs, motor vehicles, food, and alcohol.

■ ■ ■

On April 7, 2000 Diana Levine—a professional musician who played bass, guitar and piano—went to her local clinic for treatment of a migraine headache. As on previous visits, she received an intramuscular injection of Demerol for her headache and Phenergan for her nausea. Still suffering, she returned later that day and a physician assistant gave her a second dose by what is called the IV-push method. Something went wrong. Phenergan entered Levine's artery, came in contact with arterial blood, and led to gangrene. Levine's doctors were forced to amputate first her right hand, and then her entire forearm. After settling claims against the health care center and clinician, Levine sued Wyeth, the company that made Phenergan. Her claim: Wyeth's labels on Phenergen should have instructed clinicians to use the IV-drip method instead of the higher-risk IV-push method. Wyeth defended its Phenergan packaging labels, claiming they must be adequate because the Food and Drug Administration (FDA)—the federal agency charged with enforcing the Food, Drug, and Cosmetic laws—approved them. The Vermont courts rejected that claim, letting stand a $7,400,000 jury award in Levine's favor. Wyeth appealed to the Supreme Court.

Wyeth v. Levine
United States Supreme Court, 2009
129 S.Ct. 1187

Justice STEVENS delivered the Opinion of the Court.

... Directly injecting the drug Phenergan into a patient's vein creates a significant risk of catastrophic consequences.... The warnings on Phenergan's label had been deemed sufficient by the federal Food and Drug Administration (FDA) when it approved Wyeth's new drug application in 1955 and when it later approved changes in the drug's labeling. The question we must decide is whether the FDA's approvals provide Wyeth with a complete defense to Levine's tort claims. We conclude that they do not....

The evidence presented during the 5-day jury trial showed that the risk of intra-arterial injection ... can be almost entirely eliminated through the use of IV-drip, rather than IV-push, administration.... [Further evidence showed that in 1998, the agency instructed that Phenergan's final printed label "must be identical" to the FDA-approved package insert.]

The question presented by the petition is whether the FDA's drug labeling judgments "preempt state law product liability claims [which are] premised on the theory that different labeling judgments were necessary to make drugs reasonably safe for use."...

Our answer to that question must be guided by two cornerstones of our pre-emption jurisprudence. First, "the purpose of Congress is the ultimate touchstone in every pre-emption case."... Second, "[i]n all pre-emption cases, and particularly in those in which Congress has 'legislated ... in a field which the States have traditionally occupied,' ... we 'start with the assumption that the historic police powers of the States were not to be superseded by the Federal Act unless that was the clear and manifest purpose of Congress.' "...

In order to identify the "purpose of Congress" [in adopting the Food, Drug, and Cosmetic Act,] it is appropriate to briefly review the history of federal regulation of drugs and drug labeling. In 1906, Congress enacted its first significant public health law, the Federal Food and Drugs Act.... The Act, which prohibited the manufacture or interstate shipment of adulterated or misbranded drugs, supplemented the protection for consumers already provided by state regulation and common-law liability. In the 1930s, Congress became increasingly concerned about unsafe drugs and fraudulent marketing, and it enacted the Federal Food, Drug, and Cosmetic Act (FDCA).... The Act's most substantial innovation was its provision for premarket approval of new drugs....

As it enlarged the FDA's powers to "protect the public health" and "assure the safety, effectiveness, and reliability of drugs," Congress took care to preserve state law.

In 2007, after Levine's injury and lawsuit, Congress again amended the FDCA.... For the first time, it granted the FDA statutory authority to require a manufacturer to change its drug label based on safety information that becomes available after a drug's initial approval.... [The law also made] it clear that manufacturers remain responsible for updating their labels.

Wyeth first argues that Levine's state-law claims are pre-empted because it is impossible for it to comply with both the state-law duties underlying those claims and its federal labeling duties. The FDA's premarket approval of a new drug application includes the approval of the exact text in the proposed label.... There is, however, an FDA regulation that permits a manufacturer to make certain changes to its label before receiving the agency's approval. Among other things, this "changes being effected" (CBE) regulation provides that if a manufacturer is changing a label to "add or strengthen a contraindication, warning, precaution, or adverse reaction" or to "add or strengthen an instruction about dosage and administration that is intended to increase the safe use of the drug product," it may make the labeling change upon filing its supplemental application with the FDA; it need not wait for FDA approval....

Wyeth suggests that the FDA, rather than the manufacturer, bears primary responsibility for drug labeling. Yet through many amendments to the FDCA and to FDA regulations, it has remained a central premise of federal drug regulation that the manufacturer bears responsibility for the content of its label at all times. It is charged both with crafting an adequate label and with ensuring that its warnings remain adequate as long as the drug is on the market....

[W]hen the risk of gangrene from IV-push injection of Phenergan became apparent, Wyeth had a duty to provide a warning that adequately described that risk, and the CBE regulation permitted it to provide such a warning before receiving the FDA's approval....

[A]bsent clear evidence that the FDA would not have approved a change to Phenergan's label, we will not conclude that it was impossible for Wyeth to comply with both federal and state requirements....

Wyeth has offered no such evidence....

Congress did not provide a federal remedy for consumers harmed by unsafe or ineffective drugs in the 1938 statute or in any subsequent amendment. Evidently, it determined that widely available state rights of action provided appropriate relief for injured consumers....

If Congress thought state lawsuits posed an obstacle to its objectives, it surely would have enacted an express pre-emption provision at some point during the FDCA's 70-year history.... [But it did not.]

In keeping with Congress' decision not to pre-empt common-law tort suits, it appears that the FDA traditionally regarded state law as a complementary form of drug regulation. The FDA has limited resources to monitor the 11,000 drugs on the market, and manufacturers have superior access to information about their drugs, especially in the postmarketing phase as new risks emerge. State tort suits uncover unknown drug hazards and provide incentives for drug manufacturers to disclose safety risks promptly. They also serve a distinct compensatory function that may motivate injured persons to come forward with information. Failure-to-warn actions, in particular, lend force to the FDCA's premise that manufacturers, not the FDA, bear primary responsibility for their drug labeling at all times. Thus, the FDA long maintained that state law offers an additional, and important, layer of consumer protection that complements FDA regulation....

We conclude that it is not impossible for Wyeth to comply with its state and federal law obligations and that Levine's common-law claims do not stand as an obstacle to the accomplishment of Congress' purposes in the FDCA. Accordingly, the judgment of the Vermont Supreme Court [in favor of the plaintiff] is affirmed.

It is so ordered.

Justice ALITO, with whom THE CHIEF JUSTICE and Justice SCALIA Join, Dissenting.

This case illustrates that tragic facts make bad law. The Court holds that a state tort jury, rather than the Food and Drug Administration (FDA), is ultimately responsible for regulating warning labels for prescription drugs....

[T]he real issue is whether a state tort jury can countermand the FDA's considered judgment that Phenergan's FDA-mandated warning label renders its intravenous (IV) use "safe."... [D]uring his closing argument, [Levine's] attorney told the jury, "Thank God we don't rely on the FDA to ... make the safe[ty] decision. You will make the decision.... The FDA doesn't make the decision, you do."...

Federal law, however, does rely on the FDA to make safety determinations like the one it made here. The FDA has long known about the risks associated with IV-push in general and its use to administer Phenergan in particular. Whether wisely or not, the FDA has concluded—over the course of extensive, 54-year-long regulatory proceedings—that the drug is "safe" and "effective" when used in accordance with its FDA-mandated labeling. The unfortunate fact that [plaintiff's] healthcare providers ignored Phenergan's labeling may make this an ideal medical-malpractice case. But turning a common-law tort suit into a "frontal assault" on the FDA's regulatory regime for drug labeling upsets ... our conflict pre-emption jurisprudence. [The Supremacy Clause of the Constitution has been interpreted to mean that federal law will take precedence over state law, where Congress has made its intent or purpose clear.]...

Congress made its "purpose" plain in authorizing the FDA—not state tort juries—to determine when and under what circumstances a drug is "safe."...

After the FDA approves a drug, the manufacturer remains under an obligation to investigate and report any adverse events associated with the drug, and must periodically submit any new information that may affect the FDA's previous conclusions about the safety, effectiveness, or labeling of the drug, If the FDA finds that the drug is not "safe" when used in accordance with its labeling, the agency "shall" withdraw its approval of the drug. The FDA also "shall" deem a drug "misbranded" if "it is dangerous to health when used in the dosage or manner, or with the frequency or duration prescribed, recommended, or suggested in the labeling thereof."

Thus, a drug's warning label "serves as the standard under which the FDA determines whether a product is safe and effective." Labeling is "[t]he centerpiece of risk management," as it "communicates to health care practitioners the agency's formal, authoritative conclusions regarding the conditions under which the product can be used safely and effectively."... Neither the FDCA nor its implementing regulations suggest that juries may second-guess the FDA's labeling decisions....

By their very nature, juries are ill-equipped to perform the FDA's cost-benefit-balancing function. As we explained in *Riegel v. Medtronic, Inc.* (2008) juries tend to focus on the risk of a particular product's design or warning label that arguably contributed to a particular plaintiff's injury, not on the overall benefits of that design or label; "the patients who reaped those benefits are not represented in court."...

In contrast, the FDA ... consider[s] the interests of all potential users of a drug, including "those who would suffer without new medical [products]" if juries in all 50 States were free to contradict the FDA's expert determinations. And the FDA conveys its warnings with one voice, rather than whipsawing the medical community with 50 (or more) potentially conflicting ones....

To be sure, state tort suits can peacefully coexist with the FDA's labeling regime, and they have done so for decades. But this case is far from peaceful coexistence. The FDA told Wyeth that Phenergan's label renders its use "safe." But the State of Vermont, through its tort law, said: "Not so."

The state-law rule at issue here is squarely pre-empted. Therefore, I would reverse the judgment of the Supreme Court of Vermont.

QUESTIONS

1. Where does Justice Stevens place responsibility for assuring the safety of drugs? Why? What policy reasons does he mention to back up his denial of the defendant's pre-emption claim? What does he mean by the "distinct compensatory function" served by state courts deciding tort claims? How does Stevens' view compare to that of dissenting Justice Alito? What policy arguments does the dissent mention? What do you think the dissent means by "tragic facts make bad law"?

2. After this case, what advice would you give to a pharmaceutical company that is deciding how to label a new drug?

3. In 2011, the Supreme Court ruled that generic drug companies could not be sued for failing to warn patient about risks, since they had no control over the labels on their products. Should a patient therefore be allowed to sue the brand-name company when a generic is unreasonably dangerous? See *Fullington v. Pfizer*, Inc., 720 F.3d 739 (8th Cir. 2013).

GOVERNMENT REGULATION OF PRODUCT SAFETY

[Government] regulation is an imperfect substitute for the accountability, and trust, built into a market in which food producers meet the gaze of eaters and vice versa.

—MICHAEL POLLAN, In Defense of Food: An Eater's Manifesto

Some government agencies, such as Occupational Safety and Health Administration (OSHA), are located within a particular executive department, like the Department of Labor, and are led by individuals who are chosen—and can be removed—by the president. These are known as executive agencies. "Independent administrative agencies," on the other hand—the FDA, CPSC, and NHTSA, for example—are not housed within any particular branch of government. They are considered independent because they are each headed by a board of commissioners appointed for a specific term. These commissioners can be removed early only for reasons defined by Congress.

Regulation of product safety by the major government agencies is spotty at best. And, not surprisingly, even these "independent" agencies are often caught in a cross fire of criticism from both consumer groups and business interests.

Food and Drug Administration

As the Supreme Court explains in *Levine v. Wyeth,* the FDA's role has expanded since it was first created in 1906. Most of the reforms have been in response to high-profile tragedies. In 1938, for example, an early "wonder drug" marketed for strep throat in children, Elixir of Sulfanilamide, was laced with a chemical used in antifreeze and killed 107 people. Public outrage led Congress to authorize the agency to require companies to prove the safety of drugs before they could be marketed and broadened its oversight to include cosmetics and therapeutic devices. Today the FDA's jurisdiction extends to additional products: dietary supplements, food additives, blood products, products that emit radiation (such as microwaves and cell phones) and—since 2009—tobacco products. At the same time, the FDA's effectiveness in fulfilling its mission has been seriously questioned.

In 2005 the FDA created a Drug Safety Oversight Board, in response to a series of headlines about unsafe drugs that had been FDA-approved for marketing to the public. By the time *Levine v. Wyeth* was decided, Justice Stevens would comment in a footnote:

In 1955, the same year that the agency approved Wyeth's Phenergan application, an FDA advisory committee issued a report finding "conclusively" that "the budget and staff of the Food and Drug Administration are inadequate to permit the discharge of its existing responsibilities for the protection of the American public."... Three recent studies have reached similar conclusions. ("[T]he Agency suffers from serious scientific deficiencies ..."[3]); ("... There is widespread agreement that resources for postmarketing drug safety work are especially inadequate ..."[4]); ("FDA lacks a clear and effective process for making decisions about, and providing management oversight of, postmarket safety issues"[5]).

Still, the FDA has been active. In 2010, the agency severely restricted the sale of a diabetes drug, Avandia, after it was linked to heart risks. By the end of 2011, the government had persuaded its maker, GlaxoSmithKline to pay $3 billion to settle a wave of federal cases against the company for its sales and marketing practices from 1997 to 2004, including payments to doctors and manipulation of medical research to promote Avandia. In one of the worst public-health drug disasters in years a meningitis outbreak killed 50 people and sickened hundreds of others in 2012. The FDA traced the problem to steroid injections made by a New England Compounding Center. Upon inspecting the facility, it found "greenish-yellow residue on sterilization equipment, surfaces coated with levels of mold and bacteria that exceeded the company's own environmental limits, and an air-conditioner that was shut off nightly despite the importance of controlling temperature and humidity."[6] When Congress balked at the FDA's plea for new powers and more funding, the agency ran surprise raids on 30 compounding companies in the United States, finding numerous unsafe practices that could contaminate drugs in April 2013.

In May 2013 generic drug maker, Ranbaxy—a subsidiary of a Japanese pharmacy company—agreed to pay $500 million in fines to resolve claims that it sold subpar drugs and lied to the FDA.

The other major prong of FDA responsibility—assuring the safety of the American food supply—has become an almost impossible task—one complicated by the fact that it requires coordination with other agencies. The Department of Agriculture (USDA), for example, inspects meat and poultry; the FDA is responsible for inspecting everything else. The FDA cooperated with the National Marine Fisheries Services (NMFS) to ensure the safety of seafood from the Gulf following the BP *Deepwater Horizon* oil spill and with the Environmental Protection Agency (EPA) to address residues of animal drugs and pesticides in food additives.

In recent years, the agency has focused its attention on the basics: meat, fish, dairy, and produce. When 200 people became ill from *Escherichia coli*–tainted spinach in 2006, the FDA issued voluntary guidelines for handling produce. Critics noted that from 2001 to 2007, the only significant food safety regulations adopted by the agency were those ordered by Congress.

Meanwhile, the corner grocery store had become a global market. Nearly two-thirds of all fruits and vegetables and three-quarters of all seafood consumed in the United States are imported from other countries. And not all of it is safe. *Salmonella* bacteria linked to imported foods—Mexican cucumbers and papayas, pine nuts from Turkey,

---

[3]See FDA Science Board, "Report of the Subcommittee on Science and Technology: FDA Science and Mission at Risk" 2, 6 (2007), online at *http://www.fda.gov/ohrms/dockets/ac/07/briefing/2007-4329b_02_01_FDA%20 Report%20on%20Science%20and%20Technology.pdf.*

[4]National Academies, Institute of Medicine, "The Future of Drug Safety: Promoting and Protecting the Health of the Public," pp. 193–194 (2007).

[5]House Committee on Oversight and Government Reform, "Majority Staff Report, FDA Career Staff Objected to Agency Preemption Policies," 4 (2008).

[6]Sabrina Tavernise and Andrew Pollack, "FDA Details Contamination at Pharmacy," *The New York Times,* A-1, October 27, 2012.

cantaloupes from Guatemala—has sickened Americans in recent years. In 2012, some 1.5 million pounds of contaminated beef found its way to American supermarkets before it was traced to meat imported from Canada and recalled.

The FDA and USDA have been pressed to respond to repeated crises in food safety with limited resources. In addition to $417 billion worth of domestic food, the FDA regulates some $49 billion worth of imported foods.[7]

The Food Safety Modernization Act (FSMA), signed into law by President Obama in 2011, enhances the FDA's powers and requires more inspections of foreign food-processing plants and imported food, but fails to allocate additional funding. In 2013 the FDA had only enough inspectors to visit roughly 1,000 of the more than 250,000 foreign food plants that ship to the United States. According to a recent report, the FDA inspected only 2.3 percent of the 10.4 million annual food import shipments.[8]

Home-grown food has presented its own safety issues. In 2010, the FDA recalled half a billion eggs after hundreds of people contracted *Salmonella*. The outbreak was traced to two giant farms in Iowa, one of which had previously been cited for farm-labor and animal cruelty violations. Food and animal-rights activists pointed to the incident as further evidence that cheap eggs and meat come at a cost of harm to public health and the environment.[9]

In addition to expanding inspections, the FSMA of 2011 requires the Secretary of Health and Human Services to establish science-based minimum standards for the safe production and harvesting of fruits and vegetables, and requires increased inspections and reporting of information relating to food-borne contaminants.

The Global Food Supply: Genetically Modified Organisms

… Genetically modified [GM] plants (also referred to as "bioengineered," "transgenic," or "genetically engineered" organisms) have altered American agriculture. Scientists use recombinant DNA technology to remove genetic material from one plant, and insert it into another, in order to introduce a desirable trait—usually tolerance to herbicides or resistance to insects. Despite public concern about potential health and environmental impacts, by 2012 over 90 varieties of GM plants had been approved for commercialization in the United States. Roughly 94 percent of all cotton, 93 percent of all soybeans, and 88 percent of all corn planted in the United States by acreage was a GM variety.

■ ■ ■

In the next reading, Emily Montgomery, a lawyer who researches food and agricultural policy, explains some of the risks associated with GMOs. She begins by outlining some of the economic and health impacts.

---

[7]Annual Report on Food Facilities, Food Imports and Foreign Offices, U.S. Department of Health and Human Services, August 2012.

[8]Annual Report on Food Facilities, Food Imports and Foreign Offices, U.S. Department of Health and Human Services, August 2012.

[9]In 2012 their arguments would be reinforced by *The New York Times* columnist Nicholas D. Kristof, who noted that "poultry on factory farms are routinely fed caffeine, active ingredients of Tylenol and Benadryl, banned antibiotics and even arsenic." Nicholas D. Kristof, "Arsenic in Our Chicken?" *The New York Times*, A.21, April 4, 2012.

Genetically Modified Plants

Emily Montgomery[10]

The economic concerns relate mainly to cross-pollination and subsequent contamination of conventional crops by GM varieties. When contamination occurs, growers are unable to market their crops as "GM-free," export value is lost to countries that do not embrace biotech crops, and organic growers can lose organic certification for contaminated crops—resulting in lost sales, decreased revenue, and the possible loss of conventional (or heritage and heirloom) seed lines. An example of this concern come to life is the LibertyLink rice case, where an experimental strain of GM rice "cross-bred with and 'contaminated' over 30 percent of U.S. ricelands," causing futures prices of U.S. rice to fall significantly in 2006. Litigation ensued, and the developer paid out $750 million to settle claims with about 11,000 farmers for crop contamination.

Human health risks relate mainly to food safety ... [including] potential toxicity and allergenicity of GM foods. For allergenicity, there is a worry that inserting novel genes into a plant could trigger allergic reactions. This could occur either by use of genetic material from a source that is unknown to the human diet or by use of genetic material from a known allergen to produce a crop that consumers would have no reason to suspect would contain a known allergen (for instance, using a nut to modify corn). Another risk is that consumption of GM crops could lead to consumption of new toxins or increased levels of naturally occurring toxins. Some also worry that GM crops could contain fewer nutrients than non-GM counterparts.... There is no confirmed case of human disease or illness caused by GM food. Still, consumers remain worried, and some long-term health effects may be unknown given that the explosion of GM food products on grocery store shelves has been a relatively recent phenomenon.

Another category of risk centers on environmental concerns ... [including concerns about] (1) weeds and the ability for GM crops to become weeds or for wild weeds to become "superweeds"; (2) insect resistance to crops that contain biological pesticides and the creation of "superbugs"; and (3) reduced biodiversity and effects on nontarget organisms....

Some of these weed-related concerns have already become real problems in agricultural settings. Widespread adoption of glyphosate-tolerant GM crops (usually marketed as "Roundup Ready") has led to an increase in glyphosate application—which, in turn, has led to a rapid development of glyphosate-resistant weeds. There are now 11 weed species that have developed resistance to glyphosate in 26 states, and millions of acres of crops have been infested with the weeds—reducing yields, and costing farmers money in added labor and chemical costs to combat the weeds. The glyphosate-resistant weeds are especially hardy and have led to the use of herbicides that are more toxic and environmentally damaging than glyphosate....

Indeed, research and knowledge regarding GM plant impacts has not kept pace with the adoption of the technology, leading to heightened public concern.

Fear over the risks associated with GMOs crosses national boundaries. Columbia Law School professor Anu Bradford compares the regulation of GMOs in the United States and the EU in the next reading. She describes "the Brussels Effect," the "unprecedented

---

[10]Copyright © 2012 Vermont Law School; Emily Montgomery, *Vermont Law Review* 37, 2012, p. 351.

and deeply underestimated global power that the European Union is exercising through its legal institutions and standards, and how it successfully exports that influence to the rest of the world."

The Brussels Effect

Anu Bradford[11]

.... The EU and the United States take starkly opposing views on the regulation of biotechnology. The United States regards GMO products as substantially similar to products made using traditional production methods. GMO products can therefore be cultivated and marketed in the United States without extensive premarket safety studies or the need to specifically label them. In contrast, the EU subjects GMOs to extensive regulation based on their potential adverse health effects. The GMOs have to go through a lengthy approval process, which entails an evaluation of the risk the GMOs pose to human health and the environment. The evaluation is also guided by the precautionary principle, which justifies regulatory intervention in the presence of scientific uncertainty. The EU further requires that most authorized foods, ingredients, and animal feeds containing over 0.9% GMOs be labeled.

Several reasons explain the U.S.-EU regulatory divergence. The United States is the world's leading GMO producer whereas GMOs are hardly cultivated in the EU. Biotechnology is seen as a key for retaining the U.S. competitiveness in export markets, while the EU places cultural importance on small-scale farming and remains skeptical of mass production technologies. Consequently, U.S. farmers and the entire biotechnology industry are influential players in the U.S. political process, whereas farmers producing non-GMO crops wield influence in the EU. At its root, however, the divergence mirrors very different consumer preferences with respect to food safety across the Atlantic. Survey data show that 62% of Europeans are worried about the food safety risks posed by GMOs and 71% of Europeans do not want GMOs in their food, whereas U.S. consumers have shown little interest or concern for the issue. [Bradford goes on to explain the importance of the EU's stand on GMOS, i.e., how the Brussels Effect occurs.]

... For U.S. farmers, the EU is only the fifth largest export market and accounts for just 8% of U.S. agricultural exports. Many producers could thus afford to forgo the EU market and divert their trade elsewhere. At the same time, an increasing number of other countries, including Australia, Brazil, China, and Japan, are following the EU's lead and adopting mandatory labeling schemes for GMO products. This narrows the U.S. farmers' scope for trade diversion....

... [T]he United States challenged the EU's regulatory stance [with regard to GMOs] before the WTO and won a trade dispute in 2006. Yet ... the negative ruling by the WTO has done little to compromise the EU's regulation of GMOs. The EU has failed to comply with the ruling, and transatlantic trade involving GMOs remains restricted. As a result, U.S. producers of GMO varieties continue to feel the (limited) Brussels Effect due to their inability to altogether ignore the EU market and their dependence on multinational companies who prefer to cater to a single global standard and remain sensitive to potential risks and liabilities they may face in the EU....

[In its WTO challenge t]he United States claimed that the EU's alleged pursuit of food safety and concern for the health of its consumers in reality reflected its desire to protect its farmers from foreign competition. The EU defended its measures on grounds of genuine consumer preferences, which in Europe reflect deep skepticism of GMOs and growth-promoting hormones, and argued that scientific studies supported its health concerns. The WTO ruled for the United States, urging the EU to lift its import ban of hormone-treated beef and similarly approve GMO products without "undue delay." Most recently, the United States has challenged the EU's import ban of U.S. poultry that is rinsed in chlorine—a process which, according to the United States, makes poultry safe for consumption....

... [T]he WTO offers, at best, imperfect remedies ... [It] cannot compel a member state to lift its restrictive measures. For instance, the EU has maintained its import ban on hormone-treated beef, preferring to endure U.S. retaliation. The EU has also repeatedly allowed the deadline for implementing the GMO ruling to lapse, while the United States has suspended its retaliatory measures in anticipation of settlement or the EU's future compliance....

QUESTIONS

1. In the United States, regulatory oversight of GMOs is divided between three federal agencies: the FDA, USDA and the EPA. The FDA oversees GM animals; the USDA GM plants, and the EPA regulates GM plants that contain or produce pesticides. But as Martin notes, critics worry that there is "no clearly identifiable overriding guiding principle for regulating the risks of GMOs ... [and] no clear standards to guide [agency] decisions on whether a GMO should be permitted to be released into the environment." Do you think such standards are needed? Why/why not?

2. **Research:** In spring 2013, the FDA held hearings prior to deciding whether to allow AquaBounty Technologies to market a genetically engineered salmon. Find out whether the FDA allowed AquaBounty to sell what would be the first approved GM animal. If so, has the FDA allowed sellers of unaltered salmon to distinguish themselves from the GMO?

3. As we learned in Chapter 7, labeling in the United States must not be false or misleading. The FDA has already stopped dairy producers from labeling their milk as coming from cows not injected with bovine growth hormone unless they include a statement that the FDA has found that there is no difference between milk from treated and untreated cows. What are the pros and cons to this kind of "double-labeling"? Should a similar rule be applied to labeling of non-GMO food?

4. Whole Foods announced in March 2013 that all products sold in its stores would have to be labeled to indicate any genetically engineered contents. Suppose you own a new company that manufactures organic snacks. Selling to Whole Foods would be a coup, but rather than label your genetically modified ingredients, you would want your product to be certified as non-GMO. To get the certification, you would have to identify (and pay somewhat more for) conventional ingredients. Every ingredient in your product would have to be verified by affidavit as non-GMO. Too, you would probably have to invest in tinkering with your snack product, to retain its original taste and mouth feel. What would be the factors in favor of making this investment, and becoming a non-GMO certified supplier to Whole Foods?

● THE CONSUMER PRODUCT SAFETY COMMISSION

Consumers by definition, include us all. They are the largest economic group, affecting and affected by almost every public and private economic decision. Yet they are the only important group ... whose views are often not heard.

—PRESIDENT JOHN F. KENNEDY, Declaration to U.S. Congress (1962)

The Consumer Product Safety Act of 1972 created the CPSC as an independent federal regulatory agency to protect consumers from unreasonable risk of injury, illness, or death from unsafe products. Like the FDA, the agency has long been underfunded by Congress (there was only enough money for three of five potential commissioners from 1987 to 2007). Unsure of its mission, it was once described by consumer advocate Ralph Nader as "dormant for 15 years." For most of its existence the CPSC relied primarily on voluntary standards, ignoring its authority to adopt regulations and recall unsafe products. It was not until 2006 that the agency promulgated its first major safety standard, when it set minimum safeguards to make mattresses fire safe.

Increasingly, the 15,000 types of consumer products over which the CPSC has jurisdiction are imported. In response to a public outcry over high-profile product recalls in 2007—some 40 million Chinese toys and other items used by children were recalled in 2007 alone—nearly one for every household with children—Congress voted overwhelmingly for a sweeping revision of the consumer product safety laws. The Consumer Product Safety Improvement Act of 2008 (CPSIA) expands the regulatory and enforcement powers of the CPSC (e.g., greater recall authority) and imposes new obligations—including reporting requirements—on manufacturers, importers, and retailers.

Sworn in as Chair in 2009, Inez Moore Tenenbaum has reinvigorated the agency. Under her leadership, the CPSC enacted 40 final rules ranging from mandatory safety regulations for durable infant products (cribs, walkers, swings, etc.) to requirements for component parts testing for CPSC products. The agency launched the Consumer Product Safety Information Database, www.SaferProducts.gov, in March 2011 to enable consumers to search for information and report on risky products. Since then, some 4,000 businesses have registered and the CPSC has posted more than 13,000 reports of harm.

In 2011, the CPSC opened a National Product Testing and Evaluation Center, where scientists and engineers test potentially hazardous products for defects and develop testing methods to determine compliance with safety standards. Enforcement, too, has been enhanced. From 2010 to 2013, the agency secured more than $17 million in civil penalties for violating regulations such as a ban on lead paint, and for failing to report potential defects.

When the CPSC was formed in 1974, the United States imported roughly $104 billion in goods. Three decades later, that number had increased to $2 trillion. Three-quarters or more of the items recalled by the CPSC during the twenty-first century were made outside the United States. The CPSC is part of the chain of government agencies responsible for the safety of imported products—a nearly impossible job given the sheer volume. There is, for example, only one CPSC employee to perform "spot checks" in the Los Angeles area ports, where some 15 million truck-sized cargo shipments enter the country each year. While the CPSC screened more than 17,000 models of imported goods in 2012, it should not be surprising that defective products—from dangerous toys to drywall with asbestos—continue to make their way to American households.

DANGEROUS IMPORTS: CHINESE DRY WALL

Hurricanes Katrina and Rita devastated the Gulf Coast in 2005. These disasters, coinciding as they did with a boom in new housing construction, helped precipitate a shortage of drywall for the construction and reconstruction of homes in the United States. As a result, from approximately 2005 to 2008, Chinese drywall entered the U.S. market, changing hands in the chain-of-commerce, and ultimately finding its way into thousands of homes and buildings in the United States, primarily in the south. Sometime after the installation of Chinese drywall in these properties, homeowners, residents, and occupants began to notice and complain of odd odors, corrosion of metal components, failure of electronics and appliances, and in some cases, physical ailments, such as nosebleeds, skin irritation, and respiratory problems. In response, agencies like the Consumer Products Safety Commission and the Department of Housing and Urban Development began to investigate.

The situation mushroomed into the most complex litigation in American history. Multiple lawsuits involving claims by homeowners, developers, installers, retailers, realtors, brokers, suppliers, importers, and insurers were consolidated into one massive case under the direction of a federal court judge in Louisiana. Two groups of Chinese manufacturers were sued: the Tashain group and the Kanuf entities. The case was hard fought—some 1,600 record documents were filed between 2009 and 2013, and a U.S. judge traveled to China to supervise depositions (pretrial discovery).

The Tashain group refused to submit to the jurisdiction of the American courts, and as this text goes to press, continues to contest the court's jurisdiction.

The Kanuf entities, however, reached a global settlement with the various players, winning preliminary approval of the court in 2013. Earlier, in October 2011, the Knauf entities had entered into a Court-approved pilot program for remediation of homes containing drywall manufactured by Knauf. With additional funds from some of the defendants in the chain-of-commerce, the pilot program was implemented, with homes being added to and completed on a regular basis since early spring 2011.

By 2013, contractors had completed remediation of over 1,000 homes through this program. Other "notable breakthroughs" in this messy litigation included agreements by various parties to help fund the remediation efforts: Interior Exterior Building Supply, a major supplier of Chinese drywall in the Gulf Coast, agreed to provide $8 million; another supplier—Banner—promised close to half a million. The Global Settlement provides for a total payment of $70,570,000.00.[12]

QUESTIONS

1. Should producers in foreign countries be forced to answer for the safety of their products through lawsuits brought in American courts? **Research:** Find out how the court ruled on the Tashain challenges to the Chinese-Manufactured Drywall suits.

2. Suppose an American company manufactures a product in Indonesia, under dangerous or oppressive working conditions. Should foreign workers have access to American courts to hold the company accountable?

---

[12]In re Chinese-Manufactured Drywall Products Liability Litigation, 2013 W.L. 49947 (E.D. La.).

◦ NATIONAL HIGHWAY TRAFFIC SAFETY ADMINISTRATION

Created in 1970 as part of the U.S. Department of Transportation, the NHTSA's mission is to reduce deaths, injuries, and economic losses resulting from motor vehicle crashes by setting and enforcing safety performance standards, investigating defects, conducting research, and educating the public. Despite this broad mandate, its specific powers are limited. The agency has no way to track safety-related problems unless it is notified by the affected industry. In the 1990s, hundreds of people were killed or injured in rollover accidents caused by tread separation on Bridgestone and Firestone tires. But the NHTSA was not notified of the tread problem by either the carmakers or the tire makers until the companies had been sued. Finally, in 2000, the NHTSA recalled 6.5 million tires.

In 2009, the NHTSA was faced with yet another crisis: Toyotas that accelerated suddenly. Federal law requires carmakers to notify the NHTSA within five days of learning about safety defects. Toyota had waited four months before it revealed what it knew about "sticky pedal" problems. In April 2010, after three recalls issued by the carmaker and a visit to Japan by the head of the NHTSA, Toyota agreed to pay more than $16 million, what was then the largest civil penalty ever assessed against an automaker. More recalls were followed by agreements to pay more fines—twice in December 2010, and then another $17.35 million in December 2012—because the recalls were delayed. The company never admitted fault.

And the government regulator was not the only party seeking accountability from Toyota. Class action lawsuits were filed on behalf of those who had been killed or injured, and others who claimed that recalls had adversely affected the economic value of their vehicles.

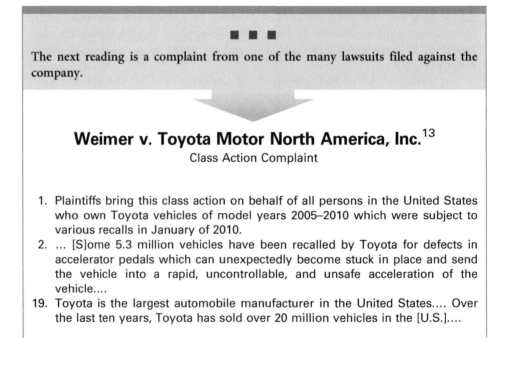

■ ■ ■

The next reading is a complaint from one of the many lawsuits filed against the company.

Weimer v. Toyota Motor North America, Inc.[13]
Class Action Complaint

1. Plaintiffs bring this class action on behalf of all persons in the United States who own Toyota vehicles of model years 2005–2010 which were subject to various recalls in January of 2010.
2. ... [S]ome 5.3 million vehicles have been recalled by Toyota for defects in accelerator pedals which can unexpectedly become stuck in place and send the vehicle into a rapid, uncontrollable, and unsafe acceleration of the vehicle....
19. Toyota is the largest automobile manufacturer in the United States.... Over the last ten years, Toyota has sold over 20 million vehicles in the [U.S.]....

---

[13]United States District Court, E.D. Louisiana, 2010. No. 10CV00219.

[In order to move forward as a "class action," certain conditions must be met. The following section explains why the plaintiffs believe their case should be "certified" as a class action.]

Class Action Allegations

28. **NUMEROSITY:** Members of the Class are so numerous that their joinder would be impracticable. The Class includes millions of owners of Toyota vehicles.... Judicial economy favors a class action mechanism instead of forcing each class member to bring a separate action individually.

29. **COMMONALITY:** Common questions of law and fact predominate over any individual questions of separate Class members. [They include the following:]
    b. Whether the defects in the vehicles recalled by Toyota render them unfit for their intended use;
    c. Whether Toyota breached their implied warranties of merchantability and fitness for a particular purpose;
    d. Whether Toyota's actions have caused damages to Plaintiffs and members of the Class...;
    g. Whether or not Toyota should be subject to punitive damages.

30. **TYPICALITY:** Plaintiffs' claims are typical of the claims of the Class Members. Plaintiffs and all Class Members have been injured by the same defective mechanism.... Plaintiffs' claims arise from the same practices and course of conduct that gives rise to the claims of the Class Members and are based on the same legal theories.

31. **ADEQUACY:** Plaintiffs willfully and adequately assert and protect the interests of the Class. Plaintiffs have retained counsel who is experienced in class actions and complex mass tort litigation. Neither Plaintiffs nor their counsel have interests contrary to or conflicting with the interests of the Class.

32. **SUPERIORITY:** A class action is superior to all other available methods for the fair and efficient adjudication of this lawsuit because individual litigation of the claims by each of the Class members is economically unfeasible and impractical. While the aggregate amount of the damages suffered by the class is in the millions of dollars, the individual damages suffered by each of the Class members as a result of the wrongful conduct by Toyota, in many cases, are too small to warrant the expense of individual lawsuits. Even if the individual damages were sufficient to warrant individual lawsuits, the court system would be unreasonably burdened by the number of cases that would be filed....

[In the next section, plaintiffs allege several alternative causes of action on which their case rests. Those legal theories—breach of implied warranty, negligence, and strict products liability—are explained later in this chapter.]

Count I: Breach of Implied Warranty

36. At the times Toyota marketed, sold, and distributed automobiles for use by Plaintiffs and Class Members, Toyota knew of the use for which the Subject Vehicles were intended and impliedly warranted the product to be of a certain quality.

37. Toyota embarked on and carried out a common scheme of marketing and selling automobiles by falsely and deceptively representing that the vehicles were safe and without defects, specifically, that the accelerator pedal of the Subject Vehicles was fit for its intended use.

38. Said representations and warranties are false, misleading, and inaccurate in that the recalled automobiles are unsafe and unreasonably dangerous due to the defective accelerator pedals.

39. The Subject Vehicles, when sold, were defective, unmerchantable, unfit for ordinary use, and unfit for the particular use for which they were sold.
40. The Subject Vehicles contain a vice or defect which renders them either absolutely useless or renders their use inconvenient and imperfect such that Plaintiffs and Class Members would not have purchased the Subject Vehicles had they known of the vice or defect.
41. The damages in question arose from the reasonably anticipated use of the product in question.
42. Toyota breached the implied warranties of merchantability and fitness for a particular purpose when the Subject Vehicles were sold to Plaintiffs and Class Members, in that the accelerator pedals are defective and have otherwise failed to function as represented and intended.
43. As a direct and proximate cause of Toyota's breach of the implied warranties of merchantability and fitness for a particular purpose, Plaintiffs and Class Members have sustained and will continue to sustain the loss of use of their vehicles, severe emotional distress, economic losses and consequential damages, and are therefore entitled to compensatory damages and equitable and declaratory relief....

Count II: Negligence

45. Toyota had a duty to Plaintiffs and Class Members to provide a safe product in design and manufacture, to notify the NHTSA, and to warn the NHTSA of the defective nature of the accelerator pedals in the Subject Vehicles.
46. Toyota breached its duty of reasonable care to Plaintiffs and Class Members by designing the accelerator pedals of the Subject Vehicles in such a manner that they were prone to becoming stuck in the depressed position and failing to return or returning extremely slowly to the idle position, thereby causing the vehicle to accelerate rapidly, uncontrollably, and dangerously.
47. Toyota breached its duty of reasonable care to Plaintiffs and Class Members by manufacturing and/or assembling the accelerator pedals of the Subject Vehicles in such a manner that they were prone to becoming stuck in the depressed position and failing to return or returning extremely slowly to the idle position, thereby causing the vehicle to accelerate rapidly, uncontrollably, as in para above and dangerously.
48. Toyota breached its duty of reasonable care to Plaintiffs and Class Members by failing to recall the Subject Vehicles at the earliest possible date and instead blaming the defect on a much less dangerous supposed "floor mat" defect.
49. As a direct and proximate result of Toyota's negligence, ... Plaintiffs and Class Members have sustained and will continue to sustain [losses.]...
50. Toyota's egregious misconduct alleged above warrants the imposition of punitive damages against Toyota to prevent such future behavior.

Count III: Products Liability

54. Toyota knew and expected the Subject Vehicles to eventually be sold to and operated by purchasers and/or eventual owners of the Subject Vehicles, including Plaintiffs and Class members; ...
55. The Subject Vehicles reached Plaintiffs without substantial change in their condition from time of completion of manufacture by Toyota.
56. The accelerator pedal defects in the Subject Vehicles could not have been contemplated by any reasonable person expected to operate the Subject

Vehicles, and, therefore, presented an unreasonably dangerous situation ... even though ... operated by expected users in a reasonable manner.

57. Toyota should have reasonably foreseen that the dangerous conditions caused by the defective accelerator pedals in the Subject Vehicles would subject Plaintiffs and Class Members to harm resulting from the defective pedals.

59. As a direct and proximate cause of Toyota's design, manufacture, assembly, marketing, and sales of the Subject Vehicles, Plaintiffs and Class Members have sustained and will continue to sustain [losses and are] therefore entitled to compensatory relief according to proof....

Prayer for Relief

WHEREFORE, Plaintiffs, individually and on behalf of the members of the Class, demand judgment in their favor and against Toyota as follows:

a.   For an Order certifying the Class pursuant to Federal Rule of Civil Procedure 23, appointing Plaintiffs as the representatives of the Class, and appointing counsel for Plaintiffs as counsel for the Class;

b.   For an award of compensatory damages...;

d.   For punitive or exemplary damages against Toyota, consistent with the degree of Toyota's reprehensibility and the resulting harm or potential harm to Plaintiffs and members of the Class, as well as an amount sufficient to punish Toyota and deter Toyota and others from similar wrongdoing;

e.   For restitution and disgorgement of profits;

f.   For an award of all costs incurred by Plaintiffs in pursuing this action;

g.   For an award of reasonable attorneys' fees;

h.   For an Order enjoining Toyota from implementing any fixes to the defect in the accelerator pedals of the Subject Vehicles without prior approval from NHTSA.

QUESTIONS

1.   What is a class action lawsuit? Why was this suit brought as a class action? How do you think such suits might benefit the judicial system? Is anyone potentially harmed by them?

2.   On what theories are the plaintiffs hoping to hold Toyota liable? What remedies do they seek?

3.   In August 2010, the Associated Press reported that initial probes by the NHTSA revealed that brakes were not applied in 35 of the 58 cases studied. What impact would you expect such findings to have on the case?

4.   The NHTSA directed the National Academy of Science to conduct a full-scale study of unintended acceleration and electronic controls across the automotive industry—an inquiry that seemed to exonerate Toyota when scientists reported in February 2011 that they could find no electronic flaws in the vehicles. What would be the likely impact of this report?

5.   In December 2012, Toyota reached a $1 billion settlement with those who sold or turned in their leased vehicles between September 2009 and December 2010. In what was the largest settlement in United States history involving automobile defects, Toyota agreed to fund research into advanced safety technologies. In January 2013, Toyota settled for an undisclosed amount a wrongful death case that was set for trial in February. As this

book goes to press hundreds of wrongful death and injury suits against Toyota are still pending. **Research:** Find out what has happened in the Toyota cases since January 2013.

■ ■ ■

Early Products Liability Law: Breach of Warranty

Today, the "product liability" theory on which the Toyota plaintiffs rest their case is a common basis for lawsuits when unsafe and dangerously defective cars, toys, drugs, and other products cause injury. But that was not always so.

The early common law had allowed few exceptions to the general rule of *caveat emptor* (buyer beware), most notably for food products. In Britain, an Act of Parliament in 1266 made it a crime to sell "corrupt wine and victuals," and American law required those who sold food intended for immediate consumption to ensure its safety or pay damages to anyone injured by it. But, prior to the twentieth century, most people injured by defective goods had little legal recourse.

The most important remedy was a suit for breach of warranty against those who sold unfit goods. For centuries, however, those claims were limited by a legal doctrine called "privity of contract," a rule that a buyer could sue only the entity from whom the item was purchased, not anyone further up the chain-of-commerce, such as a wholesale distributor or the actual manufacturer.

The Tort of Negligence

New York Court of Appeals Justice Benjamin Cardozo is widely considered the first to recognize that a person injured by an unsafe product has a right to bring a lawsuit based on negligence. In the early twentieth century he wrote an important decision, *MacPherson v. Buick Motor Co.*, allowing an injured person to sue the manufacturer of a car for a defect in its wheel. The wheel was wooden; when its spokes crumbled, the car collapsed and the plaintiff was thrown out and injured. Instead of suing the seller from whom he bought the car for breach of contract, the plaintiff sued the manufacturer for negligence. The jury ruled in his favor. On appeal, the court agreed that Buick was negligent because the car's "defects could have been discovered by a reasonable inspection, and that inspection was omitted."[14]

To win a suit for negligence, a plaintiff must establish that the defendant breached its duty of care, creating an unreasonable risk of harm, and that such careless behavior was the proximate cause of the plaintiff's injury. This is often difficult. Generally, a company will not be found negligent if it adhered to industry standards or the "state of the art" with regard to the engineering, selection of materials, production processes, assembly, and marketing of its product. Proof of reasonable quality control procedures is usually sufficient to negate a charge of negligence. A firm can also defend itself or limit the amount of damages it must pay by showing that its negligence was not the only cause of the injury—a car accident caused in part by faulty brakes and in part by drunk driving, for example—or that the plaintiff contributed to her own harm, either by assuming a known risk or acting carelessly.

---

[14]*MacPherson v. Buick Motor Co.*, 111 N.E. 1050 (N.Y. 1916).

The Tort of Strict Products Liability

Modern products liability law, the basis for Weiner's claim against Toyota, was born in mid-twentieth century. In 1963, the California Supreme Court adopted what is now called strict liability.[15] This new legal theory made it easier for injured persons to sue and harder for manufacturers who sold defective products to defend themselves. Described below in Section 402A of the Restatement of Torts (Second),[16] strict liability recognizes that there are times when losses must be allocated between two "innocent" parties: the consumer who was hurt while using a product properly and the company that was not negligent (careless) in creating it. It places the responsibility on the company for reasons articulated here by noted legal scholar William Prosser in "The Fall of the Citadel":

> *The public interest in human safety requires the maximum possible protection for the user of the product, and those best able to afford it are the suppliers…. By placing their goods upon the market, the suppliers represent to the public that they are suitable and safe for use; and by packaging, advertising and otherwise, they do everything they can to induce that belief.*[17]

RESTATEMENT OF TORTS (SECOND) SECTION 402A

1. One who sells any product in a defective condition unreasonably dangerous to the user or consumer or to his property is subject to liability for physical harm thereby caused to the ultimate user or consumer or to his property, if
   a. the seller is engaged in the business of selling such a product, and
   b. it is expected to and does reach the user or consumer without substantial change in the condition in which it is sold.
2. The rule stated in Subsection (1) applies although
   a. the seller has exercised all possible care in the preparation and sale of the product, and
   b. the user or consumer has not bought the product from or entered into any contractual relation with the seller.

Most states have adopted Section 402A of the Restatement, finding nonnegligent sellers liable for defective product designs, manufacturing ("production") defects, and failure to warn. In each case, the focus is not on the company's behavior (as it is in negligence law), but on whether the product itself is defective and unreasonably unsafe.

For example, suppose a company hires qualified engineers who design a new line of SUVs using standard techniques. No one was negligent, yet the company might be held liable if the car injures someone and a jury finds that its design was defective because the SUV was more dangerous than useful.

Or the design of a car may be perfectly safe, but something in the way a particular car is assembled causes injury—an undetected weakness in a sheet of aluminum or a glitch leading to an improperly assembled component, for example. While we expect

---

[15]*Greenman v. Yuba Power Products, Inc.,* 377 P.2d 897 (Cal. 1963).

[16]THE RESTATEMENT OF LAW is an attempt by legal scholars to summarize and "restate" the common law based on judicial precedents from around the country. Today, there is a Third Restatement of Torts. However, most states continue to follow the Second Restatement of Torts.

[17]William Prosser, "The Fall of the Citadel," *Minnesota Law Review* 50, 1966, pp. 791, 799.

companies to implement good quality control systems, we know that some production defects will occasionally slip through the cracks of any manufacturing process. Once again, strict liability burdens the company, not the consumer, with the loss, even when the company was not negligent.

A third kind of defect involves products that cannot be made completely safe but can be made safer by appropriately warning the consumer. The inadequate information about possible side effects of a drug or of the absence of other potential dangers posed by a product may result in a manufacturer's strict liability for failure to warn. This was the main defect in *Levine v. Wyeth.*

In every state, a person who sues under the Restatement must prove that the product that injured him was the proximate (or legal) cause of his harm. If the harm results from some alteration in the product (e.g., by the consumer or by someone who serviced it), the seller is not held responsible. Most states allow companies to defend themselves by proving that the plaintiff misused or abused the product in a way that the manufacturer could not have foreseen.

The Restatement (Second) does not define "defective and unreasonably dangerous product," so state courts must create their own definitions. Some use what is called the "consumer expectation" test: a product is defectively dangerous if it is dangerous to an extent beyond that which would be contemplated by the ordinary consumer who purchased it with the ordinary knowledge common to the community as to the product's characteristics. Alternatively, under the danger-utility approach adopted in other states, a product is defective if, but only if, the magnitude of the danger outweighs the utility of the product. The theory underlying this approach is that virtually all products have both risks and benefits and that there is no way to go about evaluating hazards intelligently without weighing risk against utility. When you read *Denny v. Ford,* later in this chapter, you will see how New York courts define defective and unreasonably dangerous products.

Punitive Damages

Under the common law of torts, juries are free to award an injured plaintiff all sorts of damages, not only to compensate for damaged property or out-of-pocket medical expenses, but for pain and suffering and significantly, damages designed to punish companies who disregard safety, to create incentives to make safer products and deter similar wrongdoing in the future. While some state laws limit the amount of punitive damages a jury can award, others leave the jury free to award hundreds of thousands—even millions—of dollars to punish serious wrongdoing. Not surprisingly, industry lobbyists and their attorneys have targeted punitive damage awards as a goal of "tort reform."

THE FORD PINTO CASE

In 1972 a Ford Pinto hatchback unexpectedly stalled on a freeway, erupting into flames when it was rear-ended by the car behind it. The driver, Mrs. Lilly Gray, was fatally burned, and a passenger, 13-year-old Richard Grimshaw, suffered severe and permanently disfiguring burns on his face and entire body.

Harley Copp, a former Ford engineer and executive in charge of the crash testing program who had been forced into early retirement for speaking out about safety, testified against Ford. In a trial that lasted six months, plaintiffs established the Pinto was the brainchild of Lee Iaccoca, then Vice-President of Ford, who hoped to build a car at or below 2,000 pounds to sell for no more than $2,000.

This was a rush job, designed to compete with European and Japanese models. Varying from the usual procedure, the Ford leadership team allowed styling to precede engineering and to dictate the design of the car.

Among the engineering decisions dictated by styling was the placement of the fuel tank. It was then the preferred practice in Europe and Japan to locate the gas tank over the rear axle in subcompacts because a small vehicle has less "crush space" between the rear axle and the bumper than larger cars. The Pinto's styling, however, required the tank to be placed behind the rear axle leaving only 9 or 10 inches of "crush space," far less than in any other American automobile or Ford overseas subcompact. In addition, the Pinto was designed so that its bumper was little more than a chrome strip, less substantial than the bumper of any other American car produced then or later. The Pinto's rear structure also lacked reinforcing members known as "hat sections" (2 longitudinal side members) and horizontal cross-members running between them such as were found in cars of larger unitized construction and in all automobiles produced by Ford's overseas operations. The absence of the reinforcing members rendered the Pinto less crush resistant than other vehicles. Finally, the differential housing selected for the Pinto had an exposed flange and a line of exposed bolt heads. These protrusions were sufficient to puncture a gas tank driven forward against the differential upon rear impact.

During the development of the Pinto, prototypes were built and tested.... The crash tests revealed that the Pinto's fuel system as designed could not meet the 20-mile-per-hour proposed [federal] standard....

When a prototype failed the fuel system integrity test, the standard of care for engineers in the industry was to redesign and retest it. The vulnerability of the production Pinto's fuel tank at speeds of 20 and 30-miles-per-hour fixed barrier tests could have been remedied by inexpensive "fixes," but Ford produced and sold the Pinto to the public without doing anything to remedy the defects. Design changes that would have enhanced the integrity of the fuel tank system at relatively little cost per car included the following: a single shock absorbent "flak suit" to protect the tank at $4; a tank within a tank and placement of the tank over the axle at $5.08 to $5.79; a nylon bladder within the tank at $5.25 to $8; placement of the tank over the axle surrounded with a protective barrier at a cost of $9.95 per car; ... Equipping the car with a reinforced rear structure, smooth axle, improved bumper, and additional crush space at a total cost of $15.30 would have made the fuel tank safe in a 34- to 38-mile-per-hour rear end collision by a vehicle the size of the Ford Galaxie.... If the tank had been located over the rear axle, it would have been safe in a rear impact at 50 miles per hour or more.[18]

Project engineers signed off on the design to their immediate supervisors and sent it up the chain of command, along with the crash test results. Everyone up to Mr. Iacocca approved the project, knowing the gas tank was vulnerable to puncture and that fixes were feasible at nominal cost. After a trial that lasted six months the jury awarded the plaintiffs $3.5 million in punitive damages.

---

[18]*Grimshaw v. Ford Motor Company*, 174 Cal. Rptr. 348 (Cal. Ct. App. 1981).

◦ CONTRACT LAW

Breach of Warranty and the Uniform Commercial Code

Contract law is primarily designed to encourage commerce by assuring those who freely enter into agreements that the law will protect their expectations. If one side reneges on its bargain, the other can go to court to seek a remedy that would give the plaintiff the benefit of the bargain struck.

Much of the modern American law of contracts is found in the UCC, first written in 1952 and later adopted by every state in the United States as the basic law governing the sale of goods. Under the UCC, every merchant who sells a product automatically promises that it is fit for its ordinary purpose.[19] Food should not be contaminated, hair dye should not cause one's hair to fall out, rungs of ladders should not splinter, and televisions should not explode. A merchant[20] who does not intend to make such a promise must adhere to specific rules in order to disclaim that implied warranty of merchantability.[21] A seller's promise that goods are fit for their ordinary purpose can be enforced not only by the purchaser but by members of her household as well. In some states, the warranty extends even further, protecting not only the purchaser, family, and household, but "any person who may reasonably be expected to use, consume, or be affected by the goods and who is injured" as a result of the breach.[22] Historically, the "privity of contract" rule meant that an injured party could only sue his immediate seller for breach of contract or warranty, but that requirement is no longer a bar. Today, a buyer can sue retailers, wholesalers, and manufacturers when goods are not as promised.

Since the UCC rests on a fundamental belief in the freedom to contract, the law encourages commercial parties to decide when they enter into an agreement what remedy will be available if either side breaches. If they don't make such provisions, courts deal with any breach of contract "dispassionately," giving the injured party the financial benefit it expected under the agreement—a combination of what are known as general and incidental damages. At times, the plaintiff may also win what are called "special" or consequential damages, covering the economic costs that are a "consequence" of the breach, such as lost profits while a business is shut down because a seller failed to deliver a needed machine. But juries are not free to compensate the winner for pain and suffering or to award punitive damages or attorneys' fees.

■ ■ ■

Transport Corporation of America, Inc. (TCA) operates a national trucking business out of Minnesota. In 1989, TCA decided to update the computer system it used to process incoming orders, issue dispatching assignments, and store all distribution records. TCA purchased an IBM computer system for $541,313.38 from

---

[19]UCC 2-314.

[20]Under UCC 2-104 a merchant includes (a) a person who deals in goods of the kind involved in the sale, for example, a car maker or car dealer when he sells cars; or (b) a person whose occupation indicates that he or she has special knowledge or skill regarding the good involves, for example an optometrist selling glasses; or (c) someone who hires a merchant (e.g., an agent) to act on his behalf.

[21]UCC 2-316 and Magnuson-Moss Warranty Act, 15 U.S.C. sections 2301, et seq.

[22]UCC 2-318.

Innovative Computing Corporation (ICC), a company that produces software and re-sells IBM computers. A year after the system was installed, it failed. Although it was ultimately repaired, TCA was without it for almost 34 hours and sued both the manufacturer (IBM) and the seller (ICC) on various tort and contract theories.

The lower court dismissed the suit before trial, finding that the **economic loss doctrine** barred the tort claims, and that the plaintiff was not entitled to any damages for breach of contract because the computer had been repaired. The appellate court agreed, explaining why in the following excerpt.

Transport Corporation of America v. IBM
United States Court of Appeals, Eighth Circuit, 1994
30 F.3d 953

McMILLAN, Circuit Judge.

On December 19, 1990 ... the computer system went down and one of the disk drives revealed an error code. TCA properly contacted IBM, and IBM dispatched a service person. Although TCA requested a replacement disk drive, the error code indicated that the service procedure was not to replace any components but to analyze the disk drive. TCA had restarted the computer system and did not want to shut it down for the IBM service procedure. IBM informed TCA that replacement was not necessary under the limited warranty of repair or replace, and agreed to return on December 22, 1990, to analyze the disk drive. On December 21, 1990, the same disk drive completely failed, resulting in the computer system being inoperable until December 22, 1990.

TCA alleges that the cumulative downtime for the computer system as a result of the disk drive failure was 33.91 hours. This includes the time to replace the disk drive, reload the electronic backup data, and manually re-enter data which had been entered between 2:00 a.m. and the time the system failed. TCA alleges that it incurred a business interruption loss in the amount of $473,079.46 ($468,514.46 for loss of income; $4,565.00 for loss of data and replacement media).

Economic Loss Doctrine

Minnesota courts have consistently held that the UCC should apply to commercial transactions where the product merely failed to live up to expectations and the damage did not result from a hazardous condition.... Because failure of the disk drive was contemplated by the parties and the damage was limited in scope to the computer system (into which the disk drive and its data were integrated), TCA must look exclusively to the UCC for its remedy.

IBM's Disclaimer of Implied Warranties

TCA next argues that because it was not a party to the negotiations between ICC and IBM, it is not bound by the terms of the remarketer agreement, including IBM's disclaimer of implied warranties....

The UCC as adopted in Minnesota has a privity provision that operates to extend all warranties, express or implied, to third parties who may reasonably be expected to use the warranted goods.... The seller can disclaim implied warranties ... [and these disclaimers] are extended to third party purchasers [like the plaintiff]....

The remarketer agreement between IBM and ICC included a disclaimer of "ALL OTHER WARRANTIES, EXPRESS OR IMPLIED, INCLUDING, BUT NOT LIMITED TO, THE IMPLIED WARRANTIES OF MERCHANTABILITY AND FITNESS FOR A PARTICULAR PURPOSE." As the district court correctly noted, this language complies with the requirements of [the UCC] (that is, it was in writing, conspicuous and mentioned merchantability) and thus effectively disclaimed all implied warranties.

IBM's Limited Remedy of Repair or Replace

[Next, the court must decide whether or not to enforce the "exclusive remedy" created by the parties to deal with a possible breach of contract. The UCC provides that the remedy should be enforced unless it "fails of its essential purpose."] Under Minnesota law, "[a]n exclusive remedy fails of its essential purpose if circumstances arise to deprive the limiting clause of its meaning or one party of the substantial value of its bargain."... A repair or replace clause does not fail of its essential purpose so long as repairs are made each time a defect arises....

ICC's Disclaimer of Consequential Damages Liability

[Under the UCC, a] seller may limit or exclude consequential damages unless the limitation is unconscionable.... The UCC encourages negotiated agreements in commercial transactions, including warranties and limitations.... An exclusion of consequential damages set forth in advance in a commercial agreement between experienced business parties represents a bargained-for allocation of risk that is conscionable as a matter of law....

In the agreement between ICC and TCA, TCA expressly agreed to an ICC disclaimer that stated in part "IN NO EVENT SHALL ICC BE LIABLE FOR ANY INDIRECT, SPECIAL OR CONSEQUENTIAL DAMAGES SUCH AS LOSSES OF ANTICIPATED PROFIT OR OTHER ECONOMIC LOSS IN CONNECTION WITH ... THIS AGREEMENT."

[T]he disclaimer of consequential damages was not unconscionable and ... the damages claimed by TCA, for business interruption losses and replacement media, were consequential damages. Furthermore, TCA and ICC were sophisticated business entities of relatively equal bargaining power. ICC's disclaimer was not unconscionable and TCA is therefore precluded from recovering consequential damages....

[Summary Judgment for IBM and ICC is affirmed.]

QUESTIONS

1. On what grounds did the court determine that Transport Corporation was not entitled to money damages? What might the plaintiff have done to better protect itself?

2. While it is common for businesses to limit damages, as IBM did in this case, the UCC makes it unconscionable (so shocking to the conscience that it should not be enforced) to limit damages for personal injury in the sale of products to consumers. So, for example, Ford could not give a warranty that limited its responsibility for injuries caused by a defect in one of its vehicles. Does it seem fair to distinguish consumer from commercial transactions in this way? To allow courts to "rewrite" a deal that two parties freely entered?

CONTRACT LAW AND TORT LAW

It is not uncommon for lawyers to file suit against all potential defendants (e.g., immediate seller, shipper, manufacturer, component parts maker) on several potential theories (breach of contract, negligence, and strict liability.) You can see this kind of "alternative pleading" in Weimer's complaint against Toyota. During the pretrial discovery phase of litigation, plaintiffs can gather information about the production process, injury records, and documents indicating who knew what and when—all of which help sort out which party or parties are most likely responsible, and which theories are most convincing. The rules of litigation make one or another cause of action more advantageous in particular situations. In most states, for example, the time for bringing a suit ("statute of limitations") differs for tort and contract cases. And, in all states, the general rules regarding remedies are fundamentally different for contract cases, where successful plaintiffs are generally limited to damages that would give them the economic "benefit of their bargain," and tort cases, where damages are more open-ended.

■ ■ ■

In June 9, 1986, Nancy Denny slammed on the brakes of her Ford Bronco II in an effort to avoid a deer that had walked directly into the path of her vehicle. The Bronco rolled over, and Denny was severely injured. She sued Ford, asserting negligence, strict product liability, and breach of implied warranty under the Uniform Commercial Code. The jury came back with a mixed verdict; the Bronco was not unreasonably dangerous and defective, so there was no tort liability. But, they found Ford had violated the implied warranty of merchantability—and therefore breached its contract—by selling Denny a vehicle that was not fit for its ordinary purpose. In the excerpts below, the highest court in New York has to decide whether the two legal theories—a tort action for strict product liability and a contract action for implied warranty—are really one and the same.

Denny v. Ford Motor Company
Court of Appeals of New York, 1995
639 N.Y.S.2d 250

TITONE, Judge.

The trial evidence centered on the particular characteristics of utility vehicles, which are generally made for off-road use on unpaved and often rugged terrain. Such use sometimes necessitates climbing over obstacles such as fallen logs and rocks....

Plaintiffs introduced evidence at trial to show that small utility vehicles in general, and the Bronco II in particular, present a significantly higher risk of rollover accidents than do ordinary passenger automobiles ... [and] that the Bronco II had a low stability index attributable to its high center of gravity and relatively narrow track width. The vehicle's shorter wheel base and suspension system were additional factors contributing to its instability. Ford had made minor design changes in an effort to achieve a higher stability index, but, according to plaintiffs' proof, none of the changes produced a significant improvement in the vehicle's stability.

Ford argued at trial that the design features of which plaintiffs complained were necessary to the vehicle's off-road capabilities. According to Ford, the vehicle had been intended to be used as an off-road vehicle and had not been designed to be sold as a conventional passenger automobile. Ford's own engineer stated that he would not recommend the Bronco II to someone whose primary interest was to use it as a passenger car, since the features of a four-wheel-drive utility vehicle were not helpful for that purpose and the vehicle's design made it inherently less stable.

Despite the engineer's testimony, plaintiffs introduced a Ford marketing manual which predicted that many buyers would be attracted to the Bronco II because utility vehicles were "suitable to contemporary life styles" and were "considered fashionable" in some suburban areas. According to this manual, the sales presentation of the Bronco II should take into account the vehicle's "suitab[ility] for commuting and for suburban and city driving." Additionally, the vehicle's ability to switch between two-wheel and four-wheel drive would "be particularly appealing to women who may be concerned about driving in snow and ice with their children." Plaintiffs both testified that the perceived safety benefits of its four-wheel-drive capacity were what attracted them to the Bronco II. They were not at all interested in its off-road use.

Although the products liability theory sounding in tort and the breach of implied warranty theory authorized by the UCC coexist and are often invoked in tandem, the core element of "defect" is subtly different in the two causes of action.... [T]he New York standard for determining the existence of a design defect [in strict liability cases] has required an assessment of whether "if the design defect were known at the time of manufacture, a reasonable person would conclude that the utility of the product did not outweigh the risk inherent in marketing a product designed in that manner." This standard demands an inquiry into such factors as (1) the product's utility to the public as a whole, (2) its utility to the individual user, (3) the likelihood that the product will cause injury, (4) the availability of a safer design, (5) the possibility of designing and manufacturing the product so that it is safer but remains functional and reasonably priced, (6) the degree of awareness of the product's potential danger that can reasonably be attributed to the injured user, and (7) the manufacturer's ability to spread the cost of any safety-related design changes.... The above-described analysis is rooted in a recognition that there are both risks and benefits associated with many products and that there are instances in which a product's inherent dangers cannot be eliminated without simultaneously compromising or completely nullifying its benefits.... In such circumstances, a weighing of the product's benefits against its risks is an appropriate and necessary component of the liability assessment under the policy-based principles associated with tort law.

[T]he risk/utility balancing test is a "negligence-inspired" approach, since it invites the parties to adduce proof about the manufacturer's choices and ultimately requires the fact finder to make "a judgment about [the manufacturer's] judgment."...

It is this negligence-like risk/benefit component of the defect element that differentiates strict products liability claims from UCC-based breach of implied warranty claims....

While the strict products concept of a product that is "not reasonably safe" requires a weighing of the product's dangers against its overall advantages, the UCC's concept of a "defective" product requires an inquiry only into whether the product in question was "fit for the ordinary purposes for which such goods are used."... The latter inquiry focuses on the expectations for the performance of the product when used in the customary, usual, and reasonably foreseeable manners. The cause of action is one involving true "strict" liability, since recovery may be had upon a showing that the product was not minimally safe for its expected purpose without regard to the feasibility of alternative designs or the manufacturer's "reasonableness" in marketing it in that unsafe condition.

[Next, the court explains the distinction in terms of the history of the two doctrines: Implied warranty originated in contract law, "which directs its attention to the purchaser's disappointed expectations," while strict product liability is a tort, and tort actions have traditionally been concerned with "social policy and risk allocation by means other than those dictated by the marketplace."]

As a practical matter, the distinction between the defect concepts in tort law and in implied warranty theory may have little or no effect in most cases. In this case, however, the nature of the proof and the way in which the fact issues were litigated demonstrates how the two causes of action can diverge. In the trial court, Ford took the position that the design features of which plaintiffs complain, i.e., the Bronco II's high center of gravity, narrow track width, short wheel base, and specially tailored suspension system, were important to preserving the vehicle's ability to drive over the highly irregular terrain that typifies off-road travel. Ford's proof in this regard was relevant to the strict products liability risk/utility equation, which required the fact finder to determine whether the Bronco II's value as an off-road vehicle outweighed the risk of the rollover accidents that could occur when the vehicle was used for other driving tasks.

On the other hand, plaintiffs' proof focused, in part, on the sale of the Bronco II for suburban driving and everyday road travel. Plaintiffs also adduced proof that the Bronco II's design characteristics made it unusually susceptible to rollover accidents when used on paved roads. All of this evidence was useful in showing that routine highway and street driving was the "ordinary purpose" for which the Bronco II was sold and that it was not "fit" or safe for that purpose.

Thus, under the evidence in this case, a rational fact finder could have simultaneously concluded that the Bronco II's utility as an off-road vehicle outweighed the risk of injury resulting from rollover accidents and that the vehicle was not safe for the "ordinary purpose" of daily driving for which it was marketed and sold.... Importantly, what makes this case distinctive is that the "ordinary purpose" for which the product was marketed and sold to the plaintiff was not the same as the utility against which the risk was to be weighed. It is these unusual circumstances that give practical significance to the ordinarily theoretical difference between the defect concepts in tort and statutory breach of implied warranty causes of action.... [Held: Judgment for the plaintiff affirmed. There was no error in instructing the jury to separately consider Ford's tort liability for sale of an unreasonably dangerous product and contract liability for breach of the implied warranty of merchantability.]

SIMONS, Judge, Dissenting.

In my judgment, the consumer expectation standard, appropriate to commercial sales transactions, has no place in personal injury litigation alleging a design defect and may result in imposing absolute liability on marketers of consumers' products. Whether a product has been defectively designed should be determined in a personal injury action by a risk/utility analysis....

[T]he word "defect" has no clear legal meaning....

The jury having concluded that the Bronco II was not defective for strict products liability purposes, could not logically conclude that it was defective for warranty purposes.... The warranty claim in this case was for tortious personal injury and rests on the underlying "social concern [for] the protection of human life and property, not regularity in commercial exchange."... As such, it should be governed by tort rules, not contract rules.... Accordingly, I dissent.

QUESTIONS

1. What did Nancy Denny think she was buying? What did she buy? On what legal theories did she sue? On what basis did she win?

2. Elsewhere in the decision, dissenting Judge Simons argues that the majority imposes a kind of absolute liability on a manufacturer. Is he right? What might Ford have done differently?

3. Compare this case to the Norplant case in Chapter 7. What similarities/differences do you see in the marketing campaigns? In the lawsuits?

4. Tuna fish sold in the United States generally contains small amounts of mercury, an odorless, colorless, tasteless, poisonous heavy metal. Bumble Bee promoted its tuna fish as an "excellent and safe source of high-quality protein, vitamins, minerals and omega–3 fatty acids" as well as being low in saturated fats and carbohydrates, and touted it as being "heart healthy"—with no mention of mercury. Lee P. ate roughly ten six-ounce cans of Bumble Bee tuna fish per week for two years. He bought the tuna, usually on sale, from his local grocer. When he began to experience chest pains, heart palpitations, sweatiness, dizziness, and lightheadedness, he feared a heart condition. Instead, his doctor eventually diagnosed it as mercury poisoning. In addition to lost work, he incurred medical expenses until he stopped eating tuna. (a) What legal remedies are available to Lee P.? (b) What arguments can you make on behalf of potential defendants? (c) Do an ethical analysis of Bumblebee's marketing practices. (d) Suppose you are a store manager in an "organic" grocery. How would you display tuna fish? (e) **Research:** Find out what happened in the actual case. *Porrazzo v. Bumble Bee Foods, LLC,* 822 F.Supp.2d 406 (S.D.N.Y. 2011).

■ ■ ■

An Alternative Approach

The author of the reading that closes this chapter proposes an alternative way to confront the staggering degree of damage—death,[23] injury, and disease—caused by five consumer products: alcohol, tobacco, guns, motor vehicles, and junk food. "Performance-based regulation" would place responsibility on industry, but permit the sellers to figure out how to best decrease the negative public-health consequences of their products.

---

[23]Sugarman estimates yearly deaths from these products at 690,000.

Performance-Based Regulation: Enterprise Responsibility for Reducing Death, Injury, and Disease Caused by Consumer Products

Stephen D. Sugarman[24]

In general, public health policy makers search for policy interventions on a group or population basis.... Providing communities with clean drinking water is a classic example of a population-wide measure. Mass immunization through vaccinations is another....

The typical public health perspective on problems is to promote a variety of broad policy changes designed to reduce the socially undesirable consequences. Policy changes such as banning indoor smoking, lowering speed limits, levying alcohol taxes, and restricting the number of fast food outlets in a single neighborhood are all hallmarks of conventional public health tactics aimed at these products....

Sometimes, public health leaders seek only voluntary changes by target industries. For example, a foundation connected to former president Bill Clinton recently came to an "agreement" with Pepsi, Coca-Cola, and Cadbury-Schweppes in which the three major soda companies announced that they would no longer sell certain sweetened beverages in certain schools.... Other times, rather than calling on private actors to change their behavior, public health advocates focus on the provision of new services by public agencies (like smoking cessation clinics at public hospitals, nutrition education at public schools, and safer public highways). Neither of these approaches, however, imposes legal requirements on private enterprises....

Performance-Based Regulation

In general, performance-based regulation works like this: A firm's performance target is set, either by legislation or by an administering agency running the scheme. A system of regular measurement is implemented to determine whether the firm is meeting its goal. And a penalty structure is put in place that would impose consequences if a firm fails to meet its goal....

The goal in setting the penalty levels is to induce socially efficient prevention [insofar as meeting the target may cost less for the firm than paying a fine].

In the years since the surgeon general issued his famous 1964 report on the lethal consequences of cigarettes, adult smoking prevalence rates in the United States have dropped from more than 40 percent to about 20 percent.... Earlier informational efforts have been supplemented by higher tobacco taxes, laws restricting where people can smoke, counteradvertising exposing the misconduct of tobacco companies to the public, tougher enforcement of laws barring sale to minors, restrictions on cigarette marketing campaigns, and cheaper access to more effective cessation products and programs. These policy initiatives have made a difference in curbing smoking rates.

Yet cigarettes remain widely promoted and available, and we are nowhere near the long-standing public health goal of reducing the nationwide smoking prevalence rate to below 12 percent....

Performance-based regulation attacks the issue in an altogether different way. It rests on the simple proposition that the tobacco companies themselves should be required to achieve sharply improved public health outcomes.

---

[24]Stephen D. Sugarman, "Performance-Based Regulation: Enterprise Responsibility for Reducing Death, Injury, and Disease Caused by Consumer Products," *Journal of Health Politics, Policy and Law* 34(6), 2009, pp. 1035–1077.

Imagine then, that over, say, seven years, tobacco companies were required to cut in half the number of people who smoke their products. Reducing the smoking rate to less than 10 percent would have enormously positive public-health consequences. To provide firms with the right sort of incentive, those that fail to achieve their goals would be subject to serious financial penalties.

The moral argument for this proposal is that cigarette makers—whose products kill when used as directed—should be held accountable for the death toll. The practical argument is that since tobacco companies have been so effective in enticing teens and adults to consume their products, they are also probably best positioned to figure out how to reduce the number of smokers. To be sure, cigarette makers would not be happy about having to halve the size of their businesses. But this is an industry that has been found liable for "racketeering." Besides, even if tobacco companies had only half the number of customers they now have, they could still turn a handsome profit, especially if they retained as customers their heaviest smokers....

Under my proposal, it would not matter whether a firm achieved a uniform reduction in sales from each of its brands, because the performance goal would be enterprisewide. Moreover, at least at the outset, the regulation would be indifferent as to which demographic group experienced decreased smoking rates. For example, the low-hanging fruit might consist of preventing youths from starting, keeping former smokers from restarting, and getting social smokers to quit rather than escalate to daily smoking. Notice that if firms achieved reductions in these segments of the population, they could still retain their best (i.e., heaviest-smoking) clients. Even so, the long-run public health benefits would be great.

Firms would be free to achieve their regulatory target in many different ways. One approach might be to provide smokers with subsidized access to cessation aids and programs. Alternatively, tobacco companies might increase product prices, try to convince cigarette smokers to switch to a far less dangerous alternative nicotine delivery device, or engage in advertising genuinely aimed at discouraging smoking initiation by teens. Of course, these and other tactics might be used in some combination. Given the discretion to develop their own methods, tobacco companies would likely employ some strategies that are unimaginable now. Perhaps the leading tobacco firms would cooperate in seeking to reduce smoking prevalence....

It would be possible to include a "tradable permit" feature in such a performance-based regulatory scheme.... [I]f the target reduction were 50 percent and, for example, R.J. Reynolds reduced its consumer base by more than half, it could sell that excess accomplishment to, say, Philip Morris, which could then exceed its target by the allocation it bought. Overall, the industry would have reached the public health target, and arguably in the most efficient manner....

Regulatory Alternatives

Command-and-control schemes rest on the belief that the regulator knows the best way (or at least a good way) to attack the public health problem....

[T]he major problem with this approach is that the regulator may not order the right changes, even after a number of tries, or that it will take too long to get it right. This could be because the self-interest of the regulators does not match that of the public; they may be corrupt, subject to undue influence by those being regulated, inept, or simply eager to maximize the size and budget of the agency. Even assuming the best of intentions, regulators simply may not possess or be able to acquire the information to determine the most efficient and effective changes to require. Worse yet, they may lock enterprises into outmoded and unduly costly technologies....

[Another approach is for the regulator to] try to influence the level of production or consumption of the product by imposing an excise tax or granting a subsidy.... Also in this vein, the regulator might impose a substantial license fee for a gun permit or allow consumers to claim a tax credit for purchasing a car with antilock brakes. So, too, in order to address obesity, the government might decrease subsidies for high fructose corn syrup while creating subsidies for fresh fruits and vegetables....

The success of tax and subsidy strategies in lowering the level of a dangerous activity is likely to depend [in part] ... on "elasticity of demand"—how sensitive consumers are to price, which depends in part on the price and suitability of substitute products....

[Another problem is that] taxes designed to promote public health tend to have an overbreadth problem. For example, all drinkers will have to pay more for alcohol when it costs more because of tax increases, but most of those who consume less as a result are not alcoholics or irresponsible users. Thus, public-health-based taxes will frequently suffer from "target inefficiency." Even cigarette taxes—which are great to the extent they cause people to quit, not to relapse and start smoking again, and not to start in the first place—do nothing to improve public health to the extent heavy smokers respond to the higher cost by switching from premium to lower cost brands....

[Litigation] is yet another regulatory strategy that can be employed in furtherance of public health goals....

Even though a common-law tort plaintiff normally seeks money damages only after suffering harm, the regulatory theory underlying tort litigation is that firms will take health and safety precautions in advance in hopes of avoiding lawsuits (and will even more seriously address the consequences of their products after a litigant successfully sues them or their direct competitors). Indeed, sometimes the private litigants' preferred legal remedy is an injunction to prevent ongoing or future harm....

Yet litigation has its own drawbacks. For one thing, it can be quite expensive, especially the cost of the lawyers. Second, most tort litigation is not policy oriented. It is not about identifying and blocking new dangers, such as cars that are not "crashworthy" or guns that are irresponsibly marketed. Rather, most torts cases involve routine claims such as for compensation of victims of inattentive drivers or careless property owners; or they are the hundreds or thousands (or more) follow-on claims against, say, a pharmaceutical company whose drug has already been clearly shown to have been inadequately tested)....

[P]erformance-based regulation is designed to unleash private innovation and competition. The same features that we value in the production of goods in a capitalist system can now be specifically turned toward promoting safety and health....

QUESTION

1. What does Sugarman mean by "performance-based regulation"? To what alternatives does he point? What advantages do you see to each?

CHAPTER PROBLEMS

1. The low cost, quick buzz, and sweet flavor of caffeinated and alcoholic energy drinks made them especially popular among young people. In 2010, the FDA sent letters to the makers of these "blackout in a can" beverages, warning that they were illegal—but took no other action to ban them. Within a year, Michigan and Washington states had made the drinks illegal, and in 2012, the federal Substance Abuse and

Mental Health Services Administration reported that in one year more than 12,000 E.R. visits—and as many as five deaths—were possibly linked to energy drinks. In 2013 Monster Beverages was sued by the parents of a 14-year-old who died after drinking two 24-ounce cans within 24 hours. (a) What kind of lawsuit would that be? What will the family need to prove in order to win? (b) What defenses will Monster Beverage raise? (c) **Research:** What happened in that lawsuit? (d) **Research:** Find out the legal status of alcoholic energy drinks in your home state.

2. An internal Ford memo entitled "Fatalities Associated With Crash Induced Fuel Leakage and Fires" estimated the "benefits" and "costs" of design changes to its early Pinto as follows:

Benefits: Savings—180 burn deaths, 180 serious burn injuries, and 2,100 burned vehicles Unit cost—$200,000 per death, $67,000 per injury, $700 per vehicle

Total benefits: 180 × ($200,000) plus

180 × ($67,000) plus

2,100 × ($700) = $49.53 million

Costs: Sales—11 million cars, 1.5 million light trucks

Unit cost—$11 per car, $11 per truck

Total costs: 11,000,000 × ($11) plus

1,500,000 × ($11) = $137.5 million

Assume you are a safety engineer at Ford, consulted as to the wisdom of adding $11 to the cost of manufacturing the Pinto. What recommendation would you make? Can you make use of ethical theory to argue in defense of it? Against it?

3. In some states, legal options may be limited by what is known as the **"economic loss" doctrine.** This rule, barring a party from bringing a tort suit if the only loss suffered is economic, was applied in the *TCA v. IBM* case in this chapter. (a) Apply the economic loss rule to the following scenario: AOL released a software package, AOL 5.0, in October 1999, marketing it as "risk free," "easy to use," and providing "superior benefits." But, according to thousands of subscribers, AOL 5.0 interfered with their system's communications settings so that they could no longer connect to other Internet Service Providers, run non-AOL e-mail programs, or connect to local networks. By adding or altering hundreds of files on a user's system, AOL 5.0 was said to cause instability. Subscribers could not remove the software without doing further harm to their computers. AOL has called upon its insurance company to defend it in multiple class action suits. Its insurance contract, however, requires coverage only for bodily injury or "physical damage to the tangible property of others," such as AOL users. (b) Is there anything AOL could have done to better protect itself in the process of making an insurance deal? (c) What could it have done in the process of making/selling its software? (d) **Research:** Find out what happened in *American OnLine, Inc. v. St. Paul Mercury Insurance Co.*, 207 F. Supp.2d 459 (E.D.Va. 2002).

4. DDT is a relatively cheap way to eliminate insects that threaten crops and people—including mosquitoes that spread malaria. Because it accumulates in the food chain and causes harm to humans and animals, its use has been banned in the United States since 1972. However, 23 nations continue to use it for malaria control, although most no longer use DDT for agricultural purposes. Alternative pesticides—such as pyrethroids—are two to three times more costly. By 1999, only three nations—China, Mexico, and India—still produced and exported DDT. However, when the United Nations considered a worldwide ban on DDT as part of a plan to minimize

the use of 12 toxic chemicals ("persistent organic pollutants"), some members of the public-health community were alarmed. There has been a resurgence of mosquito-borne malaria, with some 300 to 500 million new cases a year. Drugs to treat malaria are expensive and increasingly ineffective against the disease. Use ethical theory to articulate a response to this dilemma.

5. In January 2010, McNeil Consumer Health Care, a unit of Johnson & Johnson (J&J), recalled lots of Tylenol, Motrin, Benadryl, Rolaids, and aspirin in response to consumer complaints about moldy smells emanating from certain products. J&J claimed the odor was a byproduct of a chemical that leaked into the products at a company plant in Puerto Rico. FDA officials met with managers to express serious concerns about their manufacturing operations and then conducted a routine inspection of the firm's Pennsylvania plant. In May, after the FDA accused the company of using raw materials with known bacterial contamination to make certain lots of liquid Tylenol and Motrin for children in Pennsylvania, J&J issued a voluntary recall of those lots. (a) Do an ethical analysis of this scenario. (b) Can you articulate a legal claim against J&J?

6. Biotech medicines—proteins made by modifying the DNA of bacteria, yeast, or mammal cells and infused into sick patients—are the fastest growing category of health spending. Sales reached $83 billion in 2012, with hundreds of biotech products being synthesized to treat cancer, AIDS, diabetes, Alzheimer's, and a hundred other diseases. The manufacture of biotechnologies is more complex and costly than conventional medicine, and the cost to patients can run as high as $25,000–$50,000 a year. Some members of Congress have introduced legislation that would give consumers access to lower-cost copies; one would authorize the FDA to approve safe, lower-cost versions of biotechnology drugs without the full range of tests normally required for new products. Who are the stakeholders who will be affected by such legislation? What arguments can you make for or against it?

7. In 2013, the Secretary of Health and Human Services blocked the FDA's approval of the sale to adolescents without a prescription of Plan B One-Step, a contraceptive pill. This was the first time a cabinet secretary had overruled a drug-approval decision by the FDA. (a) What problems do you see with the executive branch asserting its power in this way? (b) **Research:** The courts have also been involved in the ongoing controversy over this "day after" contraception. Find out the current status of Plan B One-Step.

8. In spring 2013, the United Nations Environmental Program met to work on a global treaty to ban products and processes that release mercury into the environment as a way to reduce health hazards. One proposal would ban thimersol, a mercury-based product that has been used since the 1930s to prevent bacterial and fungal contamination in multidose vials of vaccines. If banned, the price of vaccines in developing nations will likely rise, as providers switch to single-dose vials, which cost more and require additional facilities for storage and waste disposal. **Research:** Find out how this controversy has been handled by the United Nations. How has the United States—where thimersol has not been used since the early 2000s—responded?

9. As we learned in this chapter, the FDA has limited resources to police America's food supply. In 2012, more than 250 people in 24 states were sickened by *Salmonella*-contaminated cantaloupe. Three died. In response, Oxfam America created the Equitable Food Initiative to train farmworkers to recognize and address potential food contamination problems, in return for higher pay and better working conditions. As project director Peter O'Driscoll explains, "Farm workers can be the eyes and ears

of the farm, helping to improve food safety and pest contamination." Certifications will alert consumers that growers followed food safety protocols and that workers who harvested the crop were paid and treated fairly.

Joining with its union, the United Farm Workers, Andrew & Williams, a California strawberry producer, become the first participant. The company agreed to pay its workers above-market wages in return for their added responsibilities.[25] **Research:** Find out which retailers are selling Andrew & Williamson's strawberries and whether other companies have signed on to the program. How would you evaluate its success?

CHAPTER PROJECT

Legislative Activism

1. For this project, you are asked to identify a proposed regulation related to product safety and to submit a written comment for or against the proposed rule.
   - Begin by going to the website of any of the major government regulatory agencies with responsibility for product safety (the National Highway Transportation Safety Administration at http://www.nhtsa.gov, the Environmental Protection Agency at *http://www.epa.gov*, the Consumer Product Safety Commission at *http://www.cpsc.gov*, the Food and Drug Administration at *http://www.fda.gov*, or the Federal Trade Commission at *http://www.ftc.gov*).
   - Once you have selected a government agency, locate its docket of proposed regulations. Choose one on a topic that interests you, and read through the proposal.
   - Learn as much as you can about the debate for and against the proposed regulation. Check out such consumer advocacy groups such as *http://www.citizen.org*, *http://www.consumersunion.org*, or Friends of the Earth at *http://www.foe.org*. Find the business perspectives through popular business publications, by using a database such as ABI/inform, or through a trade association such as *http://www.Phrma.org* (pharmaceutical industry) or the Business Roundtable.
   - Take a position for or against the new regulation, and submit a written comment to the regulatory agency that has proposed it. E-mail a copy of your comment to your professor.

---

[25]Stephanie Strom and Steven Greenhouse, "On the Front Lines of Food Safety," *The New York Times*, May 24, 2013.

CHAPTER 7

INTRODUCTION TO CONTRACTS

CHAPTER OUTCOMES

After reading and studying this chapter, you should be able to:

- Distinguish between contracts that are covered by the Uniform Commercial Code and those covered by the common law.

- List the essential elements of a contract.

- Distinguish among (1) express and implied contracts; (2) unilateral and bilateral contracts; (3) valid, void, voidable, and unenforceable agreements; and (4) executed and executory contracts.

- Explain the doctrine of promissory estoppel.

- Identify the three elements of enforceable quasi contract and explain how it differs from a contract.

It is impossible to overestimate the importance of contracts in the field of business. Every business, whether large or small, must enter into contracts with its employees, its suppliers, and its customers to conduct its business operations. Contract law is, therefore, an important subject for the business manager. Contract law is also basic to other fields of law treated in other parts of this book, such as agency, partnerships, corporations, sales of personal property, negotiable instruments, and secured transactions.

Even the most common transaction may involve a multitude of contracts. For example, in a typical contract for the sale of land, the seller promises to transfer title to the land, and the buyer promises to pay an agreed-upon purchase price. In addition, the seller may promise to pay certain taxes or assessments; the buyer may promise to assume a mortgage on the property or may promise to pay the purchase price to a creditor of the seller. If attorneys represent the parties, they very likely do so on a contractual basis. If the seller deposits the proceeds of the sale in a bank, he enters into a contract with the bank. If the buyer leases the property, he enters into a contract with the tenant. When one of the parties leaves his car in a parking lot to attend to any of these matters, he assumes a contractual relationship with the proprietor of the lot. In short, nearly every business transaction is based upon contract and the expectations the agreed-upon promises create. Knowing the legal requirements for making binding contracts is, therefore, essential.

DEVELOPMENT OF THE LAW OF CONTRACTS

That law arises from social necessity is clearly true of the law of contracts. The vast and complicated institution of business can be conducted efficiently and successfully only upon the certainty that promises will be fulfilled. Business must be assured not only of supplies of raw materials or manufactured goods, but also of labor, management, capital, and insurance as well. Common experience has shown that promises based solely on personal honesty or integrity do not have the reliability essential to business. Hence the development of the law of contracts, which is the law of enforceable promises.

Contract law, like law as a whole, is not static. It has undergone—and is still undergoing—enormous changes. In the nineteenth century virtually absolute autonomy in forming contracts was the rule. The law imposed contract liability only where the parties strictly complied with the required formalities. The same principle also dictated that once a contract was formed it should be enforced according to its terms and that neither party should be lightly excused from performance.

During the twentieth century, many of the formalities of contract formation were relaxed, and as a result, the law generally recognizes contractual obligations whenever the parties clearly manifest an intent to be bound. In addition, an increasing number of promises are now enforced in certain circumstances, even though they do not comply strictly with the basic requirements of a contract. While in the past contract liability was absolute and escape from liability, once assumed, was rare, presently the law allows a party to be excused from contractual duties where fraud, duress, undue influence, mistake, unconscionability, or impossibility is present. The law has expanded the nineteenth century's narrow view of contract damages to grant equitable remedies and restitution as remedies for breach of contract. The older doctrine of privity of contract, which sharply restricted which parties could enforce contract rights, has given way to the current view that permits intended third-party beneficiaries to sue in their own right.

In brief, the twentieth century left its mark on contract law by limiting the absolute freedom of contract and, at the same time, by relaxing the requirements of contract formation. Accordingly, it is now considerably easier to get into a contract and correspondingly less difficult to get out of one.

COMMON LAW

Contracts are primarily governed by State common law. An orderly presentation of this law is found in the Restatements of the Law of Contracts. The American Law Institute adopted and promulgated the first Restatement on May 6, 1932. On May 17, 1979, the institute adopted and promulgated a revised edition of the Restatement—the Restatement, Second, Contracts—which will be referred to as the Restatement. Regarded as a valuable authoritative reference work for more than seventy years, the Restatements have been extensively relied upon and quoted in reported judicial opinions.

THE UNIFORM COMMERCIAL CODE

The sale of personal property forms a substantial portion of commercial activity. Article 2 of the Uniform Commercial Code (the Code, or UCC) governs sales in all States except Louisiana. (Selected provisions of the UCC are set forth in *Appendix B* of this text.) A **sale** consists of the passing of title to goods from a seller to a buyer for a price. Section 2-106. A contract for sale includes both a present sale of goods and a contract to sell goods at a future time. Section 2-106. The Code essentially defines goods as movable personal property. Section 2-105(1). **Personal property** is any type of property other than an interest in real property (land). For example, the purchase of a television set, automobile, or textbook is considered a sale of goods. All such transactions are governed by Article 2 of the Code, but, where the Code has not specifically modified general contract law, the common law of contracts continues to apply. Section 1-103. In other words, the law of sales is a specialized part of the general law of contracts, and the law of contracts governs unless specifically displaced by the Code.

Amendments to Article 2 were promulgated in 2003 to accommodate electronic commerce and to reflect development of business practices, changes in other law, and interpretive difficulties of practical significance. Because no States had adopted them and prospects for enactment in the near future were bleak, the 2003 amendments to UCC Articles 2 and 2A were withdrawn in 2011. However, at least forty-five States have adopted the 2001 Revisions to Article 1, which applies to all of the articles of the Code.

◈ **SEE FIGURE 9-1: Law Governing Contracts**

◆ **SEE CASE 21-2**

TYPES OF CONTRACTS OUTSIDE THE CODE

General contract law governs all contracts outside the scope of the Code. Such contracts play a significant role in

◈ **FIGURE 9-1: Law Governing Contracts**

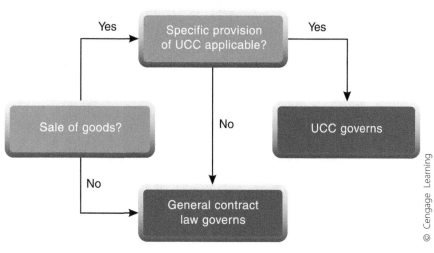

© Cengage Learning

commercial activities. For example, the Code does *not* apply to employment contracts, service contracts, insurance contracts, contracts involving **real property** (land and anything attached to it, including buildings as well as any right, privilege, or power in the real property, including leases, mortgages, options, and easements), and contracts for the sale of intangibles such as patents and copyrights. These transactions continue to be governed by general contract law.

◆ SEE CASE 9-1

DEFINITION OF A CONTRACT

A **contract** is a binding agreement that the courts will enforce. Section 1 of the Restatement more precisely defines a contract as "a promise or a set of promises for the breach of which the law gives a remedy, or the performance of which the law in some way recognizes as a duty." The Restatement provides further insight by defining a **promise** as "a manifestation of the intention to act or refrain from acting in a specified way." Restatement, Section 2.

Those promises that meet all of the essential requirements of a binding contract are contractual and will be enforced. All other promises are not contractual, and usually no legal remedy is available for a **breach** (a failure to perform properly) of these promises. The remedies provided for breach of contract (discussed in *Chapter 18*) include compensatory damages, equitable remedies, reliance damages, and restitution. Thus, a promise may be contractual (and therefore binding) or noncontractual. In other words, all contracts are promises, but not all promises are contracts.

◆ SEE FIGURE 9-2: **Contractual and Noncontractual Promises**

◆ SEE CASE 9-2

REQUIREMENTS OF A CONTRACT

The four basic requirements of a contract are as follows:

1. **Mutual assent**. The parties to a contract must manifest by words or conduct that they have agreed to enter into a contract. The usual method of showing mutual assent is by offer and acceptance.
2. **Consideration**. Each party to a contract must intentionally exchange a legal benefit or incur a legal detriment as an inducement to the other party to make a return exchange.
3. **Legality of object**. The purpose of a contract must not be criminal, tortious, or otherwise against public policy.
4. **Capacity**. The parties to a contract must have contractual capacity. Certain persons, such as those adjudicated (judicially declared) incompetent, have no legal capacity to contract, while others, such as minors, incompetent persons, and intoxicated persons, have limited capacity to contract. All others have full contractual capacity.

◆ FIGURE 9-2: **Contractual and Noncontractual Promises**

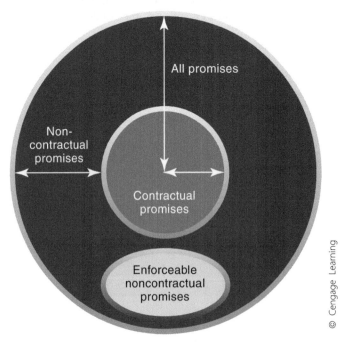

© Cengage Learning

In addition, though in some cases a contract must be evidenced by a writing to be enforceable, in most cases an oral contract is binding and enforceable. If all of these essentials are present, the promise is contractual and legally binding. If any is absent, however, the promise is noncontractual. These requirements will be separately considered in succeeding chapters.

◆ SEE FIGURE 9-3: **Validity of Agreements**

◆ SEE CASE 9-2

CLASSIFICATION OF CONTRACTS

Contracts can be classified according to various characteristics, such as method of formation, content, and legal effect. The standard classifications are (1) express or implied contracts; (2) unilateral or bilateral contracts; (3) valid, void, voidable, or unenforceable contracts; (4) executed or executory contracts; and (5) formal or informal contracts. These classifications are not mutually exclusive. For example, a contract may be express, bilateral, valid, executory, and informal.

◆ FIGURE 9-3: **Validity of Agreements**

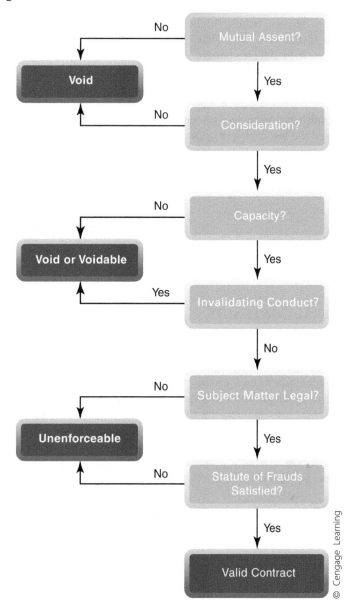

© Cengage Learning

EXPRESS AND IMPLIED CONTRACTS

Parties to a contract may indicate their assent either by express language or by conduct that implies such willingness. Thus, a contract may be (1) entirely oral; (2) partly oral and partly written; (3) entirely written; (4) partly oral or written and partly implied from the conduct of the parties; and (5) wholly implied from the conduct of the parties. The first three are known as express contracts, and the last two as implied contracts. Both express and implied contracts are genuine contracts, equally enforceable. The difference between them is merely the manner in which the parties manifest assent.

An **express contract** is therefore one in which the parties have manifested their agreement by oral or written language, or both.

An **implied contract** is one that is inferred from the parties' conduct, not from spoken or written words. Implied contracts are also called implied in fact contracts. Thus, if Elizabeth orders and receives a meal in Bill's restaurant, a promise is implied on Elizabeth's part to pay Bill the price stated in the menu or, if none is stated, Bill's customary price. Likewise, when a passenger boards a bus, a wholly implied contract is formed by which the passenger undertakes to pay the customary fare and the bus company undertakes to provide the passenger transportation.

◆ **SEE CASE 9-1**

PRACTICAL ADVICE

Whenever possible, try to use written express contracts that specify all of the important terms rather than using implied in fact contracts.

BILATERAL AND UNILATERAL CONTRACTS

In the typical contractual transaction, each party makes at least one promise. For example, if Ali says to Ben, "If you promise to mow my lawn, I will pay you ten dollars," and Ben agrees to mow Ali's lawn, Ali and Ben have made mutual promises, each undertaking to do something in exchange for the promise of the other. When a contract comes into existence by the exchange of promises, each party is under a duty to the other. This kind of contract is called a **bilateral contract**, because each party is both a *promisor* (a person making a promise) and a *promisee* (the person to whom a promise is made).

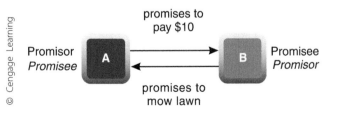

But suppose that only one of the parties makes a promise. Ali says to Ben, "If you will mow my lawn, I will pay you ten dollars." A contract will be formed when Ben has finished mowing the lawn and not before. At that time, Ali becomes contractually obligated to pay $10.00 to Ben. Ali's offer was in exchange for Ben's act of mowing the lawn, not for his promise to mow it. Because he never made a promise to mow the lawn, Ben was under no duty to mow it. This is a **unilateral contract** because only one of the parties made a promise.

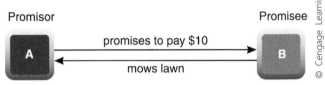

Thus, whereas a bilateral contract results from the exchange of a promise for a return promise, a unilateral contract results from the exchange of a promise either for an act or for a forbearance (refraining) from acting. If a contract is not clearly unilateral or bilateral, the courts presume that the parties intended a bilateral contract. Thus, in the previous example, if Ali says to Ben, "I will pay you ten dollars if you will mow my lawn," and Ben replies, "OK, I will mow your lawn," a bilateral contract is formed.

PRACTICAL ADVICE

Because it is uncertain whether the offeree in a unilateral contract will choose to perform, use bilateral contracts wherever possible.

VALID, VOID, VOIDABLE, AND UNENFORCEABLE CONTRACTS

By definition, a **valid contract** is one that meets all of the requirements of a binding contract. It is an enforceable promise or agreement.

A **void contract** is an agreement that does not meet all of the requirements of a binding contract. Thus, it is no contract at all; it is merely a promise or an agreement having no legal effect. An example of a void agreement is an agreement entered into by an adjudicated incompetent.

A voidable contract, on the other hand, is not wholly lacking in legal effect. A **voidable contract** is a contract, but because of the manner in which it was formed or a lack of capacity of a party to it, the law permits one or more of the parties to avoid the legal duties the contract creates. Restatement, Section 7. If the contract is avoided, both parties are relieved of their legal duties under the agreement. For instance, through intentional misrepresentation of a material fact (*fraud*), Thomas induces Regina to enter into a contract. Regina may, upon discovery of the fraud, notify Thomas that by reason of the misrepresentation she will not perform her promise, and the law will support Regina. Though not void, the contract induced by fraud is voidable at the election of Regina, the defrauded party. Thomas, the fraudulent party, has no such election. If Regina elects to avoid the contract, Thomas will be released from his promise under the agreement, although he may be liable under tort law for damages for fraud.

A contract that is neither void nor voidable may, nonetheless, be unenforceable. An **unenforceable contract** is one for the breach of which the law provides no remedy. Restatement, Section 8. For example, a contract may be unenforceable because of a failure to satisfy the requirements of the Statute of Frauds, which requires certain kinds of contracts to be evidenced by a writing to be enforceable. Also, the running of the time within which a suit may be filed, as provided in the Statute of Limitations, bars the right to bring a lawsuit for breach of contract. After that period has run, the contract is referred to as unenforceable, rather than void or voidable.

PRACTICAL ADVICE

Be careful to avoid entering into void, voidable, and unenforceable contracts.

EXECUTED AND EXECUTORY CONTRACTS

The terms *executed* and *executory* pertain to the state of performance of a contract. A contract fully performed by all of the parties to it is an **executed contract**. Strictly, an executed contract is in the present tense no contract, as all duties under it have been performed; but it is useful to have a term for a completed contract. (The word *executed* is also used to mean "signed," as in to execute or sign a certain document.)

The term **executory**, which means "unperformed," applies to situations in which one or more promises by any party to the contract are as yet unperformed or where the contract is wholly unperformed by one or more of the parties. Thus, David and Carla make a contract under which David is to sell and deliver certain goods to Carla in ten days and Carla is to pay the agreed price in thirty days. Prior to the delivery of the goods by David on the tenth day, the contract is wholly executory. Upon David's delivery of the goods to Carla, the contract is executed as to David and executory as to Carla. When Carla duly pays for the goods, the contract is wholly executed and thereby completely fulfilled.

FORMAL AND INFORMAL CONTRACTS

A **formal contract** depends upon a particular form, or mode of expression, for its legal existence. For example, at common law a promise under seal (a particular symbol that serves to authenticate an instrument) is enforceable without anything more. Another formal contract is a negotiable instrument, such as a check, which has certain legal attributes resulting solely from the special form in which it is made. A letter of credit (a promise to honor drafts or other demands for payment) is also a formal contract. Recognizances, or formal acknowledgments of indebtedness made in court, are another example of formal contracts. All other contracts, whether oral or written, are simple or **informal contracts**, as they do not depend upon formality for their legal validity.

PROMISSORY ESTOPPEL

As a general rule, promises are unenforceable if they do not meet all the requirements of a contract. Nevertheless, to avoid injustice, in certain circumstances courts enforce noncontractual promises under the doctrine of promissory estoppel. A noncontractual promise is enforceable when it is made under circumstances that should lead the promisor reasonably to expect that the promise would induce the promisee to take definite and substantial action or forbearance in reliance on the promise, and the promisee does take such action or forbearance. See *Figure 9-2*. Section 90 of the Restatement provides:

A promise which the promisor should reasonably expect to induce action or forbearance on the part of the promisee or a third person and which does induce such action or forbearance is binding if injustice can be avoided only by enforcement of the promise. The remedy granted for breach may be limited as justice requires.

For example, Gordon promises Constance not to foreclose for a period of six months on a mortgage Gordon owns on Constance's land. Constance then expends $100,000 to construct a building on the land. His promise not to foreclose is binding on Gordon under the doctrine of promissory estoppel.

◈ SEE FIGURE 9-4: **Contracts, Promissory Estoppel, and Quasi Contracts**

◆ SEE CASE 9-3

PRACTICAL ADVICE

Take care not to make promises on which others may detrimentally rely.

QUASI CONTRACTS

In addition to implied in fact contracts, there are implied in law, or quasi, contracts, which were not included in the

◆ **FIGURE 9-4: Contracts, Promissory Estoppel, and Quasi Contracts**

	Contract	Promissory Estoppel	Quasi Contract
Type of Promise	Contractual	Noncontractual	None Void Unenforceable Invalidated
Requirements	All of the essential elements of a contract	Detrimental and justifiable reliance	Benefit conferred and knowingly accepted
Remedies	Equitable Compensatory Reliance Restitution	Promise enforced to the extent necessary to avoid injustice	Reasonable value of benefit conferred

© Cengage Learning

foregoing classification of contracts because a quasi (meaning "as if") contract is not a contract at all but based in restitution. The term *quasi contract* is used because the remedy granted for quasi contract is similar to one of the remedies available for breach of contract.

A quasi contract is *not* a contract because it is based on neither an express nor an implied promise. A **contract implied in law** or quasi contract is an obligation imposed by law to avoid injustice. For example, Anna by mistake delivers to Robert a plain, unaddressed envelope containing $100 intended for Claudia. Robert is under no contractual obligation to return it. However, Anna is permitted to recover the $100 from Robert. The law imposes a quasi-contractual obligation upon Robert to prevent his unjust enrichment at Anna's expense. The elements of such a recovery are (1) a benefit conferred upon the defendant (Robert) by the plaintiff (Anna); (2) an appreciation or knowledge by the defendant (Robert) of the benefit; and (3) acceptance or retention by the defendant (Robert) of the benefit under circumstances rendering inequitable the defendant's (Robert's) retention of the benefit without compensating the plaintiff for its value.

One court has summarized the doctrine of quasi contract as follows:

Quasi contracts are not contracts at all, although they give rise to obligations more akin to those stemming from contract than from tort. The contract is a mere fiction, a form imposed in order to adapt the case to a given remedy....Briefly stated, a quasi-contractual obligation is one imposed by law where there has been no agreement or expression of assent, by word or act, on the part of either party involved. The law creates it, regardless of the intention of the parties, to assure a just and equitable result. *Bradkin v. Leverton*, 26 N.Y.2d 192, 309 N.Y.S.2d 192, 257 N.E.2d 643 (1970).

Not infrequently, courts use quasi contracts to provide a remedy when the parties have entered into a void contract, an unenforceable contract, or a voidable contract that is avoided. In such a case, the law of quasi contracts will determine the recovery permitted for any performance rendered by the parties under the invalid, unenforceable, or invalidated agreement.

◆ **SEE FIGURE 9-4: Contracts, Promissory Estoppel, and Quasi Contracts**

◆ **SEE CASE 9-4**

CHAPTER SUMMARY

DEVELOPMENT OF THE LAW OF CONTRACTS

Common Law most contracts are governed primarily by State common law, including contracts involving employment, services, insurance, real property (land and anything attached to it), patents, and copyrights

Uniform Commercial Code (UCC) Article 2 of the UCC governs the sales of goods
- *Sale* the transfer of title from seller to buyer
- *Goods* tangible personal property (personal property is all property other than an interest in land)

DEFINITION OF A CONTRACT	**Contract** binding agreement that the courts will enforce **Breach** failure to properly perform a contractual obligation
REQUIREMENTS OF A CONTRACT	**Mutual Assent** the parties to a contract must manifest by words or conduct that they have agreed to enter into a contract **Consideration** each party to a contract must intentionally exchange a legal benefit or incur a legal detriment as an inducement to the other party to make a return exchange **Legality of Object** the purpose of a contract must not be criminal, tortious, or otherwise against public policy **Capacity** the parties to a contract must have contractual capacity
CLASSIFICATION OF CONTRACTS	**Express and Implied Contracts** • *Express Contract* an agreement that is stated in words, either orally or in writing • *Implied in Fact Contract* a contract in which the agreement of the parties is inferred from their conduct **Bilateral and Unilateral Contracts** • *Bilateral Contract* a contract in which both parties exchange promises • *Unilateral Contract* a contract in which only one party makes a promise **Valid, Void, Voidable, and Unenforceable Contracts** • *Valid Contract* one that meets all of the requirements of a binding contract • *Void Contract* no contract at all; without legal effect • *Voidable Contract* a contract capable of being made void • *Unenforceable Contract* a contract for the breach of which the law provides no remedy **Executed and Executory Contracts** • *Executed Contract* a contract that has been fully performed by all of the parties • *Executory Contract* a contract that has yet to be fully performed **Formal and Informal Contracts** • *Formal Contract* an agreement that is legally binding because of its particular form or mode of expression • *Informal Contracts* all contracts other than formal contracts
PROMISSORY ESTOPPEL	**Definition** a doctrine enforcing some noncontractual promises **Requirements** a promise made under circumstances that should lead the promisor reasonably to expect that the promise would induce the promisee to take definite and substantial action, and the promisee does take such action **Remedy** a court will enforce the promise to the extent necessary to avoid injustice
QUASI CONTRACTS	**Definition** an obligation not based on contract that is imposed to avoid injustice **Requirements** a court will impose a quasi contract when (1) the plaintiff confers a benefit upon the defendant, (2) the defendant knows or appreciates the benefit, and (3) the defendant's retention of the benefit is inequitable **Remedy** the plaintiff recovers the reasonable value of the benefit she conferred upon the defendant

CASE 9-1

Contracts Outside the Code/Express and Implied Contracts
FOX v. MOUNTAIN WEST ELECTRIC, INC.
Supreme Court of Idaho, 2002
137 Idaho 703, 52 P.3d 848 2002, rehearing denied, 2002
http://scholar.google.com/scholar_case?q=52+P.3D+848&hl=en&as_sdt=2,34&case=12020421688825080366&scilh=0

Walters, J.

Lockheed Martin Idaho Technical Company ("LMITCO") requested bids for a comprehensive fire alarm system in its twelve buildings located in Idaho Falls. At a prebid meeting, MWE [Mountain West Electric, Inc.] and Fox met and discussed working together on the project. MWE was in the business of installing electrical wiring, conduit and related hookups and attachments. Fox provided services in designing, drafting, testing and assisting in the installation of fire alarm systems, and in ordering specialty equipment necessary for such projects. The parties concluded that it would be more advantageous for them to work together on the project than for each of them to bid separately for the entire job, and they further agreed that Fox would work under MWE. The parties prepared a document defining each of their roles entitled "Scope and Responsibilities."

Fox prepared a bid for the materials and services that he would provide, which was incorporated into MWE's bid to LMITCO. MWE was the successful bidder and was awarded the LMITCO fixed price contract. In May 1996, Fox began performing various services at the direction of MWE's manager. During the course of the project, many changes and modifications to the LMITCO contract were made.

A written contract was presented to Fox by MWE on August 7, 1996. A dispute between MWE and Fox arose over the procedure for the compensation of the change orders. MWE proposed a flow-down procedure, whereby Fox would receive whatever compensation LMITCO decided to pay MWE. This was unacceptable to Fox. Fox suggested a bidding procedure to which MWE objected. On December 5, 1996, Fox met with MWE to discuss the contract. No compensation arrangement was agreed upon by the parties with respect to change orders. Fox left the project on December 9, 1996, after delivering the remaining equipment and materials to MWE. MWE contracted with Life Safety Systems ("LSS") to complete the LMITCO project.

Fox filed a complaint in July 1998 seeking monetary damages representing money due and owing for materials and services provided by Fox on behalf of MWE. MWE answered and counterclaimed seeking monetary damages resulting from the alleged breach of the parties' agreement by Fox.

Following a court trial, the district court found that an implied-in-fact contract existed between the parties based on the industry standard's flow-down method of compensation. The court found in favor of MWE ... Fox appeals.

* * *

Implied-in-Fact Contract

* * *

This Court has recognized three types of contractual relationships:

First is the express contract wherein the parties expressly agree regarding a transaction. Secondly, there is the implied in fact contract wherein there is no express agreement, but the conduct of the parties implies an agreement from which an obligation in contract exists. The third category is called an implied in law contract, or quasi contract. However, a contract implied in law is not a contract at all, but an obligation imposed by law for the purpose of bringing about justice and equity without reference to the intent or the agreement of the parties and, in some cases, in spite of an agreement between the parties. It is a non-contractual obligation that is to be treated procedurally as if it were a contract, and is often refered (sic) to as quasi contract, unjust enrichment, implied in law contract or restitution.

[Citation.]

"An implied in fact contract is defined as one where the terms and existence of the contract are manifested by the conduct of the parties with the request of one party and the performance by the other often being inferred from the circumstances attending the performance." [Citation.] The implied-in-fact contract is grounded in the parties' agreement and tacit understanding. [Citation.] * * *

[UCC §] 1-205(1) defines "course of dealing" as "a sequence of previous conduct between the parties to a particular transaction which is fairly to be regarded as establishing a common basis of understanding for interpreting their expressions and other conduct."

* * *

Although the procedure was the same for each change order, in that MWE would request a pricing from Fox for the work, which was then presented to LMITCO, each party treated the pricings submitted by Fox for the change orders in a different manner. This treatment is not sufficient to establish a meeting of the minds or to establish a course of dealing when there was no "common basis of understanding for interpreting [the parties'] expressions" under [UCC §] 1-205(1).

* * * After a review of the record, it appears that the district court's findings are supported by substantial and competent, albeit conflicting, evidence. This Court will not substitute its view of the facts for the view of the district court.

Using the district court's finding that pricings submitted by Fox were used by MWE as estimates for the change orders, the conclusion made by the district court that an implied-in-fact contract allowed for the reasonable compensation of Fox logically follows and is grounded in the law in Idaho. [Citation.]

This Court holds that the district court did not err in finding that there was an implied-in-fact contract using the industry standard's flow-down method of compensation for the change orders rather than a series of fixed price contracts between MWE and Fox.

Uniform Commercial Code

Fox contends that the district court erred by failing to consider previous drafts of the proposed contract between the parties to determine the terms of the parties' agreement. Fox argues the predominant factor of this transaction was the fire alarm system, not the methodology of how the system was installed, which would focus on the sale of goods and, therefore, the Uniform Commercial Code ("UCC") should govern. Fox argues that in using the UCC various terms were agreed upon by the parties in the prior agreement drafts, including terms for the timing of payments, payments to Fox's suppliers and prerequisites to termination.

MWE contends that the UCC should not be used, despite the fact that goods comprised one-half of the contract price, because the predominant factor at issue is services and not the sale of goods. MWE points out that the primary issue is the value of Fox's services under the change orders and the cost of obtaining replacement services after Fox left the job. MWE further argues that the disagreement between the parties over material terms should prevent the court from using UCC gap fillers. Rather, MWE contends the intent and relationship of the parties should be used to resolve the conflict.

This Court in [citation], pointed out "in determining whether the UCC applies in such cases, a majority of courts look at the entire transaction to determine which aspect, the sale of goods or the sale of services, predominates." [Citation.] It is clear that if the underlying transaction to the contract involved the sale of goods, the UCC would apply. [Citation.] However, if the contract only involved services, the UCC would not apply. [Citation.] This Court has not directly articulated the standard to be used in mixed sales of goods and services, otherwise known as hybrid transactions.

The Court of Appeals in *Pittsley v. Houser*, [citation], focused on the applicability of the UCC to hybrid transactions. The court held that the trial court must look at the predominant factor of the transaction to determine if the UCC applies. [Citation.]

> The test for inclusion or exclusion is not whether they are mixed, but, granting that they are mixed, whether their predominant factor, their thrust, their purpose, reasonably stated, is the rendition of service, with goods incidentally involved (e.g., contract with artist for painting) or is a transaction of sale, with labor incidentally involved (e.g., installation of a water heater in a bathroom). This test essentially involves consideration of the contract in its entirety, applying the UCC to the entire contract or not at all.

[Citation.] This Court agrees with the Court of Appeals' analysis and holds that the predominant factor test should be used to determine whether the UCC applies to transactions involving the sale of both goods and services.

One aspect that the Court of Appeals noted in its opinion in *Pittsley*, in its determination that the predominant factor in that case was the sale of goods, was that the purchaser was more concerned with the goods and less concerned with the installation, either who would provide it or the nature of the work. MWE and Fox decided to work on this project together because of their differing expertise. MWE was in the business of installing electrical wiring, while Fox designed, tested and assisted in the installation of fire alarm systems, in addition to ordering specialty equipment for fire alarm projects.

The district court found that the contract at issue in this case contained both goods and services; however, the predominant factor was Fox's services. The district court found that the goods provided by Fox were merely incidental to the services he provided, and the UCC would provide no assistance in interpreting the parties' agreement.

This Court holds that the district court did not err in finding that the predominant factor of the underlying transaction was services and that the UCC did not apply.

* * *

This Court affirms the decision of the district court.

Definition and Requirements of a Contract
STEINBERG v. CHICAGO MEDICAL SCHOOL

Illinois Court of Appeals, 1976
41 Ill.App.3d 804, 354 N.E.2d 586
http://scholar.google.com/scholar_case?case=13765816040578352414&q=354+N.E.2d+586&hl=en&as_sdt=2,34

Dempsey, J.

In December 1973 the plaintiff, Robert Steinberg, applied for admission to the defendant, the Chicago Medical School, as a first-year student for the academic year 1974-75 and paid an application fee of $15. The Chicago Medical School is a private, not-for-profit educational institution, incorporated in the State of Illinois. His application for admission was rejected and Steinberg filed a[n] * * * action against the school, claiming that it had failed to evaluate his application * * * according to the academic entrance criteria printed in the school's bulletin. Specifically, his complaint alleged that the school's decision to accept or reject a particular applicant for the first-year class was primarily based on such nonacademic considerations as the prospective student's familial relationship to members of the school's faculty and to members of its board of trustees, and the ability of the applicant or his family to pledge or make payment of large sums of money to the school. The complaint further alleged that, by using such unpublished criteria to evaluate applicants, the school had breached the contract which Steinberg contended was created when the school accepted his application fee.

* * *

The defendant filed a motion to dismiss, arguing that the complaint failed to state a cause of action because no contract came into existence during its transaction with Steinberg inasmuch as the school's informational publication did not constitute a valid offer. The trial court sustained [ruled in favor of] the motion to dismiss and Steinberg appeals from this order.

* * *

A contract is an agreement between competent parties, based upon a consideration sufficient in law, to do or not do a particular thing. It is a promise or a set of promises for the breach of which the law gives a remedy, or the performance of which the law in some way recognizes as a duty. [Citation.] A contract's essential requirements are: competent parties, valid subject matter, legal consideration, mutuality of obligation and mutuality of agreement. Generally, parties may contract in any situation where there is no legal prohibition, since the law acts by restraint and not by conferring rights. [Citation.] However, it is basic contract law that in order for a contract to be binding the terms of the contract must be reasonably certain and definite. [Citation.]

A contract, in order to be legally binding, must be based on consideration. [Citation.] Consideration has been

defined to consist of some right, interest, profit or benefit accruing to one party or some forbearance, disadvantage, detriment, loss or responsibility given, suffered, or undertaken by the other. [Citation.] Money is a valuable consideration and its transfer or payment or promises to pay it or the benefit from the right to its use, will support a contract.

In forming a contract, it is required that both parties assent to the same thing in the same sense [citation] and that their minds meet on the essential terms and conditions. [Citation.] Furthermore, the mutual consent essential to the formation of a contract must be gathered from the language employed by the parties or manifested by their words or acts. The intention of the parties gives character to the transaction, and if either party contracts in good faith he is entitled to the benefit of his contract no matter what may have been the secret purpose or intention of the other party. [Citation.]

Steinberg contends that the Chicago Medical School's informational brochure constituted an invitation to make an offer; that his subsequent application and the submission of his $15 fee to the school amounted to an offer; that the school's voluntary reception of his fee constituted an acceptance and because of these events a contract was created between the school and himself. He contends that the school was duty bound under the terms of the contract to evaluate his application according to its stated standards and that the deviation from these standards not only breached the contract, but amounted to an arbitrary selection which constituted a violation of due process and equal protection. He concludes that such a breach did in fact take place each and every time during the past ten years that the school evaluated applicants according to their relationship to the school's faculty members or members of its board of trustees, or in accordance with their ability to make or pledge large sums of money to the school. Finally, he asserts that he is a member and a proper representative of the class that has been damaged by the school's practice.

The school counters that no contract came into being because informational brochures, such as its bulletin, do not constitute offers, but are construed by the courts to be general proposals to consider, examine and negotiate. The school points out that this doctrine has been specifically applied in Illinois to university informational publications.

* * *

We agree with Steinberg's position. We believe that he and the school entered into an enforceable contract; that the school's obligation under the contract was stated in the school's bulletin in a definitive manner and that by accepting his application fee—a valuable consideration—the school bound itself to fulfill its promises. Steinberg accepted the school's promises in good faith and he was entitled to have his application judged according to the school's stated criteria.

* * *

[Reversed and remanded.]

**CASE
9-3**

Promissory Estoppel
SKEBBA v. KASCH
Court of Appeals of Wisconsin, 2006
2006 WI App 232, 724 N.W.2d 408; review denied, 2007 WI 59
http://scholar.google.com/scholar_case?q=724+N.W.2d+408&hl=en&as_sdt=2,34&case=17278464423229519438&scilh=0

Kessler, J.

Skebba, a salesman, worked for many years for a company that eventually experienced serious financial difficulties. Kasch, with his brother, owned M.W. Kasch Co. Kasch hired Skebba as a sales representative, and over the years promoted him first to account manager, then to customer service manager, field sales manager, vice president of sales, senior vice president of sales and purchasing and finally to vice president of sales. Kasch's father was the original owner of the business, and had hired Skebba's father. Skebba's father mentored Kasch.

When M.W. Kasch Co. experienced serious financial problems in 1993, Skebba was solicited by another company to leave Kasch and work for them. When Skebba told Kasch he was accepting the new opportunity, Kasch asked what it would take to get him to stay, and noted that Skebba's leaving at this time would be viewed very negatively within the industry. Shortly thereafter, Skebba told Kasch that he needed security for his retirement and family and would stay if Kasch agreed to pay Skebba $250,000 if one of these three conditions occurred: (1) the company was sold; (2) Skebba was lawfully terminated; or (3) Skebba retired. Skebba reports, and the jury apparently found, that Kasch agreed to this proposal and Kasch promised to have the agreement drawn up. Skebba turned down the job opportunity and stayed with Kasch from December 1993 (when this discussion occurred) through 1999 when the company assets were sold.

Over the years, Skebba repeatedly asked Kasch for a written summary of this agreement; however, none was forthcoming. Eventually, Kasch sold the business. Kasch received $5.1 million dollars for his fifty-one percent share of the business when it was sold. Upon the sale of the business, Skebba asked Kasch for the $250,000 Kasch had previously promised to him, but Kasch refused, and denied ever having made such an agreement. Instead, Kasch gave Skebba a severance agreement which had been drafted by Kasch's lawyers in 1993. This agreement promised two years of salary contin-

uation on the sale of the company, but only if Skebba was not hired by the successor company and the severance agreement required a set-off against the salary continuation of any sums Skebba earned from any activity during the two years of the severance agreement. Skebba sued, alleging breach of contract and promissory estoppel.

The jury found there was no contract, but that Kasch had made a promise upon which Skebba relied to his detriment, that the reliance was foreseeable, and that Skebba was damaged in the amount of $250,000. The trial court concluded that, based on its reading of applicable case law, it could not specifically enforce the promise the jury found Kasch made to Skebba because there were other ways to measure damages. In motions after verdict, the trial court struck the jury's answer on damages, concluding that under *Hoffman* [*v. Red Owl Food Stores*], because Skebba did not prove what he would have earned had he taken the job with the other company, he could not establish what he had lost by relying on Kasch's promise and, therefore, had not proved his damages. We conclude that the trial court misread *Hoffman*. * * *

Kasch did *not* promise to pay Skebba more than Skebba would have earned at the job Skebba turned down. Kasch did *not* promise that total income to Skebba would be greater than in the turned-down job, no matter how long he remained with Kasch. Kasch *only* promised that if Skebba stayed, Kasch would pay Skebba $250,000 (the sum Skebba wanted for his retirement), at the earliest of (1) Kasch selling the business, (2) Skebba retiring, or (3) Skebba being lawfully terminated. Skebba stayed. Kasch sold the business while Skebba was still employed by Kasch. Kasch refused to pay as promised.

The purpose of promissory estoppel is to enforce promises where the failure to do so is unjust. *U.S. Oil Co., Inc. v. Midwest Auto Care Servs.*, [citation]. In this case, the trial court specifically relied on parts of *Hoffman* in determining that specific performance of the promise could not be awarded and in concluding that Skebba had not properly established damages. *Hoffman* was the first case in Wisconsin to adopt promissory estoppel. * * * [T]he *Hoffman* court explained its adoption of a cause of action based on promissory estoppel as grounded in section 90 of the Restatement of Contracts which:

> does not impose the requirement that the promise giving rise to the cause of action must be so comprehensive in scope as to meet the requirements of an offer that would ripen into a contract if accepted by the promisee. Rather the conditions imposed are:
>
> 1. Was the promise one which the promisor should reasonably expect to induce action or forbearance of a definite and substantial character on the part of the promisee?
> 2. Did the promise induce such action or forbearance?
> 3. Can injustice be avoided only by enforcement of the promise?

[Citation.]

The *Hoffman* court explains that the first two of these requirements are facts to be found by a jury or other factfinder, while the third is a policy decision to be made by the court. [Citations.] In making this policy decision, a court must consider a number of factors in determining whether injustice can only be avoided by enforcement of the promise. *U.S. Oil*, [citation]. The court in *U.S. Oil* adopted those considerations set forth in the Restatement (Second) of Contracts § 139(2), (1981):

> (a) the availability and adequacy of other remedies, particularly cancellation and restitution;
> (b) the definite and substantial character of the action or forbearance in relation to the remedy sought;
> (c) the extent to which the action or forbearance corroborates evidence of the making and terms of the promise, or the making and terms are otherwise established by clear and convincing evidence;
> (d) the reasonableness of the action or forbearance; [and]
> (e) the extent to which the action or forbearance was foreseeable by the promisor.

[Citation.]

The record does not indicate that the trial court here applied the considerations our supreme court announced in *U.S. Oil*. Instead, the trial court apparently relied on the *Hoffman* court's discussion of various damage theories that the court explained might be appropriate once the determi-

nation had been made to enforce the promise by application of promissory estoppel. * * *

* * *

A court, in fashioning a remedy, can consider any equitable *or* legal remedy which will "prevent injustice." * * *

As later commentators have noted, Wisconsin, with its landmark *Hoffman* decision, is one of a small group of states which recognizes that to fulfill the purpose of promissory estoppel—*i.e.*, prevent injustice—a court must be able to fashion a remedy that restores the promisee to where he or she would be if the promisor had fulfilled the promise. [Citation.] In this case, Skebba performed—he remained at M.W. Kasch—in reliance on Kasch's promise to pay $250,000 to him if one of three conditions occurred. Kasch enjoyed the fruits of Skebba's reliance—he kept on a top salesperson to help the company through tough financial times and he avoided the damage that he believed Skebba's leaving could have had on M.W. Kasch's reputation in the industry. Accordingly, to prevent injustice, the equitable remedy for Skebba to receive is Kasch's specific performance promised payment of the $250,000.

The record in this case, considered in light of the *U.S. Oil* tests and the jury's findings, compels specific performance of the promise because otherwise Kasch will enjoy all of the benefits of induced reliance while Skebba will be deprived of that which he was promised, with no other available remedy to substitute fairly for the promised reward. * * * In short, every factor this court requires to be considered supports enforcement of the promise through promissory estoppel. The trial court submitted the promissory estoppel cause of action to the jury. The jury concluded that the promise had been made, that Skebba relied on the promise to his detriment, and that such reliance was foreseeable by Kasch. The jury also found that Skebba's damages were the amount Skebba testified Kasch promised to pay Skebba if he was still employed when the company was sold, that is, $250,000. * * *

* * * In this case, specific performance *is* the *necessary* enforcement mechanism to prevent injustice for Skebba's reliance on the promise the jury found Kasch had made to him.

Accordingly, we conclude that the trial court erred in holding that specific performance was not available on this promissory estoppel claim. We further conclude that the trial court erred in its application of *Hoffman* to the facts of this case. We reverse and remand for further proceedings consistent with this opinion.

Order reversed and cause remanded.

CASE
9-4

Quasi Contracts
JASDIP PROPERTIES SC, LLC v. ESTATE OF RICHARDSON
Court of Appeals of South Carolina, 2011
395 S.C. 633, 720 S.E.2d 485
http://scholar.google.com/scholar_case?q=720+S.E.2d+485&hl=en&as_sdt=2,34&case=460584843454513831&scilh=0

Konduros, J.

[On May 5, 2006, Stewart Richardson (Seller) and JASDIP Properties SC, LLC (Buyer) entered into an agreement for the purchase of certain property in Georgetown, South Carolina. The purchase price for the property was to be $537,000. The buyer paid an initial earnest money deposit of $10,000. The balance was due at the closing scheduled for no later than July 28, 2006. Subsequently the seller granted the buyer extensions to the closing date in return for additional payments of $175,000 and $25,000, each to be applied to the purchase price. The buyer was unable to close in a timely fashion, and the seller rescinded the contract.

Thereafter, the buyer brought suit against the seller (1) contending that the seller would be unjustly enriched if allowed to keep the money paid despite the rescission of the agreement and (2) requesting $210,000. The $210,000 consisted of the $10,000 earnest money deposit and $200,000 in subsequent payments. The buyer later filed an amended complaint requesting $205,000, stating that the agreement permitted the seller to retain half of the $10,000 earnest money deposit.

A jury determined that neither party had breached the contract and awarded no damages on that basis. The buyer then requested a ruling by the trial court on its action for unjust enrichment. The trial court denied the buyer's claim for unjust enrichment. The buyer appealed arguing that all the evidence presented at trial, as well as the jury's verdict, supports a finding that the agreement was rescinded or abandoned and that this requires restitution of $205,000 to the buyer.]

"Restitution is a remedy designed to prevent unjust enrichment." [Citation.] ("Unjust enrichment is an equitable doctrine, akin to restitution, which permits the recovery of that amount the defendant has been unjustly enriched at the expense of the plaintiff."). "The terms 'restitution' and 'unjust enrichment' are modern designations for the older doctrine of quasi-contract." [Citation.] "[Q]uantum meruit, quasi-contract, and implied by law contract are equivalent terms for an equitable remedy." [Citation.]

"Implied in law or quasi-contract are not considered contracts at all, but are akin to restitution which permits

recovery of that amount the defendant has been benefitted at the expense of the plaintiff in order to preclude unjust enrichment." [Citation.] * * *

"To recover on a theory of restitution, the plaintiff must show (1) that he conferred a non-gratuitous benefit on the defendant; (2) that the defendant realized some value from the benefit; and (3) that it would be inequitable for the defendant to retain the benefit without paying the plaintiff for its value." [Citation.] "Unjust enrichment is usually a prerequisite for enforcement of the doctrine of restitution; if there is no basis for unjust enrichment, there is no basis for restitution." [Citation.]

Buyer seeks the $175,000 and $25,000 payments as well as the $10,000 in earnest money * * * Additionally, in its amended complaint, Buyer states that under the Agreement, Seller can only keep half of the $10,000 in earnest money and only requests a total of $205,000. An issue conceded in the trial court cannot be argued on appeal. [Citation.] Therefore, Buyer is bound by that concession and entitled to $5,000 of the earnest money at most.

The $175,000 and $25,000 payments both explicitly stated that they were towards the purchase price. Additionally, Buyer paid $10,000 in an earnest money deposit. The unappealed finding of the jury was that neither party breached the Agreement. An unchallenged ruling, right or wrong, is the law of the case. [Citation.] Based on the jury's finding that Buyer did not breach, we find Buyer is entitled to the money paid towards the purchase price as well as half of the earnest money under the theory of restitution. Buyer met the requirements to recover under the theory of restitution: (1) Buyer paid Seller $205,000 towards the purchase price and the sale did not go through despite the fact that neither party breached; (2) Seller kept the $205,000 although he also retained the Property; and (3) Seller keeping the $205,000 is inequitable because the Seller still has the Property, the jury found neither party breached, and the evidence supports that Buyer intended to go forward with the purchase. Therefore, the trial court erred in failing to find for Buyer for its claim of unjust enrichment. Accordingly, we reverse the trial court's determination that Buyer was not entitled to restitution and award Buyer $205,000.

QUESTIONS

1. Owen telephones an order to Hillary's store for certain goods, which Hillary delivers to Owen. Neither party says anything about the price or payment terms. What are the legal obligations of Owen and Hillary?

2. Minth is the owner of the Hiawatha Supper Club, which he leased for two years to Piekarski. During the period of the lease, Piekarski contracted with Puttkammer for the resurfacing of the access and service areas of the supper club. Puttkammer performed the work satisfactorily. Minth knew about the contract and the performance of the work. The work, including labor and materials, had a reasonable value of $2,540, but Puttkammer was never paid because Piekarski went bankrupt. Puttkammer brought an action against Minth to recover the amount owed to him by Piekarski. Will Puttkammer prevail? Explain.

3. Jonathan writes to Willa, stating "I'll pay you $150 if you reseed my lawn." Willa reseeds Jonathan's lawn as requested. Has a contract been formed? If so, what kind?

4. Calvin uses fraud to induce Maria to promise to pay money in return for goods he has delivered to her. Has a contract been formed? If so, what kind? What are the rights of Calvin and Maria?

5. Anna is about to buy a house on a hill. Prior to the purchase she obtains a promise from Betty, the owner of the adjacent property, that Betty will not build any structure that would block Anna's view. In reliance on this promise Anna buys the house. Is Betty's promise binding? Why or why not?

CASE PROBLEMS

6. Mary Dobos was admitted to Boca Raton Community Hospital in serious condition with an abdominal aneurysm. The hospital called upon Nursing Care Services, Inc., to provide around-the-clock nursing services for Mrs. Dobos. She received two weeks of in-hospital care, forty-eight hours of postrelease care, and two weeks of at-home care. The total bill was $3,723.90. Mrs. Dobos refused to pay, and Nursing Care Services, Inc., brought an action to recover. Mrs. Dobos maintained that she was not obligated to render payment in that she never signed a written contract, nor did she orally agree to be liable for the services. The necessity for the services, reasonableness of the fee, and competency of the nurses were undisputed. After Mrs. Dobos admitted that she or her daughter authorized the forty-eight hours of postrelease care, the trial court ordered compensation of $248 for that period. It did not allow payment of the balance, and Nursing Care Services, Inc., appealed. Decision?

7. St. Charles Drilling Co. contracted with Osterholt to install a well and water system that would produce a specified quantity of water. The water system failed to meet its warranted capacity, and Osterholt sued for breach of contract. Does the Uniform Commercial Code (UCC) apply to this contract?

8. Helvey brought suit against the Wabash County REMC (REMC) for breach of implied and express warranties. He alleged that REMC furnished electricity in excess of 135 volts to Helvey's home, damaging his 110-volt household appliances. This incident occurred more than four years before Helvey brought this suit. In defense, REMC pleads that the Uniform Commercial Code's (UCC's) Article 2 statute of limitations of four years has passed, thereby barring Helvey's suit. Helvey argues that providing electrical energy is not a transaction in goods under the UCC but rather a furnishing of services that would make applicable the general contract six-year statute of limitations. Is the contract governed by the UCC? Why?

9. Jack Duran, president of Colorado Carpet Installation, Inc., began negotiations with Fred and Zuma Palermo for the sale and installation of carpeting, carpet padding, tile, and vinyl floor covering in their home. Duran drew up a written proposal that referred to Colorado Carpet as "the seller" and to the Palermos as "the customer." The proposal listed the quantity, unit cost, and total price of each item to be installed. The total price of the job was $4,777.75. Although labor was expressly included in this figure, Duran estimated the total labor cost at $926. Mrs. Palermo in writing accepted Duran's written proposal soon after he submitted it to her. After Colorado Carpet delivered the tile to the Palermo home, however, Mrs. Palermo had a disagreement with Colorado Carpet's tile man and arranged for another contractor to perform the job. Colorado Carpet brought an action against the Palermos for breach of contract. Does the Uniform Commercial Code apply to this contract?

10. On November 1, the Kansas City Post Office Employees Credit Union merged into the Kansas City Telephone Employees Credit Union to form the Communications Credit Union (Credit Union). Systems Design and Management Information (SDMI) develops computer software programs for credit unions, using Burroughs (now Unisys) hardware. SDMI and Burroughs together offered to sell to Credit Union both a software package, called the Generic System, and Burroughs hardware. Later in November, a demonstration of the software was held at SDMI's offices, and the Credit Union agreed to purchase the Generic System software. This agreement was oral. After Credit Union was converted to the SDMI Generic System, major problems with the system immediately became apparent, so SDMI filed suit against Credit Union to recover the outstanding contract price for the software. Credit Union counterclaimed for damages based upon breach of contract and negligent and fraudulent misrepresentation. Does the Uniform Commercial Code apply to this contract?

11. Insul-Mark is the marketing arm of Kor-It Sales, Inc. Kor-It manufactures roofing fasteners, and Insul-Mark distributes them nationwide. Kor-It contracted with Modern Materials, Inc., to have large volumes of screws coated with a rust-proofing agent. The contract specified that the coated screws must pass a standard industry test and that Kor-It would pay according to the pound and length of the screws coated. Kor-It had received numerous complaints from customers that the coated screws were rusting, and Modern Materials unsuccessfully attempted to remedy the problem. Kor-It terminated its relationship with Modern Materials and brought suit for the deficient coating. Modern Materials counterclaimed for the labor and materials it had furnished to Kor-It. The trial court held that the contract (a) was for performance of a service, (b) not governed by the UCC, (c) governed by the common law of contracts, and (d) therefore, barred by a two-year statute of limitations. Insul-Mark appealed. Decision?

12. In March, William Tackaberry, a real estate agent for Weichert Co. Realtors, informed Thomas Ryan, a local developer, that he knew of property Ryan might be interested in purchasing. Ryan indicated he was interested in knowing more about the property. Tackaberry disclosed the property's identity and the seller's proposed price. Tackaberry also stated that the purchaser would have to pay Weichert a 10 percent commission. Tackaberry met with the property owner and gathered information concerning the property's current leases, income, expenses, and development plans. Tackaberry also collected tax and zoning documents relevant to the property. In a face-to-face meeting on April 4, Tackaberry gave Ryan the data he had gathered and presented Ryan with a letter calling for a 10 percent finder's fee to be paid to Weichert by Ryan upon "successfully completing and closing of title." Tackaberry arranged a meeting, held three days later, where Ryan contracted with the owner to buy the land. Ryan refused, however, to pay the 10 percent finder's fee to Weichert. Weichert sues Ryan for the finder's fee. To what, if anything, is Weichert entitled to recover? Explain.

13. Max E. Pass, Jr., and his wife, Martha N. Pass, departed in an aircraft owned and operated by Mr. Pass from Plant City, Florida, bound for Clarksville, Tennessee. Somewhere over Alabama the couple encountered turbulence, and Mr. Pass lost control of the aircraft. The plane crashed killing both Mr. and Mrs. Pass. Approximately four and a half months prior to the flight in which he was killed, Mr. Pass had taken his airplane to Shelby Aviation, an aircraft service company, for inspection and service. In servicing the aircraft, Shelby Aviation replaced both rear wing attach point brackets on the plane. Three and one half years after the crash, Max E. Pass, Sr., father of Mr. Pass and administrator of his estate, and Shirley Williams, mother of Mrs. Pass and administratrix of her estate, filed suit against Shelby Aviation. The lawsuit alleged that the rear wing attach point brackets sold and installed by Shelby Aviation were defective because they lacked the bolts necessary to secure them properly to the airplane. The plaintiffs asserted claims against the defendant for breach of express and implied warranties under Article 2 of the Uniform Commercial Code (UCC), which governs the sale of goods. Shelby Aviation contended that the transaction with Mr. Pass had been primarily for the sale of services, rather than of goods, and that consequently Article 2 of the UCC did not cover the transaction. Does the UCC apply to this transaction? Explain.

TAKING SIDES

Richardson hired J. C. Flood Company, a plumbing contractor, to correct a stoppage in the sewer line of her house. The plumbing company's "snake" device, used to clear the line leading to the main sewer, became caught in the underground line. To release it, the company excavated a portion of the sewer line in Richardson's backyard. In the process, the company discovered numerous leaks in a rusty, defective water pipe that ran parallel with the sewer line. To meet public regulations, the water pipe, of a type no longer approved for such service, had to be replaced either then or later, when the yard would have to be excavated again. The plumbing company proceeded to repair the water pipe. Though Richardson inspected the company's work daily and did not express any objection to the extra work involved in replacing the water pipe, she refused to pay any part of the total bill after the company completed the entire operation. J. C. Flood Company then sued Richardson for the costs of labor and material it had furnished.

a. What arguments would support J. C. Flood's claim for the costs of labor and material it had furnished?

b. What arguments would support Richardson's refusal to pay the bill?

c. For what, if anything, should Richardson be liable? Explain.

CHAPTER 8

Mutual Assent

CHAPTER OUTCOMES

After reading and studying this chapter, you should be able to:

- Identify the three essentials of an offer and explain briefly the requirements associated with each.

- State the seven ways by which an offer may be terminated other than by acceptance.

- Compare the traditional and modern theories of definiteness of acceptance of an offer, as shown by the common law "mirror image" rule and by the rule of the Uniform Commercial Code.

- Describe the five situations limiting an offeror's right to revoke her offer.

- Explain the various rules that determine when an acceptance takes effect.

Although each of the requirements for forming a contract is essential to its existence, mutual assent is so basic that frequently a contract is referred to as the agreement between the parties. The Restatement, Section 3, provides this definition: "An agreement is a manifestation of mutual assent on the part of two or more parties." Enforcing the contract means enforcing the agreement; indeed, the agreement between the parties is the very core of the contract.

The manner in which parties usually show mutual assent is by **offer** and **acceptance**. One party makes a proposal (offer) by words or conduct to the other party, who agrees by words or conduct to the proposal (acceptance). A contractual agreement always involves either a promise exchanged for a promise (*bilateral contract*) or a promise exchanged for an act or forbearance to act (*unilateral contract*), as manifested by what the parties communicate to one another.

An implied contract may be formed by conduct. Thus, though there may be no definite offer and acceptance, or definite acceptance of an offer, a contract exists if both parties have acted in a manner that manifests (indicates) a recognition by each of them of the existence of a contract. It may be impossible to determine the exact moment at which a contract was made.

To form the contract, the parties must manifest their agreement objectively. The important thing is what the parties indicate to one another by spoken or written words or by conduct. The law applies an **objective standard** and, therefore, is concerned only with the assent, agreement, or intention of a party as it reasonably appears from his words or actions. The law of contracts is not concerned with what a party may have actually thought or the meaning that he intended to convey, even if his subjective understanding or intention differed from the meaning he objectively indicated by word or conduct. For example, if Leslie seemingly offers to sell to Sam her Chevrolet automobile but intends to offer and believes that she is offering her Ford automobile, and Sam accepts the offer, reasonably believing it was for the Chevrolet, a contract has been formed for the sale of the Chevrolet. Subjectively, there is no agreement as to the subject matter, but objectively there is a manifestation of agreement, and the objective manifestation is binding.

The Uniform Commercial Code's (UCC or Code) treatment of mutual assent is covered in greater detail in *Chapter 21*.

OFFER

An offer is a definite proposal or undertaking made by one person to another that manifests a willingness to enter into a bargain. The person making the proposal is the **offeror**. The person to whom it is made is the **offeree**. Upon receipt, the offer confers on the offeree the power of acceptance, by which the offeree expresses her willingness to comply with the terms of the offer.

The communication of an offer to an offeree does not of itself confer any rights or impose any duties on either of the parties. The offeror, by making his offer, simply confers upon the offeree the power to create a contract by accepting the offer. Until the offeree exercises this power, the outstanding offer creates neither rights nor liabilities.

An offer may take several forms: (1) It may propose a promise for a promise. (This is an offer to enter into a bilateral contract.) An example is an offer to sell and deliver goods in thirty days in return for the promise to pay a stipulated amount upon delivery of the goods. If the offeree accepts this offer, the resulting contract consists of the parties' mutual promises, each made in exchange for the other. (2) An offer may be a promise for an act. (This is an offer to enter into a unilateral contract.) A common example is an offer of a reward for certain information or for the return of lost property. The offeree can accept such an offer only by the performance of the act requested. (3) An offer may be in the form of an act for a promise. (This is an offer to enter into an "inverted" unilateral contract.) For example, Maria offers the stated price to a clerk in a theater ticket office and asks for a ticket for a certain performance. The clerk can accept this offer of an act only by delivery of the requested ticket, which amounts, in effect, to the theater owner's promise to admit Maria to the designated performance.

ESSENTIALS OF AN OFFER

An offer need not take any particular form to have legal validity. To be effective, however, it must (1) be communicated to the offeree, (2) manifest an intent to enter into a contract, and (3) be sufficiently definite and certain. If these essentials are present, an offer that has not terminated gives the offeree the power to form a contract by accepting the offer.

COMMUNICATION

To have the mutual assent required to form a contract, the offeree must have knowledge of the offer; he cannot agree to something of which he has no knowledge. Accordingly, the offeror must communicate the offer, in an intended manner, to the offeree.

For example, Andre signs a letter containing an offer to Bonnie and leaves it on top of the desk in his office. Later that day, Bonnie, without prearrangement, goes to Andre's office, discovers that Andre is away, notices the letter on his desk, reads it, and writes on it an acceptance which she dates and signs. No contract is formed because the offer never became effective; Andre never communicated it to Bonnie. If Andre had mailed the letter, and it had gone astray in the mail, the offer would likewise never have become effective.

Not only must the offer be communicated to the offeree, but the communication must also be made or authorized by the offeror. For instance, if Joanne tells Karlene that she plans to offer Larry $600 for his piano, and Karlene promptly informs Larry of this proposal, no offer has been made. There was no authorized communication of any offer by

Joanne to Larry. By the same token, if Lance should offer to sell his diamond ring to Ed, an acceptance of this offer by Donnese would not be effective, because Lance made the offer to Ed, not to Donnese.

An offer need not be stated or communicated by words. Conduct from which a reasonable person may infer a proposal in return for either an act or a promise amounts to an offer.

An offer may be made to the general public. No person, however, can accept such an offer until and unless he has knowledge that the offer exists. For example, if a person, without knowing of an advertised reward for information leading to the return of a lost watch, gives information that leads to its return, he is not entitled to the reward. His act was not an acceptance of the offer because he could not accept something of which he had no knowledge.

INTENT

To have legal effect an offer must manifest an intent to enter into a contract. The intent of an offer is determined objectively from the words or conduct of the parties. The meaning of either party's manifestation is based upon what a reasonable person in the other party's position would have believed. The courts sometimes consider subjective intention in interpreting the parties' communications (the interpretation of contracts is discussed in *Chapter 16*).

Occasionally, a person exercises her sense of humor by speaking or writing words that—taken literally and without regard to context or surrounding circumstances—a promisee could construe as an offer. The promisor intends the promise as a joke, however, and the promisee as a reasonable person should understand it to be such. Therefore, it is not an offer. Because the person to whom it is made realizes or should realize that it is not made in earnest, it should not create a reasonable expectation in his mind. No contractual intent exists on the part of the promisor, and the promisee is or reasonably ought to be aware of that fact. If, however, the intended jest is so successful that the promisee as a reasonable person under all the circumstances believes that the joke is in fact an offer, and so believing accepts, the objective standard applies and the parties have entered into a contract.

A promise made under obvious excitement or emotional strain is likewise not an offer. For example, Charlotte, after having her month-old Cadillac break down for the third time in two days, screams in disgust, "I will sell this car to anyone for $100.00!" Lisa hears Charlotte and hands her a one hundred-dollar bill. Under the circumstances, Charlotte's statement was not an offer, if a reasonable person in Lisa's position would have recognized it merely as an overwrought, nonbinding utterance.

It is important to distinguish language that constitutes an offer from that which merely solicits or invites offers.

Such proposals, although made in earnest, lack intent and are therefore not deemed offers. As a result, a purported acceptance does not bring about a contract but operates only as an offer to accept. These proposals include preliminary negotiations, advertisements, and auctions.

■ PRACTICAL ADVICE ■

Make sure that you indicate by words or conduct what agreement you wish to enter.

◆ SEE CASE 10-1

PRELIMINARY NEGOTIATIONS If a communication creates in the mind of a reasonable person in the position of the offeree an expectation that his acceptance will conclude a contract, then the communication is an offer. If it does not, then the communication is a preliminary negotiation. Initial communications between potential parties to a contract often take the form of preliminary negotiations, through which the parties either request or supply the terms of an offer that may or may not be given. A statement that may indicate a willingness to make an offer is not in itself an offer. If Terri writes to Susan, "Will you buy my automobile for $3,000?" and Susan replies "Yes," no contract exists. Terri has not made an offer to sell her automobile to Susan for $3,000. The offeror must manifest an intent to enter into a contract, not merely a willingness to enter into negotiation.

ADVERTISEMENTS Merchants desire to sell their merchandise and thus are interested in informing potential customers about the goods, terms of sale, and the price. But if they make widespread promises to sell to each person on their mailing list, the number of acceptances and resulting contracts might conceivably exceed their ability to perform. Consequently, a merchant might refrain from making offers by merely announcing that he has goods for sale, describing the goods, and quoting prices. He is simply inviting his customers and, in the case of published advertisements, the public, to make offers to him to buy the goods. His advertisements, circulars, quotation sheets, and merchandise displays are *not* offers because (1) they do not contain a promise and (2) they leave unexpressed many terms that would be necessary to the making of a contract. Accordingly, his customers' responses are not acceptances because he has made no offer to sell.

Nonetheless, a seller is not free to advertise goods at one price and then raise the price once demand has been stimulated. Although, as far as contract law is concerned, the seller has made no offer, such conduct is prohibited by the Federal Trade Commission as well as by legislation in many States. (See *Chapter 41.*)

Moreover, in some circumstances a public announcement or advertisement may constitute an offer if the advertisement or announcement contains a definite promise of something in exchange for something else and confers a power of acceptance upon a specified person or class of persons. The typical offer of a reward is an example of a definite offer, as was shown in *Lefkowitz v. Great Minneapolis Surplus Store, Inc.* In this case, the court held that a newspaper advertisement was an offer because it contained a promise of performance in definite terms in return for a requested act.

◆ SEE CASE 10-2

AUCTION SALES The auctioneer at an auction sale does *not* make offers to sell the property that is being auctioned but invites offers to buy. The classic statement by the auctioneer is, "How much am I offered?" The persons attending the auction may make progressively higher bids for the property, and each bid or statement of a price or a figure is an offer to buy at that figure. If the bid is accepted—this customarily is indicated by the fall of the hammer in the auctioneer's hand—a contract results. A bidder is free to withdraw his bid at any time prior to its acceptance. The auctioneer is likewise free to withdraw the goods from sale *unless* the sale is advertised or announced to be without reserve.

If the auction sale is advertised or announced in explicit terms to be **without reserve**, the auctioneer may not withdraw an article or lot put up for sale unless no bid is made within a reasonable time. Unless so advertised or announced, the sale is with reserve. A bidder at either type of sale may retract his bid at any time prior to acceptance by the auctioneer. Such retraction, however, does not revive any previous bid.

DEFINITENESS

The terms of a contract, all of which the offer usually contains, must be reasonably certain so as to provide a court with a basis for determining the existence of a breach and for giving an appropriate remedy. Restatement, Section 33. It is a fundamental policy that contracts should be made by the parties and not by the courts; accordingly, remedies for breach must have their basis in the parties' contract.

However, where the parties have intended to form a contract, the courts will attempt to find a basis for granting a remedy. Missing terms may be supplied by course of dealing, usage of trade, or inference. Thus, uncertainty as to incidental matters will seldom be fatal so long as the parties intended to form a contract. Nevertheless, the more terms the parties leave open, the less likely it is that they have intended to form a contract. Because of the great variety of contracts, the terms essential to all contracts cannot be stated. In most cases, however, material terms would include the parties, subject matter, price, quantity, quality, and time of performance.

◆ SEE CASE 10-3

OPEN TERMS With respect to agreements for the sale of goods, the Code provides standards by which omitted terms may be determined, provided the parties intended to enter into a binding contract. The Code provides missing terms in a number of instances, where, for example, the contract fails to specify the price, the time or place of delivery, or payment terms. Sections 2–204(3), 2–305, 2–308, 2–309, and 2–310. The Restatement, Section 34, has adopted an approach similar to the Code's in supplying terms the parties have omitted from their contract.

Under the Code, an offer for the purchase or sale of goods may leave open particulars of performance to be specified by one of the parties. Any such specification must be made in good faith and within limits set by commercial reasonableness. Section 2–311(1). **Good faith** is defined as honesty in fact and the observance of reasonable commercial standards of fair dealing under the 2001 Revised UCC Article 1 adopted by at least forty-three States. 1–201(20). (Under the original UCC, good faith means honesty in fact in the conduct or transaction concerned. Section 1–201(19).) Commercial reasonableness is a standard determined in terms of the business judgment of reasonable persons familiar with the practices customary in the type of transaction involved and in terms of the facts and circumstances of the case.

If the price is to be fixed otherwise than by agreement and is not so fixed through the fault of one of the parties, the other party has an option to treat the contract as cancelled or to fix a reasonable price in good faith for the goods. However, where the parties intend not to be bound unless the price is fixed or agreed upon as provided in the agreement, and it is not so fixed or agreed upon, the Code provides in accordance with the parties' intent that no contractual liability exists. In such case the seller must refund to the buyer any portion of the price she has received, and the buyer must return the goods to the seller or, if unable to do so, pay the reasonable value of the goods. Section 2–305(4).

◆ SEE CASE 12-4

PRACTICAL ADVICE

To make an offer that will result in an enforceable contract, make sure you include all the necessary terms.

OUTPUT AND REQUIREMENTS CONTRACTS A buyer's agreement to purchase the entire output of a seller's factory for a stated period, or a seller's agreement to supply a buyer with all his requirements for certain goods, may appear to lack definiteness and mutuality of obligation. Such an agreement does not specify the exact quantity of goods; moreover, the seller may have some control over her output and the buyer over his requirements. Nonetheless, under the Code and the Restatement such agreements are enforceable by the application of an objective standard based upon the good faith of both parties. Thus, a seller who operated her factory for eight hours a day before entering an output agreement cannot operate her factory twenty-four hours a day and insist that the buyer take all of the output. Nor can the buyer expand his business abnormally and insist that the seller still supply all of his requirements.

DURATION OF OFFERS

An offer confers upon the offeree a power of acceptance, which continues until the offer terminates. The ways in which an offer may be terminated, *other than by acceptance*, are through (1) lapse of time; (2) revocation; (3) rejection; (4) counteroffer; (5) death or incompetency of the offeror or offeree; (6) destruction of the subject matter to which the offer relates; and (7) subsequent illegality of the type of contract the offer proposes.

LAPSE OF TIME

The offeror may specify the time within which the offer is to be accepted, just as he may specify any other term or condition in the offer. He may require that the offeree accept the offer immediately or within a **specified** period, such as a week or ten days. Unless otherwise terminated, the offer remains open for the specified period. Upon the expiration of that time, the offer no longer exists and cannot be accepted. Any subsequent purported acceptance will serve as a new offer.

If the offer states no time within which the offeree must accept, the offer will terminate after a **reasonable** time. Determining a "reasonable" period of time is a question of fact, depending on the nature of the contract proposed, the usages of business, and other circumstances of the case (including whether the offer was communicated by electronic means). Restatement, Section 41. For instance, an offer to sell a perishable good would be open for a far shorter time than an offer to sell undeveloped real estate.

PRACTICAL ADVICE

Because of the uncertainty as to what is a "reasonable time," it is advisable to specify clearly the duration of offers you make.

◆ SEE CASE 10-4

REVOCATION

An offeror generally may withdraw an offer at any time before it has been accepted, even though he has definitely promised to keep it open for a stated time. To be effective, notice of revocation of the offer must actually reach the offeree before she has accepted. If the offeror originally promises that the offer will be open for thirty days, but after five days wishes to terminate it, he may do so merely by giving the offeree notice that he is withdrawing the offer. Notice, which may be given by any means of communication, effectively terminates the offer when **received** by the offeree. A very few States, however, have adopted a rule that treats revocations the same as acceptances, thus making them effective upon dispatch. An offeror, however, may revoke an offer made to the general public only by giving to the revocation publicity equivalent to that given the offer.

Notice of revocation may be communicated indirectly to the offeree through reasonably reliable information from a third person that the offeror has disposed of the goods which he has offered for sale or has otherwise placed himself in a position which indicates an unwillingness or inability to perform the promise contained in the offer. Restatement, Section 43. For example, Jane offers to sell her portable television set to Bruce and tells Bruce that he has ten days in which to accept. One week later, Bruce observes the television set in Carl's house and is informed that Carl had purchased it from Jane. The next day Bruce sends to Jane an acceptance of the offer. There is no contract, because Jane's offer was effectively revoked when Bruce learned of Jane's inability to sell the television set to him because she had sold it to Carl.

Certain limitations, however, restrict the offeror's power to revoke the offer at any time prior to its acceptance. These limitations apply to the following five situations.

OPTION CONTRACTS

An option is a contract by which the offeror is bound to hold open an offer for a specified period of time. It must comply with all of the requirements of a contract, including *consideration* being given to the offeror by the offeree. (Consideration is discussed in *Chapter 12*.) For example, if Ann, in return for the payment of $500 to her by Bobby, grants Bobby an option, exercisable at any time within thirty days, to buy Blackacre at a price of $80,000, Ann's offer is irrevocable. Ann is legally bound to keep the offer open for thirty days, and any communication by Ann to Bobby giving notice of withdrawal of the offer is ineffective. Bobby is not bound to accept the offer, but the option contract entitles him to thirty days in which to accept.

◆ SEE CASE 12-4

FIRM OFFERS UNDER THE CODE The Code provides that a *merchant* is bound to keep an offer to buy or sell **goods** open for a stated period (or, if no time is stated, for a reasonable time) not exceeding three months, if the merchant gives assurance in a **signed writing** that the offer will be held open. Section 2–205. The Code, therefore, makes a merchant's written promise not to revoke an offer for a stated period enforceable even though no consideration is given to the offeror for that promise. A **merchant** is defined as a person (1) who is a dealer in goods of a given kind, (2) who by his occupation holds himself out as having knowledge or skill peculiar to the goods or practices involved, or (3) who employs an agent or broker whom he holds out as having such knowledge or skill. Section 2–104.

STATUTORY IRREVOCABILITY Certain offers, such as bids made to the State, municipality, or other government body for the construction of a building or some other public work, are made irrevocable by statute. Another example is pre-incorporation stock subscription agreements, which are irrevocable for a period of six months under many State incorporation statutes. See Section 6.20 of the Revised Model Business Corporation Act.

IRREVOCABLE OFFERS OF UNILATERAL CONTRACTS Where an offer contemplates a unilateral contract, that is, a promise for an act, injustice to the offeree may result if revocation is permitted after the offeree has started to perform the act requested in the offer and has substantially but not completely accomplished it. Traditionally, such an offer is not accepted and no contract is formed until the offeree has *completed* the requested act. By simply commencing performance, the offeree does not bind himself to complete performance; nor, historically, did he bind the offeror to keep the offer open. Thus, the offeror could revoke the offer at any time prior to the offeree's completion of performance. For example, Linda offers Tom $300 if Tom will climb to the top of the flagpole in the center of campus. Tom commences his ascent, and when he is five feet from the top, Linda yells to him, "I revoke."

The Restatement deals with this problem by providing that where the performance of the requested act necessarily requires the offeree to expend time and effort, the offeror is obligated not to revoke the offer for a reasonable time. This obligation arises when the offeree begins performance. If, however, the offeror does not know of the offeree's performance and has no adequate means of learning of it within a reasonable time, the offeree must exercise reasonable diligence to notify the offeror of the performance.

PRACTICAL ADVICE

When making an offer, be careful to make it irrevocable only if you so desire.

APPLYING THE LAW

Mutual Assent

FACTS Taylor and Arbuckle formed a partnership for the purpose of practicing pediatric medicine together. They found new medical office space to lease and thereafter, among other things, they set about furnishing the waiting room in a way that children would find inviting. In addition to contracting with a mural painter, they decided to purchase a high-definition flat-panel television on which they could show children's programming. On a Monday, Taylor and Arbuckle visited a local retailer with a reputation for competitive pricing, called Today's Electronics. In addition to comparing the pictures on the various models on display, the doctors discussed the pros and cons of LCD (liquid crystal display) versus plasma with the store's owner, Patel.

While they were able to narrow their options down significantly, Taylor and Arbuckle nonetheless could not decide on the exact size set to purchase because they had not yet determined the configuration of the seating to be installed in the waiting room. Sensing that the doctors were considering shopping around, Patel offered them a sizeable discount: only $999 for the forty-inch LCD screen they had chosen, or the fifty-inch plasma model they favored for only $1,299. As they were leaving the store, Patel gave the doctors his business card, on which he had jotted the model numbers and discount prices, his signature, and the notation "we assure you this offer is open through Sun., April 27."

Anxious to have the waiting room completed, Taylor and Arbuckle quickly agreed on a feasible seating arrangement for the waiting room, ordered the necessary furniture, and decided that the fifty-inch television would be too big. On Friday, April 25, Taylor returned to Today's Electronics. But before she could tell Patel that they had decided on the forty-inch LCD, Patel informed her that he could not honor the discounted prices because he no longer had in stock either model the doctors were considering.

ISSUE Is Patel free to revoke his offer notwithstanding having agreed to hold it open through the weekend?

RULE OF LAW The general rule is that an offeror may revoke, or withdraw, an offer any time before it has been accepted. However there are several limitations on an offeror's power to revoke an offer before acceptance. One of these is the Uniform Commercial Code's (UCC's) "merchant's firm offer" rule. Under the UCC, a merchant's offer to buy or sell goods is irrevocable for the stated period (or, if no period is stated, for a reasonable time) not exceeding three months, when he has signed a writing assuring the offeree that the offer will be kept open for that period. The Code defines a merchant as one who trades in the types of goods in question or who holds himself out, either personally or by way of an agent, to be knowledgeable regarding the goods or practices involved in the transaction.

APPLICATION The proposed contract between the doctors and Today's Electronics is governed by Article 2 of the Code because it involves a sale of goods, in this case a television set. Both Patel and Today's Electronics are considered merchants of televisions under the Code's definition, because Patel and his store regularly sell electronics, including television sets. Patel offered to sell to Taylor and Arbuckle either the forty-inch LCD television for $999 or the fifty-inch plasma for $1,299. By reducing his offer to a signed writing, and by promising in that writing that the stated prices were assured to be open through Sun., April 27, Patel has made a firm offer that he cannot revoke during that six-day period. Whether he still has either model in stock does not affect the irrevocability of the offer.

CONCLUSION Patel's offer is irrevocable through Sunday, April 27. Therefore Patel's attempt to revoke it is ineffective, and Taylor may still accept it.

PROMISSORY ESTOPPEL As discussed in the previous chapter, a noncontractual promise may be enforced when it is made under circumstances that should lead the promisor reasonably to expect that the promise will induce the promisee to take action in reliance on it. This doctrine has been used in some cases to prevent an offeror from revoking an offer prior to its acceptance. The Restatement provides the following rule:

An offer which the offeror should reasonably expect to induce action or forbearance of a substantial character on the part of the offeree before acceptance and which does induce such action or forbearance is binding as an option contract to the extent necessary to avoid injustice. Restatement, Section 87(2).

Thus, Ramanan Plumbing Co. submits a written offer for plumbing work to be used by Resolute Building Co. as part of Resolute's bid as a general contractor. Ramanan knows that Resolute is relying on Ramanan's bid, and in fact Resolute submits Ramanan's name as the plumbing subcontractor in the bid. Ramanan's offer is irrevocable until Resolute has a reasonable opportunity to notify Ramanan that Resolute's bid has been accepted.

REJECTION

An offeree is at liberty to accept or reject the offer as he sees fit. If the offeree decides not to accept it, he is not required to reject it formally but may simply wait until the offer terminates by the lapse of time. Through a **rejection** of an offer, the offeree manifests his unwillingness to accept. A communicated rejection terminates the power of acceptance. From the effective moment of rejection, which is the **receipt** of the rejection by the offeror, the offeree may no longer accept the offer. Rejection by the offeree may consist of express language or may be implied from language or from conduct.

COUNTEROFFER

A **counteroffer** is a counterproposal from the offeree to the offeror that indicates a willingness to contract but upon terms or conditions different from those contained in the offer. It is not an unequivocal acceptance of the original offer and, by indicating an unwillingness to agree to the terms of the offer, it operates as a rejection. It also operates as a new offer. For instance, assume that Jordan writes Chris a letter stating that he will sell to Chris a secondhand color television set for $300. Chris replies that she will pay Jordan $250 for the set. This is a counteroffer that, upon **receipt** by Jordan, terminates the original offer. Jordan may, if he wishes, accept the counteroffer and thereby create a contract for $250. If, on the other hand, Chris states in her reply that she wishes to consider the $300 offer but is willing to pay $250 at once for the set, she is making a counteroffer that does *not* terminate Jordan's original offer. In the first instance, after making the $250 counteroffer, Chris may not accept the $300 offer. In the second instance she may do so, as the manner in which she stated the counteroffer did not indicate an unwillingness to accept the original offer, and Chris therefore did not terminate it. In addition, a mere inquiry about the possibility of obtaining different or new terms is not a counteroffer and does not terminate the offer.

Another common type of counteroffer is the **conditional acceptance**, which purports to accept the offer but expressly makes the acceptance conditional upon the offeror's assent to additional or different terms. Nonetheless, it is a counteroffer and terminates the original offer. The Code's treatment of acceptances containing terms that vary from the offer are discussed later in this chapter.

Consider whether you want to make a counterproposal that terminates the original offer or whether you merely wish to discuss alternative possibilities.

DEATH OR INCOMPETENCY

The death or incompetency of either the offeror or the offeree ordinarily terminates an offer. Upon his death or incompetency the offeror no longer has the legal capacity to enter into a contract; thus, all his outstanding offers are terminated. Death or incompetency of the offeree likewise terminates the offer, because an ordinary offer is not assignable (transferable) and may be accepted only by the person to whom it was made. When the offeree dies or ceases to have legal capability to enter into a contract, no one else has the power to accept the offer. Therefore, the offer terminates.

The death or incompetency of the offeror or offeree, however, does *not* terminate an offer contained in an option.

DESTRUCTION OF SUBJECT MATTER

Destruction of the specific subject matter of an offer terminates the offer. The impossibility of performance prevents a contract from being consummated and thus terminates all outstanding offers with respect to the destroyed property. Suppose that Martina, owning a Buick automobile, offers to sell the car to Worthy and allows Worthy five days in which to accept. Three days later the car is destroyed by fire. On the following day, Worthy, without knowledge of the car's destruction, notifies Martina that he accepts her offer. There is no contract. Martina's offer was terminated by the destruction of the car.

SUBSEQUENT ILLEGALITY

One of the four essential requirements of a contract, as previously mentioned, is legality of purpose or subject matter. If performance of a valid contract is subsequently made illegal, the obligations of both parties under the contract are discharged. Illegality taking effect after the making of an offer but prior to acceptance has the same effect: the offer is legally terminated.

◆ SEE FIGURE 10-1: **Duration of Revocable Offers**

ACCEPTANCE OF OFFER

The acceptance of an offer is essential to the formation of a contract. Once an acceptance has been given, the contract is formed. An acceptance can be made only by an offeree. Acceptance of an offer for a bilateral contract requires some overt act by which the offeree manifests his assent to the

◆ FIGURE 10-1: **Duration of Revocable Offers**

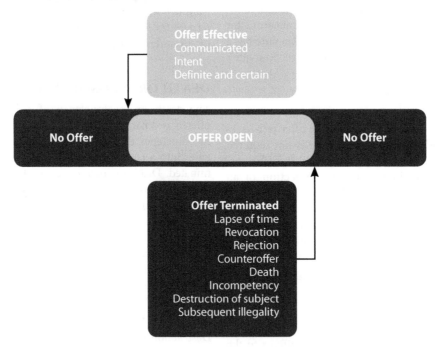

terms of the offer, such as speaking, sending a letter, or other explicit or implicit communication to the offeror. If the offer is for a unilateral contract, the offeree may refrain from acting as requested or may signify acceptance through performance of the requested act with the intention of accepting. For example, if Joy publishes an offer of a reward to anyone who returns the diamond ring which she has lost (a unilateral contract offer), and Steven, with knowledge of the offer, finds and returns the ring to Joy, Steven has accepted the offer. If, however, Steven returns the ring to Joy but in doing so disclaims the reward and says that he does not accept the offer, there is no contract. Without the intention of accepting the offer, merely doing the act requested by the offeror is not sufficient to form a contract.

A late or defective acceptance does not create a contract. After the offer has expired, it cannot be validly accepted. A late or defective acceptance, however, does manifest the offeree's willingness to enter into a contract and therefore constitutes a new offer. To create a contract based upon this offer, the original offeror must accept the new offer by manifesting his assent.

COMMUNICATION OF ACCEPTANCE

GENERAL RULE

Because acceptance manifests the offeree's assent to the offer, the offeree must communicate this acceptance to the offeror. This is the rule as to all offers to enter into bilateral contracts. In the case of an offer to enter into a unilateral contract, however, notice of acceptance to the offeror is usually not required. If, however, the offeree in a unilateral contract has reason to know that the offeror has no adequate means of learning of the performance with reasonable promptness and certainty, then the offeree must make reasonable efforts to notify the offeror of acceptance or lose the right to enforce the contract. Restatement, Section 54.

SILENCE AS ACCEPTANCE

An offeree is generally under no legal duty to reply to an offer. Silence or inaction, therefore, does *not* indicate acceptance of the offer. By custom, usage, or course of dealing, however, silence or inaction by the offeree may operate as an acceptance.

Thus, the silence or inaction of an offeree who fails to reply to an offer operates as an acceptance and causes a contract to be formed. Through previous dealings, the offeree has given the offeror reason to understand that the offeree will accept all offers unless the offeree sends notice to the contrary. Another example of silence operating as an acceptance occurs when the prospective member of a mail-order club agrees that his failure to return a notification card rejecting offered goods will constitute his acceptance of the club's offer to sell the goods.

Furthermore, if an offeror sends unordered or unsolicited merchandise to a person stating that she may purchase the goods at a specified price and that the offer will be deemed to have been accepted unless the goods are returned within a stated period of time, the offer is one for an inverted unilateral contract (i.e., an act for a promise). This practice led to abuse, however, which has prompted the Federal government as well as most States to enact statutes which provide that in such cases the offeree-recipient of the goods may keep them as a gift and is under no obligation either to return them or to pay for them.

EFFECTIVE MOMENT

As previously discussed, an offer, a revocation, a rejection, and a counteroffer are effective when they are received. An acceptance, on the other hand, is generally effective upon **dispatch**. This is true unless the offer specifically provides otherwise, the offeree uses an unauthorized means of communication, or the acceptance follows a prior rejection.

STIPULATED PROVISIONS IN THE OFFER If the offer specifically stipulates the means of communication the offeree is to use, the acceptance, to be effective, must conform to that specification. Thus, if an offer states that acceptance must be made by registered mail, any purported acceptance not made by registered mail would be ineffective. Moreover, the rule that an acceptance is effective when dispatched or sent does not apply in cases in which the offer provides that the offeror must receive the acceptance. If the offeror states that a reply must be received by a certain date or that he must hear from the offeree or uses other language indicating that the acceptance must be received by him, the effective moment of the acceptance is when the offeror receives it, not when the offeree sends or dispatches it.

PRACTICAL ADVICE

Consider whether you should specify in your offers that acceptances are valid only upon receipt.

AUTHORIZED MEANS Historically, an authorized means of communication was the means the offeror expressly authorized in the offer, or, if none was authorized, it was the means the offeror used. For example, if in reply to an offer by mail, the offeree places in the mail a letter of acceptance properly stamped and addressed to the offeror, a contract is formed at the time and place that the offeree mails the letter. This assumes, of course, that the offer at that time was open and had not been terminated by any of the methods previously discussed. The reason for this rule is that the offeror, by using the mail, impliedly authorized the offeree to use the same method of communication. It is immaterial if the letter of acceptance goes astray in the mail and is never received.

The Restatement, Section 30, and the Code, Section 2–206(1)(a), both now provide that where the language in the offer or the circumstances do not otherwise indicate, an offer to make a contract shall be construed as authorizing acceptance in any **reasonable** manner. These provisions are intended to allow flexibility of response and the ability to keep pace with new modes of communication.

◆ SEE FIGURE 10-2: **Mutual Assent**

◆ SEE CASE 10-3

UNAUTHORIZED MEANS When the offeree uses an unauthorized method of communication, the traditional rule is that acceptance is effective when and if received by the offeror, provided that he receives it within the time during which the authorized means would have arrived. The Restatement, Section 67, provides that if these conditions are met, the effective time for the acceptance relates back to the moment of dispatch.

ACCEPTANCE FOLLOWING A PRIOR REJECTION An acceptance sent after a prior rejection is not effective when sent by the offeree, but is only effective when and if the offeror receives it before he receives the rejection. Thus, when an acceptance follows a prior rejection, the first communication to be received by the offeror is the effective one. For example, Anna in New York sends by mail to Fritz in San Francisco an offer that is expressly stated to be open for ten days. On the fourth day, Fritz sends to Anna by mail a letter of rejection that is delivered on the morning of the seventh day. At noon on the fifth day, however, Fritz dispatches an overnight letter of acceptance that is received by Anna before the close of business on the sixth day. A contract was formed when Anna received Fritz's overnight letter of acceptance, as it was received before the letter of rejection.

◆ SEE FIGURE 10-3: **Offer and Acceptance**

VARIANT ACCEPTANCES

A variant acceptance—one that contains terms different from or additional to those in the offer—receives distinctly different treatment under the common law and the Code.

COMMON LAW

An acceptance must be *positive* and *unequivocal*. In that it may not change, add to, subtract from, or qualify in any way the provisions of the offer, it must be the **mirror image** of the offer. Any communication by the offeree that attempts to modify the offer is not an acceptance but is a counteroffer, which does not create a contract.

◆ FIGURE 10-2: **Mutual Assent**

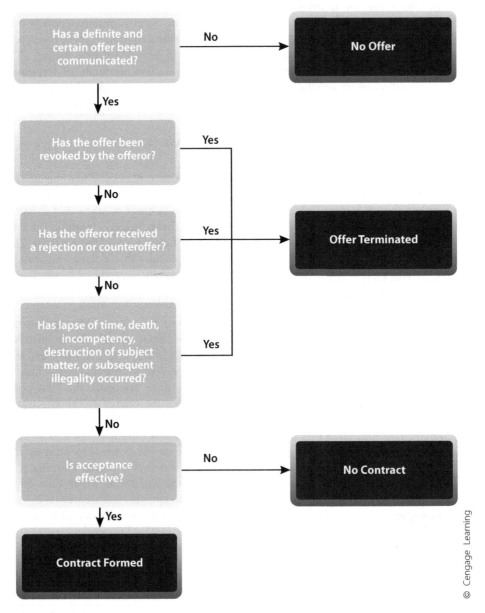

© Cengage Learning

◆ FIGURE 10-3: **Offer and Acceptance**

	Time Effective	Effect
Communications by Offeror		
Offer	Received by offeree	Creates power to form a contract
Revocation	Received by offeree	Terminates offer
Communications by Offeree		
Rejection	Received by offeror	Terminates offer
Counteroffer	Received by offeror	Terminates offer
Acceptance	Sent by offeree	Forms a contract
Acceptance after prior rejection	Received by offeror	If received before rejection forms a contract

© Cengage Learning

CODE

The Code modifies the common law "mirror image" rule, by which the acceptance cannot vary or deviate from the terms of the offer. This modification is necessitated by the realities of modern business practices. A vast number of business transactions use standardized business forms. For example, a merchant buyer sends to a merchant seller on the buyer's order form a purchase order for 1,000 dozen cotton shirts at $60.00 per dozen, with delivery by October 1 at the buyer's place of business. On the reverse side of this standard form are twenty-five numbered paragraphs containing provisions generally favorable to the buyer. When the seller receives the buyer's order, he agrees to the quantity, price, and delivery terms and sends to the buyer on his acceptance form an unequivocal acceptance of the offer. However, on the back of his acceptance form, the seller has thirty-two numbered paragraphs generally favorable to himself and in significant conflict with the buyer's form. Under the common law's *mirror image* rule, no contract would exist, for the seller has not accepted unequivocally all the material terms of the buyer's offer.

The Code in Section 2–207 attempts to alleviate this **battle of the forms** by focusing upon the intent of the parties. If the offeree expressly makes her acceptance conditioned upon assent to the additional or different terms, no contract is formed. If the offeree does not expressly make her acceptance conditional upon the offeror's assent to the additional or different terms, a contract is formed. The issue then becomes whether the offeree's different or additional terms

may become part of the contract. If both offeror and offeree are merchants, such *additional* terms may become part of the contract, provided they do not materially alter the agreement and are not objected to either in the offer itself or within a reasonable period of time. If both parties are not merchants or if the additional terms materially alter the offer, then the additional terms are merely construed as proposals to the contract. *Different* terms proposed by the offeree will not become part of the contract unless the offeror accepts them. The courts are divided over what terms a contract includes when those terms differ or conflict. Some courts hold that the offeror's terms govern; other courts, holding that the terms cancel each other out, look to the Code to provide the missing terms. Some follow a third alternative and apply the additional terms test to different terms. (See *Figure 21-4* in *Chapter 21*.)

To apply Section 2–207 to the previous example: because both parties are merchants and the acceptance was not conditional upon assent to the additional or different terms, (1) the contract will be formed without the seller's different terms unless the buyer specifically accepts them; (2) the contract will be formed without the seller's additional terms unless (a) the buyer specifically accepts them or (b) they do not materially alter the offer and the buyer does not object; and (3) depending upon the jurisdiction, either (a) the buyer's conflicting terms are included in the contract or (b) the Code provides the missing terms, as the conflicting terms cancel each other out, or (c) the additional terms test is applied.

CHAPTER SUMMARY

OFFER

ESSENTIALS OF AN OFFER	**Definition** indication of willingness to enter into a contract **Communication** offeree must have knowledge of the offer and the offer must be made by the offeror to the offeree **Intent** determined by an objective standard of what a reasonable offeree would have believed **Definiteness** offer's terms must be clear enough to provide a court with a basis for giving an appropriate remedy
DURATION OF OFFERS	**Lapse of Time** offer remains open for the time period specified or, if no time is stated, for a reasonable period of time **Revocation** generally, an offer may be terminated at any time before it is accepted, subject to the following exceptions • *Option Contract* contract that binds offeror to keep an offer open for a specified time • *Firm Offer* a merchant's irrevocable offer to sell or buy goods in a signed writing ensures that the offer will not be terminated for up to three months • *Statutory Irrevocability* offer made irrevocable by statute

- *Irrevocable Offer of Unilateral Contract* a unilateral offer may not be revoked for a reasonable time after performance is begun
- *Promissory Estoppel* noncontractual promise that binds the promisor because she should reasonably expect that the promise will induce the promisee (offeree) to take action in reliance on it

Rejection refusal to accept an offer terminates the power of acceptance
Counteroffer counterproposal to an offer that generally terminates the original offer
Death or Incompetency of either the offeror or the offeree terminates the offer
Destruction of Subject Matter of an offer terminates the offer
Subsequent Illegality of the purpose or subject matter of the offer terminates the offer

---

ACCEPTANCE OF OFFER

REQUIREMENTS
Definition positive and unequivocal expression of a willingness to enter into a contract on the terms of the offer
Mirror Image Rule except as modified by the Code, an acceptance cannot deviate from the terms of the offer

---

COMMUNICATION OF ACCEPTANCE
General Rule acceptance effective upon dispatch unless the offer specifically provides otherwise or the offeree uses an unauthorized means of communication
Stipulated Provisions the communication of acceptance must conform to the specification in the offer
Authorized Means the Restatement and the Code provide that unless the offer provides otherwise, acceptance is authorized to be in any reasonable manner
Unauthorized Means acceptance effective when received, provided that it is received within the time within which the authorized means would have arrived
Acceptance Following a Prior Rejection first communication received by the offeror is effective
Defective Acceptance does not create a contract but serves as a new offer

---

CASES

CASE 10-1	Objective Standard **CATAMOUNT SLATE PRODUCTS, INC. v. SHELDON** Supreme Court of Vermont, 2004 2003 VT 112, 845 A.2d 324 http://scholar.google.com/scholar_case?case=12161607133389120155&q=2003+VT+112&hl=en&as_sdt=2,22

Skoglund, J.

Catamount Slate Products, Inc. and its principals the Reed family appeal from a Rutland Superior Court ruling enforcing what appellees characterize as a binding, mediated settlement agreement. The trial court concluded that, at the end of their September 5, 2000 mediation, the parties had reached a binding settlement agreement. Because the Reeds lacked the requisite intent to be bound to the settlement agreement in the absence of a writing, we hold that no binding agreement was reached. * * *

The Reeds own and operate Catamount Slate, a slate quarry and mill, on 122 acres in Fair Haven, Vermont. The appellees, the Sheldons, are also Fair Haven property owners and the Reeds' neighbors. Since 1997, the parties have been litigating the Reeds' right to operate their slate business and to use the access road leading to the quarry. In 2000, with several legal actions pending, the parties agreed to try to resolve their disputes in a state-funded mediation with retired judge Arthur O'Dea serving as mediator.

Prior to the mediation, Judge O'Dea sent each party a Mediation Agreement outlining the rules governing the mediation. Paragraph nine of the Mediation Agreement stated that:

> [a]ll statements, admissions, confessions, acts, or exchanges … are acknowledged by the parties to be offers in negotiation of settlement and compromise, and as such inadmissible in evidence, and not binding upon either party unless reduced to a final agreement of settlement. Any final agreement of settlement must be in writing and signed by every party sought to be charged.

* * *

The mediation was held on September 5, 2000. Judge O'Dea began the session by reaffirming the statements made in the Mediation Agreement. After ten hours, the parties purportedly reached an agreement on all major issues. Judge O'Dea then orally summarized the terms of the resolution with the parties and counsel present. The attorneys took notes on the terms of the agreement with the understanding that they would prepare the necessary documents for signature in the coming days.

The resolution required the Reeds to pay the Sheldons $250 a month for the right to use the access road, while the Sheldons agreed to be coapplicants on Catamount Slate's pending Act 250 permit. Payments were to commence on October 1, 2000. The parties also agreed to a series of terms governing the operation of the slate quarry, including, among other things, hours of operation, number of truck trips permitted on the access road, the amount and frequency of blasting, and the location of seismic measurements. These terms were to be memorialized in two distinct documents, a Lease Agreement and a Settlement Agreement.

On September 7, 2000, two days after the mediation, the Sheldons' attorney, Emily Joselson, drafted a letter outlining the terms of the settlement and sent copies to James Leary, the Reeds' attorney, and Judge O'Dea. Within a week, Leary responded by letter concurring in some respects and outlining the issues on which the Reeds disagreed with Joselson's characterization of the settlement.

* * *

On October 1, 2000, the Reeds began paying the $250 monthly lease payments, but, since the settlement agreement was not final, the parties agreed that the money would go into an escrow account maintained by the Sheldons' counsel. The check was delivered to the Sheldons' attorney with a cover memo stating, "This check is forwarded to you with the understanding that the funds will be disbursed to your clients only after settlement agreement becomes final. Of course, if the settlement agreement does not come to fruition, then the funds must be returned to my clients." The parties

continued to exchange letters actively negotiating the remaining details of the Lease and Settlement Agreements for the better part of the next five months. Although there were others along the way, by early 2001 the only remaining issues in dispute were the location of seismic measurements and the definition of "over blast."

In February 2001, while drafts were still being exchanged, Christine Stannard, the Reeds' daughter, saw a deed and map in the Fair Haven Town Clerk's Office which led her to believe that the disputed road was not owned by the Sheldons, but was a town highway. The Reeds then refused to proceed any further with negotiating the settlement agreement. A written settlement agreement was never signed by either party.

The Sheldons responded by filing a motion to enforce the settlement agreement. * * * The trial court granted the motion, finding that the attorneys' notes taken at the end of the mediation and the unsigned drafts of the Lease and Settlement Agreements sufficiently memorialized the agreement between the parties and thus constituted an enforceable settlement agreement. * * *

The question before us is whether the oral agreement reached at mediation, when combined with the unexecuted documents drafted subsequently, constituted a binding, enforceable settlement agreement. Parties are free to enter into a binding contract without memorializing their agreement in a fully executed document. See Restatement (Second) of Contracts § 4 (1981). In such an instance, the mere intention or discussion to commit their agreement to writing will not prevent the formation of a contract prior to the document's execution. [Citations.]

"On the other hand, if either party communicates an intent not to be bound until he achieves a fully executed document, no amount of negotiation or oral agreement to specific terms will result in the formation of a binding contract." [Citation.] The freedom to determine the exact moment in which an agreement becomes binding encourages the parties to negotiate as candidly as possible, secure in the knowledge that they will not be bound until the execution of what both parties consider to be a final, binding agreement.

We look to the intent of the parties to determine the moment of contract formation. [Citation.] Intent to be bound is a question of fact. [Citation.] "To discern that intent a court must look to the words and deeds [of the parties] which constitute objective signs in a given set of circumstances." [Citation.] In [citation], the Second Circuit articulated four factors to aid in determining whether the parties intended to be bound in the absence of a fully executed document. [Citation.] The court suggested that we "consider (1) whether there has been an express reservation of the right not to be bound in the absence of a writing; whether there has been partial performance of the contract;

whether all of the terms of the alleged contract have been agreed upon; and (4) whether the agreement at issue is the type of contract that is usually committed to writing." [Citations.]

The language of the parties' correspondence and other documentary evidence presented reveals an intent by the mediation participants not to be bound prior to the execution of a final document. First, the Mediation Agreement Judge O'Dea sent to the parties prior to the mediation clearly contemplates that any settlement agreement emanating from the mediation would be binding only after being put in writing and signed. Paragraph nine of the Agreement expressly stated that statements made during mediation would not be "binding upon either party unless reduced to a final agreement of settlement" and that "any final agreement of settlement [would] be in writing and signed by every party sought to be charged." Further, Judge O'Dea reminded the parties of these ground rules at the outset of the mediation. The Reeds testified that they relied on these statements and assumed that, as indicated, they would not be bound until they signed a written agreement.

* * *

Even more compelling evidence of the Reeds' lack of intent to be bound in the absence of a writing is the statement in the cover letter accompanying the Reeds' $250 payments to the Sheldons' attorney saying, "This check is forwarded to you with the understanding that the funds will be disbursed to your clients only after settlement agreement becomes final. Of course, if the settlement agreement does not come to fruition, then the funds must be returned to my clients." This factor weighs in favor of finding that the Reeds expressed their right not to be bound until their agreement was reduced to a final writing and executed.

Because there was no evidence presented of partial performance of the settlement agreement, we next consider the third factor, whether there was anything left to negotiate. * * *

As stated by the Second Circuit in [citation], "the actual drafting of a written instrument will frequently reveal points of disagreement, ambiguity, or omission which must be worked out prior to execution. Details that are unnoticed or passed by in oral discussion will be pinned down when the understanding is reduced to writing." (internal quotations and citations omitted). [Citation.] This case is no exception. A review of the lengthy correspondence in this case makes clear that several points of disagreement and ambiguity arose during the drafting process. Beyond the location of seismic measurements and the definition of "over blast," correspondence indicates that the parties still had not reached agreement on the term and width of the lease, acceptable decibel levels and notice provisions for blasts, the definition of "truck trips," and whether all claims would be dismissed without prejudice after the execution of the agreement. Resolution of these issues was clearly important enough to forestall final execution until the language of the documents could be agreed upon. In such a case, where the parties intend to be bound only upon execution of a final document, for the court to determine that, despite continuing disagreement on substantive terms, the parties reached a binding, enforceable settlement agreement undermines their right to enter into the specific settlement agreement for which they contracted.

The fourth and final factor, whether the agreement at issue is the type of contract usually put into writing, also weighs in the Reeds' favor. Being a contract for an interest in land, the Lease Agreement is subject to the Statute of Frauds and thus generally must be in writing. * * *

* * *

In conclusion, three of the four factors indicate that the parties here did not intend to be bound until the execution of a final written document, and therefore we hold that the parties never entered into a binding settlement agreement. * * * Accordingly, the order enforcing the settlement is reversed and the case is remanded for further proceedings.

Invitations Seeking Offers
LEFKOWITZ v. GREAT MINNEAPOLIS SURPLUS STORE, INC.
Supreme Court of Minnesota, 1957
251 Minn. 188, 86 N.W.2d 689
http://scholar.google.com/scholar_case?case=1365398257799813577&q=86+N.W.2d+689&hl=en&as_sdt=2,34

Murphy, J.
This is an appeal from an order of * * * judgment award[ing] the plaintiff the sum of $138.50 as damages for breach of contract.

This case grows out of the alleged refusal of the defendant to sell to the plaintiff a certain fur piece which it had offered for sale in a newspaper advertisement. It appears from the

record that on April 6, 1956, the defendant published the following advertisement in a Minneapolis newspaper:

SATURDAY 9 AM SHARP
3 BRAND NEW
FUR COATS
Worth to $100.00

First Come
First Served
$1 EACH

On April 13, the defendant again published an advertisement in the same newspaper as follows:

SATURDAY 9 AM
2 BRAND NEW PASTEL
MINK 3-SKIN SCARFS
Selling for $89.50
Out they go
Saturday. Each … $1.00
1 BLACK LAPIN STOLE
Beautiful,
worth $139.50 … $1.00
First Come
First Served

The record supports the findings of the court that on each of the Saturdays following the publication of the above-described ads the plaintiff was the first to present himself at the appropriate counter in the defendant's store and on each occasion demanded the coat and the stole so advertised and indicated his readiness to pay the sale price of $1. On both occasions, the defendant refused to sell the merchandise to the plaintiff, stating on the first occasion that by a "house rule" the offer was intended for women only and sales would not be made to men, and on the second visit that plaintiff knew defendant's house rules. * * *

The defendant contends that a newspaper advertisement offering items of merchandise for sale at a named price is a "unilateral offer" which may be withdrawn without notice. He relies upon authorities which hold that, where an advertiser publishes in a newspaper that he has a certain quantity or quality of goods which he wants to dispose of at certain prices and on certain terms, such advertisements are not

offers which become contracts as soon as any person to whose notice they may come signifies his acceptance by notifying the other that he will take a certain quantity of them. Such advertisements have been construed as an invitation for an offer of sale on the terms stated, which offer, when received, may be accepted or rejected and which therefore does not become a contract of sale until accepted by the seller; and until a contract has been so made, the seller may modify or revoke such prices or terms. [Citations.] * * * On the facts before us we are concerned with whether the advertisement constituted an offer, and, if so, whether the plaintiff's conduct constituted an acceptance.

* * *

The test of whether a binding obligation may originate in advertisements addressed to the general public is "whether the facts show that some performance was promised in positive terms in return for something requested."

* * *

Whether in any individual instance a newspaper advertisement is an offer rather than an invitation to make an offer depends on the legal intention of the parties and the surrounding circumstances. [Citations.] We are of the view on the facts before us that the offer by the defendant of the sale * * * was clear, definite, and explicit, and left nothing open for negotiation. The plaintiff, having successfully managed to be the first one to appear at the seller's place of business to be served, as requested by the advertisement, and having offered the stated purchase price of the article, was entitled to performance on the part of the defendant. We think the trial court was correct in holding that there was in the conduct of the parties a sufficient mutuality of obligation to constitute a contract of sale.

* * *

Affirmed.

CASE 10-3

Effective Moment
OSPREY L.L.C. v. KELLY-MOORE PAINT CO., INC.
Supreme Court of Oklahoma, 1999
1999 OK 50, 984 P.2d 194
http://scholar.google.com/scholar_case?case=15066374301719252497&q=984+P.2d+194&hl=en&as_sdt=2,34

Kauger, J.
[In 1977, the defendant, Kelly-Moore Paint Company, entered into a fifteen-year commercial lease with the plaintiff, Osprey, for a property in Edmond, Oklahoma. The lease contained two five-year renewal options. The lease required that the lessee give notice of its intent to renew at least six months prior to its expiration. It also provided that the renewal "may be delivered either personally or by

depositing the same in United States mail, first class postage prepaid, registered or certified mail, return receipt requested." Upon expiration of the original fifteen-year lease, Kelly-Moore timely informed the lessor by certified letter of its intent to extend the lease an additional five years. The first five-year extension was due to expire on August 31, 1997. On the last day of the six-month notification deadline, Kelly-Moore faxed a letter of renewal notice to Osprey's office at 5:28 P.M. In addition, Kelly-Moore sent a copy of the faxed renewal notice letter by Federal Express that same day. Osprey denies ever receiving the fax, but it admits receiving the Federal Express copy of the notice on the following business day. Osprey rejected the notice, asserting that it was late, and it filed an action to remove the defendant from the premises. After a trial on the merits, the trial court granted judgment in favor of Kelly-Moore, finding that the faxed notice was effective. Osprey appealed. The Court of Civil Appeals reversed, determining that the plain language of the lease required that it be renewed by delivering notice either personally or by mail, and that Kelly-Moore had done neither. Kelly-Moore appealed.]

The precise issue of whether a faxed or facsimile delivery of a written notice to renew a commercial lease is sufficient to exercise timely the renewal option of the lease is one of first impression in Oklahoma. Neither party has cited to a case from another jurisdiction which has decided this question, or to any case which has specifically defined "personal delivery" as including facsimile delivery.

* * *

Osprey argues that: (1) the lease specifically prescribed limited means of acceptance of the option, and it required that the notice of renewal be delivered either personally or sent by United States mail, registered or certified; (2) Kelly-Moore failed to follow the contractual requirements of the lease when it delivered its notice by fax; and (3) because the terms for extending the lease specified in the contract were not met, the notice was invalid and the lease expired on August 31, 1997. Kelly-Moore counters that: (1) the lease by the use of the word "shall" mandates that the notice be written, but the use of the word "may" is permissive; and (2) although the notice provision of the lease permits delivery personally or by United States mail, it does not exclude other modes of delivery or transmission which would include delivery by facsimile. * * *

A lease is a contract and in construing a lease, the usual rules for the interpretation of contractual writings apply. * * *

Language in a contract is given its plain and ordinary meaning, unless some technical term is used in a manner meant to convey a specific technical concept. A contract term is ambiguous only if it can be interpreted as having two different meanings. * * * The lease does not appear to be ambiguous. "Shall" is ordinarily construed as mandatory and "may" is ordinarily construed as permissive. The contract clearly requires that notice "shall" be in writing. The provision for delivery, either personally or by certified or registered mail, uses the permissive "may" and it does not bar other modes of transmission which are just as effective.

The purpose of providing notice by personal delivery or registered mail is to insure the delivery of the notice, and to settle any dispute which might arise between the parties concerning whether the notice was received. A substituted method of notice which performs the same function and serves the same purpose as an authorized method of notice is not defective. Here, the contract provided that time was of the essence. Although Osprey denies that it ever received the fax, the fax activity report and telephone company records confirm that the fax was transmitted successfully, and that it was sent to Osprey's correct facsimile number on the last day of the deadline to extend the lease. The fax provided immediate written communication similar to personal delivery and, like a telegram, would be timely if it were properly transmitted before the expiration of the deadline to renew. Kelly-Moore's use of the fax served the same function and the same purpose as the two methods suggested by the lease and it was transmitted before the expiration of the deadline to renew. Under these facts, we hold that the faxed or facsimile delivery of the written notice to renew the commercial lease was sufficient to exercise timely the renewal option of the lease.

* * *

COURT OF CIVIL APPEALS OPINION VACATED; TRIAL COURT AFFIRMED.

CASE	Duration of Offers
10-4	**SHERROD v. KIDD**
	Court of Appeals of Washington, Division 3, 2007
	155 P.3d 976
	http://scholar.google.com/scholar_case?q=155+P.3d+976&hl=en&as_sdt=2,34&case=7607426217314840344&scilh=0

Sweeney, C. J.

* * *

David and Elizabeth Kidd's dog bit Mikaila Sherrod. Mikaila through her guardian ad litem (GAL) made a claim for damages. On June 14, 2005, the Kidds offered to settle the claim

for $31,837. On July 12, Mikaila through her GAL sued the Kidds. On July 20, the Kidds bumped their offer to $32,843.

The suit was subject to mandatory arbitration. The parties proceeded to arbitration on April 28, 2006. On May 5, the arbitrator awarded Mikaila $25,069.47. On May 9, the GAL wrote to the Kidds and purported to accept their last offer of $32,843, made the year before.

The GAL on Mikaila's behalf moved to enforce the settlement agreement. The court concluded the offer was properly accepted because it had not been withdrawn. And it entered judgment in the amount of the first written offer.

* * *

The Kidds contend that the trial court did not consider that implicit in its settlement offer was the GAL's forbearance in proceeding with the arbitration to its conclusion. The GAL argues that the offer was not conditioned upon the arbitration proceeding in any manner. And the offer provided no time limit for its acceptance. The GAL further claims that the consideration to create an enforceable agreement—her promise to dismiss her lawsuit—was the same when she accepted it as when it was offered. Her consideration included relinquishing her right to request a trial de novo.

An offer to form a contract is open only for a reasonable time, unless the offer specifically states how long it is open for acceptance. [Citations.] "[I]n the absence of an acceptance of an offer … within a reasonable time (where no time limit is specified), there is no contract." [Citation.]

How much time is reasonable is usually a question of fact. [Citation.] But we can decide the limits of a reasonable time if the facts are undisputed. [Citation.] And here the essential facts are not disputed.

A reasonable time "is the time that a reasonable person in the exact position of the offeree would believe to be satisfactory to the offeror." [Citation.] "The purpose of the offeror, to be attained by the making and performance of the contract, will affect the time allowed for acceptance, if it is or should be known to the offeree. In such case there is no power to accept after it is too late to attain that purpose." [Citation.] A reasonable time for an offeree to accept an offer depends on the "nature of the contract and the character of the business in which the parties were engaged." [Citation.]

Implicit in an offer (and an acceptance) to settle a personal injury suit is the party's intent to avoid a less favorable result at the hands of a jury, a judge or, in this case, an arbitrator. The defendant runs the risk that the award might be more than the offer. The plaintiff, of course, runs the risk that the award might be less than the offer. Both want to avoid that risk. And it is those risks that settlements avoid.

* * *

* * * Here, the value of this claim was set after arbitration. It was certainly subject to appeal but nonetheless set by a fact finder.

This offer expired when the arbitrator announced the award and was not subject to being accepted.

We reverse the decision of the trial judge to the contrary.

QUESTIONS

1. Ames, seeking business for his lawn maintenance firm, posted the following notice in the meeting room of the Antlers, a local lodge: "To the members of the Antlers—Special this month. I will resod your lawn for two dollars per square foot using Fairway brand sod. This offer expires July 15."

   The notice also included Ames's name, address, and signature, and specified that the acceptance was to be in writing.

   Bates, a member of the Antlers, and Cramer, the janitor, read the notice and became interested. Bates wrote a letter to Ames saying he would accept the offer if Ames would use Putting Green brand sod. Ames received this letter July 14 and wrote to Bates saying he would not use Putting Green sod. Bates received Ames's letter on July 16 and promptly wrote Ames that he would accept Fairway sod. Cramer wrote to Ames on July 10, saying he accepted Ames's offer.

   By July 15, Ames had found more profitable ventures and refused to resod either lawn at the specified price. Bates and Cramer brought an appropriate action against Ames for breach of contract. Decisions as to the respective claims of Bates and Cramer?

2. Garvey owned four speedboats named *Porpoise, Priscilla, Providence*, and *Prudence*. On April 2, Garvey made written offers to sell the four boats in the order named for $14,200 each to Caldwell, Meens, Smith, and Braxton, respectively, allowing ten days for acceptance. In which, if any, of the following four situations described was a contract formed?

   a. Five days later, Caldwell received notice from Garvey that he had contracted to sell *Porpoise* to Montgomery. The next day, April 8, Caldwell notified Garvey that he accepted Garvey's offer.

   b. On the third day, April 5, Meens mailed a rejection to Garvey which reached Garvey on the morning of the sixth day. But at 10:00 A.M. on the fourth day, Meens sent an acceptance by overnight letter to Garvey, who received it at noon on the fifth day.

   c. Smith, on April 3, replied that she was interested in buying *Providence* but declared the price asked appeared slightly excessive and wondered if, perhaps,

Garvey would be willing to sell the boat for $13,900. Five days later, having received no reply from Garvey, Smith, by letter, accepted Garvey's offer and enclosed a certified check for $14,200.

d. Braxton was accidentally killed in an automobile accident on April 9. The following day, the executor of Braxton's estate mailed an acceptance of Garvey's offer to Garvey.

3. Alpha Rolling Mill Corporation, by letter dated June 8, offered to sell Brooklyn Railroad Company two thousand to five thousand tons of fifty-pound iron rails upon certain specified terms, adding that, if the offer was accepted, Alpha Corporation would expect to be notified prior to June 20. Brooklyn Company, on June 16, by fax, referring to Alpha Corporation's offer of June 8, directed Alpha Corporation to enter an order for 1,200 tons of fifty-pound iron rails on the terms specified. The same day, June 16, Brooklyn Company, by letter to Alpha Corporation, confirmed the fax.

On June 18, Alpha Corporation, by telephone, declined to fill the order. Brooklyn Company, on June 19, wrote Alpha Corporation: "Please enter an order for 2,000 tons of rails as per your letter of the eighth. Please forward written contract. Reply." In reply to Brooklyn Company's repeated inquiries regarding whether the order for two thousand tons of rails had been entered, Alpha denied the existence of any contract between Brooklyn Company and itself. Thereafter, Brooklyn Company sued Alpha Corporation for breach of contract. Decision?

4. On April 8, Burchette received a telephone call from Bleluck, a truck dealer, who told Burchette that a new model truck in which Burchette was interested would arrive in one week. Although Bleluck initially wanted $10,500, the conversation ended after Bleluck agreed to sell and Burchette agreed to purchase the truck for $10,000, with a $1,000 down payment and the balance upon delivery. The next day, Burchette sent Bleluck a check for $1,000, which Bleluck promptly cashed.

One week later, when Burchette called Bleluck and inquired about the truck, Bleluck informed Burchette he had several prospects looking at the truck and would not sell for less than $10,500. The following day, Bleluck sent Burchette a properly executed check for $1,000 with the following notation thereon: "Return of down payment on sale of truck." After notifying Bleluck that she will not cash the check, Burchette sues Bleluck for damages. Should Burchette prevail? Explain.

5. On November 15, I. Sellit, a manufacturer of crystalware, mailed to Benny Buyer a letter stating that Sellit would sell to Buyer one hundred crystal "A" goblets at $100 per goblet and that "the offer would remain open for fifteen

(15) days." On November 18, Sellit, noticing the sudden rise in the price of crystal "A" goblets, decided to withdraw her offer to Buyer and so notified Buyer. Buyer chose to ignore Sellit's letter of revocation and gleefully watched as the price of crystal "A" goblets continued to skyrocket. On November 30, Buyer mailed to Sellit a letter accepting Sellit's offer to sell the goblets. The letter was received by Sellit on December 4. Buyer demands delivery of the goblets. What result?

6. On May 1, Melforth Realty Company offered to sell Greenacre to Dallas, Inc., for $1 million. The offer was made by a letter sent by overnight delivery and stated that the offer would expire on May 15. Dallas decided to purchase the property and sent a letter by registered first-class mail to Melforth on May 10, accepting the offer. Due to unexplained delays in the postal service, Melforth did not receive the letter until May 22. Melforth wishes to sell Greenacre to another buyer, who is offering $1.2 million for the tract of land. Has a contract resulted between Melforth and Dallas?

7. Rowe advertised in newspapers of wide circulation and otherwise made known that she would pay $5,000 for a complete set consisting of ten volumes of certain rare books. Ford, not knowing of the offer, gave Rowe all but one volume of the set of rare books as a Christmas present. Ford later learned of the offer, obtained the one remaining book, tendered it to Rowe, and demanded the $5,000. Rowe refused to pay. Is Ford entitled to the $5,000?

8. Scott, manufacturer of a carbonated beverage, entered into a contract with Otis, owner of a baseball park, whereby Otis rented to Scott a large signboard on top of the center field wall. The contract provided that Otis should letter the sign as Scott desired and would change the lettering from time to time within forty-eight hours after receipt of written request from Scott. As directed by Scott, the signboard originally stated in large letters that Scott would pay $1,000 to any ballplayer hitting a home run over the sign.

In the first game of the season, Hume, the best hitter in the league, hit one home run over the sign. Scott immediately served written notice on Otis instructing Otis to replace the offer on the signboard with an offer to pay $500 to every pitcher who pitched a no-hit game in the park. A week after receipt of Scott's letter, Otis had not changed the wording on the sign. On that day, Perry, a pitcher for a scheduled game, pitched a no-hit game while Todd, one of his teammates, hit a home run over Scott's sign. Scott refuses to pay any of the three players. What are the rights of Scott, Hume, Perry, and Todd?

9. Barnes accepted Clark's offer to sell to him a portion of Clark's coin collection. Clark forgot that his prized $20

gold piece at the time of the offer and acceptance was included in the portion that he offered to sell to Barnes. Clark did not intend to include the gold piece in the sale. Barnes, at the time of inspecting the offered portion of the collection, and prior to accepting the offer, saw the gold piece. Is Barnes entitled to the $20 gold piece?

10. Small, admiring Jasper's watch, asked Jasper where and at what price he had purchased it. Jasper replied, "I bought it at West Watch Shop about two years ago for around $85, but I am not certain as to that." Small then said, "Those fellows at West are good people and always sell good watches. I'll buy that watch from you." Jasper replied, "It's a deal." The next morning Small telephoned Jasper and said he had changed his mind and did not wish to buy the watch. Jasper sued Small for breach of contract. In defense, Small has pleaded that he made no enforceable contract with Jasper (a) because the parties did not agree on the price to be paid for the watch, and (b) because the parties did not agree on the place and time of delivery of the watch to Small. Are either, or both, of these defenses good?

11. Jeff says to Brenda, "I offer to sell you my PC for $900." Brenda replies, "If you do not hear otherwise from me by Thursday, I have accepted your offer." Jeff agrees and does not hear from Brenda by Thursday. Does a contract exist between Jeff and Brenda? Explain.

12. On November 19, Hoover Motor Express Company sent to Clements Paper Company a written offer to purchase certain real estate. Sometime in December, Clements authorized Williams to accept. Williams, however, attempted to bargain with Hoover to obtain a better deal, specifically that Clements would retain easements on the property. In a telephone conversation on January 13 of the following year, Williams first told Hoover of his plan to obtain the easements. Hoover replied, "Well, I don't know if we are ready. We have not decided; we might not want to go through with it." On January 20, Clements sent a written acceptance of Hoover's offer. Hoover refused to buy, claiming it had revoked its offer through the January 13 phone conversation. Clements then brought suit to compel the sale or obtain damages. Did Hoover successfully revoke its offer?

13. Walker leased a small lot to Keith for ten years at $1,000 a month, with a right for Keith to extend the lease for another ten-year term under the same terms except as to rent. The renewal option provided:

> Rental will be fixed in such amount as shall actually be agreed upon by the lessors and the lessee with the monthly rental fixed on the comparative basis of rental values as of the date of the renewal with rental values at this time reflected by the comparative business conditions of the two periods.

Keith sought to exercise the renewal right and, when the parties were unable to agree on the rent, brought suit against Walker. Who prevails? Why?

CASE PROBLEMS

14. The Brewers contracted to purchase Dower House from McAfee. Then, several weeks before the May 7 settlement date for the purchase of the house, the two parties began to negotiate for the sale of certain items of furniture in the house. On April 30, McAfee sent the Brewers a letter containing a list of the furnishings to be purchased at specified prices; a payment schedule, including a request for a $3,000 payment, due on acceptance; and a clause reading, "If the above is satisfactory, please sign and return one copy with the first payment."

On June 3, the Brewers sent a letter to McAfee stating that enclosed was a $3,000 check; that the original contract had been misplaced and could another be furnished; that they planned to move into Dower House on June 12; and that they wished the red desk to be included in the contract. McAfee then sent a letter dated June 8 to the Brewers, listing the items of furniture purchased.

The Brewers moved into Dower House in the middle of June. Soon after they moved in, they tried to contact McAfee at his office to tell him that there had been a misunderstanding relating to their purchase of the listed items. They then refused to pay him any more money, and he brought action to recover the balance outstanding. Will McAfee be able to collect the additional money from the Brewers?

15. The Thoelkes were owners of real property located in Orange County, which the Morrisons agreed to purchase. The Morrisons signed a contract for the sale of that property and mailed it to the Thoelkes in Texas on November 26. The next day the Thoelkes executed the contract and placed it in the mail addressed to the Morrisons' attorney in Florida. After the executed contract was mailed but before it was received in Florida, the Thoelkes called the Morrisons' attorney in Florida and attempted to repudiate the contract. Does a contract exist between the Thoelkes and the Morrisons? Discuss.

16. Lucy and Zehmer met while having drinks in a restaurant. During the course of their conversation, Lucy

apparently offered to buy Zehmer's 471.6-acre farm for $50,000 cash. Although Zehmer claims that he thought the offer was made in jest, he wrote the following on the back of a pad: "We hereby agree to sell to W. O. Lucy the Ferguson Farm complete for $50,000, title satisfactory to buyer." Zehmer then signed the writing and induced his wife Ida to do the same. She claims, however, that she signed only after Zehmer assured her that it was only a joke. Finally, Zehmer claims that he was "high as a Georgia pine" at the time but admits that he was not too drunk to make a valid contract. Decision?

17. Lee Calan Imports advertised a used Volvo station wagon for sale in the *Chicago Sun-Times*. As part of the information for the advertisement, Lee Calan Imports instructed the newspaper to print the price of the car as $1,795. However, due to a mistake made by the newspaper, without any fault on the part of Lee Calan Imports, the printed ad listed the price of the car as $1,095. After reading the ad and then examining the car, O'Brien told a Lee Calan Imports salesperson that he wanted to purchase the car for the advertised price of $1,095. Calan Imports refuses to sell the car to O'Brien for $1,095. Is there a contract? If so, for what price?

18. On May 20, cattle rancher Oliver visited his neighbor Southworth, telling him, "I know you're interested in buying the land I'm selling." Southworth replied, "Yes, I do want to buy that land, especially as it adjoins my property." Although the two men did not discuss the price, Oliver told Southworth he would determine the value of the property and send that information to him, so that Southworth would have "notice" of what Oliver "wanted for the land." On June 13, Southworth called Oliver to ask if he still planned to sell the land. Oliver answered, "Yes, and I should have the value of the land determined soon." On June 17, Oliver sent a letter to Southworth listing a price quotation of $324,000.

Southworth then responded to Oliver by letter on June 21, stating that he accepted Oliver's offer. However, on June 24 Oliver wrote back to Southworth, saying, "There has never been a firm offer to sell, and there is no enforceable contract between us." Oliver maintains that a price quotation alone is not an offer. Southworth claims a valid contract has been made. Who wins? Discuss.

19. On December 23, Wyman, a lawyer representing First National Bank & Trust (defendant), wrote to Zeller (plaintiff) stating that he had been instructed to offer a building to Zeller for sale at a price of $240,000. Zeller had previously expressed an interest in purchasing the building for $240,000. The letter also set forth details concerning interest rates and loan fees.

After receiving the letter, Zeller instructed his attorney, Jamma, to send Wyman a written counteroffer of $230,000 with interest and loan arrangements varying from the terms of the original offer. Jamma sent the written counteroffer as instructed on January 10. On the same day, Jamma telephoned Wyman and informed him of the counteroffer. Subsequently Jamma sent an acceptance of the original offer to Wyman. When Wyman refused to sell the property to him, Zeller brought an action to seek enforcement of the alleged contract. Decision?

20. First Development Corporation of Kentucky (FDCK) sought to purchase a fifteen-acre parcel of riverfront property owned by Martin Marietta. On May 9, FDCK made an offer to purchase the property for $300,000, which it submitted to Coldwell Banker, Martin Marietta's real estate agent. This offer was accompanied by an earnest money deposit evidenced by a $1,000 check payable to Coldwell Banker. The deposit was fully refundable if transfer of title to FDCK was not completed for any reason except FDCK's failure to perform. After this offer expired without being accepted, FDCK asked Don Gilmour, Coldwell Banker's account agent, to seek a counteroffer. In a letter to Gilmour, dated September 7, Martin Marietta agreed to sell the property for $550,000. The counteroffer stated it was to remain open for thirty days. Gilmour informed Pollitt, president of FDCK, of the counteroffer by telephone on September 7 and sent a copy of the letter to Pollitt, which was received on September 12.

Within days of the expiration of FDCK's original offer, Bill Harvey, president of Harmony Landing, a development company, initiated direct negotiations with Martin Marietta to purchase the riverfront parcel. These negotiations resulted in a contract being executed on September 21 or 22. During a September 21 phone call, Gilmour advised Pollitt of Harmony Landing's interest in buying the property, but Pollitt remained noncommittal during the conversation. Later that day, Pollitt, along with his partner and engineer, visited the property and discussed various studies and arrived at a decision to accept the September 7 offer from Martin Marietta. However, Pollitt did not convey this acceptance to Gilmour. Rather, he consulted his attorneys regarding a contract to accept Martin Marietta's offer.

After consulting with his attorneys, Pollitt prepared an acceptance of Martin Marietta's offer but did not put it in the mail. The next morning, Pollitt placed the acceptance in his office suite's mail depository. However, after being informed by Gilmour that Martin Marietta had accepted Harmony Landing's option on the river property, Pollitt retrieved the acceptance and personally delivered it to Gilmour at 4:15 P.M. The acceptance was returned to Pollitt and he subsequently initiated this action for temporary and permanent injunction and specific performance. The district court ruled that the $1,000 check, payable to and in the possession of Coldwell Banker during the period of this controversy was, by operation of law, converted into consideration for a thirty-day irrevocable option in favor of FDCK to purchase the riverfront property in accordance with the terms of Martin Marietta's letter of September 7. Does a contract exist between Martin Marietta and FDCK?

21. On August 12, Mr. and Mrs. Mitchell, the owners of a small secondhand store, attended Alexander's Auction, where they bought a used safe for $50. The safe, part of the Sumstad estate, contained a locked inside compartment. Both the auctioneer and the Mitchells knew this fact. Soon after the auction, the Mitchells had the compartment opened by a locksmith, who discovered $32,207 inside. The Everett Police Department impounded the money. The city of Everett brought an action against the Sumstad estate and the Mitchells to determine the owner of the money. Who should receive the money? Why?

TAKING SIDES

Cushing filed an application with the office of the Adjutant General of the State of New Hampshire for the use of the Portsmouth Armory to hold a dance on the evening of April 29. The application, made on behalf of the Portsmouth Area Clamshell Alliance, was received by the Adjutant General's office on or about March 30. On March 31 the Adjutant General mailed a signed contract after agreeing to rent the armory for the evening requested. The agreement required acceptance by the renter affixing his signature to the agreement and then returning the copy to the Adjutant General within five days after receipt. Cushing received the contract offer, signed it on behalf of the Alliance, and placed it in the outbox for mailing on April 3. At 6:30 on the evening of April 4, Cushing received a telephone call from the Adjutant General revoking the rental offer. Cushing stated during the conversation that he had already signed and mailed the contract. The Adjutant General sent a written confirmation of the withdrawal on April 5. On April 6 the Adjutant General's office received by mail from Cushing the signed contract dated April 3 and postmarked April 5.

a. What are the arguments that a binding contract exists?

b. What are the arguments that a contract does not exist or should not exist?

c. What is the proper outcome? Explain.

CHAPTER 9

CONDUCT INVALIDATING ASSENT

CHAPTER OUTCOMES

After reading and studying this chapter, you should be able to:

- Identify the types of duress and describe the legal effect of each.

- Define undue influence and identify some of the situations giving rise to a confidential relationship.

- Identify the types of fraud and the elements that must be shown to establish the existence of each.

- Define the two types of nonfraudulent misrepresentation.

- Identify and explain the situations involving voidable mistakes.

The preceding chapter considered one of the essential requirements of a contract, namely, the objective manifestation of mutual assent by each party to the other. In addition to requiring that the offer and acceptance be satisfied, the law demands that the agreement be voluntary and knowing. If these requirements are not met, then the agreement is either voidable or void. This chapter deals with situations in which the consent manifested by one of the parties to the contract is not effective because it was not knowingly and voluntarily given. These situations are considered under the headings of duress, undue influence, fraud, nonfraudulent misrepresentation, and mistake.

DURESS

A person should not be held to an agreement into which she has not entered voluntarily. Accordingly, the law will not enforce any contract induced by **duress**, which in general is any wrongful or unlawful act or threat that overcomes the free will of a party.

PHYSICAL COMPULSION

There are two basic types of duress. The first occurs when one party compels another to manifest assent to a contract through actual **physical force**, such as pointing a gun at a person or taking a person's hand and compelling him to sign a written contract. This type of duress, while extremely rare, renders the agreement **void**. Restatement, Section 174(1).

IMPROPER THREATS

The second type of duress involves the use of improper threats or acts, *including economic and social coercion*, to compel a person to enter into a contract. The threat may be explicit or may be inferred from words or conduct; in either case, it must leave the victim with no reasonable alternative. This type of duress makes the contract **voidable** at the option of the coerced party. Restatement, Section 175(2).

For example, if Lance, a landlord, induces Tamara, an infirm, bedridden tenant, to enter into a new lease on the same apartment at a greatly increased rent by wrongfully threatening to terminate Tamara's lease and evict her, Tamara can escape or *avoid* the new lease by reason of the duress exerted upon her.

With respect to the second and more common type of duress, the fact that the act or threat would not affect a person of average strength and intelligence is not determinative if it places the particular person in fear and induces him to perform an action against his will. The test is *subjective*, and the question is, did the threat actually induce assent on the part of the person claiming to be the victim of duress? Threats that would suffice to induce assent by one person may not suffice to induce assent by another. All circumstances must be considered, including the age, background, and relationship of the parties. Restatement, Section 175. Indeed, as Comment c to this section of the Restatement states,

> Persons of a weak or cowardly nature are the very ones that need protection; the courageous can usually protect themselves. Timid and inexperienced persons are

particularly subject to threats, and it does not lie in the mouths of the unscrupulous to excuse their imposition on such persons on the ground of their victims' infirmities.

Ordinarily, the acts or threats constituting duress are themselves crimes or torts. But this is not true in all cases. The acts need not be criminal or tortious to be *wrongful*; they merely need to be contrary to public policy or morally reprehensible. For example, if the threat involves a breach of a contractual duty of good faith and fair dealing or the use of the civil process in bad faith, it is improper.

Moreover, the courts have generally held that contracts induced by threats of criminal prosecution are voidable, regardless of whether the coerced party had committed an unlawful act. Likewise, threatening the criminal prosecution of a near relative, such as a son or husband, is duress, regardless of the guilt or innocence of the relative.

To be distinguished from such threats of prosecution are threats to resort to ordinary civil remedies to recover a debt due from another. Threatening to bring a civil suit against an individual to recover a debt is not wrongful. What is prohibited is threatening to bring a civil suit when bringing such a suit would be abuse of process.

PRACTICAL ADVICE

If you entered into a contract due to improper threats, consider whether you wish to void the contract. If you decide to do so, act promptly.

◆ SEE CASE 11-1

UNDUE INFLUENCE

Undue influence is the unfair persuasion of a person by a party generally in a dominant position based upon a **confidential relationship**. The law very carefully scrutinizes contracts between those in a relationship of trust and confidence that is likely to permit one party to take unfair advantage of the other. Examples are the relationships of guardian–ward, trustee–beneficiary, principal–agent, spouses to each other, parent–child, attorney–client, physician–patient, and clergy–parishioner.

A transaction induced by unfair influence on the part of the dominant party is **voidable**. The ultimate question in undue influence cases is whether the dominant party induced the transaction by influencing a freely exercised and competent judgment or by dominating the mind or emotions of a submissive party. The weakness or dependence of the person persuaded is a strong indicator of the fairness or unfairness of the persuasion. For example, Ronald, a person without business experience, has for years relied in business matters

on the advice of Nancy, who is experienced in business. Nancy, without making any false representations of fact, induces Ronald to enter into a contract with Nancy's confederate, George. The contract, however, is disadvantageous to Ronald, as both Nancy and George know. The transaction is voidable on the grounds of undue influence.

Undue influence, as previously mentioned, generally arises in the context of relationships in which one person is in a position of dominance, or is likely to be. Where such a relationship exists at the time of the transaction, and it appears that the dominant party has gained at the other party's expense, the transaction is presumed to be voidable. For example, in a legally challenged contract between a guardian and his ward, the law presumes that advantage was taken by the guardian. It is, therefore, incumbent upon the guardian to rebut this presumption. Important factors in determining whether a contract is fair are (1) whether the dominant party made full disclosure of all relevant information known to him, (2) whether the consideration was adequate, and (3) whether the dependent party received competent and independent advice before completing the transaction. Without limitation, in every situation in which a confidential relationship exists, the dominant party is held to utmost good faith in his dealings with the other.

PRACTICAL ADVICE

If you are in a confidential relationship with another person, when you enter into a contract with that person, make sure that (1) you fully disclose all relevant information about that transaction, (2) the contract is fair, and (3) the other party obtains independent advice about the transaction.

◆ SEE CASE 11-2

FRAUD

Another factor affecting the validity of consent given by a contracting party is fraud, which prevents assent from being knowingly given. There are two distinct types of fraud: fraud in the execution and fraud in the inducement.

FRAUD IN THE EXECUTION

Fraud in the execution, which is extremely rare, consists of a misrepresentation that deceives the defrauded person as to the very nature of the contract. Such fraud occurs when a person does not know, or does not have reasonable opportunity to know, the character or essence of a proposed contract because the other party misrepresents its character or essential terms. Fraud in the execution renders the transaction **void**.

For example, Abigail delivers a package to Boris, requests that Boris sign a receipt for it, holds out a simple printed form headed "Receipt," and indicates the line on which Boris is to sign. This line, which to Boris appears to be the bottom line of the receipt, is actually the signature line of a promissory note cleverly concealed underneath the receipt. Boris signs where directed without knowing that he is signing a note. This is fraud in the execution. The note is void and of no legal effect because Boris has not actually given his assent, even though his signature is genuine and appears to manifest his assent to the terms of the note. The nature of Abigail's fraud precluded consent to the signing of the note because it prevented Boris from reasonably knowing what he was signing.

FRAUD IN THE INDUCEMENT

Fraud in the inducement, generally referred to as fraud or deceit, is an intentional misrepresentation of material fact by one party to the other, who consents to enter into a contract in justifiable reliance upon the misrepresentation. Fraud in the inducement renders the contract **voidable** by the defrauded party. For example, Ada, in offering to sell her dog to Ben, tells Ben that the dog won first prize in its class in a recent national dog show. In fact, the dog had not even been entered in the show. Nonetheless, Ada's statement induces Ben to accept the offer and pay a high price for the dog. A contract exists, but it is voidable by Ben because of Ada's fraud, which induced his assent.

The requisites for fraud in the inducement are as follows:

1. a false representation
2. of a fact
3. that is material and
4. made with knowledge of its falsity and the intention to deceive (scienter) and
5. which representation is justifiably relied upon.

FALSE REPRESENTATION A basic element of fraud is a false representation or misrepresentation, that is, an assertion not in accord with the facts, made through positive statement or conduct that misleads. **Concealment** is an action intended or known to be likely to keep another from learning of a fact of which he otherwise would have learned. Active concealment is a form of misrepresentation that can form the basis for fraud, as where a seller puts heavy oil or grease in a car engine to conceal a knock. Truth may be suppressed by concealment as much as by misrepresentation.

Expressly denying knowledge of a fact, which a party knows to exist, is a misrepresentation if it leads the other party to believe that the facts do not exist or cannot be discovered. Moreover, a statement of misleading half-truth is considered the equivalent of a false representation.

As a general rule, **silence** or nondisclosure alone does *not* amount to fraud. A seller generally is not obligated to tell a purchaser everything he knows about the subject of a sale. Thus, it is not fraud when a buyer possesses advantageous information about the seller's property, of which he knows the seller to be ignorant, and does not disclose such information to the seller. Likewise, a buyer is under no duty to inform a seller of the greater value or other advantages of his property. Assume that Sid owns a farm that, as a farm, is worth $100,000. Brenda knows that there is oil under Sid's farm and knows that Sid is ignorant of this fact. Brenda, without disclosing this information to Sid, makes an offer to Sid to buy the farm for $100,000. Sid accepts the offer, and a contract is duly made. Sid, on later learning the facts, can do nothing about the matter, either at law or in equity. As one case puts it, "a purchaser is not bound by our laws to make the man he buys from as wise as himself."

PRACTICAL ADVICE
Consider bargaining with the other party to promise to give you full disclosure.

Although nondisclosure usually does not constitute a misrepresentation, in certain situations it does. One such situation arises when (1) a person fails to disclose a fact known to him, (2) he knows that the disclosure of that fact would correct a mistake of the other party as to a basic assumption on which that party is making the contract, and (3) nondisclosure of the fact amounts to a failure to act in a good faith and in accordance with reasonable standards of fair dealing. Restatement, Section 161. Accordingly, if the property at issue in the contract possesses a substantial latent (hidden) defect, one that the buyer would not discover by an ordinary examination, the seller may be obliged to reveal it. Suppose, for example, that Judith owns a valuable horse, which Judith knows is suffering from a disease only a competent veterinary surgeon might detect. Judith offers to sell this horse to Curt, but does not inform Curt about the condition of the horse. Curt makes a reasonable examination of the horse and, finding it in apparently normal condition, purchases it from Judith. Curt, on later discovering the disease in question, can have the sale set aside. Judith's silence, under the circumstances, was a misrepresentation.

PRACTICAL ADVICE
When entering into contract negotiations, first determine what duty of disclosure you owe to the other party.

In other situations, the law also imposes a duty of disclosure. For example, one may have a duty of disclosure because of prior representations, innocently made before entering into the contract, which are later discovered to be untrue. Another instance in which silence may constitute fraud is a transaction involving a fiduciary. A **fiduciary** is a person in a confidential relationship who owes a duty of trust, loyalty, and confidence to another. For example, an agent owes a fiduciary duty to his principal, as does a trustee to the beneficiary of a trust and a partner to her copartners. A fiduciary may not deal at *arm's length* but rather owes a duty to make full disclosure of all relevant facts when entering into a transaction with the other party to the relationship. In contrast, in most everyday business or market transactions, the parties are said to deal at "arm's length," meaning that they deal with each other on equal terms.

FACT The basic element of fraud is the misrepresentation of a material fact. A **fact** is an event that actually took place or a thing that actually exists. Suppose that Dale induces Mike to purchase shares in a company unknown to Mike at a price of $100 per share by representing that she had paid $150 per share for them during the preceding year, when in fact she had paid only $50.00. This representation of a past event is a misrepresentation of fact.

Actionable fraud rarely can be based on what is merely a statement of **opinion**. A representation is one of opinion if it expresses only the uncertain belief of the representer as to the existence of a fact or his judgment as to quality, value, authenticity, or other matters of judgment.

The line between fact and opinion is not an easy one to draw and in close cases presents an issue for the jury. The solution will often turn on the superior knowledge of the person making the statement and the information available to the other party. Thus, if Dale said to Mike that the shares were "a good investment," she is merely stating her opinion, and in the usual case Mike ought to regard it as no more than that. Other common examples of opinion are statements of value, such as "This is the best car for the money in town" or "This deluxe model will give you twice the wear of a cheaper model." Such exaggerations and commendations of articles offered for sale are to be expected from dealers, who are merely puffing their wares with sales talk. If, however, the representer is a professional advising a client, the courts are more likely to regard as actionable an untrue statement of opinion. When the person expressing the opinion is one who holds himself out as having expert knowledge, the tendency is to grant relief to those who have sustained loss through reasonable reliance upon the expert evaluation.

Also to be distinguished from a representation of fact is a **prediction** of the future. Predictions, which are similar to opinions in that no one can know with certainty what will happen in the future, normally are not regarded as factual statements. Likewise, promissory statements ordinarily do not constitute a basis of fraud, as a breach of promise does not necessarily indicate that the promise was fraudulently made. A promise that the promisor, at the time of making, had no intention of keeping, however, is a misrepresentation of fact. Most courts take the position that a misrepresented state of mind "is as much a fact as the state of a person's digestion." *Edgington v. Fitzmaurice*, 29 Ch.D. 459 (1885). If a dealer promises, "I will service this machine free for the next year," but at the time has no intention of doing so, his conduct is actionable if the other elements of fraud are present.

Historically, courts held that representations of **law** were not statements of fact but rather of opinion. The present trend is to recognize that a statement of law may have either the effect of a statement of fact or a statement of opinion. Restatement, Torts, Section 545. For example, a statement of law asserting that a particular statute has been enacted or repealed has the effect of a statement of fact. On the other hand, a statement as to the legal consequences of a particular set of facts is a statement of opinion. Nonetheless, such a statement may imply that the facts known to the maker are consistent with the legal conclusion stated. For example, an assertion that a company has the legal right to do business in a State may include the assurance that the company has taken all the steps required to be duly qualified. Moreover, a statement by one who is learned in the law, such as a practicing attorney, may be considered a statement of fact.

◆ SEE CASE 11-3

MATERIALITY In addition to being a misrepresentation of fact, a misrepresentation also must be material. A misrepresentation is **material** if (1) it would be likely to induce a reasonable person to manifest his assent or (2) the maker knows that it would be likely to induce the recipient to do so. Restatement, Section 162. In the sale of a racehorse, whether a certain jockey rode the horse in its most recent race may not be material, but its running time for the race probably would be. The Restatement of Contracts provides that a contract justifiably induced by a misrepresentation is voidable if the misrepresentation is either fraudulent *or* material. Therefore, a fraudulent misrepresentation does not have to be material for the recipient to obtain rescission, but it must be material if she is to recover damages. Restatement, Section 164; Restatement, Torts, Section 538.

◆ SEE CASE 11-4

KNOWLEDGE OF FALSITY AND INTENTION TO DECEIVE To establish fraud, the misrepresentation must have been known by the one making it to be false and must have been made with an intent to deceive. This element of fraud is known as *scienter*. Knowledge of falsity can consist of (1) actual knowledge, (2) lack of belief in the statement's truthfulness, or (3) reckless indifference as to its truthfulness.

JUSTIFIABLE RELIANCE A person is not entitled to relief unless he has justifiably relied upon the misrepresentation. If the misrepresentation in no way influenced the complaining party's decision, he must abide by the terms of the contract. He is not deceived if he does not rely. Justifiable reliance requires that the misrepresentation contribute substantially to the misled party's decision to enter into the contract. If the complaining party knew or it was obvious that the defendant's representation was untrue, but he still entered into the contract, he has not justifiably relied. Moreover, where the misrepresentation is fraudulent, the party who relies on it is entitled to relief even though he does not investigate the statement or is contributorily negligent in relying on it. Restatement, Torts, Sections 540, 545A. Not knowing or discovering the facts before making a contract does not constitute unjustified reliance unless it amounts to a failure to act in good faith and in accordance with reasonable standards of fair dealing. Restatement, Section 172. Thus, most courts will not allow a person who concocts a deliberate and elaborate scheme to defraud—one that the defrauded party should readily detect—to argue that the defrauded party did not justifiably rely upon the misrepresentation.

NONFRAUDULENT MISREPRESENTATION

Nonfraudulent misrepresentation is a material, false statement that induces another to rely justifiably but is made without *scienter*.

Negligent misrepresentation is a false representation that is made without due care in ascertaining its truthfulness. **Innocent misrepresentation** is a false representation made without knowledge of its falsity but with due care. To obtain relief for nonfraudulent misrepresentation, all of the other elements of fraud must be present *and* the misrepresentation must be material. The remedies that may be available for nonfraudulent misrepresentation are rescission and damages (see *Chapter 18*).

◆ SEE CASE 11-5

◈ SEE FIGURE 11-1: **Misrepresentation**

MISTAKE

A **mistake** is a belief that is not in accord with the facts. Where the mistaken facts relate to the basis of the parties' agreement, the law permits the adversely affected party to avoid or reform the contract under certain circumstances. But because permitting avoidance for mistake undermines the objective approach to mutual assent, the law has experienced considerable difficulty in specifying those circumstances that justify permitting the subjective matter of mistake to invalidate an otherwise objectively satisfactory agreement. As a result, establishing clear rules to govern the effect of mistake has proven elusive.

The Restatement and modern cases treat mistakes of law in existence at the time of making a contract no differently than mistakes of fact. For example, Susan contracts to sell a parcel of land to James with the mutual understanding that James will build an apartment house on the land. Both Susan and James believe that such a building is lawful. Unknown to them, however, the town in which the land is located had enacted an ordinance precluding such use of the land three days before they entered into the contract. This mistake of law, which the courts would treat as a mistake of fact, would lead to the consequences discussed in the following section.

◆ FIGURE 11-1: **Misrepresentation**

	Fraudulent	Negligent	Innocent
False Statement of Fact	Yes	Yes	Yes
Materiality	Yes for damages No for rescission	Yes	Yes
Fault	With knowledge and intent (*scienter*)	Without due care	Without knowledge but with due care
Reliance	Yes	Yes	Yes
Injury	Yes for damages No for rescission	Yes for damages No for rescission	Yes for damages No for rescission
Remedies	Damages Rescission	Damages Rescission	Damages Rescission

---

APPLYING THE LAW

Conduct Invalidating Assent

FACTS Gillian bought a two-year-old used car from a luxury automobile dealer for $36,000. At the time of her purchase, the odometer and title documentation both indicated that the car had 21,445 miles on it. But after just a little more than a year, the engine failed, and Gillian had to take the car to a mechanic. The problem was the water pump, which needed to be replaced. Surprised that a water pump should fail in a car with so few miles on it, the mechanic more closely examined the odometer and determined that someone had cleverly tampered with it. According to the mechanic, the car probably had about sixty thousand miles on it when Gillian bought it. At the time Gillian bought the car, the retail value for the same vehicle with sixty thousand miles on it was approximately $30,000.

Gillian decided that under these conditions she no longer wanted the car. She contacted the dealership, which strenuously denied having tampered with the odometer. In fact, the dealership's records reflect that it purchased Gillian's car at auction for $34,000, after a thorough inspection that revealed no mechanical deficiencies or alteration of the car's odometer.

ISSUE Is Gillian's contract voidable by her?

RULE OF LAW Innocent misrepresentation renders a contract voidable. Innocent misrepresentation is proven when the following elements are established: (1) a false representation, (2) of fact, (3) that is material, (4) made without knowledge of its falsity but with due care, and (5) the representation is justifiably relied upon.

APPLICATION Gillian can prove all five elements of innocent misrepresentation. First, the dealership's false representation was that the mileage on the car was 21,445, when the car actually had about sixty thousand miles on it. Second, the mileage of the car at the time of sale is an actual event not an opinion or prediction. Third, as the mileage of a used car is probably the most critical determinant of its value, this misrepresentation was material to the parties' agreed sale price, inducing the formation of the contract. Indeed, while Gillian might still have purchased this car with sixty thousand miles on it, she most certainly would have done so only at a lower price. Fourth, it is highly unlikely that the dealership was aware of the incorrect odometer reading. We know this because it paid $34,000 for the car, which should have sold for something less than $30,000 in the wholesale market if the true mileage had been known. Moreover, the dealership appears to have conducted appropriate due diligence to support both its own purchase price and the price at which it offered the car to Gillian. The odometer tampering was cleverly concealed, so much so that neither the dealerships' inspection before purchase nor Gillian's mechanic's initial inspection revealed it. Fifth, Gillian's reliance on the ostensible odometer reading is justified. The car was only two years old when she bought it, and 21,445 miles is within an average range of mileage for a used car of that age. Unless the car's physical condition or something in the title paperwork should have alerted her to an inconsistency between the stated mileage and the car's actual mileage, Gillian was entitled to rely on what appeared to be a correct odometer reading.

CONCLUSION Because all the elements of innocent misrepresentation can be shown, Gillian's contract is voidable by Gillian.

MUTUAL MISTAKE

Mutual mistake occurs when *both* parties are mistaken as to the same set of facts. If the mistake relates to a basic assumption on which the contract is made and has a material effect on the agreed exchange, then it is **voidable** by the adversely affected party unless he bears the risk of the mistake. Restatement, Section 152.

Usually, market conditions and the financial situation of the parties are not considered basic assumptions. Thus, if Gail contracts to purchase Pete's automobile under the belief that she can sell it at a profit to Jesse, she is not excused from liability if she is mistaken in this belief. Nor can she rescind the agreement simply because she was mistaken as to her estimate of what the automobile was worth. These are the ordinary risks of business, and courts do not undertake to relieve against them. But suppose that the parties contract upon the assumption that the automobile is a 2008 Cadillac with fifteen thousand miles of use, when in fact the engine is that of a cheaper model and has been run in excess of fifty thousand miles. Here, a court would likely allow a rescission because of mutual mistake of a material fact. Another example of mutual mistake of fact was presented in a California case where a noted violinist purchased two violins from a collector for $8,000, the bill of sale reading, "I have on this date sold to Mr. Efrem Zimbalist one Joseph Guarnerius violin and one Stradivarius violin dated 1717." Actually, unknown to either party, neither violin was genuine. Taken together they were worth no more than $300. The sale was voidable by the purchaser for mutual mistake. In a New Zealand case, the plaintiff purchased a "stud bull" at an auction. There were no express warranties as to "sex, condition, or otherwise." Actually, the bull was sterile. Rescission was allowed, with the court observing that it was a "bull in name only."

◆ SEE CASE 11-5

UNILATERAL MISTAKE

Unilateral mistake occurs when only one of the parties is mistaken. Courts have been hesitant to grant relief for unilateral mistake even though it relates to a basic assumption on which the party entered into the contract and has a material effect on the agreed exchange. Nevertheless, relief will be granted where the nonmistaken party knows, or reasonably should know, that such a mistake has been made (palpable unilateral mistake) or where the mistake was caused by the fault of the nonmistaken party. For example, suppose a building contractor makes a serious error in his computations and as a result submits a bid on a job that is one-half the amount it should be. If the other party knows that he made such an error, or reasonably should have known, she cannot, as a general rule, take advantage of the other's mistake by accepting the offer. In addition, many courts and the Restatement allow rescission where the effect of the unilateral mistake makes enforcement of the contract unconscionable. Section 153.

ASSUMPTION OF RISK OF MISTAKE

A party who has undertaken to bear the risk of a mistake will be unable to avoid the contract, even though the mistake (which may be either mutual or unilateral) otherwise would have permitted her to do so. This allocation of risk may occur by agreement of the parties. For instance, a ship at sea may be sold "lost or not lost." In such case the buyer is liable whether the ship was lost or not lost at the time the contract was made. There is no mistake; instead, there is a conscious allocation of risk.

Conscious ignorance may serve to allocate the risk of mistake when the parties recognize that they have limited knowledge of the facts. For example, the Supreme Court of Wisconsin refused to set aside the sale of a stone for which the purchaser paid one dollar, but which was subsequently discovered to be an uncut diamond valued at $700. The parties did not know at the time of sale what the stone was and

knew they did not know. Each consciously assumed the risk that the value might be more or less than the selling price.

PRACTICAL ADVICE
If you are unsure about the nature of a contract, consider allocating the risk of the uncertainties in your contract.

EFFECT OF FAULT UPON MISTAKE

The Restatement provides that a mistaken party's fault in not knowing or discovering a fact before making a contract does not prevent him from avoiding the contract "unless his fault amounts to a failure to act in good faith and in accordance with reasonable standards of fair dealing." Restatement, Section 157. This rule does not, however, apply to a failure to read a contract. As a general proposition, a party is held to what she signs. Her signature authenticates the writing, and she cannot repudiate that which she has voluntarily approved. Generally, one who assents to a writing is presumed to know its contents and cannot escape being bound by its terms merely by contending that she did not read them; her assent is deemed to cover unknown as well as known terms. Restatement, Section 157, Comment b.

MISTAKE IN MEANING OF TERMS

Somewhat related to mistakes of facts is the situation in which the parties misunderstand the meaning of one another's manifestations of mutual assent. A famous case involving this problem is *Raffles v. Wichelhaus*, 2 Hurlstone & Coltman 906 (1864), popularly known as the "*Peerless* Case." A contract of purchase was made for 125 bales of cotton to arrive on the *Peerless* from Bombay. It happened, however, that there were two ships by the name of *Peerless*, each sailing from Bombay, one in October and the other in December. The buyer had in mind the ship that sailed in October, while the seller reasonably believed the agreement referred to the *Peerless* sailing in December. Neither party was at fault, but both believed in good faith that a different ship was intended. The English court held that no contract existed. The Restatement, Section 20, is in accord.

There is no manifestation of mutual assent in cases in which the parties attach materially different meanings to their manifestations and neither party knows or has reason to know the meaning attached by the other. If blame can be ascribed to either party, however, that party will be held responsible. Thus, if the seller knew of two ships by the name of *Peerless* sailing from Bombay, then he would be at fault, and the contract would be for the ship sailing in October as the buyer expected. If neither party is to blame or both are to blame, there is no contract at all; that is, the agreement is void.

CHAPTER SUMMARY

DURESS **Definition** wrongful or unlawful act or threat that overcomes the free will of a party
Physical Compulsion coercion involving physical force renders the agreement void
Improper Threats improper threats or acts, including economic and social coercion, render the contract voidable

UNDUE INFLUENCE **Definition** taking unfair advantage of a person by reason of a dominant position based on a confidential relationship
Effect renders a contract voidable

FRAUD **Fraud in the Execution** a misrepresentation that deceives the other party as to the nature of a document evidencing the contract renders the agreement void
Fraud in the Inducement renders the agreement voidable if the following elements are present:
- *False Representation* positive statement or conduct that misleads
- *Fact* an event that occurred or thing that exists
- *Materiality* of substantial importance
- *Knowledge of Falsity and Intention to Deceive* called *scienter* and includes (1) actual knowledge, (2) lack of belief in statement's truthfulness, or (3) reckless indifference to its truthfulness
- *Justifiable Reliance* a defrauded party is reasonably influenced by the misrepresentation

NONFRAUDULENT MISREPRESENTATION **Negligent Misrepresentation** misrepresentation made without due care in ascertaining its truthfulness, renders agreement voidable
Innocent Misrepresentation misrepresentation made without knowledge of its falsity but with due care; renders contract voidable

MISTAKE **Definition** an understanding that is not in accord with existing fact
Mutual Mistake both parties have a common but erroneous belief forming the basis of the contract; renders the contract voidable by either party
Unilateral Mistake courts are unlikely to grant relief unless the error is known or should be known by the nonmistaken party
Assumption of Risk a party may assume the risk of a mistake
Effect of Fault upon Mistake not a bar to avoidance unless the fault amounts to a failure to act in good faith

CASES

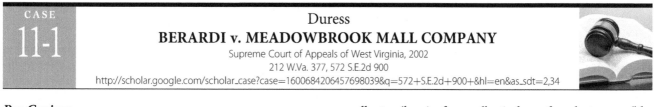

CASE 11-1

Duress
BERARDI v. MEADOWBROOK MALL COMPANY
Supreme Court of Appeals of West Virginia, 2002
212 W.Va. 377, 572 S.E.2d 900
http://scholar.google.com/scholar_case?case=1600684206457698039&q=572+S.E.2d+900+&hl=en&as_sdt=2,34

Per Curiam
Jerry A. Berardi (hereinafter referred to as "Mr. Berardi"), Betty J. Berardi, and Bentley Corporation, plaintiffs below/

appellants (hereinafter collectively referred to as "the Berardis"), seek reversal of a summary judgment granted to Meadowbrook Mall Company, an Ohio Limited Partnership, and the Cafaro Company (hereinafter referred to as "Cafaro Company"), an Ohio Corporation, defendants below/appellees (hereinafter collectively referred to as "Meadowbrook" or * * * "Cafaro Company"). * * *

Facts and Procedural History

Between 1985 and 1987, the Berardis leased space for three restaurants from Meadowbrook. In 1990, the Berardis were delinquent in their rent. Cafaro Company, an affiliate of Meadowbrook, sent a letter dated October 1, 1990, to Mr. Berardi citing the arrearages. The letter informed him that a lawsuit would be filed in Ohio requesting judgment for the total amount of the arrearages. The letter proposed that after filing the suits, a consent judgment would be forwarded to Mr. Berardi granting judgment for the full amount of arrearages. Once the consent judgment was signed by both parties and filed with the court, the letter pledged, no steps to enforce the judgment would be undertaken providing the Berardis continued to operate their three restaurants consistent with the then present payment arrangement. Mr. Berardi signed the letter on October 5, 1990. In April 1996, Meadowbrook caused to be filed in the Circuit Court of Harrison County, West Virginia, [the] * * * judgment of the Ohio lawsuits. * * * [Meadowbrook received a] lien on the Goff Building [which was owned by the Berardis, and which] impeded the refinancing [of the building by the Berardis].

Correspondence was exchanged between counsel for the parties. * * * The correspondence ultimately led, in June 1997, to the Berardis and Anthony Cafaro (an authorized agent for Meadowbrook) signing a "Settlement Agreement and Release" settling the 1990 Ohio judgments. In this document, the Berardis acknowledged the validity of the 1990 Ohio judgments and that the aggregate due under them, plus interest and leasehold charges, was $814,375.97. The Berardis agreed to pay Meadowbrook $150,000 on the date the Goff Building refinancing occurred, and also to pay Meadowbrook $100,000 plus 8.5% interest per year on the third anniversary of the initial $150,000 payment. These payments would discharge the Berardis from all other amounts due and owing. The payment of the initial $150,000 would also result in Meadowbrook releasing the lien against the Goff Building.

The agreement additionally recited:

Berardis hereby release and forever discharge Meadowbrook, its employees, agents, successors, and assigns from any and all claims, demands, damages, actions, and causes of action of any kind or nature that have arisen or may arise as a result of the leases, or Guaranties whether said claims are known or unknown, contingent, or liquidated, from the beginning of time to the effective date of the agreement. Berardis acknowledge there was no unethical behavior on behalf of Meadowbrook Mall Company, its employees, agents.

Nevertheless, on October 2, 2000, the Berardis filed a complaint against Meadowbrook alleging that Meadowbrook breached the October 1990 agreement by attempting to enforce the 1990 Ohio judgments, that Meadowbrook extorted by duress and coercion the 1997 agreement, and that Meadowbrook and other business entities had conspired to enter into extortionate agreements with their tenants. Meadowbrook filed a motion to dismiss under the 1997 settlement. * * * Meadowbrook sought summary judgment, which the circuit court granted. From this summary judgment, Berardi now appeals.

* * *

Discussion

* * *

"We begin our discussion of this issue by reiterating, at the outset, that settlements are highly regarded and scrupulously enforced, so long as they are legally sound." [Citation.] "The law favors and encourages the resolution of controversies by contracts of compromise and settlement rather than by litigation; and it is the policy of the law to uphold and enforce such contracts if they are fairly made and are not in contravention of some law or public policy." [Citations.] Those who seek to avoid a settlement "face a heavy burden" [citation] and "since * * * settlement agreements, when properly executed, are legal and binding, this Court will not set aside such agreements on allegations of duress * * * absent clear and convincing proof of such claims." [Citation.]

The Berardis contend the 1997 settlement is invalid as it was procured by "economic duress:"

The concept of "economic or business duress" may be generally stated as follows: Where the plaintiff is forced into a transaction as a result of unlawful threats or wrongful, oppressive, or unconscionable conduct on the part of the defendant which leaves the plaintiff no reasonable alternative but to acquiesce, the plaintiff may void the transaction and recover any economic loss.

[Citation.] In [citation], we emphasized that

[t]here appears to be general acknowledgment that duress is not shown because one party to the contract has driven a hard bargain or that market or other conditions now make the contract more difficult to perform by one of the parties or that financial circumstances may have caused one party to make concessions.

[Citation] "Duress is not readily accepted as an excuse" to avoid a contract. [Citation.] Thus, to establish economic duress, "in addition to their own * * * statements, the plaintiffs must produce objective evidence of their duress. The defense of economic duress does not turn only upon the subjective state of mind of the plaintiffs, but it must be reasonable in light of the objective facts presented." [Citation.]

Mr. Berardi is a sophisticated businessman who has operated a number of commercial enterprises. As of 1997, the Berardis had substantial assets and a considerable net worth. While economic duress may reach large business entities as well as the "proverbial little old lady in tennis shoes," [citation], when the parties are sophisticated business entities, releases should be voided only in "'extreme and extraordinary cases.'" [Citation.] Indeed, "where an experienced businessman takes sufficient time, seeks the advice of counsel and understands the content of what he is signing he cannot claim the execution of the release was a product of duress." [Citation.] While the presence of counsel will not *per se* defeat a claim of economic duress, "a court must determine if the attorneys had an opportunity for meaningful input under the circumstances." [Citation.]

* * *

[N]o case can be found, we apprehend, where a party who, without force or intimidation and with full knowledge of all the facts of the case, accepts on account of an unlitigated and controverted demand a sum less than what he claims and believes to be due him, and agrees to accept that sum in full satisfaction, has been permitted to avoid his act on the ground that this is duress.

[Citations.]

Moreover, the Berardis did not file their complaint until October 2, 2000. A party seeking to repudiate a release must act promptly in disavowing it once the putative duress ends

or else the party will be deemed to have ratified the agreement. [Citations.] * * *

Finally, we do not believe that any relative economic inequality between the Berardis and Meadowbrook sufficiently factor into the summary judgment calculation. We have recognized that, "in most commercial transactions it may be assumed that there is some inequality of bargaining power. * * * " [Citation.] Indeed, even when one sophisticated business entity enjoys "a decided economic advantage" over another such entity, economic duress is extremely circumscribed:

> Because an element of economic duress is * * * present when many contracts are formed or releases given, the ability of a party to disown his obligations under a contract or release on that basis is reserved for extreme and extraordinary cases. Otherwise, the stronger party to a contract or release would routinely be at risk of having its rights under the contract or release challenged long after the instrument became effective.

[Citation.]

Given the facts, the law's disfavor of economic duress, its approbation of settlements, the sophisticated nature of the parties, and the extremely high evidentiary burden the Berardis must overcome, we harbor no substantial doubt nor do we believe the circuit court abused its discretion.

* * *

Conclusion

The judgment of the Circuit Court of Harrison County is affirmed.

CASE

11-2

Undue Influence
NEUGEBAUER v. NEUGEBAUER
Supreme Court of South Dakota, 2011
804 N.W.2d 450, 2011 S.D. 64
http://scholar.google.com/scholar_case?
case=1062309080412566845&q=804+N.W.2d+450+&hl=en&num=100&as_sdt=ffffffffffe04&as_ylo=2010

Zinter, J.

Harold and Pearl Neugebauer owned a 159-acre farm the parties called the "Home Place." The Hutchinson County farm included a house, garage, granary, machine sheds, barns, silos, and a dairy barn. During their marriage, Harold handled all of the legal and financial affairs of the farm and family. In 1980, Harold died, leaving Pearl as the sole owner of the Home Place and another farm property. Following Harold's death, Lincoln, the youngest of Harold and Pearl's seven children, began farming both properties. Lincoln also resided with his mother on the Home Place.

In 1984, Lincoln and Dennis, one of Pearl's other sons, formed L & D Farms partnership for the purpose of managing the farming operation on Pearl's land. L & D Farms

entered into a ten-year lease with Pearl that included an option to purchase the Home Place for $117,000, the appraised value in 1984. In 1985, Pearl moved from the farm to a home in Parkston. In 1989, Lincoln and Dennis dissolved L & D Farms without exercising the option to purchase.

After dissolution of the partnership, Lincoln farmed Pearl's land by himself. He paid annual rent, but Lincoln and Pearl never reduced their oral farm lease to writing. Pearl trusted Lincoln and left it to him to determine how much rent to pay. Pearl did, however, expect that Lincoln would be "fair." Pearl never took any steps to determine if the $6,320 annual rent Lincoln was paying was fair.

On several occasions from 2004 to 2008, Lincoln privately consulted with attorney Keith Goehring about purchasing the

Home Place. On December 3, 2008, Lincoln took Pearl to Goehring's office to discuss the purchase. Pearl, who only had an eighth-grade education, was almost eighty-four years old and was hard of hearing. Although Lincoln and Goehring discussed details of Lincoln's proposed purchase, Pearl said virtually nothing. She later testified that she could not keep up with the conversation and did not understand the terms discussed.

On December 17, 2008, * * * Pearl and Lincoln executed a contract for deed that had been drafted by Goehring. Goehring had been retained and his fees were paid by Lincoln. Neither Lincoln nor Goehring advised Pearl that Goehring represented only Lincoln, and neither suggested that Pearl could or should retain her own legal counsel.

There is no dispute that the fair market value of the Home Place was $697,000 in 2008 when the contract for deed was executed. Under the terms of the contract, Lincoln was to pay Pearl $117,000, the farm's 1984 appraised value. The contract price was to be paid over thirty years by making annual payments of $6,902.98.

After executing the contract, Lincoln told Pearl not to tell the rest of her children about the agreement. Pearl later became suspicious that something may have been wrong with the contract. In January 2009, Pearl's children returned to Parkston for a funeral. For the first time, Pearl revealed the contract to the rest of her children, and they explained the contract to her. She began to cry and wanted the contract torn up. Pearl personally and through her children asked Lincoln to tear up the contract. Lincoln refused.

[Pearl then brought an action for rescission of the contract on the ground of undue influence. The trial court found that Lincoln had exerted undue influence and rescinded the contract. Lincoln appealed, claiming that the trial court erred in finding that the contract for deed was a product of undue influence.]

The elements [of undue influence] are: (1) a person susceptible to undue influence; (2) another's opportunity to exert undue influence on that person to effect a wrongful purpose; (3) another's disposition to do so for an improper purpose; and (4) a result clearly showing the effects of undue influence. [Citation.] The party alleging undue influence must prove these elements by a preponderance of the evidence. [Citation.]

Susceptibility to Undue Influence
Lincoln argues that no evidence supported the court's finding that Pearl was susceptible to undue influence. * * * Lincoln contends that in the absence of medical evidence of mental deficits, the court erred in finding that Pearl was susceptible to undue influence.

Concededly, "'physical and mental weakness is always material upon the question of undue influence.' Obviously,

an aged and infirm person with impaired mental faculties would be more susceptible to influence than a mentally alert younger person in good health." [Citations.] But this Court has not required medical evidence to prove susceptibility to undue influence. * * *

In this case, there was substantial non-medical evidence demonstrating Pearl's susceptibility to undue influence. Pearl had an eighth-grade education, and she lacked experience in business and legal transactions. When she signed the contract for deed, Pearl was almost eighty-four and hard of hearing. Pearl and Dennis testified that she had relied on her deceased husband to take care of all their business and legal matters during their marriage. This dependency continued after Harold's death. Pearl testified that, with the exception of her checking account and monthly expenses, she often asked her children for help with business and financial affairs, which she did not understand. * * * We also note that Lincoln admitted Pearl had some mental impairment. He told [Pearl's daughter] Cheryl that Pearl was "slipping," meaning that Pearl would say something and a few minutes later repeat herself because she had forgotten what she had said. * * *

Opportunity to Exert Undue Influence
Lincoln contends that the court's finding of opportunity to exert undue influence was erroneous because Lincoln and Pearl had no confidential relationship and Pearl had the ability to seek independent advice between the two meetings with Goehring, but chose not to do so. * * *

In this case, Pearl testified that Lincoln was her son and someone with whom she had previously lived for many years: someone she trusted to "do right." Lincoln conceded that on the date Pearl signed the contract, he knew Pearl trusted him and had confidence that he would treat her fairly in his business dealings with her. This type of trust and confidence by a mother in her son was sufficient to prove opportunity.

* * *

Disposition to Exert Undue Influence
The court's finding that Lincoln had a disposition to exert undue influence for an improper purpose was also supported. Lincoln had substantial experience in farmland transactions and real estate appreciation. He collaborated with an attorney a number of times over four years to purchase the farm and draft the necessary documents. Yet Lincoln did not have the farm appraised as he had previously done when farming the property with his brother. Instead, Lincoln set the price at a value for which it had appraised twenty-four years earlier, a price that was one-sixth of its then current value. He also took no steps to ensure that his elderly mother understood the contract terms, including the fact that considering her age and the thirty-year amortization, she would likely never receive a substantial portion of the payments.

Finally, neither Lincoln nor his attorney advised Pearl to seek legal representation. * * *

Lincoln's conduct after execution of the contract was also relevant to show disposition to exercise undue influence at the time the contract was executed. [Citation.] After this contract for deed was executed, Lincoln instructed Pearl not to tell her other children about the contract. * * *

The court finally observed that Lincoln historically took advantage of Pearl by paying her less than fair market rent under the oral lease. * * *

* * *

Result Showing Effects of Undue Influence

Finally, we see no clear error in the court finding a result clearly showing the effects of undue influence. By executing the contract for deed, Pearl sold her property for $580,000 less than its value. Not only was the contract price of $117,000 substantially below the market value of $697,000, the thirty-year payment term would have required Pearl to live to 114 years-of-age to receive the payments. * * *

We find no clear error in the circuit court's findings of fact. We affirm its conclusion that rescission was warranted. * * * The judgment of the circuit court is affirmed.

CASE 11-3

Fraud: Fact
MAROUN v. WYRELESS SYSTEMS, INC.
Supreme Court of Idaho, 2005
141 Idaho 604, 114 P.3d 974
http://scholar.google.com/scholar_case?case=18286843461461582750&hl=en&as_sdt=2&as_vis=1&oi=scholarr

Trout, J.

Tony Y. Maroun (Maroun) was employed by Amkor when he accepted an offer to work for Wyreless, a startup company. On November 20, 2000, a letter was sent from Bradley C. Robinson, president of Wyreless, to Maroun setting forth the terms of their employment agreement. The pertinent portions of the letter were as follows:

* * *

- Annual salary of $300,000.
- $300,000 bonus for successful organization of Wyreless Systems, Inc.
- 15% of the issued equity in Wyreless Systems, Inc.
- The equity and "organization bonus" will need to be tied to agreeable milestones (e.g., acquisition of Matricus, organization of management team, etc).
- Full medical benefits.
- Position of Chief Executive Officer, President and a position on the Board.
- Bonuses and incentives will need to be determined by the Board and you after the business plan has been agreed by all parties.

* * *

I would like you to have an understanding of the fund raising status. I was able to get a commitment from two investors today for a minimum of $250,000 for arrival into the WSI bank account early next week. I believe we will be able to raise an additional $350,000 during the following week. * * * If we are not successful in raising the required capital for the business the funds remaining in the account on May 1, 2001 will be

release[d] to you and Jen Gadelman (sic) as compensation beyond salaries and expenses for your efforts in developing the business.

I anticipate a starting date of employment of December 1, 2000 or as soon you (sic) can reasonably and professional (sic) resolve your responsibilities with Amkor.

Thereafter, Maroun started working for Wyreless but his employment was terminated in February 2001. Maroun then filed suit (the Wyreless suit), alleging he had not received two salary payments totaling $23,077, had not received 15% of issued equity and had not received the remainder of the $600,000 in bank account funds, alleged to be a balance of $429,145. * * * Maroun also claimed Wyreless' corporate shell should be set aside and the shareholders of Wyreless should be jointly and severally liable for any damages Wyreless caused to him. * * * After Maroun filed a motion for partial summary judgment against Wyreless on the basis that there was no dispute Maroun was owed $23,077 in unpaid wages, the parties stipulated to entry of a judgment in favor of Maroun in the amount of $23,077.

In the fall of 2002, * * * Wyreless filed a motion for summary judgment on the remaining portions of Maroun's wage claim, which included the claim for 15% of Wyreless shares and the alleged $429,145 balance of the Wyreless fund account. The district court granted the motion. * * * Maroun appealed.

* * *

Maroun argues the district court erred in granting summary judgment in favor of Robinson on the fraud claim. Fraud requires: (1) a statement or a representation of fact; (2) its falsity; (3) its materiality; (4) the speaker's knowledge of its falsity; (5) the speaker's intent that there be reliance; (6) the hearer's ignorance of the falsity of the statement; (7) reliance by the hearer; (8) justifiable reliance; and (9) resultant injury. [Citation.] In opposition to the defendants' motion for summary judgment, Maroun filed an affidavit that stated Robinson made the following representations to Maroun:

(1) That Wyreless was to be a corporation of considerable size, with initial net revenues in excess of several hundred million dollars.

(2) That Robinson would soon acquire one and one-half million dollars in personal assets, which Robinson would make available to personally guaranty payment of my compensation from Wyreless.

(3) That he would have no difficulty in obtaining the initial investments required to capitalize Wyreless as a large, world leading corporation with initial net revenues in excess of several hundred million dollars.

(4) That he had obtained firm commitments from several investors and that investment funds would be received in Wyreless' bank account in the near future.

"An action for fraud or misrepresentation will not lie for statements of future events." [Citation.] "[T]here is a general rule in [the] law of deceit that a representation consisting of [a] promise or a statement as to a future event will not serve as [a] basis for fraud…" [Citation.] Statements numbered one and two both address future events. Robinson allegedly stated Wyreless "was to be" and that he "would soon acquire." "[T]he representation forming the basis of a claim for fraud must concern past or existing material facts." [Citation.] Neither of these statements constitutes a statement or a representation of past or existing fact. A "promise or statement that an act will be undertaken, however, is actionable, if it is proven that the speaker made the promise without intending to keep it." [Citation.] There is no indication in the record that Robinson did not intend to fulfill those representations to Maroun at the time he made the statements.

"Opinions or predictions about the anticipated profitability of a business are usually not actionable as fraud." [Citation.] Statement number three appears to be merely Robinson's opinion. As to statement number four, no evidence was submitted that Robinson had not received commitments at the time he made the statement to Maroun. Accordingly, the district court's grant of summary judgment against Maroun on the fraud claim is affirmed.

* * *

[The district court's ruling on this issue is affirmed.]

| CASE 11-4 | Fraud: Materiality
REED v. KING
California Court of Appeals, 1983
145 Cal.App.3d 261, 193 Cal.Rptr. 130
http://scholar.google.com/scholar_case?case=575864357603110085&q=193+Cal.Rptr.+130&hl=en&as_sdt=2,34 | |

Blease, J.

In the sale of a house, must the seller disclose it was the site of a multiple murder?

Dorris Reed purchased a house from Robert King. Neither King nor his real estate agents (the other named defendants) told Reed that a woman and her four children were murdered there 10 years earlier. However, it seems "truth will come to light; murder cannot be hid long." (*Shakespeare, Merchant of Venice*, act II, scene II.) Reed learned of the gruesome episode from a neighbor after the sale. She sues seeking rescission and damages. King and the real estate agent defendants successfully demurred to her first amended complaint for failure to state a cause of action. Reed appeals the ensuing judgment of dismissal. We will reverse the judgment.

* * * King and his real estate agent knew about the murders and knew the event materially affected the market value of the house when they listed it for sale. They represented to Reed the premises were in good condition and fit for an "elderly lady" living alone. They did not disclose the fact of the murders. At some point King asked a neighbor not to inform Reed of that event. Nonetheless, after Reed moved in neighbors informed her no one was interested in purchasing the house because of the stigma. Reed paid $76,000, but the house is only worth $65,000 because of its past.

* * *

Does Reed's pleading state a cause of action? Concealed within this question is the nettlesome problem of the duty of disclosure of blemishes on real property which are not physical defects or legal impairments to use.

Reed seeks to state a cause of action sounding in contract, i.e., rescission, or in tort, i.e., deceit. In either event her allegations must reveal a fraud. [Citation.] "The elements of actual fraud, whether as the basis of the remedy in contract or tort, may be stated as follows: There must be (1) a *false representation* or concealment of a material fact (or, in some cases, an opinion) susceptible of knowledge, (2) made with *knowledge* of its falsity or without sufficient knowledge on the subject to warrant a representation, (3) with the *intent* to induce the person to whom it is made to act upon it, and such person must (4) act in *reliance* upon the representation (5) to his *damage*." (Original italics.) [Citation.]

The trial court perceived the defect in Reed's complaint to be a failure to allege concealment of a material fact. * * *

Concealment is a term of art which includes mere nondisclosure when a party has a duty to disclose. [Citation.] Rest.2d Contracts, § 161; Rest.2d Torts, § 551; Reed's complaint reveals only nondisclosure despite the allegation King asked a neighbor to hold his peace. There is no allegation the attempt at suppression was a cause in fact of Reed's ignorance. [Citations.] Accordingly, the critical question is: does the seller have a duty to disclose here? Resolution of this question depends on the materiality of the fact of the murders.

In general, a seller of real property has a duty to disclose: "where the seller knows of facts *materially* affecting the value or desirability of the property which are known or accessible only to him and also knows that such facts are not known to, or within the reach of the diligent attention and observation of the buyer, the seller is under a duty to disclose them to the buyer. [Citation.] This broad statement of duty has led one commentator to conclude: "The ancient maxim *caveat emptor* ('let the buyer beware') has little or no application to California real estate transactions." [Citation.]

Whether information "is of sufficient materiality to affect the value or desirability of the property * * * depends on the facts of the particular case." [Citation.] Materiality "is a question of law, and is part of the concept of right to rely or justifiable reliance." [Citation.] * * * Three considerations bear on this legal conclusion; the gravity of the harm inflicted by nondisclosure; the fairness of imposing a duty of discovery on the buyer as an alternative to compelling disclosure, and the impact on the stability of contracts if rescission is permitted.

Numerous cases have found nondisclosure of physical defects and legal impediments to use of real property are

material. [Citation.] However, to our knowledge, no prior real estate sale case has faced an issue of nondisclosure of the kind presented here.

* * *

The murder of innocents is highly unusual in its potential for so disturbing buyers they may be unable to reside in a home where it has occurred. This fact may foreseeably deprive a buyer of the intended use of the purchase. Murder is not such a common occurrence that *buyers* should be charged with anticipating and discovering this disquieting possibility.

Accordingly, the fact is not one for which a duty of inquiry and discovery can sensibly be imposed upon the buyer. Reed alleges the fact of the murders has a quantifiable effect on the market value of the premises. We cannot say this allegation is inherently wrong and, in the pleading posture of the case, we assume it to be true. If information known or accessible only to the seller has a significant and measurable effect on market value and, as is alleged here, the seller is aware of this effect, we see no principled basis for making the duty to disclose turn upon the character of the information. Physical usefulness is not and never has been the sole criterion of valuation. * * *

Reputation and history can have a significant effect on the value of realty. "George Washington slept here" is worth something, however physically inconsequential that consideration may be. Ill repute or "bad will" conversely may depress the value of property. * * *

Whether Reed will be able to prove her allegation the decade-old multiple murder has a significant effect on market value we cannot determine. If she is able to do so by competent evidence she is entitled to a favorable ruling on the issues of materiality and duty to disclose. Her demonstration of objective tangible harm would still the concern that permitting her to go forward will open the floodgates to rescission on subjective and idiosyncratic grounds.

* * *

The judgment is reversed.

CASE 11-5

Mistake/Innocent Misrepresentation
LESHER v. STRID
Court of Appeals of Oregon, 2000
165 Or.App. 34, 996 P.2d 988
http://scholar.google.com/scholar_case?case=3643927747561854317&q=996+P.2d+988&hl=en&as_sdt=2,34

Wollheim, J.
[In May 1995, the plaintiffs, Vernon and Janene Lesher, agreed to purchase an eighteen-acre parcel of real property

from defendant with the intention of using it to raise horses. In purchasing the property, the plaintiffs relied on their impression that at least four acres of the subject property had a right to irrigation from Slate Creek. The earnest money agreement to the contract provided:

D. Water Rights are being conveyed to Buyer at the close of escrow. * * * Seller will provide Buyer with a written explanation of the operation of the irrigation system, water right certificates, and inventory of irrigation equipment included in sale. [Bold in original].

The earnest money agreement also provided:

THE SUBJECT PROPERTY IS BEING SOLD "AS IS" subject to the Buyer's approval of the tests and conditions as stated herein. Buyer declares that Buyer is not depending on any other statement of the Seller or licensees that is not incorporated by reference in this earnest money contract. [Bold in original].

Before signing the earnest money agreement, the defendants presented to the plaintiffs a 1977 Water Resources Department water rights certificate and a map purporting to show an area of the subject property to be irrigated ("area to be irrigated" map), which indicated that the property carried a four-acre water right. Both parties believed that the property carried the irrigation rights and that the plaintiffs needed such rights for their horse farm. The plaintiffs did not obtain the services of an attorney or a water rights examiner before purchasing the property.

After purchasing the property and before establishing a pasture, the plaintiffs learned that the property did not carry a four-acre water right. The plaintiffs sought rescission of the contract for sale, alleging mutual mistake of fact or innocent misrepresentation regarding the existence of water rights. The trial court ruled in favor of the plaintiffs and the defendant appeals.]

Grounds for rescission on the basis of a mutual mistake of fact or innocent misrepresentation must be proved by clear and convincing evidence. [Citations.] An innocent misrepresentation of fact renders a contract voidable by a party if the party's "manifestation of assent is induced by * * * a material misrepresentation by the other party upon which the recipient is justified in relying[.]" [Citations.] A mutual mistake of fact renders a contract voidable by the adversely affected party, "where the parties are mistaken as to the facts existing at the time of the contract, if the mistake is so fundamental that it frustrates the purpose of the contract," [citation], and where the adversely affected party does not bear the risk of the mistake, [citation]. A mistake "is a state of mind which is not in accord with the facts." [Citation].

Even though it appears that the trial court did not apply the clear and convincing standard, * * * , we find that plaintiffs' evidence meets that standard. Both defendant and plaintiffs testified that they believed that the four acres of water rights were appurtenant to the subject property. Defendant does not dispute that the 1977 water rights certificate and the "area to be irrigated" map are her representation about the water right.

* * *

Plaintiffs also established by clear and convincing evidence that the existence of the four-acre water right was material and essential to the contract. Vernon testified that the motivation for the purchase was to expand his ability to raise horses from property they already owned where they had a two-acre irrigation right and that the subject property's water right was essential to the contract. Certainly, a smaller water right would limit, not expand, plaintiffs' ability to raise horses. The mistake, therefore, goes to the very essence of the contract.

We next consider defendant's arguments that plaintiffs bore the risk of that mistake. The Restatement (Second) of Contracts § 154 explains that a party bears the risk of a mistake, in part, if the risk is allocated to the party by agreement of the parties, or if the risk is allocated to the party "by the court on the ground that it is reasonable in the circumstances to do so." We find nothing in the contract that would allocate to plaintiffs the risk of a mistake as to the existence of a four-acre water right.

Defendant argues in the alternative that plaintiffs' mistake of fact is the result of defendant's misrepresentation, on which plaintiffs could not reasonably rely. An "innocent misrepresentation may support a claim for rescission of a real estate agreement if the party who relied on the misrepresentations of another establishes a right to have done so." [Citations.]

Defendant argues that her representations about the four-acre water right were extrinsic to the contract and that the contract's "as is" clause expressly excluded reliance on such extrinsic representations. * * * The "as is" clause specifically contemplated reliance on any statements by the seller that were "incorporated by reference" in the earnest money agreement. The earnest money agreement specifically referred to the conveyance of water rights.

* * *

Plaintiffs have established that both a mutual mistake of fact and an innocent misrepresentation of fact entitle them to rescission of the deed of sale.

Affirmed.

QUESTIONS

1. Anita and Barry were negotiating, and Anita's attorney prepared a long and carefully drawn contract, which was given to Barry for examination. Five days later and prior to its execution, Barry's eyes became so infected that it was impossible for him to read. Ten days thereafter and during the continuance of the illness, Anita called upon Barry and urged him to sign the contract, telling him that time was running out. Barry signed the contract despite the fact he was unable to read it. In a subsequent action by Anita, Barry claimed that the contract was not binding upon him because it was impossible for him to read and he did not know what it contained prior to his signing it. Should Barry be held to the contract?

2. **a.** Johnson tells Davis that he paid $150,000 for his farm in 2010, and that he believes it is worth twice that at the present time. Relying upon these statements, Davis buys the farm from Johnson for $225,000. Johnson did pay $150,000 for the farm in 2010, but its value has increased only slightly, and it is presently not worth $300,000. On discovering this, Davis offers to reconvey the farm to Johnson and sues for the return of his $225,000. Result?

   b. Modify the facts in (a) by assuming that Johnson had paid $100,000 for the property in 2010. What result?

3. On September 1, Adams in Portland, Oregon, wrote a letter to Brown in New York City, offering to sell to Brown one thousand tons of chromite at $48.00 per ton, to be shipped by *S.S. Malabar* sailing from Portland, Oregon, to New York City via the Panama Canal. Upon receiving the letter on September 5, Brown immediately mailed to Adams a letter stating that she accepted the offer. There were two ships by the name of *S.S. Malabar* sailing from Portland to New York City via the Panama Canal, one sailing in October and the other sailing in December. At the time of mailing her letter of acceptance Brown knew of both sailings and further knew that Adams knew only of the December sailing. Is there a contract? If so, to which *S.S. Malabar* does it relate?

4. Adler owes Panessi, a police captain, $5,000. Adler threatens that unless Panessi discharges him from the debt, Adler will disclose the fact that Panessi has on several occasions become highly intoxicated and has been seen in the company of certain disreputable persons. Panessi, induced by fear that such a disclosure would cost him his position or in any event lead to social disgrace, gives Adler a release but subsequently sues to set it aside and recover on his claim. Will Adler be able to enforce the release?

5. Harris owned a farm that was worth about $600 per acre. By false representations of fact, Harris induced Pringle to buy the farm at $1,500 per acre. Shortly after taking possession of the farm, Pringle discovered oil under the land. Harris, on learning this, sues to have the sale set aside on the ground that it was voidable because of fraud. Result?

6. On February 2, Phillips induced Miller to purchase from her fifty shares of stock in the XYZ Corporation for $10,000, representing that the actual book value of each share was $200. A certificate for fifty shares was delivered to Miller. On February 16, Miller discovered that the book value on February 2 was only $50.00 per share. Will Miller be successful in a lawsuit against Phillips? Why?

7. Doris mistakenly accused Peter's son, Steven, of negligently burning down her barn. Peter believed that his son was guilty of the wrong and that he, Peter, was personally liable for the damage, as Steven was only fifteen years old. Upon demand made by Doris, Peter paid Doris $25,000 for the damage to her barn. After making this payment, Peter learned that his son had not caused the burning of Doris's barn and was in no way responsible for its burning. Peter then sued Doris to recover the $25,000 he had paid her. Will he be successful?

8. Jones, a farmer, found an odd-looking stone in his fields. He went to Smith, the town jeweler, and asked him what he thought it was. Smith said he did not know but thought it might be a ruby. Jones asked Smith what he would pay for it, and Smith said $200, whereupon Jones sold it to Smith for $200. The stone turned out to be an uncut diamond worth $3,000. Jones brought an action against Smith to recover the stone. On trial, it was proved that Smith actually did not know the stone was a diamond when he bought it, but he thought it might be a ruby. Can Jones void the sale? Explain.

9. Decedent Judith Johnson, a bedridden, lonely woman of eighty-six years, owned outright Greenacre, her ancestral estate. Ficky, her physician and friend, visited her weekly and was held in the highest regard by Johnson. Johnson was extremely fearful of suffering and depended upon Ficky to ease her anxiety and pain. Several months before her death, she deeded Greenacre to Ficky for $10,000. The fair market value of Greenacre at this time was $250,000. Johnson was survived by two children and six grandchildren. Johnson's children challenged the validity of the deed. Should the deed be declared invalid due to Ficky's undue influence? Explain.

10. Dorothy and John Hufffschneider listed their house and lot for sale with C. B. Property. The asking price was $165,000, and the owners told C. B. that the size of the property was 6.8 acres. Dean Olson, a salesman for C. B., advertised the property in local newspapers as consisting of six acres. James and Jean Holcomb signed a contract to purchase the property through Olson after first inspecting the property with Olson and being assured by Olson that the property was at least 6.6 acres. The Holcombs never asked for or received a copy of the survey. In actuality, the lot was only 4.6 acres. The Holcombs now seek to rescind the contract. Decision?

11. In February, Gardner, a schoolteacher with no experience in running a tavern, entered into a contract to purchase for $40,000 the Punjab Tavern from Meiling. The contract was contingent upon Gardner's obtaining a five-year lease for the tavern's premises and a liquor license from the State. Prior to the formation of the contract, Meiling had made no representations to Gardner concerning the gross income of the tavern. Approximately three months after the contract was signed, Gardner and Meiling met with an inspector from the Oregon Liquor Control Commission (OLCC) to discuss transfer of the liquor license. Meiling reported to the agent, in Gardner's presence, that the tavern's gross income figures for February, March, and April were $5,710, $4,918, and $5,009, respectively. The OLCC granted the required license, the transaction was closed, and Gardner took possession on June 10. After discovering that the tavern's income was very low and that the tavern had very few female patrons, Gardner contacted Meiling's bookkeeping service and learned that the actual gross income for those three months had been approximately $1,400 to $2,000. Will a court grant Gardner rescission of the contract? Explain.

12. Christine Boyd was designated as the beneficiary of a life insurance policy issued by Aetna Life Insurance Company on the life of Christine's husband, Jimmie Boyd. The policy insured against Jimmie's permanent total disability and also provided for a death benefit to be paid on Jimmie's death. Several years after the policy was issued, Jimmie and Christine separated. Jimmie began to travel extensively, and Christine therefore was unable to keep track of his whereabouts or his state of health. Jimmie, however, continued to pay the premiums on the policy until Christine tried to cash in the policy to alleviate her financial distress. A loan previously had been made on the policy, however, leaving its cash surrender value, and thus the amount that Christine received, at only $4.19. Shortly thereafter, Christine learned that Jimmie had been permanently and totally disabled before the surrender of the policy. Aetna also was unaware of Jimmie's condition, and Christine requested that the surrendered policy be reinstated and that the disability payments be made. Jimmie died soon thereafter, and Christine then requested that Aetna pay the death benefit. Decision?

13. Plaintiff, Gibson, entered into negotiation with W. S. May, president of Home Folks Mobile Home Plaza, Inc., to buy Home Plaza Corporation. Plaintiff visited the mobile home park on several occasions, at which time he noted the occupancy, visually inspected the sewer and water systems, and asked May numerous questions concerning the condition of the business. Plaintiff, however, never requested to see the books, nor did May try to conceal them. May admits making the following representations to the plaintiff: (a) the water and sewer systems were in good condition and no major short-term expenditures would be needed; (b) the park realized a 40 percent profit on natural gas sold to tenants; and (c) usual park vacancy was 5 percent. In addition, May gave plaintiff the park's accountant-prepared income statement, which showed a net income of $38,220 for the past eight months. Based on these figures, plaintiff projected an annual net profit of $57,331.20. Upon being asked whether this figure accurately represented income of the business for the past three years, May stated by letter that indeed it did.

    Plaintiff purchased the park for $275,000. Shortly thereafter, plaintiff spent $5,384 repairing the well and septic systems. By the time plaintiff sold the park three years later, he had expended $7,531 on the wells and $8,125 on the septic systems. Furthermore, in the first year, park occupancy was nowhere near 95 percent. Even after raising rent and the charges for natural gas, plaintiff still operated at a deficit. Plaintiff sued defendant, alleging that May, on behalf of defendant, made false and fraudulent statements on which plaintiff relied when he purchased the park. Decision?

14. Columbia University brought suit against Jacobsen on two notes signed by him and his parents. The notes represented the balance of tuition he owed the University. Jacobsen counterclaimed for money damages due to Columbia's deceit or fraudulent misrepresentation. Jacobsen argues that Columbia fraudulently misrepresented that it would teach wisdom, truth, character, enlightenment,

and similar virtues and qualities. He specifically cites as support the Columbia motto: "*in lumine tuo videbimus lumen*" ("In your light we shall see light"); the inscription over the college chapel: "Wisdom dwelleth in the heart of him that hath understanding"; and various excerpts from its brochures, catalogues, and a convocation address made by the University's president. Jacobsen, a senior who was not graduated because of poor scholastic standing, claims that the University's failure to meet its promises made through these quotations constituted fraudulent misrepresentation or deceit. Decision?

15. Frank Berryessa stole funds from his employer, the Eccles Hotel Company. His father, W. S. Berryessa, learned of his son's trouble and, thinking the amount involved was about $2,000, gave the hotel a promissory note for $2,186 to cover the shortage. In return, the hotel agreed not to publicize the incident or notify the bonding company. (A bonding company is an insurer that is paid a premium for agreeing to reimburse an employer for thefts by an employee.) Before this note became due, however, the hotel discovered that Frank had actually misappropriated $6,865. The hotel then notified its bonding company, Great American Indemnity Company, to collect the entire loss. W. S. Berryessa claims that the agent for Great American told him that unless he paid them $2,000 in cash and signed a note for the remaining $4,865, Frank would be prosecuted. Berryessa agreed, signed the note, and gave the agent a cashier's check for $1,500 and a personal check for $500. He requested that the agent not cash the personal check for about a month. Subsequently, Great American sued Berryessa on the note. He defends against the note on the grounds of duress and counterclaims for the return of the $1,500 and the cancellation of the uncashed $500 check. Who should prevail? Explain.

16. Jane Francois married Victor H. Francois. At the time of the marriage, Victor was a fifty-year-old bachelor living with his elderly mother, and Jane was a thirty-year-old, twice-divorced mother of two. Victor had a relatively secure financial portfolio; Jane, on the other hand, brought no money or property to the marriage.

    The marriage deteriorated quickly over the next couple of years, with disputes centered on financial matters. During this period, Jane systematically gained a joint interest in and took control of most of Victor's assets. Three years after they married, Jane contracted Harold Monoson, an attorney, to draw up divorce papers. Victor was unaware of Jane's decision until he was taken to Monoson's office, where Monoson presented for Victor's signature a "Property Settlement and Separation Agreement." Monoson told Victor that he would need

an attorney, but Jane vetoed Victor's choice. Monoson then asked another lawyer, Gregory Ball, to come into the office. Ball read the agreement and strenuously advised Victor not to sign it because it would commit him to financial suicide. The agreement transferred most of Victor's remaining assets to Jane. Victor, however, signed it because Jane and Monoson persuaded him that it was the only way that his marriage could be saved. In October of the following year, Jane informed Victor that she had sold most of his former property and that she was leaving him permanently. Can Victor have the agreement set aside as a result of undue influence?

17. Iverson owned Iverson Motor Company, an enterprise engaged in the repair as well as the sale of Oldsmobile, Rambler, and International Harvester Scout automobiles. Forty percent of the business's sales volume and net earnings came from the Oldsmobile franchise. Whipp contracted to buy Iverson Motors, which Iverson said included the Oldsmobile franchise. After the sale, however, General Motors refused to transfer the franchise to Whipp. Whipp then returned the property to Iverson and brought this action seeking rescission of the contract. Should the contract be rescinded? Explain.

18. On February 10, Mrs. Sunderhaus purchased a diamond ring from Perel & Lowenstein for $6,990. She was told by the company's salesperson that the ring was worth its purchase price, and she also received at that time a written guarantee from the company attesting to the diamond's value, style, and trade-in value. When Mrs. Sunderhaus went to trade the ring for another, however, she was told by two jewelers that the ring was valued at $3,000 and $3,500, respectively. Mrs. Sunderhaus knew little about the value of diamonds and claims to have relied on the oral representation of the Perel & Lowenstein's salesperson and the written representation as to the ring's value. She seeks rescission of the contract or damages in the amount of the sales price over the ring's value. Decision?

19. Division West Chinchilla Ranch advertised on television that a five-figure income could be earned by raising chinchillas with an investment of only $3.75 per animal per year and only thirty minutes of maintenance per day. The minimum investment was $2,150 for one male and six female chinchillas. Division West represented to plaintiffs that chinchilla ranching would be easy and that no experience was required to make ranching profitable. Plaintiffs, who had no experience raising chinchillas, each invested $2,150 or more to purchase Division's chinchillas and supplies. After three years without earning a profit, plaintiffs sue Division for fraud. Do these facts sustain an action for fraud in the inducement?

20. William Schmalz entered into an employment contract with Hardy Salt Company. The contract granted Schmalz six months' severance pay for involuntary termination but none for voluntary separation or termination for cause. Schmalz was asked to resign from his employment. He was informed that if he did not resign, he would be fired for alleged misconduct. When Schmalz turned in his letter of resignation, he signed a release prohibiting him from suing his former employer as a consequence of his employment. Schmalz consulted an attorney before signing the release and upon signing it received $4,583.00 (one month's salary) in consideration. Schmalz now sues his former employer for the severance pay, claiming that he signed the release under duress. Is Schmalz correct in his assertion?

21. Treasure Salvors and the State of Florida entered into a series of four annual contracts governing the salvage of the *Nuestra Senora de Atocha*. The *Atocha* is a Spanish galleon that sank in 1622, carrying a treasure now worth well over $250 million. Both parties had contracted under the impression that the seabed on which the *Atocha* lay was land owned by Florida. Treasure Salvors agreed to relinquish 25 percent of the items recovered in return for the right to salvage on State lands. In accordance with these contracts, Treasure Salvors delivered to Florida its share of the salvaged artifacts. Subsequently, the U.S. Supreme Court held that the part of the continental shelf on which the *Atocha* was resting had *never* been owned by Florida. Treasure Salvors then brought suit to rescind the contracts and to recover the artifacts it had delivered to the State of Florida. Should Treasure Salvors prevail?

22. International Underwater Contractors, Inc. (IUC), entered into a written contract with New England Telephone and Telegraph Company (NET) to assemble and install certain conduits under the Mystic River for a lump sum price of $149,680. Delays caused by NET forced IUC's work to be performed in the winter months instead of during the summer as originally bid, and as a result, a major change had to be made in the system from that specified in the contract. NET repeatedly assured IUC that it would pay the cost if IUC would complete the work. The change cost IUC an additional $811,810.73; nevertheless, it signed a release settling the claim for a total sum of $575,000. IUC, which at the time was in financial trouble, now seeks to recover the balance due, arguing that the signed release is not binding because it was signed under economic duress. Is IUC correct?

23. Conrad Schaneman was a Russian immigrant who could neither read nor write the English language. In 2009 Conrad deeded (conveyed) a farm he owned to his eldest son, Laurence, for $23,500, which was the original purchase price of the property in 1979. The value of the farm in 1979 was between $145,000 and $160,000. At the time he executed the deed, Conrad was an eighty-two-year-old invalid, severely ill, and completely dependent on others for his personal needs. He weighed between 325 and 350 pounds, had difficulty breathing, could not walk more than fifteen feet, and needed a special jackhoist to get in and out of the bathtub. Conrad enjoyed a long-standing, confidential relationship with Laurence, who was his principal adviser and handled Conrad's business affairs. Laurence also obtained a power of attorney from Conrad and made himself a joint owner of Conrad's bank account and $20,000 certificate of deposit. Conrad brought this suit to cancel the deed, claiming it was the result of Laurence's undue influence. The district court found that the deed was executed as a result of undue influence, set aside the deed, and granted title to Conrad. Laurence appealed. Decision?

24. At the time of her death, Olga Mestrovic was the owner of a large number of works of art created by her late husband, Ivan Mestrovic, an internationally known sculptor and artist whose works were displayed throughout Europe and the United States. By the terms of Olga's will, all the works of art created by her husband were to be sold and the proceeds distributed to members of the Mestrovic family. Also included in the estate of Olga Mestrovic was certain real property that 1st Source Bank (the Bank), as personal representative of the estate of Olga Mestrovic, agreed to sell to Terrence and Antoinette Wilkin. The agreement of purchase and sale made no mention of any works of art, although it did provide for the sale of such personal property as a dishwasher, drapes, and French doors stored in the attic. Immediately after closing on the real estate, the Wilkins complained to the Bank of the clutter left on the premises; the Bank gave the Wilkins an option of cleaning the house themselves and keeping any personal property they desired, to which the Wilkins agreed. At the time these arrangements were made, neither the Bank nor the Wilkins suspected that any works of art remained on the premises. During cleanup, however, the Wilkins found eight drawings and a sculpture created by Ivan Mestrovic to which the Wilkins claimed ownership based upon their agreement with the Bank that, if they cleaned the real property, they could keep such personal property as they desired. Who is entitled to ownership of the artwork?

25. Ronald D. Johnson is a former employee of International Business Machines Corporation (IBM). As part of a

downsizing effort, IBM discharged Johnson. In exchange for an enhanced severance package, Johnson signed a written release and covenant not to sue IBM. IBM's downsizing plan provided that surplus personnel were eligible to receive benefits, including outplacement assistance, career counseling, job retraining, and an enhanced separation allowance. These employees were eligible, at IBM's discretion, to receive a separation allowance of two weeks' pay. However, employees who signed a release could be eligible for an enhanced severance allowance equal to one week's pay for each six months of accumulated service with a maximum of twenty-six weeks' pay. Surplus employees could also apply for alternate, generally lower-paying, manufacturing positions. Johnson opted for the release and received the maximum twenty-six weeks' pay. He then alleged, among other claims, that IBM subjected him to economic duress when he signed the release and covenant-not-to-sue, and he sought to rescind both. What will Johnson need to show in order to prove his cause of action?

TAKING SIDES

Mrs. Audrey E. Vokes, a widow of fifty-one years and without family, purchased fourteen separate dance courses from J. P. Davenport's Arthur Murray, Inc., School of Dance. The fourteen courses totaled in the aggregate 2,302 hours of dancing lessons at a cost to Mrs. Vokes of $31,090.45. Mrs. Vokes was induced continually to reapply for new courses by representations made by Mr. Davenport that her dancing ability was improving, that she was responding to instruction, that she had excellent potential, and that they were developing her into an accomplished dancer. In fact, she had no dancing ability or aptitude and had trouble "hearing the musical beat." Mrs. Vokes brought action to have the contracts set aside.

a. What are the arguments that the contracts should be set aside?

b. What are the arguments that the contracts should be enforced?

c. What is the proper outcome? Explain.

CONSIDERATION

CHAPTER OUTCOMES

After reading and studying this chapter, you should be able to:

- Define *consideration* and explain what is meant by legal sufficiency.

- Describe illusory promises, output contracts, requirements contracts, exclusive dealing contracts, and conditional contracts.

- Explain whether preexisting public and contractual obligations satisfy the legal requirement of consideration.

- Explain the concept of bargained-for exchange and whether this element is present with past consideration and third-party beneficiaries.

- Identify and discuss those contracts that are enforceable even though they are not supported by consideration.

Consideration is the primary—but not the only—basis for the enforcement of promises in our legal system. Consideration is the inducement to make a promise enforceable. The doctrine of consideration ensures that promises are enforced only in cases in which the parties have exchanged something of value in the eye of the law. Gratuitous (gift) promises, accordingly, are legally enforceable only under certain circumstances, which are discussed later in the chapter.

Consideration, or that which is exchanged for a promise, is present only when the parties intend an exchange. The consideration exchanged for the promise may be an act, a forbearance to act, or a promise to do either of these. In like manner, Section 71 of the Restatement defines consideration for a promise as (1) an act other than a promise; (2) a forbearance; (3) the creation, modification, or destruction of a legal relation; or (4) a return promise if any of these are bargained for and given in exchange for the promise.

Thus, consideration comprises two basic elements: (1) legal sufficiency (something of value) and (2) bargained-for exchange. Both must be present to satisfy the requirement of consideration. The consideration may be given to the promisor or to some other person; likewise, it may be given by the promisee or by some other person.

LEGAL SUFFICIENCY

To be legally sufficient, the consideration exchanged for the promise must be either a legal detriment to the promisee or a legal benefit to the promisor. In other words, in return for the promise the promisee must give up something of legal value or the promisor must receive something of legal value.

Legal detriment means (1) doing (or undertaking to do) that which the promisee was under no prior legal obligation to do or (2) refraining from doing (or the undertaking to refrain from doing) that which he was previously under no legal obligation to refrain from doing. On the other hand, **legal benefit** means the obtaining by the promisor of that which he had no prior legal right to obtain. Most, if not all, cases involving legal detriment to the promisee also will involve a legal benefit to the promisor. Nonetheless, the presence of either is sufficient.

ADEQUACY

Legal sufficiency has nothing to do with adequacy of consideration. Restatement, Section 79. The subject matter that the parties agree to exchange does not need to have the same or equal value; rather, the law will regard consideration as adequate if the parties have freely agreed to the exchange. The requirement of legally sufficient consideration, therefore, is not at all concerned with whether the bargain was good or bad, or whether one party received disproportionately more or less than what he gave or promised in exchange. Such facts, however, may be relevant to the availability of certain defenses (such as fraud, duress, or undue influence) or certain remedies (such as specific performance). The requirement of legally sufficient consideration is simply (1) that the parties have agreed to an exchange and (2) that, with respect to each party, the subject matter exchanged, or promised in exchange, either imposed a legal detriment upon the promisee or conferred a legal benefit upon the promisor. If the purported consideration is clearly without value, however, such that the transaction is a sham, many courts would hold that consideration is lacking.

PRACTICAL ADVICE

Be sure you are satisfied with your agreed-upon exchange, because courts will not invalidate a contract for absence of adequate consideration.

UNILATERAL CONTRACTS

In a unilateral contract, a promise is exchanged for a completed act or a forbearance to act. Because only one promise exists, only one party, the **offeror**, makes a promise and is therefore the **promisor** while the other party, the **offeree**, is the person receiving the promise and thus is the **promisee**. For example, A promises to pay B $2,000 if B paints A's house. B paints A's house.

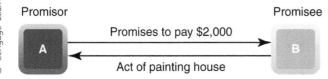

For A's promise to be binding, it must be supported by consideration consisting of either a legal detriment to B, the promisee (offeree), or a legal benefit to A, the promisor (offeror). B's having painted the house is a legal detriment to B, the promisee, because she was under no prior legal duty to paint A's house. Also, B's painting A's house is a legal benefit to A, the promisor, because A had no prior legal right to have his house painted by B.

A unilateral contract also may consist of a promise exchanged for a forbearance. To illustrate, A negligently injures B, for which B may recover damages in a tort action. A promises to pay B $5,000 if B forbears from bringing suit. B accepts by not filing suit.

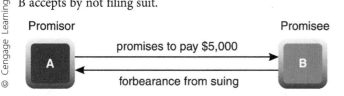

A's promise to pay B $5,000 is binding because it is supported by consideration: B, the promisee (offeree), has incurred a legal detriment by refraining from bringing suit, which he was under no prior legal obligation to refrain from doing. A, the promisor (offeror), has received a legal benefit

because she had no prior legal right to B's forbearance from bringing suit.

BILATERAL CONTRACTS

In a bilateral contract, the parties exchange promises. Thus, each party is *both* a promisor and a promisee. For example, if A (the offeror) promises (offers) to purchase an automobile from B (the offeree) for $15,000 and B promises to sell the automobile to A for $15,000 (accepts the offer), the following relationship exists:

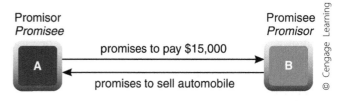

A's promise (the offer) to pay B $15,000 is binding and therefore enforceable by B, if that promise is supported by legal consideration from B (offeree), which may consist of either a legal detriment to B, the promisee, or a legal benefit to A, the promisor. B's promise to sell A the automobile is a legal detriment to B because he was under no prior legal duty to sell the automobile to A. Moreover, B's promise is also a legal benefit to A because A had no prior legal right to that automobile. Consequently, A's promise to pay $15,000 to B is supported by consideration and is enforceable.

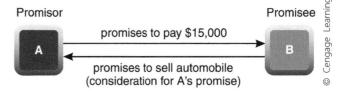

For **B's promise** (the acceptance) to sell the automobile to A to be binding, it likewise must be supported by consideration from A (offeror), which may be either a legal detriment to A, the promisee, or a legal benefit to B, the promisor. A's promise to pay B $15,000 is a legal detriment to A because he was under no prior legal duty to pay $15,000 to B. At the same time, A's promise is also a legal benefit to B because B had no prior legal right to the $15,000. Thus, B's promise to sell the automobile is supported by consideration and is enforceable.

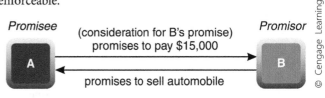

To summarize, for A's promise to B to be binding, B must support the promise with legally sufficient consideration,

◆ FIGURE 12-1: **Consideration in Unilateral and Bilateral Contracts**

Type of Contract	Offer	Acceptance	Consideration
Unilateral	Promise by A	Performance of requested act or forbearance by B	*Promise* by A *Performance* of requested act or forbearance by B
Bilateral	Promise by A	Return promise by B to perform requested act or forbearance	*Promise* by A Return *promise* by B to perform requested act or forbearance

© Cengage Learning

which requires that the promise A receives in exchange from B provide either a legal benefit to A (the promisor) or a legal detriment to B (the promisee). A, in turn, must support B's return promise with consideration for that promise to be binding on B.

Thus, in a bilateral contract each promise is the consideration for the other, a relationship that has been referred to as **mutuality of obligation**. A general consequence of mutuality of obligation is that each promisor in a bilateral contract must be bound, or neither is bound.

◆ SEE FIGURE 12-1: **Consideration in Unilateral and Bilateral Contracts**

ILLUSORY PROMISES

Words of promise that make the performance of the purported promisor entirely optional constitute no promise at all. Consequently, they cannot serve as consideration. In this section, such illusory promises will be distinguished from promises that impose obligations of performance upon the promisor and thus can be legally sufficient consideration. An **illusory promise** is a statement that is in the form of a promise but imposes no obligation upon the maker of the statement. An illusory promise is not consideration for a return promise. Thus, a statement committing the promisor to purchase such quantity of goods as she may "desire," "want," or "wish to buy" is an illusory promise because its performance is entirely optional. For example, if ExxonMobil, Inc., agrees to sell to Barnes Co. as many barrels of oil as Barnes shall choose at $40.00 per barrel, there would be no consideration: Barnes may wish or desire to buy none of the oil, yet in buying none it would fulfill its promise. An agreement containing such a promise as that made by Barnes, although accepted by both parties, does not create a contract because the promise is illusory—performance by Barnes is entirely optional, and the offer places no constraint upon its freedom. Barnes is not bound to do anything, nor can Ames reasonably expect to receive any performance. Thus, Barnes, by its promise, suffers no legal detriment and confers no

legal benefit. Consequently, Barnes's promise does not provide legally sufficient consideration for ExxonMobil's promise; thus, ExxonMobil's promise is not binding upon ExxonMobil.

◆ **SEE CASE 12-1**

PRACTICAL ADVICE

Because an agreement under which one party may perform at his discretion is not a binding contract, be sure that you make a promise and receive a promise that is not optional.

OUTPUT AND REQUIREMENTS CONTRACTS A seller's agreement to sell her entire production to a particular purchaser is called an **output contract**. It affords the seller an ensured market for her product. Conversely, a **requirements contract**, or a purchaser's agreement to buy from a particular seller all the materials of a particular kind he needs, ensures the buyer of a ready source of inventory or supplies. These contracts may or may not be accompanied by an estimate of the quantity to be sold or to be purchased. Nevertheless, these promises are not illusory. The buyer under a requirements contract does not promise to buy as much as she desires to buy but, rather, to buy as much as she *needs*. Similarly, under an output contract the seller promises to sell to the buyer the seller's entire production, not merely as much as the seller desires.

Furthermore, the Code, Section 2–306(1), imposes a good faith limitation upon the quantity to be sold or purchased under an output or requirements contract. Thus, a contract of this type involves such actual output or requirements as may occur in good faith, except that no quantity unreasonably disproportionate to any stated estimate or, in the absence of a stated estimate, to any normal prior output or requirements may be tendered or demanded. Therefore, after contracting to sell to Adler, Inc., its entire output, Benevito Company cannot increase its production from one eight-hour shift per day to three eight-hour shifts per day.

If you use an output or requirements contract, be sure to act in good faith and do not take unfair advantage of the situation.

EXCLUSIVE DEALING CONTRACTS When a manufacturer of goods grants an exclusive right to a distributor to sell its products in a designated territory, unless otherwise agreed, the manufacturer is under an implied obligation to use its best efforts to supply the goods, and the distributor must use his best efforts to promote their sale. Uniform Commercial Code (UCC) Section 2–306(2). The obligations that arise upon acceptance of an **exclusive dealing agreement** are sufficient consideration to bind both parties to the contract.

CONDITIONAL PROMISES A conditional promise is a promise the performance of which depends upon the happening or nonhappening of an event not certain to occur (the condition). A conditional promise is sufficient consideration *unless* the promisor knows at the time of making the promise that the condition cannot occur. Restatement, Section 76.

Thus, if Debbie offers to pay John $8,000 for John's automobile, provided that Debbie receives such amount as an inheritance from the estate of her deceased uncle, and John accepts the offer, the duty of Debbie to pay $8,000 to John is *conditioned* upon her receiving $8,000 from her deceased uncle's estate. The consideration moving from John to Debbie is the promise to transfer title to the automobile. The consideration moving from Debbie to John is the promise of $8,000 subject to the condition.

PREEXISTING PUBLIC OBLIGATION

The law does not regard the performance of, or the promise to perform, a preexisting legal duty, public or private, as either a legal detriment to the party under the prior legal obligation or a benefit to the other party. A **public duty** does not arise out of a contract; rather, it is imposed upon members of society by force of the common law or by statute. As illustrated in the law of torts, public duty includes the duty not to commit an assault, battery, false imprisonment, or defamation. The criminal law also imposes numerous public duties. Thus, if Cleon promises to pay Spike, the village ruffian, $100 not to abuse him physically, Cleon's promise is unenforceable because both tort and criminal law impose on Spike a preexisting public obligation to refrain from so acting.

By virtue of their public office, public officials, such as the mayor of a city, members of a city council, police officers, and firefighters, are under a preexisting obligation to perform their duties.

PREEXISTING CONTRACTUAL OBLIGATION

The performance of, or the promise to perform, a **preexisting contractual duty**, a duty the terms of which are neither doubtful nor the subject of honest dispute, is also legally insufficient consideration because the doing of what one is legally bound to do is neither a detriment to the promisee nor a benefit to the promisor. For example, Leigh and Associates employs Jason for one year at a salary of $2,000 per month and at the end of six months promises Jason that, in addition to the salary, it will pay him $3,000 if he remains on the job for the remainder of the period originally agreed upon. Leigh's promise is not binding because Jason's promise does not constitute legally sufficient consideration. If Jason's duties were changed in nature or amount, however, Leigh's promise would be binding because Jason's new duties are a legal detriment.

◆ **SEE CASE 12-2**

MODIFICATION OF A PREEXISTING CONTRACT A modification of a contract occurs when the parties to the contract mutually agree to change one or more of its terms. Under the common law, a modification of an existing contract must be supported by mutual consideration to be enforceable. In other words, the modification must be supported by some new consideration beyond that which is already owing (thus, there must be a separate and distinct modification contract). For example, Fred and Jodie agree that Fred shall put in a gravel driveway for Jodie at a cost of $2,000. Subsequently, Jodie agrees to pay an additional $1,000 if Fred will blacktop the driveway. Because Fred was not bound by the original contract to provide blacktopping, he would incur a legal detriment in doing so and is therefore entitled to the additional $1,000.

The Code has modified the common law rule for contract modification by providing that the parties can effectively modify a contract for the sale of goods without new consideration, though the Comments to this section make the modification subject to the requirement of good faith. Moreover, the Restatement has moved toward this position by providing that a modification of an executory contract is binding if it is fair and equitable in light of surrounding facts that the parties did not anticipate when the contract was made. Restatement, Section 89. A few States have followed the Code's rule by statutorily providing that the parties need provide no new consideration when modifying any contract. These States vary, however, as to whether the modification must be in writing and whether the original contract must be executory.

◆ **SEE FIGURE 12-2: Modification of a Preexisting Contract**

◆ FIGURE 12-2: **Modification of a Preexisting Contract**

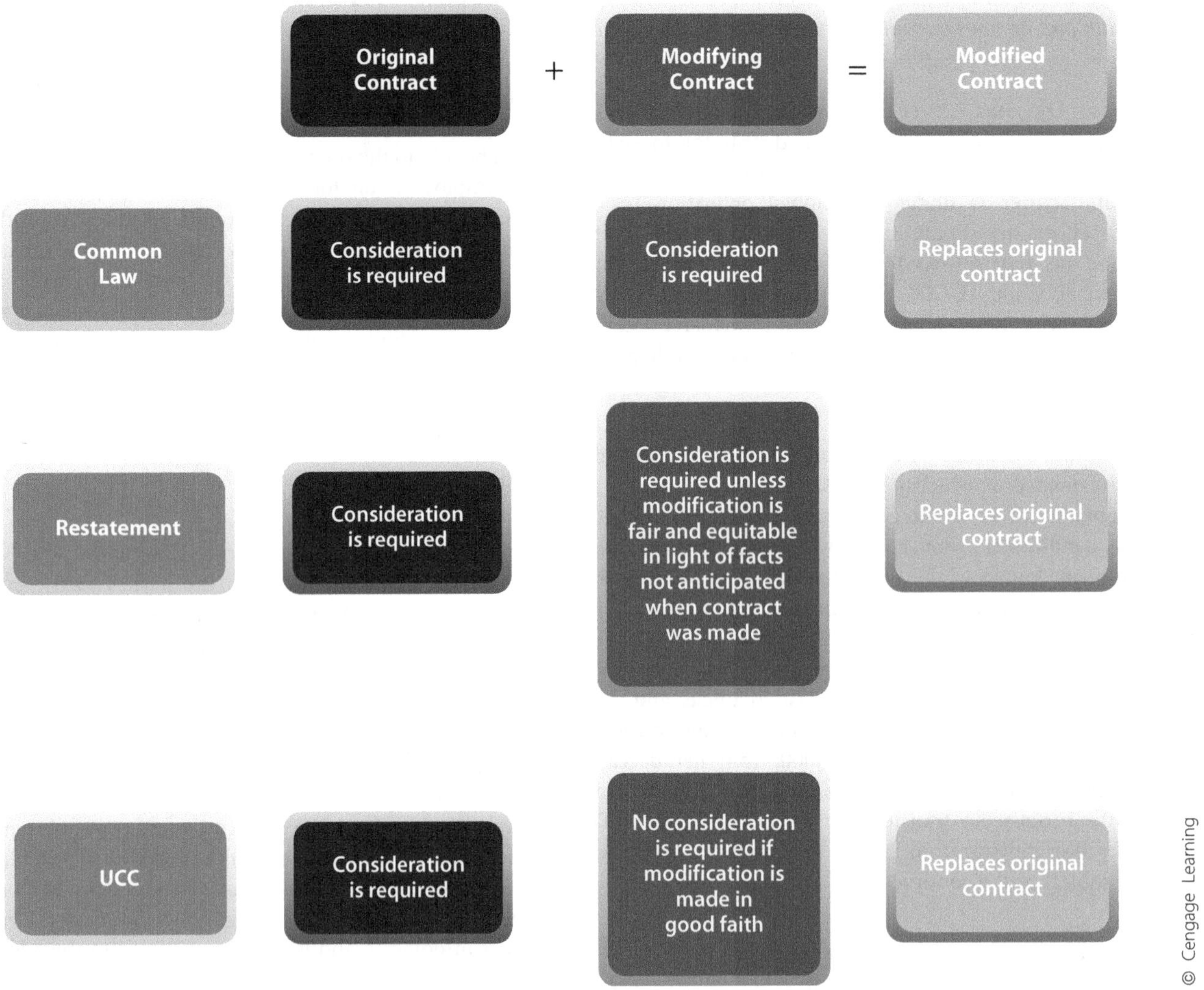

	Original Contract	+	Modifying Contract	=	Modified Contract
Common Law	Consideration is required		Consideration is required		Replaces original contract
Restatement	Consideration is required		Consideration is required unless modification is fair and equitable in light of facts not anticipated when contract was made		Replaces original contract
UCC	Consideration is required		No consideration is required if modification is made in good faith		Replaces original contract

© Cengage Learning

◆ SEE CASE 12-3

PRACTICAL ADVICE

If you modify a contract governed by the common law, be sure to provide additional consideration to make the other party's new promise enforceable.

SUBSTITUTED CONTRACTS A substituted contract results when the parties to a contract mutually agree to rescind their original contract and enter into a new one. This situation involves separate contracts: the original contract, the agreement of rescission, and the substitute contract. Substituted contracts are perfectly valid, allowing the parties effectively to discharge the original contract and to impose obligations under the new one. The rescission is binding in that each party, by giving up

his rights under the original contract, has provided consideration to the other, as long as each party still has rights under the original contract. Where the rescission and new agreement are simultaneous, the effect is the same as a contractual modification. The Restatement takes the position that the substitute contract is *not* binding unless it is fair and equitable in view of circumstances the parties did not anticipate when they made the original contract. Section 89, Comment b.

SETTLEMENT OF A LIQUIDATED DEBT A **liquidated debt** is an obligation the existence and amount of which is undisputed. Under the common law, the partial payment of a sum of money in consideration of a promise to discharge a fully matured, undisputed debt is legally *insufficient* to support the promise of discharge. To illustrate, assume that Pamela owes Julie $100, and in consideration of Pamela's paying Julie

$50.00, Julie agrees to discharge the debt. In a subsequent suit by Julie against Pamela to recover the remaining $50.00, at common law Julie is entitled to judgment for $50.00 on the ground that Julie's promise of discharge is not binding because Pamela's payment of $50.00 was no legal detriment to the promisee, Pamela, as she was under a preexisting legal obligation to pay that much and more. Consequently, the consideration for Julie's promise of discharge was legally insufficient, and Julie is not bound on her promise. If, however, Julie had accepted from Pamela any new or different consideration, such as the sum of $40.00 and a fountain pen worth $10.00 or less, or even the fountain pen with no payment of money, in full satisfaction of the $100 debt, the consideration moving from Pamela would be legally sufficient inasmuch as Pamela was under no legal obligation to give a fountain pen to Julie. In this example, consideration would also exist if Julie had agreed to accept $50.00 before the debt became due, in full satisfaction of the debt. Pamela was under no legal obligation to pay any of the debt before its due date. Consequently, Pamela's early payment would represent a legal detriment to Pamela as well as a legal benefit to Julie. The law is not concerned with the amount of the discount, as that is simply a question of adequacy for the courts to decide. Likewise, Pamela's payment of a lesser amount on the due date at an agreed-upon different place of payment would be legally sufficient consideration. The Restatement requires that the new consideration "differs from what was required by the duty in a way which reflects more than a pretense of bargain." Section 73.

SETTLEMENT OF AN UNLIQUIDATED DEBT An **unliquidated debt** is an obligation disputed as to either its existence or its amount. A promise to settle a validly disputed claim in exchange for an agreed payment or other performance is supported by consideration. Where the dispute is based upon contentions that are nonmeritorious or not made in good faith, however, the debtor's surrender of such a claim is no legal detriment to the claimant. The Restatement adopts a different position by providing that the settlement of a claim that proves invalid is consideration if at the time of the settlement (1) the claimant honestly believed that the claim was valid, or (2) the claim was in fact doubtful because of uncertainty as to the facts or the law. Section 74.

For example, in situations in which a person has requested professional services from an accountant or a lawyer and the parties reached no agreement with respect to the amount of the fee to be charged, the accountant or lawyer is entitled to receive from her client a reasonable fee for the services rendered. As no definite amount has been agreed upon, the client's obligation is uncertain; nevertheless, his legal obligation is to pay the reasonable worth of the services performed. When the accountant or lawyer sends the client a bill for services rendered, even though the amount stated in the bill is an estimate of the reasonable value of the services, the debt does not become undisputed until and unless the client agrees to pay the amount of the bill. If the client honestly disputes the amount that is owed and tenders in full settlement an amount less than the bill, acceptance of the lesser amount by the creditor discharges the debt. Thus, if Ted sends to Betty, an accountant, a check for $120 in payment of his debt to Betty for services rendered, which services Ted considered worthless but for which Betty billed Ted $600, Betty's acceptance of the check releases Ted from any further liability. Ted has given up his right to dispute the billing further, while Betty has forfeited her right to further collection. Thus, there is mutuality of consideration.

PRACTICAL ADVICE

If your contract is validly disputed, carefully consider whether to accept any payment marked "payment in full."

BARGAINED-FOR EXCHANGE

The central idea behind consideration is that the parties have intentionally entered into a bargained exchange with one another and have given to each other something in exchange for a promise or performance. "A performance or return promise is bargained for if it is sought by the promisor in exchange for his promise and is given by the promisee in exchange for that promise." Restatement, Section 71. Thus, a promise to give someone a birthday present is without consideration, as the promisor received nothing in exchange for his promise of a present.

PRACTICAL ADVICE

Because a promise to make a gift is generally not legally enforceable, obtain delivery of something that shows your control or ownership of the item to make it an executed gift.

PAST CONSIDERATION

Consideration is the inducement for a promise or performance. The element of bargained-for exchange is absent where a promise is given for a past transaction. Therefore, unbargained-for past events are not consideration, despite their designation as "past consideration." A promise made on account of something that the promisee has already done is not enforceable. For example, Noel gives emergency care to Tim's adult son while the son is ill. Tim subsequently promises to pay Noel for her services, but his promise is not binding because there is no bargained-for exchange.

◆ SEE CASE 12-4

THIRD PARTIES

Consideration to support a promise may be given to a person other than the promisor if the promisor bargains for that exchange. For example, A promises to pay B $15.00 if B delivers a specified book to C.

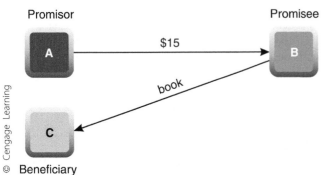

A's promise is binding because B incurred a legal detriment by delivering the book to C, as B was under no prior legal obligation to do so, and A had no prior legal right to have the book given to C. A and B have bargained for A to pay B $15.00 in return for B's delivering the book to C. A's promise to pay $15.00 is also consideration for B's promise to give the book to C.

Conversely, consideration may be given by some person other than the promisee. For example, A promises to pay B $25.00 in return for D's promise to give a radio to A.

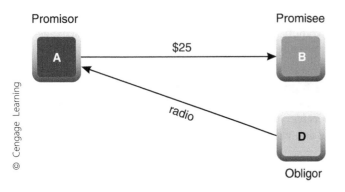

A's promise to pay $25.00 to B is consideration for D's promise to give a radio to A and vice versa.

CONTRACTS WITHOUT CONSIDERATION

Certain transactions are enforceable even though they are not supported by consideration. Such transactions include (1) promises to perform prior unenforceable obligations, (2) promises that induce detrimental reliance (promissory estoppel), (3) promises made under seal, and (4) promises made enforceable by statute.

PROMISES TO PERFORM PRIOR UNENFORCEABLE OBLIGATIONS

In certain circumstances the courts will enforce new promises to perform an obligation that originally was not enforceable or has become unenforceable by operation of law. These situations include promises to pay debts barred by the statute of limitations, debts discharged in bankruptcy, and voidable obligations. In addition, as previously indicated, some courts will enforce promises to pay moral obligations.

PROMISE TO PAY DEBT BARRED BY THE STATUTE OF LIMITATIONS Every State has a statute of limitations, which provides that legal actions must be initiated within a prescribed period after the right to bring the action arose. Actions not commenced within the specified time period, which varies among the States and also with the nature of the legal action, will be dismissed.

An exception to the past consideration rule extends to promises to pay all or part of a contractual or quasi-contractual debt barred by the statute of limitations. The new promise is binding according to its terms without consideration for a second statutory period. Any recovery under the new promise is limited to the terms contained in the new promise. Most States require that new promises falling under this rule, except those indicated by part payment, be in writing to be enforceable.

PROMISE TO PAY DEBT DISCHARGED IN BANKRUPTCY Another exception to the requirement that consideration be given in exchange for a promise to make it binding is a promise to pay a debt that has been discharged in bankruptcy. Restatement, Section 83. The Bankruptcy Act, however, imposes a number of requirements before a promise to pay a debt discharged in bankruptcy may be enforced. These requirements are discussed in *Chapter 38*.

VOIDABLE PROMISES Another promise that is enforceable without new consideration is a new promise to perform a voidable obligation that has not previously been avoided. Restatement, Section 85. The power of avoidance may be based on lack of capacity, fraud, misrepresentation, duress, undue influence, or mistake. For instance, a promise to perform an antecedent obligation made by a minor upon reaching the age of majority is enforceable without new consideration. To be enforceable, the promise itself must not be voidable. For example, if the new promise is made without knowledge of the original fraud or by a minor before reaching the age of majority, then the new promise is not enforceable.

MORAL OBLIGATION Under the common law, a promise made to satisfy a preexisting moral obligation is made for past consideration and therefore is unenforceable for lack of consideration. Instances involving such obligations include promises to pay for board and lodging previously furnished to a needy relative of the promisor, promises to pay debts owed by a relative, and an employer's promises to pay a completely disabled former employee a sum of money in addition to an award the employee has received under a workers' compensation statute. Although in many cases the moral obligation may be strong by reason of the particular facts and circumstances, no liability generally attaches to the promise.

The Restatement and a minority of States give considerable recognition to moral obligations as consideration. The Restatement provides that a promise made for "a benefit previously received by the promisor from the promisee is binding to the extent necessary to prevent injustice." Section 86. For instance, Tim's subsequent promise to Noel to reimburse her for the expenses she incurred in rendering emergency services to Tim's son is binding even though it is not supported by new consideration.

The Restatement also provides for enforcement of a moral obligation when a person promises to pay for a mistakenly conferred benefit. For example, Pam hires Elizabeth to pave her driveway, and Elizabeth mistakenly paves Chuck's driveway next door. Chuck subsequently promises to pay Pam $1,000 for the benefit conferred. Under the Restatement, Chuck's promise to pay the $1,000 is binding.

PROMISSORY ESTOPPEL

As discussed in *Chapter 9*, in certain circumstances in which detrimental reliance has occurred, the courts will enforce noncontractual promises under the doctrine of promissory estoppel. When applicable, the doctrine makes gratuitous promises enforceable to the extent necessary to avoid injustice. The doctrine applies when a promise that the promisor reasonably should expect to induce detrimental reliance does induce such action or forbearance.

Promissory estoppel does not mean that every gratuitous promise is binding simply because it is followed by a change of position on the part of the promisee. To create liability, the promisee must make the change of position in justifiable reliance on the promise. For example, Smith promises to Barclay not to foreclose on a mortgage Smith holds on Barclay's factory for a period of six months. In justifiable reliance on Smith's promise, Barclay expends $900,000 on expanding the factory. Smith's promise not to foreclose is binding on Smith under the doctrine of promissory estoppel.

The most common application of the doctrine of promissory estoppel is to charitable subscriptions. Numerous churches, memorials, college buildings, hospitals, and other structures used for religious, educational, and charitable purposes have been built with the assistance of contributions fulfilling pledges or promises to contribute to particular worthwhile causes. Although the pledgor regards herself as

making a gift for a charitable purpose and gift promises generally are not enforceable, the courts tend to enforce charitable subscription promises. Numerous reasons and theories have been advanced in support of liability: the most accepted argues that the subscription has induced a change of position by the promisee (the church, school, or charitable organization) in reliance on the promise. The Restatement, moreover, has relaxed the reliance requirement for charitable subscriptions so that actual reliance need not be shown; the probability of reliance is sufficient.

◆ SEE CASE 12-4

PROMISES MADE UNDER SEAL

Under the common law, when a person desired to bind himself by bond, deed, or solemn promise, he executed his promise under seal. He did not have to sign the document, his delivery of a document to which he had affixed his seal being sufficient. No consideration for his promise was necessary. In some States the courts still hold a promise under seal to be binding without consideration.

Nevertheless, most States have abolished by statute the distinction between contracts under seal and written unsealed contracts. In these States, the seal is no longer recognized as a substitute for consideration. The Code has also adopted this position, specifically eliminating the use of seals in contracts for the sale of goods.

PROMISES MADE ENFORCEABLE BY STATUTE

Some gratuitous promises that otherwise would be unenforceable have been made binding by statute. Most significant among these are (1) contract modifications, (2) renunciations, and (3) irrevocable offers.

CONTRACT MODIFICATIONS As mentioned previously, the UCC has abandoned the common law rule requiring that a modification of an existing contract be supported by consideration to be valid. The Code provides that a contract for the sale of goods can be effectively modified without new consideration, provided the modification is made in good faith. Section 2–209.

RENUNCIATION Under the Code, Section 1–107, any claim or right arising out of an alleged breach of contract can be discharged in whole or in part without consideration by a written waiver or renunciation signed and delivered by the aggrieved party. Under the 2001 Revised UCC Article 1, a claim or right arising out of an alleged breach may be discharged in whole or in part without consideration by agreement of the aggrieved party in an authenticated record. Section 1–306. This section is subject to the obligation of good faith and, as with all sections of Article 1, applies to a transaction to the extent that it is governed by one of the other article of the UCC. Section 1–102.

IRREVOCABLE OFFERS Under the Code, a *firm offer*, a written offer signed by a merchant offer or promising to keep open

an offer to buy or sell goods, is not revocable for lack of consideration during the time stated, not to exceed three months, or if no time is stated, for a reasonable time. Section 2–205.

◆ **SEE FIGURE 12-3: Consideration**

◆ **FIGURE 12-3: Consideration**

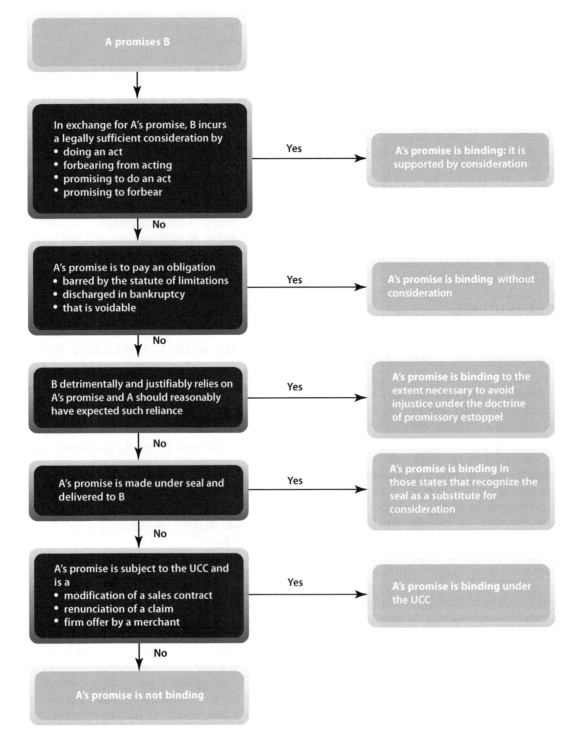

CHAPTER SUMMARY

CONSIDERATION	**Definition** the inducement to enter into a contract **Elements** legal sufficiency and bargained-for exchange
LEGAL SUFFICIENCY	**Definition** consists of either a benefit to the promisor or a detriment to the promisee • *Legal Benefit* obtaining something to which one had no prior legal right • *Legal Detriment* doing an act one is not legally obligated to do or not doing an act that one has a legal right to do **Adequacy** not required where the parties have freely agreed to the exchange **Illusory Promise** promise that imposes no obligation on the promisor; the following promises are *not* illusory: • *Output Contract* agreement to sell all of one's production to a single buyer • *Requirements Contract* agreement to buy all of one's needs from a single producer • *Exclusive Dealing Contract* grant to a franchisee or licensee by a manufacturer of the sole right to sell goods in a defined market • *Conditional Promise* a contract in which the obligations are contingent upon the occurrence of a stated event **Preexisting Public Obligations** public duties such as those imposed by tort or criminal law are neither a legal detriment nor a legal benefit **Preexisting Contractual Obligation** performance of a preexisting contractual duty is not consideration • *Modification of a Preexisting Contract* under the common law a modification of a preexisting contract must be supported by mutual consideration; under the Code a contract can be modified without new consideration • *Substituted Contracts* the parties agree to rescind their original contract and to enter into a new one; rescission and new contract are supported by consideration • *Settlement of an Undisputed Debt* payment of a lesser sum of money to discharge an undisputed debt (one whose existence or amount is not contested) does not constitute legally sufficient consideration • *Settlement of a Disputed Debt* payment of a lesser sum of money to discharge a disputed debt (one whose existence or amount is contested) is legally sufficient consideration
BARGAINED-FOR EXCHANGE	**Definition** a mutually agreed-upon exchange **Past Consideration** an act done before the contract is made is not consideration
CONTRACTS WITHOUT CONSIDERATION	**Promises to Perform Prior Unenforceable Obligations** • *Promise to Pay Debt Barred by the Statute of Limitations* a new promise by the debtor to pay the debt renews the running of the statute for a second statutory period • *Promise to Pay Debt Discharged in Bankruptcy* may be enforceable without consideration • *Voidable Promises* a new promise to perform a voidable obligation that has not been previously avoided is enforceable • *Moral Obligation* a promise made to satisfy a preexisting moral obligation is generally unenforceable for lack of consideration

Promissory Estoppel doctrine that prohibits a party from denying her promise when the promisee takes action or forbearance to his detriment reasonably based upon the promise

Promises Under Seal where still recognized, the seal acts as a substitute for consideration

Promises Made Enforceable by Statute some gratuitous promises have been made enforceable by statute; the Code makes enforceable (1) contract modifications, (2) renunciations, and (3) firm offers

CASES

CASE 12-1

Illusory Promises
VANEGAS v. AMERICAN ENERGY SERVICES
Supreme Court of Texas, 2009
302 S.W.3d 299
http://scholar.google.com/scholar_case?case=3293885797327227839&q=302+S.W.3d+299+&hl=en&as_sdt=2,34

Green, J.

In this case, we are asked to decide the enforceability of an employer's alleged promise to pay five percent of the proceeds of a sale or merger of the company to employees who are still employed at the time of the sale or merger. The employer, American Energy Services (AES), * * * was formed in the summer of 1996. AES hired the petitioners in this case (collectively, the employees) that same year. The employees allege that in an operational meeting in June 1997, they voiced concerns to John Carnett, a vice president of AES, about the continued viability of the company. The employees complained that the company required them to work long hours with antiquated equipment. The employees allege that, in an effort to provide an incentive for them to stay with the company, Carnett promised the employees, who were at-will and therefore free to leave the company at any time, that "in the event of sale or merger of AES, the original [eight] employees remaining with AES at that time would get 5% of the value of any sale or merger of AES." AES Acquisition, Inc. acquired AES in 2001. Seven of the eight original employees were still with AES at the time of the acquisition. Those remaining employees demanded their proceeds, and when the company refused to pay, the employees sued, claiming AES breached the oral agreement.

AES moved for summary judgment on [the ground] that the agreement was illusory and therefore not enforceable * * * . The employees responded that the promise represented a unilateral contract, and by remaining employed for the stated period, the employees performed, thereby making the promise enforceable. The trial court granted AES's motion for summary judgment, and the employees appealed. The court of appeals affirmed, holding that the alleged unilateral contract failed because it was not sup-

ported by at least one non-illusory promise, citing this Court's decision in *Light v. Centel Cellular Co. of Texas*, [citation]. The employees petitioned this Court for review, which we granted.

AES argues, and the court of appeals held, that our holdings in *Light* dictate the result in this case. [Citation.] In *Light*, we stated:

> Consideration for a promise, by either the employee or the employer in an at-will employment, cannot be dependent on a period of continued employment. Such a promise would be illusory because it fails to bind the promisor who always retains the option of discontinuing employment in lieu of performance. When illusory promises are all that support a purported bilateral contract, there is no contract.

> * * *

Light involved an employee's challenge to a covenant not to compete. [Citation.] * * *

We revisited the issue of illusory promises in covenants not to compete in *Sheshunoff*. * * * We reaffirmed our previous holding in *Light* that covenants not to compete in bilateral contracts must be supported by "mutual non-illusory promises." [Citation.]

Citing our holdings in *Light* and *Sheshunoff*, the court of appeals [in this case] stated that "[a] unilateral contract may be formed when one of the parties makes only an illusory promise but the other party makes a non-illusory promise. The non-illusory promise can serve as the offer for a unilateral contract, which the promisor who made the illusory promise can accept by performance." [Citation.] We agree with that statement, but the court of appeals erroneously applied those holdings to the current case.

The issue turns on the distinction between bilateral and unilateral contracts. "A bilateral contract is one in which there are mutual promises between two parties to the contract, each party being both a promisor and a promisee." [Citations.] A unilateral contract, on the other hand, is "created by the promisor promising a benefit if the promisee performs. The contract becomes enforceable when the promisee performs." [Citation.] Both *Sheshunoff* and *Light* concerned *bilateral* contracts in which employers made promises in exchange for employees' promises not to compete with their companies after termination. [Citations.] The court of appeals' explanation of these cases—describing an exchange of promises where one party makes an illusory promise and the other a non-illusory promise—describes the attempted formation of a *bilateral* contract, not a unilateral contract. [Citation.] * * *

The court of appeals held that even if AES promised to pay the employees the five percent, that promise was illusory at the time it was made because the employees were at-will, and AES could have fired all of them prior to the acquisition. [Citation.] But whether the promise was illusory at the time it was made is irrelevant; what matters is whether the promise became enforceable by the time of the breach. [Citations.] Almost all unilateral contracts begin as illusory promises. Take, for instance, the classic textbook example of a unilateral contract: "I will pay you $50 if you paint my house." The offer to pay the individual to paint the house can be withdrawn at any point prior to performance. But once the individual accepts the offer by performing, the promise to pay

the $50 becomes binding. The employees allege that AES made an offer to split five percent of the proceeds of the sale or merger of the company among any remaining original employees. Assuming that allegation is true, the seven remaining employees accepted this offer by remaining employed for the requested period of time. [Citation.] At that point, AES's promise became binding. AES then breached its agreement with the employees when it refused to pay the employees their five percent share.

Furthermore, the court of appeals' holding would potentially jeopardize all pension plans, vacation leave, and other forms of compensation made to at-will employees that are based on a particular term of service. * * *

The fact that the employees were at-will and were already being compensated in the form of their salaries in exchange for remaining employed also does not make the promise to pay the bonus any less enforceable.

* * *

AES allegedly promised to pay any remaining original employees five percent of the proceeds when AES was sold. Assuming AES did make such an offer, the seven remaining employees accepted the offer by staying with AES until the sale. Regardless of whether the promise was illusory at the time it was made, the promise became enforceable upon the employees' performance. The court of appeals erred in holding otherwise. Accordingly, we reverse the court of appeals' judgment and remand the case to the trial court for further proceedings consistent with this opinion.

| CASE 12-2 | Preexisting Obligation **DENNEY v. REPPERT** Court of Appeals of Kentucky, 1968 432 S.W.2d 647 http://scholar.google.com/scholar_case?case=14895092933351248292&q=432+S.W.2d+647&hl=en&as_sdt=2,34 | |

Myre, Special Commissioner
On June 12th or 13th, 1963, three armed men entered the First State Bank, Eubank, Kentucky, and with a display of arms and threats robbed the bank of over $30,000. Later in the day they were apprehended by State Policemen Garret Godby, Johnny Simms, and Tilford Reppert, placed under arrest, and the entire loot was recovered. Later all of the prisoners were convicted and Garret Godby, Johnny Simms, and Tilford Reppert appeared as witnesses at the trial.

The First State Bank of Eubank was a member of the Kentucky Bankers Association which provided and advertised a reward of $500.00 for the arrest and conviction of each bank robber. Hence the outstanding reward for the three bank robbers was $1,500.00. Many became claimants for the

reward and the Kentucky State Bankers Association, being unable to determine the merits of the claims for the reward, asked the circuit court to determine the merits of the various claims and to adjudge who was entitled to receive the reward or share in it. All of the claimants were made defendants in the action.

At the time of the robbery the claimants Murrell Denney, Joyce Buis, Rebecca McCollum, and Jewell Snyder were employees of the First State Bank of Eubank and came out of the grueling situation with great credit and glory. Each one of them deserves approbation and an accolade. They were vigilant in disclosing to the public and the peace officers the details of the crime, and in describing the culprits, and giving all the information that they possessed that would be useful in capturing the robbers. Undoubtedly, they performed a great service. It is in the evidence that the claimant Murrell Denney was conspicuous and energetic in his efforts to make known the robbery, to acquaint the officers as to the personal appearance of the criminals, and to give other pertinent facts.

The first question for determination is whether the employees of the robbed bank are eligible to receive or share in the reward. The great weight of authority answers in the negative. * * *

"To the general rule that, when a reward is offered to the general public for the performance of some specified act, such reward may be claimed by any person who performs such act, is the exception of agents, employees, and public officials who are acting within the scope of their employment or official duties. * * * *"

* * *

At the time of the robbery the claimants Murrell Denney, Joyce Buis, Rebecca McCollum, and Jewell Snyder were employees of the First State Bank of Eubank. They were under duty to protect and conserve the resources and moneys of the bank, and safeguard every interest of the institution furnishing them employment. Each of these employees exhibited great courage and cool bravery, in a time of stress and danger. The community and the county have recompensed them in commendation, admiration, and high praise, and the world looks on them as heroes. But in making known the robbery and assisting in acquainting the public and the officers with details of the crime and with identification of the robbers, they performed a duty to the bank and the public, for which they cannot claim a reward.

The claims of Corbin Reynolds, Julia Reynolds, Alvie Reynolds, and Gene Reynolds also must fail. According to

their statements they gave valuable information to the arresting officers. However, they did not follow the procedure as set forth in the offer of reward in that they never filed a claim with the Kentucky Bankers Association. It is well established that a claimant of a reward must comply with the terms and conditions of the offer of reward. [Citation.]

State Policemen Garret Godby, Johnny Simms, and Tilford Reppert made the arrest of the bank robbers and captured the stolen money. All participated in the prosecution. At the time of the arrest, it was the duty of the state policemen to apprehend the criminals. Under the law they cannot claim or share in the reward and they are interposing no claim to it.

This leaves the defendant, Tilford Reppert the sole eligible claimant. The record shows that at the time of the arrest he was a deputy sheriff in Rockcastle County, but the arrest and recovery of the stolen money took place in Pulaski County. He was out of his jurisdiction, and was thus under no legal duty to make the arrest, and is thus eligible to claim and receive the reward. In *Kentucky Bankers Ass'n et al. v. Cassady* [citation], it was said:

It is * * * well established that a public officer with the authority of the law to make an arrest may accept an offer of reward or compensation for acts or services performed outside of his bailiwick or not within the scope of his official duties. * * *

* * *

It is manifest from the record that Tilford Reppert is the only claimant qualified and eligible to receive the reward.

Therefore, it is the judgment of the circuit court that he is entitled to receive payment of the $1,500.00 reward now deposited with the clerk of this court.

The judgment is affirmed.

CASE
12-3

Modification of a Preexisting Contract
NEW ENGLAND ROCK SERVICES, INC. v. EMPIRE PAVING, INC.
Appellate Court of Connecticut, 1999
53 Conn App. 771, 731 A.2d 784 cert. denied, 250 Conn. 921, 738 A.2d 658
http://scholar.google.com/scholar_case?case=2815205762460431873&q=731+A.2d+784&hl=en&as_sdt=2,34

Schaller, J.
The defendants, Empire Paving, Inc. (Empire), and its bonding company, American Insurance Company, doing business as Fireman's Fund Insurance Company (Fireman's Fund), appeal from the judgment of the trial court awarding damages to the named plaintiff, New England Rock Services, Inc. (Rock Services), under a contract between the parties. The principal issue on appeal is whether the trial court improperly concluded that an agreement made by the parties on

December 9, 1995, modified an earlier contract executed by them on October 26, 1995. We affirm the judgment of the trial court.

The following facts are relevant to the disposition of this appeal. On October 26, 1995, Empire entered into a contract with Rock Services under which Rock Services would provide drilling and blasting services as a subcontractor on the Niles Hill Road sewer project on which Empire was the general contractor and the city of New London was the owner.

Pursuant to the contract, Rock Services agreed to drill and blast a certain amount of rock encountered on the sewer project. In return, Rock Services was to be paid an agreed upon price of $29 per cubic yard with an estimated amount of 5000 cubic yards, or on a time and materials basis, whichever was less.

On October 31, 1995, Rock Services commenced work on the project. From the beginning, Rock Services experienced a number of problems with the project. The primary obstacle was the presence of a heavy concentration of water on the site. The water problem hindered Rock Services' ability to complete its work as anticipated. The trial court found that it was the custom and practice in the industry for the general contractor to control the water on the site and that, on this particular job, Empire failed to control the water on the site properly. In an effort to mitigate the water problem, Rock Services attempted to "load behind the drill," a process that allows a blaster to load the drilled hole with a charge immediately after the hole is drilled, before water has the opportunity to seep into the hole. The city fire marshal, however, refused to allow Rock Services to employ this method of drilling. Thereafter, in order to complete its work, Rock Services was compelled to use the more costly and time consuming method of casing the blasting hole, a process that requires the blaster to drive a plastic casing down into the drilled hole to prevent seepage.

In late November, 1995, Rock Services advised Empire that it would be unable to complete the work as anticipated because of the conditions at the site and requested that Empire agree to amend the contract to allow Rock Services to complete the project on a time and materials basis. On December 8, 1995, Empire signed a purchase order that modified the original agreement. The modification required Empire to pay for the blasting work on a time and materials basis for the remainder of the project. Rock Services, thereafter, completed its work on the project.

Upon completion of the work, Empire refused to pay Rock Services for the remaining balance due on the time and materials agreement in the amount of $58,686.63, and Rock Services instituted this action. The trial court concluded that the later purchase order was a valid and enforceable modification of the earlier contract. The trial court found that the parties intended the purchase order to modify the earlier agreement and that Empire's assent to the modification was not made under duress but, rather, was a calculated business decision. After finding Empire's withholding of the amount due to Rock Services wrongful, the trial court awarded Rock Services damages in the amount of $58,686.63, plus interest and costs. This appeal followed.

On appeal, Empire claims that the trial court improperly found that the later purchase order was a valid and enforce-

able modification of the earlier contract. Specifically, Empire claims that the later agreement lacked the requisite consideration to be a valid and enforceable modification of the earlier contract. We disagree.

* * *

In concluding that the modification was valid and enforceable, the trial court determined that the later agreement was supported by sufficient consideration. * * *

"The doctrine of consideration is fundamental in the law of contracts, the general rule being that in the absence of consideration an executory promise is unenforceable." [Citation.] While mutual promises may be sufficient consideration to bind parties to a modification; [citations] a promise to do that which one is already bound by his contract to do is not sufficient consideration to support an additional promise by the other party to the contract. [Citations.]

"A modification of an agreement must be supported by valid consideration and requires a party to do, or promise to do, something further than, or different from, that which he is already bound to do. [Citations.] It is an accepted principle of law in this state that when a party agrees to perform an obligation for another to whom that obligation is already owed, although for lesser remuneration, the second agreement does not constitute a valid, binding contract. [Citations.] The basis of the rule is generally made to rest upon the proposition that in such a situation he who promises the additional [work] receives nothing more than that to which he is already entitled and he to whom the promise is made gives nothing that he was not already under legal obligation to give. [Citations.]"

Our Supreme Court in [citation], however, articulated an exception to the preexisting duty rule: "'[W]here a contract must be performed under burdensome conditions not anticipated, and not within the contemplation of the parties at the time when the contract was made, and the promisee measures up to the right standard of honesty and fair dealing, and agrees, in view of the changed conditions, to pay what is then reasonable, just, and fair, such new contract is not without consideration within the meaning of that term, either in law or in equity.'" * * * "'What unforeseen difficulties and burdens will make a party's refusal to go forward with his contract equitable, so as to take the case out of the general rule and bring it within the exception, must depend upon the facts of each particular case. They must be substantial, unforeseen, and not within the contemplation of the parties when the contract was made. They need not be such as would legally justify the party in his refusal to perform his contract, unless promised extra pay, or to justify a court of equity in relieving him from the contract; for they are sufficient if they are of such a character as to render the party's demand for extra pay manifestly fair, so as to rebut all inference that he is seeking to be relieved from an unsatisfactory contract, or to take advantage of the necessities of the opposite party to coerce from him a promise for further compensation. Inadequacy of the contract price which is the result of an error of judgment, and not of some excusable mistake of fact, is not sufficient.'" [Citation.] * * *

Empire argues strenuously that the water conditions on the site cannot qualify as a new circumstance that was not anticipated at the time the original contract was signed. * * *

Empire's argument, however, is misplaced. Rock Services does not argue that it was unaware of the water conditions

on the site but, rather, that Empire's failure to control or remove the water on the site constituted the new or changed circumstance. Rock Services argues that Empire's duty to control or remove the water on the job site arose in accordance with the custom and practice in the industry and, therefore, Empire's failure to control or remove the water on the site constituted a new circumstance that Rock Services did not anticipate at the time the original contract was signed.

* * *

The judgment is affirmed.

CASE 12-4

Past Condition/Promissory Estoppel
DILORENZO v. VALVE AND PRIMER CORPORATION
Appellate Court of Illinois, First District, Fifth Division, 2004
807 N.E.2d 673, 283 Ill.Dec. 68
http://scholar.google.com/scholar_case?case=258399757685586555&q=807+N.E.2d+673&hl=en&as_sdt=2,34

Reid, J.

[DiLorenzo, a forty-year employee of Valve & Primer, was also an officer, director, and shareholder of one hundred shares of stock. DiLorenzo claims that in 1987 Valve & Primer offered him a ten-year stock option that would allow DiLorenzo to purchase an additional three hundred shares at the fixed price of $250 per share. DiLorenzo claims that in reliance on that employment agreement, he stayed in his job for over nine additional years and did not follow up on any of several recruitment offers from other companies. Valve & Primer claims the 1987 employment agreement between it and DiLorenzo did not contain a stock purchase agreement. The only purported proof of the agreement is an unsigned copy of board meeting minutes of which DiLorenzo had the only copy.

In January 1996, DiLorenzo entered into a semiretirement agreement with Valve & Primer, and he attempted to tender his remaining one hundred shares pursuant to a stock redemption agreement. Shortly thereafter, Valve & Primer fired DiLorenzo. DiLorenzo argued before the trial court that, even if the purported agreement was not found to be valid, it should be enforced on promissory estoppel grounds. Valve & Primer's moved for summary judgment, which the trial court granted for lack of consideration. The trial court denied the promissory estoppel claim because of insufficient reliance. DiLorenzo appealed.]

We begin by addressing whether there was consideration for the stock options. "A stock option is the right to buy a share or shares of stock at a specified price or within a specified period." [Citation.] In order to evaluate

the nature and scope of the stock options issued to DiLorenzo, we must assume, for purposes of this portion of our discussion, that DiLorenzo's corporate minutes are valid.

"A contract, to be valid, must contain offer, acceptance, and consideration; to be enforceable, the agreement must also be sufficiently definite so that its terms are reasonably certain and able to be determined." [Citation.] "A contract is sufficiently definite and certain to be enforceable if the court is able from its terms and provisions to ascertain what the parties intended, under proper rules of construction and applicable principles of equity." [Citation.] "A contract may be enforced even though some contract terms may be missing or left to be agreed upon, but if essential terms are so uncertain that there is no basis for deciding whether the agreement has been kept or broken, there is no contract." [Citation.] A bonus promised to induce an employee to continue his employment is supported by adequate consideration if the employee is not already bound by contract to continue. [Citation.] Because we are assuming the validity of the document issuing the stock options, we now turn to whether the underlying option is supported by valid consideration so as to make it a proper contract.

"Consideration is defined as the bargained-for exchange of promises or performances and may consist of a promise, an act or a forbearance." [Citation.]

"The general principles applicable to option contracts have been long established. An option contract has two elements, an offer to do something, or to forbear, which does not become a contract until accepted; and an agreement to leave the offer open for a specified time [citation], or for a reasonable time [citation]. An option contract must be supported by sufficient consideration; and if not, it is merely an offer which may be withdrawn at any time prior to a tender of compliance. [Citation.] If a consideration of 'one dollar' or some other consideration is stated but which has, in fact, not been paid, the document is merely an offer which may be withdrawn at any time prior to a tender of compliance. The document will amount only to a continuing offer which may be withdrawn by the offeror at any time before acceptance. [Citation.] The consideration to support an option consists of 'some right, interest, profit or benefit accruing to one party, or some forbearance, detriment, loss or responsibility given, suffered or undertaken by the other' [citation]; or otherwise stated, 'Any act or promise which is of benefit to one party or disadvantage to the other * * *.' [Citation.]"

"The preexisting duty rule provides that where a party does what it is already legally obligated to do, there is no consideration because there has been no detriment." [Citation.]

Focusing on the lack of a detriment to the employee, the trial court found no valid consideration. Based upon our view of the discussion in [citation], the trial court was correct in concluding that the option contract is merely an offer which may be withdrawn at any time prior to a tender of compliance. DiLorenzo could have exercised the option the moment it was purportedly made, then immediately quit, thereby giving nothing to the employer. Though the exercise of the option would require the transfer of money for the stock, the option itself carries with it no detriment to DiLorenzo. Therefore, there was no consideration for the option.

* * *

We next address DiLorenzo's claim that he is entitled to the value of the shares of stock based upon the theory of promissory estoppel. DiLorenzo argues that the trial court misapplied the law in finding that there was insufficient reliance to support a claim for promissory estoppel. He claims that, once the trial court decided there was insufficient consideration to support the option contract, promissory estoppel should have been applied by the court to enforce the agreement as a matter of equity. DiLorenzo argues that he detrimentally relied upon Valve & Primer's promise in

that he worked at Valve & Primer for an additional period in excess of nine years in reliance on the stock option agreement. * * *

Valve & Primer responds that the trial court was correct in finding insufficient reliance to support the promissory estoppel claim. Valve & Primer argues that the DiLorenzo could not satisfy the detrimental reliance prong of the promissory estoppel elements. Though DiLorenzo claimed he did not act upon offers of employment he claims were made by other companies during the course of his employment with Valve & Primer, he presented to the trial court nothing but his own testimony in support of his claim. Valve & Primer argues that, since DiLorenzo essentially is claiming his stock option vested immediately, he cannot contend that he detrimentally relied upon the purported agreement in the corporate minutes by turning down those other opportunities. * * * For purposes of promissory estoppel, if DiLorenzo's allegations are taken as true, and the purported option vested immediately, it required nothing of him in order to be exercised other than the payment of $250 per share.

"Promissory estoppel arises when (1) an unambiguous promise was made, (2) the defendant relied on the promise, (3) the defendant's reliance on the promise was reasonable, and (4) the defendant suffered a detriment." [Citation.] Whether detrimental reliance has occurred is determined according to the specific facts of each case. [Citation.]

While we would accept that, under certain circumstances, it may be possible for a relinquishment of a job offer to constitute consideration sufficient to support a contract, this is not such a case. There is nothing in the language of the corporate minutes or any other source to be found in this record to suggest that Valve & Primer conditioned the alleged stock option on DiLorenzo's promise to remain in his employment. While the corporate minutes say the alleged grant of the stock option was intended to "retain and reward," it contains no mechanism making the retention mandatory. Since the corporate minutes lack a mandatory obligation on which DiLorenzo could have reasonably detrimentally relied, and he could have elected to buy the shares of stock immediately, DiLorenzo's decision to remain on the job for the additional period of over nine years must be viewed as a voluntary act. Under those circumstances, promissory estoppel would not apply. It was, therefore, not an abuse of discretion to grant Valve & Primer's motion for summary judgment on that issue.

* * *

Affirmed.

1. In consideration of $1,800 paid to him by Joyce, Hill gave Joyce a written option to purchase his house for $180,000 on or before April 1. Prior to April 1, Hill verbally agreed to extend the option until July 1. On May 18, Hill, known to Joyce, sold the house to Gray, who was ignorant of the unrecorded option. On May 20 Joyce sent an acceptance to Hill who received it on May 25. Is there a contract between Joyce and Hill? Explain.

2. **a.** Ann owed $2,500 to Barry for services Barry rendered to Ann. The debt was due June 30, 2013. In March 2014, the debt was still unpaid. Barry was in urgent need of ready cash and told Ann that if she would pay $1,500 of the debt at once, Barry would release her from the balance. Ann paid $1,500 and stated to Barry that all claims had been paid in full. In August 2014, Barry demanded the unpaid balance and subsequently sued Ann for $1,000. Result?

   b. Modify the facts in (a) by assuming that Barry gave Ann a written receipt stating that all claims had been paid in full. Result?

   c. Modify the facts in (a) by assuming that Ann owed Barry the $2,500 on Ann's purchase of a motorcycle from Barry. Result?

3. **a.** Judy orally promises her daughter, Liza, that she will give her a tract of land for her home. Liza, as intended by Judy, gives up her homestead and takes possession of the land. Liza lives there for six months and starts construction of a home. Is Judy bound to convey the real estate?

   b. Ralph, knowing that his son, Ed, desires to purchase a tract of land, promises to give him the $25,000 he needs for the purchase. Ed, relying on this promise, buys an option on the tract of land. Can Ralph rescind his promise?

4. George owed Keith $800 on a personal loan. Neither the amount of the debt nor George's liability to pay the $800 was disputed. Keith had also rendered services as a carpenter to George without any agreement as to the price to be paid. When the work was completed, an honest and reasonable difference of opinion developed between George and Keith with respect to the value of Keith's services. Upon receiving from Keith a bill of $600 for the carpentry services, George mailed in a properly stamped and addressed envelope his check for $800 to Keith. In an accompanying letter, George stated that the enclosed check was in full settlement of both claims. Keith indorsed and cashed the check. Thereafter, Keith unsuccessfully sought to collect from George an alleged unpaid balance of $600. May Keith recover the $600 from George?

5. The Snyder Mfg. Co., being a large user of coal, entered into separate contracts with several coal companies. In each contract it was agreed that the coal company would supply coal during the entire year in such amounts as the manufacturing company might desire to order, at a price of $55.00 per ton. In February the Snyder Company ordered one thousand tons of coal from Union Coal Company, one of the contracting parties. Union Coal Company delivered five hundred tons of the order and then notified Snyder Company that no more deliveries would be made and that it denied any obligation under the contract. In an action by Union Coal to collect $55.00 per ton for the five hundred tons of coal delivered, Snyder files a counterclaim, claiming damages of $1,500 for failure to deliver the additional five hundred tons of the order and damages of $4,000 for breach of agreement to deliver coal during the balance of the year. What contract, if any, exists between Snyder and Union?

6. On February 5, Devon entered into a written agreement with Gordon whereby Gordon agreed to drill a well on Devon's property for the sum of $5,000 and to complete the well on or before April 15. Before entering into the contract, Gordon made test borings and had satisfied himself as to the character of the subsurface. After two days of drilling, Gordon struck hard rock. On February 17, Gordon removed his equipment and advised Devon that the project had proved unprofitable and that he would not continue. On March 17, Devon went to Gordon and told Gordon that he would assume the risk of the enterprise and would pay Gordon $100 for each day required to drill the well, as compensation for labor, the use of Gordon's equipment, and Gordon's services in supervising the work, provided Gordon would furnish certain special equipment designed to cut through hard rock. Gordon said that the proposal was satisfactory. The work was continued by Gordon and completed in an additional fifty-eight days. Upon completion of the work, Devon failed to pay, and Gordon brought an action to recover $5,800. Devon answered that he had never become obligated to pay $100 a day and filed a counterclaim for damages in the amount of $500 for the month's delay based on an alleged breach of contract by Gordon. Decision?

7. Discuss and explain whether there is valid consideration for each of the following promises:

a. A and B entered into a contract for the purchase and sale of goods. A subsequently promised to pay a higher price for the goods when B refused to deliver at the contract price.

b. A promised in writing to pay a debt, which was due from B to C, on C's agreement to extend the time of payment for one year.

c. A orally promised to pay $150 to her son, B, solely in consideration of past services rendered to A by B, for which there had been no agreement or request to pay.

8. Alan purchased shoes from Barbara on open account. Barbara sent Alan a bill for $10,000. Alan wrote back that two hundred pairs of the shoes were defective and offered to pay $6,000 and give Barbara his promissory note for $1,000. Barbara accepted the offer, and Alan sent his check for $6,000 and his note, in accordance with the agreement. Barbara cashed the check, collected on the note, and one month later sued Alan for $3,000. Is Barbara bound by her acceptance of the offer?

9. Nancy owed Sharon $1,500, but Sharon did not initiate a lawsuit to collect the debt within the time prescribed by the statute of limitations. Nevertheless, Nancy promises Sharon that she will pay the barred debt. Thereafter, Nancy refuses to pay. Sharon brings suit to collect on this new promise. Is Nancy's new promise binding? Explain.

10. Anthony lends money to Frank. Frank dies without having paid the loan. Frank's widow, Carol, promises Anthony to repay the loan. Upon Carol's refusal to pay the loan, Anthony brings suit against Carol for payment of the loan. Is Carol bound by her promise to pay the loan?

11. The parties entered into an oral contract in June, under which plaintiff agreed to construct a building for defendant on a time and materials basis, at a maximum cost of $56,146, plus sales tax and extras ordered by defendant. When the building was 90 percent completed, defendant told plaintiff he was unhappy with the whole job as "the thing just wasn't being run right." The parties then on October 17 signed a written agreement lowering the maximum cost to $52,000 plus sales tax. Plaintiff thereafter completed the building at a cost of $64,155. The maximum under the June oral agreement, plus extras and sales tax, totaled $61,040. Defendant contended that he was obligated to pay only the lower maximum fixed by the October 17 agreement. Decision?

CASE PROBLEMS

12. Taylor assaulted his wife, who then took refuge in Ms. Harrington's house. The next day, Mr. Taylor entered the house and began another assault on his wife, who knocked him down and, while he was lying on the floor, attempted to cut his head open or decapitate him with an ax. Harrington intervened to stop the bloodshed, and the ax, as it was descending, fell upon her hand, mutilating it badly, but sparing Taylor his life. Afterwards, Taylor orally promised to compensate Harrington for her injury. Is Taylor's promise enforceable? Explain.

13. Jonnel Enterprises, Inc., contracted to construct a student dormitory at Clarion State College. On May 6, Jonnel entered into a written agreement with Graham and Long as electrical contractors to perform the electrical work and to supply materials for the dormitory. The contract price was $70,544.66. Graham and Long claim that they believed the May 6 agreement obligated them to perform the electrical work on only one wing of the building, but that three or four days after work was started, a second wing of the building was found to be in need of wiring. At that time Graham and Long informed Jonnel that they would not wire both wings of the building under the present contract, so a new contract was orally agreed upon by the parties. Under the new contract Graham and Long were obligated to wire both wings and were to be paid only $65,000, but they were relieved of the obligations to supply entrances and a heating system. Graham and Long resumed their work, and Jonnel made seven of the eight progress payments called for. When Jonnel did not pay the final payment, Graham and Long brought this action. Jonnel claims that the May 6 contract is controlling. Is Jonnel correct in its assertion? Why?

14. Baker entered into an oral agreement with Healey, the State distributor of Ballantine & Sons liquor products, that Ballantine would supply Baker with its products on demand and that Baker would have the exclusive agency for Ballantine within a certain area of Connecticut. Shortly thereafter the agreement was modified to give Baker the right to terminate at will. Eight months later, Ballantine & Sons revoked its agency. May Baker enforce the oral agreement? Explain.

15. PLM, Inc., entered into an oral agreement with Quaintance Associates, an executive "headhunter" service, for the recruitment of qualified candidates to be employed by PLM. As agreed, PLM's obligation to pay Quaintance

did not depend on PLM's actually hiring a qualified candidate presented by Quaintance. After several months Quaintance sent a letter to PLM, admitting that it had so far failed to produce a suitable candidate, but included a bill for $9,806.61, covering fees and expenses. PLM responded that Quaintance's services were worth only $6,060.48, and that payment of the lesser amount was the only fair way to handle the dispute. Accordingly, PLM enclosed a check for $6,060.48, writing on the back of the check "IN FULL PAYMENT OF ANY CLAIMS QUAINTANCE HAS AGAINST PLM, INC." Quaintance cashed the check and then sued PLM for the remaining $3,746.13. Decision?

16. Red Owl Stores told the Hoffman family that, upon the payment of approximately $518,000, a grocery store franchise would be built for them in a new location. Upon the advice of Red Owl, the Hoffmans bought a small grocery store in their hometown in order to get management experience. After the Hoffmans operated at a profit for three months, Red Owl advised them to sell the small grocery, assuring them that Red Owl would find them a larger store elsewhere. Although selling at that point would cost them much profit, the Hoffmans followed Red Owl's directions. In addition, to raise the money required for the deal, the Hoffmans sold their bakery business in their hometown. The Hoffmans also sold their house, and moved to a new home in the city where their new store was to be located. Red Owl then informed the Hoffmans that it would take $624,100, not $518,000, to complete the deal. The family scrambled to find the additional funds. However, when told by Red Owl that it would now cost them $654,000 to get their new franchise, the Hoffmans decided to sue instead. Should Red Owl be held to its promises? Explain.

17. Plaintiff, Brenner, entered into a contract with the defendant, Little Red School House, Ltd., which stated that in return for a non-refundable tuition of $1,080 Brenner's son could attend defendant's school for a year. When Brenner's ex-wife refused to enroll their son, plaintiff sought and received a verbal promise of a refund. Defendant now refuses to refund plaintiff's money for lack of consideration. Did mutual consideration exist between the parties? Explain.

18. Ben Collins was a full professor with tenure at Wisconsin State University in 2009. In March 2009 Parsons College, in an attempt to lure Dr. Collins from Wisconsin State, offered him a written contract promising him the rank of full professor with tenure and a salary of $55,000 for the 2009–10 academic year. The contract further provided that the College would increase his salary by $2,000 each year for the next five years. In return, Collins

was to teach two trimesters of the academic year beginning in October 2009. In addition, the contract stipulated, by reference to the College's faculty bylaws, that tenured professors could be dismissed only for just cause and after written charges were filed with the Professional Problems Committee. The two parties signed the contract, and Collins resigned his position at Wisconsin State.

In February 2011, the College tendered a different contract to Collins to cover the following year. This contract reduced his salary to $45,000 with no provision for annual increments, but left his rank of full professor intact. It also required that Collins waive any and all rights or claims existing under any previous employment contracts with the College. Collins refused to sign this new contract, and Parsons College soon notified him that he would not be employed the following year. The College did not give any grounds for his dismissal; nor did it file charges with the Professional Problems Committee. As a result, Collins was forced to take a teaching position at the University of North Dakota at a substantially reduced salary. He sued to recover the difference between the salary Parsons College promised him until 2014 and the amount he earned. Decision? Will Collins prevail? Explain.

19. Rodney and Donna Mathis (Mathis) filed a wrongful death action against St. Alexis Hospital and several physicians, arising out of the death of their mother, Mary Mathis. Several weeks before trial, an expert consulted by Mathis notified the trial court and Mathis's counsel that, in his opinion, Mary Mathis's death was not proximately caused by the negligence of the physicians. Shortly thereafter, Mathis voluntarily dismissed the wrongful death action. Mathis and St. Alexis entered into a covenant-not-to-sue in which Mathis agreed not to pursue any claims against St. Alexis or its employees in terms of the medical care of Mary Mathis. St. Alexis, in return, agreed not to seek sanctions, including attorneys' fees and costs incurred in defense of the previously dismissed wrongful death action. Subsequently, Mathis filed a second wrongful death action against St. Alexis Hospital, among others. Mathis asked the court to rescind the covenant-not-to-sue, arguing that because St. Alexis was not entitled to sanctions in connection with the first wrongful death action, there was no consideration for the covenant-not-to-sue. Are they correct in this contention? Explain.

20. Harold Pearsall and Joe Alexander were friends for more than twenty-five years. About twice a week they would get together after work and proceed to a liquor store, where they would purchase what the two liked to

refer as a "package"—a half-pint of vodka, orange juice, two cups, and two lottery tickets. Occasionally these lottery tickets would yield modest rewards of two or three dollars, which the pair would then "plow back" into the purchase of additional tickets. On December 16, Pearsall and Alexander visited the liquor store twice, buying their normal "package" on both occasions. For the first package, Pearsall went into the store alone, and when he returned to the car, he said to Alexander, in reference to the tickets, "Are you in on it?" Alexander said, "Yes." When Pearsall asked him for his half of the purchase price, though, Alexander replied that he had no money. When they went to Alexander's home, Alexander snatched the tickets from Pearsall's hand and "scratched" them, only to find that they were both worthless. Later that same evening Alexander returned to the liquor store and bought a second "package." This time, Pearsall snatched the tickets from Alexander and said that he would "scratch" them. Instead, he gave one to Alexander, and each man scratched one of the tickets. Alexander's was a $20,000 winner. Alexander cashed the ticket and refused to give Pearsall anything. Can Pearsall recover half of the proceeds from Alexander? Explain.

TAKING SIDES

Anna Feinberg began working for the Pfeiffer Company in 1966 at age seventeen. By 2004, she had attained the position of bookkeeper, office manager, and assistant treasurer. In appreciation for her skill, dedication, and long years of service, the Pfeiffer board of directors resolved to increase Feinberg's monthly salary to $4,000 and to create for her a retirement plan. The plan allowed that Feinberg would be given the privilege of retiring from active duty at any time she chose and that she would receive retirement pay of $2,000 per month for life, although the Board expressed the hope that Feinberg would continue to serve the company for many years. Feinberg, however, chose to retire two years later. The Pfeiffer Company paid Feinberg her retirement pay until 2013. The company thereafter discontinued payments.

a. What are the arguments that the company's promise to pay Feinberg $2,000 per month for life is enforceable?

b. What are the arguments that the company's promise is not enforceable?

c. What is the proper outcome? Explain.

CHAPTER 11

ILLEGAL BARGAINS

CHAPTER OUTCOMES

After reading and studying this chapter, you should be able to:

- Identify and explain the types of contracts that may violate a statute and distinguish between the two types of licensing statutes.

- Describe when a covenant not to compete will be enforced and identify the two situations in which these types of covenants most frequently arise.

- Explain when exculpatory agreements, agreements involving the commitment of a tort, and

- agreements involving public officials will be held to be illegal.

- Distinguish between procedural and substantive unconscionability.

- Explain the usual effects of illegality and the major exceptions to this rule.

An essential requirement of a binding promise or agreement is legality of objective. When the formation or performance of an agreement is criminal, tortious, or otherwise contrary to public policy, the agreement is illegal and unenforceable (as opposed to being void). The law does not provide a remedy for the breach of an unenforceable agreement and thus "leaves the parties where it finds them." It is preferable to use the term *illegal bargain* or *illegal agreement* rather than *illegal contract*, because the word *contract*, by definition, denotes a legal and enforceable agreement. The illegal bargain is made unenforceable (1) to discourage such undesirable conduct and (2) to preclude the inappropriate use of the judicial process in carrying out such socially undesirable bargains.

The Restatement avoids defining the term *illegal bargain*, instead focusing upon whether public policy should bar enforcement of the agreement. By relying upon the concept of public policy, the Restatement provides the courts with greater flexibility in determining the enforceability of questioned agreements by weighing the strength of legally recognized policies against the effect that declaring a particular bargain to be against public policy would have on the contracting parties and on the public.

This chapter will discuss (1) agreements in violation of a statute, (2) agreements contrary to public policy, and (3) the effect of illegality upon agreements.

VIOLATIONS OF STATUTES

The courts will not enforce an agreement declared illegal by statute. For example, wagering or gambling contracts are specifically declared unenforceable in most States. In addition, an agreement to violate a statute prohibiting crimes, such as murder, robbery, embezzlement, forgery, and price fixing, is unenforceable. Likewise, an agreement that is induced by criminal conduct will not be enforced. For example, if Alice enters into an agreement with Brent Co. through the bribing of Brent Co.'s purchasing agent, the agreement would be unenforceable.

LICENSING STATUTES

Every jurisdiction has laws requiring a license for those who engage in certain trades, professions, or businesses. Common examples are licensing statutes that apply to lawyers, doctors, dentists, accountants, brokers, plumbers, and contractors. Some licensing statutes mandate schooling and/or examination, while others require only financial responsibility and/or good moral character. Whether or not a person may recover for services rendered if he has failed to comply with a licensing requirement depends upon the terms or type of licensing statute. This rule pertains only to the rights of the unlicensed party to enforce the obligations of the other party.

The statute itself may expressly provide that an unlicensed person engaged in a business or profession for which a license is required shall not recover for services rendered. Absent such statutory provision, the courts commonly distinguish between those statutes or ordinances that are regulatory in character and those that are enacted merely to raise revenue through the issuance of licenses. If the statute is regulatory, a person cannot recover for professional services unless he has the required license, as long as the public policy behind the regulatory purpose clearly outweighs the person's interest in being paid for his services. Restatement, Section 181. Some courts have gone further by balancing the penalty the unlicensed party suffers against the benefit the other party receives. In contrast, if the law is for revenue purposes only, agreements for such services are enforceable.

A **regulatory** license, including those issued under statutes prescribing standards for those wishing to practice law or medicine, is a measure designed to protect the public against unqualified persons. A **revenue** license, on the other hand, does not seek to protect against incompetent or unqualified practitioners but simply to furnish revenue. An example is a statute requiring a license of plumbers but not establishing standards of competence for those who seek to follow the trade. The courts regard such legislation as a taxing measure lacking any expression of legislative intent to preclude unlicensed plumbers from enforcing their business contracts.

PRACTICAL ADVICE

Obtain all necessary licenses before beginning to operate your business.

◆ SEE CASE 13-1

GAMBLING STATUTES

In a wager the parties stipulate that one shall win and the other lose depending upon the outcome of an event in which their sole "interest" arises from the possibility of such gain or loss. All States have legislation pertaining to gambling or wagering, and U.S. courts generally refuse to recognize the enforceability of a gambling agreement. Thus, if Arnold makes a bet with Bernice on the outcome of a ball game, the agreement is unenforceable by either party. Some States, however, now permit certain kinds of regulated gambling. Wagering conducted by government agencies, principally State-operated lotteries, has come to constitute an increasingly important source of public revenues.

To be distinguished from wagers are ordinary insurance contracts in which the insured, having an "insurable interest" (discussed in *Chapter 47*), pays a certain sum of money or premium in exchange for an insurance company's promise to pay a larger amount upon the occurrence of some event, such as a fire, which causes loss to the insured. Here, the agreement compensates for loss under an existing risk; it does not create an entirely new risk. In a wager, the parties contemplate gain through mere chance, whereas in an insurance contract they seek to distribute possible loss. Furthermore, most games at fast-food restaurants and grocery store drawings have been upheld because the participants need not make a purchase to be eligible for the prize.

PRACTICAL ADVICE

Make sure that your promotions that offer prizes do not fall under State gambling statutes.

USURY STATUTES

A **usury statute** is a law establishing a maximum rate of permissible interest for which a lender and borrower of money may contract. Though, historically, every State had a usury law, a recent trend has been to limit or relax usury statutes. The maximum rates permitted vary greatly from State to State and among types of transactions. These statutes typically are general in their application, although certain specified types of transactions are exempted. For example, numerous States impose no limit on the rate of interest that may be charged on loans to corporations. Furthermore, some States permit the parties to contract for any rate of interest on loans made to individual proprietorships or partnerships for the purpose of carrying on a business. Moreover, there are not many protections remaining for typical consumer transactions, including those involving credit cards. (More than half of the States have no interest rate limits on credit card transactions. Furthermore, under Federal law, a national bank may charge the interest rate allowed in the State in which the bank is located to customers living anywhere in the United States, including States with more restrictive interest caps.)

In addition to the exceptions accorded certain designated types of borrowers, a number of States have exempted specific lenders. For example, the majority of the States have enacted installment loan laws, which permit eligible lenders a return on installment loans that is higher than the applicable general interest statute would permit. These specific lender usury statutes, which have all but eliminated general usury statutes, vary greatly but generally have included small consumer loans, corporate loans, loans by small lenders, real estate mortgages, and numerous other transactions.

For a transaction to be usurious, courts usually require evidence of the following factors: (1) a loan or forbearance (2) of money (3) which is repayable absolutely and in all events (4) for which an interest charge is exacted in excess of the interest rate allowed by law. Transactions that are really loans may not be clothed with the trappings of a sale for the purpose of avoiding the usury laws.

PRACTICAL ADVICE

When calculating interest, consider all charges, including service fees, that exceed the actual reasonable expense of making the loan.

The legal effect to be given a usurious loan varies from State to State. In a few States, the lender forfeits both principal and interest. In some jurisdictions, the lender can recover the principal but forfeits all interest. In other States, only that portion of interest exceeding the permitted maximum is forfeited. In several States, the amount forfeited is a multiple (double or treble) of the interest charged. Disposition of usurious interest already paid also varies. Some States do not allow any recovery of usurious interest paid; others allow recovery of such interest or a multiple of it.

SUNDAY STATUTES

In the absence of a statutory prohibition, the common law does not prohibit entering into contracts on Sunday. Some States, however, have legislation, referred to as **Blue Laws**, modifying this common law rule and prohibiting certain types of commercial activity on Sunday. Even in a State that prohibits contracts on Sunday, a court nonetheless will enforce a subsequent weekday ratification of a loan made on Sunday or a promise to pay for goods sold and delivered on Sunday. In addition, Blue Laws usually do not apply to activities of "necessity" and "charity."

VIOLATIONS OF PUBLIC POLICY

The reach of a statute may extend beyond its language. Sometimes, the courts, by analogy, use the statute and the policy it seeks to serve as a guide in determining the private contract rights of one harmed by a violation of the statute. In addition, the courts must frequently articulate the "public policy" of the State without significant help from statutory sources. This judicially declared public policy is very broad in scope, it often being said that agreements having "a tendency to be injurious to the public or the public good" are contrary to public policy. Thus, the term *public policy* eludes precise definition. Contracts raising questions of public policy include agreements that (1) restrain trade, (2) exempt or exculpate a party from liability for his own tortious conduct, (3) are unconscionable, (4) involve tortious conduct, (5) tend to corrupt public officials or impair the legislative process, (6) tend to obstruct the administration of justice, or (7) impair family relationships. This section will focus on the first five of these types of agreements.

COMMON LAW RESTRAINT OF TRADE

A **restraint of trade** is any contract or agreement that eliminates or tends to eliminate competition or otherwise obstructs trade or commerce. One type of restraint is a **covenant not to compete,** which is an agreement to refrain from entering into a competing trade, profession, or business.

An agreement to refrain from a particular trade, profession, or business is enforceable if (1) the purpose of the restraint is to protect a property interest of the promisee and (2) the restraint is no more extensive than is reasonably necessary to protect that interest. Restraints typically arise in two situations: the sale of a business and employment contracts.

SALE OF A BUSINESS As part of an agreement to sell a business, the seller frequently promises not to compete in that particular type of business in a *defined area* for a stated *time*. To protect the business's goodwill (an asset that the buyer has purchased), the buyer must be allowed to enforce such a covenant (promise) by the seller not to compete with the purchaser within reasonable limitations. Most litigation on this subject has involved the requirement that the restraint be no greater than is reasonably necessary. Whether the restraint is reasonable or not depends on the geographic area it covers, the time period for which it is to be effective, and the hardship it imposes on the promisor and the public.

For example, the promise of a person selling a service station business in Detroit not to enter the service station business in Michigan for the next twenty-five years is unreasonable, both as to area and time. The business interest to be protected would not include the entire State, so it is not necessary to the protection of the purchaser that the seller be prevented from engaging in the service station business in the entire State or perhaps, for that matter, in the entire city of Detroit. Limiting the area to the neighborhood in which the station is located or to a radius of a few miles probably would be adequate.

The same type of inquiry must be made about time limitations. In the sale of a service station, a twenty-five-year ban on competition from the seller would be unreasonable; a one-year ban probably would not. The court, in determining what is reasonable under particular circumstances, must consider each case on its own facts.

EMPLOYMENT CONTRACTS Salespeople, management personnel, and other employees frequently are required to sign employment contracts prohibiting them from competing with their employers during their time of employment and for some additional stated period after termination. The same is also frequently true among corporations or partnerships involving professionals, such as accountants, lawyers, investment brokers, stockbrokers, or doctors. Although the courts readily enforce a covenant not to compete during the period of employment, the promise not to compete after termination is subjected to an even stricter test of reasonableness than *[handwritten margin note: Courts enforce pending on if tort was committed intentionally (unenforceable), negligent conducted (P2 ↓)]*

that applied to noncompetition promises included in a contract for the sale of a business. One reason for this is that the employer is in a stronger bargaining position than the employee.

A court order enjoining a former employee from competing in a described territory for a stated time is the usual method by which an employer seeks to enforce the employee's promise not to compete. Before granting such injunctions, the courts insist that the employer demonstrate that the restriction is *necessary* to protect his legitimate interests, such as trade secrets or customer lists. Because issuing the injunction may place the employee out of work, the courts must carefully balance the public policy favoring the employer's right to protect his business interests against the public policy favoring full opportunity for individuals to gain employment.

Thus, one court has held unreasonable a covenant in a contract requiring a travel agency employee, after termination of her employment, to refrain from engaging in a like business in any capacity in either of two named towns or within a sixty-mile radius of those towns for two years. There was no indication that the employee had enough influence over customers to cause them to move their business to her new agency, nor was it shown that any trade secrets were involved. *United Travel Service, Inc. v. Weber*, 108 Ill. App.2d 353, 247 N.E.2d 801 (1969). Instead of refusing to enforce an unreasonable covenant, some courts, considering the action justifiable under the circumstances of the case, will reform the agreement to make it reasonable and enforceable.

Due to the rapid evolution of business practices in the Internet industry, it has been argued that noncompete agreements for Internet company employees need their own rules. *National Business Services, Inc. v. Wright* addressed the geographic scope of an Internet noncompete agreement, upholding a one-year time restriction and a territorial clause that prevented the employee from taking another Internet-related job anywhere in the United States. The court stated, "Transactions involving the Internet, unlike traditional 'sales territory' cases, are not limited by state boundaries."

PRACTICAL ADVICE

If you include a covenant not to compete to protect your property interests, be careful to select a reasonable duration and geographic scope.

◆ SEE CASE 13-2

EXCULPATORY CLAUSES

Some contracts contain an exculpatory clause that excuses one party from liability for her own tortious conduct. The courts generally agree that exculpatory clauses relieving a person from tort liability for harm caused intentionally or recklessly are unenforceable as violating public policy. On the other hand, exculpatory clauses that excuse a party from liability for harm caused by negligent conduct are scrutinized carefully by the courts, which often require that the clause be conspicuously placed in the contract and clearly written. Accordingly, an exculpatory clause on the reverse side of a parking lot claim check, which attempts to relieve the parking lot operator of liability for negligently damaging the customer's automobile, generally will be held unenforceable as against public policy.

The Restatement provides that exculpatory clauses excusing negligent conduct are unenforceable on grounds of public policy if they exempt (1) an employer from liability to an employee, (2) a public service business (such as a common carrier) from liability to a customer, or (3) a person from liability to a party who is a member of a protected class. Restatement, Section 195. For example, a railroad company will not be permitted to avoid liability for the negligent operation or maintenance of its trains.

A similar rule applies to a contractual provision unreasonably exempting a party from the legal consequences of a misrepresentation. Restatement, Section 196. Such a term is unenforceable on the grounds of public policy with respect to both fraudulent and nonfraudulent misrepresentations.

Further, where the superior bargaining position of one party has enabled him to impose upon the other party such a provision, the courts are inclined to nullify the provision. Such a situation may arise in residential leases exempting a landlord from liability for his negligence. Moreover, an exculpatory clause may be unenforceable for unconscionability.

PRACTICAL ADVICE

Because many courts do not favor exculpatory clauses, carefully limit its applicability, make sure that it is clear and understandable, put it in writing, and have it signed.

◆ SEE CASE 13-3

UNCONSCIONABLE CONTRACTS

The court may scrutinize every contract of sale to determine whether it is, in its commercial setting, purpose, and effect, **unconscionable**. The court may refuse to enforce an unconscionable contract in its entirety or any part it finds to be unconscionable. Section 2–302 of the UCC provides:

> If the court as a matter of law finds the contract or any clause of the contract to have been unconscionable at the time it was made the court may refuse to enforce the contract, or it may enforce the remainder of the

contract without the unconscionable clause, or it may so limit the application of any unconscionable clause as to avoid any unconscionable result.

Similarly, Section 208 of the Restatement parallels this provision and provides:

If a contract or term thereof is unconscionable at the time the contract is made a court may refuse to enforce the contract, or may enforce the remainder of the contract without the unconscionable term, or may so limit the application of any unconscionable term as to avoid any unconscionable result.

Neither the Code nor the Restatement defines the word *unconscionable*; however, the *New Webster's Dictionary* (Deluxe Encyclopedic Edition) defines the term as "contrary to the dictates of conscience; unscrupulous or unprincipled; exceeding that which is reasonable or customary; inordinate, unjustifiable."

The doctrine of unconscionability has been justified on the basis that it permits the courts to resolve issues of unfairness explicitly as regards that unfairness without recourse to formalistic rules or legal fictions. In policing contracts for fairness, the courts have again demonstrated their willingness to limit freedom of contract to protect the less advantaged from overreaching by dominant contracting parties. The doctrine of unconscionability has evolved through its application by the courts to include both procedural and substantive unconscionability.

Procedural unconscionability involves scrutiny for the presence of "bargaining naughtiness." In other words, was the negotiation process fair, or were there procedural irregularities, such as burying important terms of the agreement in fine print or obscuring the true meaning of the contract with impenetrable legal jargon?

Substantive unconscionability, which involves the actual terms of the contract, consists of oppressive or grossly unfair provisions, such as an exorbitant price or an unfair exclusion or limitation of contractual remedies. An all-too-common example is that involving a necessitous buyer in an unequal bargaining position with a seller, who consequently obtains an exorbitant price for his product or service. In one case, a court held unconscionable a price of $749 ($920 on time) for a vacuum cleaner that cost the seller $140. In another case the buyers, welfare recipients, purchased by time payment contract a home freezer unit for $900 that, when added to time credit charges, credit life insurance, credit property insurance, and sales tax, amounted to $1,235. The purchase resulted from a visit to the buyer's home by a salesman representing Your Shop At Home Service, Inc.; the maximum retail value of the freezer unit at time of purchase was $300. The court held the contract unconscionable and reformed it

by reducing the price to the total payment ($620) the buyers had managed to make.

Some courts hold that for a contract to be unenforceable both substantive and procedural unconscionability must be present. Nevertheless, they need not exist to the same degree; the more oppressive one is, the less evidence of the other is required.

PRACTICAL ADVICE
When negotiating a contract, keep in mind that if your bargaining techniques or the contract terms are oppressive, a court may refuse to enforce the contract in part or in full.

Closely akin to the concept of unconscionability is the doctrine of contracts of adhesion. A standard-form contract prepared by one party, an **adhesion contract** generally involves the preparer's offering the other party the contract on a "take-it-or-leave-it" basis. Such contracts are not automatically unenforceable but are subject to greater scrutiny for procedural or substantive unconscionability.

◆ SEE CASE 13-4

TORTIOUS CONDUCT

"A promise to commit a tort or to induce the commission of a tort is unenforceable on grounds of public policy." Restatement, Section 192. The courts will not permit contract law to violate the law of torts. Any agreement attempting to do so is considered contrary to public policy. For example, Andrew and Barlow Co. enter into an agreement under which Andrew promises Barlow that in return for $5,000 he will disparage the product of Barlow Co.'s competitor Cosmo, Inc., in order to provide Barlow Co. with a competitive advantage. Andrew's promise is to commit the tort of disparagement and is unenforceable as contrary to public policy.

CORRUPTING PUBLIC OFFICIALS

Agreements that may adversely affect the public interest through the corruption of public officials or the impairment of the legislative process are unenforceable. Examples include using improper means to influence legislation, to secure some official action, or to procure a government contract. Contracts to pay lobbyists for services to obtain or defeat official action by means of persuasive argument are to be distinguished from illegal influence-peddling agreements. (*Chapters 43* and *46* cover the Foreign Corrupt Practices Act, which prohibits any U.S. person—and certain foreign issuers of securities—from bribing foreign government or political officials to assist in obtaining or retaining business.)

For example, a bargain by a candidate for public office to make a certain appointment following his election is illegal.

In addition, an agreement to pay a public officer something extra for performing his official duty, such as promising a bonus to a police officer for strictly enforcing the traffic laws on her beat, is illegal. The same is true of an agreement in which a citizen promises to perform, or to refrain from performing, duties imposed on her by citizenship. Thus, a promise by Carl to pay $50 to Rachel if she will register and vote is opposed to public policy and illegal.

EFFECT OF ILLEGALITY

As a general rule, illegal contracts are unenforceable. In a few instances, however, one of the parties may be permitted to enforce all or part of the contract; whereas, under other circumstances, the courts will allow one party to recover in restitution for his performance of the illegal contract.

GENERAL RULE: UNENFORCEABILITY

In most cases when an agreement is illegal, neither party can successfully sue the other for breach or recover for any performance rendered. Whichever party is plaintiff is immaterial to the courts. As is frequently said in these cases, the court will leave the parties where it finds them.

EXCEPTIONS

The courts recognize several exceptions to the general rule regarding the effect of illegality on a contract and may, after considering the circumstances surrounding a particular contract, grant relief to one of the parties, though not to the other. The following sections will consider these exceptions.

PARTY WITHDRAWING BEFORE PERFORMANCE A party to an illegal agreement may withdraw, prior to performance, from the transaction and recover whatever she has contributed, if the party has not engaged in serious misconduct. Restatement, Section 199. A common example is recovery of money left with a stakeholder pursuant to a wager before it is paid over to the winner.

PARTY PROTECTED BY STATUTE Sometimes an agreement is illegal because it violates a statute designed to protect persons in the position of one of the parties. For example, State "Blue Sky Laws" prohibiting the sale of unregistered securities are designed primarily for the protection of investors. In such cases, even though there is an unlawful agreement, the statute usually expressly gives the purchaser the right to rescind the sale and recover the money paid.

PARTY NOT EQUALLY AT FAULT Where one of the parties is less at fault than the other, he will be allowed to recover payments made or property transferred. Restatement, Section 198. For example, this exception would apply where one party induces the other to enter into an illegal bargain through fraud, duress, or undue influence.

EXCUSABLE IGNORANCE An agreement that appears on its face to be entirely permissible, nevertheless, may be illegal by reason of facts and circumstances of which one of the parties is completely unaware. For example, a man and woman make mutual promises to marry, but unknown to the woman, the man is already married. This is an agreement to commit the crime of bigamy, and the marriage, if entered into, is void. In such case the courts permit the party who is ignorant of the illegality to maintain a lawsuit against the other party for damages.

A party also may be excused for ignorance of relatively minor legislation. Restatement, Section 180. For instance, Jones and Old South Building Co. enter into a contract to build a factory that contains specifications in violation of the town's building ordinance. Jones did not know of the violation and had no reason to know. Old South's promise to build would not be rendered unenforceable on grounds of public policy, and Jones would have a claim against Old South for damages for breach of contract.

PARTIAL ILLEGALITY A contract may be partly unlawful and partly lawful. The courts view such a contract in one of two ways. First, the partial illegality may be held to taint the entire contract with illegality, so that it is wholly unenforceable. Second, it may be possible to separate the illegal from the legal part, in which case the court will hold the illegal part unenforceable but will enforce the legal part. For example, if a contract contains an illegal covenant not to compete, the covenant will not be enforced, though the rest of the contract may be.

CHAPTER SUMMARY

VIOLATIONS OF STATUTES   **General Rule** the courts will not enforce agreements declared illegal by statute
Licensing Statutes require formal authorization to engage in certain trades, professions, or businesses
- *Regulatory License* licensing statute that is intended to protect the public against unqualified persons; an unlicensed person may not recover for services she has performed

- *Revenue License* licensing statute that seeks to raise money; an unlicensed person may recover for services he has performed

Gambling Statutes prohibit wagers, which are agreements that one party will win and the other lose depending upon the outcome of an event in which their only interest is the gain or loss

Usury Statutes establish a maximum rate of interest

Sunday Statutes prohibition of certain types of commercial activity on Sunday (also called Blue Laws)

VIOLATIONS OF PUBLIC POLICY

Common Law Restraint of Trade unreasonable restraints of trade are not enforceable
- *Sale of a Business* the promise by the seller of a business not to compete in that particular business in a reasonable geographic area for a reasonable period of time is enforceable
- *Employment Contracts* an employment contract prohibiting an employee from competing with his employer for a reasonable period following termination is enforceable provided the restriction is necessary to protect legitimate interests of the employer

Exculpatory Clauses the courts generally disapprove of contractual provisions excusing a party from liability for her own tortious conduct

Unconscionable Contracts unfair or unduly harsh agreements are not enforceable
- *Procedural Unconscionability* unfair or irregular bargaining
- *Substantive Unconscionability* oppressive or grossly unfair contractual terms

Tortious Conduct an agreement that requires a person to commit a tort is unenforceable

Corrupting Public Officials agreements that corrupt public officials are not enforceable

---

EFFECT OF ILLEGALITY

Unenforceability neither party may recover under an illegal agreement where both parties are *in pari delicto* (in equal fault)

Exceptions permit one party to recover payments
- *Party Withdrawing Before Performance*
- *Party Protected by Statute*
- *Party Not Equally at Fault*
- *Excusable Ignorance*
- *Partial Illegality*

CASES

CASE 13-1

Licensing Statutes
ALCOA CONCRETE & MASONRY v. STALKER BROS.
Court of Special Appeals of Maryland, 2010
993 A.2d 136, 191 MD. APP. 596
http://scholar.google.com/scholar_case?case=16829939965873776087&q=993+A.2d+136&hl=en&as_sdt=2,34

Rodowsky, J.

* * * At issue is whether a home improvement general contractor is contractually obligated to pay a subcontractor who was not licensed under * * * , either at the time of entering into the subcontract or when the subcontract was properly performed, but who was licensed when this suit was brought.

The subcontractor is the appellant, Alcoa Concrete and Masonry, Inc. (Alcoa or the Subcontractor). The general contractor is Stalker Brothers, Inc. (Stalker or the General Contractor), * * * . Alcoa initiated this action on September 30, 2008, in the Circuit Court for Montgomery County. Summary judgment was granted to the appellees [Stalker] * * *

The president of Alcoa affirmed that Alcoa and Stalker had done business from 2004 through 2007. In 2004, all of Alcoa's invoices were fully and timely paid. When payments in 2005 became less regular, Stalker promised to pay Alcoa when a building owned by the Brothers was sold, but full payment was not made. Alcoa continued to perform subcontract work for Stalker based on an agreement that the General Contractor would pay Alcoa $1,500 per week against invoices for past work and new work. In November 2006, Alcoa performed the cement and masonry work for Stalker on the "Cahill" job, in which Stalker represented there was sufficient profit to pay Alcoa for that subcontract and for the entire past due balance, but an indebtedness remained. In the summer of 2007, Stalker ceased paying Alcoa entirely. Alcoa claims $53,000 plus interest and attorney's fees. Appellees, through Donald Stalker's affidavit, assert that every subcontract performed by Alcoa for Stalker was "residential home improvement work" in Maryland, *i.e.*, done pursuant to a home improvement contract between the owner(s) of a residence and Stalker. Alcoa does not dispute that statement of fact.

Appellees moved for summary judgment on a number of grounds, but the circuit court granted the motion solely on the ground that the series of subcontracts were illegal and could not be enforced. The circuit court accepted appellees' argument that was based upon a venerable line of Maryland cases dealing with licensing and that is illustrated in the home improvement field principally by *Harry Berenter, Inc. v. Berman*, [citation]. In essence, these cases initially inquire whether the purpose of a business licensing statute is to raise revenue or to protect the public. If the purpose is the former, courts will enforce a contract for compensation for business activity that requires a license, even if made by an unlicensed person. But, if the purpose of the licensing requirement is to protect the public, then the Maryland cases relied upon by the appellees do not enforce contracts made by unlicensed persons who seek compensation for business activity for which a license is required.

* * *

Maryland appellate decisions have applied the revenue/regulation rule in a number of contexts. All of the cases under the Act have dealt with the contractor-owner relationship. The members of the public who were protected by the regulatory licensing requirement were the owners of the home. This Court recently again has held, applying *Harry Berenter*, that a contract between the owner of the improved premises and an unlicensed contractor would not be enforced. [Citation.] * * *

* * *

Our review fails to disclose any Maryland appellate decision directly answering whether the regulatory license rule applied in *Harry Berenter*, declaring unenforceable a home improvement contract between an owner and an unlicensed contractor, applies to a subcontract between a licensed contractor and an unlicensed subcontractor. *Harry Berenter* does recognize that, pursuant to provisions of the Act * * * , the failure to comply with certain formal contractual requirements in a home improvement contract does not invalidate the contract. [Citation.]

* * *

The authors of *Corbin on Contracts*, after reviewing the revenue/regulatory rule, state:

Even when the purpose of a licensing statute is regulatory, courts do not always deny enforcement to the unlicensed party. The statute clearly may protect against fraud and incompetence. Yet, in very many cases the situation involves neither fraud nor incompetence. The unlicensed party may have rendered excellent service or delivered goods of the highest quality. The noncompliance with the statute may be nearly harmless. The real defrauder may be the defendant who will be enriched at the unlicensed party's expense by a court's refusal to enforce the contract. Although courts have yearned for a mechanically applicable rule, most have not made one in the present instance. Justice requires that the penalty should fit the crime. Justice and sound policy do not always require the enforcement of licensing statutes by large forfeitures going not to the state but to repudiating defendants.

In most cases, the statute itself does not require such forfeitures. The statute fixes its own penalties, usually a fine or imprisonment of a minor character with a degree of discretion in the court. The added penalty of unenforceability of bargains is a judicial creation. In many cases, the court may be wise to apply this additional penalty. When nonenforcement causes great and disproportionate hardship, a court must avoid nonenforcement.

* * *

After the decision in *Harry Berenter*, in which the Court relied in part on the Restatement of Contracts, the American Law Institute adopted Restatement (Second) of Contracts (1981). Section 178 states a more flexible approach to enforceability than the rigid revenue/regulatory dichotomy. Section 178 reads:

When a Term Is Unenforceable on Grounds of Public Policy

(1) A promise or other term of an agreement is unenforceable on grounds of public policy if legislation

provides that it is unenforceable or the interest in its enforcement is clearly outweighed in the circumstances by a public policy against the enforcement of such terms.

(2) In weighing the interest in the enforcement of a term, account is taken of

    (a) the parties' justified expectations,

    (b) any forfeiture that would result if enforcement were denied, and

    (c) any special public interest in the enforcement of the particular term.

(3) In weighing a public policy against enforcement of a term, account is taken of

    (a) the strength of that policy as manifested by legislation or judicial decisions,

    (b) the likelihood that a refusal to enforce the term will further that policy.

    (c) the seriousness of any misconduct involved and the extent to which it was deliberate, and

    (d) the directness of the connection between that misconduct and the term.

We find no indication in the Act or in the Maryland cases that a policy of the Act is to protect general contractors from unlicensed subcontractors. Consequently, the fact that the Act is a regulatory measure does not bar Alcoa from recovering on its subcontracts.

* * *

Accordingly, we shall reverse the judgment of the Circuit Court for Montgomery County and remand this action for further proceedings, not inconsistent with this opinion.

CASE 13-2

Restraint of Trade
PAYROLL ADVANCE, INC. v. YATES
Missouri Court of Appeals, 2008
270 S.W.3d 428
http://scholar.google.com/scholar_case?case=12029870438647495616&q=270+S.W.3d+428&hl=en&as_sclt=2,22

Barney, J.

Payroll Advance, Inc. ("Appellant") appeals from the judgment of the trial court entered in favor of Barbara Yates ("Respondent") on Appellant's petition for injunctive relief and breach of contract of an "Employment Agreement" ("the Employment Agreement") which contains a covenant not to compete. * * *

* * *

[T]he record reveals that Appellant, a foreign corporation, is licensed to transact business in the State of Missouri and has numerous locations throughout the state, including a branch located in Kennett, Missouri. [Footnote: Appellant is "a payday loan company. [It] gives loans to clients out in the community." As best we discern the record, loans are made for short periods of time at high rates of interest. Appellant's manager testified that a payday loan company such as Appellant's is not like a bank because banks "normally [do not do] short-term loans." She also distinguished Appellant's entity from a title loan company or a debt consolidation concern.] It is customary for each of Appellant's branch offices to employ a sole employee at each branch and that sole employee is typically referred to as the manager of that particular branch. In June of 1998, Respondent was hired as the manager of the branch office in Kennett. On November 19, 1999, as a condition of her continued employment, Appellant presented Respondent with the Employment Agreement which included * * *, a provision entitled "NON-COMPETE" ("the covenant not to compete"). This provision set out:

[Respondent] agrees not to compete with [Appellant] as owner, manager, partner, stockholder, or employee in any business that is in competition with [Appellant] and within a 50 mile radius of [Appellant's] business for a period of two (2) years after termination of employment or [Respondent] quits or [Respondent] leaves employment of [Appellant].

Respondent was employed with Appellant from June of 1998 through November 8, 2007, when Respondent was apparently fired for cause.

Approximately thirty-two days after being terminated by Appellant, Respondent became employed with Check Please, one of the approximately fourteen other payday loan establishments in the area. At Check Please, Respondent performed basically the same duties such as office management and customer care as she had when employed with Appellant.

On February 7, 2008, Appellant filed its "First Amended Petition for Injunctive Relief and Breach of Contract." In this petition, Appellant brought Count I for injunctive relief to prevent Respondent from soliciting its clients for her new employer, and to stop her from using client information she purportedly obtained from her time with Appellant. Count II of the petition was for damages for breach of contract for violation of the covenant not to compete together with attorney fees and costs.

* * *

On February 14, 2008, the trial court entered its judgment which found "[n]o evidence exists that, following [Appellant's] termination of [Respondent's] ten year period of employment, [Respondent] removed any customer list or other documents from [Appellant's] place of business [or]... made any personal or other contact with any previous or present customer of [Appellant's] business or intends to do so." The trial court further determined that that if the covenant not to compete was enforced as requested, Respondent will be prohibited from engaging in employment with any payday loan business in at least 126 cities situated in Missouri, Arkansas and Tennessee ([p]resumably [Respondent] also would be prohibited from such employment within a 50-mile radius of [Appellant's] 17 other locations scattered throughout the State of Missouri. Further, [Respondent] arguably also would be prohibited from employment at a bank, savings and loan company, credit union, pawn shop or title-loan company within such geographical areas....)

Accordingly, in its discretion, the trial court found "the above result would be unreasonable under the facts and circumstances of the particular industry, agreement, and geographic location here involved." The trial court then ruled in favor of Respondent and against Appellant. The trial court also denied Respondent's request for attorney's fees and costs. This appeal followed.

* * *

"Generally, because covenants not to compete are considered to be restraints on trade, they are presumptively void and are enforceable only to the extent that they are demonstratively reasonable." [Citations.] "Noncompetition agreements are not favored in the law, and the party attempting to enforce a noncompetition agreement has the burden of demonstrating both the necessity to protect the claimant's legitimate interests and that the agreement is reasonable as to time and space." [Citation.]

There are at least four valid and conflicting concerns at issue in the law of non-compete agreements. First, the employer needs to be able to engage a highly trained workforce to be competitive and profitable, without fear that the employee will use the employer's business secrets against it or steal the employer's customers after leaving employment. Second, the employee must be mobile in order to provide for his or her family and to advance his or her career in an ever-changing marketplace. This mobility is dependent upon the ability of the employee to take his or her increasing skills and put them to work from one employer to the next. Third, the law favors the freedom of parties to value their respective interests in negotiated contracts. And, fourth, contracts in restraint of trade are unlawful.

[Citation.] "Missouri courts balance these concerns by enforcing non-compete agreements in certain limited circumstances." [Citation.] "Non-compete agreements are typically enforceable so long as they are reasonable. In practical terms, a non-compete agreement is reasonable if it is no more restrictive than is necessary to protect the legitimate interests of the employer." [Citation.] Furthermore, "[n]oncompete agreements are enforceable to the extent they can be narrowly tailored geographically and temporally." [Citation.] Lastly, it is not "necessary for the employer to show that actual damage has occurred, in order to obtain an injunction. The actual damage might be very hard to determine, and this is one reason for granting equitable relief." [Citation.]

Here, viewing the evidence in a light most favorable to the trial court's holding, [citation], it is clear the trial court took umbrage with the covenant's restrictive provisions and geographical limitations on Respondent's [Yates'] ability to find employment.

* * *

The question of reasonableness of a restraint is to be determined according to the facts of the particular case and hence requires a thorough consideration of all surrounding circumstances, including the subject matter of the contract, the purpose to be served, the situation of the parties, the extent of the restraint, and the specialization of the business.

* * *

Here, the covenant not to compete grandly declares that Respondent cannot "compete with Appellant [Payroll] as owner, manager, partner, stockholder, or employee *in any business* that is in competition with [Appellant] and within a 50 mile radius of [Appellant's] business...." (Emphasis added.) There was evidence from Appellant's representative at trial that Appellant has seventeen branch offices in Missouri and still other locations in Arkansas. If this Court interprets the plain meaning of the covenant not compete as written, the covenant not to compete would prevent Respondent not only from working at a competing business within 50 miles of the branch office in Kennett, Missouri, but Respondent would also be barred from working in a competing business within 50 miles of *any* of Appellant's branch offices. Under this interpretation, Respondent would be greatly limited in the geographic area she could work.

Additionally, the covenant not to compete bars Respondent from working at "any business that is in competition with [Appellant]." Yet, it fails to set out with precision what is to be considered a competing business and certainly does not specify that it only applies to other payday loan businesses. In that Appellant is in the business of making loans, it could be inferred that in addition to barring Respondent's employment at a different payday loan establishment the covenant not to compete also bars her from being employed anywhere loans are made including banks, credit unions, savings and loan organizations, title-loan companies, pawn shops, and other financial organizations. Such a restraint on the geographic scope of Respondent's employment and upon her type of employment is unduly burdensome and unreasonable. [Citation.]

* * *

Appellant's second point relied on asserts the trial court erred in denying its petition because

[t]he trial court erroneously applied the law in failing to modify the covenant not to compete to a geographic scope it found to be reasonable in that the court found the geographic scope to be unreasonable for the payday loan industry but failed to modify the covenant not to compete to reflect a geographic scope that would be reasonable and enforceable.

* * * This Court "recognize[s] that an unreasonable restriction against competition in a contract may be modified and enforced to the extent that it is reasonable, regardless of the covenant's form of wording." * * *

Having reviewed the record in this matter, it appears the record is devoid of a request by Appellant for modification of the covenant not to compete either in its pleadings, at trial, or in its motion for new trial before the trial court. It is settled law that "'appellate courts are merely courts of review for trial court errors, and there can be no review of matter which has not been presented to or expressly decided by the trial court.'" [Citation.]

* * *

The judgment of the trial court is affirmed.

CASE 13-3

Exculpatory Clauses
ANDERSON v. McOSKAR ENTERPRISES, INC.
Court of Appeals of Minnesota, 2006
712 N.W.2d 796
http://scholar.google.com/scholar_case?case=14986343261318628809&q=712+N.W.2d+796&hl=en&as_sdt=2,10

Shumaker, J.

Respondent McOskar Enterprises, Inc. owns and operates a fitness and health club in Monticello known as "Curves for Women." [Plaintiff] Appellant Tammey J. Anderson joined the club on April 2, 2003.

As part of the registration requirements, Anderson read an "AGREEMENT AND RELEASE OF LIABILITY," initialed each of the three paragraphs in the document, and dated and signed it. The first paragraph purported to release Curves from liability for injuries Anderson might sustain in participating in club activities or using club equipment:

In consideration of being allowed to participate in the activities and programs of Curves for Women® and to use its facilities, equipment and machinery in addition to the payment of any fee or charge, I do hereby waive, release and forever discharge Curves International Inc., Curves for Women®, and their officers, agents, employees, representatives, executors, and all others (Curves® representatives) from any and all responsibilities or liabilities from injuries or damages arriving [sic] out of or connected with my attendance at Curves for Women®, my participation in all activities, my use of equipment or machinery, or any act or omission, including negligence by Curves® representatives.

The second paragraph provided for Anderson's acknowledgment that fitness activities "involve a risk of injury" and her

agreement "to expressly assume and accept any and all risks of injury or death." After completing the registration, Anderson began a workout, primarily with machines, under the supervision of a trainer. About 15 or 20 minutes later, having used four or five machines, Anderson developed a headache in the back of her head. She contends that she told the trainer, who suggested that the problem was likely just a previous lack of use of certain muscles and that Anderson would be fine.

Anderson continued her workout and developed pain in her neck, shoulder, and arm. She informed the trainer but continued to exercise until she completed the program for that session.

The pain persisted when Anderson returned home. She then sought medical attention, eventually had a course of physical therapy, and, in June 2003, underwent a cervical diskectomy. She then started this lawsuit for damages, alleging that Curves had been negligent in its acts or omissions during her workout at the club.

Curves moved for summary judgment on the ground that Anderson had released the club from liability for negligence. The district court agreed and granted the motion. Anderson challenges the court's ruling on appeal.

* * *

It is settled Minnesota law that, under certain circumstances, "parties to a contract may, without violation of public policy, protect themselves against liability resulting from their own negligence." [Citation.] The "public interest in freedom of contract is preserved by recognizing [release and exculpatory] clauses as valid." [Citation.]

Releases of liability are not favored by the law and are strictly construed against the benefited party. [Citation.] "If the clause is either ambiguous in scope or purports to release the benefited party from liability for intentional, willful or wanton acts, it will not be enforced." [Citation.] Furthermore, even if a release clause is unambiguous in scope and is limited only to negligence, courts must still ascertain whether its enforcement will contravene public policy. On this issue, a two-prong test is applied:

> Before enforcing an exculpatory clause, both prongs of the test are examined, to-wit: (1) whether there was a disparity of bargaining power between the parties (in terms of a compulsion to sign a contract containing an unacceptable provision and the lack of ability to negotiate elimination of the unacceptable provision) ... and (2) the types of services being offered or provided (taking into consideration whether it is a public or essential service).

[Citation.]

The two-prong test describes what is generally known as a "contract of adhesion," more particularly explained in *Schlobohm*:

> It is a contract generally not bargained for, but which is imposed on the public for *necessary* service on a "take it or leave it" basis. Even though a contract is on a printed form and offered on a "take it or leave it" basis, those facts alone do not cause it to be an adhesion contract. There must be a showing that the parties were greatly disparate in bargaining power, that there was no opportunity for negotiation *and* that the services could not be obtained elsewhere.

[Citation.]

* * *

* * * There is nothing in the Curves release that expressly exonerates the club from liability for any intentional, willful, or wanton act. Thus, we consider whether the release is ambiguous in scope.

* * *

Anderson argues that the release is ambiguous because it broadly exonerates Curves from liability for "any act or omission, including negligence ... " * * *

* * *

The vice of ambiguous language is that it fails precisely and clearly to inform contracting parties of the meaning of their ostensible agreement. Because ambiguous language is susceptible of two or more reasonable meanings, each party might carry away from the agreement a different and perhaps contradictory understanding. In the context of a release

in connection with an athletic, health, or fitness activity, the consumer surely is entitled to know precisely what liability is being exonerated. A release that is so vague, general, or broad as to fail to specifically designate the particular nature of the liability exonerated is not enforceable. [Citation.]

* * * It is clear from this release that Anderson agreed to exonerate Curves from liability for negligence, that being part of the express agreement that Anderson accepted and it is solely negligence of which Curves is accused.

The unmistakable intent of the parties to the Curves agreement is that Curves at least would not be held liable for acts of negligence. * * *

* * *

Even if a release is unambiguously confined to liability for negligence, it still will be unenforceable if it contravenes public policy. Anderson contends that the Curves contract is one of adhesion characterized by such a disparity in bargaining power that she was compelled to sign it without any ability to negotiate.

But her argument is unpersuasive in view of the *Schlobohm* holding that "an adhesion contract is ... forced upon an unwilling and often unknowing public for services that cannot readily be obtained elsewhere." [Citation.] It is, according to *Schlobohm*, a contract "imposed on the public for *necessary* service on a 'take it or leave it' basis." *Schlobohm* involved a "gym or health spa" known as Spa Petite. Similar to Curves, it offered fitness services and required members to sign a contract that provided for a release of liability for negligence. The supreme court found no disparity in bargaining power between Spa Petite and the litigating member; found that there had been no showing that the spa's services were necessary or that they could not have been obtained elsewhere; and found that health and fitness clubs ordinarily are not within the public-service or public-necessity classification that make their services of great public importance and necessary for the public to obtain.

Even if there was a disparity of bargaining ability here—which has not been demonstrated—there was no showing that the services provided by Curves are necessary and unobtainable elsewhere. * * *

The Curves release did not contravene public policy, and we adopt the supreme court's conclusion in *Schlobohm*: "Here there is no special legal relationship and no overriding public interest which demand that this contract provision, voluntarily entered into by competent parties, should be rendered ineffectual." [Citation.]

* * *

The district court did not err in granting respondent's motion for summary judgment on the ground that appellant signed and agreed to a release of respondent's liability for negligence. We affirm.

CASE

13-4

Unconscionable Contract
SANCHEZ v. WESTERN PIZZA ENTERPRISES, INC.

Court of Appeal, Second District, California, 2009
90 Cal.Rptr.3d 818, 172 Cal.App.4th 154
http://scholar.google.com/scholar_case?case=18161264297915300969&q=172+Cal.App.4th+154&hl=en&as_sdt=2,10

Croskey, J.

[Octavio Sanchez works as a delivery driver at a Domino's Pizza restaurant owned by Western Pizza. He drives his own car in making deliveries. His hourly wage has ranged from the legal minimum wage to approximately $0.50 above minimum wage. Western Pizza reimburses him at a fixed rate of $0.80 per delivery regardless of the number of miles driven or actual expenses incurred. Sanchez brought this class action against Western Pizza alleging that the flat rate at which drivers were reimbursed for delivery expenses violated wage and hour laws and that the drivers were paid less than the legal minimum wage.

Sanchez and Western Pizza are parties to an undated arbitration agreement. The agreement states that (1) the execution of the agreement "is not a mandatory condition of employment"; (2) any dispute that the parties are unable to resolve informally will be submitted to binding arbitration before an arbitrator "selected from the then-current Employment Arbitration panel of the Dispute Eradication Services," and that the arbitrator must be approved by both parties; (3) the parties waive the right to a jury trial; (4) the arbitration fees will be borne by Western Pizza and, except as otherwise required by law, each party will bear its own attorney fees and costs; (5) small claims may be resolved by a summary small claims procedure; and (6) the parties waive the right to bring class arbitration. The Superior Court of Los Angeles County denied the restaurant's motion to compel arbitration, and the restaurant appealed.]

Western Pizza contends * * * the arbitration agreement is neither procedurally nor substantively unconscionable.

* * *

Procedural and substantive unconscionability must both be present to justify the refusal to enforce a contract or clause based on unconscionability. [Citation.] Procedural unconscionability focuses on oppression or unfair surprise, while substantive unconscionability focuses on overly harsh or one-sided terms. [Citations.] The more procedural unconscionability is present, the less substantive unconscionability is required to justify a determination that a contract or clause is unenforceable. Conversely, the less procedural unconscionability is present, the more substantive unconscionability is required to justify such a determination. [Citation.]

"[A] finding of procedural unconscionability does not mean that a contract will not be enforced, but rather that

courts will scrutinize the substantive terms of the contract to ensure they are not manifestly unfair or one-sided. [Citation.]...[T]here are degrees of procedural unconscionability. At one end of the spectrum are contracts that have been freely negotiated by roughly equal parties, in which there is no procedural unconscionability. Although certain terms in these contracts may be construed strictly, courts will not find these contracts substantively unconscionable, no matter how one-sided the terms appear to be. [Citation.] Contracts of adhesion that involve surprise or other sharp practices lie on the other end of the spectrum. [Citation.] Ordinary contracts of adhesion, although they are indispensable facts of modern life that are generally enforced [citation], contain a degree of procedural unconscionability even without any notable surprises, and 'bear within them the clear danger of oppression and overreaching.'" [Citation.]

"Thus, a conclusion that a contract contains no element of procedural unconscionability is tantamount to saying that, no matter how one-sided the contract terms, a court will not disturb the contract because of its confidence that the contract was negotiated or chosen freely, that the party subject to a seemingly one-sided term is presumed to have obtained some advantage from conceding the term or that, if one party negotiated poorly, it is not the court's place to rectify these kinds of errors or asymmetries." [Citation.]

* * *

The Arbitration Agreement Is Procedurally Unconscionable

Procedural unconscionability focuses on oppression or unfair surprise, as we have stated. Oppression results from unequal bargaining power when a contracting party has no meaningful choice but to accept the contract terms. [Citation.] Unfair surprise results from misleading bargaining conduct or other circumstances indicating that a party's consent was not an informed choice. [Citation.]

* * *

The arbitration agreement [in this case] states that the purpose of the agreement is "to resolve any disputes that may arise between the Parties in a timely, fair and individualized manner," but otherwise does not extol the benefits of arbitration. The arbitration agreement does not limit the limitations periods, the remedies available, or the amount of punitive damages. It states, "Except as otherwise required by law, each party shall bear its own attorney fees and costs," and therefore incorporates any statutory right to recover fees rather than creating a presumption against a fee recovery. Thus, the arbitration agreement neither contains the same types of disadvantages for employees as were present in [citation] nor fails to mention such disadvantageous terms. Moreover, the arbitration agreement expressly states that the agreement "is not a mandatory condition of employment."

We conclude, however, that the record indicates a degree of procedural unconscionability in two respects. First, * * * the inequality in bargaining power between the low-wage employees and their employer makes it likely that the employees felt at least some pressure to sign the arbitration agreement. Second, the arbitration agreement suggests that there are multiple arbitrators to choose from ("the then-current Employment Arbitration panel of the Dispute Eradication Services") and fails to mention that the designated arbitration provider includes only one arbitrator. This renders the arbitrator selection process illusory and creates a significant risk that Western Pizza as a "repeat player" before the same arbitrator will reap a significant advantage. [Citation.] These circumstances indicate that the employees' decision to enter into the arbitration agreement likely was not a free and informed decision but was marked by some degree of oppression and unfair surprise, i.e., procedural unconscionability. We therefore must scrutinize the terms of the arbitration agreement to determine whether it is so unfairly one-sided as to be substantively unconscionable.

The Arbitrator Selection Provision Is Substantively Unconscionable

"Substantively unconscionable terms may take various forms, but may generally be described as unfairly one-sided." [Citation.] "Given the lack of choice and the potential disadvantages that even a fair arbitration system can harbor for employees, we must be particularly attuned to claims that employers with superior bargaining power have imposed one-sided, substantively unconscionable terms as part of an arbitration agreement. 'Private arbitration may resolve disputes faster and cheaper than judicial proceedings. Private arbitration, however, may also become an instrument of injustice imposed on a "take it or leave it" basis. The courts must distinguish the former from the latter, to ensure that private arbitration systems resolve disputes not only with speed and economy but also with fairness.'" [Citation.]

Sanchez contends the arbitration agreement is substantively unconscionable in several respects. He cites the class arbitration waiver, the small claims provision, the absence of any provision requiring a written arbitration award, the designation of an arbitration provider consisting of a single

arbitrator, and the absence of any express provision for discovery. In light of our conclusion that the trial court properly decided that the class arbitration waiver is contrary to public policy and therefore unenforceable, we need not decide whether that provision is unconscionable. [Citation.]

* * *

* * * We conclude that the absence of express provisions requiring a written arbitration award and allowing discovery does not render the arbitration agreement unconscionable. Rather, those terms are implied as a matter of law as part of the agreement. [Citation.]

* * * We conclude that the matters authorized under the small claims provision are an ordinary incident of arbitration and that the small claims provision is not substantively unconscionable.

Finally, an arbitration agreement must provide for a neutral arbitrator. * * * In our view, the designation of a "panel" of arbitrators consisting of a single arbitrator selected by Western Pizza created a false appearance of mutuality in the selection of an arbitrator. Moreover, the effective designation of a single arbitrator in what appears to be a standard arbitration agreement applicable to a large number of corporate employees gives rise to a significant risk of financial interdependence between Western Pizza and the arbitrator, and an opportunity for Western Pizza to gain an advantage through its knowledge of and experience with the arbitrator. * * * We conclude that this provision is unfairly one-sided and substantively unconscionable.

The Entire Arbitration Agreement Is Unenforceable

A trial court may either sever an unconscionable or otherwise unlawful provision from an arbitration agreement and enforce the remainder, restrict the application of the provision so as to avoid unconscionable results, or refuse to enforce the entire agreement. [Citation.] Although a court has some discretion in this regard, a court may refuse to enforce the entire agreement only if the central purpose of the agreement is tainted by illegality. [Citation.] * * *

Whether a contract is severable in this regard is primarily a question of contract interpretation. "'Whether a contract is entire or separable depends upon its language and subject matter, and this question is one of construction to be determined by the court according to the intention of the parties.'" [Citation.] Questions of contract interpretation are subject to de novo review unless the interpretation turns on the credibility of extrinsic evidence. [Citation.]

* * *

The arbitration agreement here includes a class arbitration waiver that is contrary to public policy and an unconscionable arbitrator selection clause, as we have stated. These are important provisions that, if they were not challenged in litigation, could create substantial disadvantages for an employee seeking to arbitrate a modest claim. Although it may be true that neither of these provisions alone would justify the refusal to enforce the entire arbitration agreement [citation], we believe that these provisions considered together indicate an effort to impose on an employee a forum with distinct advantages for the employer. * * * [Thus,] we conclude that the arbitration agreement is permeated by an unlawful purpose. Accordingly, the denial of the motion to compel arbitration was proper.

QUESTIONS

1. Johnson and Wilson were the principal shareholders in Matthew Corporation, located in the city of Jonesville, Wisconsin. This corporation was engaged in the business of manufacturing paper novelties, which were sold over a wide area in the Midwest. The corporation was also in the business of binding books. Johnson purchased Wilson's shares of the Matthew Corporation and, in consideration thereof, Wilson agreed that for a period of two years he would not (a) manufacture or sell in Wisconsin any paper novelties of any kind that would compete with those sold by the Matthew Corporation or (b) engage in the bookbinding business in the city of Jonesville. Discuss the validity and effect, if any, of this agreement.

2. Wilkins, a resident of and licensed by the State of Texas as a certified public accountant (CPA), rendered service in his professional capacity in Louisiana to Coverton Cosmetics Company. He was not registered as a CPA in Louisiana. His service under his contract with the cosmetics company was not the only occasion on which he had practiced his profession in that State. The company denied liability and refused to pay him, relying upon a Louisiana statute declaring it unlawful for any person to perform or offer to perform services as a CPA for compensation until he has been registered by the designated agency of the State and holds an unrevoked registration card. Provision is made for issuance of a certificate as a CPA without examination to any applicant who holds a valid unrevoked certificate as a CPA under the laws of any other State. The statute provides further that rendition of services of the character performed by Wilkins, without registration, is a misdemeanor punishable by a fine or imprisonment in the county jail, or both. Discuss whether Wilkins would be successful in an action against Coverton seeking to recover a fee in the amount of $1,500 as the reasonable value of his services.

3. Michael is interested in promoting the passage of a bill in the State legislature. He agrees with Christy, an attorney, to pay Christy for her services in drawing up the required bill, procuring its introduction in the legislature, and making an argument for its passage before the legislative committee to which it will be referred. Christy renders these services. Subsequently, upon Michael's refusal to pay her, Christy sues Michael for damage for breach of contract. Will Christy prevail? Explain.

4. Anthony promises to pay McCarthy $10,000 if McCarthy reveals to the public that Washington is a Communist. Washington is not a Communist and never has been. McCarthy successfully persuades the media to report that Washington is a Communist and now seeks to recover the $10,000 from Anthony, who refuses to pay. McCarthy initiates a lawsuit against Anthony. What result?

5. The Dear Corporation was engaged in the business of making and selling harvesting machines. It sold everything pertaining to its business to the ABC Company, agreeing "not again to go into the manufacture of harvesting machines anywhere in the United States." The seller, which had national and international goodwill in its business, now begins the manufacture of such machines contrary to its agreement. Should the court enjoin it?

6. Charles Leigh, engaged in the industrial laundry business in Central City, employed Tim Close, previously employed in the home laundry business, as a route salesperson on July 1. Leigh rents linens and industrial uniforms to commercial customers; the soiled linens and uniforms are picked up at regular intervals by route drivers and replaced with clean ones. Every employee is assigned a list of customers. The contract of employment stated that in consideration of being employed, upon termination of his employment, Close would not "directly or indirectly engage in the linen supply business or any competitive business within Central City, Illinois, for a period of one year from the date when his employment under this contract ceases." On May 10 of the following year, Leigh terminated Close's employment for valid reasons. Thereafter, Close accepted employment with Ajax Linen Service, a direct competitor of Leigh in Central City. He commenced soliciting former customers whom he had called on for Leigh and obtained some of them as customers for Ajax. Will Leigh be able to enforce the provisions of the contract?

7. On April 30, 2013, Barack and George entered into a bet on the outcome of the 2013 Kentucky Derby. On January 28, 2014, Barack, who bet on the winner, approached George, seeking to collect the $3,000 George had wagered. George paid Barack the $3,000 wager but now seeks to recover the funds from Barack. Result?

8. Carl, a salesman for Smith, comes to Benson's home and sells him a complete set of "gourmet cooking utensils" that are worth approximately $300. Benson, an eighty-year-old man living alone in a one-room efficiency apartment, signs a contract to buy the utensils for $1,450, plus a credit charge of $145, and to make payment in ten equal monthly installments. Three weeks after Carl leaves with the signed contract, Benson decides he cannot afford the cooking utensils and has no use for them. What can Benson do? Explain.

9. Consider the same facts as in Question 8, but assume that the price was $350. Benson, nevertheless, wishes to avoid the contract based on the allegation that Carl befriended and tricked him into the purchase. Discuss.

10. Adrian rents a bicycle from Barbara. The bicycle rental contract Adrian signed provides that Barbara is not liable for any injury to the renter caused by any defect in the bicycle or the negligence of Barbara. Injured when she is involved in an accident due to Barbara's improper maintenance of the bicycle, Adrian sues Barbara for her damages. Will Barbara be protected from liability by the provision in their contract?

CASE PROBLEMS

11. Merrill Lynch employed Post and Maney as account executives. Both men elected to be paid a salary and to participate in the firm's pension and profit-sharing plans rather than take a straight commission. Thirteen years later, Merrill Lynch terminated the employment of both Post and Maney. Both men began working for a competitor of Merrill Lynch. Merrill Lynch then informed them that all of their rights in the company-funded pension plan had been forfeited pursuant to a provision of the plan that permitted forfeiture in the event an employee directly or indirectly competed with the firm. Is Merrill Lynch correct in its assertion?

12. Tovar applied for the position of resident physician in Paxton Community Memorial Hospital. The hospital examined his background and licensing and assured him that he was qualified for the position. Relying upon the hospital's promise of permanent employment, Tovar resigned from his job and began work at the hospital. He was discharged two weeks later, however, because he did not hold a license to practice medicine in Illinois as required by State law. He had taken the examination but had never passed it. Tovar claims that the hospital promised him a position of permanent employment and that by discharging him it breached their employment contract. Discuss.

13. Carolyn Murphy, a welfare recipient with very limited education and with four minor children, responded to an advertisement that offered the opportunity to purchase televisions without a deposit or credit history. She entered into a rent-to-own contract for a twenty-five-inch console color television set that required seventy-eight weekly payments of $16.00 (a total of $1,248, which was two and one-half times the retail value of the set). Under the contract, the renter could terminate the agreement by returning the television and forfeiting any payments already made. After Murphy had paid $436 on the television, she read a newspaper article criticizing the lease plan. She stopped payment and sued the television company. The television company has attempted to take possession of the set. Decision?

14. Albert Bennett, an amateur cyclist, participated in a bicycle race conducted by the United States Cycling Federation. During the race, Bennett was hit by an automobile. He claims that employees of the Federation improperly allowed the car onto the course. The Federation claims that it cannot be held liable to Bennett because Bennett signed a release exculpating the Federation from responsibility for any personal injury resulting from his participation in the race. Is the exculpatory clause effective?

15. In February, Brady contracted to construct a house for Fulghum for $206,850. Brady began construction on March 13. Neither during the negotiation of this contract nor when he began performance was Brady licensed as a general contractor as required by North Carolina law. Brady was awarded his builder's license on October 22, having passed the examination on his second attempt. At that time, he had completed two-thirds of the work on Fulghum's house. Fulghum paid Brady $204,000. Brady brought suit, seeking an additional $2,850 on the original contract and $29,000 for "additions and changes" Fulghum requested during construction. Is Fulghum liable to Brady? Explain.

16. Robert McCart owned and operated an H&R Block tax preparation franchise. When Robert became a district manager for H&R Block, he was not allowed to continue operating a franchise. So, in accordance with company policy, he signed over his franchise to his wife June. June signed the new franchise agreement, which included a covenant not to compete for a two-year period within a fifty-mile radius of the franchise territory should the H&R Block franchise be terminated, transferred, or otherwise disposed of. June and Robert were both aware of the terms of this agreement, but June chose to terminate her franchise agreement anyway. Shortly thereafter, June sent out letters to H&R Block customers, criticizing H&R Block's fees and informing them that she and Robert would establish their own tax preparation services at the same address as the former franchise location. Each letter included a separate letter from Robert detailing the tax services to be offered by the McCart's new business. Should H&R Block be able to obtain an injunction against June? Against Robert?

17. Michelle Marvin and actor Lee Marvin began living together, holding themselves out to the general public as man and wife without actually being married. The two orally agreed that while they lived together they would share equally any and all property and earnings accumulated as a result of their individual and combined efforts. In addition, Michelle promised to render her services as "companion, homemaker, housekeeper and cook" to Lee. Shortly thereafter, she gave up her lucrative career as an entertainer in order to devote her full time to being Lee's companion, homemaker, housekeeper, and cook. In return he agreed to provide for all of her financial support and needs for the rest of her life. After living together for six years, Lee compelled Michelle to leave his household but continued to provide for her support. One year later, however, he refused to provide further support. Michelle sued to recover support payments and half of their accumulated property. Lee contends that their agreement is so closely related to the supposed "immoral" character of their relationship that its enforcement would violate public policy. The trial court granted Lee's motion for judgment on the pleadings. Decision?

18. Richard Brobston was hired by Insulation Corporation of America (ICA) in 2003. Initially, he was hired as a territory sales manager but was promoted to national account manager in 2007 and to general manager in 2011. In 2013, ICA was planning to acquire computer-assisted design (CAD) technology to upgrade its product line. Prior to acquiring this technology, ICA required that Brobston and certain other employees sign employ-

ment contracts that contained restrictive covenants or be terminated and changed their employment status to "at-will" employees. These restrictive covenants provided that in the event of Brobston's termination for any reason, Brobston would not reveal any of ICA's trade secrets or sales information and would not enter into direct competition with ICA within three hundred miles of Allentown, Pennsylvania, for a period of two years from the date of termination. The purported consideration for Brobston's agreement was a $2,000 increase in his base salary and proprietary information concerning the CAD system, customers, and pricing.

Brobston signed the proffered employment contract. In October 2013, Brobston became vice president of special products, which included responsibility for sales of the CAD system products as well as other products. Over the course of the next year, Brobston failed in several respects to properly perform his employment duties and on August 13, 2014, ICA terminated Brobston's employment. In December 2014, Brobston was hired by a competitor of ICA who was aware of ICA's restrictive covenants. Can ICA enforce the employment agreement by enjoining Brobston from disclosing proprietary information about ICA and by restraining him from competing with ICA? If so, for what duration and over what geographic area?

19. Henrioulle, an unemployed widower with two children, received public assistance in the form of a rent subsidy. He entered into an apartment lease agreement with Marin Ventures that provided, "INDEMNIFICATION: Owner shall not be liable for any damage or injury to the tenant, or any other person, or to any property, occurring on the premises, or any part thereof, and Tenant agrees to hold Owner harmless for any claims for damages no matter how caused." Henrioulle fractured his wrist when he tripped over a rock on a common stairway in the apartment building. At the time of the accident, the landlord had been having difficulty keeping the common areas of the apartment building clean. Will the exculpatory clause effectively bar Henrioulle from recovery? Explain.

20. Emily was a Java programmer employed with Sun Microsystems in Palo Alto, California. Upon beginning employment, Emily signed a contract that included a noncompete clause that prevented her from taking another Java programming position with any of five companies Sun listed as "direct competitors" within three months of terminating her employment. Later that year Emily resigned and two months later accepted a position with Hewlett-Packard (HP) in Houston, Texas. HP was listed in Emily's contract as a "direct competitor," but she argues that due to the significant geographic distance between both jobs, the

contract is not enforceable. Explain whether the contract is enforceable.

21. Between 2009 and 2014, Williams purchased a number of household items on credit from Walker-Thomas Furniture Co., a retail furniture store. Walker-Thomas retained the right in its contracts to repossess an item if Williams defaulted on an installment payment. Each contract also provided that each installment payment by Williams would be credited *pro rata* to all outstanding accounts or bills owed to Walker-Thomas. As a result of this provision, an unpaid balance would remain on every item purchased until the entire balance due on all items, whenever purchased, was paid in full. Williams defaulted on a monthly installment payment in 2014, and Walker-Thomas sought to repossess all the items that Williams had purchased since 2009. Discuss.

22. Universal City Studios, Inc. (Universal) entered into a general contract with Turner Construction Company (Turner) for the construction of the Jurassic Park ride. Turner entered into a subcontract with Pacific Custom Pools, Inc. (PCP), for PCP to furnish and install all water treatment work for the project for the contract price of $959,131. PCP performed work on the project from April 2011 until June 2012 for which it was paid $897,719. PCP's contractor's license, however, was under suspension from October 12, 2011, to March 14, 2012. In addition, PCP's license had expired as of January 31, 2012, and it was not renewed until May 5, 2012. California Business and Professions Code Section 7031 provides that no contractor may bring an action to recover compensation for the performance of any work requiring a license unless he or she was "a duly licensed contractor at all times during the performance of that [work], regardless of the merits of the cause of action brought by the contractor." The purpose of this licensing law is to protect the public from incompetence and dishonesty in those who provide building and construction services. PCP brought suit against Universal and Turner, the defendants, for the remainder of the contract price. Explain who should prevail.

TAKING SIDES

EarthWeb provided online products and services to business professionals in the information technology (IT) industry. EarthWeb operated through a family of Websites offering information, products, and services for IT professionals to use for facilitating tasks and solving technology problems in a business setting. EarthWeb obtained this content primarily through licensing agreements with third parties. Schlack began his employment with EarthWeb in its New York City office. His title at EarthWeb was Vice President, Worldwide Content, and he was responsible for the content of all of EarthWeb's Websites. Schlack's employment contract stated that he was an employee at will and included a section titled "Limited Agreement Not To Compete." That section provided:

(c) For a period of twelve (12) months after the termination of Schlack's employment with EarthWeb, Schlack shall not, directly or indirectly:
    (1) work as an employee … or in any other … capacity for any person or entity that directly competes with EarthWeb. For the purpose of this section,

the term "directly competing" is defined as a person or entity or division on an entity that is
    (i) an online service for Information Professionals whose primary business is to provide Information Technology Professionals with a directory of third party technology, software, and/or developer resources; and/or an online reference library, and or
    (ii) an online store, the primary purpose of which is to sell or distribute third party software or products used for Internet site or software development.

About one year later, Schlack tendered his letter of resignation to EarthWeb. Schlack revealed at this time that he had accepted a position with ITworld.com.

a. What arguments would support EarthWeb's enforcement of the covenant not to compete?

b. What arguments would support Schlack's argument that the covenant is not enforceable?

c. Which side should prevail? Explain.

C H A P T E R 1 2

CONTRACTUAL CAPACITY

CHAPTER OUTCOMES

After reading and studying this chapter, you should be able to:

- Explain how and when a minor may ratify a contract.

- Describe the liability of a minor who (1) disaffirms a contract or (2) misrepresents his age.

- Define as necessary and explain how it affects the contracts of a minor.

- Distinguish between the legal capacity of a person under guardianship and a mentally incompetent person who is not under guardianship.

- Explain the rule governing an intoxicated person's capacity to enter into a contract and contrast this rule with the law governing minors and incompetent persons.

A binding promise or agreement requires that the parties to the agreement have contractual capacity. Everyone is regarded as having such capacity unless the law for reasons of public policy holds that the individual lacks such capacity. This essential ingredient of a contract will be discussed by considering those classes and conditions of persons who are legally limited in their capacity to contract: (1) minors, (2) incompetent persons, and (3) intoxicated persons.

MINORS

A **minor**, also called an infant, is a person who has not attained the age of legal majority. At common law, a minor was a person who was under twenty-one years of age. Today the age of majority has been changed in nearly all jurisdictions by statute, usually to age eighteen. Almost without exception, a minor's contract, whether executory or executed, is **voidable** at his or his guardian's option. Restatement, Section 14. Thus, the minor is in a favored position by having the option to disaffirm the contract or to enforce it. The adult party to the contract cannot avoid her contract with a minor. Even an "emancipated" minor, one who because of marriage or other reason is no longer subject to strict parental control, may avoid contractual liability in most jurisdictions. Consequently, businesspeople deal at their peril with minors and in situations of consequence generally require an adult to cosign or guarantee the performance of the contract. Nevertheless, most States recognize special categories of contracts that cannot be avoided (such as student loans or contracts for medical care) or that have a lower age for capacity (such as bank account, marriage, and insurance contracts).

LIABILITY ON CONTRACTS

A minor's contract is not entirely void and of no legal effect; rather, it is *voidable* at the minor's option. The exercise of this power of avoidance, called a **disaffirmance**, ordinarily releases the minor from any liability on the contract. On the other hand, after the minor becomes of age, she may choose to adopt or **ratify** the contract, in which case she surrenders her power of avoidance and becomes bound.

DISAFFIRMANCE As previously stated, a minor's contract is voidable at his or his guardian's option, conferring upon him a power to avoid liability. He, or in some jurisdictions his guardian, may, through words or conduct manifesting an intention not to abide by the contract, exercise the power to disaffirm.

In general, a minor's disaffirmance must come either during his minority or within a reasonable time after he reaches majority, as long as he has not already ratified the contract. In most States, defining a reasonable time depends upon such circumstances as the nature of the transaction, whether either party has caused the delay, and the extent to which either party has been injured by the delay. Some States, however, statutorily prescribe a time period, generally one year, in which the minor may disaffirm the contract.

A notable exception is that a sale of land by a minor cannot be disaffirmed until after he reaches his majority. But must he disaffirm immediately upon becoming an adult? In the case of a sale of land, there is a strong precedent that the minor may wait until the period of the statute of limitations has expired, if the sale involves no questions of fairness and equity.

Disaffirmance may be either *express* or *implied*. No particular form of words is essential, so long as they show an intention not to be bound. This intention also may be manifested by acts or by conduct. For example, a minor agrees to sell property to Alice and then sells that property to Brian. The sale to Brian would constitute a disaffirmance of the contract with Alice.

A troublesome yet important problem in this area, upon which the courts are not in agreement, pertains to the minor's duty upon disaffirmance. The majority hold that the minor must return any property he has received from the other party, provided he has it in his possession at the time of disaffirmance. Nothing more is required. If the minor disaffirms the purchase of an automobile and the vehicle has been wrecked, he need only return the wrecked vehicle. Other States require at least the payment of a reasonable amount for the use of the property or the amount of its depreciation while in the hands of the minor. A few States, either by statute or court ruling, recognize a duty upon the part of the minor to make *restitution*, that is, return an equivalent of what has been received in order to place the seller in approximately the same position she would have occupied had the sale not occurred.

Finally, can a minor disaffirm and recover property that his buyer has transferred to a good faith purchaser for value? Traditionally, the minor could avoid the contract and recover the property, despite the fact that the third person gave value for it and had no notice of the minority. Thus, in the case of the sale of real estate, a minor may rescind her deed of conveyance even against a good faith purchaser of the land who did not know of the minority. Regarding the sale of goods, however, this principle has been changed by Section 2–403 of the Uniform Commercial Code (UCC), which provides that a person with voidable title (e.g., the person buying goods from a minor) has power to transfer valid title to a good faith purchaser for value. For example, a minor sells his car to an individual who resells it to a used car dealership, a good faith purchaser for value. The used car dealer would acquire legal title even though he bought the car from a seller who had only voidable title.

In all significant contracts entered into with a minor, have an adult cosign or guarantee the written agreement.

◆ SEE CASE 14-1

RATIFICATION A minor has the option of ratifying a contract after reaching the age of majority. Ratification makes the contract binding *ab initio* (from the beginning). That is, the result is the same as if the contract had been valid and binding from its inception. Ratification, once effected, is final and cannot be withdrawn. Further, it must be in total, validating the entire contract. The minor can ratify the contract only as a whole, both as to burdens and benefits. He cannot, for example, ratify so as to retain the consideration he received and escape payment or other performance on his part, nor can he retain part of the contract and disaffirm the rest.

Ratification may be express, implied from conduct, or result from the failure to make a timely disaffirmance. Suppose that a minor makes a contract to buy property from an adult. The contract is voidable by the minor, and she can escape liability. But suppose that after reaching her majority, she promises to go through with the purchase. Because she has *expressly* ratified the contract she entered when she was a minor, her promise is binding, and the adult can recover for breach upon her failure to perform. In the absence of a statutory provision to the contrary, an express ratification may be oral.

Note that a minor has no power to ratify a contract while he remains a minor. A ratification cannot be based on words or conduct occurring while a minor is still underage, for his ratification at that time would be no more effective than his original contractual promise. The ratification must take place after the individual has acquired contractual capacity by attaining his majority.

Ratification, as previously stated, need not be express; it may be *implied* from the minor's conduct. Suppose that the minor, after attaining her majority, uses the property involved in the contract, undertakes to sell it to someone else, or performs some other act showing an intention to affirm the contract. She may not thereafter disaffirm the contract but is bound by it. Perhaps the most common form of implied ratification occurs when a minor, after attaining her majority, continues to use the property that she purchased as a minor. This use is obviously inconsistent with the nonexistence of the contract, and whether the contract is performed or still partly executory, it will amount to a ratification and prevent a disaffirmance by the minor. Simply keeping the goods for an unreasonable time after attaining majority also has been construed as a ratification. Although the courts are divided on the issue, payments by the minor upon reaching majority, either on principal or interest or on the purchase price of goods, have been held to amount to a ratification. Some courts require additional evidence of an intention to abide by the contract, such as an express promise to that effect or the actual use of the subject matter of the contract.

◆ SEE CASE 14-2

LIABILITY FOR NECESSARIES

Contractual incapacity does not excuse a minor from an obligation to pay for necessaries, those things that suitably and reasonably supply his personal needs, such as food, shelter, medicine, and clothing. Even here, however, the minor is liable not for the agreed price but for the *reasonable* value of the items furnished. Recovery is based on quasi contract. Thus, if a clothier sells a minor a suit that the minor needs, the clothier can successfully sue the minor. The clothier's recovery is limited, however, to the reasonable value of the suit, even if this amount is much less than the agreed-upon selling price.

Defining necessaries is a difficult problem. In general, the States regard as **necessary** those things that the minor needs to maintain himself in his particular station in life. Items necessary for subsistence and health—such as food, lodging, clothing, medicine, and medical services—are obviously included. But other less essential items, such as textbooks, school instruction, and legal advice, may be included as well. Further, many States enlarge the concept of necessaries to include articles of property and services that a minor needs to earn the money required to provide the necessities of life for himself and his dependents. Nevertheless, many States limit necessaries to items that are not provided to the minor. Thus, if a minor's guardian provides her with an adequate wardrobe, a blouse the minor purchased would not be considered a necessary. In addition, a minor is *not* liable for anything on the grounds that it is necessary unless it has been actually furnished to him and used or consumed by him. In other words, a minor may disaffirm his executory contracts for necessaries and refuse to accept the clothing, lodging, or other items or services.

Ordinarily, luxury items such as cameras, tape recorders, stereo equipment, television sets, and motorboats seldom qualify as necessaries. Whether automobiles and trucks are necessaries has caused considerable controversy, but some courts have recognized that under certain circumstances an automobile may be necessary when the minor uses it for his business activities.

◆ SEE CASE 14-3

LIABILITY FOR MISREPRESENTATION OF AGE

The States do not agree on whether a minor who has fraudulently misrepresented her age when entering into contract has the power to disaffirm. Suppose a contracting minor says that she is eighteen years of age (or twenty-one if that is the year of attaining majority) and actually looks at least that old. By the prevailing view in this country, the minor may nevertheless disaffirm the contract. Some States, however, prohibit disaffirmance if a minor misrepresents her age and the adult party, in good faith, reasonably relied upon the misrepresentation. Other States not following the majority rule either (1) require the minor to restore the other party to the position she occupied before the making of the contract or (2) allow the defrauded party to recover damages against the minor in tort.

PRACTICAL ADVICE

In all significant contracts, if you have doubts about the age of your customers, have them prove that they are of legal age.

LIABILITY FOR TORT CONNECTED WITH CONTRACT

It is well settled that minors are generally liable for their torts. There is, however, a legal doctrine providing that if a tort and a contract are so "interwoven" that the court must enforce the contract to enforce the tort action, the minor is not liable in tort. Thus, if a minor rents an automobile from an adult, he enters into a contractual relationship obliging him to exercise reasonable care and diligence to protect the property from injury. By negligently damaging the automobile, he breaches that contractual undertaking. But his contractual immunity protects him from an action by the adult based on the contract. Can the adult nonetheless recover damages on a tort theory? By the majority view, he cannot. For, it is reasoned, a tort recovery would, in effect, be an enforcement of the contract and would defeat the protection that contract law affords the minor.

A different result arises, however, when the minor departs from the terms of the agreement, as by using a rental automobile for an unauthorized purpose and in so doing negligently causing damage to the automobile. In that event, most courts would hold that the tort is independent, and the adult can collect from the minor. Such a situation would not involve the breach of a contractual duty, but rather the commission of a tort while performing an activity completely beyond the scope of the rental agreement.

INCOMPETENT PERSONS

This section discusses the contract status of incompetent persons who are under court-appointed guardianship and those who are not adjudicated incompetents.

PERSON UNDER GUARDIANSHIP

If a person is under guardianship by court order, her contracts are void and of no legal effect. Restatement, Section 13. A *guardian* is appointed by a court, generally under the terms of a statute, to control and preserve the property of a person (the **ward** or **adjudicated incompetent**) whose impaired capacity prevents her from managing her own property. Nevertheless, a party dealing with an individual under guardianship may be able to recover the fair value of any necessaries provided to the incompetent. Moreover, the contracts of the ward may be ratified by her guardian or by herself upon termination of the guardianship.

◆ SEE CASE 14-4

MENTAL ILLNESS OR DEFECT

A contract is a consensual transaction; therefore, for a contract to be valid, it is necessary that the parties have a certain level of mental capacity. If a person lacks such capacity (is mentally incompetent), he may avoid liability under the agreement (because the contract is **voidable**).

Under the traditional, cognitive ability test, a person who is lacking in sufficient mental capacity to enter into a contract is one unable to comprehend the subject of the contract, its nature, and probable consequences. To avoid the contract, he need not be proved permanently incompetent, but his mental defect must be something more than a weakness of intellect or a lack of average intelligence. In short, a person is competent unless he is unable to understand the nature and effect of his act in entering a contract. Restatement, Section 15. In this situation, the incompetent may disaffirm the contract even if the other party did not know, or had no reason to know, of the incompetent's mental condition.

A second type of mental incompetence recognized by the Restatement and some States is a mental condition that impairs a person's ability to act in a reasonable manner. Section 15. In other words, the person understands what he is doing but cannot control his behavior in order to act in a reasonable and rational way. If the contract he enters is entirely executory or grossly unfair, it is voidable. If, however, the contract is executed and fair, and the competent party had no reason to suspect the incompetency of the

other, the incompetent must restore the competent party to the *status quo* by returning the consideration he has received or its equivalent in money. If restoration to the *status quo* is impossible, avoidance will depend upon the equities of the situation.

Like minors and persons under guardianship, an incompetent person is liable for necessaries furnished him on the principle of quasi contract, the amount of recovery being the reasonable value of the goods or services. Moreover, an incompetent person may ratify or disaffirm his voidable contracts when he becomes competent or during a lucid period.

> **PRACTICAL ADVICE**
>
> *If you have doubts about the capacity of the other party to a contract, have an individual with full legal capacity cosign the contract.*

INTOXICATED PERSONS

A person may avoid any contract that he enters into if the other party has reason to know that, because of intoxication, he is unable either to understand the nature and consequences of his actions or to act in a reasonable manner. Restatement, Section 16. Such contracts are voidable, although they may be ratified when the intoxicated person regains his capacity. Slight intoxication will not destroy one's contractual capacity, but neither is it essential that one be so drunk as to be totally without reason or understanding.

The effect of intoxication on contractual capacity is similar to that accorded contracts that are voidable because of the second type of incompetency, although the courts are even more strict with contracts a party enters while intoxicated, given the idea that the condition is voluntary. Most courts, therefore, require that the intoxicated person on regaining his capacity must act promptly to disaffirm and must generally offer to restore the consideration received. Individuals who are taking prescribed medication or who are involuntarily intoxicated are treated the same as those who are incompetent under the cognitive ability test. As with incompetent persons, intoxicated persons are liable in quasi contract for necessaries furnished them during their incapacity.

◈ SEE FIGURE 14-1: **Incapacity: Minors, Nonadjudicated Incompetents, and Intoxicated**

◆ SEE CASE 14-4

◆ FIGURE 14-1: **Incapacity: Minors, Nonadjudicated Incompetents, and Intoxicated**

INCAPACITY	FULL CAPACITY
Incapacity terminates	
Contract may not be ratified	May expressly or impliedly ratify contract
Contract may be disaffirmed	Contract may be disaffirmed / Contract ratified by nondisaffirmance
	Reasonable time

© Cengage Learning

CHAPTER SUMMARY

MINORS

Definition persons who are under the age of majority (usually 18 years)

Liability on Contracts a minor's contracts are voidable at the minor's option
- *Disaffirmance* avoidance of the contract; may be done during minority and for a reasonable time after reaching majority
- *Ratification* affirmation of the entire contract; may be done upon reaching majority

Liability for Necessaries a minor is liable for the reasonable value of necessary items (those that reasonably supply a person's needs)

Liability for Misrepresentation of Age prevailing view is that a minor may disaffirm the contract

Liability for Tort Connected with Contract if a tort and a contract are so intertwined that to enforce the tort the court must enforce the contract, the minor is not liable in tort

INCOMPETENT AND INTOXICATED PERSONS

Person Under Guardianship contracts made by a person placed under guardianship by court order are void

Mental Illness or Defect a contract entered into by a mentally incompetent person (one who is unable to understand the nature and consequences of his acts) is voidable

Intoxicated Persons a contract entered into by an intoxicated person (one who cannot understand the nature and consequence of her actions) is voidable

CASES

CASE 14-1

Minors: Disaffirmance
BERG v. TRAYLOR
Court of Appeal, Second District, Division 2, California, 2007
148 Cal.App.4th 809, 56 Cal.Rptr.3d 140
http://scholar.google.com/scholar_case?case=1540939777753786246&q=56+Cal.Rptr.3d + 140&hl=en&as_sclt=2,22

Todd, J.
Appellants Meshiel Cooper Traylor (Meshiel) and her minor son Craig Lamar Traylor (Craig) appeal the judgment confirming an arbitration award in favor of Craig's former personal manager, respondent Sharyn Berg (Berg), for unpaid

commissions under a contract between Berg, Meshiel and Craig and unrepaid loans from Berg. * * *

On January 18, 1999, Berg entered into a two-page "Artist's Manager's Agreement" (agreement) with Meshiel and Craig, who was then 10 years old. Meshiel signed the agreement and wrote Craig's name on the signature page where he was designated "Artist." Craig did not sign the agreement. Pursuant to the agreement, Berg was to act as Craig's exclusive personal manager in exchange for a commission of 15 percent of all gross monies or other consideration paid to him as an artist during the three-year term of the agreement, as well as income from merchandising or promotional efforts or offers of employment made during the term of the agreement, regardless of when Craig received such monies. The agreement expressly provided that any action Craig "may take in the future pertaining to disaffirmance of this agreement, whether successful or not," would not affect Meshiel's liability for any commissions due Berg. The agreement also provided that any disputes concerning payment or interpretation of the agreement would be determined by arbitration in accordance with the rules of Judicial Arbitration and Mediation Services, Inc. (JAMS).

* * *

On or about June 13, 2001, Craig obtained a recurring acting role on the Fox Television Network show "Malcolm in the Middle" (show). On September 11, 2001, four months prior to the expiration of the agreement, Meshiel sent a certified letter to Berg stating that while she and Craig appreciated her advice and guidance, they no longer needed her management services and could no longer afford to pay Berg her 15 percent commission because they owed a "huge amount" of taxes. On September 28, 2001, Berg responded, informing appellants that they were in breach of the agreement.

* * *

In 2004, Berg filed suit against Meshiel and Craig for breach of the agreement, breach of the implied covenant of good faith and fair dealing, breach of an oral loan agreement, conversion and declaratory relief. * * *

* * *

The arbitration hearing commenced on February 7, 2005. * * * Though Meshiel and Craig's counsel failed to appear at the hearing, Meshiel personally appeared with Craig's talent agent, Steven Rice. Craig did not appear. * * *

On February 11, 2005, the arbitrator issued his award, which was served on the parties on February 14, 2005. * * * The arbitrator awarded Berg commissions and interest of $154,714.15, repayment of personal loans and interest of $5,094, and attorney fees and costs of $13,762. He also awarded Berg $405,000 "for future earnings projected on a minimum of 6 years for national syndication earnings," and stated that this part of the award would "vest and become final, as monies earned after February 7, 2005, become due and payable." * * *

[The defendants then filed a petition with the State trial court to vacate the arbitration award. Following a hearing, the trial court trial court entered a judgment in favor of Berg against Meshiel and Craig consistent with the arbitrator's award.]

* * *

Simply stated, one who provides a minor with goods and services does so at her own risk. [Citation.] The agreement here expressly contemplated this risk, requiring that Meshiel remain obligated for commissions due under the agreement regardless of whether Craig disaffirmed the agreement. Thus, we have no difficulty in reaching the conclusion that Craig is permitted to and did disaffirm the agreement and any obligations stemming therefrom, while Meshiel remains liable under the agreement and resulting judgment. Where our difficulty lies is in understanding how counsel, the arbitrator, and the trial court repeatedly and systematically ignored Craig's interests in this matter. From the time Meshiel signed the agreement, her interests were not aligned with Craig's. That no one—counsel, the arbitrator, or the trial court—recognized this conflict and sought appointment of a guardian *ad litem* for Craig is nothing short of stunning. It is the court's responsibility to protect the rights of a minor who is a litigant in court. [Citation.]

* * *

"As a general proposition, parental consent is required for the provision of services to minors for the simple reason that minors may disaffirm their own contracts to acquire such services." [Citation.] According to Family Code section 6700, "a minor may make a contract in the same manner as an adult, subject to the power of disaffirmance" * * * In turn, Family Code section 6710 states: "Except as otherwise provided by statute, a contract of a minor may be disaffirmed by the minor before majority or within a reasonable time afterwards or, in case of the minor's death within that period, by the minor's heirs or personal representative." Sound policy considerations support this provision:

> The law shields minors from their lack of judgment and experience and under certain conditions vests in them the right to disaffirm their contracts. Although in many instances such disaffirmance may be a hardship upon those who deal with an infant, the right to avoid his contracts is conferred by law upon a minor "for his protection against his own improvidence and the designs of others." It is the policy of the law to protect a minor against himself and his indiscretions and immaturity as well as against the machinations of other people and to discourage adults from contracting with an infant. Any loss occasioned by the disaffirmance of a minor's contract might have been avoided by declining to enter into the contract. [Citation.]

Berg offers two reasons why the plain language of Family Code section 6710 is inapplicable, neither of which we find persuasive. First, she argues that a minor may not disaffirm an agreement signed by a parent. * * * [This is not in accord with the law as stated in numerous cases.]

Second, Berg argues that Craig cannot disaffirm the agreement because it was for his and his family's necessities. Family Code section 6712 provides that a valid contract cannot be disaffirmed by a minor if all of the following requirements are met: the contract is to pay the reasonable value of things necessary for the support of the minor or the minor's family, the things have actually been furnished to the minor or the minor's family, and the contract is entered into by the minor when not under the care of a parent or guardian able to provide for the minor or the minor's family. These requirements are not met here. The agreement was not a contract to pay for the necessities of life for Craig or his family. While such necessities have been held to include payment for lodging [citation] and even payment of attorneys' fees [citation], we cannot conclude that a contract to secure personal management services for the purpose of advancing Craig's acting career constitutes payment for the type of necessity contemplated by Family Code section 6712. Nor is there any evidence that Meshiel was unable to provide for the family in 1999 at the time of the agreement. As such, Family Code section 6712 does not bar the minor's disaffirmance of the contract.

No specific language is required to communicate an intent to disaffirm. "A contract (or conveyance) of a minor may be avoided by any act or declaration disclosing an unequivocal intent to repudiate its binding force and effect." [Citation.] Express notice to the other party is unnecessary. [Citation.] We find that the "Notice of Disaffirmance of Arbitration Award by Minor" filed on August 8, 2005 was sufficient to constitute a disaffirmance of the agreement by Craig. * * *

We find that Craig was entitled to and did disaffirm the agreement which, among other things, required him to arbitrate his disputes with Berg. On this basis alone, therefore, the judgment confirming the arbitration award must be reversed.

* * *

Appellants do not generally distinguish their arguments between mother and son, apparently assuming that if Craig disaffirms the agreement and judgment, Meshiel would be permitted to escape liability as well. But a disaffirmance of an agreement by a minor does not operate to terminate the contractual obligations of the parent who signed the agreement. [Citation.] The agreement Meshiel signed provided that Craig's disaffirmance would not serve to void or avoid Meshiel's obligations under the agreement and that Meshiel remained liable for commissions due Berg regardless of Craig's disaffirmance. Accordingly, we find no basis for Meshiel to avoid her independent obligations under the agreement.

The judgment is reversed as to Craig and affirmed as to Meshiel.

CASE 14-2

Minors: Ratification

IN RE THE SCORE BOARD, INC.

United States District Court, D. New Jersey, 1999

238 B.R. 585

http://scholar.google.com/scholar_case?case=9690754193230293303&q=238+B.R.+585+&hl=en&as_sdt=2,34

Irenas, J.

During the Spring of 1996, Appellant Kobe Bryant ("Bryant"), then a seventeen-year old star high school basketball player, declared his intention to forego college and enter the 1996 lottery draft of the National Basketball Association. On May 8, 1996, The Score Board Inc. ("Debtor"), then a New Jersey based company in the business of licensing, manufacturing and distributing sports and entertainment-related memorabilia, contacted Bryant's Agent, Arn Tellem ("Tellem" or "Agent") in anticipation of making a deal with Bryant.

* * *

In early July 1996, after the above [initial] negotiations, Debtor prepared and forwarded a signed written licensing agreement ("agreement") to Bryant. The agreement granted Debtor the right to produce licensed products, such as trading cards, with Bryant's image. Bryant was obligated to make two personal appearances on behalf of Debtor and provide between a minimum of 15,000 and a maximum of 32,500 autographs. Bryant was to receive a $2.00 stipend for each autograph, after the first 7,500. Under the agreement, Bryant could receive a maximum of $75,000 for the autographs.

In addition to being compensated for the autographs, Bryant was entitled to receive base compensation of $10,000. Moreover, Debtor agreed to pay Bryant $5,000, of the $10,000, within ten days following receipt of the fully executed agreement. Finally, Bryant was entitled to a $5,000 bonus if he returned the agreement within six weeks.

Bryant rejected the above agreement, and on July 11, 1996, while still a minor, Bryant made a counter-offer ("counter-offer"), signed it and returned it to Debtor. The counter-offer made several changes to Debtor's agreement, including the number of autographs. Bryant also changed the amount of prepaid autographs from 7,500 to 500.

Balser claimed that he signed the counter-offer and placed it into his files. The copy signed by Debtor was subsequently misplaced, however, and has never been produced by Debtor during these proceedings. Rather, Debtor has produced a copy signed only by Bryant.

On August 23, 1996, Bryant turned eighteen. Three days later, Bryant deposited a check for $10,000 into his account from Debtor.

On or about September 1, 1996, Bryant began performing his obligations under the agreement, including autograph signing sessions and public appearances. He subsequently performed his contractual duties for about a year and a half.

By late 1997, Bryant grew reluctant to sign any more autographs under the agreement and his Agent came to the conclusion that a fully executed contract did not exist. By this time, Tellem became concerned with Debtor's financial condition because it failed to make certain payments to several other players. Debtor claims that the true motivation for Bryant's reluctance stems from his perception that he was becoming a "star" player, and that his autograph was "worth" more than $2.00.

* * *

On March 17, 1998, Debtor sent Bryant a check for $1,130 as compensation for unpaid autographs. Bryant alleges that he was entitled to $10,130, not $1,130. The Bankruptcy Court found that Bryant was owed $10,130 and the check for $1,130 was based on a miscalculation.

On March 18, 1998, Debtor filed a voluntary Chapter 11 bankruptcy petition. On March 23, 1998, Tellem returned the $1,130 check upon learning of Debtor's financial trouble. Included with the check was a letter that questioned the validity of the agreement between Bryant and Debtor.

* * * On April 20, 1998, Tellem stated that no contract existed because the counter-offer was never signed by Debtor and there was never a meeting of the minds. Tellem added that the counter-offer expired and that Kobe Bryant withdrew from the counter-offer.

Subsequently, Debtor began to sell its assets, including numerous executory contracts with major athletes, including Bryant. Bryant argued that Debtor could not do this, because he believed that a contract never existed. In the alternative, if a contract was created, Bryant contended that it was voidable because it was entered into while he was a minor.

* * *

* * * On December 21, 1998, the Honorable Gloria M. Burns ruled in her memorandum opinion that Debtor accepted Bryant's counter-offer and, therefore, a valid contract existed between Bryant and Debtor. In the alternative, the Bankruptcy Court held that even if Bryant's counter-offer was not signed by Debtor, the parties' subsequent conduct demonstrated their acceptance of the contractual obligation by performance, thereby creating an enforceable contract. Judge Burns denied Bryant's claims of mutual mistake, infancy and his motion for stay relief.

* * *

On February 2, 1999, the Bankruptcy Court entered its final orders: (1) granting Debtor's motion to assume its executory contract with Bryant and assign it to Oxxford; and (2) overruling Bryant's objection to the sale.

* * *

Bryant challenges the Bankruptcy Court's finding that he ratified the agreement upon attaining majority. Contracts made during minority are voidable at the minor's election within a reasonable time after the minor attains the age of majority. [Citations]

The right to disaffirm a contract is subject to the infant's conduct which, upon reaching the age of majority, may amount to ratification. [Citation.] "Any conduct on the part of the former infant which evidences his decision that the transaction shall not be impeached is sufficient for this purpose." [Citation.]

On August 23, 1996, Bryant reached the age of majority, approximately six weeks after the execution of the agreement. On August 26, 1996, Bryant deposited the $10,000 check sent to him from Debtor. Bryant also performed his contractual duties by signing autographs.

The Bankruptcy Court did not presume ratification from inaction as Bryant asserts. It is clear that Bryant ratified the contract from the facts, because Bryant consciously performed his contractual duties.

Bryant asserts that he acted at the insistence of his Agent, who believed that he was obligated to perform by contract. Yet, neither Bryant nor his Agent disputed the existence of a contract until the March 23, 1998, letter by Tellem. That Bryant may have relied on his Agent is irrelevant to this Court's inquiry and is proper evidence only in a suit against the Agent. To the contrary, by admitting that he acted because he was under the belief that a contract existed, Bryant confirms the existence of the contract. Moreover, it was Bryant who deposited the check, signed the autographs, and made personal appearances.

* * *

For the above reasons, Bryant's appeal of the Bankruptcy Court's orders finding that a valid and enforceable contract exists is denied.

Minors: Liability for Necessaries
ZELNICK v. ADAMS
Supreme Court of Virginia, 2002
263 Va. 601, 561 S.E.2d 711
http://scholar.google.com/scholar_case?case=13963993610436500611&q=561+S.E.2d+711+&hl=en&as_sdt=2,34

Lemons, J.

In this appeal, we consider whether a contract for legal services entered into on behalf of a minor is voidable upon a plea of infancy or subject to enforcement as an implied contract for necessaries and, if enforceable, the basis for determining value of services rendered.

Facts and Proceedings Below

Jonathan Ray Adams ("Jonathan") was born on April 5, 1980, the natural child of Mildred A. Adams ("Adams" or "mother") and Cecil D. Hylton, Jr. ("Hylton" or "father"). Jonathan's parents were never married to each other. On September 8, 1995, after highly contested litigation, an agreed order ("paternity order") was entered in Dade County, Florida, establishing Hylton's paternity of Jonathan.

Jonathan's grandfather, Cecil D. Hylton, Sr. ("Hylton Sr."), died testate [with a will] on August 25, 1989. His will established certain trusts and provided that the trustees had sole discretion to determine who qualified as "issue" under the will. * * *

The will created two separate trusts for Hylton Sr.'s grandchildren: the First Grandchildren's Charitable Trust and the Second Grandchildren's Charitable Trust ("the trusts"). Hylton Sr.'s grandchildren and great grandchildren would potentially receive distributions from the trusts in the years 2014 and 2021.

* * *

On July 11, 1996, Adams met with an attorney, Robert J. Zelnick ("Zelnick"), about protecting Jonathan's interest as a beneficiary of the trusts. She had received information leading her to believe that distributions were being made from the trusts to some of Hylton Sr.'s grandchildren. Adams told Zelnick that she contacted Jonathan's father about these alleged distributions, but she had not received a response from him. Adams explained that she had also contacted the law firm that had prepared Hylton Sr.'s will and the trustees, and no one would provide her any information about the distributions or whether the Estate would recognize Jonathan as a beneficiary. * * *

Adams explained that she could not afford to pay Zelnick's hourly fee and requested legal services on her son's behalf on a contingency fee basis. At the conclusion of the meeting, Zelnick told Adams that he was unsure whether he would take the case, but that he would investigate the matter.

Zelnick next spoke with Adams during a telephone conversation on July 18, 1996. He informed her that he had

obtained a copy of the will and reviewed it, and that he was willing to accept the case "to help her have Jonathan declared a beneficiary of the estate." Adams went to Zelnick's office the next day, July 19, 1996, where Zelnick explained that the gross amount of the estate was very large. According to Zelnick, he "wanted to make sure that she had some understanding of the size of the estate before she entered into this agreement." * * * On July 19, 1996, Adams signed a retainer agreement ("the contract") for Zelnick's firm to represent Jonathan on a one-third contingency fee basis "in his claim against the estate of Cecil D. Hylton."

* * *

In May 1997, Zelnick filed a bill of complaint for declaratory judgment, accounting and other relief on Jonathan's behalf to have Jonathan recognized as the grandchild and "issue" of Hylton Sr. for the purposes of the will and trusts. * * * A consent decree was entered on January 23, 1998, which ordered that Jonathan was "declared to be the grandchild and issue of Cecil D. Hylton" and was "entitled to all bequests, devises, distributions and benefits under the Last Will and Testament of Cecil D. Hylton and the trusts created thereunder that inure to the benefit of the grandchildren and issue of Cecil D. Hylton."

In March 1998, Jonathan's father brought a bill of complaint for declaratory judgment against Adams and Zelnick, on Jonathan's behalf, to have the contract with Zelnick declared void. Upon reaching the age of majority, Jonathan filed a petition to intervene, wherein he disaffirmed the contract. * * *

On April 6, 2000, Jonathan filed a motion for summary judgment. He asserted that the contract was "void as a matter of law" because it was not a contract for necessaries. Jonathan argued that the 1997 suit was unnecessary due to the Florida paternity decree which conclusively established Hylton's paternity. He further argued that the 1997 suit was unnecessary because the trusts could not distribute any funds until the years 2014 and 2021 and the issue was not "ripe for determination." Finally, Jonathan claimed that the contingency fee agreement was unreasonable.

The trial court granted Jonathan's motion for summary judgment and ruled that the contingency fee agreement was void. The trial court held that the contract was not binding on Jonathan because he was "in his minority" when the contract was executed. Furthermore, according to the trial court, the doctrine of necessaries did not apply to the contract "because the matter could have been adjudicated after the majority of [Jonathan], who was within a few years of his majority at the time that all of this came out."

Nonetheless, the trial court held that Zelnick was entitled to a fee under the theory of quantum meruit. * * * Zelnick testified that he spent approximately 150 to 200 hours on the case, and that in 1996–1997, his hourly rate was $200 an hour. * * *

The trial court entered judgment in favor of Zelnick in the amount of $60,000 * * * Both Zelnick and Jonathan have appealed the judgment of the trial court. * * *

Analysis
* * *

Under well and long-established Virginia law, a contract with an infant is not void, only voidable by the infant upon attaining the age of majority. [Citation.] This oft-cited rule is subject to the relief provided by the doctrine of necessaries which received thorough analysis in the case of *Bear's Adm'x v. Bear*, [citation].

In *Bear*, we explained that when a court is faced with a defense of infancy, the court has the initial duty to determine, as a matter of law, whether the "things supplied" to the infant under a contract may fall within the general class of necessaries. [Citation.] The court must further decide whether there is sufficient evidence to allow the finder of fact to determine whether the "things supplied" were in fact necessary in the instant case. If either of these preliminary inquiries is answered in the negative, the party who provided the goods or services to the infant under the disaffirmed contract cannot recover. If the preliminary inquiries are answered in the affirmative, then the finder of fact must decide, under all the circumstances, whether the "things supplied" were actually necessary to the "position and condition of the infant." If so, the party who provided the goods or services to the infant is entitled to the "reasonable value" of the things furnished. In contracts for necessaries, an infant is not bound on the express contract, but rather is bound under an implied contract to pay what the goods or services furnished were reasonably worth. [Citation.]

"[T]hings supplied," which fall into the class of necessaries, include "board, clothing and education." [Citation.] Things that are "necessary to [an infant's] subsistence and comfort, and to enable [an infant] to live according to his real position in society" are also considered part of the class of necessaries. [Citation.] * * *

Certainly, the provision of legal services may fall within the class of necessaries for which a contract by or on behalf of an infant may not be avoided or disaffirmed on the grounds of infancy. Generally, contracts for legal services related to prosecuting personal injury actions, and protecting an infant's personal liberty, security, or reputation are considered contracts for necessaries. [Citation.] "Whether attorney's services are to be considered necessaries or not depends on whether or not there is a necessity therefor. If such necessity exists, the infant may be bound. * * * If there is no necessity for services, there can be no recovery" for the services. [Citation.]

The Supreme Court of Appeals of West Virginia recently addressed this issue in a paternity action against the estate of an infant's father, brought by the infant's mother on the infant's behalf. [Citation.] The court held that contracts for legal services by infants should be regarded as contracts for necessaries in some instances because "if minors are not required to pay for legal representation, they will not be able to protect their various interests." [Citation.]

Other states have also broadened the definition of "necessaries" to include contracts for legal services for the protection of an infant's property rights. * * *

* * * The ultimate determination is an issue of fact. The trier of fact must conclude that "under all the circumstances, the things furnished were actually necessary to the position and condition of the infant * * * and whether the infant was already sufficiently supplied." [Citation.] If the contract does not fall within the "general classes of necessaries," the trial court must, as a matter of law, sustain the plea of infancy and permit the avoidance of the contract. Similarly, if the contract does fall within the "general classes of necessaries," but upon consideration of all of the circumstances, the trier of fact determines that the provision of the particular services or things was not actually necessary, the plea of infancy must be sustained. Where there is a successful avoidance of the contract, the trial court may not circumvent the successful plea of infancy by affording a recovery to the claimant on the theory of quantum meruit. However, if the plea of infancy is not sustained, the claimant is not entitled to enforcement of the express contract. Rather, as we have previously held, "even in contracts for necessaries, the infant is not bound on the express contract but on the implied contract to pay what they are reasonably worth." [Citation.]

* * *

Upon review of the record, we hold that the * * * reason stated by the trial court for holding that the necessaries doctrine did not apply, namely that the contract "was conducted while he was in his minority and he's not bound by that," is an error of law. We hold that a contract for legal services is within the "general classes of necessaries" that may defeat a plea of infancy. * * *

* * *

The trial court's determination that the necessaries doctrine did not apply was made upon motion for summary judgment filed by Jonathan. Nowhere in Jonathan's motion for summary judgment is the issue raised that the services were unnecessary at the time rendered. * * * Although Jonathan argues that the services were not necessary at all because he alleges that the Florida litigation resolved the question of his inclusion as a beneficiary under the will of Hylton Sr., the timing of the services was not even mentioned as an issue, much less as a reason for granting summary judgment. * * *

Because the trial court erred in its determination, on this record, on summary judgment, that the doctrine of necessaries did not apply, we will reverse the judgment of the trial court and remand for further proceedings, including the tak-

ing of evidence on the issue of the factual determination of necessity "under all of the circumstances." Consistent with this opinion, should the trial court upon remand hold that the doctrine of necessaries does not apply because the evidence adduced does not support the claim, the contract is avoided and no award shall be made.

Should the trial court upon remand hold that the evidence is sufficient to defeat Jonathan's plea of infancy, the trial court shall receive evidence of the reasonable value of the services rendered. * * *

Reversed and remanded.

CASE

14-4

Intoxicated Persons/Incompetent Persons
FIRST STATE BANK OF SINAI v. HYLAND
Supreme Court of South Dakota, 1987
399 N.W.2d 894
http://scholar.google.com/scholar_case?case=9646538788520684587&q=399+N.W.2d+894&hl=en&as_sdt=2,34

Henderson, J.

[Randy Hyland, unable to pay two promissory notes due September 19, 1981, negotiated with The First State Bank of Sinai (Bank) for an extension. The Bank agreed on the condition that Randy's father, Mervin, act as cosigner. Mervin, a good customer of the Bank, had executed and paid on time over sixty promissory notes within a seven-year period. Accordingly, the Bank drafted a new promissory note with an April 20, 1982, due date, which Randy took home for Mervin to sign. On April 20, 1982, the new note was unpaid. Randy, on May 5, 1982, brought the Bank a check signed by Mervin to cover the interest owed on the unpaid note and asked for another extension. The Bank agreed to a second extension, again on the condition that Mervin act as cosigner. Mervin, however, refused to sign the last note; and Randy subsequently declared bankruptcy. The Bank sued Mervin on December 19, 1982. Mervin responded that he was not liable since he had been incapacitated by liquor at the time he signed the note. He had been drinking heavily throughout this period, and in fact had been involuntarily committed to an alcoholism treatment hospital twice during the time of these events. In between commitments, however, Mervin had executed and paid his own promissory note with the Bank and had transacted business in connection with his farm. The trial court held that Mervin's contract as cosigner was void due to alcohol-related incapacity, and the Bank appealed.]

Historically, the void contract concept has been applied to nullify agreements made by mental incompetents who have contracted * * * after a judicial determination of incapacity had been entered. [Citations.] * * *

Mervin had numerous and prolonged problems stemming from his inability to handle alcohol. However, he

was not judicially declared incompetent during the note's signing. * * *

* * *

Contractual obligations incurred by intoxicated persons may be voidable. [Citation.] Voidable contracts (contracts other than those entered into following a judicial determination of incapacity * * *) may be rescinded by the previously disabled party. [Citation.] However, disaffirmance must be prompt, upon the recovery of the intoxicated party's mental abilities, and upon his notice of the agreement, if he had forgotten it. [Citation.] * * *

A voidable contract may also be ratified by the party who had contracted while disabled. Upon ratification, the contract becomes a fully valid legal obligation. [Citation.] Ratification can either be express or implied by conduct. [Citations.] In addition, failure of a party to disaffirm a contract over a period of time may, by itself, ripen into a ratification, especially if rescission will result in prejudice to the other party. [Citations.]

Mervin received both verbal notice from Randy and written notice from Bank on or about April 27, 1982, that the note was overdue. On May 5, 1982, Mervin paid the interest owing with a check which Randy delivered to Bank. This by itself could amount to ratification through conduct. If Mervin wished to avoid the contract, he should have then exercised his right of rescission. We find it impossible to believe that Mervin paid almost $900 in interest without, in his own mind, accepting responsibility for the note. His assertion that paying interest on the note relieved his obligation is equally untenable in light of his numerous past experiences with promissory notes.

* * *

We conclude that Mervin's obligation to Bank is not void. * * * Mervin's obligation on the note was voidable and his subsequent failure to disaffirm (lack of rescission) and his payment of interest (ratification) then transformed the voidable contract into one that is fully binding upon him.

We reverse and remand.

QUESTIONS

1. Michael, a minor, operates a one-man automobile repair shop. Anderson, having heard of Michael's good work on other cars, takes her car to Michael's shop for a thorough engine overhaul. Michael, while overhauling Anderson's engine, carelessly fits an unsuitable piston ring on one of the pistons, with the result that Anderson's engine is seriously damaged. Michael offers to return the sum that Anderson paid him for his work, but refuses to pay for the damage. Can Anderson recover from Michael in tort for the damage to her engine? Why?

2. Explain the outcome of each transaction.
   a. On March 20, Andy Small became seventeen years old, but he appeared to be at least twenty-one. On April 1, he moved into a rooming house in Chicago where he orally agreed to pay the landlady $300 a month for room and board, payable at the end of each month. On April 30, he refused to pay his landlady for his room and board for the month of April.
   b. On April 4, he went to Honest Hal's Carfeteria and signed a contract to buy a used car on credit with a small down payment. He made no representation as to his age, but Honest Hal represented the car to be in A-1 condition, which it subsequently turned out not to be. On April 25, he returned the car to Honest Hal and demanded a refund of his down payment.
   c. On April 7, Andy sold and conveyed to Adam Smith a parcel of real estate that he owned. On April 28, he demanded that Adam Smith reconvey the land although the purchase price, which Andy received in cash, had been spent in riotous living.

3. Jones, a minor, owned a 2012 automobile. She traded it to Stone for a 2013 car. Jones went on a three-week trip and found that the 2013 car was not as good as the 2012 car. She asked Stone to return the 2012 car but was told that it had been sold to Tate. Jones thereupon sued Tate for the return of the 2012 car. Is Jones entitled to regain ownership of the 2012 car? Explain.

4. On May 7, Roy, a minor, a resident of Smithton, purchased an automobile from Royal Motors, Inc., for $18,750 in cash. On the same day, he bought a motor scooter from Marks, also a minor, for $750 and paid him in full. On June 5, two days before attaining his majority, Roy disaffirmed the contracts and offered to return the car and the motor scooter to the respective sellers. Royal Motors and Marks each refused the offers. On June 16, Roy brought separate appropriate actions against Royal Motors and Marks to recover the purchase price of the car and the motor scooter. By agreement on July 30, Royal Motors accepted the automobile. Royal then filed a counterclaim against Roy for the reasonable rental value of the car between June 5 and July 30. The car was not damaged during this period. Royal knew that Roy lived twenty-five miles from his place of employment in Smithton and that he would probably drive the car, as he did, to provide himself transportation. Decision as to (a) Roy's action against Royal Motors, Inc., and its counterclaim against Roy; and (b) Roy's action against Marks?

5. On October 1, George Jones entered into a contract with Johnson Motor Company, a dealer in automobiles, to buy a used car for $10,850. He paid $1,100 down and, under the agreement, was to make monthly payments thereafter of $325 each. Jones was seventeen years old at the time he made the contract, but he represented to the company that he was twenty-one years old because he was afraid that if the company knew his real age, it would not sell the car to him. His appearance was that of a man of twenty-one years of age. After making the first payment on November 1, he failed to make any more payments. On December 15, the company repossessed the car under the terms provided in the contract. At that time, the car had been damaged and was in need of repairs. On December 20, George Jones became of age and at once disaffirmed the contract and demanded the return of the $1,425 he had paid on it. On refusal of the company to do so, George Jones brought an action to recover the $1,425, and the company set up a counterclaim for $1,500 for expenses it incurred in repairing the car. Who will prevail? Why?

6. Rebecca entered into a written contract to sell certain real estate to Mary, a minor, for $80,000, payable $4,000 on the execution of the contract and $800 on the first day of each month thereafter until paid. Mary paid the $4,000 down payment and eight monthly installments before attaining her majority. Thereafter, Mary made

two additional monthly payments and caused the contract to be recorded in the county where the real estate was located. Mary was then advised by her attorney that the contract was voidable. After being so advised, Mary immediately tendered the contract to Rebecca, together with a deed reconveying all of Mary's interest in the property to Rebecca. Also, Mary demanded that Rebecca return the money she had paid under the contract. Rebecca refused the tender and declined to repay any portion of the money paid to her by Mary. Can Mary cancel the contract and recover the amount paid to Rebecca? Explain.

7. Anita sold and delivered an automobile to Marvin, a minor. Marvin, during his minority, returned the automobile to Anita, saying that he disaffirmed the sale. Anita accepted the automobile and said she would return the purchase price to Marvin the next day. Later in the day, Marvin changed his mind, took the automobile without Anita's knowledge, and sold it to Chris. Anita had not returned the purchase price when Marvin took the car. On what theory, if any, can Anita recover from Marvin? Explain.

8. Ira, who in 2011 had been found innocent of a criminal offense because of insanity, was released from a hospital for the criminally insane during the summer of 2012 and since that time has been a reputable and well-respected citizen and businessperson. On February 1, 2013, Ira and Shirley entered into a contract in which Ira would sell his farm to Shirley for $100,000. Ira now seeks to void the contract. Shirley insists that Ira is fully competent and has no right to avoid the contract. Who will prevail? Why?

9. Daniel, while under the influence of alcohol, agreed to sell his 2011 automobile to Belinda for $13,000. The next morning, when Belinda went to Daniel's house with the $13,000 in cash, Daniel stated that he did not remember the transaction but that "a deal is a deal." One week after completing the sale, Daniel decides that he wishes to avoid the contract. What result?

CASE PROBLEMS

10. Langstraat, age seventeen, owned a motorcycle that he insured against liability with Midwest Mutual Insurance Company. He signed a notice of rejection attached to the policy indicating that he did not desire to purchase uninsured motorists' coverage from the insurance company. Later he was involved in an accident with another motorcycle owned and operated by a party who was uninsured. Langstraat now seeks to recover from the insurance company, asserting that his rejection was not a valid rejection because he is a minor. Can Langstraat recover from Midwest? Explain.

11. G.A.S. married his wife, S.I.S., on January 19, 2003. He began to suffer mental health problems in 2009, during which year he was hospitalized at the Delaware State Hospital for eight weeks. Similar illnesses occurred in 2011 and the early part of 2013, with G.A.S. suffering from such symptoms as paranoia and loss of a sense of reality. In early 2014, G.A.S. was still committed to the Delaware State Hospital, attending a regular job during the day and returning to the hospital at night. During this time, he entered into a separation agreement prepared by his wife's attorney.

G.A.S., however, never spoke with the attorney about the contents of the agreement; nor did he read it prior to signing. Moreover, G.A.S. was not independently represented by counsel when he executed this agreement. Can G.A.S. disaffirm the separation agreement? Explain.

12. A fifteen-year-old minor was employed by Midway Toyota, Inc. On August 18, 2012, the minor, while engaged in lifting heavy objects, injured his lower back. In October 2012 he underwent surgery to remove a herniated disk. Midway Toyota paid him the appropriate amount of temporary total disability payments ($53.36 per week) from August 18, 2012, through November 15, 2013. In February 2014 a final settlement was reached for 150 weeks of permanent partial disability benefits totaling $6,136.40. Tom Mazurek represented Midway Toyota in the negotiations leading to the agreement and negotiated directly with the minor and his mother, Hermione Parrent. The final settlement agreement was signed by the minor only. Mrs. Parrent, who was present at the time, did not object to the signing, but neither she nor anyone else of "legal guardian status" co-signed the agreement. The minor later sought to disaffirm the agreement and reopen his workers' compensation case. The workers' compensation court denied his petition, holding that Mrs. Parrent "participated fully in consideration of the offered final settlement and ... ratified and approved it on behalf of her ward to the same legal effect as if she had actually signed [it]." The minor appealed. Decision?

13. Rose, a minor, bought a new Buick Riviera from Sheehan Buick. Seven months later, while still a minor, he attempted to disaffirm the purchase. Sheehan Buick refused to accept the return of the car or to refund the purchase price. Rose, at the time of the purchase, gave all the appearance of being of legal age. The car had been used by him to carry on his school, business, and social activities. Can Rose successfully disaffirm the contract?

14. L. D. Robertson bought a pickup truck from King and Julian, doing business as the Julian Pontiac Company. Robertson, at the time of purchase, was seventeen years old, living at home with his parents, and driving his father's truck around the county to different construction jobs. According to the sales contract, he traded in a passenger car for the truck and was given $2,723 credit toward the truck's $6,743 purchase price, agreeing to pay the remainder in monthly installments. After he paid the first month's installment, the truck caught fire and was rendered useless. The insurance agent, upon finding that Robertson was a minor, refused to deal with him. Consequently, Robertson sued to exercise his right as a minor to rescind the contract and to recover the purchase price he had already paid ($2,723 credit for the car plus the one month's installment). The defendants argue that Robertson, even as a minor, cannot rescind the contract as it was for a necessary item. Are they correct?

15. Haydocy Pontiac sold Jennifer Lee an automobile for $21,552, of which $20,402 was financed with a note and security agreement. At the time of the sale Lee, age twenty, represented to Haydocy that she was twenty-one years old, the age of majority, and capable of contracting. After receiving the car, Lee allowed John Roberts to take possession of it. Roberts took the car and has not returned. Lee has failed to make any further payments on the car. Haydocy has sued to recover on the note, but Lee disaffirms the contract, claiming that she was too young to enter into a valid contract. Can Haydocy recover the money from Lee? Explain.

16. Carol White ordered a $225 pair of contact lenses through an optometrist. White, an emancipated minor, paid $100 by check and agreed to pay the remaining $125 at a later time. The doctor ordered the lenses, incurring a debt of $110. After the lenses were ordered, White called to cancel her order and stopped payment on the $100 check. The lenses could be used by no one but White. The doctor sued White for the value of the lenses. Will the doctor be able to recover the money from White? Explain.

17. Williamson, her mortgage in default, was threatened with foreclosure on her home. She decided to sell the house. The Matthewses learned of this and contacted her about the matter. Williamson claims that she offered to sell her equity for $17,000 and that the Matthewses agreed to pay off the mortgage. The Matthewses contend that the asking price was $1,700. On September 27, the parties signed a contract of sale, which stated the purchase price to be $1,800 (an increase of $100 to account for furniture in the house) plus the unpaid balance of the mortgage. The parties met again on October 10 to sign the deed. Later that day, Williamson, concerned that she had not received her full $17,000 consideration, contacted an attorney. Can Williamson set aside the sale based upon inadequate consideration and mental weakness due to intoxication?

18. Halbman, a minor, purchased a used Oldsmobile from Lemke for $11,250. Under the terms of the contract, Halbman would pay $1,000 down and the balance in $125 weekly installments. Upon making the down payment, Halbman received possession of the car, but Lemke retained the title until the balance was paid. After Halbman had made his first four payments, a connecting rod in the car's engine broke. Lemke denied responsibility, but offered to help Halbman repair it if Halbman would provide the parts. Halbman, however, placed the car in a garage where the repairs cost $637.40. Halbman never paid the repair bill.

Hoping to avoid any liability for the vehicle, Lemke transferred title to Halbman even though Halbman never paid the balance owed. Halbman returned the title with a letter disaffirming the contract and demanded return of the money paid. Lemke refused. Because the repair bill remained unpaid, the garage removed the car's engine and transmission and towed the body to Halbman's father's house. Vandalism during the period of storage rendered the car unsalvageable. Several times Halbman requested Lemke to remove the car. Lemke refused. Halbman sued Lemke for the return of his consideration, and Lemke countersued for the amount still owed on the contract. Decision?

19. On June 11, Chagnon bought a used Buick from Keser for $9,950. Chagnon, who was then a minor, obtained the contract by falsely advising Keser that he was over the age of majority. On September 25, two months and four days after reaching his majority, Chagnon disaffirmed the contract and, ten days later, returned the Buick to Keser. He then brought suit to recover the money he had paid for the automobile. Keser counterclaimed that he suffered damages as the direct result of Chagnon's false representation of his age. A trial was brought to the court, sitting without a jury, all of which culminated in a judgment in favor of Chagnon against Keser in the sum of $6,557.80. This particular sum was

arrived at by the trial court in the following manner: the trial court found that Chagnon initially purchased the Buick for the sum of $9,950 and that he was entitled to the return of his $9,950; and then, by way of setoff, the trial court subtracted from the $9,950 the sum of $3,392.20, apparently representing the difference between the purchase price paid for the vehicle and the reasonable value of the Buick on October 5, the date when the Buick was returned to Keser. Is this legally correct? Do you agree? Why?

20. On April 29, 2013, Kirsten Fletcher and John E. Marshall III jointly signed a lease to rent an apartment for the term beginning on July 1, 2013, and ending on June 30, 2014, for a monthly rent of $525 per month. At the time the lease was signed, Marshall was not yet eighteen years of age. Marshall turned eighteen on May 30, 2013. Two weeks later, the couple moved into the apartment. About two months later, Marshall moved out to attend college,

but Fletcher remained. She paid the rent herself for the remaining ten months of the lease and then sought contribution for Marshall's share of the rent plus court costs in the amount of $2,500. Can Fletcher collect from Marshall?

21. Rogers was a nineteen-year-old (the age of majority then being twenty-one) high school graduate pursuing a civil engineering degree when he learned that his wife was expecting a child. As a result, he quit school and sought assistance from Gastonia Personnel Corporation in finding a job. Rogers signed a contract with the employment agency providing that he would pay the agency a service charge if it obtained suitable employment for him. The employment agency found him such a job, but Rogers refused to pay the service charge, asserting that he was a minor when he signed the contract. Gastonia sued to recover the agreed-upon service charge from Rogers. Should Rogers be liable under his contract? If so, for how much?

TAKING SIDES

Joseph Eugene Dodson, age sixteen, purchased a used pickup truck from Burns and Mary Shrader. The Shraders owned and operated Shrader's Auto Sales. Dodson paid $14,900 in cash for the truck. At the time of sale, the Shraders did not question Dodson's age, but thought he was eighteen or nineteen. Dodson made no misrepresentation concerning his age. Nine months after the date of purchase, the truck began to develop mechanical problems. A mechanic diagnosed the problem as a burnt valve but could not be certain. Dodson, who could not afford the repairs, continued to drive the truck until one month later, when the engine "blew up." Dodson parked the vehicle in the front yard of his parents' home and contacted the Shraders to rescind the purchase of the truck and to request a full refund.

a. What arguments would support Dodson's termination of the contract?

b. What arguments would support Shrader's position that the contract is not voidable?

c. Which side should prevail? Explain.

CONTRACTS IN WRITING

CHAPTER OUTCOMES

After reading and studying this chapter, you should be able to:

- Identify and explain the five types of contracts covered by the general contract statute of frauds and the contracts covered by the Uniform Commercial Code (UCC) statute of frauds provision.

- Describe the writings that are required to satisfy the general contract and the UCC statute of frauds provisions.

- Identify and describe the other methods of complying with the general contract and the UCC statute of frauds provisions.

- Explain the parol evidence rule and identify the situations to which the rule does not apply.

- Discuss the rules that aid in the interpretation of a contract.

An **oral** contract, that is, one not written, is in every way as enforceable as a written contract unless otherwise provided by statute. Although most contracts are not required to be in writing to be enforceable, it is highly desirable that significant contracts be written. Written contracts avoid the numerous problems that proving the terms of oral contracts inevitably involves. The process of setting down the contractual terms in a written document also tends to clarify the terms and to reveal problems the parties might not otherwise foresee. Moreover, the terms of a written contract do not change over time, while the parties' recollections of the terms might.

When the parties do reduce their agreement to a complete and final written expression, the law (under the parol evidence rule) honors this document by not allowing the parties to introduce any evidence in a lawsuit that would alter, modify, or vary the terms of the written contract. Nevertheless, the parties may differ as to the proper or intended meaning of language contained in the written agreement where such language is ambiguous or susceptible to different interpretations. To ascertain the proper meaning requires an interpretation, or construction, of the contract. The rules of construction permit the parties to introduce evidence to resolve ambiguity and to show the meaning of the language employed and the sense in which both parties used it.

This chapter will examine (1) the types of contracts that must be in writing to be enforceable, (2) the parol evidence rule, and (3) the rules of contractual interpretation.

STATUTE OF FRAUDS

The statute of frauds requires that certain designated types of contracts be evidenced by a writing to be enforceable. The original statute became law in 1677, when the English Parliament adopted "An Act for Prevention of Frauds and Perjuries," commonly referred to as the statute of frauds. From the early days of U.S. history practically every State had and continues to have a statute of frauds patterned upon the original English statute.

The statute of frauds has no relation whatever to any kind of fraud practiced in the making of contracts. The common law rules relating to such fraud are discussed in *Chapter 11*. The purpose of the statute is to prevent perjured testimony in court from creating fraud in the proof of certain oral contracts, which purpose the statute accomplishes by requiring that certain contracts be evidenced by a signed writing. On the other hand, the statute does not prevent the performance of oral contracts if the parties are willing to perform. In brief, the statute relates only to the proof or evidence of a contract. It has nothing to do with the circumstances surrounding the making of a contract or with a contract's validity.

Significant contracts should be memorialized in a writing signed by both parties.

CONTRACTS WITHIN THE STATUTE OF FRAUDS

Many more types of contracts are *not* subject to the statute of frauds than are subject to it. Most oral contracts, as previously indicated, are as enforceable and valid as a written contract. If, however, a given contract is subject to the statute of frauds, the contract is said to be **within** the statute; to be enforceable, it must comply with the statute's requirements. All other types of contracts are said to be "not within" or "outside" the statute and need not comply with its requirements to be enforceable.

The following kinds of contracts are within the original English statute and remain within most State statutes; compliance requires a writing signed by the party to be charged (the party against whom the contract is to be enforced).

A sixth type of contract within the statute applied to contracts for the sale of goods. Section 2-201 of the Uniform Commercial Code (UCC) now governs the enforceability of contracts of this kind.

1. Promises to answer for the duty of another
2. Promises of an executor or administrator to answer personally for a duty of the decedent whose funds he is administering
3. Agreements upon consideration of marriage
4. Agreements for the transfer of an interest in land
5. Agreements not to be performed within one year

6. Sale of goods over $500

The various provisions of the statute of frauds apply independently. Accordingly, a contract for the sale of an interest in land also may be a contract in consideration of marriage, a contract not to be performed in one year, *and* a contract for the sale of goods.

In addition to those contracts specified in the original statute, most States require that other contracts be evidenced by a writing as well; for example, a contract to make a will, to authorize an agent to sell or purchase real estate, or to pay a commission to a real estate broker. Moreover, Article 1 of the UCC requires that a contract for the sale of securities, contracts creating certain types of security interests, and contracts for the sale of other personal property for more than $5,000 also be in writing. The 2001 Revision to Article 1 has deleted this requirement.

ELECTRONIC RECORDS

One significant impediment to e-commerce has been the questionable enforceability of contracts entered into through electronic means such as the Internet or e-mail because of the writing requirements under contract and sales law (statute of frauds). In response, the **Uniform Electronic Transactions Act (UETA)** was promulgated by the Uniform Law Commission (ULC) in July 1999 and has been adopted by forty-seven States. The three states that have not adopted the UETA, Illinois, New York, and Washington, have statutes pertaining to electronic transactions. UETA applies only to transactions between parties each of which has agreed to conduct transactions by electronic means. It gives full effect to electronic contracts, encouraging their widespread use, and develops a uniform legal framework for their implementation. UETA protects electronic signatures and contracts from being denied enforcement because of the statute of frauds. Section 7 of UETA accomplishes this by providing the following:

1. A record or signature may not be denied legal effect or enforceability solely because it is in electronic form.
2. A contract may not be denied legal effect or enforceability solely because an electronic record was used in its formation.
3. If a law requires a record to be in writing, an electronic record satisfies the law.
4. If a law requires a signature, an electronic signature satisfies the law.

Section 14 of UETA further validates contracts formed by machines functioning as electronic agents for parties to a transaction: "A contract may be formed by the interaction of electronic agents of the parties, even if no individual was aware of or reviewed the electronic agents' actions or the resulting terms and agreements." The Act excludes from its coverage wills, codicils, and testamentary trusts as well as all Articles of the UCC except Articles 2 and 2A.

In addition, Congress in 2000 enacted the **Electronic Signatures in Global and National Commerce (E-Sign)**. The Act, which uses language very similar to that of UETA, makes electronic records and signatures valid and enforceable across the United States for many types of transactions in or affecting interstate or foreign commerce. E-Sign does not generally preempt UETA. E-Sign does not require any person to agree to use or accept electronic records or electronic signatures. The Act defines transactions quite broadly to include the sale, lease, exchange, and licensing of personal property and services, as well as the sale, lease, exchange, or other disposition of any interest in real property. E-Sign defines an electronic record as "a contract or other record created, generated, sent, communicated, received, or stored by electronic means." It defines an electronic signature as "an electronic sound, symbol, or process, attached to or logically associated with a contract or other record and executed or adopted by a person with the intent to sign the record." Like UETA, E-Sign ensures that Internet and e-mail agreements will not be unenforceable because of the statute of frauds by providing that

1. a signature, contract, or other record relating to such transaction may not be denied legal effect, validity, or enforceability solely because it is in electronic form; and
2. a contract relating to such transaction may not be denied legal effect, validity, or enforceability solely because an electronic signature or electronic record was used in its formation.

To protect consumers, E-Sign provides that they must consent *electronically* to conducting transactions with electronic records after being informed of the types of hardware and software required. Prior to consent, consumers must also receive a "clear and conspicuous" statement informing consumers of their right to (1) have the record provided on paper or in nonelectronic form; (2) after consenting to electronic records, receive paper copies of the electronic record; and (3) withdraw consent to receiving electronic records.

As defined by E-Sign, an electronic agent is a computer program or other automated means used independently to initiate an action or respond to electronic records or performances in whole or in part without review or action by an individual at the time of the action or response. The Act validates contracts or other records relating to a transaction in or affecting interstate or foreign commerce formed by electronic agents so long as the action of each electronic agent is legally attributable to the person to be bound.

E-Sign specifically excludes certain transactions, including (1) wills, codicils, and testamentary trusts; (2) adoptions, divorces, and other matters of family law; and (3) the UCC other than sales and leases of goods.

SURETYSHIP PROVISION

The **suretyship** provision applies to a contractual promise by a surety (*promisor*) to a **creditor** (*promisee*) to perform the duties or obligations of a third person (**principal debtor**) if the principal debtor does not perform. Thus, if a mother tells a merchant to extend $1,000 worth of credit to her son and says, "If he doesn't pay, I will," the promise must be in writing (or have a sufficient electronic record) to be enforceable. The factual situation can be reduced to the simple statement, "If X doesn't pay, I will." The promise is said to be **collateral**, in that the promisor is not primarily liable. The mother does not promise to pay in any event; her promise is to pay only if the one primarily obligated, her son, defaults.

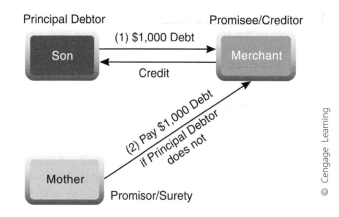

The rule applies only to cases involving three parties and two contracts. The primary contract, between the principal debtor and the creditor, creates the indebtedness. The collateral contract is made by the third person (surety) directly with the creditor, whereby the surety promises to pay the debt to the creditor in case the principal debtor fails to do so. For a complete discussion of suretyship see *Chapter 37*.

ORIGINAL PROMISE If the promisor makes an **original promise** by undertaking to become primarily liable, then the statute of frauds does not apply. For example, a father tells a merchant to deliver certain items to his daughter and says, "I will pay $400 for them." The father is not promising to answer for the debt of another; rather, he is making the debt his own. It is to the father, and the father alone, that the merchant extends credit; only from the father may the creditor seek payment. The statute of frauds does not apply, and the promise may be oral.

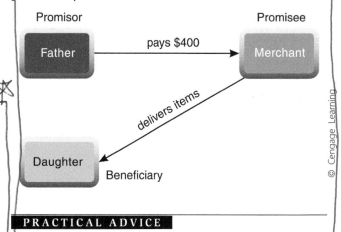

PRACTICAL ADVICE

When entering into a contract with two parties promising you that they will perform, make them both original promisors and avoid having a surety. In any event, if the contract is for a significant amount of money, have both parties sign a written agreement.

MAIN PURPOSE DOCTRINE The courts have developed an exception to the suretyship provision based on the purpose or object of the promisor, called the "main purpose doctrine" or "leading object rule." Where the object or purpose of the promisor is to obtain an economic benefit for himself, the promise is *not* within the statute. Restatement, Section 116. The expected benefit to the surety "must be such as to justify the conclusion that his main purpose in making the promise is to advance his own interest." Restatement, Section 116, Comment b. The fact that the surety received consideration for his promise or that he might receive a slight and indirect advantage is insufficient to bring the promise within the main purpose doctrine.

Suppose that a supply company has refused to furnish materials upon the credit of a building contractor. Facing a possible slowdown in the construction of his building, the owner of the land promises the supplier that if he will extend credit to the contractor, the owner will pay if the contractor does not. Here, the primary purpose of the promisor is to serve his own economic interest, even though the performance of the promise would discharge the duty of another. The intent to benefit the contractor is at most incidental, and courts will uphold oral promises of this type.

◆ SEE CASE 15-1

PROMISE MADE TO DEBTOR The suretyship provision has been interpreted not to include promises made to a debtor. For example, D owes a debt to C. S promises D that she will pay D's debt in return for valid consideration from D. Because S made the promise to the debtor (D), not the creditor, the promise may be oral. The promise is not a collateral promise to pay C if D fails to pay and thus is not a promise to discharge the obligation of another.

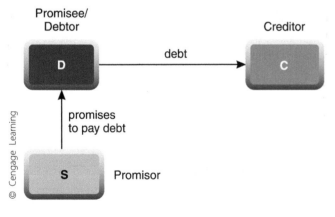

EXECUTOR-ADMINISTRATOR PROVISION

The executor-administrator provision applies to the contractual promises of an executor of a decedent's will, or to those of the administrator of his estate if the decedent dies without a will, to answer personally for a duty of the decedent. An **executor** or **administrator** is a person appointed by a court to carry on, subject to order of court, the administration of the estate of a deceased person. If the will of a decedent nominates a certain person as executor, the court customarily appoints that person. (For a more detailed discussion of executors and administrators, see *Chapter 50*.) If an executor or administrator promises to pay personally a debt of the decedent, the promise must be in writing—or in proper electronic form—to be enforceable. For example, Brian, who is Ann's son and executor of her will, recognizing that Ann's estate will not provide funds sufficient to pay all of her debts, orally promises Curtis, one of Ann's creditors, that he, Brian, will personally pay all of his mother's creditors in full in return for valid consideration from Curtis. Brian's oral promise is not enforceable. This provision does not apply to promises to pay debts of the deceased out of assets of the estate.

The executor-administrator provision is thus a specific application of the suretyship provision. Accordingly, the exceptions to the suretyship provision apply to this provision as well.

MARRIAGE PROVISION

The notable feature of the marriage provision is that it does *not* apply to mutual promises to marry. The provision applies only if a promise to marry is made in consideration for some promise other than a reciprocal promise to marry. Restatement, Section 124. If, for example, Greg and Betsy each orally promise and agree to marry each other, their agreement is not within the statute and is a binding contract between them. If, however, Greg promises to convey title to a certain farm to Betsy if she accepts his proposal of marriage, their agreement would fall within the statute of frauds.

LAND CONTRACT PROVISION

The land contract provision covers promises to transfer "any interest in land," which includes any right, privilege, power, or immunity in real property. Restatement, Section 125. Thus, all promises to transfer, buy, or pay for an interest in land, including ownership interests, leases, mortgages, options, and easements, are within the provision.

The land contract provision does not include contracts to transfer an interest in personal property. It also does not cover short-term leases, which by statute in most States are those for one year or less; contracts to build a building on a piece of land; contracts to do work on the land; or contracts to insure a building on the land.

The courts may enforce an oral contract for the transfer of an interest in land if the party seeking enforcement has so changed his position in reasonable reliance upon the contract that injustice can be prevented only by enforcing the contract. Restatement, Section 129. In applying this **part performance** exception, many States require that the transferee has paid a portion or all of the purchase price *and* either has taken possession of the real estate or has started to make valuable improvements on the land. For example, Aaron orally agrees to sell land to Barbara for $30,000. With Aaron's consent, Barbara takes possession of the land, pays Aaron $10,000, builds a house on the land, and occupies it. Several years later, Aaron repudiates the contract. The courts will enforce the contract against Aaron. On the other hand, the courts will not enforce the promise unless equity so demands.

An oral promise by a purchaser is also enforceable if the seller fully performs by conveying the property to the purchaser. As previously indicated, however, payment of part or all of the price is not sufficient in itself to remove the contract from the scope of the statute.

ONE-YEAR PROVISION

The statute of frauds requires all contracts that *cannot* be fully performed within one year of their making to be in writing or in proper electronic form. Restatement, Section 130.

THE POSSIBILITY TEST To determine whether a contract can be performed within a year, the courts ask whether it is *possible* to complete its performance within a year. The **possibility test** does not ask whether the agreement is likely to be performed within one year from the date it was formed; nor does it ask whether the parties think that performance will be within the year. The enforceability of the contract depends not on probabilities or on the actuality of subsequent events but on whether the terms of the contract make it possible for performance to occur within one year. For example, an oral contract between Alice and Bill for Alice to build a bridge, which should reasonably take three years, is enforceable if it is possible, although extremely unlikely and difficult, for Alice to perform the contract in one year. Similarly, if Alice agrees to employ Bill for life, this contract also is not within the statute of frauds. Given the possibility that Bill may die within the year (in which case the contract would be completely performed), the contract is therefore one that is *fully performable* within a year. Contracts of indefinite duration are likewise excluded from the provision. On the other hand, an oral contract to employ another person for thirteen months could not possibly be performed within a year and is unenforceable.

◆ SEE CASE 15-2

COMPUTATION OF TIME The year runs from the time the agreement is made, not from the time when the performance

is to begin. For example, on January 1, 2013, A orally hires B to work for eleven months starting on May 1, 2013. That contract will be fully performed on March 31, 2014, which is more than one year after January 1, 2013, the date the contract was made. Consequently, it is *within* the statute of frauds and unenforceable as it is oral.

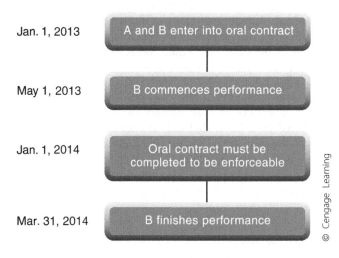

Jan. 1, 2013	A and B enter into oral contract
May 1, 2013	B commences performance
Jan. 1, 2014	Oral contract must be completed to be enforceable
Mar. 31, 2014	B finishes performance

© Cengage Learning

Similarly, a contract for a year's performance, which is to begin three days after the date on which the contract is made, is within the statute and, if oral, is unenforceable. If, however, the performance is to begin the following day or, under the terms of the agreement, could have begun the following day, the contract is not within the statute and need not be in writing, as the one year's performance would be completed on the anniversary date of the making of the contract.

FULL PERFORMANCE BY ONE PARTY Where one party to a contract has fully performed, most courts hold that the promise of the other party is enforceable, even though by its terms the performance of the contract was not possible within the period of a year. Restatement, Section 130. For example, Vince borrows $4,800 from Julie, orally promising to pay Julie $4,800 in three annual installments of $1,600. Vince's promise is enforceable, notwithstanding the one-year provision, because Julie has fully performed by making the loan.

SALE OF GOODS

The original statute of frauds, which applied to contracts for the sale of goods, has been used as a prototype for the UCC Article 2 statute of frauds provision. Section 2–201 of the UCC provides that a contract for the sale of goods for the price of *$500 or more* is not enforceable unless there is some writing or record sufficient to indicate that the parties have made a contract for sale. **Goods**, as previously indicated, are defined as movable personal property. Section 2–105(1).

The definition expressly includes growing crops and unborn animals.

ADMISSION The Code permits an oral contract for the sale of goods to be enforced against a party who in his pleading, testimony, or otherwise in court admits that a contract was made, but limits enforcement to the quantity of goods so admitted. Section 2–201(3)(b). The language "otherwise in court" may include pretrial deposition and written interrogatories of the defendant. Some courts now apply this exception to other statute of frauds provisions.

SPECIALLY MANUFACTURED GOODS The Code permits a seller to enforce an oral contract for goods specially manufactured for a buyer, but only if evidence indicates that the goods were made for the buyer and the seller can show that he made a *substantial beginning* of their manufacture prior to receiving any notice of repudiation. Section 2–201(3)(a). If goods manufactured on special order are nonetheless readily marketable in the ordinary course of the seller's business, this exception does not apply.

For example, if Jim brings an action against Robin alleging breach of an oral contract under which Robin agreed to purchase from Jim three million balloons with Robin's trademark imprinted on them at a price of $30,000, the action is not subject to the defense of the statute of frauds unless Robin can show (1) that the balloons are suitable for sale to other buyers, which is highly improbable in view of the trademark, or (2) that Jim received notice of repudiation before he had made a substantial start on the production of the balloons or had otherwise substantially committed himself to procuring them.

◆ **SEE CASE 15-3**

DELIVERY OR PAYMENT AND ACCEPTANCE Prior to the Code, delivery and acceptance of part of the goods or payment of part of the price made the entire oral contract enforceable against the buyer who had received part delivery or against the seller who had received part payment. Under the Code, such "partial performance" validates the contract only for the goods that have been accepted or for which payment has been accepted. Section 2–201(3)(c). To illustrate, Johnson orally agrees to buy one thousand watches from Barnes for $15,000. Barnes delivers three hundred watches to Johnson, who receives and accepts the watches. The oral contract is enforceable to the extent of three hundred watches ($4,500)—those received and accepted—but is unenforceable to the extent of seven hundred watches ($10,500).

◈ **SEE FIGURE 15-1: The Statute of Frauds**

◆ FIGURE 15-1: **The Statute of Frauds**

Contracts within the Statute of Frauds	Exceptions
Suretyship—a promise to answer for the duty of another	• Main purpose rule • Original promise • Promise made to debtor
Executor-Administrator—a promise to answer personally for debt of decedent	• Main purpose rule • Original promise • Promise made to debtor
Agreements made upon consideration of marriage	• Mutual promises to marry
Agreements for the transfer of an interest in land	• Part performance plus detrimental reliance • Seller conveys property
Agreements not to be performed within one year	• Full performance by one party • Possibility of performance within one year
Sale of goods for $500 or more	• Admission • Specially manufactured goods • Delivery or payment acceptance

© Cengage Learning

MODIFICATION OR RESCISSION OF CONTRACTS WITHIN THE STATUTE OF FRAUDS

Oral contracts modifying previously existing contracts are unenforceable if the resulting contract is within the statute of frauds. The reverse is also true: an oral modification of a prior contract is enforceable if the new contract is not within the statute. Thus, examples of unenforceable oral contractual modifications include an oral promise to guarantee additional duties of another, an oral agreement to substitute different land for that described in the original contract, and an oral agreement to extend an employee's contract for six months to a total of two years. On the other hand, an oral agreement to modify an employee's contract from two years to six months at a higher salary is not within the statute of frauds and is enforceable.

By extension, an oral rescission is effective and discharges all unperformed duties under the original contract. For example, Linda and Donald enter into a written contract of employment for a two-year term. Later they orally agree to rescind the contract. The oral agreement is effective, and the written contract is rescinded. Where, however, land has been transferred, an agreement to rescind the transaction constitutes a contract to retransfer the land and is within the statute of frauds.

Under the UCC, the decisive point is the contract price *after* the modification. Section 2–209(3). If the parties enter into an oral contract to sell for $450 a motorcycle to be delivered to the buyer and later, prior to delivery, orally agree that the seller shall paint the motorcycle and install new tires and that the buyer shall pay a price of $550, the modified contract is unenforceable. Conversely, if the parties have a written contract for the sale of two hundred bushels of wheat at a price of $4.00 per bushel and later orally agree to decrease the quantity to one hundred bushels at the same price per bushel, the agreement, as modified, is for a total price of $400 and thus is enforceable.

> **PRACTICAL ADVICE**
>
> *When significantly modifying an existing common law contract, make sure that consideration is given and that the modification is in writing and signed by both parties.*

COMPLIANCE WITH THE STATUTE OF FRAUDS

Even though a contract is within the statute of frauds, a sufficient *writing, memorandum,* or *record* may justify its enforcement. The writing or record need not be in any specific form, nor be an attempt by the parties to enter into a binding contract, nor represent their entire agreement: it need only comply with the requirements of the statute of frauds.

GENERAL CONTRACTS PROVISIONS

The English statute of frauds and most modern statutes of frauds require that the agreement be evidenced by a writing or record to be enforceable. The note, memorandum, or record, which may be formal or informal, must

1. specify the parties to the contract;
2. specify with reasonable certainty the subject matter and the essential terms of the unperformed promises; and
3. be signed by the party to be charged or by his agent.

The statute's purpose in requiring a writing or record is to ensure that the parties have entered into a contract. The writing or record, therefore, need not exist at the time of the litigation; showing that the memorandum once existed is sufficient.

The memorandum may be a receipt or a check. It may be such that the parties themselves view the memorandum as having no legal significance whatever, as, for example, a personal letter between the parties, an interdepartmental communication, an advertisement, or the record books of a business. The writing or record need not have been delivered to the party who seeks to take advantage of it, and it may even contain a repudiation of the oral agreement. For example, Adrian and Joseph enter into an oral agreement that Adrian will sell Blackacre to Joseph for $5,000. Adrian subsequently receives a better offer and sends Joseph a signed letter, which begins by reciting all the material terms of the oral agreement. The letter concludes, "Since my agreement to sell Blackacre to you for $5,000 was oral, I am not bound by my promise. I have since received a better offer and will accept that one." Adrian's letter constitutes a sufficient memorandum for Joseph to enforce Adrian's promise to sell Blackacre. It should be recognized that because Joseph did not sign the memorandum, the writing does not bind him. Thus, a contract may be enforceable against only one of the parties.

> **PRACTICAL ADVICE**
>
> *To avoid becoming solely liable by signing a contract before the other party signs, include a provision to the effect that no party is bound to the contract until all parties sign the contract.*

The "signature" may be initials or may even be typewritten or printed, so long as the party intended it to authenticate the writing or record. Furthermore, the signature need not be at the bottom of the page or at the customary place for a signature. The memorandum may consist of *several* papers or documents, none of which would be sufficient by itself. The several memoranda, however, must together satisfy all of the requirements of a writing or record to comply with the statute of frauds and must clearly indicate that they relate to the same transaction. Restatement, Section 132. The latter requirement can be satisfied if (1) the writings are physically attached, (2) the writings refer to each other, or (3) an examination of the writings shows them to be in reference to each other.

◆ SEE CASE 15-4

SALE OF GOODS

The statute of frauds provision under Article 2 is more liberal. For a sale of goods, Section 2–201 of the Code requires merely some writing or record

1. sufficient to indicate that a contract has been made between the parties,
2. specifying the quantity of goods to be sold, and
3. signed by the party against whom enforcement is sought or by her authorized agent or broker.

The writing or record is sufficient even if it omits or incorrectly states an agreed-upon term; however, where the quantity term is misstated, the contract can be enforced only to the extent of the quantity stated in the writing or record.

As with general contracts, several related documents may satisfy the writing or record requirement. Moreover, the signature again may be by initials or even typewritten or printed, so long as the party intended thereby to authenticate the writing or record.

In addition, the Code provides relief to a merchant who, within a reasonable time after entering into the oral contract, confirms the contract for the sale of goods by a letter or signed writing to the other party if he too is a merchant. As between **merchants**, the **written confirmation**, if sufficient against the sender, is also sufficient against the recipient unless he gives written notice of his objection within ten days after receiving the confirmation. Section 2–201(2). This means that if these requirements have been met, the recipient of the writing or record is in the same position he would have assumed by signing it; and the confirmation, therefore, is enforceable against him.

For example, Brown Co. and ATM Industries enter into an oral contract that provides that ATM will deliver twelve thousand shirts to Brown at $6.00 per shirt. Brown sends a letter to ATM acknowledging the agreement. The letter, containing the quantity term but not the price, is signed by Brown's president and is mailed to ATM's vice president for sales. Brown was bound by the contract once its authorized agent signs the letter; ATM cannot raise the defense of the statute of frauds if ATM does not object to the letter within ten days after receiving it.

PRACTICAL ADVICE

Merchants should examine written confirmations carefully and promptly to make certain that they are accurate.

EFFECT OF NONCOMPLIANCE

The English statute provided that "no action shall be brought" upon a contract to which the statute of frauds applied *and* which did not comply with its requirements. The Code, by comparison, states that the contract "is not enforceable by way of action or defense." Despite the difference in language the basic legal effect is the same: a contracting party has a defense to an action by the other party to enforce an oral contract that is within the statute and that does not comply with its requirements. In short, the oral contract is **unenforceable**.

For example, if Tia, a painter, and James, a homeowner, make an oral contract under which James is to give Tia a certain tract of land in return for her painting his house, the contract is unenforceable under the statute of frauds. It is a contract for the sale of an interest in land. Either party can repudiate and has a defense to an action by the other to enforce the contract.

FULL PERFORMANCE

After all the promises of an oral contract have been performed by all the parties, the statute of frauds no longer applies. Accordingly, neither party can have the contract set aside on the grounds that it should have been in writing. The purpose of the statute is not to prohibit the performance of oral contracts but simply to exclude oral evidence of contracts within its provisions. Courts, in other words, will not "unscramble" a fully performed contract merely because it was not in writing or a proper record. In short, the statute applies to executory contracts only.

RESTITUTION

A party to a contract that is unenforceable because of the statute of frauds may have, nonetheless, acted in reliance upon the contract. In such a case the party may recover in restitution the benefits he conferred upon the other in relying upon the unenforceable contract. Thus, if Wilton makes an oral contract to furnish services to Rochelle that are not to be performed within a year and Rochelle discharges Wilton after three months, Wilton may recover as restitution the value of the services he rendered during the three months. Most courts require, however, that the party seeking restitution not be in default.

PROMISSORY ESTOPPEL

A growing number of courts have used the doctrine of promissory estoppel to displace the requirement of a writing by enforcing oral contracts within the statute of frauds where the party seeking enforcement has reasonably and foreseeably relied upon a promise in such a way that injustice can be avoided only by enforcing the promise. Restatement, Section 139. This section is essentially identical to Section 90 of the Restatement, which, as discussed in *Chapter 12*, dispenses with the requirement of consideration, although the comments to Section 139 state that "the requirement of consideration is more easily displaced than the requirement of a writing." The remedy granted is limited, as justice requires, and depends upon such factors as the availability of other remedies; the foreseeability, reasonableness, and substantiality of the reliance; and the extent to which reliance corroborates evidence of the promise.

PAROL EVIDENCE RULE

A contract reduced to writing and signed by the parties is frequently the result of many conversations, conferences, proposals, counterproposals, letters, and memoranda and sometimes is the product of negotiations conducted, or partly conducted, by agents of the parties. Any given stage in the negotiations may have produced tentative agreements that were superseded (or regarded as such by one of the parties) by subsequent negotiations. Offers may have been made and withdrawn, either expressly or by implication, or forgotten in the give-and-take of negotiations. Ultimately, though, the parties prepare and sign a final draft of the written contract, which may or may not include all of the points that were discussed and agreed upon during the negotiations. By signing the agreement, however, the parties have declared it to be their contract; and the terms it contains represent the contract they have made. As a rule of substantive law, neither party is later permitted to show that the contract they made differs from the terms and provisions that appear in the written agreement. This rule, which also applies to wills and deeds, is called the parol evidence rule.

THE RULE

When a contract is expressed in a writing that is intended to be the complete and final expression of the rights and duties of the parties, parol evidence of *prior* oral or written negotiations or agreements of the parties, or their *contemporaneous* oral agreements that vary or change the written contract, are not admissible. The word *parol* means literally "speech" or "words." The term **parol evidence** refers to any evidence, whether oral or in writing, which is outside the written contract and not incorporated into it either directly or by reference.

The parol evidence rule applies only to an *integrated* contract; that is, one contained in a certain writing or writings to which the parties have assented as the statement of the complete agreement or contract between them. When a contract is thus integrated, the courts will not permit parol evidence of any prior or contemporaneous agreement to vary, change, alter, or modify any of the terms or provisions of the written contract. Restatement, Section 213.

A writing may contain a **merger clause**, which states that the writing is intended to be the complete and final expression of the agreement between the parties. Most courts consider a merger clause to be conclusive proof of an integrated contract, while a few courts view a merger clause only as evidence of an integrated contract.

The reason for the parol evidence rule is that the parties, by reducing their entire agreement to writing, are regarded as having intended the writing that they signed to include the whole of their agreement. The terms and provisions contained in the writing are there because the parties intended them to be there. Conversely, any provision not in the writing is regarded as having been omitted because the parties intended that it should not be a part of their contract. In safeguarding the contract as made by the parties, the rule excluding evidence that would tend to change, alter, vary, or modify the terms of a written agreement applies to all integrated written contracts and deals with what terms are part of the contract. The rule differs from the statute of frauds, which governs what contracts must be evidenced by a writing to be enforceable.

PRACTICAL ADVICE

If your contract is intended to be the complete and final agreement, make sure that all terms are included and state your intention that the writing is complete and final. If you do not intend the writing to be complete or final, make sure that you so indicate in the writing itself.

◆ SEE CASE 15-4

◆ SEE CASE 15-5

SITUATIONS TO WHICH THE RULE DOES NOT APPLY

The parol evidence rule, in spite of its name, is neither an exclusionary rule of evidence nor a rule of construction or interpretation; rather, it is a rule of substantive law that defines the limits of a contract. Bearing this in mind, as well as the reason underlying the rule, it should be clear that the rule does *not* apply to any of the following:

1. A contract that is partly written and partly oral; that is, one in which the parties do not intend the writing to be their entire agreement.
2. A clerical or *typographical error* that obviously does not represent the agreement of the parties. Where, for example, a written contract for the services of a skilled mining engineer provides that his rate of compensation is to be $7.00 per day, a court of equity would permit reformation (correction) of the contract to rectify the mistake upon a showing that both parties intended the rate to be $700 per day.
3. Evidence showing the lack of *contractual capacity* of one of the parties, such as proof of minority, intoxication, or mental incompetency. Such evidence would not tend to vary, change, or alter any of the terms of the written agreement, but rather would show that the written agreement was voidable or void.
4. A *defense* of fraud, misrepresentation, duress, undue influence, mistake, illegality, or unconscionability. Though evidence establishing any of these defenses would not purport to vary, change, or alter any of the terms of the written agreement, it would show such agreement to be voidable, void, or unenforceable.
5. A *condition precedent* to which the parties agreed orally at the time they executed the written agreement and to which they made the entire agreement subject. Again, such evidence does not tend to vary, alter, or change any of the terms of the agreement, but rather shows whether the entire written agreement, unchanged and unaltered, ever became effective. For example, if John signs a subscription agreement to buy stock in a corporation to be formed and delivers the agreement to Thompson with the mutual understanding that it is not to be binding unless the other persons financially responsible under it shall each agree to buy at least an equivalent amount of such stock, John is permitted to show by parol evidence this condition.
6. A *subsequent mutual rescission or modification* of the written contract. Parol evidence of a later agreement does not tend to show that the integrated writing did not represent the contract between the parties at the time it was made. Parties to an existing contract, whether written or oral, may agree to change the terms of their contract as they see fit, or to cancel it completely, if they so desire.
7. Parol evidence is admissible to explain *ambiguous* terms in the contract. To enforce a contract, it is necessary to understand its intended meaning. Nevertheless, such interpretation is not to alter, change, or vary the terms of the contract.
8. The rule does not prevent a party from proving the existence of a separate, distinct contract between the same parties.

SUPPLEMENTAL EVIDENCE

Although a written agreement may not be contradicted by evidence of a prior agreement or of a contemporaneous agreement, under the Restatement, Section 216, and the Code, Section 2–202, a written contract may be explained or supplemented by (1) course of dealing between the parties, (2) usage of trade, (3) course of performance, or (4) evidence of consistent additional terms, unless the parties intended the writing to be a complete and exclusive statement of their agreement.

A **course of dealing** is a sequence of previous conduct between the parties under an agreement that the court reasonably may regard as establishing a common basis of understanding for interpreting their expressions and other conduct.

A **usage of trade** is a practice or method of dealing, regularly observed and followed in a place, vocation, or trade.

Course of performance refers to the manner and extent to which the respective parties to a contract have accepted without objection successive tenders of performance by the other party.

The Restatement and the Code permit *supplemental consistent evidence* to be introduced into a court proceeding, but only if it does not contradict a term or terms of the original agreement and probably would not have been included in the original contract.

◈ **SEE FIGURE 15-2: Parol Evidence Rule**

INTERPRETATION OF CONTRACTS

Although the written words or language in which the parties embodied their agreement or contract may not be changed by parol evidence, the ascertainment (determination) of the meaning to be given the written language is outside the scope of the parol evidence rule. Though written words embody the terms of the contract, words are but symbols. If their meaning is unclear, the courts may clarify this meaning by applying rules of interpretation or construction and by using extrinsic (external) evidence, where necessary.

The Restatement, Section 200, defines **interpretation** as the ascertainment of the meaning of a promise or agreement or a term of the promise or agreement. Where the language in a contract is unambiguous, the courts will not accept extrinsic evidence tending to show a meaning different from that which the words clearly convey. Its function being to interpret and construe written contracts and documents, the

◆ **FIGURE 15-2: Parol Evidence Rule**

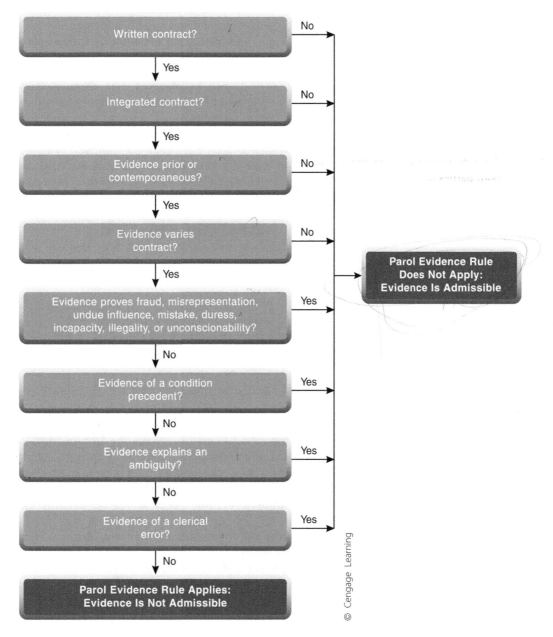

court adopts rules of interpretation to apply a legal standard to the words contained in the agreement. The courts will attempt to interpret a contract in accordance with the intent of the parties. If the subjective intent of the parties fails to provide a clear interpretation, the courts will make an objective interpretation. Among the rules that aid interpretation are the following:

1. Words and other conduct are interpreted in the light of all the circumstances, and the principal purpose of the parties, if ascertainable, is given great weight.

2. A writing is interpreted as a whole, and all writings that are part of the same transaction are interpreted together.

3. Unless a different intention is manifested, language that has a commonly accepted meaning is interpreted in accordance with that meaning.

4. Unless a different intention is manifested, technical terms and words of art are given their technical meanings.

5. Wherever reasonable, the manifestations of intention of the parties to a promise or agreement are interpreted as

consistent with each other and with any relevant course of performance, course of dealing, or usage of trade.

6. An interpretation that gives a reasonable, lawful, and effective meaning to all the terms is preferred over an interpretation that leaves a part unreasonable, unlawful, or of no effect.

7. Specific terms and exact terms are given greater weight than general language.

8. Separately negotiated or added terms are given greater weight than standardized terms or other terms not separately negotiated.

9. Express terms, course of performance, course of dealing, and usage of trade are weighted in that order.

10. Where a term or promise has several possible meanings, it will be interpreted against the party who supplied the contract or the term. Restatement, Sections 201, 202, and 203.

11. Where written provisions are inconsistent with typed or printed provisions, the written provision is given prefer-

ence. Likewise, typed provisions are given preferences to printed provisions.

12. If the amount payable is set forth in both figures and words and the amounts differ, the words control the figures.

It may be observed that, through the application of the parol evidence rule (where properly applicable) and the above rules of interpretation and construction, the law not only enforces a contract but, in so doing, exercises great care that the contract being enforced is the one the parties made and that the sense and meaning of the parties' intentions are carefully ascertained and given effect.

PRACTICAL ADVICE
Take care to ensure that your contracts are complete and understandable, especially if you drafted the contract.

CHAPTER SUMMARY

STATUTE OF FRAUDS

CONTRACTS WITHIN THE STATUTE OF FRAUDS

Rule contracts within the statute of frauds must be evidenced by a writing to be enforceable

Electronic Records full effect is given to electronic contracts and signatures

Suretyship Provision applies to promises to pay the debts of others
- *Promise Must Be Collateral* promisor must be secondarily, not primarily, liable
- *Main Purpose Doctrine* if primary object is to provide an economic benefit to the surety, then the promise is not within the statute

Executor-Administrator Provision applies to promises to answer personally for duties of decedents

Marriage Provision applies to promises made in consideration of marriage but not to mutual promises to marry

Land Contract Provision applies to promises to transfer any rights, privileges, powers, or immunities in real property

One-Year Provision applies to contracts that cannot be performed within one year
- *The Possibility Test* the criterion is whether it is possible, not likely, for the agreement to be performed within one year
- *Computation of Time* the year runs from the time the agreement is made
- *Full Performance by One Party* makes the promise of the other party enforceable under majority view

Sale of Goods a contract for the sale of goods for the price of $500 or more must be evidenced by a writing or record to be enforceable
- *Admission* an admission in pleadings, testimony, or otherwise in court makes the contract enforceable for the quantity of goods admitted
- *Specially Manufactured Goods* an oral contract for specially manufactured goods is enforceable
- *Delivery or Payment and Acceptance* validates the contract only for the goods that have been accepted or for which payment has been accepted

Modification or Rescission of Contracts within the Statute of Frauds oral contracts modifying existing contracts are unenforceable if the resulting contract is within the statute of frauds

METHODS OF COMPLIANCE	**General Contract Law** the writing(s) or record must

General Contract Law the writing(s) or record must
- specify the parties to the contract
- specify the subject matter and essential terms
- be signed by the party to be charged or by her agent

Sale of Goods provides a general method of compliance for all parties and an additional one for merchants
- *Writing(s) or Record* must (1) be sufficient to indicate that a contract has been made between the parties, (2) be signed by the party against whom enforcement is sought or by her authorized agent, and (3) specify the quantity of goods to be sold
- *Written Confirmation* between merchants, a written confirmation that is sufficient against the sender is also sufficient against the recipient unless the recipient gives written notice of his objection within ten days

EFFECT OF NONCOMPLIANCE

Oral Contract within Statute of Frauds is unenforceable

Full Performance statute does not apply to executed contracts

Restitution is available in a quasi contract for benefits conferred in reliance on the oral contract

Promissory Estoppel oral contracts will be enforced in cases in which the party seeking enforcement has reasonably and justifiably relied on the promise and the court can avoid injustice only by enforcement

PAROL EVIDENCE RULE

Statement of Rule when parties express a contract in a writing that they intend to be the complete and final expression of their rights and duties, evidence of their prior oral or written negotiations or agreements of their contemporaneous oral agreements that vary or change the written contract are not admissible

Situations to Which the Rule Does Not Apply
- a contract that is not an integrated document
- correction of a typographical error
- showing that a contract was void or voidable
- showing whether a condition has in fact occurred
- showing a subsequent mutual rescission or modification of the contract

Supplemental Evidence may be admitted
- *Course of Dealing* previous conduct between the parties
- *Usage of Trade* practice engaged in by the trade or industry
- *Course of Performance* conduct between the parties concerning performance of the particular contract
- *Supplemental Consistent Evidence*

INTERPRETATION OF CONTRACTS

Definition the ascertainment of the meaning of a promise or agreement or a term of the promise or agreement

Rules of Interpretation include the following:
- all the circumstances are considered and the principal purpose of the parties is given great weight

- a writing is interpreted as a whole
- commonly accepted meanings are used unless the parties manifest a different intention
- wherever possible, the intentions of the parties are interpreted as consistent with each other and with course of performance, course of dealing, or usage of trade
- technical terms are given their technical meaning
- specific terms are given greater weight than general language
- separately negotiated terms are given greater weight than standardized terms or those not separately negotiated
- the order for interpretation is express terms, course of performance, course of dealing, and usage of trade
- where a term has several possible meanings, the term will be interpreted against the party who supplied the contract or term
- written provisions are given preference over typed or printed provisions, and typed provisions are given preference over printed provisions
- if an amount is set forth in both words and figures and they differ, words control figures

CASES

CASE 15-1

Suretyship/Main Purpose Rule
ROSEWOOD CARE CENTER, INC. v. CATERPILLAR, INC.
Supreme Court of Illinois, 2007
226 Ill.2d 559, 877 N.E.2d 1091, 315 Ill. Dec. 762
http://scholar.google.com/scholar_case?case=14227814297099210378&q=877+N.E.2d+1091&hl=en&as_sclt=2,22

Burke, J.

[On January 3, 2002, Caterpillar contacted HSM Management Services (HSM), the management agent for Plaintiff, Rosewood Care Center, Inc. (Rosewood), a skilled nursing facility. Caterpillar requested that Rosewood admit Betty Jo Cook, an employee of Caterpillar, on a "managed care basis (fixed rate)." HSM advised Caterpillar that Rosewood would not admit Cook on those terms. Shortly thereafter, on January 10, Dr. Norma Just, Caterpillar's employee in charge of medical care relating to workers' compensation claims, contacted HSM. Just told HSM that Cook had sustained a work-related injury and was receiving medical care at Caterpillar's expense under the workers' compensation laws. Just requested that Cook be admitted to Rosewood for skilled nursing care and therapy, and stated that the cost of Cook's care would be 100 percent covered and paid directly by Caterpillar to Rosewood with a zero deductible and no maximum limit. Just further advised HSM that Cook had been precertified for four weeks of care. Just asked that Rosewood send the bills for Cook's care to Caterpillar's workers' compensation division. On January 20, "Sue" from Dr. Just's office telephoned HSM and confirmed approval for Cook's transfer from the hospital to Rosewood. On January 30, Sue reconfirmed, via telephone, Caterpillar's authorization for Cook's care and treatment in accordance with the January 10 agreement, except that Sue now advised HSM that Cook was precertified for two weeks of care instead of the original four weeks. On January 30, Cook was admitted to Rosewood. Upon her admission, Cook signed a document entitled "Assignment of Insurance Benefits" as required by law. In this document, Cook assigned any insurance benefits she might receive to Rosewood and acknowledged her liability for any unpaid services. Caterpillar, through its health care management company, continued to orally "authorize" care for Cook and did so on February 8, February 25, March 11, March 21, April 8, April 18, May 16, and June 4. Cook remained at Rosewood until June 13, 2002. The total of Rosewood's charges for Cook's care amounted to $181,857. Caterpillar never objected to the bills being sent to it for Cook's care, nor did it ever advise Rosewood that treatment was not authorized. However, Caterpillar ultimately refused to pay for services rendered to Cook.

The plaintiff filed an action against Caterpillar seeking reimbursement for the services provided to Cook while she was a patient at Rosewood. In response, Caterpillar moved to dismiss the complaint, arguing that the alleged promise to pay for Cook's care was not enforceable because it was not in writing as required by the statute of frauds. The trial court granted Caterpillar's motion for summary judgment and Rosewood appealed. The appellate court reversed and remanded.]

* * *

In general, the statute of frauds provides that a promise to pay the debt of another, i.e., a suretyship agreement, is unenforceable unless it is in writing. * * *

* * *

The plain object of the statute is to require higher and more certain evidence to charge a party, where he does not receive the substantial benefit of the transaction, and where another is primarily liable to pay the debt or discharge the duty; and thereby to afford greater security against the setting up of fraudulent demands, where the party sought to be charged is another than the real debtor, and whose debt or duty, on performance of the alleged contract by such third person, would be discharged. [Citation.]

* * *

II. "Main Purpose" or "Leading Object" Rule
* * * According to Rosewood, Caterpillar's promise falls outside the statute of frauds pursuant to the "main purpose" or "leading object" rule. Under this rule, when the "main purpose" or "leading object" of the promisor/surety is to subserve or advance its own pecuniary or business interests, the promise does not fall within the statute. [Citation.] As section 11 of the Restatement (Third) of Suretyship & Guaranty states:

A contract that all or part of the duty of the principal obligor to the obligee shall be satisfied by the secondary obligor is not within the Statute of Frauds as a promise to answer for the duty of another if the consideration for the promise is in fact or apparently desired by the secondary obligor mainly for its own economic benefit, rather than the benefit of the principal obligor. [Citation.]

The reason for the "main purpose" or "leading object" rule has been explained:

Where the secondary obligor's main purpose is its own pecuniary or business advantage, the gratuitous or sentimental element often present in suretyship is eliminated, the likelihood of disproportion in the values exchanged between secondary obligor and obligee is reduced, and the commercial context commonly provides evidentiary safeguards. Thus, there is less need for cautionary or evidentiary formality than in other secondary obligations. [Citations.]

* * *

It is clear * * * that the "main purpose" or "leading object" rule, as set out in the Restatements, has been a part of Illinois law since 1873. We note that the majority of jurisdictions have adopted this rule as well. [Citations.]

Applying this rule in the case at bar, Caterpillar denies that the "main purpose" for its alleged promise to Rosewood was to promote its own interest. Caterpillar also denies that it received any benefit from the agreement. Alternatively, Caterpillar argues that we should remand this cause for further proceedings to determine the "main purpose" or "leading object" of its promise.

Whether the "main purpose" or "leading object" of the promisor is to promote a pecuniary or business advantage to it is generally a question for the trier of fact. [Citation.] * * * Here, a decision on what was Caterpillar's "main purpose" or "leading object" in making the promise cannot be made based on the allegations in the complaint. * * * The determination must be made by the trier of fact based on evidence to be presented by the parties. * * *

III. Whether a Suretyship Was Created in This Case
* * * Rosewood argues that no suretyship was created by Caterpillar's promise. According to Rosewood, Caterpillar contracted directly with Rosewood, became liable for its own commitment, and received benefits as a result.

A suretyship exists when one person undertakes an obligation of another person who is also under an obligation or duty to the creditor/obligee. [Citation.] Specifically, "[a] contract is not within the Statute of Frauds as a contract to answer for the duty of another unless the promisee is an obligee of the other's duty, the promisor is a surety for the other, and the promisee knows or has reason to know of the suretyship relation." [Citation.] * * *

* * *

The question of whether Caterpillar's promise was a suretyship or not, like the question regarding Caterpillar's "main purpose" or "leading object," cannot be determined on the basis of allegations in Rosewood's complaint. This question is a factual one to be made based on evidence to be presented by the parties. Accordingly, this issue must also be resolved by the circuit court on remand.

One-Year Provision
MACKAY v. FOUR RIVERS PACKING CO.

Supreme Court of Idaho, 2008

179 P.3d 1064

http://scholar.google.com/scholar_case?case=3479455732652915832&q=179+P.+3d+1064+&hl=en&as_sdt=2,34

Jones, J.

Four Rivers operates an onion packing plant near Weiser, Idaho. Randy Smith, the general manager of Four Rivers, hired Stuart Mackay as a field man during the summer of 1999 to secure onion contracts from growers in the area. Four Rivers began experiencing financial difficulties in late 1999. All employees, including Mackay, were laid off at this time because one of the owners of Four Rivers filed suit to prevent the company from conducting business. When the lawsuit was resolved, Smith rehired Mackay as a field man. According to Mackay, Four Rivers offered him a long-term employment contract in March of 2000 to continue working as a field man up to the time of his retirement. Mackay claims he accepted the long-term offer of employment and advised Four Rivers that he may not retire for approximately ten years, at around age 62.

Four Rivers denies extending such an offer to Mackay. According to Four Rivers, the owners informed Randy Smith in 2000 that they did not know whether the company would be in business the next fall due to continuing financial difficulties. In 2001, Mackay asked Four Rivers for a written contract of employment. He refused to sign the agreement that was prepared because it gave Four Rivers the right to terminate his employment at will. Subsequent efforts to arrive at a written employment agreement were unsuccessful.

* * *

On March 7, 2003, Smith terminated Mackay's employment relationship without notice * * * [claiming that] Mackay's performance was not satisfactory because he was not meeting with growers with the frequency or regularity necessary to obtain the quantity of onions necessary to keep Four Rivers' packing plant operational on a full-time basis, resulting in the closure of the packing plant in February 2003. Four Rivers claims its employees, including Mackay, were laid off at this time as a result of the early closure. Mackay claims Four Rivers closed due to the price of onions at the time. Mackay applied for unemployment benefits in 2003, stating in his application that he was laid off due to company financial difficulties. Smith states he offered to rehire Mackay in a different position later that year, and Mackay declined.

Mackay filed a complaint on August 24, 2004, claiming Four Rivers breached his employment contract * * * . Four Rivers answered, alleging that Mackay was an "at will" employee. Further, it asserted an affirmative defense that a contract such as that claimed by Mackay is null, void, and unenforceable as violating Idaho Code § 9-505 because the agreement could not be performed within one year of its making. Four Rivers moved for summary judgment in October 2006, and the district court granted its motion. The court concluded the alleged contract could not be performed by its terms within one year and would therefore be invalid in the state of Idaho. Thus, it granted summary judgment with regard to Mackay's breach of contract claim. * * * Plaintiff subsequently filed a motion for reconsideration, which the district court denied, resulting in this appeal.

* * *

The parties disagree regarding the proper application of Idaho's Statute of Frauds. According to Mackay, the long-standing rule in Idaho is that where an agreement depends upon a condition which may ripen within a year, even though it may not mature until much later, the agreement does not fall within the Statute. Since the alleged contract here contains a term that it will last until Mackay retires, and Mackay could have retired within the first year, the oral contract does not violate the Statute. * * *

Four Rivers denies entering into a long-term contract of employment, and * * * claims the contract violates [the] Idaho [Statute of Frauds] * * *

Idaho's Statute of Frauds provision * * * provides that "an agreement that by its terms is not to be performed within a year from the making thereof" is invalid, unless the same or some note or memorandum thereof, be in writing and subscribed by the party charged, or by his agent. [Citation.] * * * Under the prevailing interpretation, the enforceability of a contract under the one-year provision does not turn on the actual course of subsequent events, nor on the expectations of the parties as to the probabilities. [Citation.] Contracts of uncertain duration are simply excluded, and the provision covers only those contracts whose performance cannot possibly be completed within a year. [Citation.]

Leading treatises follow this general rule. It is well settled that the oral contracts invalidated by the Statute because they are not to be performed within a year include only those which *cannot* be performed within that period. [Citation.] A promise which is not likely to be performed within a year, and which in fact is not performed within a year, is not within the Statute, if at the time the contract is made there is a possibility in law and in fact that full performance such as the parties intended may be completed before the expiration of a year. [Citation.] The question is not what the probable, or expected, or actual, performance of the contract was, but whether the contract, according to the reasonable interpretation of its terms, required that it could not be performed within the year. [Citation.] Further, a promise which is performable at or until the happening of any specified contingency which may or may not occur within a year is not within the Statute. [Citation.]

Idaho cases are in accord. A contract which is capable of being performed and might have been fully performed and terminated within a year does not fall within the Statute. [Citation.] Where the termination of a contract is dependent upon the happening of a contingency which may occur within a year, although it may not happen until the expiration of a year, the contract is not within the Statute, since it may be performed within a year. [Citations.]

In this case, the district court applied the *Burton* decision and found that the alleged oral contract could not, by its terms, be completed within a year. In *Burton*, the plaintiff alleged there was an implied contract, which guaranteed her employment until she reached retirement, at age 65. * * *

This case differs. In this case, Mackay alleges the term of the contract is until retirement. * * * Unlike the contract in *Burton*, which specified "until age 65," the alleged contract term in this case is indefinite. Thus, the district court erred when it held *Burton* applied to preclude enforcement of the contract alleged in this case.

Rather, this case falls under the general rule cited in numerous Idaho cases and in the Restatement (Second) of Contracts. For the purposes of summary judgment, we must take as true Mackay's allegation that the contract was to last "until retirement." Since Mackay could have retired within one year under the terms of the alleged contract, this contract is outside Idaho's Statute of Frauds provision. * * * Since the event at issue here—Mackay's retirement—could possibly have occurred within one year, the Statute does not bar evidence of such contract.

* * *

We vacate the district court's order granting summary judgment against Mackay * * * and remand the case for further proceedings consistent with this opinion. * * *

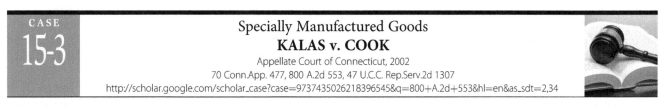

CASE 15-3

Specially Manufactured Goods
KALAS v. COOK
Appellate Court of Connecticut, 2002
70 Conn.App. 477, 800 A.2d 553, 47 U.C.C. Rep.Serv.2d 1307
http://scholar.google.com/scholar_case?case=9737435026218396545&q=800+A.2d+553&hl=en&as_sdt=2,34

Peters, J.
Pursuant to a long-standing oral agreement, a print shop manufactured and delivered written materials designed by the buyer for the buyer's use and sale. After the buyer's death, the executor of her estate refused to pay for the last deliveries of these materials to the buyer. The principal issue in this appeal is whether the statute of frauds, as codified in the Uniform Commercial Code, [citation], bars enforcement of the oral agreement. * * * [W]e agree with the [trial] court's conclusion that, under the circumstances of this case, the seller is entitled to be paid.

The plaintiff, Barbara H. Kalas, owner of the print shop, filed a complaint against the defendant, Edward W. Cook, executor of the estate of the buyer, Adelma G. Simmons. The plaintiff alleged that the defendant, in breach of the obligations contained in an oral contract with Simmons for the sale of goods, had refused to pay for goods delivered to her. The defendant denied these allegations and interposed a number of special defenses, including a defense under the statute of frauds. * * *

The trial court held that the transaction between the plaintiff and the deceased was a sale of goods as that term is defined in [UCC] § 2–105. That determination has not been

challenged on appeal. As a contract for the sale of goods, its enforcement was not precluded by the statute of frauds provision. * * * Accordingly, the court rendered a judgment in favor of the plaintiff in the amount of $24,599.38. The defendant has appealed.

The facts found by the trial court, which are currently uncontested, establish the background for the court's judgment. The plaintiff, doing business as Clinton Press of Tolland, operated a printing press and, for several decades, provided written materials, including books and pamphlets for Simmons. Simmons ordered these materials for use and sale at her farm, known as Caprilands Herb Farm (Caprilands). The defendant has not suggested that these materials could have been sold on the open market.

Due to limited space at Caprilands, the plaintiff and Simmons agreed that the written materials would remain stored at the plaintiff's print shop until Simmons decided that delivery was necessary. The materials were delivered either routinely, based on Simmons' ordinary need for materials, or upon her request for a special delivery. After each delivery, the plaintiff sent an invoice requesting payment by Simmons. These invoices were honored.

In 1991, the town of Tolland acquired the land on which the plaintiff resided. In early 1997, the plaintiff was notified that she would have to vacate the property by the end of that calendar year. Upon receiving that notice, the plaintiff decided to close her business. The plaintiff and Simmons agreed that the materials printed for Caprilands and stored at the plaintiff's print shop would be delivered on an accelerated basis. * * *

On December 3, 1997, after several months of deterioration of her physical health, Simmons died. * * * The plaintiff submitted a claim against the estate for $24,599.38 for unpaid deliveries to Caprilands. These deliveries took place from February 12, 1997 to December 11, 1997, with the last two deliveries occurring after Simmons' death.

* * *

On appeal, the defendant argues that the oral contract was invalid * * * because a writing was required by [UCC] § 2–201. This argument is unpersuasive. * * *

* * *

* * * Contracts for the sale of goods * * * are governed by [UCC] § 2–201. [Citations.]

Under [UCC] § 2–201, oral agreements for the sale of goods at a price of $500 or more are presumptively unenforceable. [Citations.] The applicable provisions in this case, however, are other subsections of [UCC] § 2-201.

Under [UCC] § 2–201 (3) (a), an oral contract for the sale of goods is enforceable if the goods in question are "specially manufactured." In determining whether the specially manufactured goods exception applies, courts generally apply a four part standard: "(1) the goods must be specially made for the buyer; (2) the goods must be unsuitable for sale to others in the ordinary course of the seller's business; (3) the seller must have substantially begun to

have manufactured the goods or to have a commitment for their procurement; and (4) the manufacture or commitment must have been commenced under circumstances reasonably indicating that the goods are for the buyer and prior to the seller's receipt of notification of contractual repudiation." [Citation.] In applying this standard, "courts have traditionally looked to the goods themselves. The term 'specially manufactured,' therefore, refers to the nature of the particular goods in question and not to whether the goods were made in an unusual, as opposed to the regular, business operation or manufacturing process of the seller." [Citations.]

Printed material, particularly that, as in this case, names the buyer, has been deemed by both state and federal courts to fall within the exception set out for specially manufactured goods. [Citations.]

It is inherent in the court's findings that the printed materials in the present case were specially manufactured goods. The materials were printed specifically for Caprilands. The materials included brochures and labels with the Caprilands name, as well as books that were written and designed by Simmons. The plaintiff testified that the books were printed, as Simmons had requested, in a rustic style with typed inserts and hand-drawn pictures. Therefore, none of these materials was suitable for sale to others. It is undisputed that, at the time of breach of the alleged contract, goods printed for Simmons already had been produced.

We conclude that, in light of the nature of the goods at issue * * * this case falls within the exception for specially manufactured goods. To be enforceable, the agreement for their production was, therefore, not required to be in writing under [UCC] § 2-201 (3) (a). Accordingly, we affirm the judgment of the court. * * * [Citations.]

CASE
15-4

Writing/Parol Evidence
ESTATE OF JACKSON v. DEVENYNS
Supreme Court of Wyoming, 1995
892 P.2d 786
http://scholar.google.com/scholar_case?case=11233159489095516955&q=892+P.2d.786&hl=en&as_sdt=2,34

Golden, J.

Appellants, personal representatives of the estate of George Herbert Jackson, appeal the probate court's order of conveyance in favor of appellees. Appellants claim a writing signed by George Jackson purporting to sell seventy-nine acres, reserve approximately one acre, and sell machinery is unenforceable because the agreement does not sufficiently describe the property as required by * * * the statute of

frauds. Following appellees' petition * * * , the probate court determined the writing satisfied the statute of frauds, was enforceable, and ordered the estate's personal representatives to perform the contract.

We hold the agreement's property description is insufficient to meet the requirements of the statute of frauds and reverse the order of conveyance.

* * *

Facts

On February 9, 1993, George Jackson (Jackson) and his neighbors, Karen and Steve Devenyns (Devenyns), drafted and signed a document which reads as follows:

> George Jackson agrees to sell 79 acres and machinery to Steve and Karen Devenyns for $120,000.00.
>
> * * *
>
> George want[s] to keep yard intact which is area 66′ × 114′ as well as area around house approximately 1.3 acres 168′ × 325′.
>
> Devenyns ha[ve] first option to buy on property George will provide title insurance and survey house and approximately 1.3 acre from total. This survey can be done within 5 months.
>
> These matters were discussed by both parties on 2/9/93 and agreed upon
>
> Steve Devenyns
>
> George H. Jackson

Jackson died on May 8, 1993. After the attorney for Jackson's estate refused the Devenyns' request to honor the contract, the Devenyns petitioned for an order of conveyance. * * *

The estate objected to the petition, contending the property description did not comply with the statute of frauds' requirement that the document itself sufficiently describe the property to be conveyed. The estate filed a motion, * * * objecting to proposed testimony as violative of the parol evidence rule, the statute of frauds * * * . However, the probate court heard testimony from witnesses for the Devenyns and considered parol evidence to determine whether the document satisfied the statute of frauds.

* * *

From parol evidence, the probate court determined that Jackson had used words of ownership referring to the eighty acres of real property he owned in Park County, Wyoming, and that Jackson did not own any other real property in the world. The probate court further found that Jackson had conveyed his seventy-nine acre farm, but had reserved out an approximate one acre parcel containing Jackson's house and yard. The probate court held that the reserved one acre could be satisfactorily determined by a surveyor using the dimensions found on page two of the agreement, and the sketch found on page three, as well as from assistance of witnesses who testified at the hearing that they could point out the specific area based on conversations with Jackson. The probate court held the agreement was enforceable and ordered conveyance by the estate to the Devenyns. This appeal followed.

Discussion

Statute of Frauds

* * *

A written memorandum purporting to convey real estate must sufficiently describe the property so as to comply with the requirements of the statute of frauds and permit specific performance. [Citation.]

* * *

* * * This Court's decision in *Noland* [citation] concluded that a valid contract to convey land must expressly contain a description of the land, certain in itself or capable of being rendered certain by reference to an extrinsic source which the writing itself designates. [Citation.] *Noland* expressly prohibited supplying the writing's essential provisions by inferences or presumptions deduced from oral testimony. [Citation.]

Parol Evidence

The parties both recognize that the central issue is the adequacy of the property description supplied in the agreement to satisfy the statute of frauds. The estate contends the probate court improperly relied upon parol evidence in deciding the document had sufficiently described Jackson's property in satisfaction of the statute of frauds. The general rule for Wyoming is that parol evidence is admissible to identify described property, but parol evidence may not supply a portion of the description. [Citation.]

This writing insufficiently describes the property it purports to convey, to reserve, and for which it grants an option to purchase. All three of these land transactions fall under the statute of frauds and each must be sufficiently definite in description to satisfy the statute of frauds or, as a matter of law, the contract is void because an essential term has been omitted. [Citation.] We also note that if the description of the property reserved out of the tract to be conveyed is indefinite and uncertain, then the general description of the land to be conveyed is indefinite and the entire conveyance must fail. [Citation.]

* * *

When a writing only states the total acreage without any description of the location of the land involved, the statute of frauds' requirement that the subject matter be reasonably certain is not satisfied and the contract is void. [Citation.] Without the prohibited supplied inference of ownership, the present description only provides the total acreage, does not provide any certainty that this particular tract was intended to be conveyed and, consequently, is too uncertain to be enforced. [Citations.]

The descriptions for the property reserved and for the option also fail to satisfy the statute of frauds. The reserved property boundaries can only be ascertained by witnesses actually directing a surveyor on-site according to the witnesses' memory of Jackson's boundary description. Parol evidence cannot supply a portion of the description. [Citation.] The option granted in the document does not provide any description at all, leaving unclear for what property an option was granted.

Conclusion

The parol evidence received in this case reveals that fraud is not a concern and leaves no doubt as to the identity of the property involved, but the property was not described in the

agreement and the agreement cannot be enforced. The legislative policy justifying the statute of frauds requires this Court to test not what the parties to the contract know, but what they put in the contract as the description. A description cannot be supplied by parol proof because that allows in the harm which the statute was intended to prevent. The probate court erred as a matter of law in accepting parol evidence to describe the land.

In view of our decision that the contract is unenforceable under the statute of frauds, * * * [t]he order of conveyance is reversed.

CASE 15-5

Parol Evidence
JENKINS v. ECKERD CORPORATION

District Court of Appeal of Florida, First District, 2005
913 So.2d 43
http://scholar.google.com/scholar_case?case=12402686802007965629&hl=en&as_sdt=2&as_vis=1&oi=scholarr

Van Nortwick, J.

In January 1991, Sandhill and K & B Florida Corporation (K & B), a pharmaceutical retailer, entered into the subject lease (K & B Lease) providing for the rental of a parcel of real property located in the Gulf Breeze Shopping Center in Gulf Breeze, Florida. Shortly before the execution of the K & B Lease, Sandhill had leased space in the shopping center to Delchamps, Inc., a regional supermarket chain, as a so called "anchor" tenant in the shopping center. Article 2B of the K & B Lease referred to the Delchamps lease and provided, in pertinent part, as follows:

Article 2

* * *

B. Lessor represents to Lessee that Lessor has entered into leases with the following named concerns: with Delchamps, Inc. (Delchamps) for a minimum of 45,000 square feet for supermarket grocery store and that Lessor will construct and offer for lease individual retail shops for a minimum of 21,000 square feet for various retail uses, all located and dimensioned shown on the attached Plot Plan,... Lessor further represents that said Delchamps lease is for leasing and paying rent by Delchamps as designated hereinabove in the Shopping Center, all as shown on the Plot Plan, Exhibit "A", * * * *The continued leasing and payment of rent for their store in the Shopping Center by Delchamps is part of the consideration to induce Lessee to lease and pay rent for its store, as hereinafter described on the Leased Premises as a part of the Shopping Center. Accordingly, should Delchamps fail or cease to lease and pay rent for its store in the Shopping Center during the*

Lease Term as hereinafter set out, Lessee shall have the right and privilege of: (a) cancelling this Lease and of terminating all of its obligations hereunder at any time thereafter upon written notice by Lessee to Lessor, and such cancellation and termination shall be effective ninety (90) days after the mailing of such written notice; … It is specifically understood that Lessor shall be obligated to immediately notify Lessee in writing should Delchamps fail or cease to lease and pay rent for such a store in the Shopping Center during the primary term of this Lease, but any failure of Lessor to notify Lessee thereof shall in no way deprive Lessee of its privilege of cancelling this Lease and terminating all of its obligation hereunder.

(Emphasis added [by court]).

Article 29A of the K & B Lease contained an integration clause which provided that "[t]his lease contains all of the agreements made between the parties hereto and may not be modified orally or in any manner other than by an agreement in writing signed by the parties hereto or their heirs, legal representatives, successors, transferees, or assigns." The Delchamps lease included an assignment provision which granted Delchamps "the right, at any time after the commencement of the term hereof, to assign this lease …"

In August 1997, Rite Aid, Incorporated (Rite Aid), another drugstore operator, acquired K & B and continued to operate the drugstore in the shopping center under the K & B Lease as a Rite Aid store. In September 1997, Jitney Jungle Stores of America, Inc. (Jitney Jungle), another grocery store operator, acquired the capital stock of Delchamps and continued the operation of the Delchamps grocery store in the shopping center. In 1998, Eckerd acquired certain drugstore properties from Rite Aid, including the drugstore in the shopping center. The K & B Lease was assigned to Eckerd, which began operating an Eckerd drugstore in the leased premises. In October 1999, Jitney Jungle, and its affiliates, including Delchamps, filed for bankruptcy protection under Chapter 11 of the United States Bankruptcy Code. Thereafter, an order was entered in the bankruptcy proceeding approving Delchamps' assignment of its lease in the shopping center to Bruno's Supermarkets, Inc. (Bruno's). Since the assignment, Bruno's has occupied the leased premises under the assigned Delchamps lease and has operated a Bruno's grocery store there. Sandhill failed to provide notice to, or obtain consent from, Eckerd of this assignment.

* * * On June 22, 2001, Eckerd notified Sandhill that, because Delchamps had ceased to lease and pay rent for its store in the shopping center, pursuant to article 2B of the K & B Lease, Eckerd was cancelling its lease effective September 20, 2001. Eckerd continued to pay rent due under the lease through October 2001.

In December 2001, Sandhill filed suit against Eckerd for an alleged breach of the shopping center lease, * * *

At trial, Sandhill sought to introduce testimony relating to its negotiations of the K & B Lease to explain the parties' intent in drafting the allegedly ambiguous language of article 2B. [The district court prohibited the introduction of this evidence under the parol evidence rule.]

* * *

At the close of Sandhill's case, Eckerd moved for, and the trial court granted, a directed verdict in favor of Eckerd. * * *

The trial court also awarded Eckerd $16,026.04 in damages reflecting the amount of rent payments made by Eckerd for the period from September 20, 2001, to October 31, 2001. This appeal ensued.

* * *

It is a fundamental rule of contract interpretation that a contract which is clear, complete, and unambiguous does not require judicial construction. [Citations.]

* * *

In the case on appeal, the trial court concluded, and we agree, that article 2B of the K & B Lease clearly and unambiguously gave the lessee the option to cancel the lease if Delchamps ceased to lease and pay rent for the use of its store. As is clear from article 2B itself, the subject language was an inducement for the drugstore tenant to lease in the shopping center. * * *

* * *

Sandhill argues that the trial court erred in applying the parol evidence rule and refusing to allow the introduction of extrinsic evidence in interpreting article 2B of the K & B Lease. Sandhill correctly acknowledges that, if a contract provision is "clear and unambiguous," a court may not consider extrinsic or "parol" evidence to change the plain meaning set forth in the contract. [Citation.] Sandhill contends that parol evidence was admissible below since the lease is incomplete and contains a latent ambiguity. [Citations.] A latent ambiguity arises when a contract on its face appears clear and unambiguous, but fails to specify the rights or duties of the parties in certain situations. [Citation.] Sandhill submits that, while the reference in article 2B of the K & B Lease to the Delchamps lease may be "unambiguous" when read literally, this reference was not "clear" or "complete" with regard to the operation of the lease should the Delchamps lease be assigned. We cannot agree.

The operation of the parol evidence rule encourages parties to embody their complete agreement in a written contract and fosters reliance upon the written contract. "The parol evidence rule serves as a shield to protect a valid, complete and unambiguous written instrument from any verbal assault that would contradict, add to, or subtract from it, or affect its construction." [Citation.] The parol evidence rule presumes that the written agreement that is sought to be modified or explained is an integrated agreement; that is, it represents the complete and exclusive instrument setting forth the parties' intended agreement. [Citation.] The concept of integration is based on a presumption that the parties to a written contract intended that writing "to be the sole expositor of their agreement." [Citation.] The terms of an integrated written contract can be varied by extrinsic evidence only to the extent that the terms are ambiguous and are given meaning by the extrinsic evidence. [Citation.]

Here, * * * the K & B Lease contains a so-called merger or integration clause. Although the existence of a merger clause does not *per se* establish that the integration of the agreement is total, [citation], a merger clause is a highly persuasive statement that the parties intended the agreement to be totally integrated and generally works to prevent a party from introducing parol evidence to vary or contradict the written terms. * * * Here, we find that the K & B Lease is an integrated agreement complete in all essential terms.

Further, Article 2B is not in the least unclear or incomplete. It contains no latent or patent ambiguity. Although article 2B does not mention assignment by Delchamps, it unambiguously grants the lessee the right to terminate the K & B Lease if Delchamps ceases to lease and pay rent for its store in the shopping center *for any reason*. * * * Accordingly, the trial court correctly ruled that it could not admit extrinsic evidence.

* * *

AFFIRMED.

QUESTIONS

1. Rafferty was the principal shareholder in Continental Corporation, and, as a result, he received the lion's share of Continental's dividends. Continental Corporation was eager to close an important deal for iron ore products to use in its business. A written contract was on the desk of Stage Corporation for the sale of the iron ore to Continental. Stage Corporation, however, was cautious about signing the contract; and it did not sign until Rafferty called Stage Corporation on the telephone and stated that if Continental Corporation did not pay for the ore, he would. Business reversals struck Continental Corporation, and it failed. Stage Corporation sues Rafferty. What defense, if any, has Rafferty?

2. Green was the owner of a large department store. On Wednesday, January 26, he talked to Smith and said, "I will hire you as sales manager in my store for one year at a salary of $48,000; you are to begin work next Monday." Smith accepted and started work on Monday, January 31. At the end of three months, Green discharged Smith. On May 15, Smith brings an action against Green to recover the unpaid portion of the $28,000 salary. Is Smith's employment contract enforceable?

3. Rowe was admitted to the hospital suffering from a critical illness. He was given emergency treatment and later underwent surgery. On at least four occasions, Rowe's two sons discussed with the hospital the payment for services it was to render. The first of these four conversations took place the day after Rowe was admitted. The sons informed the treating physician that their father had no financial means but that they themselves would pay for such services. During the other conversations, the sons authorized whatever treatment their father needed, assuring the hospital that they would pay for the services. After Rowe's discharge, the hospital brought this action against the sons to recover the unpaid bill for the services rendered to their father. Are the sons' promises to the hospital enforceable? Explain.

4. Ames, Bell, Cain, and Dole each orally ordered LCD (liquid crystal display) televisions from Marvel Electronics Company, which accepted the orders. Ames's television was to be encased in a specially designed ebony cabinet. Bell, Cain, and Dole ordered standard televisions described as "Alpha Omega Theatre." The price of Ames's television was $1,800, and the televisions ordered by Bell, Cain, and Dole were $700 each. Bell paid the company $75.00 to apply on his purchase; Ames, Cain, and Dole paid nothing. The next day, Marvel sent Ames, Bell, Cain, and Dole written confirmations captioned "Purchase Memorandum," numbered 12345, 12346, 12347, and 12348, respectively, containing the essential terms of the oral agreements. Each memorandum was sent in duplicate with the request that one copy be signed and returned to the company. None of the four purchasers returned a signed copy. Ames promptly called the company and repudiated the oral contract, which it received before beginning manufacture of the set for Ames or making commitments to carry out the contract. Cain sent the company a letter reading in part, "Referring to your Contract No. 12347, please be advised I have canceled this contract. Yours truly, (Signed) Cain." The four televisions were duly tendered by Marvel to Ames, Bell, Cain, and Dole, all of whom refused to accept delivery. Marvel brings four separate actions against Ames, Bell, Cain, and Dole for breach of contract. Decide each claim.

5. Moriarty and Holmes enter into an oral contract by which Moriarty promises to sell and Holmes promises to buy Blackacre for $100,000. Moriarty repudiates the contract by writing a letter to Holmes in which she states accurately the terms of the bargain, but adds "our agreement was oral. It, therefore, is not binding upon me, and I shall not carry it out." Thereafter, Holmes sues Moriarty for specific performance of the contract. Moriarty interposes the defense of the statute of frauds, arguing that the contract is within the statute and, hence, unenforceable. What result? Discuss.

6. On March 1, Lucas called Craig on the telephone and offered to pay him $190,000 for a house and lot that Craig owned. Craig accepted the offer immediately on the telephone. Later in the same day, Lucas told Annabelle that if she would marry him, he would convey to her the property he then owned, which was the subject of the earlier agreement. On March 2, Lucas called Penelope and offered her $25,000 if she would work for him for the year commencing March 15, and she agreed. Lucas and Annabelle were married on June 25. By this time, Craig had refused to convey the house to Lucas. Thereafter, Lucas renounced his promise to convey the property to Annabelle. Penelope, who had been working for Lucas, was discharged without cause on July 5; Annabelle left Lucas and instituted divorce proceedings.

   What rights, if any, have—

   a. Lucas against Craig for his failure to convey the property?

   b. Annabelle against Lucas for failure to convey the house to her?

   c. Penelope against Lucas for discharging her before the end of the agreed term of employment?

7. Clay orally promises Trent to sell him five crops of potatoes to be grown on Blackacre, a farm in Minnesota, and Trent promises to pay a stated price for them on delivery. Is the contract enforceable?

8. Grant leased an apartment to Epstein for the term May 1, at $750 a month "payable in advance on the first day of each and every month of said term." At the time the lease was signed, Epstein told Grant that he received his salary on the tenth of the month and that he would be unable to pay the rent before that date each month. Grant replied that would be satisfactory. On June 2, due to Epstein's not having paid the June rent, Grant sued Epstein for such rent. At the trial, Epstein offered to prove the oral agreement as to the date of payment each month. Is the oral evidence admissible?

9. Rachel bought a car from the Beautiful Used Car Agency under a written contract. She purchased the car in reliance on Beautiful's agent's oral representations that it had never been in a wreck and could be driven at least two thousand miles without adding oil. Thereafter, Rachel discovered that the car had, in fact, been previously wrecked and rebuilt, that it used excessive quantities of oil, and that Beautiful's agent was aware of these facts when the car was sold. Rachel brings an action to rescind the contract and recover the purchase price. Beautiful objects to the introduction of oral testimony concerning representations of its agent, contending that the written contract alone governed the rights of the parties. Explain whether Rachel should succeed.

10. In a contract drawn up by Booke Company, it agreed to sell and Yermack Contracting Company agreed to buy wood shingles at $950 per bunch. After the shingles were delivered and used, Booke Company billed Yermack Company at $950 per bunch of nine hundred shingles. Yermack Company refused to pay because it thought the contract meant $950 per bunch of one thousand shingles. Booke Company brought action to recover on the basis of $950 per bunch of nine hundred shingles. The evidence showed that there was no applicable custom or usage in the trade and that each party held its belief in good faith. Decision?

11. Halsey, a widower, was living without family or housekeeper in his house in Howell, New York. Burns and his wife claim that Halsey invited them to give up their house and business in Andover, New York, to live in his house and care for him. In return, they allege, he promised them the house and its furniture upon his death. Acting upon this proposal, the Burnses left Andover, moved into Halsey's house, and cared for him until he died five months later. No deed, will, or memorandum exists to authenticate Halsey's promise. McCormick, the administrator of the estate, claims the oral promise is unenforceable under the statute of frauds. Explain whether McCormick is correct.

12. Amos orally agrees to hire Elizabeth for an eight-month trial period. Elizabeth performs the job magnificently, and after several weeks Amos orally offers Elizabeth a six-month extension at a salary increase of 20 percent. Elizabeth accepts the offer. At the end of the eight-month trial period, Amos discharges Elizabeth, who brings suit against Amos for breach of contract. Is Amos liable? Why?

CASE PROBLEMS

13. Ethel Greenberg acquired the ownership of the Carlyle Hotel on Miami Beach. Having had little experience in the hotel business, she asked Miller to participate in and counsel her operation of the hotel, which he did. He claims that because his efforts produced a substantial profit, Ethel made an oral agreement for the continuation of his services. Miller alleges that in return for his services, Ethel promised to marry him and to share the net income resulting from the operation of the hotel. Miller maintains that he rendered his services to Ethel in reliance upon her promises. The couple planned to wed in the fall, but Ethel, due to physical illness, decided not to marry. Miller sued for damages for Ethel's breach of their agreement. Is the oral contract enforceable? Discuss.

14. Dean was hired on February 12 as a sales manager of the Co-op Dairy for a minimum period of one year with the dairy agreeing to pay his moving expenses. By February 26, Dean had signed a lease, moved his family from Oklahoma to Arizona, and reported for work. After he worked for a few days, he was fired. Dean then brought this action against the dairy for his salary for the year, less what he was paid. The dairy argues that the statute of frauds bars enforcement of the oral contract because the contract was not to be performed within one year. Is the dairy correct in its assertion?

15. Alice solicited an offer from Robett Manufacturing Company to manufacture certain clothing that Alice intended to supply to the government. Alice contends that in a telephone conversation Robett made an oral offer that she

immediately accepted. She then received the following letter from Robett, which, she claims, confirmed their agreement:

> Confirming our telephone conversation, we are pleased to offer the 3,500 shirts at $14.00 each and the trousers at $13.80 each with delivery approximately ninety days after receipt of order. We will try to cut this to sixty days if at all possible.
>
> This, of course, as quoted f.o.b. Atlanta and the order will not be subject to cancellation, domestic pack only.
>
> Thanking you for the opportunity to offer these garments, we are
> Very truly yours,
> Robett Manufacturing Co., Inc.

Is the agreement enforceable against Robett?

16. David and Nancy Songer planned to travel outside the United States and wanted to acquire medical insurance prior to departure. They spoke with an agent of Continental who requested that Nancy Songer undergo a medical examination based on a statement that she had a heart murmur. She promptly complied, and the Songers later met with the agent to complete the application. David Songer signed the application and tendered a check for the first six months' premium. The Songers also claim that the agent stated that a "binder" was in effect such that policy coverage was available immediately. The agent subsequently denied making this statement, relying, instead, on a clause in the contract that required home office acceptance. The Songers left the United States and sixty days later inquired as to the status of their application. At approximately the same time, Continental denied the application and sent a refund to the Songers. Nancy Songer was then severely injured in an automobile accident. When Continental refused to honor the policy, the Songers claimed that the oral representation constituted part of the contract due to the vagueness of the policy "acceptance" language. Is the evidence regarding the oral representations admissible?

17. Yokel, a grower of soybeans, had sold soybeans to Campbell Grain and Seed Company and other grain companies in the past. Campbell entered into an oral contract with Yokel to purchase soybeans from him. Promptly after entering into the oral contract, Campbell signed and mailed to Yokel a written confirmation of the oral agreement. Yokel received the written confirmation but neither signed it nor objected to its content. Campbell now brings this action against Yokel for breach of contract upon Yokel's failure to deliver the soybeans. Should Yokel be considered a merchant and thus bound by Campbell's written confirmation?

18. Presti claims that he reached an oral agreement with Wilson by telephone in October 2013 to buy a horse for $60,000. Presti asserts that he sent Wilson a bill of sale and a postdated check, which Wilson retained. Presti also claims that Wilson told him that he wished not to consummate the transaction until January 1, 2014, for tax reasons. The check was neither deposited nor negotiated. Wilson denies that he ever agreed to sell the horse or that he received the check and bill of sale from Presti. Presti's claim is supported by a copy of his check stub and by the affidavit of his executive assistant, who says that he monitored the telephone call and prepared and mailed both the bill of sale and the check. Wilson argues that the statute of frauds governs this transaction, and because there was no writing, the contract claim is barred. Is Wilson correct? Explain.

19. Louie E. Brown worked for the Phelps Dodge Corporation under an oral contract for approximately twenty-three years. In 2013, he was suspended from work for unauthorized possession of company property. In 2014, Phelps Dodge fired Brown after discovering that he was using company property without permission and building a trailer on company time. Brown sued Phelps Dodge for benefits under an unemployment benefit plan. According to the plan, "in order to be eligible for unemployment benefits, a laid-off employee must: (1) Have completed 2 or more years of continuous service with the company, and (2) Have been laid off from work because the company had determined that work was not available for him." The trial court held that the wording of the second condition was ambiguous and should be construed against Phelps Dodge, the party who chose the wording. A reading of the entire contract, however, indicates that the plan was not intended to apply to someone who was fired for cause. What is the correct interpretation of this contract?

20. Katz offered to purchase land from Joiner, and, after negotiating the terms, Joiner accepted. On October 13, over the telephone, both parties agreed to extend the time period for completing and mailing the written contract until October 20. Although the original paperwork deadline in the offer was October 14, Katz stated he had inserted that provision "for my purpose only." All other provisions of the contract remained unchanged. Accordingly, Joiner completed the contract and mailed it on October 20. Immediately after, however, Joiner sent Katz an overnight letter stating that "I have signed and returned contract, but have changed my mind. Do not wish to sell property." Joiner now claims an oral modification of a

contract within the statute of frauds is unenforceable. Katz counters that the modification is not material and therefore does not affect the underlying contract. Explain who is correct.

21. When Mr. McClam died, he left the family farm, heavily mortgaged, to his wife and children. To save the farm from foreclosure, Mrs. McClam planned to use insurance proceeds and her savings to pay off the debts. She was unwilling to do so, however, unless she had full ownership of the property. Mrs. McClam wrote her daughter, stating that the daughter should deed over her interest in the family farm to her mother and promising that all the children would inherit the farm equally upon their mother's death. The letter further explained that if foreclosure occurred, each child would receive very little, but if they complied with their mother's plan, each would eventually receive a valuable property interest upon her death. Finally, the letter stated that all the other children had agreed to this plan. Consequently, the daughter also agreed. Years later, Mrs. McClam tries to convey the farm to her son Donald. The daughter challenges, arguing that the mother is contractually bound to convey the land equally to all of the children. Donald says this was an oral agreement to sell land and is unenforceable. The daughter argues that the letter satisfies the statute of frauds, making the contract enforceable. Who gets the farm? Explain.

22. Butler Brothers Building Company sublet all of the work in a highway construction contract to Ganley Brothers, Inc. Soon thereafter, Ganley brought this action against Butler for fraud in the inducement of the contract. The contract, however, provided: "The contractor [Ganley] has examined the said contracts … , knows all the requirements, and is not relying upon any statement made by the company in respect thereto." Can Ganley introduce into evidence the oral representations made by Butler?

23. Shane Quadri, contacted Don Hoffman, an employee of Al J. Hoffman & Co. (Hoffman Agency), to procure car insurance. Later, Quadri's car was stolen on October 25 or 26. Quadri contacted Hoffman, who arranged with Budget Rent-a-Car for a rental car for Quadri until his car was recovered. Hoffman authorized Budget Rent-a-Car to bill the Hoffman Agency. Later, when the stolen car was recovered, Hoffman telephoned Goodyear and arranged to have four new tires put on Quadri's car to replace those damaged during the theft. Budget and Goodyear sued Hoffman for payment of the car rental and tires. Is Hoffman liable on his oral promise to pay for the car rental and the four new tires?

24. Thomson Printing Company is a buyer and seller of used machinery. On April 10, the president of the company, James Thomson, went to the surplus machinery department of B.F. Goodrich Company in Akron, Ohio, to examine some used equipment that was for sale. Thomson discussed the sale, including a price of $9,000, with Ingram Meyers, a Goodrich employee and agent. Four days later, on April 14, Thomson sent a purchase order to confirm the oral contract for purchase of the machinery and a partial payment of $1,000 to Goodrich in Akron. The purchase order contained Thomson Printing's name, address, and telephone number, as well as certain information about the purchase, but did not specifically mention Meyers or the surplus equipment department. Goodrich sent copies of the documents to a number of its divisions, but Meyers never learned of the confirmation until weeks later, by which time the equipment had been sold to another party. Thomson Printing brought suit against Goodrich for breach of contract. Goodrich claimed that no contract had existed and that at any rate the alleged oral contract could not be enforced because of the statute of frauds. Is the contract enforceable? Why?

25. On July 5, 2003, Richard Price signed a written employment contract as a new salesman with the Mercury Supply Company. The contract was of indefinite duration and could be terminated by either party for any reason upon fifteen days' notice. Between 2003 and 2011, Price was promoted several times. In 2008, Price was made vice president of sales. In September 2011, however, Price was told that his performance was not satisfactory and that if he did not improve he would be fired. In February 2014, Price received notice of termination. Price claims that in 2008 he entered into a valid oral employment contract with Mercury Supply Company wherein he was made vice president of sales for life or until he should retire. Is the alleged oral contract barred by the one-year provision of the statute of frauds?

26. Plaintiffs leased commercial space from the defendant to open a florist shop. After the lease was executed, the plaintiffs learned that they could not place a freestanding sign along the highway to advertise their business because the Deschutes County Code allowed only one freestanding sign on the property, and the defendant already had one in place. The plaintiffs filed this action, alleging that defendant had breached the lease by failing to provide them with space in which they could erect a freestanding sign. Paragraph 16 of the lease provides as follows: "Tenant shall not erect or install any signs visible

from outside the leased premises with out [sic] the previous written consent of the Landlord." Explain whether this evidence is admissible.

27. Jesse Carter and Jesse Thomas had an auto accident with a driver insured by Allstate. Carter and Thomas hired attorney Joseph Onwuteaka to represent them. Mr. Onwuteaka sent a demand letter for settlement of plaintiffs' claims to Allstate's adjustor, Ms. Gracie Weatherly. Mr. Onwuteaka claims Ms. Weatherly made, and he orally accepted, settlement terms on behalf of the plaintiffs. When Allstate did not honor the agreements, Carter and Thomas filed a suit for breach of contract. Discuss the enforceability of the oral agreement.

28. Mary Iacono and Carolyn Lyons had been friends for almost thirty-five years. Mary suffers from advanced rheumatoid arthritis and is in a wheelchair. Carolyn invited Mary to join her on a trip to Las Vegas, Nevada, for which Carolyn paid. Mary contended she was invited to Las Vegas by Carolyn because Carolyn thought Mary was lucky. Sometime before the trip, Mary had a dream about winning on a Las Vegas slot machine. Mary's dream convinced her to go to Las Vegas, and she accepted Carolyn's offer to split "50–50" any gambling winnings. Carolyn provided Mary with money for gambling. Mary and Carolyn started to gamble but after losing $47.00, Carolyn wanted to leave to see a show. Mary begged Carolyn to stay, and Carolyn agreed on the condition that Carolyn put the coins into the machines because doing so took Mary too long. Mary agreed and led Carolyn to a dollar slot machine that looked like the machine in her dream. The machine did not pay on the first try. Mary then said, "Just one more time," and Carolyn looked at Mary and said, "This one's for you, Puddin." They hit the jackpot, winning $1,908,064 to be paid over a period of twenty years. Carolyn refused to share the winnings with Mary. Is Mary entitled to one-half of the proceeds? Explain.

TAKING SIDES

Stuart Studio, an art studio, prepared a new catalog for the National School of Heavy Equipment, a school run by Gilbert and Donald Shaw. When the artwork was virtually finished, Gilbert Shaw requested Stuart Studio to purchase and supervise the printing of twenty-five thousand catalogs. Shaw told the art studio that payment of the printing costs would be made within ten days after billing and that if the "National School would not pay the full total that he would stand good for the entire bill." Shaw was chairman of the board of directors of the school, and he owned 100 percent of its voting stock and 49 percent of its nonvoting stock. The school became bankrupt, and Stuart Studio was unable to recover the sum from the school. Stuart Studio then brought an action against Shaw on the basis of his promise to pay the bill.

a. What are the arguments that Shaw is not liable on his promise?

b. What are the arguments that Shaw is liable on his promise?

c. Is Shaw obligated to pay the debt in question? Explain.

THIRD PARTIES TO CONTRACTS

CHAPTER OUTCOMES

After reading and studying this chapter, you should be able to:

- Distinguish between an assignment of rights and a delegation of duties.

- Identify (1) the requirements of an assignment of contract rights and (2) those rights that are not assignable.

- Identify those situations in which a delegation of duties is not permitted.

- Distinguish between an intended beneficiary and an incidental beneficiary.

- Explain when the rights of an intended beneficiary vest.

Whereas prior chapters considered contractual situations essentially involving only two parties, this chapter deals with the rights or duties of third parties, namely, persons who are not parties to the contract but who have a right to, or an obligation for, its performance. These rights and duties arise either by (1) an assignment of the rights of a party to the contract, (2) a delegation of the duties of a party to the contract, or (3) the express terms of a contract entered into for the benefit of a third person. In an assignment or delegation, the third party's rights or duties arise after the contract is made, whereas in the third situation, the third-party beneficiary's rights arise at the time the contract was formed. We will consider these three situations in that order.

ASSIGNMENT OF RIGHTS

Every contract creates both rights and duties. A person who owes a duty under a contract is an **obligor**, while a person to whom a contractual duty is owed is an **obligee**. For instance, Ann promises to sell to Bart an automobile for which Bart promises to pay $10,000 in monthly installments over the next three years. Ann's right under the contract is to receive payment from Bart, whereas Ann's duty is to deliver the automobile. Bart's right is to receive the automobile; his duty is to pay for it.

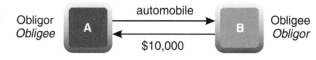

An **assignment of rights** is the voluntary transfer to a third party of the rights arising from the contract. In the

above example, if Ann were to transfer her right under the contract (the installment payments due from Bart) to Clark for $8,500 in cash, this would constitute a valid assignment of rights. In this case, Ann would be the **assignor**, Clark would be the **assignee**, and Bart would be the **obligor**.

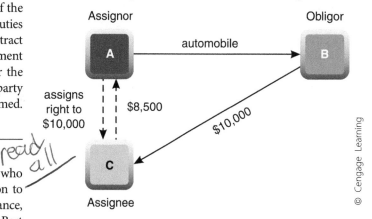

An effective assignment terminates the assignor's right to receive performance by the obligor. After an assignment, only the assignee has a right to the obligor's performance.

On the other hand, if Ann and Doris agree that Doris should deliver the automobile to Bart, this would constitute a delegation, not an assignment, of duties between Ann and Doris. A **delegation of duties** is a transfer to a third party of a contractual obligation. In this instance, Ann would be the **delegator**, Doris would be the **delegatee**, and Bart would be the **obligee**. Delegations of duties are discussed later in this chapter.

LAW GOVERNING ASSIGNMENTS

The law governing assignments arises principally from the common law of contracts, Article 2 of the Uniform Commercial Code (UCC), and Article 9 of the UCC. Article 2 applies to assignments of rights under a contract for the sale of goods. Article 9 covers all assignments made to secure the performance of an obligation *and* all assignments involving rights to payment for goods sold or leased or for services rendered.

REQUIREMENTS OF AN ASSIGNMENT

The Restatement defines an assignment of a right as a "manifestation of the assignor's intention to transfer it by virtue of which the assignor's right to performance by the obligor is extinguished in whole or in part and the assignee acquires a right to such performance." Section 317(1). No special form or particular words are necessary to create an assignment. Any words that fairly indicate an intention to make the assignee the owner of the right are sufficient. For instance, Eve delivers to Harold a writing addressed to Mary stating, "Pay Harold for his own use $1,000 out of the amount you owe me." This writing is a legally sufficient assignment. Restatement, Section 325, Illustration 1.

Unless otherwise provided by statute, an assignment may be oral. The UCC imposes a writing requirement on all assignments beyond $5,000. Section 1–206. The 2001 Revision to Article 1, however, has deleted this requirement. In addition, Article 9 requires certain assignments to be in writing.

Consideration is not required for an effective assignment. Consequently, gratuitous assignments are valid and enforceable. By giving value for the assignment, the assignee manifests his assent to the assignment as part of the bargained-for exchange. On the other hand, when the assignment is gratuitous, the assignee's assent is not always required. Any assignee, however, who has not assented to an assignment, may disclaim the assignment within a reasonable time after learning of its existence and terms. Restatement, Section 327. No particular formality is required for the disclaimer, which renders the assignment inoperative from the beginning.

REVOCABILITY OF ASSIGNMENTS When the assignee gives consideration in exchange for an assignment, a contract exists between the assignor and the assignee. Consequently, the assignor may not revoke the assignment without the assignee's assent. A gratuitous assignment, in contrast, is revocable by the assignor and is terminated by her death, incapacity, or subsequent assignment of the right, unless she has made an effective delivery of the assignment to the assignee by transferring a deed or other document evidencing the right, such as a stock certificate or savings passbook. Delivery also may consist of physically delivering a signed, written assignment of the contract right.

A gratuitous assignment is also rendered irrevocable if, prior to the attempted revocation, the donee-assignee receives payment of the claim from the obligor, obtains a judgment against the obligor, or obtains a new contract with the obligor. For example, Nancy owes Howard $50,000. Howard signs a written statement granting Paul a gratuitous assignment of his rights from Nancy but dies prior to delivering to Paul the signed, written assignment of the contract right. The assignment is terminated and therefore ineffective. On the other hand, had Howard delivered the signed, written assignment to Paul before he died, the assignment would have been effective and irrevocable.

PRACTICAL ADVICE

Be sure to make irrevocable assignments of only those rights you wish to transfer.

PARTIAL ASSIGNMENTS A partial assignment is a transfer of a portion of the contractual rights to one or more assignees. Although partial assignments were not enforceable at early common law, such assignments now are permitted and are enforceable. The obligor, however, may require all the parties entitled to the promised performance to litigate the matter in one action, thus ensuring that all parties are present and thereby avoiding the undue hardship of multiple lawsuits. For example, Jack owes Richard $2,500. Richard assigns $1,000 to Mildred. Neither Richard nor Mildred can maintain an action against Jack if Jack objects, unless the other is joined in the lawsuit against Jack.

RIGHTS THAT ARE ASSIGNABLE

As a general rule, most contract rights, including rights under an option contract, are assignable. The most common contractual right that may be assigned is the right to the payment of money, such as an account receivable or interest due or to be paid. The right to property other than money, such as goods or land, is also frequently assignable.

RIGHTS THAT ARE NOT ASSIGNABLE

To protect the obligor or the public interest, some contract rights are not assignable. These nonassignable contract rights include those that (1) materially change the obligor's duty or materially increase the risk or burden upon the obligor, (2) transfer highly personal contract rights, (3) are validly prohibited by the contract, or (4) are prohibited by statute or public policy. Restatement, Section 317(2).

ASSIGNMENTS THAT MATERIALLY INCREASE THE DUTY, RISK, OR BURDEN An assignment is ineffective when performance by the obligor to the assignee would differ materially from her performance to the assignor; that is, when the assignment would significantly change the nature or extent of the obligor's duty. Thus, an automobile liability insurance policy issued to Alex is not assignable by Alex to Betty. The risk assumed by the insurance company was liability for Alex's negligent operation of the automobile. Liability for operation of the same automobile by Betty would be a risk entirely different from the one that the insurance company had assumed. Similarly, Alex would not be allowed to assign to Cynthia, the owner of a twenty-five-room mansion, his contractual right to have Betty paint his small, two-bedroom house. Clearly, such an assignment would materially increase Betty's duty of performance. By comparison, the right to receive monthly payments under a contract may be assigned, for mailing the check to the assignee costs no more than mailing it to the assignor. Moreover, if a contract explicitly provides that it may be assigned, then rights under it are assignable even if the assignment would change the duty, risk, or burden of performance on the obligor. Restatement, Section 323(1).

ASSIGNMENTS OF PERSONAL RIGHTS Where the rights under a contract are highly personal, in that they are limited to the person of the obligee, such rights are not assignable. An extreme example of such a contract is an agreement of two persons to marry one another. The prospective groom obviously cannot transfer to some third party the prospective bride's promise to marry him. A more typical example of a contract involving personal rights would be a contract between a teacher and a school. The teacher could not assign to another teacher her right to a faculty position. Similarly, a student who is awarded a scholarship cannot assign his right to some other person.

◆ SEE CASE 16-1

EXPRESS PROHIBITION AGAINST ASSIGNMENT Contract terms prohibiting assignment of rights under the contract are strictly construed. Moreover, most courts interpret a general prohibition against assignments as a mere promise not to assign. As a consequence, the prohibition, if violated, gives the obligor a right to damages for breach of the terms forbidding assignment but does *not* render the assignment ineffective.

Section 322(1) of the Restatement provides that, unless circumstances indicate the contrary, a contract term prohibiting assignment of the contract bars only the delegation to the assignee (delegatee) of the assignor's (delegator's) duty of performance, not the assignment of rights. Thus, Abe and Bill contract for the sale of land by Bill to Abe for $300,000 and provide in their contract that Abe may not assign his rights under it. Abe pays Bill $300,000 and thereby fully performs his obligations under the contract. Abe then assigns his rights to Cheryl, who is entitled to receive the land from Bill (the obligor) despite the contractual prohibition of assignment.

UCC Section 2-210(2) provides that a right to damages for breach of the whole contract or a right arising out of the assignor's due performance of his entire obligation can be assigned despite a contractual provision to the contrary. UCC Section 2-210(3) provides that, unless circumstances indicate the contrary, a contract term prohibiting assignment of the contract bars only the delegation to the assignee (delegatee) of the assignor's (delegator's) duty of performance, not the assignment of rights. UCC Section 9-406 makes generally ineffective any term in a security agreement restricting the assignment of a security interest in any right to payment for goods sold or leased or for services rendered.

◆ SEE CASE 16-2

PRACTICAL ADVICE
Consider including in your contract a provision prohibiting the assignment of any contractual rights without your written consent and making ineffective any such assignment.

ASSIGNMENTS PROHIBITED BY LAW Various Federal and State statutes, as well as public policy, prohibit or regulate the assignment of certain types of contract rights. For instance, assignments of future wages are subject to statutes, some of which prohibit such assignments altogether while others require them to be in writing and subject to certain restrictions. Moreover, an assignment that violates public policy will be unenforceable even in the absence of a prohibiting statute.

RIGHTS OF THE ASSIGNEE

OBTAINS RIGHTS OF ASSIGNOR The general rule is that an assignee **stands in the shoes** of the assignor. He acquires the rights of the assignor, but no new or additional rights, and takes the assigned rights with all of the defenses, defects, and infirmities to which they would be subject, were the assignor to bring an action against the obligor. Thus, in an action brought by the assignee against the obligor, the obligor may plead fraud, duress, undue influence, failure of consideration, breach of contract, or any other defense against the assignor arising out of the original contract. The obligor also may assert rights of setoff or counterclaim arising against the assignor out of entirely separate matters, provided they arose prior to his receiving notice of the assignment.

The Code permits the buyer under a contract of sale to agree as part of the contract that he will not assert against an assignee any claim or defense that the buyer may have against the seller if the assignee takes the assignment for value, in good faith, and without notice of conflicting claims or of certain defenses. UCC Section 9-403. Such a provision in an agreement renders the seller's rights more marketable. The Federal Trade Commission, however, has invalidated such waiver of defense provisions in consumer credit transactions. (This rule is discussed more fully in *Chapter 27.*) Article 9 reflects this rule by essentially rendering waiver-of-defense clauses ineffective in consumer transactions. UCC Section 9–403(d). Most States also have statutes protecting buyers in consumer transactions by prohibiting waiver of defenses.

◆ **SEE CASE 16-3**

NOTICE To be valid, notice of an assignment does not have to be given to the obligor. Nonetheless, giving such notice is advisable because an assignee will lose his rights against an obligor who pays the assignor without notice of the assignment: to compel an obligor to pay a claim a second time, when she was not notified that a new party was entitled to payment would be unfair. For example, Donald owes Gary $1,000 due on September 1. Gary assigns the debt to Paula on August 1, but neither he nor Paula informs Donald. On September 1, Donald pays Gary. Donald is fully discharged from his obligation, whereas Gary is liable for $1,000 to Paula. On the other hand, if Paula had given notice of the assignment to Donald before September 1 and Donald had paid Gary nevertheless, Paula would then have the right to recover the $1,000 from either Donald or Gary.

Furthermore, notice cuts off any defenses based on subsequent agreements between the obligor and assignor. Moreover, as already indicated, notice precludes subsequent setoffs and counterclaims of the obligor that arise out of entirely separate matters.

PRACTICAL ADVICE
Upon receiving an assignment of a contractual right, promptly notify the obligor of the assignment.

IMPLIED WARRANTIES OF ASSIGNOR

An implied warranty is an obligation imposed by law upon the transfer of property or contract rights. In the absence of an express intention to the contrary, an assignor who receives value makes the following implied warranties to the assignee with respect to the assigned right:

1. that he will do nothing to defeat or impair the assignment;
2. that the assigned right actually exists and is subject to no limitations or defenses other than those stated or apparent at the time of the assignment;
3. that any writing evidencing the right delivered to the assignee or exhibited to him as an inducement to accept the assignment is genuine and what it purports to be; and
4. that the assignor has no knowledge of any fact that would impair the value of the assignment.

Thus, Eric has a right against Julia and assigns it for value to Gwen. Later, Eric gives Julia a release. Gwen may recover damages from Eric for breach of the first implied warranty.

EXPRESS WARRANTIES OF ASSIGNOR

An **express warranty** is an explicitly made contractual promise regarding property or contract rights transferred. The assignor is further bound by any express warranties he makes to the assignee with respect to the right assigned. The assignor does not, however, guarantee that the obligor will pay the assigned debt or otherwise perform, unless such a guarantee is explicitly stated.

PRACTICAL ADVICE
Consider obtaining from the assignor an express warranty that the contractual right is assignable and guaranteeing that the obligor will perform the assigned obligation.

SUCCESSIVE ASSIGNMENTS OF THE SAME RIGHT

The owner of a right could conceivably make successive assignments of the same claim to different persons. Assume that Barney owes Andrea $1,000. On June 1, Andrea for value assigns the debt to Carlos. Thereafter, on June 15, Andrea assigns it to David, who in good faith gives value and has no knowledge of the prior assignment by Andrea to Carlos. If the assignment is subject to Article 9, then that article's priority rules will control, as discussed in *Chapter 37.* Otherwise, the priority is determined by the common law. The majority rule in the United States is that the **first assignee in point of time** (here, Carlos) prevails over subsequent assignees. By comparison, in England and in a minority of the States, the first assignee to notify the obligor prevails.

The Restatement adopts a third view. A prior assignee is entitled to the assigned right and its proceeds to the exclusion of a subsequent assignee, *except* where the prior assignment is revocable or voidable by the assignor or where the subsequent assignee in good faith and without knowledge of the prior assignment gives value and obtains one of the following: (1) payment or satisfaction of the obligor's duty, (2) a judgment against the obligor, (3) a new contract with the obligor, or (4) possession of a writing of a type customarily accepted as a symbol or evidence of the right assigned. Restatement, Section 342.

DELEGATION OF DUTIES

As indicated, contractual duties are *not* assignable, but their performance generally may be *delegated* to a third person. A **delegation of duties** is a transfer of a contractual obligation to a third party. For example, Anthony promises to sell Bella a new automobile, for which Bella promises to pay $10,000 by monthly installments over the next three years. If Anthony and Donald agree that Donald should deliver the automobile to Bella, this would not constitute an assignment but would be a delegation of duties between Anthony and Donald. In this instance, Anthony would be the **delegator**, Donald would be the **delegatee**, and Bella would be the **obligee**.

A delegation of duty does not extinguish the delegator's obligation to perform, because Anthony remains liable to Bella. When the delegatee accepts, or assumes, the delegated duty, both the delegator and delegatee are held liable to the obligee for performance of the contractual duty.

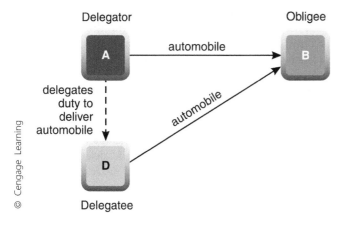

DELEGABLE DUTIES

Although contractual duties generally are delegable, a delegation will not be permitted if

1. the nature of the duties is personal in that the obligee has a substantial interest in having the delegator perform the contract;
2. the performance is expressly made nondelegable; or
3. the delegation is prohibited by statute or public policy.

Restatement, Section 318 and UCC Section 2–210. The courts will examine a delegation more closely than an assignment because a delegation compels the nondelegating party to the contract (the obligee) to receive performance from a party with whom she has not dealt.

For example, a schoolteacher may not delegate her performance to another teacher, even if the substitute is equally competent, because this is a contract that is personal in nature. In the frequently quoted words of an English case: "You have a right to the benefit you contemplate from the character, credit and substance of the person with whom you contract." On the other hand, under a contract in which performance involves no peculiar or special skill and in which no personal trust or confidence is involved, the party may

delegate the performance of his duty. For example, the duty to pay money, to deliver fungible goods such as corn, or to mow a lawn is usually delegable.

◆ **SEE CASE 16-4**

PRACTICAL ADVICE

When it is important that the other party to a contract personally perform his contractual obligations, consider including a term in the contract prohibiting any delegation of duties without written consent.

DUTIES OF THE PARTIES

Even when permitted, a delegation of a duty to a third person still leaves the delegator bound to perform. If the delegator desires to be discharged of the duty, she is allowed to enter into an agreement by which she obtains the consent of the obligee to substitute a third person (the delegatee) in her place. This is a **novation**, whereby the delegator is discharged and the third party becomes directly bound upon his promise to the obligee.

Though a delegation authorizes a third party to perform a duty for the delegator, a delegatee becomes liable for performance only if he assents to perform the delegated duties. Thus, if Frank owes a duty to Grace, and Frank delegates that duty to Henry, Henry is not obligated to either Frank or Grace to perform the duty unless Henry agrees to do so. Nevertheless, if Henry promises either Frank (the delegator) or Grace (the obligee) that he will perform Frank's duty, Henry is said to have **assumed the delegated duty** and becomes liable to both Frank and Grace for nonperformance. Accordingly, when duties are both delegated and assumed, both the delegator and the delegatee are liable to the obligee for proper performance of the original contractual duty. The delegatee's promise to perform creates contract rights in the obligee who may bring an action against the delegatee as a third party beneficiary of the contract between the delegator and the delegatee. (Third-party contracts are discussed later in this chapter.)

The question of whether a delegatee has assumed delegated duties frequently arises in the following ambiguous situation: Marty and Carol agree to an assignment of Marty's contract with Bob. The Code clearly resolves this ambiguity by providing that, unless the language or circumstances indicate the contrary, an assignment of "the contract," or of "all my rights under the contract," or an assignment in similar general terms is an assignment of rights *and* a delegation of performance of the assignor's duties; its acceptance by the assignee constitutes a promise by her to perform those duties. Section 2–210(4). The Restatement, Section 328, has also adopted this position. For example, Cooper Oil Co. has a contract to deliver oil to Halsey. Cooper Oil Co. delivers to Lowell Oil Co. a writing assigning to Lowell Oil Co. "all Cooper

APPLYING THE LAW

Third Parties to Contracts

FACTS Monica signed a twelve-month lease with Grand-ridge Apartments in Grand City. But after only two months she received a promotion that required her to move to Lakeville, three hundred miles away. Mindful of her lease obligation, she found an acquaintance, Troy, to rent the apartment for the remaining ten months. Troy promised Monica he would pay the rent directly to the landlord each month and would clean the place up before moving out at the end of the lease term.

After moving in, Troy personally delivered a check for the rent to the landlord each month until four months later when he lost his job, at which point he stopped paying rent altogether. The landlord evicted Troy and, as he was unable to find another suitable tenant, he sued Monica for the rent owed on the remainder of the lease. Monica claimed the landlord should have sued Troy.

ISSUE Is Monica liable for the remaining lease payments?

RULE OF LAW Performance of a contract obligation generally may be delegated to a third person who is willing to assume the liability. However, such a delegation by the obligor does not extinguish the obligor/delegator's duty to perform the contract. If the delegator wishes to be discharged from the contract prospectively, she should enter into a new agreement with the obligee, in which the obli-gee consents to the substitution of a third party (the dele-gatee) in the delegator's place. This is called a novation.

APPLICATION The lease is a contract obligation. Monica is the obligor, and the landlord is the obligee. Here, Monica delegated her performance under the lease to Troy. Troy assumed liability for the lease payments by agreeing to pay the rent. However, even though a valid delegation has been made, Monica is not relieved of her duty to pay the rent. Instead, both Troy and Monica are now obligated to the landlord for the remaining lease term.

Had Monica entered into a novation with the landlord, only Troy would be liable for the remaining rent. But the facts do not support finding a novation. Troy made the rent payments directly to the landlord, who ultimately evicted Troy from the apartment. Therefore, the landlord was aware that Troy had taken possession of the apartment and that Troy may have taken on some responsibility for rent payments. At most, the landlord tacitly consented to the informal assignment and delegation of the lease to Troy. However, the landlord never agreed to substitute Troy for Monica and thereby to release Monica from her legal obligations under the lease.

CONCLUSION In a suit by the landlord, Monica is responsible for the remaining rent payments.

Oil Co.'s rights under the contract." Lowell Oil Co. is under a duty to Halsey to deliver the oil called for by the contract, and Cooper Oil Co. is liable to Halsey if Lowell Oil Co. does not perform. It should also be recalled that the Restatement and the Code provide that a clause prohibiting an assignment of "the contract" is to be construed as barring only the delegation to the assignee (delegatee) of the assignor's (delegator's) performance, unless the circumstances indicate the contrary.

THIRD-PARTY BENEFICIARY CONTRACTS

A contract in which a party (the **promisor**) promises to render a certain performance not to the other party (the **promisee**) but to a third person (the **beneficiary**) is called a third-party beneficiary contract. The third person is not a party to the contract but is merely a beneficiary of it. Such contracts may be divided into two types: (1) intended beneficiary and (2) incidental beneficiary. An **intended beneficiary** is intended by the two parties to the contract (the promisor and promisee) to receive a benefit from the performance of their agreement. Accordingly, the courts generally permit intended beneficiaries to enforce third-party contracts. For example, Abbott promises Baldwin to deliver an automobile to Carson if Baldwin promises to pay $10,000. Carson is the intended beneficiary.

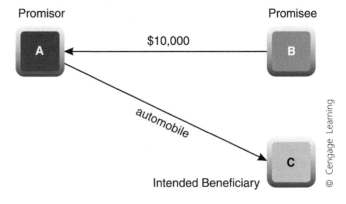

In an **incidental beneficiary** contract, the third party is not intended to receive a benefit under the contract.

Accordingly, courts do not enforce the third party's right to the benefits of the contract. For example, Abbott promises to purchase and deliver to Baldwin an automobile for $10,000. In all probability, Abbott would acquire the automobile from Davis. Davis would be an incidental beneficiary and would have no enforceable rights against either Abbott or Baldwin.

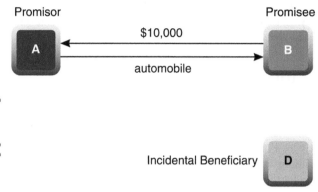

INTENDED BENEFICIARY

Unless otherwise agreed between the promisor and promisee, a beneficiary of a promise is an intended beneficiary if the parties intended this to be the result of their agreement. Restatement, Section 302. There are two types of intended beneficiaries: (1) donee beneficiaries and (2) creditor beneficiaries.

DONEE BENEFICIARY A third party is an intended donee beneficiary if the promisee's purpose in bargaining for and obtaining the agreement with the promisor is to make a gift of the promised performance to the beneficiary. The ordinary life insurance policy illustrates this type of contract. The insured (the promisee) makes a contract with an insurance company (the promisor) that promises, in consideration of premiums paid to it by the insured, to pay upon the death of the insured a stated sum of money to the named beneficiary, who is an intended donee beneficiary.

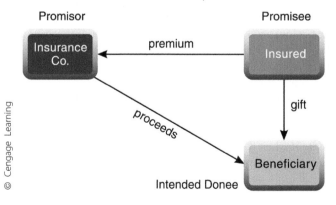

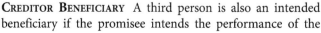

CREDITOR BENEFICIARY A third person is also an intended beneficiary if the promisee intends the performance of the promise to satisfy a legal duty he owes to the beneficiary, who is a creditor of the promisee. The contract involves consideration moving from the promisee to the promisor in exchange for the promisor's engaging to pay a debt or to discharge an obligation the promisee owes to the third person.

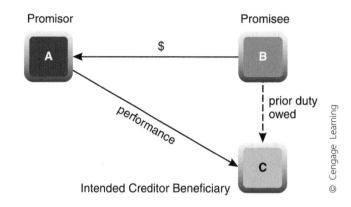

To illustrate, in a contract for the sale by Wesley of his business to Susan, Susan promises Wesley that she will pay all of his outstanding business debts, as listed in the contract. Here, Wesley's creditors are creditor beneficiaries. Similarly, in the classic *Lawrence v. Fox*, 20 N.Y. 268 (1859), Holly loaned Fox $300 in consideration for Fox's promise to pay that sum to Lawrence, a creditor of Holly. Fox failed to pay Lawrence, who sued Fox for the $300. The court held for Lawrence, who was permitted to recover as a third-party creditor beneficiary to the contract between Holly and Fox.

◆ **SEE CASE 16-5**

RIGHTS OF INTENDED BENEFICIARY An intended *donee* beneficiary may enforce the contract only against the promisor. He cannot maintain an action against the promisee, as the promisee was under no legal obligation to him. An intended *creditor* beneficiary, however, may enforce the contract against either or both parties. If Willard owes Lola $500, and Julie contracts with Willard to pay this debt to Lola, Willard is not thereby relieved of his liability to Lola. If Julie breaks the contract, Lola, as a creditor beneficiary, may sue her. In addition, Lola may sue Willard as her debtor. If Lola should obtain judgments against both Julie and Willard, she is, of course, entitled to collect only one judgment. If Lola recovers against Willard, Willard has a right of reimbursement from Julie, the promisor. Restatement, Section 310.

VESTING OF RIGHTS A contract for the benefit of an intended beneficiary confers upon that beneficiary rights that she may enforce. Until these rights **vest** (take effect), however, the promisor and promisee may, by later agreement, vary or completely discharge them. The States vary considerably as to when vesting occurs. Some hold that vesting takes place immediately upon the making of the contract. In others, vesting occurs when the third party learns of the contract and assents to it. In another group of States, vesting requires the third party to change his position in reliance upon the promise made for his benefit. The Restatement has adopted the following position: If the contract between the promisor and promisee provides that they may not vary its terms without the consent of the beneficiary, such a provision is effective. Otherwise, the parties to the contract may rescind or vary the contract unless the intended beneficiary (1) has brought an action upon the promise, (2) has changed her position in reliance upon it, or (3) has assented to the promise at the request of the promisor or promisee. Restatement, Section 311.

On the other hand, the promisor and promisee may provide that the benefits will *never* vest. For example, Mildred purchases an insurance policy on her own life, naming her husband as beneficiary. Her policy, as such policies commonly do, reserves to Mildred the right to change the beneficiary or even to cancel the policy entirely.

PRACTICAL ADVICE

To avoid uncertainty, consider specifying in the contract whether there are any third-party beneficiaries and, if so, who they are, what their rights are, and when their rights vest.

DEFENSES AGAINST BENEFICIARY In an action by the intended beneficiary of a third-party contract to enforce the promise, the promisor may assert any defense that would be available to her if the action had been brought by the promisee. The rights of the third party are based upon the promisor's contract with the promisee. Thus, the promisor may assert the absence of mutual assent or consideration, lack of capacity, fraud, mistake, and the like against the intended beneficiary. Once an intended beneficiary's rights have vested, however, the promisor may not assert the defense of contractual modification or rescission.

INCIDENTAL BENEFICIARY

An incidental third-party beneficiary is a person whom the parties to a contract did not intend to benefit but who nevertheless would derive some benefit from its performance. For instance, a contract to raze an old, unsightly building and replace it with a costly, modern house would benefit the owner of the adjoining property by increasing his property's value. He would have no rights under the contract, however, as the benefit to him would be unintended and incidental.

A third person who may benefit incidentally from the performance of a contract to which he is not a party has no rights under the contract. Neither the promisee nor the promisor intended that the third person benefit. Assume that for a stated consideration George promises Kathy that he will purchase and deliver to Kathy a brand-new Sony television of the latest model. Kathy pays in advance for the television. George does not deliver the television to Kathy. As an incidental beneficiary, Cosmos Appliances, Inc., the local exclusive Sony dealer, has no rights under the contract, although performance by George would produce a sale from which Cosmos would benefit.

CHAPTER SUMMARY

ASSIGNMENT OF RIGHTS   **Definition of Assignment** voluntary transfer to a third party of the rights arising from a contract so that the assignor's right to performance is extinguished
- *Assignor* party making an assignment
- *Assignee* party to whom contract rights are assigned
- *Obligor* party owing a duty to the assignor under the original contract
- *Obligee* party to whom a duty of performance is owed under a contract

Requirements of an Assignment include intent but not consideration
- *Revocability of Assignment* when the assignee gives consideration, the assignor may not revoke the assignment without the assignee's consent
- *Partial Assignment* transfer of a portion of contractual rights to one or more assignees

Assignability most contract rights are assignable, except
- assignments that materially increase the duty, risk, or burden upon the obligor
- assignments of personal rights
- assignments expressly forbidden by the contract
- assignments prohibited by law

Rights of Assignee the assignee stands in the shoes of the assignor
- *Defenses of Obligor* may be asserted against the assignee
- *Notice* is not required but is advisable

Implied Warranty obligation imposed by law upon the assignor of a contract right

Express Warranty explicitly made contractual promise regarding contract rights transferred

Successive Assignments of the Same Right the majority rule is that the first assignee in point of time prevails over later assignees; minority rule is that the first assignee to notify the obligor prevails

---

DELEGATION OF DUTIES

Definition of Delegation transfer to a third party of a contractual obligation
- *Delegator* party delegating his duty to a third party
- *Delegatee* third party to whom the delegator's duty is delegated
- *Obligee* party to whom a duty of performance is owed by the delegator and delegatee

Delegable Duties most contract duties may be delegated, *except*
- duties that are personal
- duties that are expressly nondelegable
- duties whose delegation is prohibited by statute or public policy

Duties of the Parties
- *Delegation* delegator is still bound to perform original obligation
- *Novation* contract, to which the obligee is a party, substituting a new promisor for an existing promisor, who is consequently no longer liable on the original contract and is not liable as a delegator

---

THIRD-PARTY BENEFICIARY CONTRACTS

Definition a contract in which one party promises to render a performance to a third person (the beneficiary)

Intended Beneficiaries third parties intended by the two contracting parties to receive a benefit from their contract
- *Donee Beneficiary* a third party intended to receive a benefit from the contract as a gift
- *Creditor Beneficiary* a third person intended to receive a benefit from the agreement to satisfy a legal duty owed to her
- *Rights of Intended Beneficiary* an intended donee beneficiary may enforce the contract against the promisor; an intended creditor beneficiary may enforce the contract against either or both the promisor and the promisee
- *Vesting of Rights* if the beneficiary's rights vest, the promisor and promisee may not thereafter vary or discharge these vested rights
- *Defenses against Beneficiary* in an action by the intended beneficiary of a third-party contract to enforce the promise, the promisor may assert any defense that would be available to her if the action had been brought by the promisee

Incidental Beneficiary third party whom the two parties to the contract have no intention of benefiting by their contract and who acquires no rights under the contract

CASES

CASE
16-1

Rights That Are Not Assignable: Personal Rights
REISER v. DAYTON COUNTRY CLUB COMPANY
United States Court of Appeals, Sixth Circuit, 1992
972 F.2d 689
http://scholar.google.com/scholar_case?case=6023421001644754391&q=972+F.2d+689&hl=en&as_sdt=2,34

Joiner, J.
[The Dayton Country Club Company (the Club) offers many social activities to its members. The privilege to play golf at the Club, however, is reserved to a special membership category for which additional fees are charged. The Club chooses golfing memberships from a waiting list of members according to detailed rules, regulations, and procedures. Magness and Redman were golfing members of the Club. Upon their filing for bankruptcy, their trustee sought to assign by sale their golf rights to (1) other members on the waiting list, (2) other members not on the waiting list, or (3) the general public, provided the purchaser first acquired membership in the Club. The bankruptcy court found that the Club's rules governing golf membership were essentially anti-assignment provisions and therefore the estate could not assign rights contained in the membership agreement. On appeal to the district court, the bankruptcy court's ruling was affirmed. The district court added that this case was not a lease but rather a "non-commercial dispute over the possession of a valuable membership in a recreational and social club."]

* * *

* * * [T]he contracts involve complex issues and multiple parties: the members of the club, in having an orderly procedure for the selection of full golfing members; the club itself, in demonstrating to all who would become members that there is a predictable and orderly method of filling vacancies in the golfing roster; and more particularly, persons on the waiting list who have deposited substantial sums of money

based on an expectation and a developed procedure that in due course they, in turn, would become full golfing members.

If the trustee is permitted to assume and assign the full golf membership, the club would be required to breach its agreement with the persons on the waiting list, each of whom has contractual rights with the club. It would require the club to accept performance from and render performance to a person other than the debtor. * * *

* * *

The contracts creating the complex relationships among the parties and others are not in any way commercial. They create personal relationships among individuals who play golf, who are waiting to play golf, who eat together, swim and play together. They are personal contracts and Ohio law does not permit the assignment of personal contracts. [Citation.]

So-called personal contracts, or contracts in which the personality of one of the parties is material, are not assignable. Whether the personality of one or both parties is material depends on the intention of the parties, as shown by the language which they have used, and upon the nature of the contract.

* * *

Therefore, we believe that the trustee's motion to assign the full golf membership should be denied. We reach this conclusion because the arrangements for filling vacancies proscribe assignment, the club did not consent to the assignment and sale, and applicable law excuses the club from accepting performance from or rendering performance to a person other than the debtor.

CASE
16-2

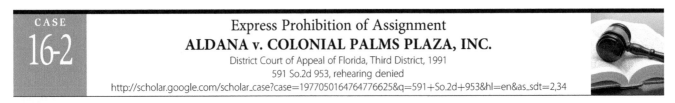

Express Prohibition of Assignment
ALDANA v. COLONIAL PALMS PLAZA, INC.
District Court of Appeal of Florida, Third District, 1991
591 So.2d 953, rehearing denied
http://scholar.google.com/scholar_case?case=1977050164764776625&q=591+So.2d+953&hl=en&as_sdt=2,34

Per Curiam
The appellant, Robert Aldana, appeals an adverse summary judgment in favor of appellee, Colonial Palms Plaza, Inc. and an order awarding Colonial Palms Plaza, Inc. attorney's fees pursuant to the offer of judgment rule. We reverse.

Colonial Palms Plaza, Inc. [Landlord], entered into a lease agreement with Abby's Cakes On Dixie, Inc. [Tenant] for

commercial space in a shopping center. The lease included a provision in which Landlord agreed to pay Tenant a construction allowance of up to $11,250 after Tenant satisfactorily completed certain improvements to the rented premises.

Prior to the completion of the improvements, Tenant assigned its right to receive the first $8,000 of the construction allowance to Robert Aldana [Assignee]. In return,

Assignee loaned Tenant $8,000 to finance the construction. Assignee recorded the assignment and sent notice to the assignment by certified mail to Landlord.

When Tenant completed the improvements to the rented premises, Landlord ignored the assignment and paid Tenant the construction allowance. Assignee sued Landlord for the money due pursuant to the assignment. The trial court granted Landlord's motion for summary judgment.

The trial court also awarded Landlord attorney's fees pursuant to the offer of judgment rule, [citation], and costs pursuant to [citation].

Landlord relies on an anti-assignment clause in the lease agreement to argue that the assignment was void and unenforceable. The clause states in part:

> TENANT agrees not to assign, mortgage, pledge, or encumber this Lease, in whole or in part, or to sublet the whole or any part of the DEMISED PREMISES, or to permit the use of the whole or any part of the DEMISED PREMISES by any licensee or concessionaire, without first obtaining the prior, specific written consent of LANDLORD at LANDLORD'S sole discretion. * * * Any such assignment, encumbrance or subletting without such consent shall be void and shall at LANDLORD'S option constitute a default.

* * *

Assignee argues * * * that under ordinary contract principles, the lease provision at issue here does not prevent the assignment of the right to receive contractual payments. We agree.

So far as pertinent here, the lease provides that "TENANT agrees not to assign * * * this Lease, in whole or in part. * * * " Tenant did not assign the lease, but instead assigned a right to receive the construction allowance.

The law in this area is summarized in Restatement (Second) of Contracts, §322(1), as follows:

> Unless the circumstances indicate the contrary, a contract term prohibiting assignment of "the contract" bars only the delegation to an assignee of the performance by the assignor of a duty or condition.

As a rule of construction, in other words, a prohibition against assignment of the contract (or in this case, the lease) will prevent assignment of contractual duties, but does not prevent assignment of the right to receive payments due—unless the circumstances indicate the contrary. [Citations.]

Landlord was given notice of the assignment. Delivery of the notice of the assignment to the debtor fixes accountability of the debtor to the assignee. [Citation.] Therefore, Landlord was bound by the assignment. [Citation.] The trial court improperly granted final summary judgment in favor of Landlord and the judgment must be reversed. Consequently, the trial court's award of attorney's fees and costs to Landlord must also be reversed. The cause is remanded for further proceedings consistent herewith.

Reversed and remanded.

CASE 16-3

Rights of the Assignee
MOUNTAIN PEAKS FINANCIAL SERVICES, INC. v. ROTH-STEFFEN

Court of Appeals of Minnesota, 2010
778 N.W.2d 380
http://scholar.google.com/scholar_case?q=778+N.W.2d+380&hl=en&as_sdt=2,
34&case=11662901939297878943&scilh=0

Bjorkman, J.

In May 1998, appellant Catherine Roth-Steffen graduated from law school with over $100,000 in school loans from more than a dozen lenders. Of this total, Roth-Steffen received $20,350 from the Missouri Higher Education Loan Authority (MOHELA) CASH Loan program through loans disbursed in 2005 and 2007. As of November 5, 1998, Roth-Steffen had incurred interest on these loans (MOHELA loan) in the amount of $3,043.28. Roth-Steffen listed the balance of $23,401.28 in a loan consolidation application she submitted in December 1998. She requested that the MOHELA loan not be consolidated with her other loans.

In February 2003, MOHELA assigned ownership of the MOHELA loan to Guarantee National Insurance Company

(GNIC), which, in turn, assigned the loan for collection to respondent Mountain Peaks Financial Services, Inc. (Mountain Peaks). [Mountain Peaks commenced a collection action claiming that it holds the MOHELA loan and that it is entitled to judgment in the amount of the outstanding balance, $23,120.52, and additional interest at the rate of 2.54% from July 19, 2007. In response, Roth-Steffen asserted that the action is barred by Minnesota's six-year statute of limitations for collection on promissory notes. The district court granted summary judgment in favor of Mountain Peaks, determining that Mountain Peaks (1) owns Roth-Steffen's loan, (2) is a valid assignee of MOHELA's right, and (3) under the federal Higher Education Act is not to be subject to any state statutes of limitation.]

Enacted in 1965, the Higher Education Act was the first comprehensive government program designed to provide scholarships, grants, work-study funding, and loans for students to attend college [and graduate school]. [Citations.] Pursuant to the act, the federal government makes loans and guarantees loans made by private lenders. [Citation.] In 1991, in response to rising loan defaults and an unfavorable legal ruling, Congress adopted the Higher Education Technical Amendments. [Citation.]

The amendments eliminate all statutes of limitation on actions to recover on defaulted student loans for certain classes of lenders. [Citation.] These lenders are defined in section 1091a:

* * *

(B) a guaranty agency that has an agreement with the Secretary under section 1078(c) of this title that is seeking the repayment of the amount due from a borrower on a loan made under part B of this subchapter after such guaranty agency reimburses the previous holder of the loan for its loss on account of the default of the borrower; * * *

[Citation.] For convenience, we refer to the entities described in this statute as "named lenders."

Mountain Peaks argues that it is exempt from Minnesota's statutes of limitation because it is a valid assignee of MOHELA, a lender that has an agreement with the Secretary of Education under [section] 1091a(a)(2)(B). Roth-Steffen acknowledges that MOHELA is a named lender but argues that because Congress did not expressly identify assignees as named lenders, section 1091a does not preempt state statutes of limitation for claims asserted by assignees of named lenders.

* * *

Section 1091a does not, by its terms, extend its statutes-of-limitation exemption to assignees of named lenders. Nor does the statute expressly preclude application of the exemption to assignees. * * *

* * *

But courts interpreting federal statutes must also presume that Congress intended to preserve the common law * * *

The common law of most states, including Minnesota, has long recognized that "[a]n assignment operates to place the assignee in the shoes of the assignor, and provides the assignee with the same legal rights as the assignor had before assignment." [Citation]; *see generally* Restatement (Second) of Contracts § 317 (1981) (Assignment of a Right). Contractual rights and duties are generally assignable, including the rights to receive payment on debts, obtain nonmonetary performance, and recover damages. Restatement (Second) of Contracts § 316 (1981). But an assignor may not transfer rights that are personal, such as recovery for personal injuries or performance under contracts that involve personal trust or confidences. [Citation]; *see generally* Restatement (Second) of Contracts § 317 cmt. c. Under the common law, a contractual right to recover student-loan debt is assignable and does not fall within the personal-rights exclusion to the assignment rule.

* * *

* * * Because Congress legislated with a full knowledge of the common law of assignment, all contractual rights of the named lenders, including the protection from state statutes of limitations, should transfer to their assignees. * * *

We conclude that section 1091a of the Higher Education Act applies to assignees of named lenders. Mountain Peaks is an assignee of a named lender, therefore this action is not time-barred by any Minnesota statute of limitations.

CASE
16-4

Delegation of Duties
PUBLIC SERVICE COMMISSION OF MARYLAND v. PANDA-BRANDYWINE, L.P.

Court of Appeals of Maryland, 2003
375 Md. 185, 825 A.2d 462
http://scholar.google.com/scholar_case?case=14283409950595264869&q=825+a.2d+462&hl=en&as_sdt=2,34

Wilner, J.
PEPCO [Potomac Electric Power Company] is an electric utility serving the metropolitan Washington, D.C. area. Panda [Panda-Brandywine, L.P.] is a "qualified facility" (QF) under the Public Utility Regulatory Policies Act of 1978 [citation]. * * *

* * *

In August, 1991, PEPCO and Panda entered into a PPA [power purchase agreement] calling for (1) the construction by Panda of a new 230-megawatt cogenerating power plant in

Prince George's County, (2) connection of the facility to PEPCO's high voltage transmission system by transmission facilities to be built by Panda but later transferred without cost to PEPCO, and (3) upon commencement of the commercial operation of the plant, for PEPCO to purchase the power generated by that plant for a period of 25 years. The plant was built at a cost of $215 million, financed mostly through loans.

The PPA is 113 pages in length, single-spaced, and is both detailed and complex. In it, PEPCO was given substantial authority to review, influence, and, in some instances, determine important aspects of both the construction and operation of the Panda facility. * * *

* * *

Section 19.1 of the PPA provided, with certain exceptions not relevant here, that "neither this Agreement, nor any of the rights or obligations hereunder, may be assigned, transferred, or delegated by either Party, without the express prior written consent of the other Party, which consent shall not be unreasonably withheld...." * * *

* * *

In 1999, the General Assembly passed the Electric Consumer Choice and Competition Act of 1999 [citation], calling for the restructuring of the electric industry in an effort to promote competition in the generation and delivery of electricity * * * PEPCO's proposed restructuring involved a complete divestiture of its electric generating assets and its various PPAs, to be accomplished by an auction. * * *

The sale to the winning bidder was to be accomplished by an Asset Purchase and Sale Agreement (APSA) that included a number of PPAs to which PEPCO was a party and specifically the PPA with Panda. * * *

* * *

[Under the APSA] the buyer was authorized to take all actions that PEPCO could lawfully take under the PPA without further approval from PEPCO * * * .

* * *

* * * [O]n June 7, 2000, SEI was declared the winning bidder. On September 27, 2000, the PSC [Public Service Commission] entered an order (Order No. 76472) declaring, among other things, that the provisions in the APSA did not constitute an assignment or transfer within the meaning of §19.1 of the Panda PPA, that PEPCO was not assigning "significant obligations and rights under the PPA," that Panda would not be harmed by the transaction, and that the APSA did not "fundamentally alter[]" the privity of contract between Panda and PEPCO. It thus concluded that Panda's consent to the proposed APSA was not required. * * *

Panda sought judicial review in the Circuit Court for Montgomery County. That court found that the APSA * * * effected an assignment of Panda's PPA. It reversed the PSC order * * * .

* * *

* * * PEPCO appealed [and the] court concluded that, through the APSA, PEPCO effectively and improperly delegated its duties under the PPA to SEI. It added that the APSA amounted to an assignment because it extinguished PEPCO's right to performance from Panda—a right that was transferred to SEI. * * * We granted cross-petitions for *certiorari* to consider whether the Court of Special Appeals erred * * * .

* * *

By prohibiting both nonconsensual assignment and delegation, the PPA recognizes a nuance, or distinction, that is occasionally overlooked. In a bilateral contract, each party ordinarily has both rights and duties—the right to expect performance from the other party to the contract and the duty to perform what the party has agreed to perform. Although both are often the subject of transfer, the law does distinguish between them, using the term "assignment" to refer to the transfer of contractual rights and the term "delegation" to refer to the transfer of contractual duties. * * *

Restatement §317 defines the assignment of a right as "a manifestation of the assignor's intention to transfer it by virtue of which the assignor's right to performance by the obligor is extinguished in whole or in part and the assignee acquires a right to such performance." Section 317(2) permits a contractual right to be assigned unless (a) "the substitution of a right of the assignee for the right of the assignor would materially change the duty of the obligor, or materially increase the burden or risk imposed on him by his contract, or materially impair his chance of obtaining return performance, or materially reduce its value to him," (b) the assignment is forbidden by statute or is inoperative on grounds of public policy, or (c) "*assignment is validly precluded by contract.*" (Emphasis added).

Section 318 speaks to the delegation of performance. Section 318(1) allows an obligor to delegate the performance of a contractual duty "unless the delegation is contrary to public policy *or the terms of his promise.*" (Emphasis added.) Section 318(2) provides that, unless otherwise agreed, a promise requires performance by a particular person "only to the extent that the obligee has a substantial interest in having that person perform or control the acts promised." Finally, §318(3) states that, "unless the obligee agrees otherwise, neither delegation of performance nor a contract to assume the duty made with the obligor by the person delegated discharges any duty or liability of the delegating obligor."

Although using somewhat different language, we have adopted those principles. In *Macke Co. v. Pizza of Gaithersburg*, [citation], we held that "in the absence of a contrary provision ... rights and duties under an executory bilateral contract may be assigned and delegated, subject to the exception that duties under a contract to provide personal services may never be delegated, nor rights be assigned under a contract where *delectus personae* was an ingredient of the bargain."

These general statements, both in §§317 and 318 and in *Macke* regarding the extent to which rights may be assigned and duties of performance may be delegated are, as noted, subject to any valid contractual provision prohibiting assignment or delegation. Section 19.1 of the PPA very clearly prohibits both the assignment of rights and the delegation of duties of performance, absent express written consent. The issue, then, is not whether PEPCO can make such an assignment or delegation but only whether it has, in fact, done so. The answer to that lies in the effect that the [provisions of the APSA] have on the contractual relationship between PEPCO and Panda.

* * *

* * * The APSA involves a great deal more than merely a resale of electricity purchased from Panda and even more than the effective substitution of one customer for another. Much of Panda's control over its own facility and business was subject to the approval and cooperation of PEPCO; indeed, to a large extent, the operation of the facility was, in many important respects, almost a joint venture. In agreeing to that kind of arrangement, Panda necessarily was relying on its perceptions of PEPCO's competence and

managerial style. One does not ordinarily choose a business partner by auction or lottery, and there is no evidence that Panda did so in this case. Paraphrasing §318(2) of the Restatement, Panda has "a substantial interest in having [PEPCO] perform or control the acts promised." Under [the APSA], that control has been delegated irrevocably to SEI—a stranger to Panda—with the ability of SEI to delegate it to others.

* * * Virtually none of the rights and responsibilities transferred to SEI under [the APSA] are permitted under §19.1 of the PPA. * * * We hold that [the APSA] constitutes an assignment of rights and obligations under the PPA in contravention of §19.1 of that agreement and that it is therefore invalid and unenforceable.

* * *

[Judgment affirmed.]

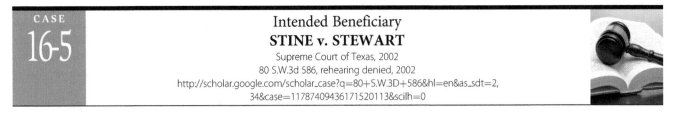

CASE

16-5

Intended Beneficiary
STINE v. STEWART

Supreme Court of Texas, 2002
80 S.W.3d 586, rehearing denied, 2002
http://scholar.google.com/scholar_case?q=80+S.W.3D+586&hl=en&as_sdt=2,
34&case=11787409436171520113&scilh=0

Per Curiam

On April 26, 1984, [Mary] Stine loaned her daughter [Mary Ellen Stewart] and son-in-law [William] Stewart $100,000 to purchase a home. In return, the Stewarts jointly executed a promissory note for $100,000, payable on demand to Stine. The note required interest payments at a floating rate adjusted every six months to one percent below the prime rate. It also required the Stewarts to pay the interest on the first of each month as it accrued on the unpaid principal. The Stewarts did not give a security interest or mortgage to secure the note. The Stewarts eventually paid $50,000 on the note, leaving $50,000, together with unpaid accrued interest, due.

The Stewarts divorced on October 2, 1992. The couple executed an Agreement Incident to Divorce * * * which disposed of marital property, including the home the agreement identifies as the Lago Vista property. The agreement provides that Stewart could lease the house, but if Stewart sold it, he agreed that "any monies owing to [Stine] are to be paid in the current principal sum of $50,000.00." The agreement further states:

The parties agree that with regard to the note to Mary Nelle Stine, after application of the proceeds of the [Lago Vista property], if there are any amounts owing to [Stine] the remaining balance owing to her will be appropriated 50% to NANCY KAREN STEWART and 50% to WILLIAM DEAN STEWART, JR. and said 50% from each party will be due and payable upon the deter-

mination that the proceeds from the sale of said residence are not sufficient to repay said $50,000.00 in full.

Stine did not sign the agreement.

On November 17, 1995, Stewart sold the Lago Vista property for $125,000, leaving $6,820.21 in net proceeds. Stewart did not pay these proceeds to Stine and did not make any further payments on the $50,000 principal. Consequently, on July 27, 1998, Stine sued Stewart for breaching the agreement. * * *

After a bench trial, the trial court concluded that Stine was an intended third-party beneficiary of the agreement and that Stewart breached the agreement when he refused to pay Stine as the agreement required. The trial court awarded Stine $28,410 in damages * * * from Stewart.

The court of appeals reversed the judgment and rendered judgment for Stewart. [Citation.] The court of appeals concluded that, because the agreement does not show that the Stewarts intended to confer a gift to Stine, Stine was not an intended third-party donee beneficiary of the agreement. [Citation.] Additionally, the court of appeals concluded that Stine was not an intended third-party creditor beneficiary of the agreement. [Citation.] * * *

A third party may recover on a contract made between other parties only if the parties intended to secure a benefit to that third party, and only if the contracting parties entered into the contract directly for the third party's benefit. [Citation.] A third party does not have a right to enforce the contract if she received only an incidental benefit. [Citation.] "A court will not create a third-party beneficiary contract by implication." [Citation.] Rather, an agreement must clearly and fully express an intent to confer a direct benefit to the third party. [Citation.] To determine the parties' intent, courts must examine the entire agreement when interpreting a contract and give effect to all the contract's provisions so that none are rendered meaningless. [Citation.]

To qualify as an intended third-party beneficiary, a party must show that she is either a "donee" or "creditor" beneficiary of the contract. [Citation.] An agreement benefits a "donee" beneficiary if, under the contract, "the performance promised will, when rendered, come to him as a pure donation." [Citation]; *see also* Restatement (Second) of Contracts §302(1)(b). In contrast, an agreement benefits a "creditor" beneficiary if, under the agreement, "that performance will come to him in satisfaction of a legal duty owed to him by the promisee." [Citation]; *see also* Restatement (Second) of Contracts §302(1)(a). This duty may be an indebtedness, contractual obligation or other legally enforceable commitment owed to the third party. [Citation.]

Stine contends that she has standing to sue for breach of the agreement as a third-party beneficiary, because the Stewarts intended to secure a benefit to her—that is, the payment of the remaining balance under the note. Stine also argues that whether or not limitations expired on enforcing the note, she was still a third-party creditor beneficiary because the debt remained an existing, legal obligation. Moreover, Stine contends, the agreement "acknowledges" the $50,000 debt owed to her because it recognizes that the note exists and requires the Stewarts to pay any amounts due under the note when Stewart sells the Lago Vista property. * * *

Stewart responds that Stine does not have standing to sue under the agreement, because she is only an incidental beneficiary. Stewart argues that the agreement was not entered into directly and primarily for Stine's benefit, and the agreement does not fully and clearly express the intent to confer a benefit to Stine. * * * Moreover, Stewart contends that the agreement does not acknowledge the original note,

because it does not contain unequivocal language that revives the expired debt. * * *

We agree with the court of appeals' determination that Stine was not an intended third-party donee beneficiary of the agreement. [Citation.] But, we conclude that Stine is a third-party creditor beneficiary. The agreement expressly provides that the Stewarts intended to satisfy an obligation to repay Stine the $50,000 that the Stewarts owed her. Specifically, the agreement refers to the monies owed to Stine as "the current principal sum of $50,000." Then, the agreement states that Stewart agreed to pay the property sale net proceeds "with regard to the note" to Stine. The agreement further provides that, if the property sale net proceeds did not cover the amount owed to Stine, the remainder would be immediately due and payable from the Stewarts, with each owing one half. Thus, the agreement expressly requires the Stewarts to satisfy their existing obligation to pay Stine. [Citation.]

* * *

Furthermore, contrary to Stewart's argument, a third-party beneficiary does not have to show that the signatories executed the contract *solely* to benefit her as a non-contracting party. Rather, the focus is on whether the contracting parties intended, at least in part, to discharge an obligation owed to the third party. [Citation.] Here, the entire agreement is obviously not for Stine's sole benefit. However, certain provisions in the agreement expressly state the Stewarts' intent to pay Stine the money due to her.

* * *

The agreement's language clearly shows that Stewart intended to secure a benefit to Stine as a third-party creditor beneficiary. The agreement also acknowledges the existence of a legal obligation owed to Stine and thus revives it as an enforceable obligation. Consequently, Stewart breached the agreement when he refused to pay Stine the money owed to her as the agreement requires. * * * Accordingly, we reverse the court of appeals' judgment and remand this case to the trial court to render judgment consistent with this opinion. [Citation.]

QUESTIONS

1. On December 1, Euphonia, a famous singer, contracted with Boito to sing at Boito's theater on December 31 for a fee of $45,000 to be paid immediately after the performance.
   a. Euphonia, for value received, assigns this fee to Carter.
   b. Euphonia, for value received, assigns this contract to sing to Dumont, an equally famous singer.

   c. Boito sells his theatre to Edmund and assigns his contract with Euphonia to Edmund. State the effect of each of these assignments.

2. The Smooth Paving Company entered into a paving contract with the city of Chicago. The contract contained the clause "contractor shall be liable for all damages to buildings resulting from the work performed." In the

process of construction, one of the bulldozers of the Smooth Paving Company struck and broke a gas main, causing an explosion and a fire that destroyed the house of John Puff. Puff brought an action for breach of the paving contract against the Smooth Paving Company to recover damages for the loss of his house. Can Puff recover under this contract? Explain.

3. Anne, who was unemployed, registered with the Speedy Employment Agency. A contract was then made under which Anne, in consideration of such position as the Agency would obtain for her, agreed to pay the Agency one-half of her first month's salary. The contract also contained an assignment by Anne to the Agency of one-half of her first month's salary. Two weeks later, the Agency obtained a permanent position for Anne with the Bostwick Co. at a monthly salary of $1,900. The agency also notified Bostwick of the assignment by Anne. At the end of the first month, Bostwick paid Anne her salary in full. Anne then quit and disappeared. The Agency now sues Bostwick Co. for $950 under the assignment. Who will prevail? Explain.

4. Georgia purchased an option on Greenacre from Pamela for $10,000. The option contract contained a provision by which Georgia promised not to assign the option contract without Pamela's permission. Georgia, without Pamela's permission, assigns the contract to Michael. Michael seeks to exercise the option, and Pamela refuses to sell Greenacre to him. Must Pamela sell the land to Michael?

5. Julia contracts to sell to Hayden, an ice cream manufacturer, the amount of ice Hayden may need in his business for the ensuing three years to the extent of not more than 250 tons a week at a stated price per ton. Hayden makes a corresponding promise to Julia to buy such an amount of ice. Hayden sells his ice cream plant to Clark and assigns to Clark all Hayden's rights under the contract with Julia. Upon learning of the sale, Julia refuses to furnish ice to Clark. Clark sues Julia for damages. Decision?

6. Brown enters into a written contract with Ideal Insurance Company under which, in consideration of her payment of the premiums, the insurance company promises to pay State College the face amount of the policy, $100,000, on Brown's death. Brown pays the premiums until her death. Thereafter, State College makes demand for the $100,000, which the insurance company refuses to pay upon the ground that State College was not a party to the contract. Can State College successfully enforce the contract?

7. Grant and Debbie enter into a contract binding Grant personally to do some delicate cabinetwork. Grant

assigns his rights and delegates performance of his duties to Clarence.

a. On being informed of this, Debbie agrees with Clarence, in consideration of Clarence's promise to do the work, that Debbie will accept Clarence's work, if properly done, instead of the performance promised by Grant. Later, without cause, Debbie refuses to allow Clarence to proceed with the work, though Clarence is ready to do so, and makes demand on Grant that Grant perform. Grant refuses. Can Clarence recover damages from Debbie? Can Debbie recover from Grant?

b. Instead, assume that Debbie refuses to permit Clarence to do the work, employs another carpenter, and brings an action against Grant, claiming as damages the difference between the contract price and the cost to employ the other carpenter. Explain whether Debbie will prevail.

8. Rebecca owes Lewis $2,500 due on November 1. On August 15, Lewis assigns this right for value received to Julia, who gives notice on September 10 of the assignment to Rebecca. On August 25, Lewis assigns the same right to Wayne, who in good faith gives value and has no prior knowledge of the assignment by Lewis to Julia. Wayne gives Rebecca notice of the assignment on August 30. What are the rights and obligations of Rebecca, Lewis, Julia, and Wayne?

9. Lisa hired Jay in the spring, as she had for many years, to set out in beds the flowers Lisa had grown in her greenhouses during the winter. The work was to be done in Lisa's absence for $300. Jay became ill the day after Lisa departed and requested his friend, Curtis, to set out the flowers, promising to pay Curtis $250 when Jay received his payment. Curtis agreed. Upon completion of the planting, an agent of Lisa's, who had authority to dispense the money, paid Jay, and Jay paid Curtis. Within two days it became obvious that the planting was a disaster. Everything set out by Curtis had died of water rot because he had operated Lisa's automatic watering system improperly.

   May Lisa recover damages from Curtis? May she recover damages from Jay? If so, does Jay have an action against Curtis?

10. Caleb, operator of a window-washing business, dictated a letter to his secretary addressed to Apartments, Inc., stating, "I will wash the windows of your apartment buildings at $4.10 per window to be paid upon completion of the work." The secretary typed the letter, signed Caleb's name, and mailed it to Apartments, Inc. Apartments, Inc., replied, "Accept your offer."

Caleb wrote back, "I will wash them during the week commencing July 10 and direct you to pay the money you will owe me to my son, Bernie. I am giving it to him as a wedding present." Caleb sent a signed copy of the letter to Bernie.

Caleb washed the windows during the time stated and demanded payment to him of $8,200 (2,000 windows at $4.10 each), informing Apartments, Inc., that he had changed his mind about having the money paid to Bernie. What are the rights of the parties?

CASE PROBLEMS

11. McDonald's has an undeviating policy of retaining absolute control over who receives new franchises. McDonald's granted to Copeland a franchise in Omaha, Nebraska. In a separate letter, it also granted him a right of first refusal for future franchises to be developed in the Omaha–Council Bluffs area. Copeland then sold all rights in his six McDonald's franchises to Schupack. When McDonald's offered a new franchise in the Omaha area to someone other than Schupack, Schupack attempted to exercise the right of first refusal. McDonald's would not recognize the right in Schupack, claiming that it was personal to Copeland and, therefore, nonassignable without its consent. Schupack brought an action for specific performance, requiring McDonald's to accord him the right of first refusal. Is Schupack correct in his contention?

12. In 1952, the estate of George Bernard Shaw granted to Gabriel Pascal Enterprises, Limited, the exclusive rights to produce a musical play and a motion picture based on Shaw's play *Pygmalion*. The agreement contained a provision terminating the license if Gabriel Pascal Enterprises did not arrange for well-known composers, such as Lerner and Loewe, to write the musical and produce it within a specified time. George Pascal, owner of 98 percent of the Gabriel Pascal Enterprise's stock, attempted to meet these requirements but died in July 1954 before negotiations had been completed. In February 1954, however, while the license had two years yet to run, Pascal sent a letter to Kingman, his executive secretary, granting to her certain percentages of his share of the profits from the expected stage and screen productions of *Pygmalion*. Subsequently, Pascal's estate arranged for the writing and production of the highly successful *My Fair Lady*, based on Shaw's *Pygmalion*. Kingman then sued to enforce Pascal's gift assignment of the future royalties. Decision?

13. Northwest Airlines leased space in the terminal building at the Portland Airport from the Port of Portland. Crosetti entered into a contract with the Port to furnish janitorial services for the building, which required Crosetti to keep the floor clean, to indemnify the Port against loss due to claims or lawsuits based upon Crosetti's failure to perform, and to provide public liability insurance for the Port and Crosetti. A patron of the building who was injured by a fall caused by a foreign substance on the floor at Northwest's ticket counter brought suit for damages against Northwest, the Port, and Crosetti. Upon settlement of this suit, Northwest sued Crosetti to recover the amount of its contribution to the settlement and other expenses on the grounds that Northwest was a third-party beneficiary of Crosetti's contract with the Port to keep the floors clean and, therefore, within the protection of Crosetti's indemnification agreement. Will Northwest prevail? Why?

14. Tompkins-Beckwith, as the contractor on a construction project, entered into a subcontract with a division of Air Metal Industries. Air Metal procured American Fire and Casualty Company to be surety on certain bonds in connection with contracts it was performing for Tompkins-Beckwith and others. As security for these bonds, on January 3, Air Metal executed an assignment to American Fire of all accounts receivable under the Tompkins-Beckwith subcontract. On November 26 of that year, Boulevard National Bank lent money to Air Metal. To secure the loans, Air Metal purported to assign to the bank certain accounts receivable it had under its subcontract with Tompkins-Beckwith.

In June of the following year, Air Metal defaulted on various contracts bonded by American Fire. On July 1, American Fire served formal notice on Tompkins-Beckwith of Air Metal's assignment. Tompkins-Beckwith acknowledged the assignment and agreed to pay. In August Boulevard National Bank notified Tompkins-Beckwith of its assignment. Tompkins-Beckwith refused to recognize the bank's claim and, instead, paid all remaining funds that had accrued to Air Metal to American Fire. The bank then sued to enforce its claim under Air Metal's assignment. Is the assignment effective? Why?

15. The International Association of Machinists (the union) was the bargaining agent for the employees of Powder Power Tool Corporation. On August 24, the union and

the corporation executed a collective bargaining agreement providing for retroactively increased wage rates for the corporation's employees effective as of April 1. Three employees who were working for Powder before and for several months after April 1, but who were not employed by the corporation when the agreement was executed on August 24, were paid to the time their employment terminated at the old wage scale. The three employees assigned their claims to Springer, who brought this action against the corporation for the extra wages. Decision?

16. In March, Adrian Saylor sold government bonds owned exclusively by him and with $6,450 of the proceeds opened a savings account in a bank in the name of "Mr. or Mrs. Adrian M. Saylor." In June of the following year, Saylor deposited the additional sum of $2,132 of his own money in the account. There were no other deposits and no withdrawals prior to Saylor's death a year later. Is the balance of the account on Saylor's death payable wholly to Adrian Saylor's estate, wholly to his widow, or half to each?

17. Linda King was found liable to Charlotte Clement as the result of an automobile accident. King, who was insolvent at the time, declared bankruptcy and directed her attorney, Prestwich, to list Clement as an unsecured creditor. The attorney failed to carry out this duty, and consequently King sued him for legal malpractice. When Clement pursued her judgment against King, she received a written assignment of King's legal malpractice claim against Prestwich. Clement has attempted to bring the claim, but Prestwich alleges that a claim for legal malpractice is not assignable. Decision?

18. Rensselaer Water Company contracted with the city of Rensselaer to provide water to the city for use in homes, public buildings, industry, and fire hydrants. During the term of the contract, a building caught fire. The fire spread to a nearby warehouse and destroyed it and its contents. The water company knew of the fire but failed to supply adequate water pressure at the fire hydrant to extinguish the fire. The warehouse owner sued the water company for failure to fulfill its contract with the city. Can the warehouse owner enforce the contract? Explain.

19. While under contract to play professional basketball for the Philadelphia 76ers, Billy Cunningham, an outstanding player, negotiated a three-year contract with the Carolina Cougars, another professional basketball team. The contract with the Cougars was to begin at the expiration of the contract with the 76ers. In addition to a signing bonus of $125,000, Cunningham was to receive under the new contract a salary of $100,000 for the first year, $110,000 for the second, and $120,000 for the third. The contract also stated that Cunningham "had special, exceptional and unique knowledge, skill and ability as a basketball player" and that Cunningham therefore agreed the Cougars could enjoin him from playing basketball for any other team for the term of the contract. In addition, the contract contained a clause prohibiting its assignment to another club without Cunningham's consent. In 1971 the ownership of the Cougars changed, and Cunningham's contract was assigned to Munchak Corporation, the new owners, without his consent. When Cunningham refused to play for the Cougars, Munchak Corporation sought to enjoin his playing for any other team. Cunningham asserts that his contract was not assignable. Was the contract assignable? Explain.

20. Pauline Brown was shot and seriously injured by an unknown assailant in the parking lot of National Supermarkets. Pauline and George Brown brought a negligence action against National, Sentry Security Agency, and T. G. Watkins, a security guard and Sentry employee. Sentry had a security contract with National. The Browns maintained that the defendants have a legal duty to protect National's customers both in the store and in the parking lot, and that this duty was breached. The defendants denied this allegation. What will the Browns have to prove to prevail? Explain.

21. Members of Local 100, Transport Workers Union of America (TWU), began an 11-day mass transit strike that paralyzed the life and commerce of the city of New York. Plaintiffs are engaged in the practice of law as a profession, maintaining offices in Manhattan. Plaintiffs sue both individually and on behalf of all other professional and business entities (the class) that were damaged as a consequence of the defendants' willful disruption of the service provided by the public transportation system of the City of New York. The law firm sought to recover as a third-party beneficiary of the collective bargaining agreement between the union and New York City. The agreement contains a no-strike clause and states that the TWU agreed to cooperate with the city to provide a safe, efficient, and dependable mass transit system. As a member of the public which depends on the public transit system and which employs dozens of persons who need the public transit system to get to and from work, plaintiffs argue that they are within the class of persons for whose benefit the TWU has promised to provide "dependable transportation service." Are the members of the class action suit entitled to recover? Explain.

22. On behalf of himself and other similarly situated options investors, Rick Lockwood sued defendant, Standard &

Poor's Corporation (Standard & Poor's), for breach of contract. Lockwood alleged that he and other options investors suffered lost profits on certain options contracts because Standard & Poor's failed to correct a closing stock index value. Standard & Poor's compiles and publishes two composite stock indexes, the "S&P 100" and the "S&P 500" (collectively the S&P indexes). The S&P indexes are weighted indexes of common stocks primarily listed for trading on the New York Stock Exchange (NYSE). Standard & Poor's licenses its S&P indexes to the Chicago Board Options Exchange (CBOE) to allow the trading of securities options contracts (S&P index options) based on the S&P indexes (the license agreement). S&P index options are settled by the Options Clearing Corporation (OCC). The exercise settlement values for S&P index options are the closing index values for the S&P 100 and S&P 500 stock market indexes as reported by Standard & Poor's to OCC following the close of trading on the day of exercise.

In his complaint, Lockwood alleged that at approximately 4:12 P.M. on Friday, December 15, 1989, the last trading day prior to expiration of the December 1989 S&P index options contracts, the NYSE erroneously reported a closing price for Ford Motor Company common stock. Ford Motor Company was one of the composite stocks in both the S&P 100 and S&P 500. At approximately 4:13 P.M., Standard & Poor's calculated and disseminated closing index values for the S&P 100 and S&P 500 stock market indexes based on the erroneous price for Ford stock. The NYSE reported a corrected closing price for Ford Motor at approximately 4:18 P.M. Standard & Poor's corrected the values of the S&P 100 and S&P 500 stock market indexes the following Monday, December 18, 1989. In the meantime, however, OCC automatically settled all expiring S&P index options according to the expiration date of Saturday, December 16, 1989. OCC used the uncorrected closing index values to settle all expiring S&P index options. Due to the error, Lockwood alleges that the S&P 100 index was overstated by 0.15 and he lost $105. Lockwood claimed investors in S&P 500 index options suffered similar losses. Lockwood filed a class action on behalf of "all holders of long put options and all sellers of short call options on the S&P 100 or S&P 500 … which were settled based on the closing index values for December 15, 1989, as reported by Standard & Poor's," claiming that the options holders could recover in contract as third-party beneficiaries of the license agreement between Standard & Poor's and the CBOE. Are the members of the class action suit entitled to recover? Explain.

TAKING SIDES

Pizza of Gaithersburg and The Pizza Shops (Pizza Shops) contracted with Virginia Coffee Service (Virginia) to install vending machines in each of their restaurants. One year later, the Macke Company (a provider of vending machines) purchased Virginia's assets, and the vending machine contracts were assigned to Macke. Pizza Shops had dealt with Macke before but had chosen Virginia because they preferred the way it conducted its business. When Pizza Shops attempted to terminate their contracts for vending services, Macke brought suit for damages for breach of contract.

a. What arguments would support Pizza Shop's termination of the contracts?

b. What arguments would support Macke's suit for breach of contract?

c. Which side should prevail? Explain.

PERFORMANCE, BREACH, AND DISCHARGE

CHAPTER OUTCOMES

After reading and studying this chapter, you should be able to:

- Identify and distinguish among the various types of conditions.

- Distinguish between full performance and tender of performance.

- Explain the difference between material breach and substantial performance.

- Distinguish among a mutual rescission, substituted contract, accord and satisfaction, and novation.

- Identify and explain the ways discharge may be brought about by operation of law.

The subject of discharge of contracts concerns the termination of contractual duties. In earlier chapters we have seen how parties may become bound to a contract. It is also important to know how a person may become unbound from a contract. For although contractual promises are made for a purpose, and the parties reasonably expect this purpose to be fulfilled by performance, performance of a contractual duty is only one method of discharge.

Whatever causes a binding promise to cease to be binding constitutes a discharge of the contract. In general, there are four kinds of discharge: (1) performance by the parties, (2) material breach by one or both of the parties, (3) agreement of the parties, and (4) operation of law. Moreover, many contractual promises are not absolute promises to perform but rather are conditional; that is, they are dependent upon the happening or nonhappening of a specific event. After a discussion of conditions, the four kinds of discharge will be covered.

CONDITIONS

A **condition** is an event whose happening or nonhappening affects a duty of performance under a contract. Some conditions must be satisfied before any duty to perform arises; others terminate the duty to perform; still others either limit or modify the duty to perform. A promisor inserts conditions into a contract for her protection and benefit. Furthermore, the more conditions to which a promise is subject, the less content the promise has. For example, a promise to pay $8,000, provided that such sum is realized from the sale of

an automobile, provided the automobile is sold within sixty days, and provided that the automobile, which has been stolen, can be found, is clearly different from, and worth considerably less than, an unconditional promise by the same promisor to pay $8,000.

A fundamental difference exists between the breach or nonperformance of a contractual promise and the failure or nonhappening of a condition. A breach of contract subjects the promisor to liability. It may or may not, depending upon its materiality, excuse nonperformance by the nonbreaching party of his duty under the contract. The happening or nonhappening of a condition, on the other hand, either prevents a party from acquiring a right to performance by the other party or deprives him of such a right, but subjects neither party to any liability.

Conditions may be classified by *how* they are imposed: express conditions, implied-in-fact conditions, or implied-in-law conditions (also called constructive conditions). They also may be classified by *when* they affect a duty of performance: conditions concurrent, conditions precedent, or conditions subsequent. These two ways of classifying conditions are not mutually exclusive; for example, a condition may be constructive and concurrent or express and precedent.

PRACTICAL ADVICE

Consider using conditions to place the risk of the nonoccurrence of critical, uncertain events on the other party to the contract.

EXPRESS CONDITION

An **express condition** is explicitly set forth in language. No particular form of words is necessary to create an express condition, so long as the event to which the performance of the promise is made subject is clearly expressed. An express condition is usually preceded by such words as "provided that," "on condition that," "if," "subject to," "while," "after," "upon," or "as soon as."

The basic rule applied to express conditions is that they must be fully and literally performed before the conditional duty to perform arises. Where application of the full and literal performance test would result in a forfeiture, however, the courts usually apply to the completed portion of the condition a *substantial satisfaction* test, as discussed later in this chapter under the section titled "Substantial Performance."

SATISFACTION OF A CONTRACTING PARTY The parties to a contract may agree that performance by one of them will be to the satisfaction of the other, who will not be obligated to pay for such performance unless he is satisfied. This is an express condition to the duty to pay for the performance. Assume that tailor Melissa contracts to make a suit of clothes to Brent's satisfaction, and that Brent promises to pay Melissa $850 for the suit if he is satisfied with it when completed. Melissa completes the suit using materials ordered by Brent. Though the suit fits Brent beautifully, he tells Melissa that he is not satisfied with it and refuses to accept or pay for it. If Brent's dissatisfaction is honest and in good faith, even if it is unreasonable, Melissa is not entitled to recover $850 or any amount from Brent by reason of the nonhappening of the express condition. Where satisfaction relates to a matter of personal taste, opinion, or judgment, the law applies the **subjective satisfaction** standard: if the promisor in good faith is dissatisfied, the condition has not occurred.

If the contract does not clearly indicate that satisfaction is subjective, or if the performance contracted for relates to mechanical fitness or utility, the law assumes an **objective satisfaction** standard. For example, the objective standard would apply to the sale of a building or standard goods, such as steel, coal, or grain. In such cases, the question would not be whether the promisor was actually satisfied with the performance by the other party but whether, as a reasonable person, he ought to be satisfied.

◆ SEE CASE 17-1

PRACTICAL ADVICE

In your contracts based on satisfaction, specify which standard— subjective satisfaction or objective satisfaction—should apply to each contractual duty of performance.

SATISFACTION OF A THIRD PARTY A contract may condition the duty of one contracting party to accept and pay for the performance of the other contracting party upon the approval of a third party who is not a party to the contract. For example, building contracts commonly provide that before the owner is required to pay, the builder shall furnish a certificate of the architect stating that the building has been constructed according to the plans and specifications. Although the owner is paying for the building, not for the certificate, he must have both the building and the certificate before he is obligated to pay. The duty of payment was made expressly conditional upon the presentation of the certificate.

IMPLIED-IN-FACT CONDITIONS

Implied-in-fact conditions are similar to express conditions, in that they must fully and literally occur and in that the parties understand them to be part of the agreement. They differ in that they are not stated in express language; rather, they are necessarily inferred from the terms of the contract, the nature of the transaction, or the conduct of the parties. Thus, if Fernando, for $1,750, contracts to paint Peggy's house any color Peggy desires, it is necessarily implied in fact that Peggy will inform Fernando of the desired color before Fernando begins to paint. The notification of choice of color is an implied-in-fact condition, an operative event that must occur before Fernando is subject to the duty of painting the house.

IMPLIED-IN-LAW CONDITIONS

An **implied-in-law condition**, or a **constructive condition**, is imposed by law to accomplish a just and fair result. It differs from an express condition and an implied-in-fact condition in two ways: (1) it is not contained in the language of the contract or necessarily inferred from the contract, and (2) it need only be substantially performed. For example, Melinda contracts to sell a certain tract of land to Kelly for $18,000, but the contract is silent as to the time of delivery of the deed and payment of the price. The law will imply that the respective performances are not independent of one another; consequently, the courts will treat the promises as mutually dependent and will therefore hold that a delivery or tender of the deed by Melinda to Kelly is a condition to Kelly's duty to pay the price. Conversely, Melinda's duty to deliver the deed to Kelly is conditioned upon the payment or tender of $18,000 by Kelly to Melinda. If the contract specifies a sale on credit, however, giving Kelly thirty days after delivery of the deed within which to pay the price, these conditions are not implied by law because the parties have expressly agreed to make their respective duties of performance independent of each other.

CONCURRENT CONDITIONS

Concurrent conditions occur when the mutual duties of performances are to take place simultaneously. As indicated previously in the discussion of implied-in-law conditions, in the absence of an agreement to the contrary, the law assumes that the respective performances under a contract are concurrent conditions.

CONDITIONS PRECEDENT

A **condition precedent** is an event that must occur before performance under a contract is due. For instance, if Gail is to deliver shoes to Mike on June 1, with Mike's duty to pay for the shoes on July 15, Gail's delivery of the shoes is a condition precedent to Mike's performance. Similarly, if Seymour promises to buy Edna's land for $50,000, provided Seymour can obtain financing in the amount of $40,000 at 10 percent interest or less for thirty years within sixty days of signing the contract, Seymour's obtaining the specified financing is a condition precedent to his duty. If the condition is satisfied, Seymour is bound to perform; if it is not, he is not so bound. Seymour, however, is under an implied-in-law duty to use his best efforts to obtain financing under these terms.

CONDITIONS SUBSEQUENT

A **condition subsequent** is an event that terminates an existing duty. For example, where goods are sold under terms of "sale or return," the buyer has the right to return the goods to the seller within a stated period but is under an immediate duty to pay the price unless she and the seller have agreed upon credit. A return of the goods, which operates as a condition subsequent, terminates the duty to pay the price. Conditions subsequent occur very infrequently in contract law, while conditions precedent are quite common.

DISCHARGE BY PERFORMANCE

Discharge by performance is undoubtedly the most frequent method of discharging a contractual duty. If a promisor exactly performs his duty under the contract, he is no longer subject to that duty.

Every contract imposes upon each party a duty of good faith and fair dealing in its performance and its enforcement. Restatement, Section 205. As discussed in *Chapter 21*, the Uniform Commercial Code imposes a comparable duty. Section 1–203; Revised Section 1–304.

Tender is an offer by one party—who is ready, willing, and able to perform—to the other party to perform his obligation according to the terms of the contract. Under a bilateral contract, the refusal or rejection of a tender of performance may be treated as a repudiation that excuses or discharges the tendering party from further duty of perfor-

mance under the contract. For example, on the due date of contractual performance, George arrives at Thelma's house prepared to do plumbing work under their contract. Thelma, however, refuses to allow George to enter the premises. George is therefore discharged from performing the contract and has a legal claim against Thelma for material breach.

If a debtor owes money on several accounts and tenders to his creditor less than the total amounts due, the debtor has the right to designate the account or debt to which the payment is to be applied, and the creditor must accept this direction. If the debtor does not direct the application of the payment, the creditor may apply it to any account owing to him by the debtor or distribute it among several such accounts.

DISCHARGE BY BREACH

Breach of contract is the unexcused failure of a party to perform her promise. While breach of contract always gives rise to a cause of action for damages by the aggrieved (injured) party, it may have a more important effect: an uncured (uncorrected) *material* breach by one party operates as an excuse for nonperformance by the other party and discharges the aggrieved party from any further duty under the contract. If, on the other hand, the breach is not material, the aggrieved party is not discharged from the contract, although she may recover money damages. Under the Code, *any* deviation discharges the aggrieved party.

MATERIAL BREACH

An unjustified failure to perform *substantially* the obligations promised in a contract constitutes a **material breach**. The key is whether, despite the breach, the aggrieved party obtained substantially what he bargained for or whether the breach significantly impaired his rights under the contract. A material breach discharges the aggrieved party from his duty of performance. For instance, Esta orders a custom-made, tailored suit from Stuart to be made of wool; but Stuart instead makes the suit of cotton. Assuming that the labor component of this contract predominates and thus the contract is not considered a sale of goods, Stuart has materially breached the contract. Consequently, Esta not only is discharged from her duty to pay for the suit but may also recover money damages from Stuart due to his breach.

Although there are no clear-cut rules as to what constitutes a material breach, the Restatement, Section 241, lists a number of relevant factors:

In determining whether a failure to render or to offer performance is material, the following circumstances are significant:

(a) the extent to which the injured party will be deprived of the benefit which he reasonably expected;

(b) the extent to which the injured party can be adequately compensated for the part of that benefit of which he will be deprived;

(c) the extent to which the party failing to perform or to offer to perform will suffer forfeiture;

(d) the likelihood that the party failing to perform or to offer to perform will cure his failure, taking account of all the circumstances including any reasonable assurances;

(e) the extent to which the behavior of the party failing to perform or to offer to perform comports with standards of good faith and fair dealing.

An *intentional* breach of contract is generally held to be material. Moreover, a failure to perform a promise promptly is a material breach if "**time is of the essence**," that is, if the parties have clearly indicated that a failure to perform by the stated time is material; otherwise, the aggrieved party may recover damages only for the loss caused by the delay.

Finally, the parties to a contract may, within limits, specify what breaches are to be considered material.

PRACTICAL ADVICE

If the timely performance of a contractual duty is important, use a "time-is-of-the-essence" clause to make failure to perform promptly a material breach.

PREVENTION OF PERFORMANCE One party's substantial interference with or **prevention of performance** by the other generally constitutes a material breach that discharges the other party to the contract. For instance, Craig prevents an architect from giving Maud a certificate that is a condition to Craig's liability to pay Maud a certain sum of money. Craig may not then use Maud's failure to produce a certificate as an excuse for his nonpayment. Likewise, if Harold has contracted to grow a certain crop for Rafael, and Rafael plows the field and destroys the seedlings after Harold has planted the seed, his interference with Harold's performance discharges Harold from his duty under the contract. It does not, however, discharge Rafael from his duty under the contract.

PERFECT TENDER RULE The Code greatly alters the common law doctrine of material breach by adopting what is known as the **perfect tender rule**. This rule, which is discussed more fully in *Chapter 22*, essentially provides that *any* deviation from the promised performance in a sales contract under the Code constitutes a material breach of the contract and discharges the aggrieved party from his duty of performance. Thus, if a seller of camera accessories delivers to a buyer ninety-nine of the one hundred ordered pieces, or ninety-nine correct accessories and one incorrect

accessory, the buyer may rightfully reject the improper delivery.

SUBSTANTIAL PERFORMANCE

If a party substantially, but not completely, performs her obligations under a contract, the common law generally will allow her to obtain the other party's performance, less any damages caused by the partial performance. Thus, in the specially ordered suit illustration discussed in the previous section, if Stuart, the tailor, used the correct fabric but improperly used black buttons instead of blue, Stuart would be permitted to collect from Esta the contract price of the suit less the damage, if any, caused to Esta by the substitution of the wrongly colored buttons. The doctrine of substantial performance assumes particular importance in the construction industry in cases in which a structure is built on the aggrieved party's land. Consider the following: Kent Construction Co. builds a $300,000 house for Martha but deviates from the specifications, causing Martha $10,000 in damages. If this breach were considered material, then Martha would not have to pay for the house that is now on her land. This would clearly constitute an unjust forfeiture on Kent's part. Therefore, because Kent's performance is substantial, the courts would probably not deem the breach material. As a result, Kent would be able to collect $290,000 from Martha.

ANTICIPATORY REPUDIATION

A breach of contract, as discussed, is a failure to perform the terms of a contract. Although it is logically and physically impossible to fail to perform a duty before the date on which that performance is due, a party nonetheless may announce before the due date that she will not perform, or she may commit an act that makes her unable to perform. Either act repudiates the contract, which notifies the other party that a breach is imminent. Such repudiation before the performance date fixed by the contract is called an **anticipatory repudiation**. The courts, as shown in the leading case of *Hochster v. De La Tour*, view it as a breach that discharges the nonrepudiating party's duty to perform and permits her to bring suit immediately. Nonetheless, the nonbreaching party may wait until the time the performance is due, to see whether the repudiator will retract his repudiation and perform his contractual duties. To be effective, the retraction must come to the attention of the injured party before she materially changes her position in reliance on the repudiation or before she indicates to the repudiator that she considers the repudiation to be final. If the retraction is effective and the repudiator does perform, then there is a discharge by performance; if he does not perform, there is a material breach.

APPLYING THE LAW

Performance, Breach, and Discharge

FACTS Davis manages commercial real estate. In April, Davis contracted with Bidley to acquire and plant impatiens in the flowerbeds outside fourteen office properties that Davis manages. Bidley verbally agreed to buy and plant the impatiens by May 31, for a total of $10,000. Bidley purchased the necessary plants from Ackerman, who delivered them to Bidley on May 26. Bidley completed the planting at thirteen of the office buildings by May 29, but because another job took much longer than anticipated, Bidley was unable to finish planting the flowers outside the fourteenth office building until June 1. When he received Bidley's invoice, Davis refused to pay any of the $10,000.

ISSUE Has Bidley's committed a material breach of the contract so as to discharge Davis's performance under the contract?

RULE OF LAW Breach of contract is defined as a wrongful failure to perform. An uncured material breach discharges the aggrieved party's performance, serving as an excuse for the aggrieved party's nonperformance of his obligations under the contract. A breach is material if it significantly impairs the aggrieved party's contract rights. When a breach relates to timing of performance, failure to promptly perform a contract as promised is considered a material breach only if the parties have agreed that "time is of the essence," in other words that the failure to perform on time is material. If, on the other hand, the

aggrieved party does get substantially that for which he bargained, the breach is not material. In such a case the aggrieved party is not discharged from the contract but has a right to collect damages for the injury sustained as a result of the breach.

APPLICATION Bidley failed to plant all of the flowers by May 31 as he promised. Therefore, he has breached the contract. However, Bidley's breach is not material. There is no indication that the parties agreed that time was of the essence nor that there was any compelling reason the plants had to be in the ground by May 31. They simply agreed on May 31 as the date for performance.

Furthermore, Davis has gotten substantially that for which he bargained. In fact, as of May 31, Bidley had completed the planting at thirteen of the office buildings and had commenced the work at the fourteenth. One day later, the entire job was done. Given that Bidley's late performance did not significantly impair Davis's rights under the contract, the breach is not material. Therefore, Davis is entitled only to recover any damages he can prove were suffered as a result of Bidley's late performance.

CONCLUSION Bidley's breach is not material. Davis is not discharged from performance and must pay the $10,000 owed under the contract, less the value of any damages caused by the one-day delay in planting flowers at one office building.

◆ **SEE CASE 17-2**

PRACTICAL ADVICE

If the other party to a contract commits an anticipatory breach, carefully consider whether it is better to sue immediately or to wait until the time performance is due.

MATERIAL ALTERATION OF WRITTEN CONTRACT

An unauthorized alteration or change of any of the material terms or provisions of a written contract or document is a discharge of the entire contract. To be a discharge, the alteration must be material and fraudulent and must be the act of a party to the contract or someone acting on his behalf. An alteration is material if it would vary any party's legal relations with the maker of the alteration or would adversely

affect that party's legal relations with a third person. Restatement, Section 286. An unauthorized change in the terms of a written contract by a person who is not a party to the contract does not discharge the contract.

DISCHARGE BY AGREEMENT OF THE PARTIES

The parties to a contract may by agreement discharge each other from performance under the contract. They may do this by rescission, substituted contract, accord and satisfaction, or novation.

MUTUAL RESCISSION

A **mutual rescission** is an agreement between the parties to terminate their respective duties under the contract. Literally a contract to end a contract, it must contain all the essentials of a contract. In rescinding an executory, bilateral contract, each party furnishes consideration in giving up his rights under the contract in exchange for the other party's relinquishment of his rights under the contract. Where one party has already fully performed, a mutual rescission may not be binding at common law because of lack of consideration.

SUBSTITUTED CONTRACT

A **substituted contract** is a new contract accepted by both parties in satisfaction of their duties under the original contract. Restatement, Section 279. A substituted contract immediately discharges the original duty and imposes new obligations. For example, the Restatement, Section 279, gives the following illustration:

> A and B make a contract under which A promises to build on a designated spot a building, for which B promises to pay $100,000. Later, before this contract is performed, A and B make a new contract under which A is to build on the same spot a different building, for which B is to pay $200,000. The new contract is a substituted contract and the duties of A and B under the original contract are discharged.

ACCORD AND SATISFACTION

An **accord** is a contract by which an obligee promises to accept a stated performance in satisfaction of the obligor's existing contractual duty. Restatement, Section 281. The performance of the accord is called a **satisfaction**, and it discharges the original duty. Thus, if Ted owes Alan $500 and the parties agree that Ted shall paint Alan's house in satisfaction of the debt, the agreement is an accord. The debt, however, is not discharged until Ted performs the accord by painting Alan's house.

◆ SEE CASE 17-3

NOVATION

A **novation** is a substituted contract that involves an agreement among *three* parties to substitute a new promisee for the existing promisee, or to replace the existing promisor with a new one. Restatement, Section 280. A novation discharges the old obligation by creating a new contract in which there is either a new promisee or a new promisor. Thus, if Barbie owes Anson $500, and Anson, Barbie, and Cameron agree that Cameron will pay the debt and Barbie will be discharged, the novation is the substitution of the new promisor Cameron for Barbie. Alternatively, if the three parties agree that Barbie will pay $500 to Dontaya instead of to Anson, the novation is the substitution of a new promisee (Dontaya for Anson). In each instance, the debt Barbie owes to Anson is discharged.

DISCHARGE BY OPERATION OF LAW

This chapter has considered various ways by which contractual duties may be discharged. In all of these cases, the discharge resulted from the action of one or both of the parties to the contract. This section examines discharge brought about by the operation of law.

IMPOSSIBILITY

"Contract liability is strict liability ... [and an] obligor is therefore liable for in damages breach of contract even if he is without fault and even if circumstances have made the contract more burdensome or less desirable than he had anticipated." Restatement, Introductory Note to Chapter 11. Historically, the common law excused a party from contractual duties for **objective impossibility**; that is, for situations in which no one could render the performance. If, by comparison, a particular contracting party is unable to perform because, for instance, of financial inability or lack of competence, this **subjective impossibility** does not excuse the promisor from liability for breach of contract. For example, the Christys entered into a written contract to purchase an apartment house from Pilkinton for $30,000. Pilkinton tendered a deed to the property and demanded payment of the unpaid balance of $29,000 due on the purchase price. Because of a decline in their used car business, the Christys, who did not possess and could not borrow the unpaid balance, asserted that it was impossible for them to perform their contract. The court held for Pilkinton, identifying a distinction between objective impossibility, which amounts to saying, "the thing cannot be done," and subjective impossibility—"I cannot do it." The latter, which is illustrated by a promisor's financial inability to pay, does not discharge the contractual duty. *Christy v. Pilkinton*, 224 Ark. 407, 273 S.W.2d 533 (1954).

The **death** or **incapacity** of a person who has contracted to render *personal services* discharges his contractual duty due to objective impossibility. Restatement, Section 262. For example, a singer unable to perform a contractual engagement because of a severe cold is excused from performance, as is a pianist or violinist who is unable to perform because of a hand injury.

DESTRUCTION OF SUBJECT MATTER Destruction of the subject matter or of the agreed-upon means of performance of a contract, without the fault of the promisor, is also excusable impossibility. "Subject matter" here means specific subject matter. Suppose that Alice contracts to sell to Gary five office chairs at an agreed price. Alice has one hundred of these chairs in stock, out of which she expects to deliver five to Gary. Before she can do so, fire destroys the entire stock of one hundred chairs. Though not at fault, Alice is not excused from performance. This was not a contract for the sale of specific goods; consequently, Alice could perform the contract by delivering to Gary any five chairs of the kind and grade specified in the contract. Her failure to do so will render her liable to Gary for breach of contract. Suppose, now, that Alice and Gary make a contract for Alice to manufacture these five chairs in her factory but that prior to their manufacture, fire destroys the factory. Again, Alice is not at fault. Although the chairs are available from other manufacturers, the destruction of the factory discharges Alice's duty to deliver the chairs. Suppose further that Alice and Gary enter into a contract under which Alice is to sell to Gary the particular desk that she uses in her private office. This desk, and no other, is the specific subject matter of the contract. If, before the sale is completed, this desk is destroyed by fire without Alice's fault, it is then impossible for Alice to perform. The contract is therefore discharged.

PRACTICAL ADVICE

Use a clause in your contract specifying which events will excuse the nonperformance of the contract.

SUBSEQUENT ILLEGALITY If the performance of a contract that was legal when formed becomes illegal or impractical by reason of a subsequently enacted law, the duty of performance is discharged. Restatement, Section 264. For example, Jill contracts to sell and deliver to Fred ten cases of a certain whiskey each month for one year. A subsequent prohibition law makes the manufacture, transportation, or sale of intoxicating liquor unlawful. The contractual duties that Jill has yet to perform are discharged.

FRUSTRATION OF PURPOSE Where, after a contract is made, a party's principal purpose is substantially frustrated without his fault by the occurrence of an event the nonoccurrence of which was a basic assumption on which the contract was made, his remaining duties to render performance are discharged, unless the party has assumed the risk. Restatement, Second 265. This rule developed from the so-called coronation cases. When, upon the death of his mother, Queen Victoria, Edward VII became King of England, impressive coronation ceremonies were planned, including a procession along a designated route through certain streets in London. Owners and lessees of buildings along the route made contracts to permit the use of rooms with a view on the date scheduled for the procession. The King, however, became ill, and the procession did not take place. The purpose for using the rooms having failed, the rooms were not used. Numerous suits were filed, some by landowners seeking to hold the would-be viewers liable on their promises, and some by the would-be viewers seeking to recover money they paid in advance for the rooms. The principle involved was novel, but

from these cases evolved the **frustration of purpose doctrine**, under which a contract is discharged if supervening circumstances make impossible the fulfillment of the purpose that both parties had in mind, unless one of the parties has contractually assumed that risk.

COMMERCIAL IMPRACTICABILITY The Restatement, Section 261, and the Code, Section 2–615, have relaxed the traditional test of objective impossibility by providing that performance need not be actually or literally impossible, but that commercial impracticability will excuse nonperformance. This does not mean mere hardship or an unexpectedly increased cost of performance. A party will be discharged from performing his duty only when a supervening event not caused by his fault makes his performance impracticable. Moreover, the nonoccurrence of the subsequent event must have been a "basic assumption" both parties made when entering into the contract, neither party having assumed the risk that the event would occur. Commercial impracticability could include

> a severe shortage of raw materials or of supplies due to a contingency such as war, embargo, local crop failure, unforeseen shutdown of major sources of supply or the like, which either causes a marked increase in cost or altogether prevents the seller from securing supplies necessary to his performance. UCC Section 2–615, Comment 4.

◆ **SEE CASE 17-4**

PRACTICAL ADVICE

Clearly state the basic assumptions of your contract and which risks are assumed by each of the parties.

BANKRUPTCY

Bankruptcy is a discharge of a contractual duty by operation of law available to a debtor who, by compliance with the requirements of the Bankruptcy Code, obtains an order of discharge by the bankruptcy court. It is applicable only to obligations that the Code provides are dischargeable in bankruptcy. The subject of bankruptcy is treated in *Chapter 38*.

STATUTE OF LIMITATIONS

At common law a plaintiff was not subject to any time limitation within which to bring an action. Now, however, all States have statutes providing such a limitation. The majority of courts hold that the running of the period of the statute of limitations does not operate to discharge the obligation, but only to bar the creditor's right to bring an action.

◆ **SEE FIGURE 17-1: Discharge of Contracts**

◆ FIGURE 17-1: **Discharge of Contracts**

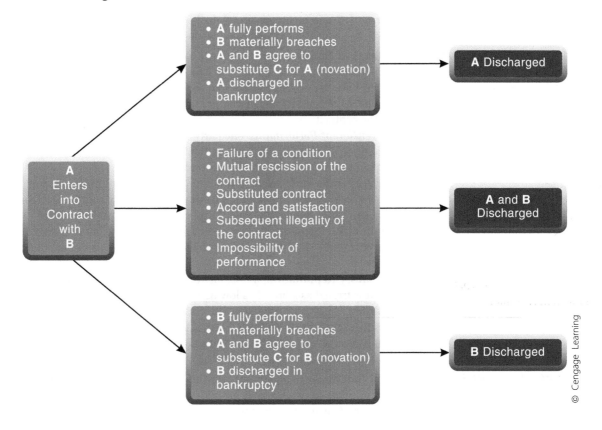

© Cengage Learning

CHAPTER SUMMARY

CONDITIONS

Definition of a Condition an event whose happening or nonhappening affects a duty of performance

Express Condition contingency explicitly set forth in language

- *Satisfaction* express condition making performance contingent upon one party's approval of the other's performance
- *Subjective Satisfaction* approval based upon a party's honestly held opinion
- *Objective Satisfaction* approval based upon whether a reasonable person would be satisfied

Implied-in-Fact Conditions contingency understood by the parties to be part of the agreement, though not expressed

Implied-in-Law Conditions contingency not contained in the language of the contract but imposed by law; also called a constructive condition

Concurrent Conditions conditions that are to take place at the same time

Conditions Precedent an event that must or must not occur before performance is due

Conditions Subsequent an event that terminates a duty of performance

DISCHARGE BY PERFORMANCE	**Discharge** termination of a contractual duty **Performance** fulfillment of a contractual obligation resulting in a discharge

DISCHARGE BY BREACH

Definition of Breach a wrongful failure to perform the terms of a contract that gives rise to a right to damages by the injured party

Material Breach nonperformance that significantly impairs the injured party's rights under the contract and discharges the injured party from any further duty under the contract

- *Prevention of Performance* one party's substantial interference with or prevention of performance by the other; constitutes a material breach and discharges the other party to the contract
- *Perfect Tender Rule* standard under the Uniform Commercial Code that a seller's performance under a sales contract must strictly comply with contractual duties and that any deviation discharges the injured party

Substantial Performance performance that is incomplete but that does not defeat the purpose of the contract; does not discharge the injured party but entitles him to damages

Anticipatory Repudiation an inability or refusal to perform, before performance is due, that is treated as a breach, allowing the nonrepudiating party to bring suit immediately

Material Alteration of Written Contract a material and fraudulent alteration of a written contract by a party to the contract; discharges the entire contract

DISCHARGE BY AGREEMENT OF THE PARTIES

Mutual Rescission an agreement between the parties to terminate their respective duties under the contract

Substituted Contract a new contract accepted by both parties in satisfaction of the parties' duties under the original contract

Accord and Satisfaction substituted duty under a contract (accord) and the discharge of the prior contractual obligation by performance of the new duty (satisfaction)

Novation a substituted contract involving a new third-party promisor or promisee

DISCHARGE BY OPERATION OF LAW

Impossibility performance of contract cannot be done
- *Subjective Impossibility* the promisor—but not all promisors—cannot perform; does not discharge the promisor
- *Objective Impossibility* no promisor is able to perform; generally discharges the promisor
- *Destruction of Subject Matter* will discharge contract if it occurs without the promisor's fault
- *Subsequent Illegality* if performance becomes illegal or impractical as a result of a change in the law, the duty of performance is discharged
- *Frustration of Purpose* principal purpose of a contract cannot be fulfilled because of a subsequent event
- *Commercial Impracticability* where performance can be accomplished only under unforeseen and unjust hardship, the contract is discharged under the Code and the Restatement

Bankruptcy discharge available to a debtor who obtains an order of discharge by the bankruptcy court

Statute of Limitations after the statute of limitations has run, the debt is not discharged, but the creditor cannot maintain an action against the debtor

CASES

CASE
17-1

Express Conditions: Satisfaction
SILVESTRI v. OPTUS SOFTWARE, INC.
Supreme Court of New Jersey, 2003
175 N.J. 113, 814 A.2d 602
http://scholar.google.com/scholar_case?q=814+A.2d+602&hl=en&as_sdt=2,34&case=3846111007491599697&scilh=0

LaVecchia, J.

This is a breach of contract action. Defendant Optus Software, Inc. ("Optus" or "the company"), a small computer software company, hired plaintiff Michael Silvestri as its Director of Support Services, responsible for supervising the provision of technical support services to the company's customers. Silvestri's two-year employment contract [commencing on January 4, 1999 at an annual salary of $70,000] contained a clause that reserved to the company the right to terminate his employment for failure to perform to the company's satisfaction (the "satisfaction clause").

Nine months into the contract, Silvestri was terminated under the satisfaction clause by the chief executive officer of Optus, Joseph Avellino. Silvestri filed this action, contending that the company's dissatisfaction was objectively unreasonable and that therefore his termination was a breach of the employment contract. The trial court granted summary judgment to the company. The Appellate Division reversed, however, holding that an employer must meet an objective standard for satisfaction in order to invoke a right to terminate pursuant to a satisfaction clause in an employment contract.

The question presented then is whether the employer's satisfaction is subject to an objective or subjective evaluation. We conclude that, absent language to the contrary, a subjective assessment of personal satisfaction applies and that the trial court's grant of summary judgment to the company was appropriate. * * *

* * * Silvestri was charged with supervision of the support services staff, responsibility for communication with resellers of the Optus computer software to end-users, and coordination of ongoing training for support staff and resellers of the company's products in order to maintain their proficiency in assisting end-users. * * *

[During the first six months of his employment Silvestri enjoyed the full support of Joseph Avellino, the CEO of Optus. Avellino's attitude started to change during the summer months of 1999, when several clients and resellers communicated to Avellino their disappointment with the performance and attitude of the support services staff generally, and several complaints targeted Silvestri specifically. Avellino informed Silvestri of those criticisms. On September

17, 1999, Avellino terminated Silvestri under the satisfaction clause.]

* * *

Silvestri did not assert that there was any reason for his termination other than Avellino's genuine dissatisfaction with his performance. Rather, Silvestri challenged the reasonableness of that dissatisfaction. He portrayed Avellino as a meddling micro-manager who overreacted to any customer criticism and thus could not reasonably be satisfied. * * *

* * *

Agreements containing a promise to perform in a manner satisfactory to another, or to be bound to pay for satisfactory performance, are a common form of enforceable contract. [Citation.] Such "satisfaction" contracts are generally divided into two categories for purposes of review: (1) contracts that involve matters of personal taste, sensibility, judgment, or convenience; and (2) contracts that contain a requirement of satisfaction as to mechanical fitness, utility, or marketability. [Citation.] The standard for evaluating satisfaction depends on the type of contract. Satisfaction contracts of the first type are interpreted on a subjective basis, with satisfaction dependent on the personal, honest evaluation of the party to be satisfied. [Citation.] Absent language to the contrary, however, contracts of the second type—involving operative fitness or mechanical utility—are subject to an objective test of reasonableness, because in those cases the extent and quality of performance can be measured by objective tests. [Citation]; Restatement (Second) of Contracts §228; [citation].

A subjective standard typically is applied to satisfaction clauses in employment contracts because "there is greater reason and a greater tendency to interpret [the contract] as involving personal satisfaction," rather than the satisfaction of a hypothetical "reasonable" person. [Citations.]

In the case of a high-level business manager, a subjective test is particularly appropriate to the flexibility needed by the owners and higher-level officers operating a competitive enterprise. [Citation.] When a manager has been hired to share responsibility for the success of a business entity, an employer is entitled to be highly personal and idiosyncratic in judging the employee's satisfactory performance in advancing the enterprise. [Citations.]

The subjective standard obliges the employer to act "honestly in accordance with his duty of good faith and fair dealing," [citation], but genuine dissatisfaction of the employer, honestly held, is sufficient for discharge. [Citation.]

Although broadly discretionary, a satisfaction-clause employment relationship is not to be confused with an employment-at-will relationship in which an employer is entitled to terminate an employee for any reason, or no reason, unless prohibited by law or public policy. [Citation.] In a satisfaction clause employment setting, there must be honest dissatisfaction with the employee's performance. * * * If * * * the employer's dissatisfaction is honest and genuine, even if idiosyncratic, its reasonableness is not subject to second guessing under a reasonable-person standard. In other words, standing alone, mere dissatisfaction is sufficient so long as it does not mask any other reason for the adverse employment action.

* * *

We hold that a subjective test of performance governs the employer's resort to a satisfaction clause in an employment contract unless there is some language in the contract to suggest that the parties intended an objective standard. There is no such language here. * * *

Turning then to application of the subjective test in this setting, * * * we conclude that the entry of summary judgment in favor of defendants was appropriate. * * *

The judgment of the Appellate Division is reversed and the matter remanded for entry of summary judgment in favor of defendants.

CASE

17-2

Anticipatory Breach
HOCHSTER v. DE LA TOUR
Queen's Bench of England, 1853
2 Ellis and Blackburn Reports 678

Lord Campbell, C. J.
[On April 12, 1852, Hochster contracted with De La Tour to serve as a guide for De La Tour on his three-month trip to Europe, beginning on June 1 at an agreed-upon salary. On May 11, De La Tour notified Hochster that he would not need Hochster's services. He also refused to pay Hochster any compensation. Hochster brings this action to recover damages for breach of contract.]

On this motion * * * the question arises, Whether, if there be an agreement between A. and B., whereby B. engages to employ A. on and from a future day for a given period of time, to travel with him into a foreign country as a [guide], and to start with him in that capacity on that day, A. being to receive a monthly salary during the continuance of such service, B. may, before the day, refuse to perform the agreement and break and renounce it, so as to entitle A. before the day to commence an action against B. to recover damages for breach of the agreement; A. having been ready and willing to perform it, till it was broken and renounced by B.

* * *

If the plaintiff has no remedy for breach of the contract unless he treats the contract as in force, and acts upon it down to the 1st June, 1852, it follows that, till then, he must enter into no employment which will interfere with his promise "to start with the defendant on such travels on the day and year" and that he must then be properly equipped in all respects as a [guide] for a three months' tour on the continent of Europe. But it is surely much more rational, and more for the benefit of both parties, that, after the renunciation of the agreement by the defendant, the plaintiff should be at liberty to consider himself absolved from any future performance of it, retaining his right to sue for any damage he has suffered from the breach of it. Thus, instead of remaining idle and laying out money in preparations which must be useless, he is at liberty to seek service under another employer, which would go in mitigation of the damages to which he would otherwise be entitled for a breach of the contract. It seems strange that the defendant after renouncing the contract, and absolutely declaring that he will never act under it, should be permitted to object that faith is given to his assertion, and that an opportunity is not left to him of changing his mind. * * *

* * * The man who wrongfully renounces a contract into which he has deliberately entered cannot justly complain if he is immediately sued for a compensation in damage by the man whom he has injured: and it seems reasonable to allow an option to the injured party, either to sue immediately, or to wait till the time when the act was to be done, still holding it as prospectively binding for the exercise of this option, which may be advantageous to the innocent party, and cannot be prejudicial to the wrongdoer.

Judgment for plaintiff.

CASE

17-3

Accord and Satisfaction

MCDOWELL WELDING & PIPEFITTING, INC. v. UNITED STATES GYPSUM CO.

Supreme Court of Oregon, 2008

345 OR. 272, 193 P.3d 9

http://scholar.google.com/scholar_case?q=193+P.3d+9&hl=en&as_sdt=2,34&case=8212741394978818508&scilh=0

Kistler, J.

Defendant United States Gypsum (U.S. Gypsum) was constructing a new plant in Columbia County. Defendant B E & K Construction Co. (B E & K) was the general contractor on that project. B E & K subcontracted with plaintiff [McDowell Welding & Pipefitting, Inc.] to perform work on the project. During construction, defendants asked plaintiff to perform additional tasks, over and above plaintiff's contractual obligations, and defendants promised to pay plaintiff for doing so. After plaintiff completed its work on the project, the parties disagreed over the amount that defendants owed for the additional work that plaintiff had performed.

Plaintiff filed this action against defendants, alleging breach of contract and related claims. All of plaintiff's claims arose out of the modification to the construction contract. B E & K's answer included an affirmative defense [and counterclaim] captioned "Compromise and Settlement," alleging that plaintiff had agreed to settle its claims against defendants [for a total payment of $896,000.] * * *

B E & K filed a motion asking the trial court to bifurcate the proceedings and try its counterclaim before trying plaintiff's claims against it. * * * The trial court granted B E & K's motion.

After the trial court granted B E & K's motion, plaintiff filed a demand for a jury trial, which B E & K moved to strike. B E & K reasoned that, because its counterclaim was equitable, plaintiff had no right to a jury trial on the counterclaim. The trial court granted B E & K's motion to strike plaintiff's jury trial demand and, sitting as the trier of fact, found that plaintiff had accepted defendants' offer to settle its claims in return for defendants' promise to pay plaintiff $800,000. [Court's footnote: Although defendants alleged that they promised to pay plaintiff $896,000 in return for plaintiff's promise to release its claims against them, defendants proved and the trial court found that defendants had promised to pay only $800,000.]

Based on its resolution of defendants' counterclaim, the trial court entered a limited judgment directing defendants to tender $800,000 to the court clerk and directing plaintiff, after defendants tendered that sum, to execute releases of its claims against defendants. After the trial court entered the limited judgment, defendants tendered $800,000 to the court clerk and then moved for summary judgment on plaintiff's claims against them. The trial court granted defendants' motion and entered a general judgment that dismissed

plaintiff's claims with prejudice. The plaintiff appealed, claiming a state constitutional right to a jury trial on the factual issues that the defendant's counterclaim had raised. A divided Court of Appeals affirmed the trial court's judgment. The Oregon Supreme Court allowed the plaintiff's petition for review.

As we discuss more fully below, a settlement agreement may take one of three forms: an executory accord, an accord and satisfaction, or a substituted contract. As we also discuss below, when the Oregon Constitution was adopted, only a court of equity would enforce an executory accord. The law courts would not enforce executory accords because they suspended the underlying obligation; they did not discharge it. By contrast, an accord and satisfaction and a substituted contract discharged the underlying obligation, albeit for different reasons, and both were enforceable in the law courts. It follows that the question whether the agreement that gave rise to defendants' counterclaim would have been cognizable in law or equity turns, at least initially, on whether it is an executory accord, an accord and satisfaction, or a substituted contract. We first describe the distinctions among those types of settlement agreements before considering which type of settlement agreement defendants alleged.

An executory accord is "an agreement for the future discharge of an existing claim by a substituted performance." [Citation.] Usually, an executory accord is a bilateral agreement; the debtor promises to pay an amount in return for the creditor's promise to release the underlying claim. When the parties enter into an executory accord, the underlying claim "is not [discharged] until the new agreement is performed. The right to enforce the original claim is merely suspended, and is revived by the debtor's breach of the new agreement." [Citation.]

Because an executory accord does not discharge the underlying claim but merely suspends it, the law courts refused to allow it to be pleaded as a bar to the underlying claim. [Citations.] Once the promised performance occurs, the accord has been executed or satisfied and the underlying claim is discharged, resulting in an accord and satisfaction. [Citation.] [Court's footnote: An accord and satisfaction may occur in one of two ways: "The two parties may first make an accord executory, that is, a contract for the future discharge of the existing claim by a substituted performance still to be rendered. When this executory contract is fully performed as agreed, there is said to be an accord and satisfaction, and the previously existing claim is discharged. It is quite possible, however, for the parties to make an accord and satisfaction without any preliminary accord executory or any other executory contract of any kind. [For example, a] debtor may offer the substituted performance in satisfaction of his debt and the creditor may receive it, without any binding promise being made by either party." [Citation.] Because an accord and satisfaction discharges the underlying claim, that defense is legal, not equitable. [Citation.]

Finally, the parties may enter into a substituted contract; that is, the parties may agree to substitute the new agreement for the underlying obligation. [Citation.] A substituted contract differs from an executory accord in that the parties intend that entering into the new agreement will immediately discharge the underlying obligation. [Citations.] A substituted contract discharges the underlying obligation and could be asserted as a bar to an action at law. [Citation.]

With that background in mind, we turn to the question whether defendants pleaded an executory accord, an accord and satisfaction, or a substituted contract. Here, defendants alleged that they agreed to pay plaintiff $896,000 in exchange for a release of plaintiff's claims against them. Defendants did not allege that they had paid plaintiff the promised sum—an allegation necessary for an accord and satisfaction. [Citations.] Nor did they allege that, by entering into the settlement agreement, they extinguished the underlying obligation—an allegation necessary to allege a substituted contract. [Citations.] Rather, defendants alleged that plaintiff agreed to release its claims only after defendants made the promised payment. In short, defendants alleged an executory accord.

* * *

[The Oregon constitutional right to a jury trial in civil cases does not extend to the defendants' counterclaim of an executory accord. We affirm the Court of Appeals decision on the plaintiff's jury trial claim but reverse its decision on a subsidiary issue regarding prejudgment interest.]

CASE
17-4

Impossibility
NORTHERN CORP. v. CHUGACH ELECTRICAL ASSOCIATION
Supreme Court of Alaska, 1974
518 P.2d 76
http://scholar.google.com/scholar_case?q=518+P.2d+76&hl=en&as_sdt=2,34&case=2017068664150967540&scilh=0

Boochever, J.

[Northern Corporation entered into a contract with Chugach in August 1966 to repair and upgrade the upstream face of Cooper Lake Dam in Alaska. The contract required Northern to obtain rock from a quarry site at the opposite end of the lake and to transport the rock to the dam during the winter across the ice on the lake. In December 1966, Northern cleared the road on the ice to permit deeper freezing, but thereafter water overflowed on the ice, preventing the use of the road. Northern complained of the unsafe condition of the lake ice, but Chugach insisted on performance. In March 1967, one of Northern's loaded trucks broke through the ice and sank. Northern continued to encounter difficulties and ceased operations with the approval of Chugach. On January 8, 1968, Chugach notified Northern that it would be in default unless all rock was hauled by April 1. After two more trucks broke through the ice, causing the deaths of the drivers, Northern ceased operations and notified Chugach that it would make no more attempts to haul across the lake. Northern advised Chugach it considered the contract terminated for impossibility of performance and commenced suit to recover the cost incurred in attempting to complete the contract.]

* * *

The focal question is whether the * * * contract was impossible of performance. The September 27, 1966 directive specified that the rock was to be transported "across Cooper Lake to the dam site when such lake is frozen to a sufficient depth to permit heavy vehicle traffic thereon," and * * * specified that the hauling to the dam site would be done during the winter of 1966–67. It is therefore clear that the parties contemplated that the rock would be transported across the frozen lake by truck. Northern's repeated efforts to perform the contract by this method during the winter of 1966–67 and subsequently in February 1968, culminating in the tragic loss of life, abundantly support the trial court's findings that the contract was impossible of performance by this method.

Chugach contends, however, that Northern was nevertheless bound to perform, and that it could have used means other than hauling by truck across the ice to transport the rock. The answer to Chugach's contention is that * * * the parties contemplated that the rock would be hauled by truck once the ice froze to a sufficient depth to support the weight of the vehicles. The specification of this particular method of performance presupposed the existence of ice frozen to the requisite depth. Since this expectation of the parties was never fulfilled, and since the provisions relating to the means of performance was clearly material, Northern's duty to perform was discharged by reason of impossibility.

There is an additional reason for our holding that Northern's duty to perform was discharged because of impossibility. It is true that in order for a defendant to prevail under the original common law doctrine of impossibility, he had to show that no one else could have performed the contract. However, this harsh rule has gradually been eroded, and the Restatement of Contracts has departed from the early common law rule by recognizing the principle of "commercial impracticability." Under this doctrine, a party is discharged from his contract obligations, even if it is technically possible to perform them, if the costs of performance would be so disproportionate to that reasonably contemplated by the parties as to make the contract totally impractical in a commercial sense. * * * Removed from the strictures of the common law, "impossibility" in its modern context has become a coat of many colors, including among its hues the point argued here—namely, impossibility predicated upon "commercial impracticability." This concept—which finds expression both in case law * * * and in other authorities * * * is grounded upon the assumption that in legal contemplation something is impracticable when it can only be done at an excessive and unreasonable cost. As stated in *Transatlantic Financing Corp. v. United States* [citation]

> * * * The doctrine ultimately represents the ever-shifting line, drawn by courts hopefully responsive to commercial practices and mores, at which the community's interest in having contracts enforced according to their terms is outweighed by the commercial senselessness of requiring performance. * * *

* * *

In the case before us the detailed opinion of the trial court clearly indicates that the appropriate standard was followed. There is ample evidence to support its findings that "[t]he ice haul method of transporting riprap ultimately selected was within the contemplation of the parties and was part of the basis of the agreement which ultimately resulted in amendment No. 1 in October 1966," and that that method was not commercially feasible within the financial parameters of the contract. We affirm the court's conclusion that the contract was impossible of performance.

QUESTIONS

1. A–1 Roofing Co. entered into a written contract with Jaffe to put a new roof on the latter's residence for $1,800, using a specified type of roofing, and to complete the job without unreasonable delay. A–1 undertook the work within a week thereafter, but when all the roofing material was at the site and the labor 50 percent completed, the premises were totally destroyed by fire caused by lightning. A–1 submitted a bill to Jaffe for $1,200 for materials furnished and labor performed up to the time of the destruction of the premises. Jaffe refused to pay the bill, and A–1 now seeks payment from Jaffe. Should A–1 prevail? Explain.

2. By contract dated January 5, Rebecca agreed to sell to Nancy, and Nancy agreed to buy from Rebecca, a certain parcel of land then zoned commercial. The specific intent of Nancy, which was known to Rebecca, was to erect a manufacturing plant on the land; and the contract stated that the agreement was conditioned upon Nancy's ability to construct such a plant upon the land. The closing date for the transaction was set for April 1. On February 15, the city council rezoned the land from commercial to residential, which precluded the erection of the plant. As the closing date drew near, Nancy made it known to Rebecca that she did not intend to go through with the purchase because the land could no longer be used as intended. On April 1, Rebecca tendered the deed to Nancy, who refused to pay Rebecca the agreed purchase price. Rebecca brought an action against Nancy for breach of their contract. Can Rebecca enforce the contract?

3. The Perfection Produce Company entered into a written contract with Hiram Hodges for the purchase of three hundred tons of potatoes to be grown on Hodge's farm in Maine at a stipulated price per ton. Although the land would ordinarily produce one thousand tons and the planting and cultivation were properly done, Hodges was able to deliver only one hundred tons because an unprecedented drought caused a partial crop failure. Perfection accepted the one hundred tons but paid only 80 percent of the stipulated price per ton. Hodges sued the produce company to recover the unpaid balance of the agreed price for the one hundred tons of potatoes accepted by Perfection. Perfection counterclaimed against Hodges for his failure to deliver the remaining two hundred tons. Who will prevail? Why?

4. On November 23, Sylvia agreed to sell to Barnett her Buick automobile for $7,000, delivery and payment to be made on December 1. On November 26, Barnett informed Sylvia that he wished to rescind the contract and would pay Sylvia $350 if Sylvia agreed. She agreed

and took the $350 cash. On December 1, Barnett tendered to Sylvia $6,650 and demanded that she deliver the automobile. Sylvia refused and Barnett initiated a lawsuit. May Barnett enforce the original contract?

5. Webster, Inc., dealt in automobile accessories at wholesale. Although he manufactured a few items in his own factory, among them windshield wipers, Webster purchased most of his inventory from a large number of other manufacturers. In January, Webster entered into a written contract to sell Hunter two thousand windshield wipers for $4,900, delivery to be made June 1. In April, Webster's factory burned to the ground, and Webster failed to make delivery on June 1. Hunter, forced to buy windshield wipers elsewhere at a higher price, is now trying to recover damages from Webster. Will Hunter be successful in its claim?

6. Erwick Construction Company contracted to build a house for Charles. The specifications called for the use of Karlene Pipe for all plumbing. Erwick, however, got a better price on Boynton Pipe and substituted the equally good Boynton Pipe for Karlene Pipe. Upon inspection, Charles discovered the change, and he now refuses to make the final payment. The contract price was for $200,000, and the final payment is $20,000. Erwick now brings suit seeking the $20,000. Will Erwick succeed in its claim?

7. Green owed White $3,500, which was due and payable on June 1. White owed Brown $3,500, which was due and payable on August 1. On May 25, White received a letter signed by Green stating, "If you will cancel my debt to you, in the amount of $3,500, I will pay, on the due date, the debt you owe Brown, in the amount of $3,500." On May 28, Green received a letter signed by White stating, "I received your letter and agree to the proposals recited therein. You may consider your debt to me canceled as of the date of this letter." On June 1, White, needing money to pay his income taxes, made a demand upon Green to pay him the $3,500 due on that date. Is Green obligated to pay the money demanded by White?

8. By written contract Ames agreed to build a house on Bowen's lot for $165,000, commencing within ninety days of the date of the contract. Prior to the date for beginning construction, Ames informed Bowen that he was repudiating the contract and would not perform. Bowen refused to accept the repudiation and demanded fulfillment of the contract. Eighty days after the date of the contract, Bowen entered into a new contract with Curd for $162,000. The next day, without knowledge or notice of Bowen's contract with Curd, Ames began construction. Bowen ordered Ames from the premises

and refused to allow him to continue. Will Ames be able to collect damages from Bowen? Explain.

9. Judy agreed in writing to work for Northern Enterprises, Inc., for three years as superintendent of Northern's manufacturing establishment and to devote herself entirely to the business, giving it her whole time, attention, and skill, for which she was to receive $72,000 per annum, in monthly installments of $6,000. Judy worked and was paid for the first twelve months, when, through no fault of her own or Northern's, she was arrested and imprisoned for one month. It became imperative for Northern to employ another, and it treated the contract with Judy as breached and abandoned, refusing to permit Judy to resume work upon her release from jail. What rights, if any, does Judy have under the contract?

10. The Park Plaza Hotel awarded its valet and laundry concession to Larson for a three-year term. The contract contained the following provision: "It is distinctly understood and agreed that the services to be rendered by Larson shall meet with the approval of the Park Plaza Hotel, which shall be the sole judge of the sufficiency and propriety of the services." After seven months, the hotel gave a month's notice to discontinue services based on the failure of the services to meet its approval. Larson brought an action against the hotel, alleging that its dissatisfaction was unreasonable. The hotel defended upon the ground that subjective or personal satisfaction may be the sole justification for termination of the contract. Who is correct? Explain.

11. Schlosser entered into an agreement to purchase a cooperative apartment from Flynn Company. The written agreement contained the following provision:

> This entire agreement is conditioned on Purchaser's being approved for occupancy by the board of directors of the Cooperative. In the event approval of the Purchaser shall be denied, this agreement shall thereafter be of no further force or effect.

When Schlosser unilaterally revoked her "offer," Flynn sued for breach of contract. Schlosser claims the approval provision was a condition precedent to the existence of a binding contract and, thus, she was free to revoke. Decision?

12. Jacobs, owner of a farm, entered into a contract with Earl Walker in which Walker agreed to paint the buildings on the farm. As authorized by Jacobs, Walker acquired the paint from Jones with the bill to be sent to Jacobs. Before the work was completed, Jacobs without good cause ordered Walker to stop. Walker made offers to complete the job, but Jacobs declined to permit

Walker to fulfill his contract. Jacobs refused to pay Jones for the paint Walker had acquired for the job. Explain whether Jones and Walker will be successful in an action against Jacobs for breach of contract.

CASE PROBLEMS

13. On August 20, Hildebrand entered into a written contract with the city of Douglasville whereby he was to serve as community development project engineer for three years at an "annual fee" of $19,000. This salary figure could be changed without affecting the other terms of the contract. One of the provisions for termination of the contract was written notice by either party to the other at any time at least ninety days prior to the intended date of termination. The contract listed a substantial number of services and duties Hildebrand was to perform for the city; among the lesser duties were (1) keeping the community development director (Hildebrand's supervisor) informed at all times of his whereabouts and how he could be contacted, and (2) attending meetings at which his presence was requested. Two years later, on September 20, by which time Hildebrand's fee had risen to $1,915.83 per month, the city fired Hildebrand effective immediately, citing "certain material breaches … of the … agreement." The city specifically charged that he did not attend the necessary meetings although requested to do so and seldom if ever kept his supervisor informed of his whereabouts and how he could be contacted. Will Hildebrand prevail in a suit against the mayor and city for damages in the amount of $5,747.49 because of the city's failure to give him ninety days' notice prior to termination?

14. Walker & Co. contracted to provide a sign for Harrison to place above his dry cleaning business. According to the contract, Harrison would lease the sign from Walker, making monthly payments for thirty-six months. In return, Walker agreed to maintain and service the sign at its own expense. Walker installed the sign in July, and Harrison made the first rental payment. Shortly thereafter, someone hit the sign with a tomato. Harrison also claims he discovered rust on its chrome and little spider webs in its corners. Harrison repeatedly called Walker for the maintenance work promised under the contract, but Walker did not respond immediately. Harrison then notified Walker that due to Walker's failure to perform the maintenance services, he held Walker in material breach of the contract. A week later, Walker sent out a crew, which did all of the requested maintenance services. Has Walker committed a material breach of contract? Explain.

15. Barta entered into a written contract to buy the K&K Pharmacy, located in the local shopping center. Included in the contract was a provision stating that "this Agreement shall be contingent upon Buyer's ability to obtain a new lease from Landlord for the premises presently occupied by Seller. In the event Buyer is unable to obtain a lease satisfactory to Buyer, this Agreement shall be null and void." Barta planned to sell "high traffic" grocery items such as bread, milk, and coffee to attract customers to his drugstore. A grocery store in the local shopping center, however, held the exclusive right to sell grocery items. Barta, therefore, could not obtain a leasing agreement meeting his approval. Barta refused to close the sale. In a suit by K&K Pharmacy against Barta for breach of contract, who will prevail? Explain.

16. Victor Packing Co. (Victor) contracted to supply Sun Maid Raisin Growers 1,800 tons of raisins from the current year's crop. After delivering 1,190 tons of raisins by August, Victor refused to supply any more. Although Victor had until the end of the crop season to ship the remaining 610 tons of raisins, Sun Maid treated Victor's repeated refusals to ship any more raisins as a repudiation of the contract. To prevent breaching its own contracts, Sun Maid went into the marketplace to "cover" and bought the raisins it needed. Unfortunately, between the time Victor refused delivery and Sun Maid entered the market, disastrous rains had caused the price of raisins to skyrocket. May Sun Maid recover from Victor the difference between the contract price and the market price before the end of the current crop year?

17. In May, Watts was awarded a construction contract, based on its low bid, by the Cullman County Commission. The contract provided that it would not become effective until approved by the State director of the Farmers Home Administration (now part of the U.S. Department of Agriculture Rural Development Office). In September construction still had not been authorized, and Watts wrote to the County Commission requesting a 5 percent price increase to reflect seasonal and inflationary price increases. The County Commission countered with an offer of 3.5 percent. Watts then wrote the commission, insisting on a 5 percent increase and stating that if this was not agreeable, it was withdrawing its original bid. The commission obtained another company to

perform the project, and on October 14, informed Watts that it had accepted the withdrawal of the bid. Watts sued for breach of contract. Explain whether Watts will prevail and why or why not.

18. K&G Construction Co. was the owner of and the general contractor for a housing subdivision project. Harris contracted with the company to do excavating and earth-moving work on the project. Certain provisions of the contract stated that (a) K&G was to make monthly progress payments to Harris, (b) no such payments were to be made until Harris obtained liability insurance, and (c) all of Harris's work on the project must be performed in a workmanlike manner. On August 9, a bulldozer operator, working for Harris, drove too close to one of K&G's houses, causing the collapse of a wall and other damage. When Harris and his insurance carrier denied liability and refused to pay for the damage, K&G refused to make the August monthly progress payment. Harris, nonetheless, continued to work on the project until mid-September, when the excavator ceased its operations due to K&G's refusal to make the progress payment. K&G had another excavator finish the job at an added cost of $1,450. It then sued Harris for the bulldozer damage, alleging negligence, and also for the $1,450 damages for breach of contract. Harris claims that K&G defaulted first, having no legal right to refuse the August progress payment. Did K&G default first? Explain.

19. Mountain Restaurant Corporation (Mountain) leased commercial space in the ParkCenter Mall to operate a restaurant called Zac's Grill. The lease specified that the lessee shall "at all times have a nonexclusive and nonrevocable right, together with the other tenants and occupants of ... the shopping center, to use the parking area ... for itself, its customers and employees." Zac's Grill was to be a fast-food restaurant where tables were anticipated to "turn over" twice during lunch. Zac's operated successfully until parking close to the restaurant became restricted. Two other restaurants opened and began competing for parking spaces, and the parking lot would become full between 12:00 and 12:30 P.M. Parking, however, was always available at other areas of the mall. Business declined for Zac's, which fell behind on the rent due to ParkCenter until finally the restaurant closed. Mountain claims that it was discharged from its obligations under the lease because of material breach. Is Mountain correct? Explain.

20. In late 2010 or early 2011, the plaintiff, Lan England, agreed to sell 258,363 shares of stock to the defendant, Eugene Horbach, for $2.75 per share, resulting in a total price of $710,498.25. Although the purchase money was to be paid in the first quarter of 2011, the defendant

made periodic payments on the stock at least through September 2011. The parties met in May of 2012 to finalize the transaction. At this time, the plaintiff believed that the defendant owed at least $25,000 of the original purchase price. The defendant did not dispute that amount. The parties then reached a second agreement whereby the defendant agreed to pay to the plaintiff an additional $25,000 and to hold in trust 2 percent of the stock for the plaintiff. In return, the plaintiff agreed to transfer the stock and to forego his right to sue the defendant for breach of the original agreement.

In December 2013, the plaintiff made a demand for the 2 percent stock, but the defendant refused, contending that the 2 percent agreement was meant only to secure his payment of the additional $25,000. The plaintiff sued for breach of the 2 percent agreement. Prior to trial, the defendant discovered additional business records documenting that he had, before entering into the second agreement, actually overpaid the plaintiff for the purchase of the stock. The defendant asserts the plaintiff could not enforce the second agreement as an accord and satisfaction because (a) it was not supported by consideration, and (b) it was based upon a mutual mistake that the defendant owed additional money on the original agreement. Is the defendant correct in his assertions? Explain.

21. An artist once produced a painting now called *The Plains of Meudon*. For a while, the parties in this case thought that the artist was Theodore Rousseau, a prominent member of the Barbizon school, and that the painting was quite valuable. With this idea in mind, the Kohlers consigned the painting to Leslie Hindman, Inc. (Hindman), an auction house. Among other things, the consignment agreement between the Kohlers and Hindman defined the scope of Hindman's authority as agent. First, Hindman was obliged to sell the painting according to the conditions of sale spelled out in the auction catalog. Those conditions provided that neither the consignors nor Hindman made any warranties of authenticity. Second, the consignment agreement gave Hindman extensive and exclusive discretionary authority to rescind sales if in its "sole discretion" it determined that the sale subjected the company or the Kohlers to any liability under a warranty of authenticity.

Despite having some doubts about its authenticity, Thune was still interested in the painting but wanted to have it authenticated before committing to its purchase. Unable to obtain an authoritative opinion about its authenticity before the auction, Leslie Hindman and Thune made a verbal agreement that Thune could return the painting within approximately thirty days of the auction if he was the successful bidder and if an expert then determined that Rousseau had not painted it. Neither Leslie Hindman nor anyone else at Hindman told the Kohlers about the questions concerning the painting or about the side agreement between Thune and Hindman. At the auction, Thune prevailed in the bidding with a high bid of $90,000, and he took possession of the painting without paying. He then sent it to an expert in Paris who decided that it was not a Rousseau. Thune returned the painting to Hindman within the agreed upon period. Explain whether the Kohlers would be successful in a lawsuit against either Hindman, Inc., or Thune.

TAKING SIDES

Associated Builders, Inc., provided labor and materials to William M. Coggins and Benjamin W. Coggins, doing business as Ben & Bill's Chocolate Emporium, to complete a structure on Main Street in Bar Harbor, Maine. After a dispute arose regarding compensation, Associated and the Cogginses executed an agreement stating that there existed an outstanding balance of $70,000 and setting forth the following terms of repayment:

> It is agreed that, two payments will be made by the Cogginses to Associated Builders as follows: Twenty Five Thousand Dollars ($25,000.00) on or before June 1, 2012, and Twenty Five Thousand Dollars ($25,000.00) on or before June 1, 2013. No interest will be charged or paid providing payments are made as agreed. If the payments are not made as agreed then interest shall accrue at 10% per annum figured from the date of default. It is further agreed that Associated Builders will forfeit the balance of Twenty Thousand Dollars and No Cents ($20,000.00) providing the above payments are made as agreed.

The Cogginses made their first payment in accordance with the agreement. The second payment, however, was delivered three days late on June 4, 2013. Claiming a breach of the contract, Associated contended that the remainder of the original balance of $20,000, plus interest and cost, were now due.

a. What arguments would support Associated's claim for $20,000?

b. What arguments would support the claim by the Cogginses that they were not liable for $20,000?

c. For what damages, if any, are the Cogginses liable? Explain.

CHAPTER 16

CONTRACT REMEDIES

CHAPTER OUTCOMES

After reading and studying this chapter, you should be able to:

- Explain how compensatory damages and reliance damages are computed.

- Define (1) nominal damages, (2) incidental damages, (3) consequential damages, (4) foreseeability of damages, (5) punitive damages, (6) liquidated damages, and (7) mitigation of damages.

- Define the various types of equitable relief and explain when the courts will grant such relief.

- Explain how restitutionary damages are computed and identify the situations in which restitution is available as a contractual remedy.

- Identify and explain the limitations on contractual remedies.

[handwritten: ★ question 8 on mock final ★ read all]

When one party to a contract breaches the contract by failing to perform his contractual duties, the law provides a remedy for the injured party. Although the primary objective of contract remedies is to compensate the injured party for the loss resulting from the breach, it is impossible for any remedy to equal the promised performance. To an injured party a court can give as relief what it regards as an equivalent of the promised performance.

This chapter will examine the most common judicial remedies available for breach of contract: (1) monetary damages, (2) the equitable remedies of specific performance and injunction, and (3) restitution. Sales of goods are governed by Article 2 of the Uniform Commercial Code (UCC), which provides specialized remedies that are discussed in *Chapter 25*.

2. the **reliance interest**, which is his interest in being reimbursed for loss caused by reliance on the contract by being put in a position as good as the one he would have been in had the contract not been made; or

3. the **restitution interest**, which is his interest in having restored to him any benefit that he has conferred on the other party. Restatement, Section 344.

The expectation interest is protected by the contract remedies of compensatory damages, specific performance, and injunction. The reliance interest is protected by the contractual remedy of reliance damages, while the restitution interest is protected by the contractual remedy of restitution.

PRACTICAL ADVICE
Consider including in your contracts a provision for the arbitration of contract disputes.

INTERESTS PROTECTED BY CONTRACT REMEDIES

Contract remedies are available to protect one or more of the following interests of the injured party:

1. the **expectation interest**, which is his interest in having the benefit of his bargain by being put in a position as good as the one he would have occupied had the contract been performed;

MONETARY DAMAGES

A judgment awarding monetary damages is the most frequently granted judicial remedy for breach of contract. Monetary damages, however, will be awarded only for losses that are foreseeable, established with reasonable certainty, and unavoidable. The equitable remedies discussed in this chapter are discretionary and are available only if monetary damages are inadequate.

Consider including in your contracts a provision for the recovery of attorneys' fees in the event of breach of contract.

COMPENSATORY DAMAGES

The right to recover compensatory money damages for breach of contract is always available to the injured party. Restatement, Section 346. The purpose in allowing **compensatory damages** is to place the injured party in a position as good as the one she would have occupied had the other party performed under the contract. This involves compensating the injured party for the dollar value of the benefits she would have received had the contract been performed less any savings she experienced by not having to perform her own obligations under the contract. Because these damages are intended to protect the injured party's expectation interest, or the value she expected to derive from the contract, the amount of compensatory damages is generally computed as follows:

> **Loss of value**
> **− Loss or cost avoided by injured party**
> **+ Incidental damages**
> **+ Consequential damages**
> **= Compensatory damages**

LOSS OF VALUE In general, loss of value is the *difference between the value of the promised performance* of the breaching party *and the value of the actual performance* rendered by the breaching party.

> **Value of promised performance**
> **− Value of actual performance**
> **= Loss of value**

If the breaching party renders no performance at all, then the loss of value is the value of the promised performance. If defective or partial performance is rendered, the loss of value is the difference between the value that the full performance would have had and the value of the performance actually rendered. Thus, where there has been a breach of warranty, the injured party may recover the difference between the value the goods would have had, if they had been as warranted, and the value of the goods in the condition in which the buyer received them. To illustrate, Victor sells an automobile to Joan and expressly warrants that it will get forty-five miles per gallon, but the automobile gets only twenty miles per gallon. The automobile would have been worth $24,000 had it been as warranted, but it is worth only $20,000 as delivered. Joan would recover $4,000 in damages for loss of value.

In addition to loss of value, the injured party may also recover for all other losses actually suffered, subject to the limitation of foreseeability discussed in a subsequent section. These damages include incidental and consequential damages.

COST AVOIDED The recovery by the injured party, however, is reduced by any cost or loss she has avoided by not having to perform. For example, Clinton agrees to build a hotel for Debra for $11,250,000 by September 1. Clinton breaches by not completing construction until October 1. As a consequence, Debra loses revenues for one month in the amount of $400,000 but saves operating expenses of $60,000. She therefore may recover damages for $340,000. Similarly, in a contract in which the injured party has not fully performed, the injured party's recovery is reduced by the value to him of the performance he promised but did not render. For example, Clinton agrees to convey land to Debra in return for Debra's promise to work for Clinton for two years, but she repudiates the contract before Clinton has conveyed the land. Clinton's recovery for loss from Debra is reduced by the value to Clinton of the land.

INCIDENTAL DAMAGES **Incidental damages** are damages that arise directly out of the breach, such as costs incurred to acquire the nondelivered performance from some other source. For example, Agnes employs Benton for nine months for $40,000 to supervise construction of a factory, but fires him without cause after three weeks. Benton, who spends $850 in reasonable fees attempting to find comparable employment, may recover $850 in incidental damages, in addition to any other actual loss he may suffer.

CONSEQUENTIAL DAMAGES **Consequential damages** include lost profits and injury to person or property resulting from defective performance. Thus, if Tracy leases to Sean a defective machine that causes him $40,000 in property damage and $120,000 in personal injuries, Sean may recover, in addition to damages for loss of value and incidental damages, $160,000 as consequential damages.

If you are the provider of goods or services, consider including a contractual provision for the limitation or exclusion of consequential damages. If you are the purchaser of goods or services, avoid such limitations.

NOMINAL DAMAGES

An action to recover damages for breach of contract may be maintained even though the plaintiff has not sustained or cannot prove any injury or loss resulting from the breach. Restatement, Section 346. In such a case, he will be permitted to recover **nominal damages**—a small sum fixed without regard to the amount of loss. For example, Edward contracts to sell and deliver goods to Florence for $1,000. Edward refuses to deliver the goods as agreed, and so breaks the contract. Florence, however, is able to purchase goods of the same kind and quality elsewhere for $1,000 without incurring any incidental damages. As a result, although Edward has violated Florence's rights under the contract, Florence has suffered no actual loss. Consequently, if Florence, as she may, should sue Edward for breach of contract, she would recover a judgment for nominal damages only. Nominal damages are also available where loss is actually sustained but cannot be proved with reasonable certainty.

RELIANCE DAMAGES

As an alternative to compensatory damages, the injured party may seek reimbursement for foreseeable loss caused by his reliance upon the contract. The purpose of **reliance damages** is to place the injured party in a position as good as the one he would have held, had the contract *not been made.* Reliance damages include expenses incurred in preparing to perform, in actually performing, or in forgoing opportunities to enter into other contracts. An injured party may prefer damages for reliance to compensatory damages when he is unable to establish his lost profits with reasonable certainty. For example, Donald agrees to sell his retail store to Gary, who spends $750,000 acquiring inventory and fixtures. Donald then repudiates the contract, and Gary sells the inventory and fixtures for $735,000. Neither party can establish with reasonable certainty what profit Gary would have made; Gary, therefore, may recover from Donald as damages the loss of $15,000 he sustained on the sale of the inventory and fixtures plus any other costs he incurred in entering into the contract. An injured party may choose reliance damages instead of compensatory damages when the contract is itself unprofitable. In such a case, however, if the breaching party can prove with reasonable certainty the amount of the loss, it will be subtracted from the injured party's reliance damages.

DAMAGES FOR MISREPRESENTATION

The basic remedy for misrepresentation is rescission (avoidance) of the contract, though when appropriate, the courts also will require restitution. At common law, an alternative remedy to rescission is a suit for damages. The Code liberalizes the common law by not restricting a defrauded party to an election of remedies; that is, the injured party may both rescind the contract by restoring the other party to the status quo and recover damages or obtain any other remedy available under the Code. UCC Section 2–721. In most States, the measure of damages for misrepresentation depends upon whether the misrepresentation was fraudulent or nonfraudulent.

FRAUD A party induced by fraud to enter into a contract may recover general damages in a tort action. A minority of States allows the injured party to recover, under the "**out-of-pocket**" rule, general damages equal to the difference between the value of what she has received and the value of what she has given for it. The great majority of States, however, under the "**benefit-of-the-bargain**" rule, permits the intentionally defrauded party to recover general damages that are equal to the difference between the value of what she has received and the value of the fraudulent party's performance as represented. The Restatement of Torts provides the fraudulently injured party with the option of either out-of-pocket or benefit-of-the-bargain damages. Section 549. To illustrate, Emily intentionally misrepresents the capabilities of a printing press and thereby induces Melissa to purchase the machine for $20,000. The value of the press as delivered is $14,000, but if the machine had performed as represented, it would be worth $24,000. Under the out-of-pocket rule, Melissa would recover $6,000, whereas under the benefit-of-the-bargain rule, she would recover $10,000.

In addition to a recovery of general damages under one of the measures just discussed, consequential damages may be recovered to the extent they are proved with reasonable certainty and to the extent they do not duplicate general damages. Moreover, where the fraud is gross, oppressive, or aggravated, punitive damages are permitted.

◆ **SEE CASE 18-1**

NONFRAUDULENT MISREPRESENTATION Where the misrepresentation is negligent, the deceived party may recover general damages—under the out-of-pocket measure—and consequential damages. Restatement of Torts, Section 552B. Some States, however, permit the recovery of general damages under the benefit-of-the-bargain measure for negligent misrepresentation. Where the misrepresentation is neither fraudulent nor negligent, however, the Restatement limits damages to the out-of-pocket measure. Section 552C.

PUNITIVE DAMAGES

Punitive damages are monetary damages in addition to compensatory damages awarded to a plaintiff in certain situations involving willful, wanton, or malicious conduct. Their purpose is to punish the defendant and thus discourage him and others from similar wrongful conduct. The purpose of allowing contract damages, on the other hand, is to compensate the plaintiff for the loss that he has sustained because of the defendant's breach of contract. Accordingly, the Restatement provides that punitive damages are *not* recoverable for a breach of contract unless the conduct constituting the breach is also a tort for which the plaintiff may recover punitive damages. Restatement, Section 355.

◆ **SEE CASE 18-1**

LIQUIDATED DAMAGES

A contract may contain a **liquidated damages** provision by which the parties agree in advance to the damages to be paid in event of a breach. Such a provision will be enforced if it amounts to a reasonable forecast of the loss that may or does result from the breach. If, however, the sum agreed upon as liquidated damages bears no reasonable relationship to the amount of probable loss that may or does result from breach, it is unenforceable as a penalty. (A penalty is a contractual provision designed to deter a party from breaching her contract and to punish her for doing so.) Restatement, Section 356, Comment a states,

> The parties to a contract may effectively provide in advance the damages that are to be payable in the event of breach as long as the provision does not disregard the principle of compensation. The enforcement of such provisions for liquidated damages saves the time of courts, juries, parties and witnesses and reduces the expense of litigation. This is especially important if the amount in controversy is small. However, the parties to a contract are not free to provide a penalty for its breach. The central objective behind the system of contract remedies is compensatory, not punitive.

By examining the substance of the provision, the nature of the contract, and the extent of probable harm to the promisee that a breach may reasonably be expected to cause, the courts will determine whether the agreed amount is proper as liquidated damages or unenforceable as a penalty. If a liquidated damage provision is not enforceable, the injured party nevertheless is entitled to the ordinary remedies for breach of contract.

To illustrate, Reliable Construction Company contracts with Equerry to build a grandstand at Equerry's racecourse at a cost of $1,330,000, to have it completed by a certain date, and to pay Equerry, as liquidated damages, $5,000 per day for every day's delay beyond that date in completing the grandstand. The stipulated sum for delay is liquidated damages and not a penalty because the amount is reasonable. If, instead, the sum stipulated had been $40,000 per day, it obviously would have been unreasonable and therefore a penalty. Provisions for liquidated damages are sometimes found in contracts for the sale of a business, in which the seller agrees not to reenter the same business within a reasonable geographic area and time period. Actual damages resulting from the seller's breach of his agreement ordinarily would be difficult to ascertain, and the sum stipulated, if reasonable, would be enforced as liquidated damages.

◆ **SEE CASE 18-2**

PRACTICAL ADVICE

Consider including a contractual provision for reasonable liquidated damages, especially where damages will be difficult to prove.

LIMITATIONS ON DAMAGES

To accomplish the basic purposes of contract remedies, the law imposes the limitations of foreseeability, certainty, and mitigation upon monetary damages. These limitations are intended to ensure that damages can be taken into account at the time of contracting, that damages are compensatory and not speculative, and that damages do not include loss that could have been avoided by reasonable efforts.

FORESEEABILITY OF DAMAGES A contracting party is generally expected to consider foreseeable risks when entering into the contract. Therefore, compensatory or reliance damages are recoverable only for loss that the party in breach had reason to foresee as a *probable* result of such breach when the contract was made; conversely, the breaching party is not liable for loss that was not foreseeable when the parties entered into the contract. The test of foreseeability is *objective*, based upon what the breaching party had reason to foresee. Loss may be deemed foreseeable as a probable result of a breach by following from the breach (1) in the ordinary course of events or (2) as a result of special circumstances, beyond the ordinary course of events, which the party in breach had reason to know. Restatement, Section 351(2). Moreover, "[a] court may limit damages for foreseeable loss by excluding recovery for loss of profits, by allowing recovery only for loss incurred in reliance, or otherwise if it concludes that in the circumstances justice so requires in order to avoid disproportionate compensation." Restatement, Section 351(3).

The leading case on the subject of foreseeability of damages is *Hadley v. Baxendale*, decided in England in 1854. In this case, the plaintiffs operated a flourmill at Gloucester. Their mill was compelled to cease operating because of a broken crankshaft attached to the steam engine that furnished power to the mill. It was necessary to send the broken shaft to a foundry located at Greenwich so that a new shaft could be made. The plaintiffs delivered the broken shaft to the defendants, who were common carriers, for immediate transportation from Gloucester to Greenwich, but did not inform the defendants that operation of the mill had ceased because of the nonfunctioning crankshaft. The defendants received the shaft, collected the freight charges in advance, and promised to deliver the shaft for repairs the following day. The defendants, however, did not make delivery as promised; as a result, the mill did not resume operations for several days, causing the plaintiffs to lose profitable sales. The defendants contended that the loss of profits was too remote, and therefore unforeseeable, to be recoverable. Nonetheless, the jury, in awarding damages to the plaintiffs, was permitted to take into consideration the loss of these profits. The appellate court reversed the decision and ordered a new trial on the ground that the plaintiffs had never communicated to the defendants the special circumstances that caused the loss of profits, namely, the continued stoppage of the mill while awaiting the return of the repaired crankshaft. A common carrier, the court reasoned, would not reasonably have foreseen that the plaintiffs' mill would be shut down as a result of delay in transporting the broken crankshaft.

On the other hand, if the defendants in *Hadley v. Baxendale* had been informed that the shaft was necessary for the operation of the mill, or otherwise had reason to know this fact, they would be liable for the plaintiffs' loss of profit during that period of the shutdown caused by their delay. Under these circumstances, the loss would be the "foreseeable" and "natural" result of the breach.

Should a plaintiff's expected profit be extraordinarily large, the general rule is that the breaching party will be liable for such special loss only if he had reason to know of it. In any event, the plaintiff may recover for any ordinary loss resulting from the breach. Thus, if Madeline breaches a contract with Jane, causing Jane, due to special circumstances, $10,000 in damages where ordinarily such a breach would result in only $6,000 in damages, Madeline would be liable to Jane for $6,000, not $10,000, provided that Madeline was unaware of the special circumstances causing Jane the unusually large loss.

PRACTICAL ADVICE

Be sure to inform the other party to the contract of any "special circumstances" beyond the ordinary course of events that could result from a breach of contract.

CERTAINTY OF DAMAGES Damages are not recoverable for loss beyond an amount that the injured party can establish with reasonable certainty. Restatement, Section 352. If the injured party cannot prove a particular element of her loss with reasonable certainty, she nevertheless will be entitled to recover the portion of her loss that she can prove with reasonable certainty. The certainty requirement creates the greatest challenge for plaintiffs seeking to recover consequential damages for lost profits on related transactions. Plaintiffs attempting to prove lost profits caused by breach of a contract to produce a sporting event or to publish a new book experience similar difficulties.

MITIGATION OF DAMAGES Under the doctrine of mitigation of damages, the injured party may not recover damages for loss that he could have avoided with reasonable effort and

without undue risk, burden, or humiliation. Restatement, Section 350. Thus, if James is under a contract to manufacture goods for Kathy, and Kathy repudiates the contract after James has commenced performance, James will not be allowed to recover for losses he sustains by continuing to manufacture the goods if to do so would increase the amount of damages. The amount of loss that James reasonably could have avoided is deducted from the amount that otherwise would be recoverable as damages. On the other hand, if the goods were almost completed when Kathy repudiated the contract, completing the goods might mitigate the damages, because the finished goods may be resalable whereas the unfinished goods may not. UCC Section 2–704(2).

Similarly, if Harvey contracts to work for Olivia for one year for a weekly salary and is wrongfully discharged by Olivia after two months, Harvey must use reasonable efforts to mitigate his damages by seeking other employment. If, after such efforts, he cannot obtain other employment of the same general character, he is entitled to recover full pay for the contract period that he is unemployed. He is not obliged to accept a radically different type of employment or to accept work at a distant place. For example, a person employed as a schoolteacher or accountant who is wrongfully discharged is not obliged, in order to mitigate damages, to accept available employment as a chauffeur or truck driver. If Harvey does not seek other employment, then if Olivia proves with reasonable certainty that employment of the same general character was available, Harvey's damages are reduced by the amount he could have earned.

◆ **SEE CASE 3-3**

PRACTICAL ADVICE

If the other party to the contract breaches, be sure to make reasonable efforts to avoid or mitigate damages.

REMEDIES IN EQUITY

At times, damages based on the expectation interest, reliance interest, or restitution interest will not adequately compensate an injured party. In these cases, equitable relief in the form of specific performance or an injunction may be available to protect the injured party's interest.

The remedies of specific performance and an injunction are not a matter of right but rest in the discretion of the court. Consequently, they will not be granted where:

1. there is an adequate remedy at law;
2. it is impossible to enforce them, as where the seller has already conveyed the subject matter of the contract to an innocent third person;

3. the terms of the contract are unfair;
4. the consideration is grossly inadequate;
5. the contract is tainted with fraud, duress, undue influence, mistake, or unfair practices;
6. the terms of the contract are not sufficiently certain; or
7. the relief would cause unreasonable hardship.

A court may grant specific performance or an injunction despite a provision for liquidated damages. Restatement, Section 361. Moreover, a court will grant specific performance or an injunction even though a term of the contract prohibits equitable relief, if denying such relief would cause unreasonable hardship to the injured party. Restatement, Section 364(2).

Another equitable remedy is **reformation**, a process whereby the court "rewrites" or "corrects" a written contract to make it conform to the true agreement of the parties. The purpose of reformation is not to make a new contract for the parties but rather to express adequately the contract they have made for themselves. The remedy of reformation is granted when the parties agree on a contract but write it in a way that inaccurately reflects their actual agreement. For example, Acme Insurance Co. and Bell agree that for good consideration Acme will issue an annuity paying $500 per month. Through a clerical error, the annuity policy is issued for $50.00 per month. A court of equity, upon satisfactory proof of the mistake, will reform the policy to provide for the correct amount—$500 per month. In addition, as discussed in *Chapter 13*, in cases in which a covenant not to compete is unreasonable, some courts will reform the agreement to make it reasonable and enforceable.

SPECIFIC PERFORMANCE

Specific performance is an equitable remedy that compels the defaulting party to perform her contractual obligations. Ordinarily, where a seller breaches her contract for the sale of **personal property**, the buyer has a sufficient remedy at law. If, however, the personal property contracted for is rare or unique, this remedy is inadequate. Examples of such property would include a famous painting or statue, an original manuscript or a rare edition of a book, a patent, a copyright, shares of stock in a closely held corporation, or an heirloom. Articles of this kind cannot be purchased elsewhere. Accordingly, should the seller breach her contract for the sale of any such article, money damages will not adequately compensate the buyer. Consequently, in these instances, the buyer may avail herself of the equitable remedy of specific performance.

Although courts of equity will grant specific performance in connection with contracts for the sale of personal property only in exceptional circumstances, they will always grant it in cases involving breach of contract for the sale of **real property**. The reason for this is that every parcel of land is considered unique. Consequently, if the seller refuses to convey title to the real estate contracted for, the buyer may seek the aid of a court of equity to compel the seller to convey the title. Most courts of equity will likewise compel the buyer in a real estate contract to perform at the suit of the seller. Courts of equity will not grant specific performance of contracts for personal services. In the first place, enforcing such a decree may be difficult if not impossible. In the second place, it is against the policy of the courts to force one person to work for or to serve another against his will, even though the person has contracted to do so, in that such enforcement would closely resemble involuntary servitude. For example, if Carmen, an accomplished concert pianist, agrees to appear at a certain time and place to play a specified program for Rudolf, a court would not issue a decree of specific performance upon her refusal to appear.

◆ **SEE CASE 18-3**

INJUNCTIONS

The **injunction**, as used as a contract remedy, is a formal court order enjoining (commanding) a person to refrain from doing a specific act or to cease engaging in specified conduct. A court of equity, at its discretion, may grant an injunction against breach of a contractual duty where damages for a breach would be inadequate. For example, Clint enters into a written contract to give Janice the right of first refusal on a tract of land he owns. Clint, however, subsequently offers the land to Blake without first offering it to Janice. A court of equity may properly enjoin Clint from selling the land to Blake. Similarly, valid covenants not to compete may be enforced by an injunction.

An employee's promise of exclusive personal services may be enforced by an injunction against serving another employer as long as the probable result will not be to deprive the employee of other reasonable means of making a living. Restatement, Section 367. Suppose, for example, that Allan makes a contract with Marlene, a famous singer, under which Marlene agrees to sing at Allan's theater on certain dates for an agreed fee. Before the date of the first performance, Marlene makes a contract with Craig to sing for Craig at his theater on the same dates. Although, as already discussed, Allan cannot secure specific performance of his contract by Marlene, a court of equity will, on suit by Allan against Marlene, issue an injunction against her, ordering her not to sing for Craig.

In cases in which the services contracted for are not unusual or extraordinary, the injured party cannot obtain injunctive relief. His only remedy is an action at law for damages.

◆ **SEE CASE 18-4**

RESTITUTION

One remedy that may be available to a party to a contract is restitution. **Restitution** is the act of returning to the aggrieved party the consideration, or its value, which he gave to the other party. The purpose of restitution is to restore the injured party to the position he occupied before the contract was made. Therefore, the party seeking restitution must return what he has received from the other party.

Restitution is available in several contractual situations: (1) as an alternative remedy for a party injured by breach, (2) for a party in default, (3) for a party who may not enforce a contract because of the statute of frauds, and (4) for a party wishing to rescind (avoid) a voidable contract.

PARTY INJURED BY BREACH

A party is entitled to restitution if the other party totally breaches the contract by nonperformance or repudiation. Restatement, Section 373. For example, Benedict agrees to sell land to Beatrice for $60,000. After Beatrice makes a partial payment of $15,000, Benedict wrongfully refuses to transfer title. As an alternative to damages or specific performance, Beatrice may recover the $15,000 in restitution.

PARTY IN DEFAULT

Where a party, after having partly performed, commits a breach by nonperformance or repudiation that discharges the other party's duty to perform, the party in default is entitled to restitution for any benefit she has conferred in excess of the loss she has caused by her breach. Restatement, Section 374. For example, Nathan agrees to sell land to Lilly for $160,000, and Lilly makes a partial payment of $15,000. Lilly then repudiates the contract. Nathan sells the land to Murray in good faith for $155,000. Lilly may recover from Nathan in restitution the part payment of the $15,000 *less* the $5,000 damages Nathan sustained because of Lilly's breach, which equals $10,000.

STATUTE OF FRAUDS

A party to a contract that is unenforceable because of the statute of frauds may, nonetheless, have acted in reliance upon the contract. In such a case, that party may recover in restitution the benefits she conferred upon the other in relying upon the unenforceable contract. In most States, the party seeking restitution must not be in default. Thus, if Wilton makes an oral contract to furnish services to Rochelle that are not to be performed within a year, and Rochelle discharges Wilton after three months, Wilton may recover as restitution the value of the services he rendered during the three months.

VOIDABLE CONTRACTS

A party who has rescinded or avoided a contract for lack of capacity, duress, undue influence, fraud in the inducement, nonfraudulent misrepresentation, or mistake is entitled to restitution for any benefit he has conferred upon the other party. Restatement, Section 376. For example, Samuel fraudulently induces Edith to sell land for $160,000. Samuel pays the purchase price, and Edith conveys the land. Discovering the fraud, Edith may disaffirm the contract and recover the land as restitution. Generally, the party seeking restitution must return any benefit that he has received under the agreement; however, as discussed in *Chapter 14* (which deals with contractual capacity), this is not always the case.

◆ **SEE FIGURE 18-1: Contract Remedies**

LIMITATIONS ON REMEDIES
ELECTION OF REMEDIES

If a party injured by a breach of contract has more than one remedy available to him, his manifesting a choice of one of them, such as bringing suit, does not prevent him from seeking another remedy unless the remedies are inconsistent and the other party materially changes his position in reliance on the manifestation. Restatement, Section 378. For example, a party who seeks specific performance, an injunction, or restitution may be entitled to incidental damages for delay in performance. Damages for total *breach*, however, are inconsistent with the remedies of specific performance, injunction, and restitution. Likewise, the remedy of specific performance or an injunction is inconsistent with that of restitution.

With respect to contracts for the sale of goods, the Code rejects any doctrine of election of remedies. Thus, the remedies it provides are essentially cumulative, including all of the available remedies for breach. Whether one remedy precludes another depends on the facts of the individual case. UCC Section 2–703, Comment 1.

◆ **SEE CASE 18-1**

LOSS OF POWER OF AVOIDANCE

A party with a power of avoidance for lack of capacity, duress, undue influence, fraud, misrepresentation, or mistake may lose that power if (1) she affirms the contract, (2) she delays unreasonably in exercising the power of disaffirmance, or (3) the rights of third parties intervene.

AFFIRMANCE A party who has the power to avoid a contract for lack of capacity, duress, undue influence, fraud in the inducement, nonfraudulent misrepresentation, or mistake will lose that power by affirming the contract. Affirmance occurs

◆ FIGURE 18-1: **Contract Remedies**

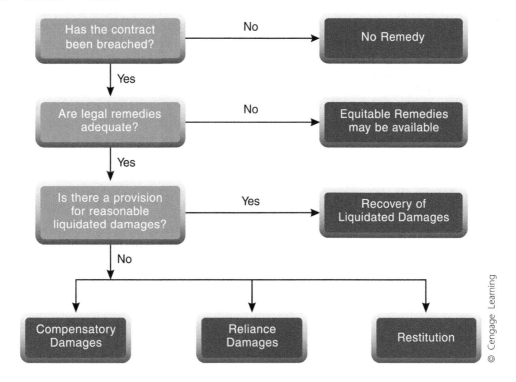

when the party, with full knowledge of the facts, either declares his intention to proceed with the contract or takes some other action from which such intention may reasonably be inferred. Thus, suppose that Pam was induced to purchase a ring from Sally through Sally's fraudulent misrepresentation. If, after learning the truth, Pam undertakes to sell the ring to Janet or else does something that is consistent only with her ownership of the ring, she may no longer rescind the transaction with Sally. In the case of incapacity, duress, or undue influence, affirmance is effective only after the circumstances that made the contract voidable cease to exist. In the case of fraudulent misrepresentation, the defrauded party may affirm only after he knows of the misrepresentation. If the misrepresentation is nonfraudulent or a mistake is involved, the defrauded or mistaken party may affirm only after he knows or should know of the misrepresentation or mistake.

PRACTICAL ADVICE

If you have the power to avoid a contract, do not affirm the contract unless you are sure you wish to relinquish your right to rescind the contract.

DELAY   The power of avoidance may be lost if the party who has the power does not rescind within a reasonable time after the circumstances that made the contract voidable have ceased to exist. Determining a reasonable time depends upon all the circumstances, including the extent to which the delay enables the party with the power of avoidance to speculate at the other party's risk. To illustrate, a defrauded purchaser of stock cannot wait unduly to see whether the market price or value of the stock appreciates sufficiently to justify retaining the stock.

RIGHTS OF THIRD PARTIES   The intervening rights of third parties further limit the power of avoidance and the accompanying right to restitution. If A transfers property to B in a transaction that is voidable by A, and B sells the property to C (a good faith purchaser for value) before A exercises her power of avoidance, A will lose the right to recover the property.

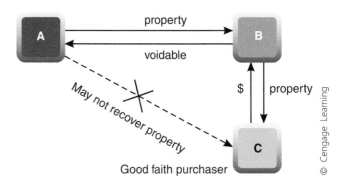

Thus, if C, a third party who is a good faith purchaser, acquires an interest in the subject matter of the contract before A has elected to rescind, no rescission is permitted. Because the transaction is voidable, B acquires a voidable title to the property. Upon a sale of the property by B to C, who is a purchaser in good faith and for value, C obtains good title and is allowed to retain the property. As both A and C are innocent, the law will not disturb the title held by C, the good faith purchaser. In this case, as in all cases in which rescission is not available, A's only recourse is against B.

The one notable exception to this rule is the situation involving a sale, *other than a sale of goods*, by a minor who subsequently wishes to avoid the transaction, in which the property has been retransferred to a good faith purchaser. Under this special rule, a good faith purchaser is deprived of the protection generally provided such third parties. Therefore, the third party in a transaction not involving goods, real property being the primary example, is no more protected from the minor's disaffirmance than is the person dealing directly with the minor.

CHAPTER SUMMARY

MONETARY DAMAGES

Compensatory Damages contract damages placing the injured party in a position as good as the one he would have held had the other party performed; equals loss of value minus loss avoided by injured party plus incidental damages plus consequential damages
- *Loss of Value* value of promised performance minus value of actual performance
- *Cost Avoided* loss or costs the injured party avoids by not having to perform
- *Incidental Damages* damages arising directly out of a breach of contract
- *Consequential Damages* damages not arising directly out of a breach but arising as a foreseeable result of the breach

Nominal Damages a small sum awarded when a contract has been breached but the loss is negligible or unproved

Reliance Damages contract damages placing the injured party in as good a position as she would have been in had the contract not been made

Damages for Misrepresentation
- *Benefit-of-the-Bargain Damages* difference between the value of the fraudulent party's performance as represented and the value the defrauded party received
- *Out-of-Pocket Damages* difference between the value given and the value received

Punitive Damages are generally *not* recoverable for breach of contract

Liquidated Damages reasonable damages agreed to in advance by the parties to a contract

Limitations on Damages
- *Foreseeability of Damages* potential loss that the party now in default had reason to know of when the contract was made
- *Certainty of Damages* damages are not recoverable beyond an amount that can be established with reasonable certainty
- *Mitigation of Damages* injured party may not recover damages for loss he could have avoided by reasonable effort

REMEDIES IN EQUITY

Availability only in cases in which there is no adequate remedy at law

Types
- *Specific Performance* court decree ordering breaching party to render promised performance
- *Injunction* court order prohibiting a party from doing a specific act
- *Reformation* court order correcting a written contract to conform with the original intent of the contracting parties

RESTITUTION

Definition of Restitution restoration of the injured party to the position she was in before the contract was made

Availability

- *Party Injured by Breach* if the other party totally breaches the contract by nonperformance or repudiation
- *Party in Default* for any benefit conferred in excess of the loss caused by the breach
- *Statute of Frauds* where a contract is unenforceable because of the statute of frauds, a party may recover the benefits conferred on the other party in reliance on the contract
- *Voidable Contracts* a party who has avoided a contract is entitled to restitution for any benefit conferred on the other party

---

LIMITATIONS ON REMEDIES

Election of Remedies if remedies are not inconsistent, a party injured by a breach of contract may seek more than one

Loss of Power of Avoidance a party with the power to avoid a contract may lose that power by

- affirming the contract
- delaying unreasonably in exercising the power of avoidance
- being subordinated to the intervening rights of third parties

---

CASES

CASE

18-1

Election of Remedies/Punitive Damages
MERRITT v. CRAIG
Court of Special Appeals of Maryland, 2000
130 Md.App. 350, 746 A.2d 923, certiorari denied, 359 Md. 29, 753 A.2d 2
http://scholar.google.com/scholar_case?q=746+A.2d+923&hl=en&as_sdt=2,34&case=10339288125936808164&scilh=0

Davis, J.

In the fall of 1995, during their search for a new residence, appellants [Benjamin and Julie Merritt] inspected Craig's property located at Pergin Farm Road in Garrett County [Maryland]. After viewing the residence, appellants advised Craig that they were interested in purchasing the property; however, their offer was contingent upon a satisfactory home inspection. On November 5, 1995, appellants, their inspector, and appellee's husband Mark Craig conducted an inspection of the basement area of the residence, during which there was an examination of cistern and water supply pipes. The examination revealed that the cistern had been used to store a water supply reserve, but was not currently utilized.

The inspector advised appellants that the system he had observed was one which utilized a submersible pump in the well from which water flowed to a pressure tank in the basement. The pressure tank distributed water through the internal piping system of the house. There were also two water lines that entered into the basement area. One of the lines came from an 800-foot well that was located on the property, and the other line came from a well located on the adjacent property. The well located on the adjacent property supplied water to both appellants' residence and a guest house owned by Craig. The existence of the adjacent well was not disclosed to appellants.

On December 2, 1995, a contract of sale for the property was executed between appellants and Craig, along with a "Disclosure Statement" signed by Craig on June 9, 1994, and acknowledged by appellants on November 2, 1995, affirming that there were no problems with the water supply to the dwelling. Between November 5, 1995 and June 1996, Craig caused the water line from the guest house to appellants' residence to be cut, and the cistern reactivated to store water from the existing well on appellants' lot. On May 18, 1996, Craig's husband advised Dennis Hannibal, one of the real estate agents involved in the deal, that he had spent $4,196.79 to upgrade the water system on appellants' property and to restore the cistern and remove appellants' house from the second well on Craig's guest house property. On

June 14, 1996, appellants and Craig had settlement on the property. Later that afternoon, Craig's husband, without appellants' knowledge, excavated the inside wall of appellants' house and installed a cap to stop a leaking condition on the water line that he had previously cut.

Subsequently, appellants, while attempting to fill a water bed, noticed that the water supply in their well had depleted. On July 13, 1996, appellants met with Craig to discuss a solution to the water failure problem, believing that Craig was responsible for cutting a water line to their house. Appellants agreed with Craig to conduct a flow test to the existing well and contribute money for the construction of a new well. On October 29, 1996, the well was drilled and produced only one half gallon of water per minute. On December 13, appellants paid for the drilling of a second well on their property, but it failed to produce water. In January appellants contacted a plumber, Robert Warnick, who confirmed that the line from the guest house well to appellants' residence had been cut flush with the inside surface of the basement wall and cemented closed. Appellants continued to do further work on the house in an effort to cure the water problem.

On February 11, 1997, appellants brought suit against Craig and other appellees in the Circuit Court for Garrett County, seeking rescission of the deed to the property and contract of sale, along with compensatory and punitive damages. During the course of the trial, the judge dismissed appellants' claim for rescission on the ground that they had effectively waived their right to rescission. * * * At the close of trial, the jury returned a verdict in favor of appellants and awarded compensatory damages in the amount of $42,264.76. Appellants were also awarded punitive damages in the amount of $150,000. Subsequently, appellants filed a motion to alter or amend the judgment requesting the court to grant rescission of the contract of sale and the deed, which the circuit court denied on June 17, 1998.

* * *

* * * Under Maryland law, when a party to a contract discovers that he or she has been defrauded, the party defrauded has either "a right to retain the contract and collect damages for its breach, or a right to rescind the contract and recover his or her own expenditures," not both. [Citations.] "These rights [are] inconsistent and mutually exclusive, and the discovery put[s] the purchaser to a prompt election." [Citation.] "A plaintiff seeking rescission must demonstrate that he [or she] acted promptly after discovery of the ground for rescission," otherwise the right to rescind is waived. [Citations.] * * *

In the case *sub judice* [before the court], appellants claim that they were entitled to a rescission of the subject contract of sale and deed and incidental damages. Appellants also

claim that they were entitled to compensatory and punitive damages arising from Craig's actions. Appellants, however, may not successfully rescind the contract while simultaneously recovering compensatory and punitive damages. Restitution is "a party's unilateral unmaking of a contract for a legally sufficient reason, such as the other party's material breach" and it in effect "restores the parties to their precontractual position." [Citation.] The restoration of the parties to their original position is incompatible with the circumstance when the complaining party is, at once, relieved of all obligations under the contract while simultaneously securing the windfall of compensatory and punitive damages beyond incidental expenses.

* * *

In sum, although whether appellants promptly repudiated the contract was not squarely before the court, we are not persuaded by appellees' assertion that appellants did not seek rescission in a timely fashion. We hold that, under the facts of this case, appellants must elect the form of relief, i.e., damages or rescission * * *

* * *

We hold that * * * the appellants are entitled to be awarded punitive damages resulting from Craig's actions. A "[p]laintiff seeking to recover punitive damages must allege in detail in the complaint the facts that indicate the entertainment by defendant of evil motive or intent." [Citation.] The Court of Appeals has held that "punitive damages may only be awarded in such cases where 'the plaintiff has established that the defendant's conduct was characterized by evil motive, intent to injure, ill will or fraud. * * *'" [Citation.] In cases of fraud that arise out of a contractual relationship, the plaintiff would have to establish actual malice to recover punitive damages. [Citation.] Finally, we have stated that "actual or express malice requires an intentional or willful act (or omission) * * * and 'has been characterized as the performance of an act without legal justification or excuse, but with an evil or rancorous motive influenced by hate, the purpose being to deliberately and willfully injure the plaintiff.'" [Citation.]

* * *

The jury believed that the representations made by Craig were undertaken with actual knowledge that the representations were false and with the intention to deceive appellants. * * * Moreover, the record reflects that the jury could reasonably infer Craig's intention to defraud appellants by her representation in the Disclosure Statement that there were no problems with the water supply, and by subsequently making substantial changes in the water system by cutting off a water line which supplied water to appellants' residence immediately after appellants' inspector examined the system. Therefore, we hold that the circuit court was not in error in finding facts from the record sufficient to support an award of punitive damages.

Craig also challenges the punitive damages award on the basis that the amount of the award was excessive. * * *

In the case at hand, the trial judge undertook the appropriate review of the jury's award. It is clear from the court's comments at the hearing that the court's decision not to disturb the jury's verdict was based on the evidence presented at trial and was not excessive. * * * Craig's conduct toward appellants was reprehensible and fully warranted punitive damages. Her conduct in willfully misrepresenting the condition of the water system in the Disclosure Statement, coupled with her actions and those of her husband in interfering and diverting the water flow subsequent to the inspection and

sale of the property, constitute egregious conduct. As a result of Craig's conduct, appellants were forced to employ extreme water conservation practices due to an insufficient water supply and they attempted to ameliorate the problem by having two new wells drilled on the property which proved to be unproductive. Moreover, the lack of water supply to appellants' property clearly reduced its market value. * * *

* * *

* * * Consequently, should appellants seek compensatory and punitive damages on remand, appellants' actual knowledge, coupled with the intent to deceive, is a sufficient factual predicate for submission of punitive damages to the jury.

Judgment of the circuit court reversed; case remanded for further proceedings consistent with this opinion.

CASE 18-2

Liquidated Damages

ARROWHEAD SCHOOL DISTRICT NO. 75, PARK COUNTY, MONTANA, v. KLYAP

Supreme Court of Montana, 2003
318 Mont. 103, 79 P.3d 250

http://scholar.google.com/scholar_case?case=643756738100095281 &q=79+p.3d+250&hl=en&as_sdt=2,34

Nelson, J.

Arrowhead School District No. 75 (District) is located in Park County south of Livingston [Montana]. The District consists of one school, Arrowhead School (School).

For the 1997–98 school year, the School employed about eleven full-time teachers and several part-time teachers. During that school year, the School employed Klyap as a new teacher instructing math, language arts, and physical education for the sixth, seventh, and eighth grades. In addition, Klyap, through his own initiative, helped start a sports program and coached flag football, basketball, and volleyball.

* * * [T]he School offered Klyap a contract for the 1998–99 school year on or about June 15, 1998, which he accepted by signing on or about June 30, 1998. This contract provided for a $20,500 salary and included the liquidated damages clause at issue here. The clause calculated liquidated damages as a percentage of annual salary determined by the date of breach; a breach of contract after July 20, 1998, required payment of 20% of salary as damages. Klyap also signed a notice indicating he accepted responsibility for familiarizing himself with the information in the teacher's handbook which also included the liquidated damages clause.

* * *

* * * On August 12, [Klyap] informed the School that he would not be returning for the 1998–99 school year even though classes were scheduled to start on August 26. As a result of Klyap's decision not to teach at the School, the

School sought to enforce the liquidated damages clause in Klyap's teaching contract for the stipulated amount of $4,100, 20% of the $20,500 salary. * * *

After Klyap resigned, the School attempted to find another teacher to take Klyap's place. Although at the time that Klyap was offered his contract the School had 80 potential applicants, only two viable applicants remained available. Right before classes started, the School was able to hire one of those applicants, a less experienced teacher, at a salary of $19,500.

* * * After a bench trial, the District Court determined the clause was enforceable * * * because the damages suffered by the School [were] impractical and extremely difficult to fix. Specifically, the court found the School suffered damages because it had to spend additional time setting up an interview committee, conducting interviews, training the new, less experienced teacher, and reorganizing the sports program. The District Court also found that all these activities took away from the other school and administrative duties that had been scheduled for that time and that the new teacher missed all the staff development training earlier that year. Finally, the court found that such clauses are commonly used in Montana and that the School had routinely and equitably enforced the clause against other teachers. After concluding that the School took appropriate steps to mitigate its damages, the court awarded judgment in favor of the School in the amount of $4,100. * * *

* * *

The fundamental tenet of modern contract law is freedom of contract; parties are free to mutually agree to terms governing their private conduct as long as those terms do not conflict with public laws. [Citation.] This tenet presumes that parties are in the best position to make decisions in their own interest. Normally, in the course of contract interpretation by a court, the court simply gives effect to the agreement between the parties in order to enforce the private law of the contract. [Citation.] When one party breaches the contract, judicial enforcement of the contract ensures the nonbreaching party receives expectancy damages, compensation equal to what that party would receive if the contract were performed. [Citations.] By only awarding expectancy damages rather than additional damages intended to punish the breaching party for failure to perform the contract, court enforcement of private contracts supports the theory of efficient breach. In other words, if it is more efficient for a party to breach a contract and pay expectancy damages in order to enter a superior contract, courts will not interfere by requiring the breaching party to pay more than was due under their contract. [Citation.]

Liquidated damages are, in theory, an extension of these principles. Rather than wait until the occurrence of breach, the parties to a contract are free to agree in advance on a specific damage amount to be paid upon breach. [Citation.] This amount is intended to predetermine expectancy damages. Ideally, this predetermination is intended to make the agreement between the parties more efficient. Rather than requiring a post-breach inquiry into damages between the parties, the breaching party simply pays the nonbreaching party the stipulated amount. Further, in this way, liquidated damages clauses allow parties to estimate damages that are impractical or difficult to prove, as courts cannot enforce expectancy damages without sufficient proof.

* * *

In order to determine whether a clause should be declared a penalty, courts attempt to measure the reasonableness of a liquidated damages clause. * * * As indicated by * * * § 356 of the RESTATEMENT (SECOND) OF CONTRACTS (1965) (hereinafter RESTATEMENT § 356), the threshold indicator of reasonableness is whether the situation involves damages of a type that are impractical or extremely difficult to prove. * * *

According to RESTATEMENT § 356 and other treatises, damages must be reasonable in relation to the damages the parties anticipated when the contract was executed or in relation to actual damages resulting from the breach.

* * *

* * * Liquidated damages in a personal service contract induce performance by an employee by predetermining compensation to an employer if the employee leaves. However, the employer clearly prefers performance by the specific employee because that employee was chosen for hire. The preference for performance by a specific person is reflected in the rule that personal service contracts are not assignable. Further, because personal service contracts are not enforceable by specific performance, [citation], liquidated damages are an appropriate way for employers to protect their interests. * * *

* * *

After reviewing the facts of this case, we hold that while the 20% liquidated damages clause is definitely harsher than most, it is still within Klyap's reasonable expectations and is not unduly oppressive. First, as the School pointed out during testimony, at such a small school teachers are chosen in part depending on how their skills complement those of the other teachers. Therefore, finding someone who would provide services equivalent to Klyap at such a late date would be virtually impossible. This difficulty was born out when only two applicants remained available and the School hired a teacher who was less experienced than Klyap. As a teacher, especially one with experience teaching at that very School, Klyap would have to be aware of the problem finding equivalent services would pose.

Second, besides the loss of equivalent services, the School lost time for preparation for other activities in order to attempt to find equivalent services. * * * Further, the new teacher missed all the staff development training earlier that year so individual training was required. And finally, because Klyap was essential to the sports program, the School had to spend additional time reorganizing the sports program as one sport had to be eliminated with Klyap's loss. These activities all took away from the other school and administrative duties that had been scheduled for that time. * * *

Finally, although the School testified it had an intent to secure performance and avoid the above damages by reason of the clause, * * * , such an intent does not turn a liquidated damages clause into a penalty unless the amount is unreasonably large and therefore not within reasonable expectations. * * *

Therefore, because as a teacher Klyap would know teachers are typically employed for an entire school year and would know how difficult it is to replace equivalent services at such a small rural school, it was within Klyap's reasonable expectations to agree to a contract with a 20% of salary liquidated damages provision for a departure so close to the start of the school year.

* * * Accordingly, we hold the District Court correctly determined that the liquidated damages provision was enforceable.

[Affirmed.]

CASE
18-3
Specific Performance
REAL ESTATE ANALYTICS, LLC v. VALLAS
Court of Appeal, Fourth District, Division 1, California, 2008
160 Cal.App.4th 463, 72 Cal.Rptr.3d 835, review denied 2008
http://scholar.google.com/scholar_case?case=16761955053572987435&q=72+cal.rptr.3d+835&hl=en&as_sdt=2,34

Haller, J.

Real Estate Analytics, LLC (REA) is a limited liability company formed by Troy Shadian. In January 2004, Shadian and his business partner, Roshan Bhakta, became interested in [Theodore Tee] Vallas's 14.13-acre property (the Lanikai Lane property) located in Carlsbad [California] near the Pacific Coast Highway. The property contained a mobilehome park with 147 individual mobilehomes and numerous amenities, including a pool, playground, laundry facilities, and a long winding street. Vallas leased the property to a mobilehome park operator, which managed the park and subleased the spaces to residents who owned their mobilehomes. The lease began in 1951 and terminates in 2013.

* * *

* * * [I]n March 2004, REA and Vallas entered into a written purchase and sale agreement. Under the agreement, the sales price was $8.5 million, with REA to pay an immediate $100,000 deposit, and then pay $2.9 million at closing. In return, Vallas agreed to finance the remaining $5.5 million, with the unpaid balance to be paid over a five-year period, with the balance due on April 1, 2009.

REA's primary goal in purchasing the property was to make a profit for its investors. One proposed business model was to subdivide the property and sell the subdivided lots to the property's mobilehome park residents. Shadian and Bhakta intended to make a substantial monetary profit through this investment.

* * *

[On June 14 Vallas cancelled the contract. The next day REA brought a breach of contract action seeking specific performance. The court, sitting without a jury, found Vallas breached the contract but refused to grant specific performance and instead awarded REA damages of $500,000, reflecting the difference between the contract price and the fair market value at the time of the breach.]

* * * [T]he court declined to award specific performance based on its finding that damages would provide REA adequate relief. * * * [T]he court found specific performance was not appropriate because REA purchased the property "solely as a commodity" to earn "money for their investors," and not because of the "uniqueness" of the property itself.

* * *

REA contends the court erred in refusing to order specific performance of the parties' real estate contract.

* * *

To obtain specific performance after a breach of contract, a plaintiff must generally show: (1) the inadequacy of his legal remedy; (2) an underlying contract that is both reasonable and supported by adequate consideration; (3) the existence of a mutuality of remedies; (4) contractual terms which are sufficiently definite to enable the court to know what it is to enforce; and (5) a substantial similarity of the requested performance to that promised in the contract. [Citations.] * * *

In this case, the court refused to specifically enforce the contract based on its finding that the first element (inadequacy of legal remedy) was not satisfied because REA sought to purchase the property as an investment, and not for some particular use of the land. REA contends this finding was incorrect as a matter of law and, alternatively, unsupported by the evidence.

It is a familiar legal principle that a damage award is generally an inadequate remedy for a breach of real estate contract, and therefore courts routinely grant a plaintiff's request for specific performance. [Citation.] This rule arose in medieval England where land ownership was a primary indicator of the owner's social status and voting rights. [Citations.] * * *

Although these historical reasons no longer apply, most jurisdictions have continued the rules requiring special treatment of land sale contracts, reflecting the enduring view that: (1) each parcel of land is unique and therefore there can be no adequate replacement after a breach; and (2) monetary damages are difficult to calculate after a party refuses to complete a land sales contract, particularly expectation damages. (See Rest.2d Contracts, § 360.) * * * [L]egislatures and the courts have largely adhered to the rule that specific performance is the appropriate remedy upon a breach of a real estate contract.

In California, these principles are embodied in section 3387. Section 3387 states:

> It is to be presumed that the breach of an agreement to transfer real property cannot be adequately relieved by pecuniary compensation. In the case of a single-family dwelling which the party seeking performance intends to occupy, this presumption is conclusive. In all other cases, this presumption is a presumption affecting the burden of proof.

By imposing a conclusive presumption for certain residential transactions, the Legislature decided that monetary damages can never be satisfactory compensation for a buyer who intends to live at a single-family home, regardless of the circumstances. But by establishing a rebuttable presumption with respect to other property, the Legislature left open the possibility that damages can be an adequate remedy for a breach of a real estate contract. The rebuttable presumption shifts the burden of proof to the breaching party to prove the adequacy of the damages. By so doing, the Legislature intended that a damages remedy for a nonbreaching party to a commercial real estate contract is the exception rather than the rule.

* * *

* * * By imposing a rebuttable presumption on the inadequacy of remedy element for certain types of purchases, the Legislature necessarily contemplated that there may be circumstances when the presumption that damages are inadequate can be overcome. * * *

But the specific issue presented here is not whether a defendant can ever rebut the inadequacy of remedy presumption. The issue is whether Vallas did so in this case. And on this issue, we agree with REA that Vallas did not make a sufficient evidentiary showing to establish damages were adequate to compensate REA for the breach. * * * Although it did not need to do so, REA produced strong evidence to support the presumption. This evidence showed that the Lanikai Lane property is unique in terms of its size, location, and existing use—it consists of 14.13 acres near the Pacific Ocean and contains an established mobilehome community. The property has ocean views and is close to several desirable local beaches, two major vacation resorts, the Del Mar racetrack, expensive neigh-borhoods, and major transportation routes. REA's evidence also showed that Lanikai Lane is unique in terms of the potential profits resulting from ownership because of its existing use (mobilehome park) on a long-term lease that would terminate in 2013, and the fact that existing residents would like to obtain ownership interests in the property. REA purchased the property for investment purposes, and it intended to obtain the highest return on this investment by subdividing the property and selling it to the existing residents of the park, which could result in substantial profits.

Given the statutory presumption that damages were inadequate and the largely undisputed evidence strongly supporting this presumption, Vallas had a high threshold to satisfy his burden to show damages would be an adequate remedy. * * *

* * *

* * * Thus, although REA did not necessarily intend to benefit from its personal or commercial *use* of the land, the land did have a particular unique value because of the manner in which it could be used to earn profits upon a resale. * * * Missing from the court's analysis was the recognition that to rebut the presumption that damages are an inadequate remedy, the defendant must come forward with evidence showing that damages will fully compensate the plaintiff for the breach. The record in this case was bereft of any such evidence.

Judgment reversed. The court is ordered to enter a new judgment granting specific performance and to strike the alternate damages remedy. * * *

CASE 18-4

Injunctions
MADISON SQUARE GARDEN CORP., ILL. v. CARNERA
United States Court of Appeals, Second Circuit, 1931
52 F.2d 47
http://scholar.google.com/scholar_case?q=52+F.2d+47&hl=en&as_sdt=2,34&case=133326573442361100&scilh=0

Chase, J.

Suit by plaintiff, Madison Square Garden Corporation, against Primo Carnera, defendant. From an order granting an injunction against defendant, defendant appeals.

On January 13, 1931, the plaintiff and defendant by their duly authorized agents entered into the following agreement in writing:

1. Carnera agrees that he will render services as a boxer in his next contest (which contest, hereinafter called the "First Contest," shall be with the winner of the proposed Schmeling-Stribling contest, or, if the same is drawn, shall be with Schmeling, and shall be deemed to be a contest for the heavyweight championship title; provided, however, that, in the event of the inability of the Garden to cause Schmeling or Stribling, as the case may be, to perform the terms of his agreement with the Garden calling for such contest, the Garden shall be without further liability to Carnera) exclusively under the auspices of the Garden, in the United States of America, or the Dominion of Canada, at such time, not, however, later than midnight of September 30, 1931, as the Garden may direct. * * *

9. Carnera shall not, pending the holding of the First Contest, render services as a boxer in any major

boxing contest, without the written permission of the Garden in each case had and obtained. A major contest is understood to be one with Sharkey, Baer, Campolo, Godfrey, or like grade heavyweights, or heavyweights who shall have beaten any of the above subsequent to the date hereof. If in any boxing contest engaged in by Carnera prior to the holding of the First Contest, he shall lose the same, the Garden shall at its option, to be exercised by a two weeks' notice to Carnera in writing, be without further liability under the terms of this agreement to Carnera. Carnera shall not render services during the continuance of the option referred to in paragraph 8 hereof for any person, firm or corporation other than the Garden. Carnera shall, however, at all times be permitted to engage in sparring exhibitions in which no decision is rendered and in which the heavyweight championship title is not at stake, and in which Carnera boxes not more than four rounds with any one opponent. * * *

Thereafter the defendant, without the permission of the plaintiff, written or otherwise, made a contract to engage in a boxing contest with the Sharkey mentioned in paragraph 9 of the agreement above quoted, and by the terms thereof the contest was to take place before the first contest mentioned in the defendant's contract with the plaintiff was to be held.

The plaintiff then brought this suit to restrain the defendant from carrying out his contract to box Sharkey, and obtained the preliminary injunction order, from which this appeal was taken. Jurisdiction is based on diversity of citizenship and the required amount is involved.

The District Court has found on affidavits which adequately show it that the defendant's services are unique and extraordinary. A negative covenant in a contract for such personal services is enforceable by injunction where the damages for a breach are incapable of ascertainment. [Citations.]

The defendant points to what is claimed to be lack of consideration for his negative promise, in that the contract is inequitable and contains no agreement to employ him. It is true that there is no promise in so many words to employ the defendant to box in a contest with Stribling or Schmeling, but the agreement read as a whole binds the plaintiff to do just that, providing either Stribling or Schmeling becomes the contestant as the result of the match between them and can be induced to box the defendant. The defendant has agreed to "render services as a boxer" for the plaintiff exclusively, and the plaintiff has agreed to pay him a definite percentage of the gate receipts as his compensation for so doing. The promise to employ the defendant to enable him to earn the compensation agreed upon is implied to the same force and effect as though expressly stated. * * * [Citations.]

As we have seen, the contract is valid and enforceable. It contains a restrictive covenant which may be given effect. Whether a preliminary injunction shall be issued under such circumstances rests in the sound discretion of the court. [Citations.] The District Court, in its discretion, did issue the preliminary injunction and required the plaintiff as a condition upon its issuance to secure its own performance of the contract in suit with a bond for $25,000 and to give a bond in the sum of $35,000 to pay the defendant such damages as he may sustain by reason of the injunction. Such an order is clearly not an abuse of discretion. Order affirmed.

QUESTIONS

1. Edward, a candy manufacturer, contracted to buy one thousand barrels of sugar from Marcia. Marcia failed to deliver, and Edward was unable to buy any sugar in the market. As a direct consequence he was unable to make candies to fulfill unusually lucrative contracts for the Christmas trade.
   a. What damages is Edward entitled to recover?
   b. Would it make any difference if Edward had told Marcia that he wanted the sugar to make candies for the Christmas trade and that he had accepted lucrative contracts for delivery for the Christmas trade?

2. Daniel agreed to erect an apartment building for Steven for $12 million and that Daniel would suffer a deduction of $12,000 per day for every day of delay. Daniel was twenty days late in finishing the job, losing ten days because of a strike and ten days because the material suppliers were late in furnishing materials. Daniel claims that he is entitled to payment in full (a) because the agreement as to $12,000 a day is a penalty and (b) because Steven has not shown that he has sustained any damage. Discuss each contention and decide.

3. Sharon contracted with Jane, a shirtmaker, for one thousand shirts for men. Jane manufactured and delivered five hundred shirts, which were paid for by Sharon. At the same time, Sharon notified Jane that she could not use or dispose of the other five hundred shirts and

directed Jane not to manufacture any more under the contract. Nevertheless, Jane proceeded to make up the other five hundred shirts and tendered them to Sharon. Sharon refused to accept the shirts, and Jane then sued for the purchase price. Is she entitled to the purchase price? If not, is she entitled to any damages? Explain.

4. Stuart contracts to act in a comedy for Charlotte and to comply with all theater regulations for four seasons. Charlotte promises to pay Stuart $1,800 for each performance and to allow Stuart one benefit performance each season. It is expressly agreed "Stuart shall not be employed in any other production for the period of the contract." During the first year of the contract, Stuart and Charlotte have a terrible quarrel. Thereafter, Stuart signs a contract to perform in Elaine's production and ceases performing for Charlotte. Charlotte seeks (a) to prevent Stuart from performing for Elaine, and (b) to require Stuart to perform his contract with Charlotte. What result?

5. Louis leased a building to Pam for five years at a rental of $1,000 per month, Pam depositing $10,000 as security for performance of all her promises in the lease, which was to be retained by Louis in case of any breach on Pam's part. Pam defaulted in the payment of rent for the last two months of the lease. Louis refused to return any of the deposit, claiming it as liquidated damages. Pam sued Louis to recover $8,000 (the $10,000 deposit less the amount of rent due Louis for the last two months). What amount of damages should Pam be allowed to collect from Louis? Explain.

6. In which of the following situations is specific performance available as a remedy?
   a. Mary and Anne enter into a written agreement under which Mary agrees to sell and Anne agrees to buy for $100 per share one hundred shares of the three hundred shares outstanding of the capital stock of the Infinitesimal Steel Corporation, whose shares are not listed on any exchange and are closely held. Mary refuses to deliver when tendered the $10,000.
   b. Modifying (a), assume that the subject matter of the agreement is stock of the United States Steel Corporation, which is traded on the New York Stock Exchange.

   c. Modifying (a), assume that the subject matter of the agreement is undeveloped farmland of little commercial value.

7. On March 1, Joseph sold to Sandra fifty acres of land in Oregon, which Joseph at the time represented to be fine black loam, high, dry, and free of stumps. Sandra paid Joseph the agreed price of $140,000 and took from him a deed to the land. Subsequently discovering that the land was low, swampy, and not entirely free of stumps, Sandra nevertheless undertook to convert the greater part of the land into cranberry bogs. After one year of cranberry culture, Sandra became entirely dissatisfied, tendered the land back to Joseph, and demanded from Joseph the return of the $140,000. Upon Joseph's refusal to repay the money, Sandra brings an action against him to recover the $140,000. What judgment?

8. James contracts to make repairs to Betty's building in return for Betty's promise to pay $12,000 upon completion of the repairs. After partially completing the repairs, James is unable to continue. Betty refuses to pay James and hires another builder, who completes the repairs for $5,000. The building's value to Betty has increased by $10,000 as a result of the repairs by James, but Betty has lost $500 in rents because of the delay caused by James's breach. James sues Betty. How much, if any, may James recover in restitution from Betty?

9. Linda induced Sally to enter into a purchase of a home theater receiver by intentionally misrepresenting the power output to be seventy-five watts when in fact the unit delivered only forty watts. Sally paid $450 for the receiver. Receivers producing forty watts generally sell for $200, whereas receivers producing seventy-five watts generally sell for $550. Sally decides to keep the receiver and sue for damages. How much may Sally recover in damages from Linda?

10. Virginia induced Charles to sell his boat to her by misrepresentation of material fact upon which Charles reasonably relied. Virginia promptly sold the boat to Donald, who paid fair value for it and knew nothing concerning the transaction between Virginia and Charles. Upon discovering the misrepresentation, Charles seeks to recover the boat. What are Charles's rights against Virginia and Donald?

CASE PROBLEMS

11. Felch was employed as a member of the faculty of Findlay College under a contract that permitted dismissal only for cause. He was dismissed by action of the President and Board of Trustees, which did not comply with

a contractual provision for dismissal that requires a hearing. Felch requested the court to grant specific performance of the contract and require Findlay College to continue Felch as a member of the faculty and to pay him the salary agreed upon. Is Felch entitled to specific performance? Explain.

12. Copenhaver, the owner of a laundry business, contracted with Berryman, the owner of a large apartment complex, to allow Copenhaver to own and operate the laundry facilities within the apartment complex. Berryman subsequently terminated the five-year contract with Copenhaver with forty-seven months remaining. Within six months, Copenhaver placed the equipment into use in other locations and generated at least as much income as he would have earned at Berryman's apartment complex. He then filed suit, claiming that he was entitled to conduct the laundry operations for an additional forty-seven months and that through such operations he would have earned a profit of $13,886.58, after deducting Berryman's share of the gross receipts and other operating expenses. Decision?

13. Billy Williams Builders and Developers (Williams) entered into a contract with Hillerich under which Williams agreed to sell to Hillerich a certain lot and to construct on it a house according to submitted plans and specifications. The house built by Williams was defectively constructed. Hillerich brought suit for specific performance of the contract and for damages resulting from the defective construction and delay in performance. Williams argued that Hillerich was not entitled to have both specific performance and damages for breach of the contract because the remedies were inconsistent and Hillerich had to elect one or the other. Explain whether Williams is correct in this assertion.

14. Developers under a plan approved by the city of Rye had constructed six luxury cooperative apartment buildings and were to construct six more. To obtain certificates of occupancy for the six completed buildings, the developers were required to post a bond with the city to ensure completion of the remaining buildings. The developers posted a $100,000 bond upon which the defendant, Public Service Mutual Insurance Company, as guarantor or surety, agreed to pay $200 for each day after the contractual deadline that the remaining buildings were not completed. After the contractual deadline, more than five hundred days passed without completion of the buildings. The city claims that its inspectors and employees will be required to devote more time to the project than anticipated because it has taken extra years to complete. It also claims that it will lose tax revenues for the years the buildings are not completed. Should the city prevail in its suit against the developers and the insurance company to recover $100,000 on the bond? Explain.

15. Kerr Steamship Company sent a telegram at a cost of $26.78 to the Philippines through the Radio Corporation of America. The telegram, which contained instructions in unintelligible code for loading cargo on one of Kerr's ships, was mislaid and never delivered. Consequently, the ship was improperly loaded and the cargo was lost. Kerr sued the Radio Corporation for $6,675.29 in profits lost on the cargo because of the Radio Corporation's failure to deliver the telegram. Should Kerr be allowed to recover damages from Radio? Explain.

16. El Dorado Tire Company fired Bill Ballard, a sales executive. Ballard had a five-year contract with El Dorado but was fired after only two years of employment. Ballard sued El Dorado for breach of contract. El Dorado claimed that any damages due to breach of the contract should be mitigated because of Ballard's failure to seek other employment after he was fired. El Dorado did not provide any proof showing the availability of comparable employment. Explain whether El Dorado is correct in its contention.

17. California and Hawaiian Sugar Company (C and H) is an agricultural cooperative in the business of growing sugarcane in Hawaii and transporting the raw sugar to its refinery in California for processing. Because of the seasonal nature of the sugarcane crop, availability of ships to transport the raw sugar immediately after harvest is imperative. After losing the services of the shipping company it had previously used, C and H decided to build its own ship, a Macababoo, which had two components, a tug and a barge. C and H contracted with Halter Marine to build the tug and with Sun Ship to build the barge. In finalizing the contract for construction of the barge, both C and H and Sun Ship were represented by senior management and by legal counsel. The resulting contract called for a liquidated damages payment of $17,000 per day that delivery of the completed barge was delayed. Delivery of both the barge and the tug were significantly delayed. Sun Ship paid the $17,000 per day liquidated damages amount and then sued to recover it, claiming that without the liquidated damages provision, C and H's legal remedy for money damages would have been significantly less than that paid by Sun Ship pursuant to the liquidated damages provision. Decision?

18. Bettye Gregg offered to purchase a house from Head & Seeman, Inc. (seller). Though she represented in writing that she had between $15,000 and $20,000 in equity in another home that she would pay to the seller after she sold the other home, she knew that she did not have such equity. In reliance upon these intentionally fraudulent representations, the seller accepted Gregg's offer and the parties entered into a land contract. After taking occupancy, Gregg failed to make any of the contract payments. The seller's investigations then revealed the fraud. Head & Seeman then brought suit seeking rescission of the

contract, return of the real estate, and restitution. Restitution was sought for the rental value for the five months of lost use of the property and the seller's out-of-pocket expenses made in reliance upon the bargain. Gregg contends that under the election of remedies doctrine, the seller cannot both rescind the contract and recover damages for its breach. Is Gregg correct? Explain.

19. Watson agreed to buy Ingram's house for $355,000. The contract provided that Watson deposit $15,000 as earnest money and that "in the event of default by the Buyer, earnest money shall be forfeited to Seller as liquidated damages, unless Seller elects to seek actual damages or specific performance." Because Watson did not timely comply with all of the terms of the contract, nine months after the Watson sale was to occur, Ingram sold the house to a third party for $355,000. Is Ingram entitled to Watson's $15,000 earnest money as liquidated damages? Explain.

TAKING SIDES

Sanders agreed in writing to write, direct, and produce a motion picture on the subject of lithography (a method for printing using stone or metal) for the Tamarind Lithography Workshop. After the completion of this film, *Four Stones for Kanemitsu*, litigation arose concerning the parties' rights and obligations under their agreement. Tamarind and Sanders resolved this dispute by a written settlement agreement that provided for Tamarind to give Sanders a screen credit stating: "A Film by Terry Sanders." Tamarind did not comply with this agreement and failed to include the agreed-upon screen credit for Sanders.

Sanders sued Tamarind seeking damages for breach of the settlement agreement and specific performance to compel Tamarind's compliance with its obligation to provide the screen credit.

a. What arguments would support Sander's claim for specific performance in addition to damages?

b. What arguments would support Tamarind's claim that Sanders was not entitled to specific performance in addition to damages?

c. Which side's arguments are most convincing? Explain.

CHAPTER 17

Whistleblowing
Conflict of Loyalties

© Ryan McVay/The Image Bank/Getty Images

Physical courage is remarkably widespread in [the U.S.] population.... Moral and intellectual courage are not in nearly so flourishing a state.... These forms of courage ... threaten or violate loyalty, group identity.... They are, intrinsically, outside the range of consensus.

—MARILYNNE ROBINSON, Novelist and Essayist

I don't see myself as a hero, because what I'm doing is self-interested: I don't want to live in a world where there's no privacy and therefore no room for intellectual exploration and creativity.

—EDWARD SNOWDEN, 29-year-old whistleblower
of National Security Agency surveillance

This chapter is about people who feel morally driven to call attention to problems they see at work—often at the risk of disturbing the status quo, alienating others, and bringing damaging repercussions upon themselves and their families. It is about being caught between conflicting loyalties—to one's employer, and to one's conscience—the dilemma faced by a person who must decide whether to become a "whistleblower."

Whistleblowers are people who decide to report unethical or illegal activities, usually activities under the control of their employers. They may be working for private companies, nonprofit organizations, or for the government. They may disclose information inside or outside their organizations—to supervisors, regulators, or to the media. What unites all whistleblowing is the urge to bring a disturbing situation to light, the urge to bring about some corrective change. The motivating issues range from airline, nuclear, and environmental safety to the kinds of investment practices that led the Securities and Exchange Commission to go after Goldman Sachs for its role in the financial crisis that began in 2007.

This chapter explains the legal doctrine known as **employment-at-will,** which gives employers broad discretion to fire employees "for a good reason, a bad reason, or no reason at all." Although twentieth-century exceptions to this rule have blunted its harshness, the cases demonstrate that whistleblowers often experience retaliation and have little recourse under the common law. Statutes passed in all 50 states provide some protection for employees, but wide variation exists among them; we will look at one of them. Next, we will learn about the critical role of whistleblowers in the food industry. We consider how First Amendment freedom of speech has been interpreted by the

Supreme Court to limit the right of public employees to blow the whistle. Finally, we look at the False Claims Act, which provides financial incentives to report fraud against the government, and we learn about the personal experiences of so-called *qui tam* whistleblowers under that law.

Whistleblowing can wreak havoc. Those who insist that bad news must be heard may damage the reputations of their employers, and risk having their own careers destroyed. In this chapter we see that in spite of the costs, we may yet appreciate the role of the dissenters in serving the public interest when the checkpoints of our systems fail us.

■ ■ ■

In 1993, Dr. Donn Milton was hired by a nonprofit scientific research organization, IIT Research Institute (IITRI), to oversee a contract with the federal government. By 1995, his responsibilities widened as he was promoted to vice president of IITRI's Advanced Technology Group. Like other nonprofits, IITRI had been established with a public mission and was classified as tax exempt. As Dr. Milton discovered, however, the organization was "abusing its tax-exempt status by failing to report … taxable income generated by the substantial portion of … business that did not constitute scientific research in the public interest."

Donn Milton, Dr., v. IIT Research Institute
Fourth Circuit Court of Appeals, 1998
138 F.3d 519

WILKINSON, Chief Judge.

Milton voiced his concerns to IITRI management, to no avail. In 1995, after similar allegations by a competitor, IITRI initiated an internal examination of the issue. In connection with this inquiry, IITRI received an outside opinion letter concluding that the IRS could well deem some of IITRI's projects unrelated business activities and that the income from these activities was likely taxable. Milton urged the President of IITRI, John Scott, to take action in response to the letter, but Scott refused. Milton raised the issue with IITRI's Treasurer, who agreed that IITRI was improperly claiming unrelated business income as exempt income and promised to remedy the problem after Scott's then-imminent retirement. However, this retirement did not come to pass [and the treasurer took no action]. Finally, in November 1996, when Scott falsely indicated to IITRI's board of governors that IITRI had no problem with unrelated business income, Milton reported the falsity of these statements to Lew Collens, Chairman of the Board of IITRI, and informed Collens of the opinion letter.

On January 1, 1997, Scott called Milton at home and informed him that he had been relieved of his Group Vice President title and demoted. On February 12, 1997, Milton's attorney contacted IITRI about the demotion, alleging that it was unlawful retaliation for informing management of IITRI's unlawful practices. Two days later … Milton received a letter from Collens terminating his employment with IITRI.

[The general legal rule is that employees can be fired with or without cause, but there is an exception: Under the tort of "wrongful discharge," an employee can argue that the firing clearly conflicts with "public policy."]

Milton filed suit against IITRI for wrongful discharge....

Maryland has recognized a "narrow exception" to the general rule of at-will employment: "discharge may not contravene a clear mandate of public policy." Maryland courts have found such a mandate only in limited circumstances: (1) "where an employee has been fired for refusing to violate the law ..." and (2) "where [an] employee has been terminated for exercising a specific legal right or duty...."

Milton makes no claim that he was asked to break the law. He had no role in preparing IITRI's submissions to the IRS and no responsibility for their content. Instead, Milton claims he was fired for fulfilling his fiduciary duty as a corporate officer to inform IITRI's Board of activities injurious to the corporation's long-term interests....

Maryland law does provide a wrongful discharge cause of action for employees who are terminated because they perform their "statutorily pre-scribed duty." However, this exception to the norm of at-will employment has been construed narrowly by the Maryland courts and is not available in Milton's case.... [I]n *Thompson v. Memorial Hospital* (D. Md. 1996), the court ... held that, because a hospital employee was not chargeable with the hospital's regulatory duty to report misadministration of radiation, he did not state a claim for wrongful discharge when he was fired for making such a report. By contrast, in *Bleich v. Florence Crittenden Services* (Md. 1993), the court recognized that an educator terminated for filing a report of child abuse and neglect, as she was explicitly required to do by Maryland law, did state a claim for wrongful discharge. These cases indicate that, for Milton to recover, it is not enough that someone at IITRI was responsible for correcting its tax fil-ings or that the corporation may have been liable for tax fraud. This responsi-bility was never Milton's, nor did he face any potential liability for failing to discharge it, so his claim fails.

Milton argues that his fiduciary obligations as an officer of IITRI supply the legal duty that was missing in *Thompson* and that supported the cause of action in *Bleich*. But in fact Milton labored under no "specific legal duty," to report IITRI's tax fraud to the Board. He points to no statute or other legal source that imposes on him a specific duty to report, and the broad fiduciary obligations of "care and loyalty" he alleges are simply too general to qualify as a specific legal duty that will support the claim that his discharge violates a "clear mandate of public policy." Recognizing whistleblower protection for every corporate officer fired in the wake of a disagreement over an employer's business practices would transform this "narrow exception" into a broad one indeed.

This search for a specific legal duty is no mere formality. Rather it limits judi-cial forays into the wilderness of discerning "public policy" without clear direc-tion from a legislative or regulatory source.

[Judgment of dismissal affirmed.]

QUESTIONS

1. In legal terms, why did Milton lose?

2. The court here expresses concern that, if Dr. Milton were permitted to win, it would open a "Pandora's box," with "every corporate officer fired in the wake of a disagreement over an employer's business practices" a potential successful plaintiff. Reframe this argument. What is at stake here for employers?

3. This case is about conflicting loyalties. Make a list of the stakeholders (those primarily affected by the situation). Now describe the various links of loyalty—who felt responsible to whom? Analyze the situation using the ethical theories and the information about corporate governance in Chapter 1. Did Milton do the right thing?

■ ■ ■

EMPLOYMENT-AT-WILL

The right of an employee to quit the services of the employer, for whatever reason, is the same as the right of the employer, for whatever reason, to dispense with the services of such employee.

—JUSTICE HARLAN in *Adair v. U.S.*, 208 U.S. 161 (1908)

The Law, in its majestic equality, forbids the rich, as well as the poor, to sleep under the bridges, to beg in the streets, and to steal bread.

—ANATOLE FRANCE

Employment-at-will is a legal rule that developed in the nineteenth century, giving employers unfettered power to "dismiss their employees at will for good cause, for no cause, or even for cause morally wrong, without being thereby guilty of a legal wrong."[1] The economic philosophy of laissez-faire provided theoretical support for employment-at-will. Its legal underpinnings consisted mainly of "freedom of contract," the idea that individuals are free to choose how to dispose of what they own, including their labor, as they see fit, and that the voluntary contractual promises they make are legitimately enforceable.

Exceptions under Statutes

The earliest adjustments to the doctrine of employment-at-will were made as workers fought for the right to organize and form unions. In 1935, they were guaranteed these rights, and not long after, the U.S. Supreme Court announced that an employer could not use employment-at-will as a means of "intimidat[ing] or coerc[ing] its employees with respect to their self organization."[2] In other words, employees could not be fired as punishment for attempting to organize themselves into unions. Although at this writing only a fairly narrow slice of the U.S. workforce is unionized,[3] collective bargaining agreements typically cut against employment-at-will, protecting workers from being fired except for "good cause."

---

[1] *Payne v. Webster & Atlantic R.R. Co.*, 81 Tenn. 507, 519–20 (1884).

[2] *NLRB v. Jones & Laughlin Steel Corp.*, 301 U.S. 1, 45–46 (1937).

[3] According to the Bureau of Labor Standards, the union membership rate in 2012 was 11.3 percent, with some 14.4 million wage and salary workers belonging to unions. If we look at only private sector workers, we see they represent 6.6 percent of the workforce today, compared with 35 percent in 1950.

Beginning in the 1960s, federal civil rights laws created remedies against employers who fire workers because of their race, national origin, color, religion, sex, age, or disability.[4] In the 1970s and 1980s, federal and state statutes included protection from retaliation for employees who report violations of environmental or workplace safety laws, for example.[5]

Today, many federal statutes include provisions compensating employees who have been punished for whistleblowing. For example, environmental, workplace safety, and antidiscrimination laws carrying whistleblower protections, as does the 2010 Affordable Care Act ("Obamacare"). In the wake of scandals and the implosion of major firms such as Enron and Worldcom, in 2002 Congress passed corporate fraud reform legislation with whistleblower provisions protecting those who report financial misconduct in publicly traded companies. This law, known as Sarbanes-Oxley (SOX), was strengthened and expanded after the housing crisis and the economic meltdown of 2007–2009 in the Dodd-Frank reform legislation, which again includes whistleblower protections. While these federal laws covering whistleblowers are numerous, and apply to those who work for both the government and private companies, each one attaches to a specific federal law, and to a limited set of circumstances.

A relatively small subset of the labor force, the approximately 2.8 million employees who work for the federal government, can look to the Whistleblower Protection Enhancement Act (WPEA), passed in a rare bipartisan way in 2012. The WPEA strengthens the 1989 Whistleblower Protection Act (WPA), covering federal employees who report waste, fraud, and abuse, but which had been interpreted narrowly over the years by judges who were clearly hostile to it. From 1994 through 2012, whistleblowers' track record at the single available court to hear their cases was 3–224. Judges had read the WPA to mean that federal employees would lose their cases if they disclosed to a supervisor, blew the whistle while carrying out their job duties, or revealed the consequences of a policy decision, for instance. Since 1999, they had requiring employees to present "undeniable, uncontestable or incontrovertible proof" of the accuracy of their disclosures in order to qualify for protection. The new WPEA ends these judge-made limitations and significantly improves protection for federal employees who blow the whistle. For example, it bans retaliation against employees who challenge government censorship of scientific material. However, the protections of this new law do not cover employees working for the national security apparatus.

Exceptions under Case Law

The common law has also evolved to create exceptions to the employment-at-will rule. In some states, courts have set limits by means of contract law. There are two main approaches: (1) to imply a promise of "good faith and fair dealing" in the contract of employment or (2) to imply contractual terms (not to dismiss except for good cause,

---

[4]For example, *Civil Rights Act of 1964,* 42 U.S.C. Sec. 2000e–2a (1976); *Age Discrimination in Employment Act of 1967,* 29 U.S.C. Sec. 623(a) (1976); and *Americans with Disabilities Act,* 42 U.S.C. Sec. 12112(b)(5)(A). Civil rights laws are discussed in more detail in Chapter 4. Most states have similar laws, and some of these go further than the federal statutes, protecting employees against discrimination on the basis of family status or sexual orientation, for example.

[5]Federal laws include the *Toxic Substances Control Act,* 15 U.S.C. Sec. 2622(a) (1988); *Occupational Safety and Health Act,* Sec. 660(c)(1) (1988); *Water Pollution Control Act,* 33 U.S.C. Sec. 1367(a) (1988); *Safe Drinking Water Act,* 42 U.S.C.A. Sec. 300j–9(i)(1); *Energy Reorganization Act,* 42 U.S.C. Sec. 5851(a)(3) (1982); *Solid Waste Disposal Act,* 42 U.S.C. Sec. 6971(a) (1982); *Comprehensive Environmental Response, Compensation, and Liability Act,* Sec. 99610(a); and *Clean Air Act* Sec. 7622(a).

for instance) from an employer's handbook, policy statement, or behavior. However, fewer than a dozen states use the first approach. And, although the second approach has been recognized by most states, employers are on notice, and unlikely to make any express or implied promises that might be interpreted to cut against employment-at-will. In fact, they are more likely to promise the reverse, as in the following paragraph, recommended for inclusion in employment handbooks for law firms:

> *Your employment with the Firm is voluntarily entered into and you are free to resign at any time. Similarly, the Firm is free to conclude an employment relationship with you where it believes it is in the Firm's best interest at any time. It should be recognized that neither you, nor we, have entered into any contract of employment, express or implied. Our relationship is and will be always one of voluntary employment "at will."*[6]

Tort law has also made inroads into employment-at-will, offering a plaintiff the chance to convince a jury to award substantial money damages. For more than four decades, most U.S. state courts have been shaping the tort of "wrongful discharge," a firing that contradicts "public policy"—in other words, a dismissal that undermines what is beneficial to society in general.

The problem has been how to define public policy.[7] As with contract law, this exception to employment-at-will developed simultaneously in several states, producing a crazy quilt of varying rules. Most state courts are comfortable looking to the legislature—to laws that have already been passed—for guidance. For instance, they will protect from retaliation employees who have simply exercised their legal rights to file a worker's compensation or a sexual harassment claim,[8] or who have merely performed their legal duty to serve on a jury.[9] And, if employers put their employees "between a rock and a hard place," expecting them to participate in breaking the law or be fired, most courts would again see a violation of public policy, triggering the tort of wrongful discharge.[10] For example, suppose you were an employee of BP in Louisiana, and your supervisor told you to delete safety and engineering files related to the government investigation of the 2010 oil spill in the Gulf of Mexico. Once subpoenas were issued, destroying those files would amount to obstruction of justice. So, if you refused to destroy them and were fired for that, in most states you would succeed in a suit for wrongful discharge.

But some states still do not recognize the tort at all. In New York, for instance, while an employer could be fined for refusing to allow an employee time for jury service, the employee could not then sue for wrongful discharge.[11] As we have seen, other jurisdictions, such as Maryland, are conservative in identifying violations of public policy.

---

[6]Victor Schachter, "The Promise of Partnership," *National Law Journal*, October 8, 1984, p. 15.

[7]Public policy is generally understood to mean that which benefits society as a whole. But this is a fuzzy concept indeed and very likely to mirror the personal and political beliefs of individual judges. As one commentator put it, "Public policy is the unruly horse of the law."

[8]*Frampton v. Central Indiana Gas Co.*, 297 N.E.2d 425 (Indiana 1973). Plaintiff fired for filing a worker's compensation claim.

[9]*Reuther v. Fowler & Williams*, 386 A.2d 119 (Pa. 1978). Plaintiff fired for jury service.

[10]For example, in *Petermann v. Intl. Brotherhood of Teamsters*, 344 P.2d 25 (1969), plaintiff was instructed by his employer to lie when testifying before a legislative investigatory committee. He refused and was fired. The court allowed his suit for wrongful discharge, describing public policy as "that principle of law which holds that no citizen can lawfully do that which has a tendency to be injurious to the public or against the public good." Id. at 27.

[11]*Di Blasi v. Traffax Traffic Network*, 681 N.Y.S.2d 147 (N.Y. App. Div 1998); *In re Eigner*, 39 Misc.3d 1214 (N.Y. Sup. Ct. 2013).

Inconsistencies like these complicate the risk for whistleblowers. They have noticed a troubling situation at work. It may be illegal; it may be "merely" unethical; it may be one they are expected to participate in; it may be one they are expected to ignore; it may involve a statute that carries protection for whistleblowers; it may not. Whistleblowers react first and must worry about the reach of "public policy" later. Characteristically unable to remain passive in the face of what they believe is wrong, they speak out. Research reveals that whistleblowers are typically long-term, highly loyal employees who feel strongly that their companies should do the right thing, and who tend to disclose to outsiders only after trying to make headway internally.[12] The whistleblower profile is such that, if nothing is done to respond to their internal complaints, they often feel compelled to disclose to authorities outside the company—even to the media. In any case, they are taking the chance that they will not be covered under the wrongful discharge exception to employment-at-will. As one commentator put it, effectively, those who blow the whistle "very often must choose between silence and driving over a cliff."[13]

SOX AND DODD-FRANK: WHISTLEBLOWING ON FINANCIAL FRAUD

In 2002, in reaction to a series of corporate and accounting scandals in which investors lost billions and firms like Enron, Worldcom, and Arthur Anderson imploded, Congress passed the Sarbanes-Oxley Act (SOX).[14] Under SOX, senior management of publicly traded companies must individually certify the accuracy of financial information, boards of directors have more oversight responsibilities, and internal and independent "audit committees" must be established. SOX protects whistleblowers: Publicly held corporations cannot retaliate against an employee who provides information or assists in investigating conduct that the employee "reasonably believes" to be securities fraud. And under SOX, a public company must establish a process giving its employees the option to report internally, and in confidence, to its audit committee.

SOX whistleblower provisions also cover subsidiaries, contractors, and agents of public companies. So, for example, a small accounting firm working under contract with a publicly traded firm could be liable for retaliation against an employee who reported accounting irregularities to the Securities and Exchange Commission (SEC). The illegal conduct reported doesn't have to be on the part of the company for which the whistleblower works. In one recent case, a FedEx courier was suspended after she alerted the local sheriff's office that a FedEx customer was using FedEx to commit mail fraud. Earlier, she had made a series of reports about suspicious packages, but her dispatcher refused to pass them onto the fraud department; she was protected under SOX.[15]

Passed in response to the housing market and financial crisis of 2007–2008, the Dodd-Frank Wall Street Reform and Consumer Protection Act of 2010 rewards individuals who help the SEC uncover securities violations, including violations of the Foreign

---

[12]Marlene Winfield, "Whistleblowers as Corporate Safety Net," in *Whistleblowing: Subversion or Corporate Citizenship?* 21, 22 (New York: St. Martin's Press,1994).

[13]Joseph Henkert, "Management's Hat Trick: Misuse of 'Engineering Judgment' in the Challenger Incident," *Journal of Business Ethics* 10, 1991, pp. 617, 619.

[14]*18 U.S.C.A. § 1514A.*

[15]*Funke v. Federal Express Corp.*, ARB No. 09-004, ALJ No. 2007-SOX-043 (ARB July 8, 2011).

Corrupt Practices Act (making it a crime for American citizens or companies to bribe foreign officials). Under Dodd-Frank those who initiate reports to the SEC leading to a recovery exceeding $1 million receive a share between 10 percent and 30 percent of the amount recovered. The SEC has reported some 3,000 tips in 2012 alone.

While Dodd-Frank defines whistleblowers as those reporting to the SEC, the section of the law protecting whistleblowers against retaliation covers a broader range of conduct, including internal reporting. Richard Kramer, Vice President of Human Resources for Trans-Lux, reported irregularities in the company's pension practices to his Board of Directors. Later, he also sent a letter to the SEC. Shortly afterward, Trans-Lux fired Kramer and the entire HR department. He sued, claiming a violation of Dodd-Frank. A federal court has allowed the case to go forward, despite the company's argument that Kramer's "internal report" was not covered by the whistleblower law.[16]

Whistleblowing and Professional Ethics

THE MAYOR:	We shall expect you, on further investigation, to come to the conclusion that the situation is not nearly as pressing or as dangerous as you had at first imagined.
DR. STOCKMANN:	Oh! You expect that of me, do you?
THE MAYOR:	Furthermore we will expect you to make a public statement expressing your faith in the management's integrity and in their intention to take thorough and conscientious steps to remedy any possible defects.
DR. STOCKMANN:	But that's out of the question, Peter. No amount of patching or tinkering can put this matter right; I tell you I know! It is my firm and unalterable conviction—
THE MAYOR:	As a member of the staff you have no right to personal convictions.
DR. STOCKMANN:	(With a start) No right to—?
THE MAYOR:	Not as a member of the staff—no! As a private individual—that's of course another matter. But as a subordinate in the employ of the Baths you have no right to openly express convictions opposed to those of your superiors.
DR. STOCKMANN:	This is too much! Do you mean to tell me that as a doctor—a scientific man—I have no right to—!
THE MAYOR:	But this is not purely a scientific matter; there are other questions involved—technical and economic questions.
DR. STOCKMANN:	To hell with all that! I insist that I am free to speak my mind on any and all questions![17]

---

[16] 2012 WL 4444820 (D. Conn. 2012).
[17] Henrik Ibsen, *An Enemy of the People.*

■ ■ ■

In the next case, the plaintiff is a doctor caught in a conflict between what her employer expects her to do, and what she feels is in line with her professional ethical responsibilities.

Pierce v. Ortho Pharmaceutical Corp.
Supreme Court of New Jersey, 1980
417 A.2d 505

Pollock, J.

This case presents the question whether an employee-at-will has a cause of action against her employer to recover damages for the termination of her employment following her refusal to continue a project she viewed as medically unethical....

Ortho specializes in the development and manufacture of therapeutic and reproductive drugs. Dr. Pierce is a medical doctor who was first employed by Ortho in 1971 as an Associate Director of Medical Research. She signed no contract except a secrecy agreement, and her employment was not for a fixed term. She was an employee-at-will. In 1973, she became the Director of Medical Research/Therapeutics, one of three major sections of the Medical Research Department. Her primary responsibilities were to oversee development of therapeutic drugs and to establish procedures for testing those drugs for safety, effectiveness, and marketability. Her immediate supervisor was Dr. Samuel Pasquale, Executive Medical Director.

In the spring of 1975, Dr. Pierce was the only medical doctor on a project team developing loperamide, a liquid drug for treatment of diarrhea in infants, children, and elderly. The proposed formulation contained saccharin. Although the concentration was consistent with the formula for loperamide marketed in Europe, the project team agreed that the formula was unsuitable for use in the United States.[18] An alternative formulation containing less saccharin might have been developed within approximately three months.

By March 28, however, the project team, except for Dr. Pierce, decided to continue with the development of loperamide [without reducing the amount of saccharin]. That decision was made apparently in response to a directive from the Marketing Division of Ortho. This decision meant that Ortho would file an investigational new drug application (IND) with the Federal Food and Drug Administration (FDA), continuing laboratory studies on loperamide, and begin work on a formulation....

Dr. Pierce continued to oppose the work being done on loperamide at Ortho. On April 21, 1975, she sent a memorandum to the project team expressing her disagreement with its decision to proceed.... In her opinion, there was no justification for seeking FDA permission to use the drug in light of medical controversy over the safety of saccharin.

---

[18]The group's toxicologist, for instance, noted that saccharin was a "slow carcinogen"; it had produced benign and malignant tumors in test animals after 17 years. The harm it might cause would be obvious only after a long period of time, and "any intentional exposure of any segment of the human population to a potential carcinogen is not in the best interest of public health of the Ortho Pharmaceutical Corporation."

Dr. Pierce met with Dr. Pasquale on May 9 and informed him that she disagreed with the decision to file an IND with the FDA.... She concluded that the risk that saccharin might be harmful should preclude testing the formula on children or elderly persons, especially when an alternative formulation might soon be available....

After their meeting on May 9, Dr. Pasquale informed Dr. Pierce that she would no longer be assigned to the loperamide project. On May 14, Dr. Pasquale asked Dr. Pierce to choose other projects.... She felt she was being demoted, even though her salary would not be decreased. Dr. Pierce [submitted a] letter of resignation.... [This is called "constructive discharge," the legal equivalent of being fired.]

Dr. Pierce claimed damages for the termination of her employment. Her complaint alleged: "The Defendant, its agents, servants and employees requested and demanded Plaintiff follow a course of action and behavior which was impossible for Plaintiff to follow because of the Hippocratic oath she had taken, because of the ethical standards by which she was governed as a physician, and because of the regulatory schemes, both federal and state, statutory and case law, for the protection of the public in the field of health and human well-being, which schemes Plaintiff believed she should honor."

... Under the common law, in the absence of an employment contract, employers or employees have been free to terminate the employment relationship with or without cause....

Commentators have questioned the compatibility of the traditional at-will doctrine with the realities of modern economics and employment practices.... The common law rule has been modified by the enactment of labor relations legislation [prohibiting employers from firing workers because they organize or join a union]....

Recently [many] states have recognized a common law cause of action for employees-at-will who were discharged for reasons that were in some way "wrongful." The courts in those jurisdictions have taken varied approaches, some recognizing the action in tort, some in contract. Nearly all jurisdictions link the success of the wrongful discharged employee's action to proof that the discharge violated public policy....

In recognizing a cause of action to provide a remedy for employees who are wrongfully discharged, we must balance the interests of the employee, the employer, and the public. Employees have an interest in knowing they will not be discharged for exercising their legal rights. Employers have an interest in knowing they can run their businesses as they see fit as long as their conduct is consistent with public policy. The public has an interest in employment stability and in discouraging frivolous lawsuits by dissatisfied employees.

Although the contours of an exception are important to all employees-at-will, this case focuses on the special considerations arising out of the right to fire an employee-at-will who is a member of a recognized profession. One writer has described the predicament that may confront a professional employed by a large corporation: Consider, for example, the plight of an engineer who is told that he will lose his job unless he falsifies his data or conclusions, or unless he approves a product which does not conform to specifications or meet minimum standards ... and the predicament of an accountant who is told to falsify his employer's profit and loss statement in order to enable the employer to obtain credit.

Employees who are professionals owe a special duty to abide not only by federal and state law, but also by the recognized codes of ethics of their professions. That duty may oblige them to decline to perform acts required by their employers. However, an employee should not have the right to prevent his or her employer from pursuing its business because the employee perceives that a particular business decision violates the employee's personal morals, as distinguished from the recognized code of ethics of the employee's profession.

We hold that an employee has a cause of action for wrongful discharge when the discharge is contrary to a clear mandate of public policy. The sources of public policy include legislation; administrative rules, regulations or decisions; and judicial decisions. In certain instances, a professional code of ethics may contain an expression of public policy. However, not all such sources express a clear mandate of public policy. For example, a code of ethics designed to serve only the interests of a profession or an administrative regulation concerned with technical matters probably would not be sufficient. Absent legislation, the judiciary must define the cause of action in case-by-case determinations.... [U]nless an employee-at-will identifies a specific expression of public policy, he may be discharged with or without cause.

[B]efore loperamide could be tested on humans, an IND had to be submitted to the FDA to obtain approval for such testing. The IND must contain complete manufacturing specifications, details of pre-clinical studies [testing on animals] which demonstrate the safe use of the drug, and a description of proposed clinical studies. The FDA then has 30 days to withhold approval of testing. Since no IND had been filed here, and even giving Dr. Pierce the benefit of all doubt regarding her allegations, it is clear that clinical testing of loperamide on humans was not imminent.

Dr. Pierce argues that by continuing to perform research on loperamide she would have been forced to violate professional medical ethics expressed in the Hippocratic oath. She cites the part of the oath that reads: "I will prescribe regimen for the good of my patients according to my ability and my judgment and never do harm to anyone." Clearly, the general language of the oath does not prohibit specifically research that does not involve tests on humans and that cannot lead to such tests without governmental approval.

We note that Dr. Pierce did not rely on or allege violation of any other standards, including the "codes of professional ethics" advanced by the dissent. Similarly, she did not allege that continuing her research would constitute an act of medical malpractice or violate any statute....

The case would be far different if Ortho had filed the IND, the FDA had disapproved it, and Ortho insisted on testing the drug on humans....

[I]mplicit in Dr. Pierce's position is the contention that Dr. Pasquale and Ortho were obliged to accept her opinion. Dr. Pierce contends, in effect, that Ortho should have stopped research on loperamide because of her opinion about the controversial nature of the drug.

Dr. Pierce espouses a doctrine that would lead to disorder in drug research.... Chaos would result if a single doctor engaged in research were allowed to determine, according to his or her individual conscience, whether a project should continue. An employee does not have a right to continued employment when he or she refuses to conduct research simply because it would contravene his or her personal morals. An employee-at-will who refuses to work for an employer in answer to a call of conscience should recognize that other employees and their employer might heed a different call. However, nothing in this opinion should be construed to restrict the right of an employee-at-will to refuse to work on a project that he or she believes is unethical....

Under these circumstances, we conclude that the Hippocratic oath does not contain a clear mandate of public policy that prevented Dr. Pierce from continuing her research on loperamide. To hold otherwise would seriously impair the ability of drug manufacturers to develop new drugs according to their best judgment.

The legislative and regulatory framework pertaining to drug development reflects a public policy that research involving testing on humans may proceed with FDA approval. The public has an interest in the development of drugs, subject to the approval of a responsible management and the FDA, to protect and promote the health of mankind....

[Appellate division judgment for the plaintiff is reversed and the case is remanded.]

Pashman, J., Dissenting.

The majority's analysis recognizes that the ethical goals of professional conduct are of inestimable social value. By maintaining informed standards of conduct, licensed professions bring to the problems of their public responsibilities the same expertise that marks their calling. The integrity of codes of professional conduct that result from this regulation deserves judicial protection from undue economic pressure. Employers are a potential source of this pressure, for they can provide or withhold until today, at their whim, job security and the means of enhancing a professional's reputation. Thus, I completely agree with the majority's ruling that "an employee has a cause of action for wrongful discharge when the discharge is contrary to a clear mandate of public policy" as expressed in a "professional code of ethics."

The Court pronounces this rule for the first time today. One would think that it would therefore afford plaintiff an opportunity to seek relief within the confines of this newly announced cause of action. By ordering the grant of summary judgment for defendant, however, the majority apparently believes that such an opportunity would be an exercise in futility. I fail to see how the majority reaches this conclusion. There are a number of detailed, recognized codes of medical ethics that proscribe participation in clinical experimentation when a doctor perceives an unreasonable threat to human health. Any one of these codes could provide the "clear mandate of public policy" that the majority requires.

Three other points made by the majority require discussion.... The first is the majority's characterization of the effect of plaintiff's ethical position. It appears to believe that Dr. Pierce had the power to determine whether defendant's proposed development program would continue at all. This is not the case, nor is plaintiff claiming the right to halt defendant's developmental efforts. [P]laintiff claims only the right to her professional autonomy. She contends that she may not be discharged for expressing her view that the clinical program is unethical or for refusing to continue her participation in the project. She has done nothing else to impede continued development of defendant's proposal; moreover, it is undisputed that defendant was able to continue its program by reassigning personnel. Thus, the majority's view that granting doctors a right to be free from abusive discharges would confer on any one of them complete veto power over desirable drug development, is ill-conceived.

The second point concerns the role of governmental approval of the proposed experimental program. In apparent ignorance of the past failures of official regulation to safeguard against pharmaceutical horrors, the majority implies that the necessity for administrative approval for human testing eliminates the need for active, ethical professionals within the drug industry. But we do not know whether the United States Food and Drug Administration (FDA) would be aware of the safer alternative to the proposed drug when it would pass upon defendant's application for the more hazardous formula. The majority professes no such knowledge. We must therefore assume the FDA would have been left in ignorance. This highlights the need for ethically autonomous professionals within the pharmaceutical industry....

The final point to which I must respond is the majority's observation that plaintiff expressed her opposition prematurely, before the FDA had approved clinical experimentation. Essentially, the majority holds that a professional employee may not express a refusal to engage in illegal or clearly unethical conduct until his actual participation and the resulting harm is imminent. This principle grants little protection to the ethical autonomy of professionals that the majority proclaims. Would the majority have Dr. Pierce wait until the first infant was placed before her, ready to receive the first dose of a drug containing 44 times the concentration of saccharin permitted in 12 ounces of soda?

I respectfully dissent.

QUESTIONS

1. The *Pierce* majority announces a new "cause of action in New Jersey for wrongful discharge when the discharge is contrary to a clear mandate of public policy." Such a mandate, it goes on to say, could be found in a professional code of ethics, yet Dr. Pierce had failed to identify one in her complaint with enough specificity. How does the dissenting judge respond to this point?

2. What is the procedure for obtaining FDA approval of a new drug? Do you agree with the majority that when Dr. Pierce stopped working on the loperamide project, the risk to human test subjects was not "imminent"?

3. Surveying the interests at stake in the case, the *Pierce* majority states:

   [W]e must balance the interests of the employee, the employer, and the public. Employees have an interest in knowing they will not be discharged for exercising their legal rights. Employers have an interest in knowing they can run their businesses as they see fit as long as their conduct is consistent with public policy. The public has an interest in employment stability and in discouraging frivolous lawsuits by dissatisfied employees.

   Are there any important stakeholder interests not mentioned here?

4. The dissent mentions "past failures of official regulation to safeguard against pharmaceutical horrors." There have been more recent failures. Since 2000, the diet drug Fen-Phen led to lung and heart disorders, the antidepressant Paxil caused birth defects in children whose mothers took Paxil while pregnant, and the painkiller Vioxx was found to double the risk of heart attack. In each instance, the pharmaceutical firms had evidence suggesting serious problems with drugs that were in development or had already been brought to market. By the time Merck recalled Vioxx in late 2004, there were congressional hearings underway. A doctor in the FDA's Office of Drug Safety, David Graham, told Congress that Vioxx may have caused as many as 55,000 deaths. Graham charged his agency with being "incapable of protecting America" against dangerous drugs. A study led by Dr. Graham that looked at the cardiovascular risks of taking Vioxx was supposed to be published in a prestigious medical journal, but was pulled at the last minute after Dr. Graham received a warning from his supervisor. FDA management then began a smear campaign, with anonymous claims that his study could reflect scientific misconduct, and that Graham "bullied" his staff.

   Research: Fearing his job was at risk, Graham sought help from the whistleblower support organization, the Government Accountability Project. Find out what happened. What accusations did Graham make against the FDA in 2010, regarding the diabetes drug Avandia?

5. Agencies such as the FDA (Food and Drug Administration), the FAA (Federal Aviation Administration), or the EPA (Environmental Protection Agency)

depend on corporations to generate accurate data to use in analyzing safety risks. Because government resources are limited, it must rely on companies to do their own tests, and to share all relevant results. Business decisions to hold back adverse information from regulators can be both fatal and expensive. Consider Toyota's problems with sudden acceleration. In 2009 Toyota apparently learned of problems with sticking accelerators and dangerous floor mats months before it was forced to recall more than 2.3 million cars and was hit with the largest fine in the history of the National Highway Traffic Safety Administration (NHTSA). Action had been taken in Europe and Canada before the problem was even acknowledged in the United States.

6. The dissent in *Pierce* mentions the need to protect "professional autonomy." What does this phrase mean? What connection might professional autonomy have with the U.S. safety regulatory scheme?

7. In 1986, responding to the *Pierce* decision of its supreme court, the New Jersey legislature adopted *The Conscientious Employee Protection Act,*[19] shielding from retaliation employees who object to, or refuse to participate in, "any activity, policy or practice which the employee reasonably believes to be incompatible with a clear mandate of public policy concerning the public health, safety or welfare." What would have been the likely outcome had Dr. Pierce sued under this new law?

8. **Research:** By 2000, every state in the United States had adopted whistle-blower protection statutes of some type. Locate one such law from your home state. Under what circumstances are whistleblowers protected? Are private sector as well as government employees covered? Does coverage under the statute exclude the possibility of suing in tort?

WINSTON V. BANK OF AMERICA

What matters ... is not what a person is, but how closely his many personae mesh with the organizational ideal; not his willingness to stand by his actions, but his agility in avoiding blame; not what he stands for, but whom he stands with in the labyrinths of his organization.

—ROBERT JACKALL, Moral Mazes: Bureaucracy and Managerial Work

Michael G. Winston was a high-powered executive in organizational management. After successful stints at Motorola, McDonnell Douglas, and Lockheed, he headed worldwide leadership and organizational strategy at Merrill Lynch in New York. In May 2005, as the mortgage wave was cresting, Winston began working for Countrywide Financial, the subprime lending giant, where he was soon promoted to managing director and enterprise chief leadership officer, responsible for helping the company continue to grow and to groom better managers.

---

[19]*N.J.S.A.* 34:19-1 et. seq.

But within a few months, something happened that made Winston worry about his new employer. In the Countrywide parking lot one day, he noticed an employee's vanity license plate that read "Fund 'Em." Winston approached him, saying, "I'm not familiar with that expression. What's this about?" The employee responded that it was about funding all loans, the company's growth strategy for 2006. Winston then asked, "What if the person has no job? " "Fund 'em" was the answer. "What if the person has no assets?" Again the answer was: "Fund 'em."

Winston immediately reported this "anything-goes" strategy to the chief production officer of Countrywide Home Loans. "I told him that you need to focus on customer satisfaction, on the quality of the loan portfolio and on building leaders who would focus their people on that," he said. "I wrote him a very comprehensive proposal on how to reward people properly."

Winston reported another issue the following year. It involved a droplet-laden orange-pink mist that began seeping into his office. Nauseated, he left the building with his employees. As people began reporting symptoms of illness and fears about going back to work, Winston tried to find out whether company officials were going to do anything about the strange occurrence. He was told it was a "one-off event." Winston then placed a call to California OSHA. Soon after that, his budget was frozen, he was relocated repeatedly, and he began to be uninvited to meetings.

About two months later, Winston found himself again at odds with company policy, when he refused to misrepresent Countrywide's corporate governance practices in a report to Moody's ratings agency. Moody's had expressed concerns about executive pay and succession planning: "We view governance as a credit challenge that constrains future ratings improvement at Countrywide." Winston was asked by the company president to refute that and to outline Countrywide's extensive succession planning, but Winston said he couldn't do that, since he had never seen documentation of such a plan. "I'm not your guy," he told the president.

Winston stayed on at Countryside, but he was marginalized, with only two people reporting to him, down from close to two hundred. When Bank of America bought out the company in 2008, he was told that there were no positions available for him postmerger, and he was let go.

Michael Winston sued for wrongful termination, and in February 2011 won a jury verdict of $3.8 million, which was reversed on appeal. Meanwhile, Winston has been trying, without success, to find work in line with his experience. "I want to do my part to promote vision-driven, values-based leadership that is a force for good," he has said. "The devastation caused by Countrywide to me, my family, my team, the work force, customers, shareholders, taxpayers and citizens around the world is incalculable."

By 2003, Countrywide Financial's low-income loan business had grown to $600 billion, and by 2006 the company financed a bigger share of mortgages than any other single lender: 20 percent of all mortgages in the United States. Countrywide's subprime documents revealed a policy of lending to families with as little as $1,000 of disposable income. When Bank of America took over Countrywide in 2008, it agreed to pay $8.7 billion to settle a multistate lawsuit brought by state attorneys general against Countrywide based on predatory lending practices. In April 2013, a $500 million class action lawsuit by borrowers was settled. A federal lawsuit against the company—under which the United States sought billions of dollars in damages—was still pending in June 2013.

■ ■ ■

Montana: Wrongful Discharge from Employment Act[20]

Purpose

This part sets forth certain rights and remedies with respect to wrongful discharge. Except as limited in this part, employment having no specified term may be terminated at the will of either the employer or the employee on notice to the other for any reason considered sufficient by the terminating party.

Definitions

In this part, the following definitions apply:

(2) "Discharge" includes a constructive discharge ... and any other termination of employment, including resignation, elimination of the job, layoff for lack of work, failure to recall or rehire, and any other cutback in the number of employees for a legitimate business reason.

(3) "Employee" means a person who works for another for hire. The term does not include a person who is an independent contractor....

(5) "Good cause" means reasonable job-related grounds for dismissal based on a failure to satisfactorily perform job duties, disruption of the employer's operation, or other legitimate business reason. The legal use of a lawful product by an individual on the employer's premises during nonworking hours is not a legitimate business reason....

(7) "Public policy" means a policy in effect at the time of the discharge concerning the public health, safety, or welfare established by constitutional provision, statute, or administrative rule.

Elements of Wrongful Discharge

A discharge is wrongful only if:

1. it was in retaliation for the employee's refusal to violate public policy or for reporting a violation of public policy;
2. the discharge was not for good cause and the employee had completed the employer's probationary period of employment; or
3. the employer violated the express provisions of its own written personnel policy.

Remedies

1. If an employer has committed a wrongful discharge, the employee may be awarded lost wages and fringe benefits for a period not to exceed four years from the date of discharge, together with interest thereon....
2. The employee may recover punitive damages otherwise allowed by law if it is established by clear and convincing evidence that the employer engaged in actual fraud or actual malice in the discharge of the employee [for refusing to violate public policy or for reporting a violation of public policy].

---

[20]39 *Montana Code Annotated* Chapter 2, Part 9. Puerto Rico has been the only other U.S. jurisdiction that has passed equivalent legislation.

Exemptions

This part does not apply to a discharge:

1. that is subject to any other state or federal statute that provides a procedure or remedy for contesting the dispute. Such statutes include those that prohibit discharge for filing complaints, charges, or claims with administrative bodies or that prohibit unlawful discrimination based on race, national origin, sex, age, handicap, creed, religion, political belief, color, marital status, and other similar grounds.
2. of an employee covered by a written collective bargaining agreement or a written contract of employment for a specific term.

Preemption of Common-Law Remedies

Except as provided in this part, no claim for discharge may arise from tort or express or implied contract.

QUESTIONS

1. How would the *Milton* case have been decided had this law been in effect in Maryland? How would Dr. Pierce have fared under it? Michael Winston?

2. What parts of this law seem to benefit employees? Employers?

3. The state laws protecting whistleblowers vary enormously, but none of them protect whistleblowers who turn to the media first. Why do you think that is so? Does that seem like sound policy to you? Does it encourage or discourage ethical behavior?

■ ■ ■

○ Blowing the Whistle for Food Safety

The first item in this section is a case study written by Paul Leighton, Professor of Sociology, Anthropology, & Criminology at Eastern Michigan University. It should be read and discussed in segments as indicated.

Ken Kendrick and the Peanut Corporation of America

Paul Leighton

Ken Kendrick was tired of the long commute to his job as a laboratory technician for a food safety testing company. Along his route to work in Texas, The Peanut Corporation of America (PCA) was opening a processing plant and hiring employees. Kendrick applied and became an assistant manager for production with a $12 an hour salary. Food safety was not part of his job—nor was it anyone else's job. That bothered Kendrick because the plant "looked like something out of the 1950s" and was "disgusting."

PCA—a "low cost" provider—had purchased a former pig slaughterhouse and sausage factory that had sat vacant for 30 years. The roof leaked in multiple locations and the walls had openings that let in rodents, both of which increase the likelihood of salmonella. Generally, salmonella is caused by animal feces, and water causes the bacteria to grow and spread. Infections last four to seven days, causing diarrhea, fever, abdominal cramps, and vomiting. While most people recover from this bacterial assault without treatment, it can lead to hospitalization and death in the elderly, infants and those with weakened immune systems. Problems with leaks had been repeatedly brought to management's attention, Kendrick learned, but the response was a series of temporary fixes; requests for money to do more were unequivocally denied in multipage emails laced with profanity.

A number of Good Manufacturing Practice standards mitigate the threat of salmonella, but they were not required by regulations or law—and PCA ignored almost all of them. Food should go through a "kill step" to reduce pathogens to a safe level, but PCA cooked the peanuts just to get to the right color, not to kill bacteria. Food that has been through a kill step should be segregated from raw product, but PCA's plant and processes allowed for cross-contamination. The plant did no environmental testing, which means swabbing work surfaces and machinery to see if pathogens are present. PCA also did no regular testing of its finished product, even though PCA's materials and CEO Stewart Parnell's emails to customers claimed it had "state-of-the-art Food Safety techniques."

Kendrick also realized that PCA was defrauding customers. An order for 44,000 pounds of high grade Valencia peanuts was mixed 50–50 with lower grade nuts under orders from management. The business customer was not getting what it paid for, and it was subsequently creating a misbranded product so retail customers who paid for expensive organic Valencia peanut butter also got something less. Both of these circumstances, Kendrick knew, were in violation of the Food, Drug and Cosmetic Act (21 USC §331a).

QUESTIONS

1. If you were in Kendrick's shoes, what ethical issues might you confront?

2. Which, if any, issues would you raise with management? How assertively would you push these issues?

3. Which, if any, outside agencies, organizations and/or defrauded customers would you tell? Explain your decision to be silent or the rationale for which outside group(s) you would contact.

■ ■ ■

Kendrick raised a variety of safety/salmonella issues with his manager and occasionally with Parnell, but was told that the company could not afford to fix the big problems with the plant and its equipment. A potentially major customer inspected the plant and refused to purchase from PCA partly because they did no environmental testing. That allowed Kendrick to start a rudimentary Quality Assurance program. But he realized the program was meant to be more symbolic than substantive, and Kendrick's heart sank when another manager suggested to him that they would get better results and win the contract if he microwaved the sponges before sending them to the lab for testing.

QUESTIONS

1. If you were Kendrick, what would you do now?

2. If you were Kendrick's supervisor, what would you do?

■ ■ ■

Kendrick anonymously alerted the customer of the Valencia peanuts and asked them to say they had discovered it on their own: "I need my job and would be fired very quickly for telling you this, but I do not want you to be ripped off as I have some ethics left." He also anonymously emailed the Texas Department of Health about conditions in the plant, but they never followed up. After three months, Kendrick left PCA.

In 2008, the Centers for Disease Control (CDC) started tracking a multi-state outbreak of salmonella that public health officials painstakingly traced back to PCA's facility in Blakely, Georgia. PCA issued a series of denials as the investigation became more focused and more damning. Kendrick was following the recalls and the outbreak carefully. His granddaughter was sick and only wanted comfort food: Austin peanut butter crackers. It never occurred to him that a company as large and reputable as Kellogg would buy from PCA, but then he noticed the Austin snack crackers on the recall list.

QUESTIONS

1. What does "I need my job and would be fired very quickly for telling you this, but I have some ethics left" mean to you? In Kendrick's shoes, what lines would you resist crossing?

2. At this point, there were hospitalizations, hundreds of confirmed cases of salmonella poisoning and some deaths. Given that attention was only focused on the Blakely plant and no one was even mentioning the Texas plant, would you say something about it? Why/why not? If so, to whom? Would you go public?

■ ■ ■

Kendrick sent hundreds of warning emails to state departments of health, companies that were recalling products, and to the media. He wanted the Texas plant closed because every week they remained open, they were shipping thousands of pounds of contaminated product—food that would make people sick and eventually cause another death. Someone at Safe Tables Our Priority (now STOP Foodborne Illness) listened and got Kendrick on *Good Morning America*, where he started to tell his story and put the Texas plant in the spotlight.

It turned out that PCA had never registered the Plainview plant with the Texas Department of Health, so there had never been a sanitation inspection. When the FDA finally inspected it, they found six leaks in the ceiling, numerous dead mice and mouse droppings, and "what appeared to be a bird's nest." The Texas Department of State Health Services noted that the plant's ventilation system sucked debris from a crawl space infested with dead mice and mouse droppings and blew it over the production areas. In closing the plant, they relied on state law authorizing such action for "a condition that poses an immediate and serious threat to human life or health." Three hundred jobs were lost.

According to the CDC, the outbreak caused nine deaths and 714 cases of confirmed illness; 166 people were hospitalized. There were 11,000 to 20,700 total cases. Congress held a hearing, passed the Food Safety Modernization Act (FSMA), and four years later the Dept. of Justice returned a 76 count indictment against top PCA employees. They had falsified a number of Certificates of Analysis to show a negative result for salmonella when it was positive, and they shipped many lots of product in spite of positive tests for salmonella. The indictment charged them with intentionally releasing adulterated and misbranded food, mail and wire fraud for false statements, and obstruction of justice.

People in Kendrick's community were angry with him because they lost jobs when the plant closed. An introverted, "regular guy," he was having a difficult time in the national spotlight. Although he was now known as a whistleblower, Kendrick did not identify with that term, equating it with a "prison snitch." He lost his job, separated from his wife, lost his house and suffers from depression. Several potential employers have told him during interviews that they will not hire a whistleblower.

"It's been depressing and taken a terrible toll," Kendrick says, but he would do it again: "people were dying and kids were suffering permanent consequences like a kidney transplant, so I had no choice. Morally, I had no choice. How could I live with myself if I did nothing?"

QUESTIONS

1. Why do Kendrick and the public see whistleblowing as negative—like "snitching"? How do Kendrick's actions differ from those of a "prison snitch"? What might be a basis for distinguishing between the right and the wrong time to disclose negative information?

2. Should managers want employees to report negative information to their supervisors? If so, what could they create to encourage this?

3. In cases where whistleblowing supports a public good, what changes should be made in social perception, media, and/or public policy to encourage people to do the right thing?

Food Safety Modernization Act of 2010

After a spate of tragedies in which hundreds of people were sickened and some died, and after whistleblowers like Ken Kendrick made explicit the connections between those tragedies and reckless corporate behavior, the problem of food safety came sharply into focus.[21] Bereaved parents turned into dedicated activists. Nancy Donley, for example, whose six-year-old son Alex died in 1993 from *Escherichia coli*–contaminated ground beef, became the president of STOP Foodborne Illness and a leading proponent of food safety in Washington. As parents buttonholed lawmakers, whistleblowers triggered media exposes and nonprofit groups pushed hard for protective legislation. Hearings were held, and, finally, in 2010, a new law was passed.

The *Food Safety Modernization Act* (FSMA[22]), the first major overhaul of the nation's food security system in 80 years, authorizes the FDA to require science-based safety controls of the food producers under its jurisdiction. For the first time, food importers must verify that foreign suppliers are using adequate safety controls, and the FDA, which had previously relied on voluntary recalls by food producers, now has the power to make recalls mandatory.

The *FSMA* includes protection for whistleblowers. If an employee reports, refuses to participate in, or testifies about a potential violation of this law, an employer "engaged in the manufacture, processing, packing, transporting, distribution, reception, holding, or importation of food" is prohibited from firing or otherwise discriminating against the whistleblower "with respect to compensation, terms, conditions, or privileges of

---

[21]According to CDC estimates, every year approximately 1 out of 6 people in the United States will suffer from foodborne illness; 128,000 will be hospitalized and 3,000 will die.

[22]*Food Safety Modernization Act*, Pub. L. No. 110-353, 124 Stat. 3885 (2011).

employment." Employees are protected from retaliation whether or not their disclosures are directly related to their job responsibilities. And they are protected when they disclose information that they "reasonably believe" violates the law. This important aspect of the FSMA allows whistleblowers protection if they have a sincere, rationally based belief that a violation exists, even if, ultimately, they are mistaken.

There are some significant exceptions to the broad coverage of the FSMA, however. While vegetable, fruits, nuts, dairy, and seafood are within the FDA jurisdiction, the Secretary of Agriculture controls the quality of meat, poultry, and eggs. Many activists are concerned about this, given that some of the most severe problems with food safety are found in slaughterhouses, and involve the treatment of cattle and chickens. In the next reading, we see how efforts to expose these problems have met resistance.

Anti-Whistleblower Laws

The Government Accountability Project (GAP) is the nation's leading whistleblower protection organization. One of the programs within GAP is its Food Integrity Campaign (FIC), which focuses on "alter[ing] the relationship of power between the food industry and consumers [and] protecting the rights of those who speak out against the practices that compromise food integrity."

Amanda Hitt, Director of GAP's Food Integrity Campaign, here describes the controversial anti-whistleblower laws known as "Ag Gag," which make it illegal to record undercover videos showing animal cruelty.

"Ag Gag" and Food Integrity

Amanda Hitt

On February 17, 2008, over 140 million pounds of ground beef destined for consumers and the national school lunch program was recalled following the release of undercover video taken by the Humane Society of the United States. Prompting the largest meat recall in history, the HSUS footage of Hallmark-Westland Slaughter Facility in Chino California depicted countless acts of animal cruelty and revealed threats to the food supply.[23] The fallout from the Chino investigation not only shook consumer confidence in the safety of meat, but also sounded alarms within the meat industry that undercover investigations could have devastating impact on profits.

Recordings of animal slaughter facilities and on-farm abuse continued to surface, with each expose resulting in heightened scrutiny. The unwanted attention prompted a meat and poultry industry response in the form of state by state legislation. The industries lobbied for whistleblower suppression laws, commonly known as Ag Gag, which would criminalize not only undercover documentation of animal abuse but also any recordings of public health violations occurring in agricultural facilities.

Ag Gag proponents are primarily associated with large industrial agriculture firms, meat producers, and farm bureaus. They argue that the legislation protects the freedom to farm without interference and that, taken out of context, many routine and legal practices carried out on the modern farm will be subject to

---

[23]The videos showed workers forcibly moving "downer" animals—those that are too weak to stand on their own—in violation of federal law. Downer animals are thought to be at higher risk for Mad Cow disease, which, transmitted to humans through the meat, causes devastating and life-threatening neurological injury.

misinterpretation. They cast doubt on both the authenticity and the editing of the digital documentation, claiming that the videos give viewers the false impression that normal farm practices are somehow abusive or illegal.

Opponents of Ag Gag are a varied coalition of organizations representing animal welfare, labor, public health, consumers, human rights, civil liberties, and the environment. These groups maintain that undercover video brings necessary accountability and transparency to otherwise hidden wrongful practices. They believe that whistleblowers play an important role in bringing about appropriate regulation of the agriculture industry, especially given the weak inspector force. Beyond advocating for animal welfare, these groups contend that whistleblowers shine light on both the labor and environmental violations that have long been associated with factory farming. Civil rights advocates also voice constitutional concerns about Ag Gag with respect to first amendment free speech rights and the bills' impacts on investigative journalism.

In 2011, Ag Gag bills were introduced in Florida, Iowa, Minnesota, and New York. These bills either stalled or failed to pass their respective state legislative sessions. However, they would be reintroduced in 2012 and joined by 10 more antiwhistleblower bills from Florida, Illinois, Indiana, Tennessee, Missouri, Nebraska, Minnesota, New York, Iowa and Utah. Challenged by animal welfare activists, workers' rights groups, and free speech advocates, all but two of these bills—Iowa's and Utah's—failed.

Although individual state bills varied in approach, they all had strikingly similar language and their seemingly coordinated introductions into state houses led many to speculate that the bills were based on a model created by the American Legislative Exchange Council (ALEC), an industry-funded group that drafts state laws to meet corporate agendas. Noticeably, the state Ag Gag bills mirrored language in the 2003 ALEC-inspired "Animal and Ecological Terrorism Act" that broadly labels even nonviolent animal rights activism as terrorism.

Ag Gag language employs one or more of three prohibitions. The earliest bills attempted to criminalize any video or recording of any agricultural facility. Overly broad, they ran afoul of constitutional rights to free speech. Later bills, like the one that passed in Iowa, narrowed their focus to prohibit "agricultural fraud." Agricultural fraud criminalizes gaining access to an animal facility by false pretenses (e.g. falsification of an employment application). Newer bills, like the one introduced in New Hampshire, include "mandatory reporting," requiring whistleblowers to report animal abuse and turn over videotapes and other documentation within 24 hours or face prosecution. Proponents of Ag Gag maintain that mandatory reporting language was introduced to insure that animals would get immediate help if they were witnessed being harmed. But animal welfare advocates cast doubt on that argument, suggesting that such provisions make it impossible to carry out the kind of long-term, in-depth investigations that would demonstrate systemic abuse. Opponents also point out that the 24 hour window is not enough time for a potential whistleblower to seek legal assistance before deciding to blow the whistle.

Ag Gag not only challenges the consumer's right to know, but also the employee's right to tell. In large-scale agriculture, the workers' voice is seldom heard. The majority of meat industry workers are low-wage immigrants with little or no ability to speak out against company wrongdoing. Often the first line of defense against threats to the food system, these workers are rarely in a position to speak out against workplace threats to themselves, much less speak out against abuses to animals. When it comes to bringing horrific truths to light, undercover footage and audio are often the most effective outlet for whistleblowers who otherwise risk retaliation. And when disputes arise about what's really happening behind closed doors, video is the ultimate arbiter of truth.

Whistleblower exposés involving the use of undercover video include:

Chicken "Fecal Soup": USDA grader Hobart Bartley, who was transferred and demoted in 1985 after repeatedly warning the Department of Agriculture about unsanitary conditions at a Missouri poultry plant, came to GAP and exposed the industry practice of soaking thousands of chicken carcasses in a giant "chiller" (with dried blood, feces and hair floating in among the dead birds) in order to increase their selling weight. His disclosure garnered national attention when undercover footage was aired on CBS *60 Minutes*.

Food Lion: Food Lion grocery chain whistleblower employees reported abuses of food safety standards in the early 1990s. Food Lion practices included grinding expired meat into sausage, washing off meat that was greenish and slimy, soaking poultry in bleach to conceal spoilage, and putting tomato sauce on expired chicken then selling the altered product at a higher price. These whistleblower concerns were shared with ABC. With the benefit of undercover video, the whistleblowers were vindicated.

USDA Public Health Veterinarian Dr. Dean Wyatt: In 2009 Dean Wyatt made multiple complaints to USDA supervisors about animal welfare and violations of the Humane Methods of Slaughter Act. Wyatt voiced his concerns at a swine facility in Oklahoma, and for his complaints was relocated to a veal plant in Vermont. Similar issues arose in Vermont and an undercover video taken by the Humane Society of the United States substantiated Wyatt's disclosures of wrongdoing.

QUESTIONS

1. The author notes that Ag Gag laws have been successfully passed in Utah and in Iowa. **Research**: Find these statutes. Do they contain the three provisions mentioned in the article? Has there been any litigation related to either law? Have additional Ag Gag laws been passed in other states since 2013?

2. The author points to the "American Legislative Exchange Council (ALEC), an industry-funded group that drafts state laws to meet corporate agendas," as having created the template for Ag Gag legislation. **Research**: Who funds ALEC? What is its operating budget? What is its stated philosophy? What other legislative templates has ALEC drafted?

3. GAP describes itself as a nonpartisan, public interest group. **Research**: Who funds GAP? What is its operating budget? What is its stated philosophy? What kinds of initiatives is GAP now pursuing?

4. Consider how ethical theory would apply to the Ag Gag scenario. Who are the stakeholders? How would the passage of Ag Gag laws look through the lens of free market ethics? Utilitarianism? Deontology Virtue Ethics? The Ethic of Care?

NATIONAL LABOR RELATIONS BOARD RULES ON NEW MEDIA

In recent rulings, the National Labor Relations Board (NLRB) has stated the right to discuss working conditions freely and without fear of retaliation should exist online just as it should at the work site. According to the Board, if these kinds of conversations are legally protected "at the watercooler," they must be protected on Facebook too. "All we're doing is applying traditional rules to a new technology," Board Chairman Mark G. Pearse has said. The issue in the new media cases is typically whether online remarks amount to "concerted activity"—or the efforts workers make to discuss work-related matters, efforts that might lead to the creation of a union.

The NLRB rulings strike a balance. On the one hand, an employee simply indulging in a lone rant online would not be protected. A reporter for an Arizona newspaper's Twitter comments included: "What?!?!?! No overnight homicide…. You're slacking Tucson." and "You stay homicidal, Tucson." He was fired, and the Board found his tweets were not protected "concerted activity." There was no sympathy either for a bartender who hadn't received a raise for years, and expressed the wish on Facebook that his "redneck" customers would choke on glass as they drive home drunk.

But broad workplace bans on "disrespectful" of "inappropriate" online comments have been found to be illegal interference with "concerted activity" if they discourage employees from discussing wages, benefits, or working conditions. At a nonprofit agency in upstate New York, a caseworker threatened to complain that her coworkers were slacking. Another caseworker went on Facebook and wrote, "My fellow co-workers, how do you feel?" There were some angry, expletive-laden responses. Those who had engaged in the Facebook exchange were fired for violating the agency's policy on harassment. In this case the NLRB found the online speech was protected under the labor law as "concerted activity" for mutual aid.

Some of these decisions are causing discomfort on part of businesses who see the Board as applying mid–twentieth-century law to twenty-first-century technology. Too, the NLRB rulings on "concerted activity" apply not only to unionized workers, but to all those in private sector employment.

PUBLIC EMPLOYEES AND FREEDOM OF SPEECH

What I was surprised at was the silence, the collective silence by so many people that had to be involved, that had to have seen something or heard something.

—SGT. SAMUEL PROVANCE, Key Witness in government
investigation of Abu Ghraib Prison Abuse

Citizens with a conscience are not going to ignore wrongdoing simply because they'll be destroyed for it: the conscience forbids it. Instead, these draconian responses simply build better whistleblowers.

—EDWARD SNOWDEN, Former National Security Agency
contractor who disclosed highly classified documents
detailing American government surveillance

People who work for the government or for any of its branches—such as police officers, air traffic controllers, and those employed by government-supported institutions such as hospitals or schools—are called public employees. For almost 200 years, public employees were thought to have no greater speech rights than those who worked in the private sector. The leading case, which dates back to the nineteenth century, involved a police officer who was fired for publicly criticizing the management of his department. He sued to get his job back, relying on his free speech rights. Judge Oliver Wendell Holmes refused his claim, stating, "The petitioner may have a constitutional right to talk politics, but he has no constitutional right to be a policeman."[24]

---

[24]*McAuliffe v. Mayor of New Bedford,* 29 N.E. 517 (1892).

Then, in 1968, the Supreme Court reinterpreted the First Amendment of the U.S. Constitution to give public employees at least limited speech protections. Marvin Pickering, a public school teacher, was fired for publishing a letter in the local paper critical of the Board of Education's allocation of funds to its athletic program. He sued, losing in the lower courts. On appeal, however, the Court ruled in his favor. In *Pickering v. Board of Education,*[25] the Court weighed "the interests of the teacher, as a citizen, in commenting upon matters of public concern" against the "interest of the State, as an employer, in promoting the efficiency of the public services it performs through its employees." On balance, Pickering's free speech interests were greater. The Court noted that a public employee could not be punished for speaking out on matters of public concern unless the employer could demonstrate that the employee's statements caused substantial interference with the performance of his own duties or with the functioning of the workplace.

In 1983, in *Connick v. Myers,*[26] the Supreme Court clarified and reinterpreted *Pickering.* Sheila Myers had distributed at her place of employment a questionnaire that inquired not only about internal matters, such as an office transfer policy, but also about matters of public concern, including pressure put on employees to work on certain political campaigns. Before applying the *Pickering* test, the Court ruled that it would first have to determine whether a public employee's speech was related to matters of public concern, thus creating a new obstacle for plaintiffs in these cases. Ms. Myers's questionnaire was tinged with just enough public interest to be examined under the *Pickering* test, although a statement limited to internal matters would not be. She lost, however, because the government demonstrated that her questionnaire interfered with working relationships by causing a "mini-insurrection" that could have disrupted the office.

■ ■ ■

In 2006, the Supreme Court revisited the *Pickering* rule, making it even more difficult for public employees to successfully argue their free speech rights had been violated. The facts of the case were as follows: Richard Ceballos began working as a deputy district attorney in Los Angeles County in 1989. By 2000, he was a "calendar" attorney, supervising other lawyers in the DA's office. In February of that year, a defense attorney contacted Ceballos to tell him he would be challenging a search warrant because it was based on "inaccuracies" in the supporting affidavit. Ceballos agreed to investigate. When he went to the location described in the warrant as a "long driveway," he found a separate road. Although the affidavit described tire tracks that led from a stripped-down truck to the premises to be searched, Ceballos found a road surface that would make it difficult or impossible to leave visible tire tracks.

After a telephone conversation with the affiant—a deputy sheriff—Ceballos told his supervisors that the case should be dismissed because there were serious misrepresentations in the affidavit supporting the search warrant. He repeated the same concerns in a memorandum. Then, at a heated meeting with his supervisors and with the sheriff who had made the statements in the warrant, Ceballos was

[25]391 U.S. 563 (1968).

[26]*Connick v. Myers,* 461 U.S. 138 (1983).

sharply reprimanded. Later, he claims, he experienced a series of retaliations, including being reassigned, transferred, and denied promotion.

He sued, claiming those actions violated his First Amendment rights.

Garcetti v. Ceballos
U.S. Supreme Court, 2006
547 U.S. 410

Justice KENNEDY Delivered the Opinion of the Court.

Pickering and the cases decided in its wake identify two inquiries to guide interpretation of the constitutional protections accorded to public employee speech. The first requires determining whether the employee spoke as a citizen on a matter of public concern. If the answer is no, the employee has no First Amendment cause of action.... If the answer is yes, then the possibility of a First Amendment claim arises. The question becomes whether the relevant government entity had an adequate justification for treating the employee differently from any other member of the general public....

When a citizen enters government service, the citizen by necessity must accept certain limitations on his or her freedom ... Government employers, like private employers, need a significant degree of control over their employees' words and actions; without it, there would be little chance for the efficient provision of public services....

At the same time, the Court has recognized that a citizen who works for the government is nonetheless a citizen. The First Amendment limits the ability of a public employer to leverage the employment relationship to restrict, incidentally or intentionally, the liberties employees enjoy in their capacities as private citizens. So long as employees are speaking as citizens about matters of public concern, they must face only those speech restrictions that are necessary for their employers to operate efficiently and effectively....

[T]he First Amendment interests at stake extend beyond the individual speaker ... [to include] the public's interest in receiving the well-informed views of government employees engaging in civic discussion ... [and] the necessity for informed, vibrant dialogue in a democratic society....

With these principles in mind we turn to the instant case....

The controlling factor in Ceballos' case is that his expressions were made pursuant to his duties as a calendar deputy. That consideration—the fact that Ceballos spoke as a prosecutor fulfilling a responsibility to advise his supervisor about how best to proceed with a pending case—distinguishes Ceballos' case ... We hold that when public employees make statements pursuant to their official duties, the employees are not speaking as citizens for First Amendment purposes, and the Constitution does not insulate their communications from employer discipline.

The significant point is that the memo was written pursuant to Ceballos' official duties.... Contrast, for example, the expressions made by the speaker in *Pickering,* whose letter to the newspaper had no official significance and bore similarities to letters submitted by numerous citizens every day.

Ceballos did not act as a citizen when he went about conducting his daily professional activities, such as supervising attorneys, investigating charges, and preparing filings. In the same way he did not speak as a citizen by writing a memo that addressed the proper disposition of a pending criminal case. When he went to work and performed the tasks he was paid to perform, Ceballos acted as a government employee. The fact that his duties sometimes required him to speak or write does not mean his supervisors were prohibited from evaluating his performance.

This result is consistent with our precedents' attention to the potential societal value of employee speech.... First Amendment claims based on government employees' work product does not prevent them from participating in public debate. The employees retain the prospect of constitutional protection for their contributions to the civic discourse.... This prospect of protection, however, does not invest them with a right to perform their jobs however they see fit.

Our holding likewise is supported by the emphasis of our precedents on affording government employers sufficient discretion to manage their operations. Employers have heightened interests in controlling speech made by an employee in his or her professional capacity.... Supervisors must ensure that their employees' official communications are accurate, demonstrate sound judgment, and promote the employer's mission. Ceballos' memo is illustrative. It demanded the attention of his supervisors and led to a heated meeting with employees from the sheriff's department. If Ceballos' superiors thought his memo was inflammatory or misguided, they had the authority to take proper corrective action....

Proper application of our precedents thus leads to the conclusion that the First Amendment does not prohibit managerial discipline based on an employee's expressions made pursuant to official responsibilities. Because Ceballos' memo falls into this category, his allegation of unconstitutional retaliation must fail....

Justice STEVENS, Dissenting.

The proper answer to the question "whether the First Amendment protects a government employee from discipline based on speech made pursuant to the employee's official duties," is "Sometimes," not "Never." Of course a supervisor may take corrective action when such speech is "inflammatory or misguided," But what if it is just unwelcome speech because it reveals facts that the supervisor would rather not have anyone else discover?

[P]ublic employees are still citizens while they are in the office. The notion that there is a categorical difference between speaking as a citizen and speaking in the course of one's employment is quite wrong. Over a quarter of a century has passed since then-Justice Rehnquist, writing for a unanimous Court, rejected "the conclusion that a public employee forfeits his protection against governmental abridgment of freedom of speech if he decides to express his views privately rather than publicly." ... [It] is senseless to let constitutional protection ... hinge on whether [words] fall within a job description. Moreover, it seems perverse to fashion a new rule that provides employees with an incentive to voice their concerns publicly before talking frankly to their superiors.

Justices SOUTER, STEVENS and GINSBERG, Dissenting.

Open speech by a private citizen on a matter of public importance lies at the heart of expression subject to protection by the First Amendment.... At the other extreme, a statement by a government employee complaining about nothing beyond treatment under personnel rules raises no greater claim to constitutional protection against retaliatory response than the remarks of a private employee.... In between these points lies a public employee's speech unwelcome to the government but on a significant public issue. Such an employee speaking as a citizen, that is, with a citizen's interest, is protected from reprisal unless the statements are too damaging to the government's capacity to conduct public business to be justified by any individual or public benefit thought to flow from the statements. *Pickering v. Board of Ed. of Township High School Dist.* (1968)....

This significant, albeit qualified, protection of public employees who irritate the government is understood to flow from the First Amendment, in part, because a government paycheck does nothing to eliminate the value to an individual of speaking on public matters, and there is no good reason for categorically discounting a speaker's interest in commenting on a matter of public concern just because the government employs him.... [and in part on] the value to the public of receiving the opinions and information that a public employee may disclose. "Government employees are often in the best position to know what ails the agencies for which they work." *Waters v. Churchill,* (U.S. 1994).

The reason that protection of employee speech is qualified is that it can distract co-workers and supervisors from their tasks at hand and thwart the implementation of legitimate policy, the risks of which grow greater the closer the employee's speech gets to commenting on his own workplace and responsibilities. It is one thing for an office clerk to say there is waste in government and quite another to charge that his own department pays full-time salaries to part-time workers....

... [I]t stands to reason that a citizen may well place a very high value on a right to speak on the public issues he decides to make the subject of his work day after day. Would anyone doubt that a school principal evaluating the performance of teachers for promotion or pay adjustment retains a citizen's interest in addressing the quality of teaching in the schools? ... Would anyone deny that a prosecutor like Richard Ceballos may claim the interest of any citizen in speaking out against a rogue law enforcement officer, simply because his job requires him to express a judgment about the officer's performance? (But the majority says the First Amendment gives Ceballos no protection, even if his judgment in this case was sound and appropriately expressed.)

Indeed, the very idea of categorically separating the citizen's interest from the employee's interest ignores the fact that the ranks of public service include those who share the poet's "object ... to unite [m]y avocation and my vocation." These citizen servants are the ones whose civic interest rises highest when they speak pursuant to their duties, and these are exactly the ones government employers most want to attract....

The interest at stake is as much the public's interest in receiving informed opinion as it is the employee's own right to disseminate it. This is ... true when an employee's job duties require him to speak about such things: when, for example, a public auditor speaks on his discovery of embezzlement of public funds, when a building inspector makes an obligatory report of an attempt to bribe him, or when a law enforcement officer expressly balks at a superior's order to violate constitutional rights he is sworn to protect. (The majority, however, places all these speakers beyond the reach of First Amendment protection against retaliation.)...

Justice BREYER, Dissenting.

The facts present two special circumstances that together justify First Amendment review.

First, the speech at issue is professional speech—the speech of a lawyer. Such speech is subject to independent regulation by canons of the profession. Those canons provide an obligation to speak in certain instances....

Second, the Constitution itself here imposes speech obligations upon the government's professional employee. A prosecutor has a constitutional obligation to learn of, to preserve, and to communicate with the defense about exculpatory and impeachment evidence in the government's possession. [Exculpatory evidence is evidence that proves innocence. Ceballos believed that what he learned about the affidavit was exculpatory.]

I would apply the *Pickering* balancing test here. With respect, I dissent.

QUESTIONS

1. The majority adds a threshold requirement to the analysis of First Amendment claims for public employees. According to *Pickering* and its progeny (cases interpreting *Pickering),* the first determination was whether the employee spoke as a citizen on a matter of public concern. If no, then the employee would have no First Amendment protection. If yes, the balancing test would be applied to the facts. Here in *Garcetti,* the Court sets up an additional threshold barrier for plaintiffs: Where public employee speech is found to be pursuant to official duties, it lacks First Amendment protection. How does the majority argue in favor of this new requirement? What arguments do the dissenters make for alternative methods of analysis?

2. Dissenting Justices Souter, Stevens, and Ginsburg write: "When constitutionally significant interests clash, resist the demand for winner-take-all; try to make adjustments that serve all of the values at stake." Think about the values that underlie each portion of this opinion. Which values are most prominent for Justice Kennedy with the majority? For Justice Stevens in dissent? Which values are framed in the dissent led by Souter? What value does Breyer mention?

3. In a part of *Garcetti* not included in this text, Justice Kennedy writes that government employees can turn to "the powerful network of legislative enactments—such as whistleblower protection laws and labor codes—available to those who seek to expose wrongdoing." Dissenting Justice Souter counters that these laws are not uniform and do not exist in all states. Where they do exist, do they tend to protect employees? In Mississippi, police officers were fired for reporting that a fellow officer had beaten a "restrained prisoner." They sued under federal constitutional and state whistleblower law. The court ruled that, because they had reported through the chain of command as their job duties required, they were doing so pursuant to their official duties and their speech was not protected under *Garcetti.* And because they were reporting through the chain of command, the Mississippi state whistleblower statute too did not protect them. State law would have protected the officers had they reported the misconduct through an investigative agency such as the district attorney instead of to their commanding officers. *Williams v. Riley,* 481 F. Supp. 2d 582 (N.D. Miss. 2007).

   (a) **Research:** Find a public employee whistleblower case that made claims both under *Garcetti* and under state whistleblower law. What were the facts? Was the federal constitutional claim successful? The state law claim?

   (b) If the police officers who were fired after reporting to their supervisors that some of their coworkers were physically beating restrained prison inmates had instead gone straight to the media, their actions would not have been pursuant to their official duties. Does *Garcetti* create a perverse incentive to go public with workplace grievances and concerns?

4. Consider the following scenarios drawn from the news. If these whistle-blowers sued, would they succeed in their federal constitutional free speech claims? Why or why not?

   a. The April 5, 2010, explosion at the Massey Energy's Upper Big Branch Mine in West Virginia was the worst coal mining disaster in 40 years. Fellow coal miners and family members of the 29 miners killed described the deadly conditions in the mine during the months leading up to the blast at a House of Representatives Committee on Education and Labor hearing in May 2010. Gary Quarles, a coal miner for 34 years and father of a miner killed in the blast, testified about the role of federal government inspectors at Upper Big Branch, stating that "MSHA [Mine Safety and Health Administration] inspections at Massey did little to protect miners. We absolutely looked to MSHA for leadership, particularly on safety issues, but MSHA has let us down many times." Quarles blamed MSHA for only conducting inspections during the day shift, ignoring safety during evenings, nights and weekends. A federal mine inspector complained about this to her supervisors and was fired.

   b. Gregory Williams was the football coach and athletic director at Dallas Independent School District's (DISD's) Pinkston High School. Coach Williams began asking questions about irregular budgetary procedures and confusing balance statements in his athletic budget. Unsatisfied with the answers he got from the principal and office manager, Williams sent a memo to the principal protesting the unorthodox way funds were being managed and spent at the school. Four days later, the principal removed Williams as athletic director. His contract for the next year was not renewed.

   c. Adis M. Vila was the Vice President for External and Legal Affairs at Miami Dade Community College (MDCC). She told MDCC administrators (who had authority to investigate and take corrective action) about concerns regarding three potentially illegal/unethical projects at the college: (1) an advertising contract between MDCC and a vendor that was not bid competitively as required by Florida law, (2) a proposal for MDCC to purchase the Freedom Tower for $10 million, and (3) the proposed use of college funds to illustrate a poetry book for the daughter of a college trustee. Vila received notice that she would not be renewed.

   d. Chief of Police proposed to change the staffing of the police department. While the supervisors were still together, Sgt. Mills voiced her objections to the plan to reduce the number of crime prevention officers under her command. Mills was on duty and in uniform at the time. She was later admonished for failure to work through the chain of command, removed from her supervisory position, and assigned to patrol duties.

■ ■ ■

FALSE CLAIMS ACT *QUI TAM* WHISTLEBLOWERS

We have seen to what extent the law might—or might not—protect whistleblowers from retaliation by their employers. But another legal approach is to give individuals an incentive to become whistleblowers in the first place, rewarding them for speaking out against wrongdoing. This is the premise of the federal False Claims Act, a more than 150-year-old response to fraud against the government. It was first enacted in 1863 during the Civil

War, when profiteers were selling rancid food rations and artillery shells filled with sawdust to the Union army. Private citizens who came forward to report such abuses and successfully filed suit were eligible for 50 percent of damages.

Plaintiffs who initiate cases under the False Claims Act are called *qui tam,* an abbreviation of a Latin phrase meaning "who sues on behalf of the king as well as for himself." The law has been amended several times, including in 1986 when it was brought to light that up to 10 percent of the federal budget was being drained by fraud, particularly in defense and health-care contracts. Under the 1986 amendments, *qui tam* cases are mutually advantageous to the Justice Department, which can receive triple damages, and to whistleblowers, who can be awarded from 15 to 25 percent of the amount recovered, depending on the value of the evidence they provide.[27]

Qui tam and Fraud in Health Care

According to the Kaiser Family Foundation, in 2009 the United States spent 17.6 percent of its gross domestic product on health care, more than double the percentages spent by Spain, Italy, Australia, Britain, or Japan. American health-care costs continue to skyrocket, and fraud in the health-care industry contributes as much as 10 percent of these costs.

In 2012, the Department of Justice (DOJ) recovered some $5 billion in fraud, more than half of that—$3.3 billion—thanks to whistleblowers. The health-care industry has been a particular target. Among those companies paying multimillion dollar fines for defrauding the government: Mylan (overcharging for generic drugs), McKesson (inflating prescription drug prices), Odyssey Health Care (overbilling for unnecessary hospice care). In the largest health-care fraud settlement in U.S. history, GlaxoSmithKline agreed in July 2012 to pay $3 billion to resolve charges that it had illegally marketed nine drugs, failed to report safety data, and engaged in false price reporting practices. Two billion dollars of the settlement was to resolve claims made under the False Claims Act and state laws. And Abbott Laboratories, a global health-care company, agreed to pay $1.5 billion to resolve civil and criminal charges that it had unlawfully promoted the prescription drug Depakote for unapproved uses and then submitted the charges to government health-care programs. Criminal fines and forfeitures, civil penalties, and whistleblower awards totaling $84 million were all part of the settlement.

EXPERIENCES OF *QUI TAM* WHISTLEBLOWERS AGAINST THE PHARMACEUTICAL INDUSTRY

In May 2010 three academics in public health[28] wrote an article[29] summarizing their investigation of the motivations and experiences of health-care industry whistleblowers under the False Claims Act. Focusing on successful prosecutions taken up by the Department of Justice against pharmaceutical companies, they analyzed data gleaned from 40-minute interviews with 26 individuals who became *qui tam* plaintiffs between

[27]Whistleblowers can recover even more—between 25 and 30 percent of the amount recovered—if the government declines to join the lawsuit.

[28]Aaron Kesselheim, M.D., J.D., M.P.H., instructor at Harvard Medical School and faculty member in the Department of Medicine at Brigham and Women's Hospital, David Studdert LL.B., Sc.D., M.P.H with a joint appointment at Melbourne Law School and the Melbourne School of Population Health, and Michelle Mello, J.D., Ph.D., M.Phil Associate Director of the Program in Law and Public Health at Harvard University.

[29]"Whistleblowers' Experiences in Fraud Litigation against Pharmaceutical Companies," 362 *N.E. J. Med.* 19, 1832–39 (May 13, 2010).

January 2001 and March 2009. Their study yields valuable insights about whistle-blowers, more nuanced than the common stereotypes depicting them as either "heroes struggling against corporate greed, [enduring] hardships and retaliation," or people with questionable motives who reap excessive rewards for disloyal behavior.

Here are some of the findings: Virtually all of the "insiders"—those who worked for the company against whom they eventually became *qui tam* plaintiffs—attempted to fix the situation first from within, "talking to their superiors, filing an internal complaint, or both." These individuals were either told the behavior was legal, or had their complaints dismissed "with accompanying demands that [they] do what they were told."

As for the motivations of these whistleblowers, only 6 of the 26 said they had intended from the start to use the *qui tam* process; the rest were advised to do so as they considered bringing suit for other reasons—unfair employment practices, for example. None stated that financial reward was what motivated them to get involved. Instead, they reported being driven by a mix of these factors: integrity, altruism, public safety, and self-preservation—with integrity the most frequently mentioned reason. Potential risks to public health was a concern for about one third of the respondents.

The majority described the process of working with the government to gather evidence for a *qui tam* case as grueling. More than half were actively involved in these efforts, wearing wires to covertly record conversations, and secretly copying files. One respondent described spending "thousands of hours" on the case over five years; another said the first few years demanded "probably 30 hours a week."

For nearly all of the *qui tam* plaintiffs in this study, the personal toll was "substantial and long-lasting." Of those who worked for the company at the time of the investigation, 82 percent experienced retaliation with devastating effects on their careers. After settlement, only 2 of the 22 "inside" plaintiffs continued to work in the pharmaceutical industry. And there were harsh effects on their personal lives. Six of the respondents experienced divorce, marital stress, or other family difficulties while they were going through the *qui tam* process. About half reported health disorders, including panic attacks, asthma, insomnia, and generalized anxiety.

All of the respondents received a share of the damages recovered by the government. Their rewards ranged from $100,000 to $42 million; the median was $3 million. Yet for the majority, the financial payoff was not worth it "relative to the time they spent on the case and the disruption and damage to their careers."

Despite all of this, most of the respondents—22 of the 26—remained convinced that "what they did was important for ethical ... psychological or spiritual reasons."

CHAPTER PROBLEMS

1. Kenneth Abbott, a former contractor who worked for British Petroleum, claims the company violated state and federal laws and its own internal policy by failing to maintain crucial safety documents related to one of its deepwater production facilities in the Gulf of Mexico. The project, called BP Atlantis, is one of the largest and deepest underwater oil and gas platforms in the world. Abbott, who had been hired to oversee BP databases, discovered Atlantis had been operating without the majority of the engineer-certified documents required by law and by BP's own procedures, and that

the platform was at risk for a catastrophic disaster even more massive than the spill that was triggered by the deadly Deepwater Horizon explosion in early 2010. Abbott reported his concerns to BP management. His contract was abruptly terminated. He later made reports to a former federal judge who was serving as an ombudsman to take complaints about BP operations following a ruptured pipeline incident in Prudhoe Bay. BP has issued this statement in response to Abbott's allegations:

> As CEO Tony Hayward constantly makes clear, safe and reliable operations are his number 1 priority for BP and the company has a very strong record of safe and reliable operations in the Gulf of Mexico.... The Atlantis field has been in service since October 2007 and has safely produced many millions of barrels of oil. The platform was successfully maintained through the course of two major hurricanes in 2008. Its safety, operation, and performance record is excellent.

Assume Kenneth Abbott sues. How would he fare under the law in Maryland? New Jersey? Montana? Assume a whistleblower in the federal Minerals Management Service (MMS) reported these concerns to his supervisor. How would she fare under *Garcetti*?

2. What would you do if you were the supervisor in the following situation: Your company has a rule forbidding armored truck drivers from leaving the truck unattended. Even if pulled over by someone who appears to be a police officer, drivers are to show a card explaining that the driver will follow the police to the stationhouse. Kevin Gardner is one of your drivers. At a scheduled stop at a bank, he waited in the vehicle while his coworker was in the bank. Suddenly he spotted a woman, whom he recognized as the manager, running out of the bank screaming, "Help me!" Chasing her was a man with a knife. Seeing nobody coming to help the manager, Gardner got out of the truck, locking the door behind him. Gardner lost sight of the manager, but walked toward the suspect who had already grabbed another employee, Kathy Martin, who Gardner recognized. The suspect put the knife to Martin's throat and dragged her back into the bank. Gardner followed them into the bank where he observed his partner with his gun drawn and aimed at the suspect. While his partner distracted the suspect, Gardner and a bank customer tackled the suspect and disarmed him. The police arrived immediately thereafter and took custody of the suspect. Ms. Martin was unharmed. Find out what happened in the case on which this is based: *Gardner v. Loomis Armored Inc.*, 913 P.2d 377 (Washington 1996).

3. Jane Akre and her husband, Steve Wilson, award-winning broadcast journalists, were recruited by Fox News to do investigative reports. With a deep voice in its promotional commercial, Fox promoted the two as the Mod Squad, "The Investigators, uncovering the truth, getting results, protecting you!" Akre and Wilson were promised that Fox would support them in their work, never caving into advertisers' pressure or altering a disturbing news story. In 1997 the team began investigating the use of bovine growth hormone (BGH) in the dairy farming industry. BGH, a Monsanto product, is used to enhance production; it is controversial because it is linked to cancer. In a four-part series, Akre and Wilson uncovered information about BGH health risks and unethical marketing practices. Having learned of the series, Monsanto's legal department sent a series of threatening letters to Fox, casting aspersions of the journalists' integrity: "Consider thoroughly what is at stake and the enormous damage that can be done by the reckless presentation of unsupported speculation as fact and the equally reckless publication of unsupported accusations ..." Fox had Akre rewrite the BGH story 83 times over nine months, and finally fired the "Mod Squad." They sued under Florida whistleblower law, which protects employees who experience retaliation

for refusing to participate in or reporting illegal activity. A jury awarded Akre and Wilson $425,000. How would they have fared under Maryland law? New Jersey? Montana? What are the ethical issues in this case? What happened on appeal? See *New World Communications of Tampa, Inc. v. Akre,* 866 So. 2d 1231 (Florida 2003).

4. The vast majority of the hamburger produced in the United States comes from Beef Products International (BPI). Much of the BPI meat includes a low-cost filler made from fatty meat scraps that are heated to remove most of the fat, then treated with ammonium hydroxide gas that supposedly kills bacteria such as *E. coli* and *Salmonella.* Kit Foshee, a quality control manager for BPI for 10 years, blew the whistle about these safety claims, calling them misleading. According to Fonshee, BPI would manipulate test results by artificially raising pH levels and by avoiding effective test methods. "All they wanted was a test to give a negative result," he claimed.

   Once ammonia-treated ground beef was dubbed "pink slime" by a former United States Department of Agriculture official, and once it became known that the substance was being served in school lunches, BPI faced major consumer outrage. As of March 2012, after an online petition quickly garnered more than 200,000 signatures, the USDA announced that schools could "opt out" of pink slime.

   Research:

   (a) Kit Fonshee was fired. What can you find out about the lawsuit he brought against his former employer?

   (b) In September 2012, Kit Foshee was named—along with ABC News, journalists Diane Sawyer, Jim Avila, and others—as defendants in a defamation lawsuit filed by BPI. There are several defenses to defamation: (1) the information put forth by the defendant was true, (2) the information was an opinion, and (3) the information was in the public interest. In addition, the media has a First Amendment–based argument. A case against a news organization cannot go forward unless the plaintiff can offer proof of "actual malice." Actual malice would be present if ABC knew Foshee's information was false and broadcast it anyway, or if ABC had "recklessly disregarded" whether his information was true or false—by failing to check sources, for example. Considering these legal rules, do you think BPI's defamation case against Foshee and ABC New and its broadcast journalists will succeed? If not, why do you think BPI decided to file it?

5. As of June 2013, the largest award given to a single whistleblower in U.S. history went to Cheryl Eckard, a quality assurance manager for GlaxoSmithKline. Sent to visit a GSK plant in Puerto Rico, Ms. Eckard discovered complaints that different drugs were being mixed in the same bottle—one boy had been given a double dose of the antidepressant Paxil, for instance—and there had been no effort to recall product or correct the reason for the mix-ups. Her recommendations were strong: stop all shipments from the plant, suspend manufacturing to allow time to resolve the product mix-ups, and notify the FDA. These suggestions were ignored. According to her *qui tam* lawsuit, Ms. Eckard's supervisors were preoccupied with preparing for an FDA inspection that would clear the way for approval of two new drugs. Eventually, after several more trips to the plant in Puerto Rico, Eckard told her boss she could no longer "participate in a cover-up of the quality assurance and compliance problems." She was terminated in 2003. She herself went to the FDA's San Juan office to detail her concerns in August of 2003.

   (a) **Research:** Find out what kind of case Cheryl Eckard won, and how much she was awarded.

   (b) What could GlaxoSmithKline done instead to avoid this expensive outcome?

6. The National Labor Relations Board has issued reports recently regarding employer policies on employee use of social media. Wal-Mart was praised for its policy which prohibits "inappropriate posting that may include discriminatory remarks, harassment and threats of violence or similar inappropriate or unlawful conduct." On the other hand, the Board was critical of General Motors' policy, which stated "offensive, demeaning, abusive or inappropriate remarks are as out of place online as they are in the office." Why do you think the Wal-Mart policy was viewed as acceptable, but the GM policy was not?

7. Should immigrant guest workers have whistleblower protection? Consider this: There are approximately 24 million U.S. workers in the "low-skilled" temporary economy, in farm fields, hotels, restaurants, on construction sites, and in landscaping. There are also some 66,000 "guestworkers," immigrants with temporary "H-2B" visas, who also participate in this sector of the economy. Here is one of their stories: After arriving from Mexico on an H-2B visa, Ana Diaz peeled crawfish for a Wal-Mart supplier in Louisiana, where she and her fellow guest workers endured 24-hour shifts without overtime pay. They were locked into the plant, and threatened with being beaten with a shovel if they would not work faster. When workers complained, their boss threatened violence against them and their families. According to the National Guestworker Alliance, this kind of severe abuse, from wage theft to forced labor, is common. As of 2013, business interests were lobbying through immigration reform to quadruple the number of H-2B visas issued.

   (a) Who are the stakeholders in this situation? What are their interests? What would be their arguments, pro and con, regarding whistleblower protection for guest workers?

   (b) **Research:** In 2013, Senator Richard Blumenthal introduced an amendment to the Senate immigration bill that would give H-2B guest workers whistleblower protection. It received some bipartisan support. What happened to this aspect of immigration reform?

8. Edward Snowden was 29 years old when he became one of most notorious whistleblowers in the history of military intelligence. A high school dropout who completed a GED, Snowden was fascinated by computers and became extremely tech-savvy. Granted a top-secret clearance, he held jobs at different times at both the National Security Agency (NSA) and one of its contractors. At the time he blew the whistle, he was working for a defense contractor earning almost $200,000 a year, and had access to huge amounts of secret information. Over time, Snowden had become increasingly uncomfortable about the ways in which he believed NSA surveillance networks were violating the privacy of American citizens.

   In a videotaped interview he gave to journalists in 2013, Snowden described noticing "disturbing" things on a "frequent basis." When he would ask questions about what he saw, he would encounter indifference. Eventually he decided his comfortable life was helping to build an "architecture of oppression," and he made the decision to disclose what the U.S. government was doing.

   Research:

   (a) What was it that Snowden disclosed?

   (b) What are the various opinions on Snowden's disclosures and whether antiterrorism surveillance is violating the privacy rights of American citizens? Check Republican, Democratic, journalist, pundit, and public opinion polling. Where do you stand on this?

   (c) What happened to Edward Snowden?

9. Seven months after the U.S. space shuttle *Columbia* crashed in August 2003, a report on the causes of the disaster was released. It had been a gargantuan effort. Some 25,000 workers had gathered more than 84,000 pieces of debris evidence by walking slowly across eastern Texas and western Louisiana. According to the final report, the "broken safety culture" inside NASA was at least as much to blame for the crash as the chunk of foam tile that blew a hole in the wing of *Columbia* just after liftoff. Engineers, hoping a high-risk rescue might be possible, had asked management for outside assistance in getting photos of the damage, but these requests were rejected:

> As much as the foam, what helped to doom the shuttle and its crew, even after liftoff, was not a lack of technology or ability … but missed opportunities and a lack of leadership and open-mindedness in management. The accident "was probably not an anomalous, random event, but rather likely rooted to some degree in NASA's history and the human spaceflight program's culture."[30]

Similar problems appear to have affected the CIA in the months leading up to the U.S. invasion of Iraq. According to a scathing Congressional report released in July 2004, key assessments used to justify the war were not supported by the government's own evidence:

> Among the central findings, endorsed by all nine Republicans and eight Democrats on the committee, were that a culture of "group think" in intelligence agencies left unchallenged an institutional belief that Iraq had illicit weapons; and that intelligence agencies too often failed to acknowledge the limited, ambiguous and even contradictory nature of their information about Iraq and illicit arms.[31]

Studies have shown that, within large organizations, there is a tendency to go along with the majority. Most people are not likely to challenge the value of the task at hand, or the way in which the task at hand is being accomplished. This reality, combined with the pressures that affect an organization from the outside—time and money pressures in the case of NASA's Columbia shuttle, political pressures in the case of the United States in Iraq—can obscure good judgment.

What kind of policies and practices might have the effect of changing an organizational culture to make it more receptive to ideas and opinions that go against the grain?

10. Consider the following comparison between how work is viewed in the United States and how it is viewed in the European Union:

> In the United States, work is mostly defined as having a job (or being self-employed). Jobs are the entry tickets to provision—health insurance, pension benefits, and social security. As feminists and critical race theorists have explained, work also includes homemaking, childcare work, unwaged work, and invisible work. Despite these multiple understandings of work, our political system, our cultural values, and our law are still largely predicated on the assumption that full citizens contribute to the country through waged work. As many scholars have explained, work confers not only self-sufficiency, then, but also dignity, standing in society, and membership in the social structure....

---

[30]John Schwartz and Matthew Wald, "Report on Loss of Shuttle Focuses on NASA Blunders," *The New York Times*, August 27, 2003.

[31]Douglas Jehl, "Senators Assail C.I.A. Judgments on Iraq's Arms as Deeply Flawed," *The New York Times*, July 10, 2004.

Work is far more than a market exchange of labor for dollars.... Other than in family relationships, nowhere in life do people invest so much of their time, their passion, and their imagination.

[Yet] U.S. law treats the employment relation as if it were nothing more than a market transaction, as if labor were nothing more than a commodity....

The acceptance of a relatively high unemployment rate in the United States as business-as-usual is philosophically linked to our commitment to the doctrine of employment-at-will. Other countries with lower unemployment rates are not only more committed to job-saving measures in the event of financial downturns, but also have erected a legal architecture that imposes more checks on discharge to begin with.... Most countries outside the United States require just cause for discharge, although they typically permit layoffs for economic reasons as well, usually requiring notice and severance packages, at least for mass layoffs.... Some countries adhere to an even more rigorous standard, limiting employer discretion to discharge. Germany, for example, prohibits discharge except for cause or "urgent social need," reflecting the country's view that job security is a legal entitlement....

Worker training and investment in human capital are perhaps the most important sorts of programs for countries that hope to compete effectively in a global market, and the United States lags far behind its European neighbors in such investments.... Employers [in the European Union] have discretion to hire and fire as necessary to respond to business cycles, but workers enjoy generous unemployment benefits and a commitment to worker training....

Countries that conceptualize work as a fundamental right recognize a species of property interest held by the worker in his or her job. Thus, employers must justify interference with the right, and notice and severance pay obligations are triggered where infringement is unavoidable. The U.S. rule clashes with the lived experience of workers, who believe that the jobs in which they have invested blood, sweat, and tears, often over a lengthy period of time, belong to them....

Why does the law treat work as if it does not matter? Because in U.S. work law, property rights trump labor. Capital investment matters; work does not. The human costs of that policy choice have never been clearer.[32]

Research: Find a country that has enshrined the right to work in its constitution. How would you expect employers to treat whistleblowers in that country? Find out how whistleblowers have in fact been treated.

Chapter Project

Stakeholder Ethics Role-Play

Guidelines: Appendix D

Name the stakeholders in this business ethics dilemma. Discuss possible choices for Nash in the light of law and ethical theory.

---

[32]Marion Crain, "Work Matter," *Kansas Journal of Law & Public Policy* 19(3). Spring 2010.

Desperate Air[33]

Desperate Air Corporation (DAC) flies routes along the U.S. East Coast. DAC acquired a number of hotels and undeveloped properties five years ago as part of a short-lived diversification strategy. DAC has recently experienced substantial losses, has a negative cash flow. Bankruptcy looms as a possibility unless high labor costs can be reduced and consumer confidence restored.

Benton Williams has just been brought in as CEO to revitalize DAC. Williams began by cutting back on middle management and by placing a one-year moratorium on hiring MBAs. Middle managers terminated by DAC and other airlines are having a tough time finding equivalent jobs.

DAC owns a large, undeveloped oceanfront property on the east coast of Florida. Williams directs George Nash, DAC's vice president of real estate, to find a buyer for the property to generate badly needed cash. After some effort, Nash identifies Fledgling Industries, a relatively new developer of retirement villas, as a good prospect. Fledgling is interested in finding a property on which it could build a complex of high-rise retirement condos featuring elaborate walking trails and outside recreational facilities.

DAC had conducted a full environmental audit of the property six months earlier and had discovered no problems. A copy of this report was given to the Fledgling representative, who also walked over the property and discovered no problems. The representative asked, "Anything I should know about?" Nash replied, "No problems."

As the negotiations progressed with Fledgling, Nash was approached by a longtime friend at DAC, Laura Devitt, who told him that there was now some highly toxic waste on the property. She said she heard this might be true through the rumor mill at the firm and that she had been curious enough to check things out. Walking around on the property one day, she had found several partially buried metal containers marked DANGER/BIOHAZARD. RADIOACTIVE MEDICAL WASTE. The containers were rusted where they were exposed; two were cracked, and their liquid contents were seeping onto the ground. Laura told Nash she wanted him to know about this because she was worried that innocent people could be hurt if the sale went through.

Nash contacted Williams, but before he could mention the containers to him, Williams interrupted and told him it was vital that the sale closed and that it be done as soon as possible. Nash consulted with a DAC lawyer who told him that under Florida law it is not necessary to disclose the existence of hazardous waste on commercial property as long as there hasn't been a fraudulent misstatement about the condition of the property.

Nash was troubled. Should he mention the hazardous materials to the Fledgling representative before he closed the sale? He knew Fledgling had been considering some other similar properties, and Nash thought that if he mentioned the toxic spill problem Fledgling would probably not go through with the sale. At the least, disclosure could delay the sale for months while the spill was investigated and potential liability problems considered. Nash figured that he would be unlikely ever to deal with Fledgling again regarding future real estate deals because DAC did not own any other properties that fit Fledgling's business needs.

The question of whether to close the sale immediately bothered Nash enough that he talked to his wife about it, and then prayed about what to do.

---

[33]This case was written by the late and much-beloved Professor Thomas Dunfee of the Wharton School at the University of Pennsylvania and is reprinted with his permission.

Valuing Diversity
Stereotyping versus Inclusion

Like and *difference* are quickening words, brooding and hatching. *Better* and *worse* are eggsucking words. They leave only the shell.

—URSULA LE GUIN

The events of 9/11 made "immigrant" synonymous with "terrorist."

—RUBEN J. GARCIA, "Ghost Workers in an Interconnected World" (2003)

Our obligation is to define the liberty of all, not to mandate our own moral code.

—JUSTICE ANTHONY KENNEDY, *Lawrence v. Texas* (2003)

Despite civil rights laws and Supreme Court rulings that span half a century, the remnants of past discriminatory practices survive. They can be seen in the difficulties that continue to plague small businesses owned by minorities and women, in the wage gap between men and women, in the differential treatment of whites and people of color who seek mortgages and homes, and in a national workforce in which jobs are still by and large segregated by race and gender. Stereotypes continue to create social and economic hardships for many in our society. In the early decades of the new millennium, the threat of terrorism and the globalization of business and labor have created new strains and concerns. These pressures, coupled with an economic crisis that began to unfold in 2007, have revived a national debate over immigration policies and the rights of noncitizens who live among us. By the time you read this text, there may even be major reform of the nation's immigration laws.

This chapter opens with a case that is one of the most controversial in years: the Supreme Court decision on same-sex marriage. The Equal Protection Clause of the U.S. Constitution and federal laws against discrimination based on race, religion, sex, national origin, and disability provide the legal backdrop. Readings that explore the importance of the workplace (especially to the most vulnerable) and the work–family dilemma round out the chapter.

Edith Windsor and Thea Spyer met in New York City in 1963 and began a long-term relationship. They registered as domestic partners when New York City gave that right to same-sex couples in 1993. Concerned about Spyer's health, the couple traveled to Canada in 2007 to marry, then came back to New York to live. The State of New York recognized their Ontario marriage as valid. When Spyer died in 2009, Windsor paid $363,053 in estate taxes and sought a refund. The Internal Revenue Service denied the refund, concluding that, under the Defense of Marriage Act [DOMA], Windsor was not a "surviving spouse." Windsor sued, arguing that DOMA was unconstitutional. In the case that follows, the Supreme Court explains why Windsor is right:

United States v. Windsor
United States Supreme Court, 2013
133 S.Ct. 2675

Justice KENNEDY ...

In 1996, as some States were beginning to consider the concept of same-sex marriage, and before any State had acted to permit it, Congress enacted the Defense of Marriage Act (DOMA)....

[Section 3 of DOMA amends federal law to define 'marriage' as] ... "only a legal union between one man and one woman as husband and wife, and the word 'spouse' [to refer only] to a person of the opposite sex who is a husband or a wife."...

When at first Windsor and Spyer longed to marry, neither New York nor any other State granted them that right.... [But gradually t]he limitation of lawful marriage to heterosexual couples, which for centuries had been deemed both necessary and fundamental, came to be seen in New York and certain other States as an unjust exclusion....

... DOMA, because of its reach and extent, departs from ... [a long] history and tradition of reliance on state law to define marriage....

The States' interest in defining and regulating the marital relation, subject to constitutional guarantees, stems from the understanding that marriage is more than a routine classification for purposes of certain statutory benefits. Private, consensual sexual intimacy between two adult persons of the same sex may not be punished by the State, and it can form "but one element in a personal bond that is more enduring." *Lawrence v. Texas (U.S. 2003)....* New York sought to give further protection and dignity to that bond. For same-sex couples who wished to be married, the State acted to give their lawful conduct a lawful status. This status is a far-reaching legal acknowledgment of the intimate relationship between two people, a relationship deemed by the State worthy of dignity in the community equal with all other marriages. It reflects both the community's considered perspective on the historical roots of the institution of marriage and its evolving understanding of the meaning of equality.

DOMA seeks to injure the very class New York seeks to protect. By doing so it violates basic due process and equal protection principles applicable to the Federal Government.... The Constitution's guarantee of equality "must at the very least mean that a bare congressional desire to harm a politically unpopular group cannot" justify disparate treatment of that group....

The history of DOMA's enactment and its own text demonstrate that interference with the equal dignity of same-sex marriages, a dignity conferred by the States in the exercise of their sovereign power, was more than an incidental effect of the federal statute. It was its essence. The House Report announced its conclusion that "it is both appropriate and necessary for Congress to do what it can to defend the institution of traditional heterosexual marriage...." The House concluded that DOMA expresses "both moral disapproval of homosexuality, and a moral conviction that heterosexuality better comports with traditional (especially Judeo–Christian) morality." The stated purpose of the law was to promote an "interest in protecting the traditional moral teachings reflected in heterosexual-only marriage laws." Were there any doubt of this far-reaching purpose, the title of the Act confirms it: The Defense of Marriage.

DOMA's operation in practice confirms this purpose.... DOMA writes inequality into the entire United States Code. The particular case at hand concerns the estate tax, but DOMA is more than a simple determination of what should or should not be allowed as an estate tax refund. Among the over 1,000 statutes and numerous federal regulations that DOMA controls are laws pertaining to Social Security, housing, taxes, criminal sanctions, copyright, and veterans' benefits.

DOMA's principal effect is to identify a subset of state-sanctioned marriages and make them unequal. The principal purpose is to impose inequality, not for other reasons like governmental efficiency.... [DOMA] places same-sex couples in an unstable position of being in a second-tier marriage. The differentiation demeans the couple, whose moral and sexual choices the Constitution protects ... and whose relationship the State has sought to dignify. And it humiliates tens of thousands of children now being raised by same-sex couples. The law in question makes it even more difficult for the children to understand the integrity and closeness of their own family and its concord with other families in their community and in their daily lives....

The power the Constitution grants it also restrains. And though Congress has great authority to design laws to fit its own conception of sound national policy, it cannot deny the liberty protected by the Due Process Clause of the Fifth Amendment.

... [T]he principal purpose and the necessary effect of this law are to demean those persons who are in a lawful same-sex marriage. This requires the Court to hold, as it now does, that DOMA is unconstitutional as a deprivation of the liberty of the person protected by the Fifth Amendment of the Constitution.

Justice SCALIA, dissenting.

... As I have observed before, the Constitution does not forbid the government to enforce traditional moral and sexual norms.... [It] neither requires nor forbids our society to approve of same-sex marriage, much as it neither requires nor forbids us to approve of no-fault divorce, polygamy, or the consumption of alcohol.

However, even setting aside traditional moral disapproval of same-sex marriage (or indeed same-sex sex), there are many perfectly valid—indeed, downright boring—justifying rationales for this legislation. Their existence ought to be the end of this case. For they give the lie to the Court's conclusion that only those with hateful hearts could have voted "aye" on this Act....

To choose just one of these defenders' arguments, DOMA avoids difficult choice-of-law issues that will now arise absent a uniform federal definition of marriage.... Imagine a pair of women who marry in Albany and then move to Alabama, which does not "recognize as valid any marriage of parties of the same sex." Ala.Code § 30-1-19(e)(2011). When the couple files their next federal tax return, may it be a joint one? Which State's law controls, for federal-law purposes: their State of celebration (which recognizes the marriage) or their State of domicile (which does not)? (Does the answer depend on whether they were just visiting in Albany?) Are these questions to be answered as a matter of federal common law, or perhaps by borrowing a State's choice-of-law rules? If so, *which* State's? And what about States where the status of an out-of-state same-sex marriage is an unsettled question under local law? DOMA avoided all of this uncertainty by specifying which marriages would be recognized for federal purposes. That is a classic purpose for a definitional provision....

... [T]o defend traditional marriage is not to condemn, demean, or humiliate those who would prefer other arrangements, any more than to defend the Constitution of the United States is to condemn, demean, or humiliate other constitutions.... In the majority's judgment, any resistance to its holding is beyond the pale of reasoned disagreement. To question its high-handed invalidation of a presumptively valid statute is to act (the majority is sure) with *the purpose* to "disparage," "injure," "degrade," "demean," and "humiliate" our fellow human beings, our fellow citizens, who are homosexual. All that, simply for supporting an Act that did no more than codify an aspect of marriage that had been unquestioned in our society for most of its existence—indeed, had been unquestioned in virtually all societies for virtually all of human history. It is one thing for a society to elect change; it is another for a court of law to impose change by adjudging those who oppose it *hostes humani generis,* enemies of the human race.

Justice ALITO, dissenting.

It is beyond dispute that the right to same-sex marriage is not deeply rooted in this Nation's history and tradition. In this country, no State permitted same-sex marriage until the Massachusetts Supreme Judicial Court held in 2003 that limiting marriage to opposite-sex couples violated the State Constitution. Nor is the right to same-sex marriage deeply rooted in the traditions of other nations. No country allowed same-sex couples to marry until the Netherlands did so in 2000....

The family is an ancient and universal human institution. Family structure reflects the characteristics of a civilization, and changes in family structure and in the popular understanding of marriage and the family can have profound effects. Past changes in the understanding of marriage—for example, the gradual ascendance of the idea that romantic love is a prerequisite to marriage—have had far-reaching consequences. But the process by which such consequences come about is complex, involving the interaction of numerous factors, and tends to occur over an extended period of time....

At present, no one—including social scientists, philosophers, and historians—can predict with any certainty what the long-term ramifications of widespread acceptance of same-sex marriage will be. And judges are certainly not equipped to make such an assessment....

... Windsor and the United States are really seeking to have the Court resolve a debate between two competing views of marriage.

The first and older view, which I will call the "traditional" or "conjugal" view, sees marriage as an intrinsically opposite-sex institution. [The members of Congress who have defended DOMA] note that virtually every culture, including many not influenced by the Abrahamic religions, has limited marriage to people of the opposite sex.... [and attempt] to explain this phenomenon by arguing that the institution of marriage was created for the purpose of channeling heterosexual intercourse into a structure that supports child rearing. Others explain the basis for the institution in more philosophical terms. They argue that marriage is essentially the solemnizing of a comprehensive, exclusive, permanent union that is intrinsically ordered to producing new life, even if it does not always do so.... While modern cultural changes have weakened the link between marriage and procreation in the popular mind, there is no doubt that, throughout human history and across many cultures, marriage has been viewed as an exclusively opposite-sex institution and as one inextricably linked to procreation and biological kinship.

The other, newer view is what I will call the "consent-based" vision of marriage, a vision that primarily defines marriage as the solemnization of mutual commitment—marked by strong emotional attachment and sexual attraction—between two persons. At least as it applies to heterosexual couples, this view of marriage now plays a very prominent role in the popular understanding of the institution.... Proponents of same-sex marriage argue that because gender differentiation is not relevant to this vision, the exclusion of same-sex couples from the institution of marriage is rank discrimination.

The Constitution does not codify either of these views of marriage.... Because our constitutional order assigns the resolution of questions of this nature to the people, I would not presume to enshrine either vision of marriage in our constitutional jurisprudence.

For these reasons, I would hold that § 3 of DOMA does not violate the Fifth Amendment. I respectfully dissent.

QUESTIONS

1. In your view, what is marriage really about: An intimate relationship? An economic partnership? A way to raise children? An institution that allows the state to "privatize dependency" by making spouses legally responsible for caring for each other and their children? Which Justice in *Windsor* comes closest to your own vision? To what extent does your vision affect how you feel about same-sex marriage?

2. What is at stake for opponents of same-sex marriage?

3. In March 2013, after a four-year review of the scientific literature, the American Academy of Pediatrics issued a policy statement that says same-sex marriage helps guarantee rights, benefits and long-term security for children. **Research:** Find out what the research shows about the impact of same-sex marriage on children.

4. **Research:** Find *Loving v. Virginia*, the 1967 Supreme Court case that held that statutes barring marriage across racial lines were unconstitutional. Did the Court employ any of the same arguments made by the majority in *Windsor?*

5. As this book goes to press, the following nations recognize same-sex marriage or marriage-like partnerships: Argentina, Belgium, Brazil, Canada, Denmark, France, Iceland, Ireland, Netherlands, New Zealand, Norway, Portugal, South Africa, Spain, Sweden, the United Kingdom, and Uruguay. What impact might wide-scale recognition of same-sex marriage have on business?

6. **Research:** When this case was decided, 11 states and the District of Columbia recognized same-sex marriage, and other states and municipalities recognized domestic partnerships but not marriage among same-sex couples. Find out how your state or municipality deals with same-sex partnerships.

7. **Research:** As this book goes to press, reaction to the *Windsor* decision is already in motion. In July 2013, the ACLU bought suit on behalf of 23 plaintiffs, challenging a Pennsylvania law that permits marriage only between a man and a woman and that denies the validity of same-sex marriages from other states. This case is the first of an expected wave of similar lawsuits.

And on the other side of the issue, in Indiana the governor is pushing for a state constitutional amendment outlawing same-sex marriage. What can you find out about the progress of such efforts at the state level—both in favor and against same-sex marriage—in the wake of *Windsor?*

■ ■ ■

EQUAL PROTECTION

[N]or shall any State deprive any person of life, liberty or property, without due process of law; nor deny to any person within its jurisdiction the equal protection of the law.

—FOURTEENTH AMENDMENT, United States Constitution

The Equal Protection Clause of the United States Constitution rests on the central notion that government must be reasonable, not arbitrary. It can sometimes treat classes of people differently, but only if the classification rests upon some difference that has a fair and substantial relation to the goal or purpose of the laws, so that "all persons in similar circumstances shall be treated alike." In other words, to treat two groups differently, the government must show that it has a strong enough reason for doing so. The strength of the government's justification varies depending on the type of discrimination involved.

Suppose the state of California passed a law that allowed all 16-year-olds, except those of Mexican ancestry, to apply for drivers' licenses. This law would discriminate between groups (Mexicans vs. non-Mexicans) that are otherwise similarly situated: They are all 16 years old, and they all want to get a driver's license. It distinguishes them based on an "immutable" characteristic, one that people can do nothing to change but has been used historically to oppress groups of people: their ethnicity. This kind of discrimination would be subjected to **"strict scrutiny"** by the courts. To satisfy the requirements of equal protection, California would have to prove that its law serves a very strong or **"compelling" state interest,** and that it is narrowly tailored. In other words, if California can achieve its important goal(s) in a less discriminatory way, it must. Strict scrutiny has been applied only to **suspect classifications,** such as race and ethnicity, and in cases where the classification infringes on such **fundamental freedoms** as the right of free speech or religion or the right to vote. It sets such a high barrier that few cases in our entire history have met the strict scrutiny standard. The best known case was the *Korematsu* decision, in which the Supreme Court upheld an executive order issued by President Franklin Roosevelt that sent Japanese Americans to live in internment camps during World War II.[1]

When the government discriminates in a way that is neither based on race or ethnicity nor involves a fundamental right, equal protection analysis is much looser and permits the **state action** so long as it has a **rational relationship** to a **valid government purpose.** For example, suppose the Chicago Department of Health decided to inspect restaurants of more than 1,000 square feet twice a year, while inspecting smaller restaurants only annually. The classification—larger versus smaller eating establishments—is not suspect, and there is no fundamental right to operate an unclean restaurant.

---

[1]*Korematsu v. United States*, 323 U.S. 214 (1944). In an effort to ameliorate the results of this later-regretted decision, Congress in 1988 ordered $20,000 in reparations to be paid to each living survivor of the detention camps. 50 U.S.C. App. §1989(b)(1988).

The enforcement program would probably be upheld as well tailored to promote a legitimate state goal. Most legislation can pass the rational relationship test.

Some classifications—notably gender—receive what has come to be known as **intermediate or heightened scrutiny,** a level of judicial inquiry that falls somewhere between strict scrutiny and the minimal rational relationship. When government treats males one way and females another, the courts must determine if there is a **substantial government reason** for the difference. If not, it will rule that the classification violates equal protection.

At times, government action that appears to be neutral, in fact may more negatively impact on one group than another. For example, a law granting veterans' preferences for government jobs would tend to favor men over women, simply because a higher percentage of men than women have served in the armed services. Under judicial interpretations of the Equal Protection Clause, such "facially neutral" laws are acceptable unless there is proof of an intent to discriminate against the group that is harmed by them.

■ ■ ■

The city of Hazleton is nestled in the coal mining region of northeastern Pennsylvania. After the September 11, 2001, terrorist attacks, many Latino families—legal and undocumented—left New York and New Jersey, seeking a better life, employment, and affordable housing in Hazleton. The sudden influx led to a sharp rise in population from 23,000 residents in 2000 to an estimated 30,000–33,000 by 2006. Although immigrants supported the local economy as consumers, renters, and taxpayers, the City adopted a series of ordinances aimed at combating what many viewed as the problems created by the presence of "illegal aliens." The ordinances (hereinafter, IIRA) made it unlawful to employ or rent to illegal aliens.

The following lawsuit challenged the IIRA on two grounds: that federal immigration law "preempted" the town's right to pass its own laws and that the IIRA violated the Equal Protection Clause. The case was filed by multiple plaintiffs: Pedro Lozano, a lawful permanent resident of the United States, who immigrated in January 2002 after 35 years as an officer in Colombia's National Police; Jose Luis and Rosa Lechuga, who immigrated illegally to the United States from Mexico in 1982 to forge a better life for themselves and their children (and who became lawful permanent residents through an amnesty program in the late 1980s); and several John Does who had lived in Hazleton unlawfully for a number of years. One of them, an architect in Colombia, had moved to Hazleton with his wife of 28 years. They were joined by the Hazleton Hispanic Business Association and other organizations.

Lozano v. City of Hazleton
United States District Court, M.D. Pennsylvania, 2007
496 F.Supp.2d 477

MUNLEY, District Judge.

Generally, under federal law, aliens can be present in the country as: 1) lawfully admitted non-immigrants, i.e., visitors, those in the country temporarily; and 2) lawful immigrants, lawful permanent residents, referred to sometimes as "green card holders." (Lawfully admitted for permanent residence status can be attained in various ways, including family or employment characteristics, the "green card lottery" or relief such as asylum.)

A third category of aliens present in the country are "undocumented aliens" who lack lawful immigration status. These aliens may have overstayed their time in the United States or may have entered the country illegally. The number of these individuals is approximately twelve million. Hazleton's use of the term "illegal alien" evidently is aimed at these individuals....

The equal protection "clause prohibits states from intentionally discriminating between individuals on the basis of race." "To prove intentional discrimination by a facially neutral policy, a plaintiff must show that the relevant decisionmaker (e.g., a state legislature) adopted the policy at issue 'because of,' not merely 'in spite of,' its adverse effects upon an identifiable group."...

Plaintiffs point to the testimony of immigration expert Marc Rosenblum, Ph.D., to argue that IIRA will "exacerbate the phenomenon of 'defensive hiring,' " the practice by which employers choose not to hire individuals who "might be illegal." ... Plaintiffs contend that these actions would more likely affect Latinos than members of other groups, since employers and landlords would ... operate on the assumption that illegal aliens are most likely Latinos....

No evidence indicates that Mayor Barletta approved of the ordinances because of their potential discriminatory impact.... [Therefore no] equal protection violation exists on those grounds.

As another ground for an equal protection challenge, plaintiffs have argued that IIRA improperly allows the City to consider race, ethnicity or national origin in enforcing it.... [T]he ordinances do not implicate a fundamental right or use a suspect classification ... since they declare that no complaint that uses race, ethnicity or national origin will be enforced. The plaintiffs also do not contend that they implicate a fundamental right, such as marriage. We need not examine the policy using strict scrutiny. Accordingly, our equal protection analysis must only explore whether IIRA has "a rational relationship to a legitimate state interest." We agree with the defendant that the ordinances meet this standard. As its interest in passing this legislation, the City claims that it was motivated by a desire to protect public safety by limiting the crimes committed by illegal immigrants in the city and to safeguard community resources expended on policing, education and health care. The City presented evidence that some crimes were committed by illegal aliens. Assuming that the City has the right to regulate the presence of illegal aliens in the city, the City program that provides penalties for those who employ or provide housing for undocumented persons in the City is rationally related to the aim of limiting the social and public safety problems caused by the presence of people without legal authorization in the City. We therefore find that Ordinance [IIRA] does not on its face violate the plaintiffs' right to the equal protection of the laws....

QUESTIONS

1. Although plaintiffs lost their equal protection argument, they won their case on other grounds. The trial court found that the Hazleton ordinance was invalid because it was preempted by federal immigration law. That holding was affirmed on appeal, 620 F.3d 170 (3d Cir. 2010). Who are the stakeholders in the Hazleton immigration debate? How does the Hazleton ordinance impact them? If you had been on Hazleton's City Council, how would you have voted? Why?

2. In 2007, when the Hazleton case was decided, 41 states adopted some kind of immigration laws. Most were aimed at discouraging undocumented

immigrants—by restricting the right to obtain a driver's license or the right to medical and other state aid. But it was Arizona's tough stance, signed into law in April 2010, that revved up the national debate. Faced with an estimated 460,000 illegal immigrants, miles of desert-border with Mexico, and what it deemed inadequate federal enforcement, Arizona took matters into its own hands. The new law required "aliens" to carry registration documents, empowered state law officers to arrest persons who could be deported, and required law officers to verify the immigration status of anyone violating a local law if they reasonably suspected the person was in the state illegally. And—much like Hazleton—Arizona went after workers. The law made it a misdemeanor for "an unauthorized alien to knowingly apply for work, solicit work in a public place or perform work as an employee or independent contractor in Arizona."

Arizona's law was challenged all the way to the Supreme Court, which found most of the law to be invalid because it interfered with the operation of federal law. Under then current federal law, only an employer—not the employee—could be held criminally responsible for hiring an unauthorized immigrant. In ruling to overturn the Arizona law, the majority explained that immigration policy can affect trade, investment, tourism and diplomatic relations for the entire Nation, and so must be uniform, and established at the federal level. Dissenting Justice Scalia argued "if securing its territory in this fashion is not within the power of Arizona, we should cease referring to it as a sovereign State." *United States v. Arizona*, 132 S.Ct. 2492 (2012). Should states be permitted to create their own immigration policies?

3. While some states were following Arizona's lead, others moved in the opposite direction. A growing number of city governments—from Trenton, New Jersey to San Francisco, California—have adopted community identification cards. The cards are meant to help illegal immigrants by easing access to services and to locations that require identification, such as public libraries, medical centers, charitable organizations, and public recreation areas. **Research:** Find out if your state or municipality has recently adopted any immigration laws. What are they?

4. Illegal immigrants are not eligible for Social Security benefits or the earned income tax credit. Since 1996, however, they can get a special Individual Tax Identification Number (ITIN) that enables them to pay federal taxes without a Social Security number. In 2011, the IRS processed some 2.9 million ITIN tax returns. What are the pros and cons of this approach?

5. E-Verify is an electronic system jointly operated by the Department of Homeland Security and the Social Security Administration. Most federal contractors and subcontractors doing work in the United States must use it, and it has become mandatory for employers in some states, including Arizona. Critics point to the time and resources that business must spend on E-Verify as burdensome to employers, and note that results are not always accurate due to name changes, variations of spelling, and system errors. One provision of an immigration reform bill being debated in 2013 would require all employers in the country within five years to use the E-Verify system. **Research:** Find out who supported this proposal and who opposed it. What were the arguments on either side? Has it become law?

6. **Research:** Mayor Barletta justified the ordinance with the claim that the influx of illegal immigrants to Hazelton was causing more crime there. The same argument was used to justify the Arizona law. What can you find out about the relationship between increased illegal immigration and criminal activity?

7. **Research:** Laws like the one in Hazelton, Pennsylvania, have been passed in towns across the country. In 2010, voters in Fremont, Nebraska, approved an ordinance requiring all renters to apply for an occupancy permit, and denying permits to illegal immigrants. This ordinance was challenged, and a federal District Court judge ruled that the part denying housing permits to people not in the U.S. legally was discriminatory. In June 2013 the 8th Circuit decided this case on appeal. What happened?

■　■　■

IS THE UNITED STATES "POST-RACIAL"?

Post-Racial America is a theoretical environment where the United States is void of racial preference, discrimination, and prejudice. (Wikipedia, June 29, 2010)

- **Poverty rate:** At no point since 1959 has the poverty rate for African Americans been less than double that of whites. According to the Kaiser Family Foundation website, the 61 million Americans living below the poverty line in 2012 included 13 percent of all white Americans, 35 percent of black Americans, and 33 percent of Hispanic Americans.
- **Wealth:** The gap in wealth between white and black Americans nearly doubled during the Great Recession. According to Census Bureau figures released in 2012, White Americans had 22 times ($110,729) the wealth of African Americans ($4,995), and 15 times that of Hispanic Americans ($7,424). Much of this is due to disparity in home ownership, and HUD reported in 2013 that discrimination in both rentals and home ownership persists. African Americans and Latinos have suffered the greatest declines in homeownership rates since the housing bust in 2007 and are more likely than whites to be turned down for mortgages.
- **Employment:** Although some people of color have ascended to the ranks of the professional class, African Americans and Latinos still disproportionately tend to occupy lower paying and lower status jobs while their unemployment rates exceed that of whites. The situation is most dire for African Americans, whose unemployment rate has been roughly double that of whites since the early 1970s.
- **Health:** African Americans have double the rates of white Americans of preventable hospitalizations and die younger and more often of heart disease, according to the Centers for Disease Control and Prevention in 2013.

○ THE CIVIL RIGHTS ACT OF 1964

It shall be unlawful for an employer to fail or refuse to hire or to discharge any individual or otherwise discriminate against any individual with respect to his compensation, terms, conditions, or privileges of employment because of such individual's race, color, religion, sex or national origin.

—TITLE VII, The Civil Rights Act of 1964[2]

---

[2] 42 U.S.C.A. § 2000(e).

Gradually, over time, the courts began to expand the meaning of the Constitutional right to equal protection—ruling in *Brown v. Board of Education* in 1954, for example, that segregated schools were unequal. But only the government is constrained by that clause. For almost a century after the Civil War, there was no federal law against discrimination by private individuals or businesses, and state laws were uneven in their scope and application.

After a decade of protest against segregation and in the wake of the assassination of President John F. Kennedy, the U.S. Congress passed comprehensive civil rights legislation that, for the first time, would address discrimination in the private sector, banning it in public accommodations (Title II) (hotels, motels, restaurants), in federally assisted programs (Title VII), and in employment (Title VII). The Fair Housing Act of 1968 extended protection against discrimination to rentals and home ownership, and Title IX of the Education Amendments of 1972 banned discrimination in education on the basis of sex.

Title VII, the provision dealing with employment, has no mention of the hot-button issues that emerged in the decades after its passage—affirmative action, sexual harassment, and same-sex marriage. Its mandate appears to be relatively straightforward: to end discrimination. Yet Title VII has been interpreted as banning not only outright differential treatment, but also practices that appear to be neutral (height and weight standards, educational requirements, for example), but which disproportionately disadvantage members of one race, sex, or religion ("disparate impact discrimination"). It empowers courts to correct discrimination when they find it: to order companies to hire, promote, adjust raises or benefits, or otherwise compensate those who have been wronged.

Affirmative Action

Four decades ago, when the Civil Rights Act was first enacted, some believed that to achieve equality within a reasonable time the nation would have to do more than simply end past discriminatory practices. In September 1965, President Lyndon B. Johnson signed Executive Order 11246, requiring companies that contracted with the federal government to "act affirmatively" to ameliorate the effects of past race discrimination. Many employers, either because they sought federal contracts or because they wanted to avoid Title VII liability, devised plans allowing race and gender to positively affect hiring or promotion decisions.

The seminal case on affirmative action in industry reached the U.S. Supreme Court in 1979. It grew out of an affirmative action plan adopted by Kaiser Aluminum and its unions five years earlier. At the time, fewer than 2 percent of Kaiser's skilled craft workers were black, even though the local workforce was approximately 39 percent black, largely due to past discriminatory practices. As a remedy, Kaiser agreed to establish a program to train production workers to fill craft openings and to earmark 50 percent of the openings for blacks. During the first year, seven black and six white trainees were selected from the plant. Brian Weber, a white man, was not, despite the fact that he had more seniority than any of the seven black trainees. He sued, arguing for a literal interpretation of the Civil Rights Act that would outlaw Kaiser's affirmative action plan because it did not treat whites the same as blacks. The Court rejected his claim in an opinion by Justice Brennan:

> *The purposes of [Kaiser Aluminum's affirmative action] plan mirror those of [Title VII of the Civil Rights Act.] Both were designed to break down old patterns of racial segregation and hierarchy. Both were structured to "open employment opportunities for Negroes in occupations that have been traditionally closed to them...."*

> *At the same time, the plan does not unnecessarily trammel the interests of the white employees. The plan does not require the discharge of white workers and their replacement with new black hires.... Nor does the plan create an absolute bar to the advancement of white employees; half of those trained in the program will be white. Moreover, the plan is a temporary measure; it is not intended to maintain racial balance, but simply to eliminate a manifest racial imbalance.* Steelworkers v. Weber, *443 U.S. 193 (1979).*

When the government takes race into account, even for purposes of affirmative action, the courts will scrutinize its classification to see if it violates the right to equal protection. This has occurred, for example, when cities create programs that give preferences to minority or female-owned contractors and when public universities consider race as an admissions factor.

■ ■ ■

For more than two decades Texas has been trying to assure greater diversity at its universities. The Top Ten Percent Law, adopted in 1997, guarantees admission to any public state college to all students in the top 10% of their Texas high school class. In addition, the flagship University of Texas relied on various special admissions procedures, including the one at issue in the next case, adopted for the entering class of 2004 to ensure a "critical mass" of minority students. Each applicant is scored based on both academic factors and personal factors which include, among others, race. Abigail Fisher, a white high school student, challenged the admissions process as violating her right to equal protection.

Fisher v. Texas
United States Supreme Court, 2013
133 S. Ct. 2411

Justice KENNEDY, delivered the opinion of the Court.

... Located in Austin, Texas, on the most renowned campus of the Texas state university system, the University is one of the leading institutions of higher education in the Nation. Admission is prized and competitive. In 2008, when petitioner sought admission to the University's entering class, she was 1 of 29,501 applicants. From this group 12,843 were admitted, and 6,715 accepted and enrolled. Petitioner was denied admission....

... In *Bakke*, [the first Supreme Court case dealing with affirmative action in higher education] the Court considered a system used by the medical school of the University of California at Davis. From an entering class of 100 students the school had set aside 16 seats for minority applicants. In holding this program impermissible under the Equal Protection Clause Justice Powell's opinion stated certain basic premises. First, "decisions based on race or ethnic origin by faculties and administrations of state universities are reviewable under the Fourteenth Amendment."... Any racial classification must meet strict scrutiny, for when government decisions "touch upon an individual's race or ethnic background, he is entitled to a judicial determination that the burden he is asked to bear on that basis is precisely tailored to serve a compelling governmental interest."

Next, Justice Powell identified one compelling interest that could justify the consideration of race: the interest in the educational benefits that flow from a diverse student body....

The attainment of a diverse student body ... serves values beyond race alone, including enhanced classroom dialogue and the lessening of racial isolation and stereotypes....

In *Gratz* [a 2003 case upholding affirmative action at the University of Michigan] and *Grutter*, [a companion case upholding affirmative action in law school admissions] the Court endorsed the precepts stated by Justice Powell....

[Justice Kennedy next explains the rules for affirmative action that grow out of *Baake, Gratz, and Grutter*.]

"... [A] race-conscious admissions program cannot use a quota system,"... but instead must "remain flexible enough to ensure that each applicant is evaluated as an individual and not in a way that makes an applicant's race or ethnicity the defining feature of his or her application...."

... [J]udicial review must begin from the position that "any official action that treats a person differently on account of his race or ethnic origin is inherently suspect."...

Once the University has established that its goal of diversity is consistent with strict scrutiny, however, there must still be a further judicial determination that the admissions process meets strict scrutiny in its implementation. The University must prove that the means chosen by the University to attain diversity are narrowly tailored to that goal ... [I]t remains at all times the University's obligation to demonstrate, and the Judiciary's obligation to determine, that admissions processes "ensure that each applicant is evaluated as an individual and not in a way that makes an applicant's race or ethnicity the defining feature of his or her application." ...

[S]trict scrutiny imposes on the university the ultimate burden of demonstrating, before turning to racial classifications, that available, workable race-neutral alternatives do not suffice.

Rather than perform this searching examination, however, the Court of Appeals held petitioner could challenge only "whether [the University's] decision to reintroduce race as a factor in admissions was made in good faith." And in considering such a challenge, the court would "presume the University acted in good faith" and place on petitioner the burden of rebutting that presumption.... [This was not strict scrutiny.]

Strict scrutiny must not be "'strict in theory, but fatal in fact,'" ... But the opposite is also true. Strict scrutiny must not be strict in theory but feeble in fact. In order for judicial review to be meaningful, a university must make a showing that its plan is narrowly tailored to achieve the only interest that this Court has approved in this context: the benefits of a student body diversity that "encompasses a ... broa[d] array of qualifications and characteristics of which racial or ethnic origin is but a single though important element." The judgment of the Court of Appeals is vacated, and the case is remanded for further proceedings consistent with this opinion....

Justice THOMAS, concurring.

... "Purchased at the price of immeasurable human suffering, the equal protection principle reflects our Nation's understanding that [racial] classifications ultimately have a destructive impact on the individual and our society."

... Aside from *Grutter*, the Court has recognized only two instances in which a "[p]ressing public necessity" may justify racial discrimination by the government.

First, in *Korematsu,* the Court recognized that protecting national security may satisfy this exacting standard.... Second, [in *Wygant v. Jackson Bd. of Ed.*] the Court has recognized that the government has a compelling interest in remedying past discrimination for which it is responsible ....

... [T]he pursuit of diversity as an end is nothing more than impermissible "racial balancing." ... Therefore, the *educational benefits* allegedly produced by diversity must rise to the level of a compelling state interest in order for the program to survive strict scrutiny.

Unfortunately for the University, the educational benefits flowing from student body diversity—assuming they exist—hardly qualify as a compelling state interest. Indeed, the argument that educational benefits justify racial discrimination was advanced in support of racial segregation in the 1950's, but emphatically rejected by this Court. And just as the alleged educational benefits of segregation were insufficient to justify racial discrimination then, see *Brown v. Board of Education,* (1954), the alleged educational benefits of diversity cannot justify racial discrimination today....

The University asserts, for instance, that the diversity obtained through its discriminatory admissions program prepares its students to become leaders in a diverse society.... The segregationists likewise defended segregation on the ground that it provided more leadership opportunities for blacks. This argument was unavailing.... Indeed, no court today would accept the suggestion that segregation is permissible because historically black colleges produced Booker T. Washington, Thurgood Marshall, Martin Luther King, Jr., and other prominent leaders....

The University also asserts that student body diversity improves interracial relations. In this argument, too, the University repeats arguments once marshaled in support of segregation....

Finally, while the University admits that racial discrimination in admissions is not ideal, it asserts that it is a temporary necessity because of the enduring race consciousness of our society ... [again echoing] the hollow justifications advanced by the segregationists. But these arguments too were unavailing. The Fourteenth Amendment views racial bigotry as an evil to be stamped out, not as an excuse for perpetual racial tinkering by the State....

My view of the Constitution is the one advanced by the plaintiffs in *Brown*: "[N]o State has any authority under the equal-protection clause of the Fourteenth Amendment to use race as a factor in affording educational opportunities among its citizens."... The Constitution does not pander to faddish theories about whether race mixing is in the public interest.... All applicants must be treated equally under the law, and no benefit in the eye of the beholder can justify racial discrimination....

I would overrule *Grutter* and hold that the University's admissions program violates the Equal Protection Clause because the University has not put forward a compelling interest that could possibly justify racial discrimination.

... I also believe that its use of race has little to do with the alleged educational benefits of diversity. I suspect that the University's program is instead based on the benighted notion that it is possible to tell when discrimination helps, rather than hurts, racial minorities.... The worst forms of racial discrimination in this Nation have always been accompanied by straight-faced representations that discrimination helped minorities.

Slaveholders argued that slavery was a "positive good" that civilized blacks and elevated them in every dimension of life....

A century later, segregationists similarly asserted that segregation was not only benign, but good for black students. They argued, for example, that separate schools protected black children from racist white students and teachers....

Following in these inauspicious footsteps, the University would have us believe that its discrimination is likewise benign. I think the lesson of history is clear enough: Racial discrimination is never benign....

I note that racial engineering does in fact have insidious consequences. There can be no doubt that the University's discrimination injures white and Asian applicants who are denied admission because of their race. But I believe the injury to those admitted under the University's discriminatory admissions program is even more harmful.

Blacks and Hispanics admitted to the University as a result of racial discrimination are, on average, far less prepared than their white and Asian classmates....

Tellingly, neither the University nor any of the 73 *amici* briefs in support of racial discrimination has presented a shred of evidence that black and Hispanic students are able to close this substantial gap during their time at the University....

Furthermore, the University's discrimination does nothing to increase the number of blacks and Hispanics who have access to a college education generally. Instead, the University's discrimination has a pervasive shifting effect. The University admits minorities who otherwise would have attended less selective colleges where they would have been more evenly matched. But, as a result of the mismatching, many blacks and Hispanics who likely would have excelled at less elite schools are placed in a position where underperformance is all but inevitable.... Setting aside the damage wreaked upon the self-confidence of these overmatched students, there is no evidence that they learn more at the University than they would have learned at other schools for which they were better prepared. Indeed, they may learn less....

Moreover, the University's discrimination "stamp[s] [blacks and Hispanics] with a badge of inferiority." It taints the accomplishments of all those who are admitted as a result of racial discrimination. ... [and] all those who are the same race as those admitted as a result of racial discrimination.

For the foregoing reasons, I would overrule *Grutter*. However, because the Court correctly concludes that the Court of Appeals did not apply strict scrutiny, I join its opinion.

Justice GINSBURG, dissenting.

... Petitioner urges that Texas' Top Ten Percent Law and race-blind holistic review of each application achieve significant diversity, so the University must be content with those alternatives. I have said before and reiterate here that only an ostrich could regard the supposedly neutral alternatives as race unconscious....

Texas' percentage plan was adopted with racially segregated neighborhoods and schools front and center stage.... It is race consciousness, not blindness to race, that drives such plans. As for holistic review, if universities cannot explicitly include race as a factor, many may "resort to camouflage" to "maintain their minority enrollment."... [I would affirm the lower court's holding that the Texas procedure is constitutional, without remanding for further review.]

QUESTIONS

1. Justice Kennedy begins his analysis by saying he takes three precedent cases as "given for purposes of deciding this case" they are *Bakke, Grutter,* and *Gratz.* What rules does he say those cases set forth? Why would Justice Thomas not "take them as given?"

2. Longtime advocate of affirmative action in higher education Lee C. Bollinger wrote this after the *Fisher* decision: "There is a moral and constitutional difference between policies that take into account the realities of America's troubled racial history, and pernicious forms of discrimination like Jim Crow laws."[3] Do you agree? How would Justice Thomas respond? Justice Ginsberg?

3. Some argue that society should focus on making higher education more accessible and affordable to those students who are economically disadvantaged, regardless of race. Do you agree?

4. **Research:** A number of states have outlawed race and gender-based affirmative action in government contracts and/or public education. A voter initiative in Michigan, for example, led to a ban of racial preferences in admissions to public universities. However, a legal challenge to the ban was upheld by a federal appeals court in *Schuette v. Coalition to Defend Affirmative Action* (2012). Shortly before this text went to press, the Supreme Court agreed to hear an appeal. Find out how the Court ruled.

5. Find out about the admissions policy at your school. Is race a factor? Economic hardship? Do you think the policy would withstand strict scrutiny? If not, how would you change it?

■ ■ ■

Religion

The impetus for the passage of Title VII was clearly the movement for civil rights for African Americans, and race discrimination remains the most common claim made to the Equal Employment Opportunity Commission (EEOC), the federal agency responsible for enforcing the law. But in recent years, charges based on religion and national origin have become increasingly common.

■ ■ ■

Kimberlie Webb is a practicing Muslim, employed by the City of Philadelphia as a police officer since 1995. On February 11, 2003, Webb requested permission from her commanding officer to wear a khimar or hijaab—the traditional headcover worn by Muslim women—while in uniform and on duty. Webb's headscarf would cover neither her face nor her ears, only her head and the back of her neck. Her request was denied because Police Department Directive 78 prescribes the approved Philadelphia police uniforms and equipment, and does not authorize any religious symbols or garb as part of the uniform.

Webb filed a complaint of religious discrimination under Title VII of the 1964 Civil Rights Act. While the matter was pending, she arrived at work wearing her headscarf, refused to remove it and was sent home. After repeating this three times, she was charged with insubordination and suspended for 13 days.

---

[3]Lee C. Bollinger, "A Long Slow Drift From Racial Justice," *The New York Times*, op-ed. June 25, 2013.

Webb v. City of Philadelphia

United States Court of Appeals, Third Circuit, 2009
562 F.3d 256

SCIRICA, Chief Judge.

In this employment discrimination case, the issue on appeal is whether a police officer's request to wear religious garb with her uniform could be reasonably accommodated without imposing an undue burden upon the City of Philadelphia. On the facts presented, the District Court held it could not.... We agree....

Title VII of the 1964 Civil Rights Act prohibits employers from discharging or disciplining an employee based on his or her religion. "Religion" is defined as "all aspects of religious observance and practice, as well as belief...." To establish a prima facie case of religious discrimination, the employee must show: (1) she holds a sincere religious belief that conflicts with a job requirement; (2) she informed her employer of the conflict; and (3) she was disciplined for failing to comply with the conflicting requirement. Once all factors are established, the burden shifts to the employer to show either it made a good-faith effort to reasonably accommodate the religious belief, or such an accommodation would work an undue hardship upon the employer and its business.

Title VII religious discrimination claims often revolve around the question of whether the employer can show reasonable accommodation would work an undue hardship. An accommodation constitutes an "undue hardship" if it would impose more than a *de minimis* cost on the employer....

[Next the court refers to precedents involving challenges to other dress and grooming codes. In the first, police officer Edward Johnson objected to a rule requiring male officers to wear their hair neat, clean, trimmed above their ears and without falling below the front of their headgear.]

In *Kelley v. Johnson (1976),* the Supreme Court characterized a police department's "[c]hoice of organization, dress, and equipment for law enforcement personnel...[as] a decision entitled to [a] ... presumption of legislative validity."... [In another case, the Court] found "the traditional outfitting of personnel in standardized uniforms encourages the subordination of personal preferences and identities in favor of the overall group mission." [For that reason, uniform policies are allowed.]

Our most recent decision in this area is *Fraternal Order of Police Newark Lodge No. 12 v. City of Newark* (3d Cir.1999). ... The Newark police department forbade police officers from growing beards but granted medical exceptions for beards as required by the Americans with Disabilities Act.... Two Muslim police officers, whose religion required they grow beards, filed suit contending their First Amendment rights were infringed upon by the no-beards policy. We agreed, holding that the police department must create a religious exemption to its "no-beards" policy to parallel its secular [medical] one....

Webb's religious beliefs are sincere, her employer understood the conflict between her beliefs and her employment requirements, and she was disciplined for failing to comply with a conflicting official requirement. Thus, the burden shifts and the City must establish that to reasonably accommodate Webb (that is, allow her to wear a headscarf with her uniform) would constitute an undue hardship. The City offered no accommodation, contending any accommodation would impose an undue hardship.

In the City's view, at stake is the police department's impartiality, or more precisely, the perception of its impartiality by citizens of all races and religions whom the police are charged to serve and protect. If not for the strict enforcement of Directive 78, the City contends, the essential values of impartiality, religious neutrality, uniformity, and the subordination of personal preference would be severely damaged to the detriment of the proper functioning of the police department. In the words of Police Commissioner Sylvester Johnson, uniformity "encourages the subordination of personal preferences in favor of the overall policing mission" and conveys "a sense of authority and competence to other officers inside the Department, as well as to the general public."

Commissioner Johnson identified and articulated the police department's religious neutrality (or the appearance of neutrality) as vital in both dealing with the public and working together cooperatively.... Commissioner Johnson's testimony was not contradicted or challenged by Webb at any stage in the proceedings....

As a paramilitary entity, the Philadelphia Police Department requires "a disciplined rank and file for efficient conduct of its affairs." Commissioner Johnson's thorough and uncontradicted reasons for refusing accommodations are sufficient to meet the more than *de minimis* cost of an undue burden....

[The District Court's dismissal of this case is affirmed.]

QUESTIONS

1. How does Philadelphia Police Directive 78 differ from the "No beards" policy at issue in the *Fraternal Order of Police* case? Why is that difference legally significant? Does it seem ethically distinguishable to you? Why or why not?

2. How would you deal with each of the following as head of human resources: (a) L, hired to work as a saleswoman/model, adheres to the store's "Look Policy," which directs associates to wear clothes similar to the brand sold. At the time, that consisted of very short skirts, ripped-up jeans, and slightly revealing tops—in short, sporty, laid-back California beach-style clothes that were sexy, form-fitting, and designed to show off body contours. Within a relatively short time, L is promoted. Several months later she converts to an Apostolic religion, which has dress regulations: below-the-knee skirts, forearms covered, no revealing cleavage. She begins to come to work in long skirts and loose fitting, long-sleeved shirts. (b) The new CEO of Jiffy-Lube decides to improve customer relations by implementing a grooming code that requires customer-contact employees to be clean-shaven and wear their hair neatly trimmed. Richard has been a practicing Rastafarian for a decade. His religion does not permit him to shave or cut his hair. He has worked as a technician at Jiffy-Lube for several years on both the upper and lower bays. The lower bay is colder, more dangerous, and it is harder to take breaks. Richards prefers the upper bay, where he also works as greeter, salesman, and cashier.

3. Dress and grooming codes have also been challenged as discriminatory on the basis of sex or race. Gender-specific rules are generally acceptable if based on social norms, unless they place an unfair burden on one sex. So, for example, having a "business dress" rule that requires men to wear ties and women to wear dresses or skirts would be legal, but requiring only one sex to wear a uniform would not. What problems can you identify with any of the following? (a) Bank does not allow male employees to wear earrings. (b) Casino hires men and women as cocktail waiters. Women are required to wear three-inch high heels and make-up; men are allowed to wear any "dress shoe." (c) A pizza company will make no exceptions to its rule that drivers

must be clean shaven. Sixty percent of African American men have a skin condition characterized by severely painful shaving bumps. The condition is cured by growing a beard.

4. As we saw in the *Webb* case, Title VII requires employers to reasonably accommodate the religious practices of employees, unless doing so would cause an undue hardship to the company. How would you handle the following: (a) A worker who has recently been promoted to driver for your company (United Parcel Service) has refused to make deliveries between sunset on Friday, his Sabbath, and sunset on Saturday. (b) One of your employees insists that her religion requires her to convert others; she persists in bringing religious tracts to the office, even though co-workers are annoyed when they find them in their workspace.

■ ■ ■

National Origin

During the past four decades, the United States has experienced the largest wave of immigration in its history, with at least one-third of new immigrants coming from Mexico. Census Bureau figures show that nearly 12.8 percent of the 308 million people living in the United States in 2010 were born somewhere else. Increasingly, the new migrants are finding homes throughout the country from the upper Midwest to the Rocky Mountain states, as well as the more traditional landing spots along the borders and coasts.

In an economy still adjusting to globalization, the information revolution, and the shift from production to services, there is widespread debate about the new influx of foreign-born workers. Here we look at one site of that contest: rules requiring English as the only language to be used at a workplace.

EEOC GUIDELINE ON ENGLISH-ONLY WORKPLACE RULES

1. An English-only rule that applies at all times is considered "a burdensome term and condition of employment" [in violation of Title VII] and
2. An English-only rule that applies only at certain times does not violate Title VII if the employer can justify the rule by showing business necessity.

Rationale for Rules

1. English-only policies may "create an atmosphere of inferiority, isolation, and intimidation" that could make a "discriminatory working environment";
2. English-only rules adversely impact employees with limited or no English skills ... by denying them a privilege enjoyed by native English speakers: the opportunity to speak at work;
3. English-only rules create barriers to employment for employees with limited or no English skills;
4. English-only rules prevent bilingual employees whose first language is not English from speaking in their most effective language; and the risk of discipline and termination for violating English-only rules falls disproportionately on bilingual employees as well as persons with limited English skills.

■ ■ ■

When the city of Altus, Oklahoma, adopted an English-only rule for its employees, 29 workers complained to the EEOC. All are Hispanic, the only significant national-origin minority group affected by the policy. All are bilingual, each speaking fluent English and Spanish. Unable to resolve the dispute, the EEOC granted them a right to sue. The trial court, however, threw out their case, granting summary judgment that would allow the city to enforce its new regulations. The employees appealed. Their claim: rights under Title VII of the Civil Rights Act of 1964 and the First Amendment to the U.S. Constitution were violated.

Maldonado v. City of Altus
U.S. Court of Appeals, Tenth Circuit, 2006
433 F.3d 1294

HARTZ, Circuit Judge.

In the spring of 2002 the City's Street Commissioner, Defendant Holmes Willis, received a complaint that because Street Department employees were speaking Spanish, other employees could not understand what was being said on the City radio. Willis informed the City's Human Resources Director, Candy Richardson, of the complaint, and she advised Willis that he could direct his employees to speak only English when using the radio for City business.

Plaintiffs claim that Willis instead told the Street Department employees that they could not speak Spanish at work at all and informed them that the City would soon implement an official English-only policy....

In July 2002 the City promulgated the following official policy:

To insure effective communications among and between employees and various departments of the City, to prevent misunderstandings and to promote and enhance safe work practices, all work related and business communications during the work day shall be conducted in the English language with the exception of those circumstances where it is necessary or prudent to communicate with a citizen, business owner, organization, or criminal suspect in his or her native language due to the person or entity's limited English language skills. The use of the English language during work hours and while engaged in City business includes face to face communication of work orders and directions as well as communications utilizing telephones, mobile telephones, cellular telephones, radios, computer or e-mail transmissions, and all written forms of communications.... This policy does not apply to strictly private communications between co-workers while they are on approved lunch hours or breaks or before or after work hours while the employees are still on City property if City property is not being used for the communication ... [or to] strictly private communication between an employee and a family member.... Employees are encouraged to be sensitive to the feelings of their fellow employees, including a possible feeling of exclusion if a co-worker cannot understand what is being said in his or her presence when a language other than English is being utilized....

Plaintiffs allege that the policy created a hostile environment for Hispanic employees, causing them "fear and uncertainty in their employment," and subjecting them to racial and ethnic taunting. They contend "that the English-only rule created a hostile environment because it pervasively—every hour of every work day—burdened, threatened, and demeaned the [Plaintiffs] because of their Hispanic origin." Plaintiffs each stated in their affidavits:

> The English-only policy affects my work environment every day. It reminds me every day that I am second-class and subject to rules for my employment that the Anglo employees are not subject to....

Evidence of ethnic taunting included Plaintiffs' affidavits stating that they had "personally been teased and made the subject of jokes directly because of the English-only policy...." [Plaintiff Tommy] Sanchez also testified that an Altus police officer taunted him about not being allowed to speak Spanish by saying, "Don't let me hear you talk Spanish." As evidence that such taunting was not unexpected by management, Lloyd Lopez recounted in his deposition that Street Commissioner Willis told ... him [and an Hispanic co-worker] that he was informing them of the English-only policy in private because Willis had concerns about "the other guys making fun of [them]."

I. Discussion of Civil Rights Violations: Disparate Impact

... One might say that Plaintiffs have not been subjected to an unlawful employment practice because they are treated identically to non-Hispanics. They claim no discrimination with respect to their pay or benefits, their hours of work, or their job duties. And every employee, not just Hispanics, must abide by the English-only policy....

[But in] *Griggs v. Duke Power Co.* (1971) the Supreme Court held that Title VII "proscribes not only overt discrimination but also practices that are fair in form, but discriminatory in operation." These kinds of claims, known as disparate-impact claims, "involve employment practices that are facially neutral in their treatment of different groups but that in fact fall more harshly on one group than another and cannot be justified by business necessity."...

Plaintiffs have produced evidence that the English-only policy created a hostile atmosphere for Hispanics in their workplace.... [A]ll the Plaintiffs stated that they had experienced ethnic taunting as a result of the policy and that the policy made them feel like second-class citizens....

[According to the Supreme Court in the *Griggs* case] the touchstone is business necessity. If an employment practice which operates to [discriminate against a protected minority] cannot be shown to be related to job performance, the practice is prohibited.

Defendants' evidence of business necessity in this case is scant. As observed by the district court, "[T]here was no written record of any communication problems, morale problems, or safety problems resulting from the use of languages other than English prior to implementation of the policy." And there was little undocumented evidence. Defendants cited only one example of an employee's complaining about the use of Spanish prior to implementation of the policy ... "[and city officials] could give no specific examples of safety problems resulting from the use of languages other than English...." Moreover, Plaintiffs produced evidence that the policy encompassed lunch hours, breaks, and private phone conversations; and Defendants conceded that there would be no business reason for such a restriction....

[Held] In our view, the record contains sufficient evidence of intent to create a hostile environment that the summary judgment on those claims must be set aside...[and the plaintiffs may proceed to trial on their Title VII claims.]

II. First Amendment Claims

... Perhaps the City's English-only rule suffers from First Amendment shortcomings. But on the evidence and contentions presented by Plaintiffs, their challenge fails.... They have not shown that their speech precluded by the English-only rule includes communications on matters of public concern. Nor have they produced evidence that the English-only rule was intended to limit communications on matters of public concern [as required by the Supreme Court precedent case, *Pickering*.]...

Here, we do not question that Plaintiffs take pride in both their Hispanic heritage and their use of the Spanish language, nor do we question the importance of that pride. What we do question, because there is no supporting evidence, is that by speaking Spanish at work they were intending to communicate that pride, much less "to inform [an] issue [so] as to be helpful ... in evaluating the conduct of government."... **[Held:** plaintiff's First Amendment claims are dismissed.]

SEYMOUR. J., concurring [in Part I, Discrimination] and dissenting [in Part II, First Amendment.]

... [I] part company with the majority in determining whether Plaintiffs' speech touched on a matter of public concern.... [It is] reasonable to assume that the alleged "content" of Plaintiffs' speech, namely, their choice to converse in Spanish rather than English, is pride in their cultural and ethnic identity and heritage. Plaintiffs have thus indicated that their desire to speak Spanish is, itself, a matter of public concern.

In arguing that their choice of language is itself a statement of public concern, Plaintiffs find support in *Hernandez v. New York* (1991), [where the Supreme Court] recognized the power of language (as well as a person's decision to speak a particular language as opposed to another) to convey special meaning as well as to engender conflict and disclose bigotry.

> ... [A] person's choice of language can convey a message—and a powerful one at that.... [L]anguage choice and ethnic or cultural identity can be inextricably intertwined both in the mind of the speaker and in the minds of those who hear him....

Mr. Sanchez himself characterized the content of the prohibited speech as an expression of community identity and ethnic heritage, of solidarity and pride, in the face of contravening forces. In other words, an apter analogy may be wearing a tee-shirt proclaiming "proud to be a Yankees fan" to a rally for the Boston Red Sox, because that analogy describes the context as well as the content of the speech.

With respect to context, the record contains evidence of months of tension between Hispanic and non-Hispanic City employees. Prior to the adoption of the English-only policy, several Hispanic employees had filed complaints of discrimination and retaliation. The City, in response, had hired an outside human resources consultant.... Numerous individuals, both Hispanic and non-Hispanic, were involved in an ongoing and evolving discussion on race relations, and ... all levels of City government were involved, including the mayor, the City administrator, the City's director of human resources, and many City department heads and supervisors.... [T]he general public was aware of and interested in the English-only policy and its effects.... In one [news] article, the mayor was quoted as referring to the Spanish language as "garbage." That he later claimed in his deposition to have been misquoted is irrelevant to the question of whether his misquote further inflamed public debate over the English-only policy and its perceived intent. Moreover, the mayor's testimony that he eventually apologized to the City council for the misquote, underscores the seriousness and the pervasiveness of the whole issue, namely, the apparently degenerating relations between Hispanics and non-Hispanics in the City of Altus. At a certain point then, this dispute evolved from a situation involving City employees to a wider discussion of discrimination, race relations, and the power of expressions of ethnic identity to elicit strong emotions on either side.

In sum, this is not a case about a single employee wearing a tee-shirt proclaiming "proud to be Hispanic!" or "proud to be Irish!" or "proud to be Vietnamese!" This is a case about a large group of employees (twenty-nine Hispanic City employees) desiring to wear such tee-shirts when an even larger number of their fellow employees are wearing (or perceived to be wearing) tee-shirts proclaiming "annoyed by Hispanics!" or "sick and tired of the Irish!" or "threatened by Vietnamese!" The record suggests this was a situation in which the right to speak one's chosen language became an expression of pride and resistance and identity....

[I]t is important to remember what this case is not about. This is not a case involving the sole complaint of one employee in a City with no history of racial tensions. This is not a case involving one employee's complaint against one or two of his supervisors. This is a case involving more than two dozen employees in a diverse workforce in a City with a recent history of racial and national origin discrimination complaints. This is a case in which the City, fully cognizant of that history, nonetheless adopted a broadly-sweeping policy that its director of human resources admitted in her deposition testimony could offend Hispanic employees and further inflame racial tensions. This is a case in which we have upheld, for summary judgment purposes, Plaintiffs' race and national origin discrimination claims against the City for restricting the very speech Plaintiffs want to use. In light of these facts, it seems incorrect to characterize Plaintiffs' expression of pride in their ethnic identity as reflecting merely "personal" or "internal" grievances. It is also difficult to see how that expression of pride does not add to the public debate on diversity or "sufficiently inform" the public that there are two equally vocal and passionate sides to that debate.... To the contrary, plaintiffs have expressed a desire to speak Spanish in order to sustain their community's history of linguistic and ethnic diversity and to preserve that history in the everyday details of their lives. The City's ban on Spanish from the workplace creates a public space where Spanish speakers arguably do not feel welcome. In such a context, it is not hard to imagine the power of a simple "buenos dias" to convey resistance to that effort and hope for the future.... [I dissent.]

QUESTIONS

1. Who might be hurt by English-only rules? Who tends to benefit? Can such rules create or reinforce stereotypes?

2. Articulate the kind of discrimination claim made by the plaintiffs in this case. What will they have to prove at trial? How will the city defend itself? How important is it that Plaintiffs are all bilingual?

3. Would there be a business necessity for requiring airline pilots to speak English in all air traffic communications within the United States? Having computer software salespeople speak English in all management meetings? What about an English-only rule for workers on a semiconductor assembly line or an airline baggage handling area? Is there ever a business necessity for requiring English to be spoken during non-work hours?

4. What reasons might an employer have for preferring to hire people who don't speak English? What ethical issues might arise in such circumstances?

5. Title IX prohibits discrimination on the basis of race, color, religion, sex, or national origin in education. Should a school be allowed to prohibit students from speaking a language other than English in school? Should it matter whether it is a public or private school? See *Rubio v. Turner Unified School District No. 202,* 453 F. Supp.2d 1295 (D. Kansas, 2006) and *Silva v. St. Anne's Catholic School,* 595 F.Supp.2d 1171 (D.Kan.2009).

6. Dissenting Judge Seymour mentions the history behind the adoption of the city's English-only policy, a history fraught with conflict. Can you think of a way this litigation might have been avoided? Suppose you were the HR consultant hired to lead discussions on a possible English-only policy for the city. Who would you try to bring into the conversation? How might you enable the different stakeholders to become active, respectful participants? What information might you want to access to assist their decision-making process?

■ ■ ■

Sex Discrimination

Sexual Harassment   Sexual harassment has a familiar ring today. But the notion that any type of private discrimination based on sex could be grounds for lawsuits was new at the time the Civil Rights Act of 1964 was under consideration by Congress. Then, opponents of the law attempted to block its passage by amending it to cover "sex," a ploy they believed would expose the whole concept of the law as absurd. Their strategy backfired; the Civil Rights Act did pass, and sex discrimination became illegal almost as an ironic afterthought. Yet the law made no mention of sexual harassment and never identified it as a form of sex discrimination. By the late 1970s, successful plaintiffs had convinced the courts that what feminist lawyer Catharine MacKinnon described as the "unwanted imposition of sexual requirements in the context of a relationship of unequal power" must indeed be classified as sex discrimination—an understanding that receives widespread support today.

Hostile Environment: Proving a **Prima Facie Case**   What has been called " *quid pro quo*" harassment—sexual favors in exchange for something concrete such as a job or a raise—is easily identifiable as illegal sex discrimination and employers are automatically responsible for such "tangible" employment retaliation. Much harder to define and far more controversial are situations involving what has come to be known as "hostile environment" sexual harassment.

As is true in every civil lawsuit, a plaintiff's first burden is to demonstrate the possibility of winning by offering evidence to support each element of her claim. This is called a *prima facie* case. The defendant will then offer contrary evidence, witnesses who can discredit the plaintiff's allegations or support the defendant's own claims and affirmative defenses. To make out a *prima facie* case of hostile environment sexual harassment, a plaintiff must show that (1) she is a member of a protected group, (2) she was the subject of unwelcome sexual harassment, (3) the harassment occurred because of her sex, and (4) the harassment was sufficiently severe or pervasive to alter the terms and conditions of her employment.

Member of a Protected Group   The first element is easy to prove in most cases. The Supreme Court has made clear that men, as well as women, are "protected" by Title VII—so long as they are targeted based on their maleness or femaleness—and that a supervisor can be responsible for sexually harassing a person of the same sex. Each of the other elements, however, have created knotty problems for the lower courts.

Unwelcomeness   Plaintiffs must prove that the behavior that creates a hostile environment is not welcome. As courts try to determine "welcomeness," they consider the entire range of circumstances. They may take into account, for example, a plaintiff's manner of speaking, behaving, or dressing. For a female plaintiff, this could mean that the tight fit of her sweaters or her taste in jokes may be viewed as "provocative," as inviting the behavior of which she complains.

Some have argued that the standard used to measure hostile environment and whether a victim found it unwelcome is male-biased. While studies have repeatedly demonstrated that there is a great disparity between the way men and women view being approached sexually at work—men are typically flattered; women insulted—many in our society make the assumption that women tend to enjoy and welcome sexualized behavior. The law allows that assumption to be overcome, but the burden of proof is on the plaintiff. At the same time, courts have said that although men are stereotypically thought to always welcome women's advances, a male plaintiff has the right to prove that a woman's advances were in fact unwelcome.

Because of ... One's Sex   Since hostile environment suits are essentially claims of sex discrimination, a plaintiff must establish that whatever harassment took place did so "because of" her sex. This element can be proven even if the particular plaintiff is not targeted. In one case the court found harassment based on sex where the office atmosphere was akin to a "guys locker room," rife with sexually explicit comments not aimed directly at the plaintiff.[4]

This requirement is hardest to meet when both harasser and harassed are of the same sex. Some same-sex claims sound relatively familiar: for example, a male supervisor makes sexual advances, motivated by sexual desire, toward a male subordinate, or a female supervisor is professional and friendly with her male employees, but constantly treats other women in the workplace with hostility. In those cases, it is relatively easy for a judge to find that the treatment is "based on sex."

Courts are not in agreement as to how to deal with cases involving complaints that co-workers mistreat an employee because he or she is *perceived to be gay*. Some consider differential treatment of an "effeminate" male to be "because of" his sex, since the individual was punished for deviating from gender stereotypes. This view follows the logic of *Price Waterhouse v. Hopkins,*[5] where the Supreme Court ruled that it was discriminatory

---

[4]*Gallagher v. C.H. Robinson Worldwide,* Inc. 567 F.3d 263 (6th Cir. 2009).
[5]*Price Waterhouse v. Hopkins,* 490 U.S. 228 (1989).

HIGHLIGHTS IN THE EVOLVING LAWS OF SEX HARRASSMENT

- **Congress Sets the Stage:** In 1964, Title VII of the Civil Rights Act was passed, outlawing discrimination in hiring, firing, and terms and conditions of employment based on race, color, religion, sex, or national origin. There is no mention of sexual harassment.

- **Early Lower Court Cases:** The first reported case of sexual harassment was filed by two women who resigned because of constant sexual advances from their boss. The court denied their claim, describing the supervisor's conduct as "nothing more than a personal proclivity, peculiarity, or mannerism." *Corne v. Bausch & Lomb*, 390 F.Supp. 161 (D. Ariz., 1975). But in a breakthrough case, a woman whose job was abolished after she repulsed the sexual advances of her boss sued and won. ("But for her womanhood the woman would not have lost her job.") *Barnes v. Costle*, 561 F.2d 983 (D.C. Cir. 1977).

- **EEOC Posts Guidelines:** In 1980, EEOC outlined two types of illegal sexual harassment: *quid pro quo* and hostile environment. *Quid pro quo* refers to demands for sexual favors with threats attached; either the victim gives in or loses a tangible job benefit—even the job itself. Hostile environment refers to behavior that creates an intimidating or abusive workplace atmosphere.

- **Supreme Court Speaks:** In its first case involving sexual harassment, the Court recognized a claim for the hostile environment form where behavior is "sufficiently severe or pervasive to alter the conditions of the victim's employment and create an abusive working environment," *Meritor Savings Bank v. Vinson*, 106 S.Ct. 2399 (1986). In a later case, the Supreme Court explained that a victim need not prove psychological injury to win, "so long as the environment would reasonably be perceived, and is perceived, as hostile or abusive." *Harris v. Forklift Systems*, 510 U.S. 17 (1993).

- **Supreme Court and Employer Liability:** In 1998, the Court clarified that employers are liable for misuse of supervisory authority—whether or not threats are carried out. Where tangible employment retaliation—for example, termination, demotion, or undesirable reassignment—is carried out or even threatened, the employer is automatically liable. In cases where a plaintiff claims a hostile environment exists, the employer can successfully defend by proving (1) it took reasonable care to prevent and correct promptly any sexually harassing behavior, and (2) the employee "unreasonably failed to take advantage of any preventive or corrective opportunities." *Faragher v. City of Boca Raton* 118 S.Ct. 2275 (1998) and *Burlington Industries v. Ellerth*, 118 S.Ct. 2257 (1998).

- **Same-Sex Harassment:** A year later, the Supreme Court held that Title VII protects men as well as women, and the fact that both plaintiff and defendant are of the same sex does not necessarily prevent a claim of sex discrimination. *Oncale v. Sundowner Offshore Services, Inc.*, 118 S.Ct. 998 (1999).

- **Constructive Discharge:** When a supervisor's official act precipitates a constructive discharge—making the abusive working environment so intolerable that a reasonable person would be compelled to resign—the employer is strictly liable ("aggravated hostile environment"). *Pennsylvania State Police v. Suders*, 124 S.Ct. 2342 (2004).

- **A Truncated Definition of "Supervisor":** A company is not strictly liable for sexual or racial harassment unless the person responsible had authority to "hire, fire, demote, promote, transfer or discipline." *Vance v. Ball State University*, 133 S.Ct. 2434 (2013). Justice Breyer joined the three female Justices in a vigorous dissent, labeling this ruling a "remarkable resistance to the thrust of our prior decisions, workplace realities, and the EEOC's Guidance."

to deny a woman a partnership because she was not sufficiently feminine and "needed to go to charm school." Other judges argue that such findings stretch Title VII beyond its intended scope by effectively outlawing discrimination based on sexual orientation.

Sufficiently Severe or Pervasive   Case law tells us that an employee does not have to put up with discriminatory intimidation, ridicule, and insult so severe or pervasive that it creates an abusive working environment. Courts are supposed to determine when this standard has been met by looking at all—the "totality" of—the circumstances including:

> *[The] frequency of the discriminatory conduct; its severity; whether it is physically threatening or humiliating, or a mere offensive utterance; and whether it unreasonably interferes with an employee's work performance. [S]imple teasing, offhand comments, and isolated incidents (unless extremely serious) will not amount to discriminatory changes in the terms and conditions of employment.*[6]

But which factors to consider, and how to weigh them, is a matter of dispute among the various federal courts of appeals. One federal trial judge explains:

> *The question of what is "sufficiently severe" sexual harassment is complicated because: (a) courts routinely remind plaintiffs that "Title VII is not a federal civility code," (b) the modern notion of acceptable behavior ... has been coarsening over time; therefore, (c) what courts implicitly ask the "Title VII victim" to tolerate as mere "boorish behavior" or "workplace vulgarity" must, once placed in the contemporary context, account for any "Slouch Toward Gomorrah" societal norms might take. At the same time, this entire area of law is enervated by vague, almost circular standards.... [I]f behavior offends the particular judge ... then it must be "discriminatory."...*
>
> *As the case law has grown to show, determining the intensity/quantity of sexual gesturing, touching, bantering, and innuendo that it takes to render a work environment sexually hostile is now no less difficult than "trying to nail a jellyfish to the wall."...*[7]

Vicki Schultz has been a strong advocate for changes that would make the workplace more equitable and hospitable to women. In the next reading, Schultz is critical of employer attempts to wipe out sexual harassment by harshly and promptly punishing harassers—a process she dubs "sanitization," and which she believes causes problems of its own, further distancing us from real solutions to gender inequality.

The Sanitized Workplace[8]

Vicki Schultz

... [T]he focus on sexual conduct has encouraged organizations to treat harassment as a stand-alone phenomenon—a problem of bad or boorish men who oppress or offend women—rather than as a symptom of larger patterns of sex segregation and inequality....

[T]he emphasis on eliminating sexual conduct encourages employees to articulate broader workplace harms as forms of sexual harassment, obscuring more structural problems that may be the true source of their disadvantage. Thus, women may

---

[6]*Harris v. Forklift Systems, Inc.*, 510 U.S. 17 (1993).

[7]*Breda v. Wolf Camera, Inc.*, 148 F.Supp.2d 1371 (S.D.Ga. 2001).

[8]*Vicki Schultz*, "The Sanitized Workplace," 112 Yale L. J. 2061 (2003). Reprinted by permission of The Yale Law Journal Company and William S. Hein Company from *The Yale Law Journal*, Vol. 112, pages 2061–2193.

complain about sexual jokes, when their real concern is a caste system that relegates them to low-status, low-pay positions.... Even more worrying is the prospect that some employees may make allegations of sexual harassment that disproportionately disadvantage racial and sexual minorities.... [W]hite women who enjoy sexual banter and flirtation with their white male co-workers may regard the same conduct as a form of sexual harassment when it comes from men of color. Heterosexual men who willingly engage in sexual horseplay with men whom they regard as heterosexual may be quick to label the same overtures as harassment when they come from openly gay men. [This suggests] that one-size-fits-all, acontextual prohibitions on sexual conduct may give individual employees, and management as a whole, too much power to enforce sexual conformity in the name of pursuing a project of gender equality that has been all but abandoned.

The truth is that managers cannot succeed in banishing sexuality from the workplace: They can only subject particular expressions of it to surveillance and discipline. Although some groups suffer more than others when this occurs, everyone loses.... With the decline of civil society, the workplace is one of the few arenas left in our society where people from different walks of life can come to know one another well. Because people who work together come into close contact with each other for extended periods for the purpose of achieving common goals, work fosters extraordinarily intimate relationships of both the sexually charged and the more platonic varieties.... We cannot expect diverse groups of people to form close bonds and alliances—whether sexual or nonsexual—if they must be concerned that reaching out to one another puts them at risk of losing their jobs or their reputations....

The larger question is whether we as a society can value the workplace as a realm alive with personal intimacy, sexual energy, and "humanness" more broadly. The same impulse that would banish sexuality from the workplace also seeks to suppress other "irrational" life experiences such as birth and death, sickness and disability, aging, and emotion of every kind. But the old Taylorist dream of the workplace as a sterile zone in which workers suspend all their human attributes while they train their energies solely on production doesn't begin to reflect the rich, multiple roles that work serves in people's lives. For most people, working isn't just a way to earn a livelihood. It's a way to contribute something to the larger society, to struggle against their limits, to make friends and form communities, to leave their imprint on the world, and to know themselves and others in a deep way.... [W]ork isn't simply a sphere of production. It is also a source of citizenship, community, and self-understanding.

Just as individual employees may express themselves or embroider intimate relations through sexual language and conduct, so too may employees as a group resort to sexual interactions to alleviate stress or boredom on the job, to create vital forms of community and solidarity with each other, or to articulate resistance to oppressive management practices. Research suggests that workplace romance may even increase productivity in some circumstances.

Contrary to prevailing orthodoxy, such uses of workplace sexuality do not always harm or disadvantage women: A lot depends on the larger structural context in which the sexuality is expressed. As a well-accepted body of systematic social science research demonstrates, women who enter jobs in which they are significantly underrepresented often confront hostility and harassment from incumbent male workers, and in some settings the men use sexual conduct as a means of marking the women as "different" and out of place. However, a new body of sociological research suggests that women who work in more integrated, egalitarian settings often willingly participate and take pleasure in sexualized interactions—probably because their numerical strength gives them the power to help shape the sexual norms and culture to their own liking. Rather than presuming that women will always find sexual conduct offensive, this research suggests that we should ensure that women are fully integrated into equal jobs and positions of authority, thus giving them the power to decide for themselves what kind of work cultures they want to have....

I would like to see organizations abandon sensitivity training in favor of incorporating their harassment policies into broader efforts to achieve integration and equality throughout the firm. Along similar lines, I urge that employers forgo measures to prohibit or discourage sexual or dating relationships among employees and refuse to intervene, just as they do with nonsexual friendships, unless there is clear evidence that a particular relationship is undermining specific organizational goals.... In my view, employees and supervisors should be free to work together to create a variety of different work cultures—including more and less sexualized ones—so long as that process occurs within a larger context of structural equality that provides all women and men the power to shape those cultures....

The contemporary drive to sanitize the workplace came about through a complex interplay of forces in which feminists, judges, HR managers, lawyers, and the news media all helped create an understanding that sexuality disadvantages women and disrupts productivity. In my view, we can only hope to halt the sanitization process by articulating a more appealing vision in which sexuality and intimacy can coexist with, and perhaps even enhance, gender equality and organizational rationality....

QUESTIONS

1. Schultz favors broad efforts to achieve integration and equality throughout the firm. What do you think she means by this? Can you give examples?
2. **Research:** Schultz mentions "the old Taylorist dream of the workplace as a sterile zone." Who was Frederick Taylor? What about his life's achievement would lead Schultz to describe his dream as "sterile"? What is Schultz's vision of work?

Bending the Gender Stereotypes

A person is defined as transgendered precisely because of the perception that his or her behavior transgresses gender stereotypes.

—JUDGE BARKET, *Glenn v. Brumby*, 2011

QUILTBAG: " [an acronym standing for] Queer/Questioning, Undecided, Intersex, Lesbian, Transgender/Transsexual, Bisexual, Allied/Asexual, Gay/Genderqueer."
http://queerdictionary.tumblr.com/post/3899608042/quiltbag

Sex, gender, and sexuality are terms whose meanings have been contested and reconceptualized in the past few decades. Social scientists and feminist theorists, for example, generally use "sex" to refer to one's biological sex, labeling people "male" or "female" depending on their chromosomes, hormones, and anatomical features. Sex, they argue, is distinguishable from "gender" (whether one is masculine or feminine), because gender is the meaning that a particular society gives to one's sex. Whether one is "feminine" may depend, for example, on whether one takes care of children—even though, biologically, both males and females are capable of caring for children. This is often called the social construction of gender.

Interpreting the Civil Rights Act's ban on "discrimination on the basis of sex," courts have had to decide what Congress meant by sex. Federal courts have consistently held that "sex" refers to one's biological sex, whether discrimination occurred because one is male or female, or because of gender stereotyping. The statute has rarely been interpreted to protect against discrimination based on one's sexual orientation or affiliations (homosexuality, bisexuality, heterosexuality). This means that, except in those states and localities with laws banning discrimination based on sexual orientation, an employer can refuse to hire a woman because she is a lesbian, a man because he is gay.

■ ■ ■

The next case presents yet another nuance in the realm of sex discrimination. Peter Oiler alleges that he was fired from his job because he cross-dresses and impersonates a woman when he is off duty. This, he claims, illegally discriminates on the basis of sexual stereotyping.

Oiler v. Winn-Dixie Louisiana, Inc.
U.S. District Court, Louisiana, 2002
2002 WL 31098541

AFRICK, District Judge.

In 1979, plaintiff, Peter Oiler, was hired by defendant, Winn-Dixie, as a loader. In 1981, he was promoted to yard truck driver and he later became a road truck driver. As a road truck driver, plaintiff delivered groceries from Winn-Dixie's grocery warehouse in Harahan, Louisiana, to grocery stores in southern and central Louisiana and Mississippi.

Plaintiff is a heterosexual man who has been married since 1977. The plaintiff is transgendered. He is not a transsexual and he does not intend to become a woman.... He is a male cross-dresser [or] transvestite.

When he is not at work, plaintiff appears in public approximately one to three times per month wearing female clothing and accessories. In order to resemble a woman, plaintiff wears wigs and makeup, including concealer, eye shadow, foundation, and lipstick ... skirts, women's blouses, women's flat shoes, and nail polish. He shaves his face, arms, hands, and legs. He wears women's underwear and bras and he uses silicone prostheses to enlarge his breasts. When he is cross-dressed as a woman, he adopts a female persona and he uses the name "Donna."...

While cross-dressed, he attended support group meetings, dined at a variety of restaurants in Kenner and Metairie, visited night clubs, went to shopping malls, and occasionally attended church services. He was often accompanied by his wife and other friends, some of whom were also cross-dressed.

On October 29, 1999, plaintiff told Gregg Miles, a Winn-Dixie supervisor, that he was transgendered.... [W]hen plaintiff did not resign voluntarily, Winn-Dixie discharged him ... because [of concerns that] if Winn-Dixie's customers learned of plaintiff's lifestyle, i.e., that he regularly cross-dressed and impersonated a woman in public, they would shop elsewhere and Winn-Dixie would lose business. Plaintiff did not cross-dress at work and he was not terminated because he violated any Winn-Dixie on-duty dress code. He was never told ... that he was being terminated for appearing or acting effeminate at work, i.e., for having effeminate mannerisms or a high voice. Nor did any Winn-Dixie manager ever tell plaintiff that he did not fit a male stereotype or assign him work that stereo-typically would be performed by a female....

In *Ulane v. Eastern Airlines, Inc.* (7th Cir. 1984) a male airline pilot was fired when, following sex reassignment surgery, she attempted to return to work as a woman.... The *Ulane* court stated that:

The phrase in Title VII prohibiting discrimination based on sex, in its plain meaning, implies that it is unlawful to discriminate against women because they are women and against men because they are men. The words of Title VII do not outlaw discrimination against a person who has a sexual identity disorder, i.e., a person born with a male body who believes himself to be a female, or a person born with a female body who believes herself to be male; a prohibition against discrimination based on an individual's sex is not synonymous with a prohibition based on an individual's sexual identity disorder or discontent with the sex into which they were born....

In 1964, when Title VII was adopted, there was no debate on the meaning of the phrase "sex." In the social climate of the early sixties, sexual identity and sexual orientation related issues remained shrouded in secrecy and individuals having such issues generally remained closeted. Thirty-eight years later, however, sexual identity and sexual orientation issues are no longer buried and they are discussed in the mainstream. Many individuals having such issues have opened wide the closet doors.

Despite the fact that the number of persons publicly acknowledging sexual orientation or gender or sexual identity issues has increased exponentially since the passage of Title VII, the meaning of the word "sex" in Title VII has never been clarified legislatively. From 1981 through 2001, thirty-one proposed bills have been introduced in the United States Senate and the House of Representatives which have attempted to amend Title VII and prohibit employment discrimination on the basis of affectional or sexual orientation. None have passed....

Plaintiff argues that his termination by Winn-Dixie was not due to his cross-dressing as a result of his gender identity disorder, but because he did not conform to a gender stereotype....

After much thought and consideration of the undisputed facts of this case, the Court finds that this is not a situation where the plaintiff failed to conform to a gender stereotype. Plaintiff was not discharged because he did not act sufficiently masculine or because he exhibited traits normally valued in a female employee, but disparaged in a male employee. Rather, the plaintiff disguised himself as a person of a different sex and presented himself as a female for stress relief and to express his gender identity. The plaintiff was terminated because he is a man with a sexual or gender identity disorder who, in order to publicly disguise himself as a woman, wears women's clothing, shoes, underwear, breast prostheses, wigs, makeup, and nail polish, pretends to be a woman, and publicly identifies himself as a woman named "Donna."...

This is not just a matter of an employee of one sex exhibiting characteristics associated with the opposite sex. This is a matter of a person of one sex assuming the role of a person of the opposite sex....

In holding that defendant's actions are not proscribed by Title VII, the Court recognizes that many would disagree with the defendant's decision and its rationale. The plaintiff was a long-standing employee of the defendant. He never cross-dressed at work and his cross-dressing was not criminal or a threat to public safety.

Defendant's rationale for plaintiff's discharge may strike many as morally wrong. However, the function of this Court is not to raise the social conscience of defendant's upper level management, but to construe the law in accordance with proper statutory construction and judicial precedent. The Court is constrained by the framework of the remedial statute enacted by Congress and it cannot, therefore, afford the luxury of making a moral judgment.... [**Held:** plaintiff's suit is dismissed.]

QUESTIONS

1. On what basis did Oiler lose his case?

2. Assume that this case was appealed and that a majority of the appeals court agreed with Judge Africk. Write a dissenting opinion.

3. Increasingly, courts are grappling with cases involving persons who identify themselves as transgendered or as having a "gender identity disorder" that causes them to identify with a gender other than the one they were assigned at birth. How would you deal with each of these scenarios: (a) You are Dean at Yeshiva University, an orthodox Jewish university whose parents, alumni, and financial supporters tend to be socially conservative. One of your faculty members—a literature professor—has just been tenured after five years of teaching as a male. He writes you a letter, indicating that he will be teaching as a woman. "Jay" will be "Joy," from now on. The President of your university suggests that you place Joy on fully paid leave until she can find a position elsewhere. However, she does not want to find another job. (b) One of your employees, a "male" editor, has started to come to work dressed as a woman, and informs you that he is undergoing gender transition therapy. Other workers are uncomfortable with him using the female restroom, and several have made comments about how disruptive it is to have him presenting as a woman. *Glenn v. Brumby,* 663.F.3d 1312 (11th Cir. 2011) (c) You are the human relations director at a small company in Indiana. The company has a dress code that requires male employees to maintain a "conservative, socially acceptable general appearance, with hair above the collar and without earrings or other piercings." Recently you have received customer complaints that one of your sales associates has been wearing earrings, makeup, and long hair. When you call him in to speak to you, he explains that he suffers from gender identity disorder, and has continued the transition from male to female that he began before being hired. *Creed v. Family Express Corp.* 2009 WL 35237 (N.D. Ind.)

4. **Research:** In 1993 Minnesota became the first state to explicitly protect transgendered persons from discrimination. By 2013, 15 other states, the District of Columbia, and more than 150 cities and counties had passed similar laws. Find out whether or not your local or state civil rights laws protect persons who are discriminated against because of their (a) sexual orientation, (b) sexual identity (e.g., transgendered) or (c) gender performance (e.g., cross-dressing).

■ ■ ■

WORK–LIFE BALANCE

There's no such thing as work-life balance.... There are work-life choices, and you make them, and they have consequences.

—JACK WELCH, Former CEO of General Electric Company

Our current system has been built upon myths of autonomy and independence and thus fails to reflect the vulnerable as well as dependent nature of the human condition.

—MARTHA ALBERTSON FINEMAN

Some economists believe that the wage gap between men and women is explained neither by discrimination nor by occupational segregation, but by the fact that many women choose to spend more time with their families than developing their careers. They point to human capital studies showing that when workers take time off (e.g., to have or raise children, to care for elderly parents) they earn less money than workers who don't interrupt their careers. Not surprisingly, it is more often women who leave their jobs, work part time, and work less, and so earn lower wages.

Other experts argue that the wage gap is a result of discrimination and is also affected by the degree to which women—more than men—must cope with work that takes place outside of the workplace, especially child- and elder-care. While some of this may be freely chosen, they believe, stereotyping and the lack of options factor in heavily.

Joan Williams, director of the WorkLife Law Institute at Hastings Law School, coined the phrase "the maternal wall," a play on the "glass ceiling," as a way of describing subtle discrimination against women who become mothers. She explains that sociologists have found that our image of a "good mother" is someone who is always available to her children, while a "good father" is a man who provides for his family. As a result, a woman who works part time to spend time with her family is often seen as only an adequate worker, but has status as a good mother; a man who does the same loses status as both worker and father.

FAMILY RESPONSIBILITY DISCRIMINATION

Two years after she was hired by Wellpoint, Inc., an insurance company in Maine, Laurie Chadwick was promoted. In her new position, she earned six years of stellar performance evaluations and was encouraged by her supervisor, Nanci Miller, to apply for a promotion. Unbeknown to Miller, Chadwick was the mother of an 11-year-old son and 6-year-old triplets. Her husband worked the night shift, serving as primary caretaker. After Chadwick's interview, and before a decision was made, Miller learned about Chadwick's family situation. Her response: "Bless you!" Then she promoted another woman—one with less impressive performance evaluations and no children. Asked to explain, Miller told Chadwick, "It was nothing you did or didn't do. It was just that you're going to school, you have the kids, and you just have a lot on your plate right now." While federal law does not specifically outlaw "caregiver discrimination" Chadwick pursued her case based on a theory of illegal sex discrimination based on the stereotype that "a woman, because she is a woman, will neglect her job responsibilities in favor of her presumed childcare responsibilities." The court agreed: "Women have the right to prove that mettle in the work arena without the burden of stereotypes regarding whether they can fulfill their responsibilities."[9]

Discrimination against those with family responsibilities is not unusual. The Center for WorkLife Law database contains nearly 3,000 cases involving caregivers. One oft-cited study shows the bias: It found that when subjects were given almost-identical resumes (one was a mother, the other wasn't) the mother was 79 percent less likely to be hired, 100 percent less likely to be promoted, offered an average of $11,000 less in salary, and held to higher performance and punctuality standards.[10]

Nor does such discrimination harm only women. Consider these reports to the hotline run by the Center for WorkLife Law: A factory worker was disciplined for failing to show up for overtime work on a weekend because no one else could stay with his wife, who had cancer and was severely depressed; a lumber company management trainee, warned that he would be "cutting his own throat" if he took leave to care for his sick father, was fired when he took the leave; a police sergeant who took two months leave under the Family and Medical Leave Act to care for his newborn was denied a promotion. By law, the men in those cases had a right to take leaves.

A recent report documents a new wrinkle involving elder-care: Roughly 42 percent of U.S. workers provided elder-care from 2007 to 2012, with responsibilities falling disproportionately on women and low-wage workers.[11] And, like other caregivers, those who care for aging parents or friends are subject to discrimination both blatant—leaves denied, retaliation for exercising legal rights under the FMLA—and subtle—labeling workers as "lackadaisical" or hyper-scrutinizing them.

Legislating Family Leave

While Title VII made it illegal for employers to discriminate on the basis of gender ("sex"), the courts interpreted it as allowing employers to single out and discriminate on the basis of pregnancy. In one highly criticized case, the Supreme Court upheld an employee disability plan that provided insurance for sickness and accidents, but excluded coverage for complications arising from pregnancy. The Court explained why Title VII's ban on sex discrimination was not violated:

> [A]n exclusion of pregnancy from a disability-benefits plan providing general coverage is not a gender-based discrimination at all....[T]he selection of risks covered by the Plan did not operate, in fact to discriminate against women.... The Plan, in effect ... is nothing more than an insurance package, which covers some risks, but excludes others....[12]

---

[9]*Chadwick v. Wellpoint, Inc.* 561 F.3d 38 (1st Cir. 2009).

[10]Steven Bernard, et al., "Cognitive Bias and the Motherhood Penalty," *Hastings Law Journal* 59, 2007–2008, p. 1359.

[11] Joan C. Williams, Robin Devaux, and Patricija Petrac (Center for Worklife Law) and Lynn Feinberg (AARP Public Policy Institute), "Protecting Family Caregivers from Employment Discrimination" (Insight on the Issues 68, August, 2012), AARP Public Policy Institute.

[12]*General Electric Co. v. Gilbert,* 429 U.S. 125 (1976).

Congress reacted to the Court's interpretation of Title VII by amending the law in 1978 to make it clear that discrimination on the basis of pregnancy was illegal. The amendments, known as the **Pregnancy Discrimination Act** of 1978, provide:

Women affected by pregnancy, childbirth, and related medical conditions shall be treated the same for all employment-related purposes, including receipt of benefits under fringe benefit programs, as other persons not so affected but similar in their ability or inability to work.

Under this law, pregnant workers are to be treated like any other workers. But an argument can be made that a law that makes it illegal to fire a woman simply because she is pregnant does not go far enough. It affords no protection, for example, to a pregnant employee who is fired for excessive absenteeism by a company that similarly dismisses ill or injured workers who miss too many days at work. Nor does it address the need for time to care for a healthy newborn or accommodate other family responsibilities.

In 1993, Congress passed, and President Clinton signed into law, the **Family and Medical Leave Act**, excerpted below. Note the format of the legislation: It begins with a section that lays out Congress' reasons for adopting it ("Findings and Purposes"), followed by the parts that create enforceable rights ("Leave Requirements.")

Family and Medical Leave Act

29 United States Code Annotated 2601, et seq.

Section 2601 Findings and Purposes: Congress finds that—

1. the number of single-parent households and two-parent households in which the single parent or both parents work is increasing significantly;
2. it is important for the development of children and the family unit that fathers and mothers be able to participate in early childrearing and the care of family members who have serious health conditions;
3. the lack of employment policies to accommodate working parents can force individuals to choose between job security and parenting;
4. there is inadequate job security for employees who have serious health conditions that prevent them from working for temporary periods;
5. due to the nature of the roles of men and women in our society, the primary responsibility for family caretaking often falls on women, and such responsibility affects the working lives of women more than it affects the working lives of men; and
6. employment standards that apply to one gender only have serious potential for encouraging employers to discriminate against employees and applicants for employment who are of that gender.

Section 2612(a)1: Leave Requirements

Entitlement to leave
[A]n eligible employee shall be entitled to a total of 12 workweeks of leave during any 12-month period for one or more of the following:

(A) Because of the birth of a son or daughter of the employee and in order to care for such son or daughter.
(B) Because of the placement of a son or daughter with the employee for adoption or foster care.

(C) In order to care for the spouse, or a son, daughter, or parent, of the employee, if such spouse, son, daughter, or parent has a serious health condition.

(D) Because of a serious health condition that makes the employee unable to perform the functions of the position of such employee.

(E) Because of any qualifying exigency ... arising out of the fact that the spouse, or a son, daughter, or parent of the employee is [deployed overseas or notified of an impending call to be deployed overseas] in the Armed Forces.

Section 2614 (b)(1): Restoration to Position and Special Rules

The law guarantees that an employee who returns from a leave can go back to his or her position, or one with equivalent benefits, pay, and conditions, without losing any benefits that had accrued prior to the leave, although without gaining any seniority while they were on leave.

[There are some exceptions. Those within a firm's top 10 percent of salaried employees within a 75-mile radius, for example, can be denied restoration to the job after a leave if:]

A. such denial is necessary to prevent substantial and grievous economic injury to the operations of the employer;

B. the employer notifies the employee of the intent of the employer to deny restoration on such basis at the time the employer determines that such injury would occur; and

C. in any case in which the leave has commenced, the employee elects not to return to employment after receiving such notice.

The FMLA and Department of Labor regulations also provide that employees have a right to use their leave time by taking intermittent or reduced time health leaves if medically necessary. The employer, however, may temporarily transfer the employee to a different, comparably paid position. Leave for new-child care must be taken all at once, unless both employee and employer agree to some other arrangement. Employees must give whatever notice of their intention to take leave is possible and reasonable considering the circumstances (e.g., 30 days' notice before birth or placement of an adopted child), and make reasonable efforts to schedule medical treatment to cause the least possible disruption to the employer. Employers are required to maintain coverage under group health plans for employees on leave.

The **Injured Servicemember Leave Act** allows up to twenty-six weeks of leave in a 12-month period to care for a next-of-kin servicemember with a serious injury or illness. "Servicemember" means any current member of the armed forces including the National Guard or Reserves, or a member on temporary disability. "Qualified exigencies" for which leave is guaranteed include participation in official ceremonies, family support or assistance programs, and attending to special child care needs required by overseas deployment.

QUESTIONS

1. Look at the statutory provisions that explain the FMLA leave requirements. Do they seem well crafted to respond to the findings set forth by Congress in the law?

2. Does the law require employers to give paid family or medical leave? Does it permit paid leave?

3. Look back at the *Windsor* case that opens this chapter. What impact would you expect that case to have on the FMLA?

4. Does Congress address any stereotypes about caregivers? How responsive is the law to changes in our ideas about family? Who benefits from the law? Is anyone harmed? Can you think of any changes that would make it more responsive to the needs of caregivers? **Research:** The FMLA Inclusion Act would expand the list of covered relationships. Find out who would be covered and whether the bill, proposed in April 2013, has been passed.

5. **Research:** Of 173 nations surveyed by Harvard/McGill Universities in 2007, only five did not provide some form of paid leave to all new mothers: Lesoto, Liberia, Papua New Guinea, Swaziland, and the United States. (a) Find out about an organization that advocates for or against such leave in the United States. What arguments do they give for their positions? Are they persuasive? (b) In 2002, California became the first state to enact a comprehensive paid family leave law. Since then, only New Jersey, Rhode Island, and Colorado have passed similar state laws. The National Partnership for Women and Families has drafted a bill for a similar law.[13] Find out the current status of such proposals in your state.

6. **Research:** According to the Bureau of Labor Statistics in 2013 only 61 percent of U.S. workers—and only 40 percent of service workers—have paid sick leave. (a) The proposed *Healthy Families Act* would change that. Find out whether that bill has become law. (b) Only a handful of states—and a growing number of cities—guaranteed paid sick leave in 2013. Find out if yours is one of them. If not, what efforts are being made to pass such laws in your state or the municipality closest to you? (c) Check out *Slate*'s online map of countries that require paid sick leave.

7. **Research:** In some states, laws have been introduced that would pre-empt cities from passing their own sick or family leave laws. Find out if your state is one of them. What concerns would motivate such laws?

Reasonable Accommodation of Disabled Workers

Society first confined people with disabilities in almshouses, and then in institutions. Alone and ignored, people with disabling conditions experienced life in a Hobbesian state of nature: an existence, "solitary, poor, nasty, brutish, and short."... Until 1973, Chicago prohibited persons who were "deformed" and "unsightly" from exposing themselves to public view.... In 1975, when federal legislation finally required states receiving federal educational funds to serve all school-aged children with disabilities, 1.75 million children were not receiving any schooling, and an estimated 2.5 million were in programs that did not meet their needs.

—MARK C. WEBER[14]

In 1990 Congress adopted the Americans with Disabilities Act (ADA). Hailed by some as the most important legislation since the Civil Rights Acts of 1964, the ADA is patterned

---

[13]Heymann, J., Earle, A., and Hayes, J. (2007). The Work, Family, and Equity Index: How Does the United States Measure Up? Montreal, QC, and Boston, MA: Project on Global Working Families. Retrieved June 10, 2010 from http://www.mcgill.ca/files/ihsp/WFEI2007FEB.pdf.

[14]"Exile and the King: Integration, Harassment, and the Americans With Disabilities Act," *Maryland Law Review* 63, 2004, p. 162.

on an earlier law that prohibited discrimination against persons with handicaps in government-funded programs. It is a bold stroke to eliminate barriers in employment, education, housing, transportation, and public accommodations.

The ADA also takes aim at another problem: society's accumulated myths and fears about disability and disease. The law makes it illegal for employers to discriminate against a qualified person on the basis of disability and requires firms to make "reasonable accommodation" so that the disabled are given more opportunity to enter the mainstream.

The concept of reasonable accommodation is broad and flexible—but is not intended to impose an "undue hardship" on a business. It encompasses both physical changes to buildings (e.g., broadening aisles and doorways and lowering shelves to make them accessible to those in wheelchairs) and adjustments in the ways people work (e.g., flexible work schedules or modified job descriptions). While Title VII speaks of ending discrimination, the ADA does that and more: It sometimes requires employers to alter the jobs themselves.

Wherever reasonably possible, physical obstacles—the absence of ramps to enter buildings, narrow seating in theaters, the arrangement of furniture and machinery in some workplaces—must be replaced or altered to make business and public places accessible to disabled customers, clients, and employees.

The following definitions are excerpted from the law.

Equal Opportunity for Individuals with Disabilities (Americans with Disabilities Act)

42 United States Code Annotated §12102

The term **disability** means, with respect to an individual (A) a physical or mental impairment that substantially limits one or more of the major life activities of such individual; (B) a record of such an impairment; or (C) being regarded as having such an impairment.

"**Major life activities**" include, but are not limited to, caring for oneself, performing manual tasks, seeing, hearing, eating, sleeping, walking, standing, lifting, bending, speaking, breathing, learning, reading, concentrating, thinking, communicating and working.

The term **qualified individual with a disability** means an individual with a disability who, with or without reasonable accommodation, can perform the essential functions of the employment position that such individual holds or desires.... [C]onsideration shall be given to the employer's judgment as to what functions of a job are essential, and if an employer has prepared a written description before advertising or interviewing applicants for the job, this description shall be considered evidence of the essential functions of the job.

The term **reasonable accommodation** may include (A) making existing facilities used by employees readily accessible to and usable by individuals with disabilities; and (B) job restructuring, part-time or modified work schedules, reassignment to a vacant position, acquisition or modification of equipment or devices, appropriate adjustment or modifications of examinations, training materials or policies, the provision of qualified readers or interpreters, and other similar accommodations....

The term **undue hardship** means an action requiring significant difficulty or expense, when considered in light of the [following]: In determining whether an accommodation would impose an undue hardship on a covered entity, factors to be considered include (i) the nature and cost of the accommodation needed under this chapter; (ii) the overall financial resources of the facility or facilities involved in the provision of the reasonable accommodation; the number of persons employed at such facility; the effect on expenses and resources, or the impact otherwise of such accommodation upon the operation of the facility; (iii) the overall financial resources of the covered entity; the overall size of the business of a covered entity with respect to the number of its employees; the number, type, and location of its facilities; and (iv) the type of operation or operations of the covered entity, including the composition, structure, and functions of the workforce of such entity; the geographic separateness, administrative, or fiscal relationship of the facility or facilities in question to the covered entity.

In 2008, Congress amended the ADA to overturn Supreme Court decisions that had narrowed the broad scope of protection the act was supposed to offer. As amended, the law requires courts to construe the definition of "disability" in favor of broad coverage of individuals; clarifies that a person meets the definition of "disabled" if he or she has any impairment that substantially limits even one major life activity; and that persons with such impairments are covered, even if their disability is episodic or in remission.

QUESTIONS

1. EEOC-promulgated guidelines for interpreting the ADA make it clear that while pregnancy is not *per se* a disability, "a pregnancy-related impairment that substantially limits a major life activity is a disability" requiring a reasonable accommodation. As a supervisor, how would you deal with each of the following: (a) a receptionist at your company is pregnant, and experiencing severe morning sickness. She wants to "flex" her hours to come in at noon; (b) A doctor has certified that a male airline ticket agent has an impairment that restricts his ability to lift more than 20 pounds for several months; (c) A doctor has certified that a pregnant airline ticket agent cannot lift more than 15 pounds for the duration of her pregnancy.

2. **Research:** During the past three decades, as technology evolves, the courts have helped define the extent to which a particular business must change to accommodate the disabled. (a) Should courts consider a website to be a "public space" that must reasonably accommodate the disabled? See, for example, the allegations that Target's website was inadequate in *National Federation of the Blind v. Target Corporation*, 2009 WL 2390261 (N.D. Cal. 2009) and the pressure on Netflix to make its video streaming more accessible to the hearing impaired in *National Ass'n. of the Deaf v. Netflix, Inc.*, 869 F.Supp.2d 196 (D.Mass. 2012). (b) What kind of access to ATMs do the blind need? Find out what happened in a suit against the company that owns and operates some 47,500 ATMs nationwide. *Massachusetts v. ETrade Access Inc.*, 2013 WL 1167474 (D. Mass. 2013). (c) Amazon.com is attempting to flood the market with its Kindle e-readers, often donating directly to schools around the country. Neither the Kindle devices nor their content are accessible to students with certain visual or print disabilities. Find out about the negotiations between Amazon and the National Federation of the Blind over Kindles.

3. **Research:** In a lawsuit filed in 2006, the U.S. Treasury was accused of violating the Rehabilitation Act (the law that preceded the ADA) by failing to issue paper currency that was readily distinguishable by blind and visually impaired people. Of the 180 nations that issue paper currency, only the United States prints bills

identical in size and color in all denominations. Raised symbols enable the blind to distinguish bills printed by Canada, Argentina, China, and Israel. New bills are constantly being printed—especially $1 bills—and the United States made major design changes in 1996. (a) Should the government do another redesign to address the needs the blind or visually impaired? (b) To see how the court ruled, read *American Council of the Blind v. Paulson,* 525 F.3d 1256 (D.C. Cir. 2008).

4. **Research:** The United Nations Convention on the Rights of Persons with Disabilities, adopted in 2006, is the first human rights treaty to be adopted in the twenty-first century and the first to be signed by the United States (2009) in many years. By summer 2013, some 129 nations had ratified the treaty—but the United States was not one of them. Find out why not? Has the treaty been ratified by the U.S. since this book went to press? Compare the provisions of the Convention to the Americans with Disabilities Act. Would the U.S. have to do more to meet its treaty obligations?

GENDER INEQUITY: A GLOBAL PERSPECTIVE

When women's status in society improves, history shows, hunger is reduced. Olivier De Schutter, the United Nations Special Rapporteur on the Right to Food, is charged with prodding governments to do more to ensure that citizens are not deprived of their basic human right to food. The following reading helps explain why he believes that "sharing power with women is a shortcut to reducing hunger and malnutrition, and is the single most effective step to realizing the right to food."[15] It was published on March 4, 2013, the day De Schutter issued a major report on "Gender and The Right to Food."

The Feminization of Farming

Olivier De Schutter[16]

Across the developing world, millions of people are migrating from farms to cities in search of work. The migrants are mostly men. As a result, women are increasingly on the front lines of the fight to sustain family farms. But pervasive discrimination, gender stereotypes and women's low social standing have frustrated these women's rise out of poverty and hunger.

Discrimination denies small-scale female farmers the same access men have to fertilizer, seeds, credit, membership in cooperatives and unions, and technical assistance. That deters potential productivity gains. But the biggest barriers don't even have to do with farming—and yet they have a huge impact on food security.

As sole or principal caregivers, women and girls often face a heavy burden of unremunerated household chores like cooking, cleaning, fetching water, collecting firewood and caring for the very young and the elderly. These uncompensated activities are equivalent to as much as 63 percent of gross domestic product in India and Tanzania. But they result in lost opportunities for women, who don't have

[15]United Nations Human Rights, Office of the High Commissioner Press Release, March 4, 2013.

[16]Published as an Op-ed in *The New York Times*, March 4, 2013.

the time to attend classes, travel to markets to sell produce or do other activities to improve their economic prospects....

[De Schutter next explains that progress in women's education did more than any other driver to increase food security, globally, over the period 1970–95. But, even governments that understand the connections between gender, poverty, and education, don't always do enough. He points to continued lack of education for girls in several Asian countries that offer stipends to keep girls in school. The reason: lack of adequate sanitation facilities and paucity of female teachers that discourages socially conservative parents who don't want their daughters to be taught by men; government failure to prevent farmers from pulling their children, usually girls first, from school to till the fields.]

Countries like Indonesia have introduced *microfinance* programs to help women pursue small-business ideas instead of housework. But creditworthy women are sometimes used as intermediaries to obtain loans for businesses run by their male relatives.

In a report to the United Nations Human Rights Council that is being released today, [March 2013] I urge a comprehensive, rights-based approach focused on removing legal discrimination and on improving public services—child care, water supplies, sanitation and energy sources—to reduce the burden on women who farm. But such an approach must also systematically challenge the traditional gender roles that burden women with household chores in the first place.

In Bangladesh, a program begun in 2002 by a nonprofit group, Building Resources Across Communities, shows how this might be achieved. It provided women with poultry (easier to raise than pigs, cows, goats and sheep); subsidized legal and health services; clean water and sanitary latrines, and a temporary daily stipend to tide over extremely poor women who were working as maids for extra income, so that they could focus on farming. The program also secured support from local elites, who among other things could help ensure that the women's children were enrolled in school.

In the Philippines, a conditional cash-transfer program, started in 2008, covers 3 million households. Aiming to improve women's access to obstetric care, and to improve spending on children's health and education, the program includes a "gender action plan" that requires that bank accounts be set up in women's names (which protects their control of the money and prevents fraud); trains women on their rights with respect to domestic violence, child care, nutrition and other areas; and trains fathers to share responsibility as caregivers.

In Yunnan Province in western China, women's groups were enlisted for a rural road-maintenance program in 2009. ...The women were able to work while maintaining other income-generating activities like raising pigs or selling vegetables. They also got training to improve their agricultural productivity.

Recognizing the burden that the feminization of global farming places on women requires us to overturn longstanding gender norms that have kept women down even as they feed more and more of the world. The most effective strategies to empower women who tend farm and family—and to alleviate hunger in the process—are to remove the obstacles that hinder them from taking charge of their lives.

QUESTIONS

1. What are the "gender norms" that keep women down? Do you think those norms are still a problem in the United States, or only in developing nations?

2. What role might the United States play in helping to make the fundamental right to be free from hunger a reality?

CHAPTER PROBLEMS

1. Belem was born in Mexico. Her father left for the United States to do farmwork in Sacramento. When Belem was nine, she and her mother made a dangerous desert crossing into the United States, to reunite the family in California. Now in her twenties, Belem considers the United States her home. Benjamin was born in Chile, and was brought to the United States when he was nine months old. An accomplished student and musician, he didn't learn about his undocumented status until after high school graduation, when his mother finally explained why he lacked a Social Security number. Like Belem, Benjamin feels that he belongs to the United States. These are typical stories of young undocumented immigrants, most of whom were brought to this country by their parents. The so-called Dreamers, who dream of having full acceptance in the place they feel is their home, have been the focus of President Obama's first step toward immigration reform. Just five months before the 2012 election, President Obama created *Deferred Action for Childhood Arrivals* (DACA). It defers for two years the deportation of those under 31 who arrived in the United States before turning 16 and have lived here for at least five years, have no serious criminal record, and either hold a high school diploma, are in school, or have been honorably discharged from the armed services.

   By 2013, a dozen states allowed illegal immigrants to qualify for state-resident tuition at state colleges. But a half dozen other states—including Arizona and Indiana—explicitly bar illegal immigrants from qualifying for in-state tuition. And in 2012, private donors created a scholarship fund for illegal immigrants ("Dream Fellowships") at the City University of New York system. Consider each of these approaches to the Dreamers from the perspective of the various ethical theories described in Chapter 1.

2. Title VII of the Civil Rights Act of 1964 bans discrimination in pay and other compensation based on race, color, religion, sex, or national origin. And the **Equal Pay Act of 1963** makes it illegal for employers to pay men and women different wages for doing the same job (except to the extent that wage differentials are based on seniority, merit, or factors "other than sex"). Yet, half a century later, there is still a wage gap. In 2012, the national median earnings for women working fulltime, year round was $37,110, or 77 percent of what men working fulltime, year round earned. The wage gap is even greater for African American women and Latinas. **Research:** (a) Use the interactive map on the website of the *National Committee for Pay Equity* to compare wages by race and gender in your state. (b) The proposed *Fair Pay Act* targets the effects of occupational segregation; it seeks to end wage discrimination against those who work in jobs dominated by women or minorities by establishing equal pay for equivalent work. Another proposed law, the *Paycheck Fairness Act,* calls for voluntary guidelines to help employers evaluate—and pay—jobs more fairly. Find out the current status of these bills. What arguments can you make for and against each of them?

3. Suppose your company allows employees to schedule themselves to leave work early to engage in community service, including coaching children's league-teams. Should the company also grant similar rights to parents to spend time with their own children? **Research** (a) Does any federal law require such treatment? (b) Find out if there are laws in your state or city that mandate time-off for family-related activities, and/or for other admirable reasons, such as to become an organ or blood donor, to

provide volunteer emergency and/or disaster services. (c) If you were head of HR, what kind of leave policies would you create?

4. **Research:** Is there still a glass ceiling in the United States? As of 2013, in key technology jobs like computer systems design and electronic production, men outnumbered women by more than two to one. *Business Insider* reported in 2013 that women's share of venture capital was roughly 4.4 percent. Why do these disparities linger? Can you imagine a strategy for change?

5. Fewer than 5 percent of Fortune 500 CEOs were women although they made up 36 percent of Business School students in 2012. Women held only 16.6 percent of board of director seats on Fortune 500 companies, with women of color holding far fewer (3.3 percent) of those seats. Throughout 2013, the European Union debated a measure that would require 40 percent of a company's directors be women. (a) What are the pros and cons of this approach? (b) Do you think the United States should adopt a similar rule? (c) **Research:** Has the proposal been adopted by the EU?

6. **Research:** Find a company that has tried to create a corporate culture that supports men or women in caretaking responsibilities. [*Hint: Working Mother* magazine yearly identifies the top family-friendly companies. *Warning:* Companies apply for this honor.] What are the characteristics of its program? Compare its work–family benefits to those of other companies in the same business sector. Now check the company's financials. Is the "progressive" firm you've located also a successful one? Is it one you would want to work for?

7. Business places a high value on flexibility and "availability" of workers. But those qualities may unfairly stress those at both ends of the salary scale. Workers with hourly jobs—in restaurants, retail, health care, for example—typically find their hours are fluctuating, scarce, and unpredictable. "Availability" allows businesses to offer employment when they need to hire, and to cut back whenever it makes economic sense to do so. At the high end, "flexibility" often means professionals—with their fixed salaries and benefits—are pressured to be willing to work as many hours as possible and to bring work home, even at the cost of family and personal lives. Should employees have some voice in redefining the qualities that make them valuable? What might be the mechanism for doing this?

8. **Research:** Donnicia had worked as an account representative for three years when she took a leave to give birth to her first child. Four months later, she called her supervisor to say she was getting ready to return to work, was breastfeeding, and wanted to know if she would be able to use a breast pump when she returned. She was told "no." The next time she called, she learned that someone else had been hired to fill her position. Does this violate any law? See *EEOC v. Houston Funding II, Ltd.*, 717 F.3d 425 (5th Cir. 2013).

9. Many seasonal, mostly small businesses, such as seafood processors, amusement parks, hotels, and landscapers, depend on the federal H-2B program, which governs foreign migrants (except those in agricultural work). In order to hire temporary workers under this program, employers must assert that there are no U.S. citizens available to do the jobs. They must also pay a guest worker's transportation costs to and from their home country. Who benefits from the H-2B program? Who is disadvantaged by it?

10. In the 1970s, two-thirds of the farmworkers in the United States were Americans, one-third were foreign migrants. A decade later those numbers had reversed. Some 85,000 farmworkers are guaranteed minimum wages under the H-2A visa program. Mexican guest workers—brought on buses for limited time periods—are praised by the growers as hardworking, efficient, and reliable, not to mention easy to supervise. Local workers, although citizens, may never have worked in the fields. African

American laborers in Vidalia, Georgia, recently sued a large onion grower, Stanley Farms, claiming they were paid less than Mexican guest workers. A similar suit in a nearby county alleged that American plaintiffs had been fired because of their race and national origin, given less desirable jobs, and fewer work opportunities. **Research:** Find out what has happened to those lawsuits. What is the AFL-CIO's position on farmworkers?

CHAPTER PROJECT

Alternative Dispute Resolution: Cyberbullying

Guidelines: Appendix E

Witness Statement: Jonathan Scarlatti

I was thrilled when I was accepted with a full scholarship to Ratgut University last year. It was my first choice, mostly because of its music school. I've been playing oboe since I was seven. I love it. All through high school I had been performing in the band. We won two regional competitions. I had been thinking about a career as a classical musician, but I was also getting interested in jazz. My scholarship was from Ratgut's music school, one of the top five in the country. So I was happy about the financial package, and glad that Ratgut is only a half hour from home. My high school boyfriend Will and I are still close. I didn't want to break up with him just because I was going to college. I'm gay. I came out to my parents in my junior year of high school. I've been out on Facebook, and I blog about my life on a couple of LGBT sites.

I first heard about my Ratgut University roommate the summer before classes started. He sounded nice—outgoing, decent. He listed skateboarding as a hobby, and break-dancing. From the time I met Hunter Pratt he was always with a couple of other students, and about to go out somewhere, usually a party. I never saw him study. But then I never really saw him much at all. He would come in late after I was asleep. He'd be sleeping when I was awake. In the beginning of the semester, even though our room was cramped, we were managing to give each other enough space, and I felt pretty comfortable. A couple of nights, when I knew Hunter was going to be out, I had Will stay with me.

But then I found out what was really going on. My roommate is a homophobe, and cruel. He was twittering about how I was gay and I was hooking up with another "gay dude" in the dorm. And he was spying on me! He set up a webcam in our room, and while he and another student watched from their room, he was streaming video of me and Will together for the world to see.

This happened a few days ago. I've been really depressed. I feel like the whole university—the whole universe—is laughing at me. I haven't been able to study or practice. I don't want to go out of the room, but the room feels creepy too—*there's no place I want to be.* Sometimes I think of revenge—like I think of pouring pink paint all over Hunter's stuff, but that wouldn't change anything. I know this isn't over, either. He's just waiting for his next chance to humiliate me.

Witness Statement: Hunter Pratt

I'm a finance major at Ratgut University. Last year a bunch of seniors from my high school were accepted too, and we've been hanging together since we got to campus.

I'm a good student, but I'm also the kind of person who likes to be with people. I'm a great break-dancer and I'm good at most sports. In a crowd, I'm usually the one who's

making people laugh. I have more friends than I can handle really, but that's a good thing. I'm a tech geek and I'm all over the net—twitter, Facebook, all that stuff.

I just pulled off my best prank ever. Before I even got to college I was checking out my roommate, Jonathan Scarlatti. He's a classical music freak, and I found out he's a fag. I have nothing against gays, it's their business. But living with one was weird! He was always either studying or playing his oboe. At first I didn't think he had any life at all, and then it turns out he's got this boyfriend, and this boyfriend is coming to Ratgut for a weekend.

So here's what I did: I tweeted the news: "Roommate asked for the room until midnight. Keep posted if you want to see him making out with a dude!" Then I set up my webcam in the room so it was aimed at Jonathan's bed but hidden. I left, I went to the game, I ate dinner, and later my friend Meghan and I watched the webcam from her dorm room. We were laughing ourselves sick. I streamed the action out to a few of our friends. People were sending each other their favorite parts. We stayed up the whole night. It was great!

Assume that Jonathan Scarlatti has complained to the Resident Assistant of his dormitory, who has in turn reported this incident to Ratgut University's Disciplinary Board

This scenario is based on the events surrounding the suicide of Tyler Clementi, a freshman student at Rutgers University who jumped off the George Washington Bridge on September 22, 2010, after his roommate uploaded videos of him having sexual relations with a man.